lonely

D0194298

Discover
USA

Experience the best
of the USA

This edition written and researched by

Regis St Louis,
Amy C Balfour, Sandra Bao, Michael Benanav, Greg Benchwick,
Sara Benson, Alison Bing, Catherine Bodry, Celeste Brash,
Gregor Clark, Lisa Dunford, Ned Friary, Michael Grosberg, Adam
Karlin, Mariella Krause, Carolyn McCarthy, Brendan Sainsbury,
Caroline Sieg, Adam Skolnick, Ryan Ver Berkmoes, Mara
Vorhees, Karla Zimmerman

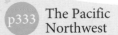

The Pacific Northwest p333

Boston & New England p157

New York City p51

Chicago p127

Washington, DC p95

California p367

The Grand Canyon & the Southwest p291

New Orleans & the South p203

Florida p253

Contents

Contents

Discover USA

In Focus

Survival Guide

● ● ●

The Best of the Rest 421

This Is the USA

Enormous in size and staggeringly diverse, the USA harbors astounding wonders. The sheer variety is simply breathtaking, from teeming city streets to mountains, coastlines and forests.

It has brimming metropolises whose names alone conjure a million different notions. Start with Los Angeles, Las Vegas, Chicago, Miami, Boston and New York City, then look more closely. The American quilt unfurls in all its surprising variety, revealing the red-hot music scene of Memphis, the easygoing charms of antebellum Savannah, the eco-consciousness of free-spirited Portland and the magnificent waterfront of San Francisco.

This is a country of road trips and great open skies. Four million miles of highway lead past red-rock deserts, below towering mountain peaks and across fertile wheat fields that roll toward the horizon. The scenic country lanes of New England, the lush rainforests of the Pacific Northwest and the Spanish moss–draped backdrop of the Deep South are a few fine starting points for the great American road trip.

Cuisine is another highlight of the American experience. New York locals get their fix of bagels and lox at century-old delis on the Upper West Side while, several states away, pancakes and fried eggs disappear under the clatter of cutlery at 1950s-style diners. Plates of fresh lobster served off Maine piers, oysters and champagne in California wine bars, beer and deep-dish pizza at Chicago pubs – there are so many ways to dine à la Americana.

The world's third-largest nation has made tremendous contributions to the arts. From the jazz of New Orleans to the country of Nashville, plus bluegrass, hip-hop and rock and roll, America has invented sounds that are integral to modern music. Cities such as Chicago and New York have become veritable drawing boards for the great architects of the modern era, while Hollywood continues to inspire.

> 66
> Look closely, and the American quilt unfurls in all its surprising variety
> 99

Comet Falls, Mt Rainier National Park (p353)
PETER HAIGH/GETTY IMAGES ©

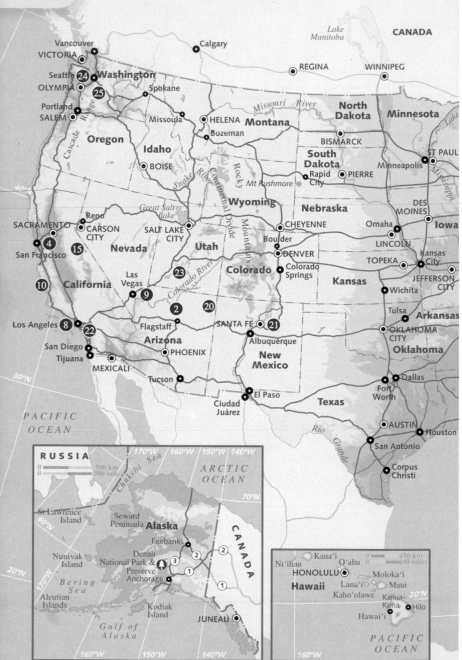

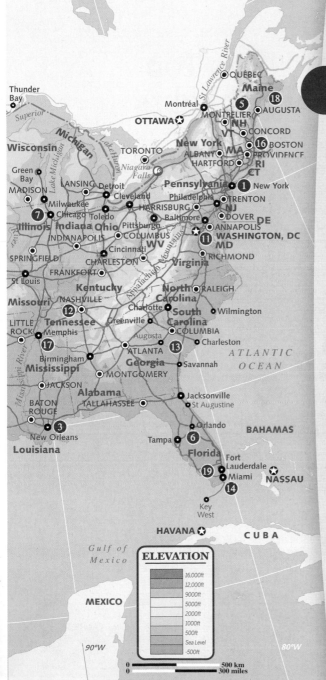

25
Top Highlights

1. New York City
2. Grand Canyon National Park
3. New Orleans
4. San Francisco & Wine Country
5. New England in Fall
6. Walt Disney World
7. Chicago
8. Los Angeles
9. Las Vegas
10. Pacific Coast Highway
11. Washington, DC
12. Nashville
13. Deep South
14. Miami
15. Yosemite National Park
16. Boston & Cape Cod
17. Memphis & Graceland
18. Coastal Maine
19. Everglades National Park
20. Native American Sites
21. Santa Fe
22. Disneyland
23. Zion & Southern Utah National Parks
24. Seattle
25. Mount Rainier National Park

25 USA's Top Highlights

New York City

Home to striving artists, hedge-fund moguls and immigrants from every corner of the globe, New York City (p51) is constantly reinventing itself. It remains a world center for fashion, theater, food, music, publishing, advertising and finance. A staggering number of museums, parks and ethnic neighborhoods are scattered through the five boroughs, so do as every New Yorker does and hit the streets. Every block reflects the character and history of this dizzying kaleidoscope, and on even a short walk you can cross continents.

WITOLD SKRYPCZAK/GETTY IMAGES ©

Grand Canyon National Park

You've seen pictures and heard about it from everyone else but is it worth the hype? The answer is a resounding yes. The Grand Canyon (p300) is vast and its age nearly incomprehensible: it took six million years for the canyon to form, while some rocks exposed along its walls are two billion years old. Peer over the edge to confront the great power and mystery of this earth we live on. Once you've seen it, no other natural phenomenon will quite compare.

New Orleans

While the rest of us eat to live, New Orleanians live to eat. The French, Spanish, Filipinos, Haitians, former Yugoslavians, Irish and Lord-knows-who-else have all contributed to the gastro amalgamation, making New Orleans (p212) one of the USA's most food-centric cities. Sure, there's unique history, gorgeous architecture and amazing music, but a visit inevitably ends up being all about the food. For the true taste of N'awlins, eat with the locals in Riverbend, Uptown, Faubourg Marigny and the Bywater. Below: Gumbo, a popular New Orleans dish

The Best...
Hiking

SOUTH KAIBAB
Stupendous panoramas along one of the prettiest hikes inside the Grand Canyon. (p301)

MARIN COUNTY
Hike amid towering redwoods, then watch the sun set over the Pacific. (p412)

WONDERLAND TRAIL
The 93-mile jewel of Mt Rainier National Park, with lush alpine scenery and abundant wildlife. (p353)

ACADIA NATIONAL PARK
Maine's coastal beauty offers sea cliffs, craggy shorelines and boulder-strewn peaks. (p198)

The Best...
Wine Regions

NAPA VALLEY
With more than 200 vineyards, Napa is synonymous with world-class winemaking. (p413)

COLUMBIA RIVER VALLEY
This scenic valley outside Seattle produces superb Syrahs and Chardonnays. (p364)

WALLA WALLA
Home to scores of wineries, picturesque scenery and talented restaurateurs, this is a top spot to wine and dine. (p364)

SANTA YNEZ & SANTA MARIA VALLEYS
Head north of Santa Barbara in Southern California to the rolling hills of vineyards made famous in the film *Sideways*. (p420)

4 San Francisco & Wine Country

Amid the clatter of old-fashioned trams and thick fog that sweeps in by night, the diverse neighborhoods of San Francisco (p397) invite long days of wandering, with indie shops, world-class restaurants and bohemian nightlife. If you can tear yourself away, the lush, rolling vineyards of Napa, Sonoma and the Russian River Valley lie just north of the city. Touring wineries, drinking great wine and lingering over farm-to-table meals – it's all part of the great Wine Country experience.

5 New England in Fall

Watching the leaves change color is an epic event in New England (p160). See autumn's fire light up Boston and Cambridge, up through Portsmouth and New Hampshire and all the way to Maine's Acadia National Park. Or head inland to Vermont, where entire hillsides blaze in brilliant crimsons, oranges and yellows. Covered bridges and white-steeple churches form the backdrop to leaf-peeping heaven.

Walt Disney World

Walt Disney World (p266) pulls out all the stops to deliver the exhilarating sensation that *you* are the most important character in the show. Despite all the rides and entertainment, the real magic is watching your own child swell with belief after they've made Goofy laugh, been curtsied to by Cinderella and guarded the galaxy with Buzz Lightyear.

Right: Cinderella's Castle

Chicago

The Windy City (p127) will blow you away with its cloud-scraping architecture, lakefront beaches and world-class museums – but its true mojo is its blend of high culture and earthy pleasures. Is there another metropolis that dresses its Picasso sculpture in local sports-team gear? Where residents are as likely to queue for hot dogs as for some of North America's top restaurants? While the winters are long and brutal, come summer Chicago fetes the arrival of warm days with a magnificent array of food and music festivals that make fine use of its striking waterfront.

Los Angeles

The entertainment capital of the world, Los Angeles (p376) is much more than a two-dimensional movie town. To start, this is the city of oddball haven Venice Beach; art galleries and dining in Santa Monica; indie-loving neighborhoods Los Feliz and Silverlake; surf-loving beaches such as Malibu; and rugged and wild Griffith Park. Dig deeper and you'll find museums displaying all kinds of ephemera, a cultural renaissance happening downtown, and vibrant multi-ethnic 'hoods where great food lies just around the corner. Below: Venice Beach (p386)

The Best...
Museums

NEW YORK CITY
Spend days ploughing through the city's museums and you'll barely even scratch the surface. (p60)

WASHINGTON, DC
Treasured halls dedicated to outer space, history and art – plus woolly mammoths. (p104)

SAN FRANCISCO
From futuristic design at the MH de Young (p403) to American counterculture at the Beat Museum (p400).

CHICAGO
Home to a treasure trove of great art, including the spectacular Art Institute of Chicago, plus loads of small galleries. (p137)

Las Vegas

Sin City (p312) is a neon-fueled ride through the nerve center of America's strike-it-rich fantasies. See billionaires' names gleam from the marquees of luxury hotels. Hear a raucous soundscape of slot machines, clinking martini glasses, and the hypnotic beats of DJs spinning till dawn. Sip cocktails under palm trees and play blackjack by the pool. Visit Paris, the Wild West and a tropical island, all in one night. It's all here and it's all open 24 hours – for the price of a poker chip and a little bit of luck. Below: The Strip, Las Vegas

The Best...
Scenic Drives

BLUE RIDGE PARKWAY
Mountainous scenery plus great hiking and wildlife-watching in the southern Appalachian Mountains. (p239)

OVERSEAS HIGHWAY
An engineering masterpiece, this highway traverses the Florida Keys, with splendid scenery along the way. (p281)

NATCHEZ TRACE PARKWAY
An incredibly lush drive between Tennessee and Mississippi, sprinkled with historic sites. (p237)

PACIFIC COAST HIGHWAY
Wild and remote beaches with clifftop views overlooking crashing waves. (p417)

Pacific Coast Highway

Stunning coastal highways (p417) wind their way down the US's West Coast, from Canada all the way to the Mexican border, offering dramatic scenery that's hard to match anywhere in the world. You'll get clifftop views over crashing waves, and pass sunlit rolling hills, fragrant eucalyptus forests and lush redwoods, wild and remote beaches, idyllic towns and fishing villages, and primeval rainforest. Amid the remote natural beauty you can mix things up with big-city adventures, dipping into Seattle, Portland, San Francisco and Los Angeles.

Washington, DC

A city of soaring monuments, wide boulevards and neoclassical architecture, Washington, DC (p95), was built to grand scale after America's independence. Besides being the political nexus of the US, it has some of the nation's finest museums (many with free admission), packed with fine art, Native American lore, spacecraft, dinosaurs and Americana. DC also offers great options for dining, drinking and exploring, in areas such as historic Georgetown and verdant Rock Creek Park.

Right: The Capitol (p112)

CHRIS CHEADLE/GETTY IMAGES ©

Nashville

Nicknamed 'Music City,' Nashville (p232) is home to a head-spinning variety of sounds – from homespun country ballads to hands-in-the-air Southern rock, wide-eyed jazz improvisations, toe-stomping bluegrass and down-and-dirty blues. You'll find all this and more amid the honky-tonks, college bars and nightclubs in town. Even restaurants host live music, so you won't have to go far to hear the local (and often international) talent. Come for the love of music, and bring an appetite: hearty Southern cooking is a Nashville specialty. Above: Tootsie's Orchid Lounge (p236)

Deep South

Steeped in history and complex regional pride, the Deep South (p203) is the US at its most fascinating, from the moss-draped Georgia swamps to the juke joints of the Mississippi Delta to the French-speaking enclaves of the Louisiana bayou. Famous for its slow pace, the Deep South is all about enjoying life's small pleasures: nibbling on Cajun crawfish at an old-school New Orleans eatery, strolling Savannah's antebellum alleys or sipping sweet tea on a Charleston porch with new friends. Left: Swamp alligators

Miami

How does one city get so lucky? Most content themselves with one or two admirable attributes, but Miami (p270) seems to have it all. Beyond the stunning beaches and Art Deco Historic District, there's culture at every turn. In smoky dance halls, Havana expats dance to Cuban music, while in fashionable nightclubs, fiery-eyed Brazilian models move to Latin beats. Old men clack dominos in the park and, to top it off, street vendors and restaurants dish out flavors from the Caribbean, Cuba, Argentina and Spain. Below: South Beach, Miami (p272)

14

The Best...
Historic Sites

BOSTON
The ghosts of the past live on in the cobblestone streets and house museums of historic Boston. (p166)

SANTA FE
Time-travel to the 1600s amid adobe buildings and scenic public squares. (p324)

WASHINGTON, DC
See where history was made in the White House, on Capitol Hill and on the National Mall. (p95)

SAVANNAH
Explore antebellum mansions, a former pirate prison and an island fort that played a pivotal role in the Civil War. (p242)

The Best...
National Parks

OLYMPIC NATIONAL PARK
A sprawling wilderness of temperate virgin rainforest and rugged coastline, with adventure activities galore. (p355)

GREAT SMOKY MOUNTAINS NATIONAL PARK
A much-loved and bio-diverse woodland in southern Appalachia. (p237)

YELLOWSTONE NATIONAL PARK
Geysers, geothermal springs, giant moose and towering peaks: prepare to be awed. (p433)

CANYONLANDS NATIONAL PARK
Go for hiking, rafting or four-wheel driving amid stunning red-rock scenery. (p322)

Yosemite National Park

The iconic glacier-carved valley in Yosemite National Park (p415) never fails to get hearts racing, even when the crowds are bumper-to-bumper in summer. In spring, get drenched by the spray of thundering snow-melt waterfalls, then twirl to your mental score of *The Sound of Music* in high-country meadows awash with wildflowers and enlivened by the occasional bear. Yosemite's scenery is intoxicating, with dizzying rock walls and formations, and ancient giant sequoia trees. It's also a place of solitude, space and nary an exhaust pipe – 1100 sq miles of utter wilderness for you to roam and explore. Above: Chipmunks in Yosemite

ABOVE: JUDY BELLAH/GETTY IMAGES © LEFT: CROW CAROL RUKLISS, PHOTOGRAPHER/GETTY IMAGES ©

Boston & Cape Cod

Start by tracing the footsteps of early Tea Partiers like Paul Revere and Sam Adams on Boston's famed Freedom Trail (p175). After following the road through American Revolutionary War history, romp around the campus of Harvard University (p174) and do a little 'rebel'-rousing yourself at one of the city's famed clubs. Then cool off by hitting the beaches of the Cape Cod National Seashore, joining a whale-watching cruise and getting lost in the wild dunes of Provincetown. Above: Humpback whale

Memphis & Graceland

In the early 1900s, Memphis (p226) became a hub for the emerging and utterly transfixing sound of what came to be known as 'the blues.' Fifty years later, it's where American rock and roll was born. Today the music lives on in the carnivalesque riot of Beale St, with rock, blues, jazz and country playing late into the night. By day, see where musical history was made at Sun Studio, and check out the extravagance of Elvis' Graceland (p229). Left: Sun Studio (p228)

Coastal Maine

Marked by fingerlike peninsulas and picturesque inlets, the rugged Maine coast offers ample rewards. The charming harbor city of Portland (p196) is home to decadent seafood restaurants, colorful nightlife and plentiful opportunities to get out on the water. Drive north, stopping at seaside villages and feast-worthy lobster shacks en route to photogenic Boothbay Harbor, before heading to Acadia National Park, a magnificent reserve with coastal mountains and craggy shores that are paradise for hikers and kayakers. Below: Acadia National Park (p198)

The Best...
Beaches

MALIBU
Great surf and lovely scenery abound in this iconic SoCal spot. (p382)

SOUTH BEACH
Famous the world over, Miami's South Beach has pretty sands adorned with beautiful bodies. (p272)

CAPE COD NATIONAL SEASHORE
Massive sand dunes, picturesque lighthouses and cool forests invite endless exploring. (p179)

SAN DIEGO
Coronado for white sand, Pacific and Mission Beaches for people-watching and fish tacos. (p391)

The Best...
Architecture

NEW YORK CITY
There's as much happening overhead as there is on the streets, from the spiraling Guggenheim (p92) to the majestic Brooklyn Bridge (p65).

CHICAGO
Birthplace of the skyscraper and home of the nation's tallest buildings. (p127)

MIAMI
Miami's Art Deco Historic District is a Technicolor dream come true, with the world's largest collection of deco buildings. (p270)

LOS ANGELES
Frank Gehry's Walt Disney Concert Hall (p377) and the hilltop Getty Center (p382) are scene-stealers.

Everglades National Park

19

Not quite the fetid swamp full of people-eating alligators you might have heard about, the Everglades (p279) is actually a rich ecosystem of eight distinct habitats – including cypress groves, coastal prairies and mangrove systems – with a great variety of wildlife, from bottlenose dolphins to bald eagles. The best viewing is during the dry season (December to April). You can visit on foot or by kayak, bicycle or guided boat tour, and it makes an easy add-on to a trip to Miami or the Keys. Right: Shark Valley (p280), the Everglades

WITOLD SKRYPCZAK/GETTY IMAGES ©

EMILY RIDELL/GETTY IMAGES ©

20 Native American Sites

The Southwest (p291) is Native American country, with a fantastic array of sites covering both the distant past and the present. In New Mexico, you can visit the ancient clifftop homes of the Puebloan peoples who lived among this dramatic and rocky landscape before mysteriously abandoning it. For living cultures, pay a visit to the Navajo Nation, where you can hire a guide and trek to the bottom of the sacred Canyon de Chelly, stay overnight on reservation land and buy handicrafts directly from Native American artisans. Left: Cliff dwellings at Mesa Verde National Park (p320)

Zion & Southern Utah National Parks

With red-rock canyons, sculpturelike rock formations and towering massifs, Southern Utah has some of the most memorable scenery in the Southwest. Zion National Park (p321) is home to 85% of Utah's flora and fauna, though it's better known for towering canyon walls and dramatic hikes through gallery-like tunnels and up to majestic heights. Bryce Canyon National Park (p319), with its strange, spirelike rock formations, is mesmerizing beneath the amber glow of sunset. There are other great geological wonders inside the aptly named Arches and Canyonlands National Parks. Below: Zion National Park

21

JEREMY WOODHOUSE/GETTY IMAGES ©

22 Disneyland

No matter your age, it's hard not to be swept away by Disneyland (p389). Stroll through Main Street, an idyllic turn-of-the-century town with barbershop quartets and penny arcades, then mingle with princesses beneath Sleeping Beauty Castle or hurtle through darkness at frightening speeds on Space Mountain. There's an Old West theme town, adventure-style outings à la Indiana Jones, nightly fireworks in summer, and pirates aplenty.

Santa Fe

For a glimpse back in time in this 400-year-old city, start at the central plaza (a former bullfighting ring), fronted by the striking 17th-century Palace of the Governors (p325) and a slew of history museums. Santa Fe unfolds in captivating variety: galleries, art museums – including the Georgia O'Keeffe Museum (p324) – Spanish Colonial churches, shops selling Native American crafts and jewelry, plus cafes, bars and restaurants, some tucked inside historic adobe buildings. Below: New Mexico Museum of Art (p325)

ALAN COPSON/GETTY IMAGES ©

The Best...
Foodie Cities

NEW YORK CITY
Whether you crave steak frites, sushi or gourmet hot dogs, globe-trotting Gotham has you covered. (p82)

CHICAGO
Great Greek, Thai and molecular gastronomy, famous deep-dish pizzas and much more. (p147)

SAN FRANCISCO
Real-deal taquerias and trattorias, sprawling farmers markets and critically acclaimed California cooking. (p407)

NEW ORLEANS
Down-home cooking served just right, with jambalaya, beignets, gumbo and Cajun crawfish. (p220)

The Best...
Live Music

CHICAGO
World-class blues and jazz players (p151), plus huge events like the Chicago Blues Fest. (p43)

NEW ORLEANS
The Big Easy has a sound-track as intoxicating as the city itself – room-filling big-band jazz, funk, blues, zydeco and indie rock. (p222)

NASHVILLE
You'll find country crooning, heart-pounding rock and jazz, bluegrass and blues on the bright stages of Nashville. (p236)

AUSTIN
Texas' favorite little city hosts one of the world's biggest music fests, though no matter when you visit, you'll find dizzying live-music choices. (p436)

Seattle

Seattle (p342) is a cutting-edge Pacific Rim city with an uncanny habit of turning locally hatched ideas into global brands. It's earned its place in the pantheon of US metropolises, with a world-renowned music scene, a mercurial coffee culture and a penchant for internet-driven innovation. But while Seattle's trendsetters rush to unearth the next big thing, city traditionalists guard its soul with distinct urban neighborhoods, a home-grown food culture and what is arguably the nation's finest public market at Pike Place. Right: Space Needle (p347), Seattle Center

LAWRENCE WORCESTER/GETTY IMAGES ©

RENE FREDERICK/GETTY IMAGES ©

25 Mount Rainier National Park

Visible from Seattle and unobstructed by other peaks, Mt Rainier's (p353) overwhelming presence has long enraptured the inhabitants who live in its shadow. Encased in a 368-sq-mile national park, the mountain's forested foothills harbor numerous hiking trails and swaths of flower-carpeted meadows. When the clouds magically disappear during long, clear days in July and August, it becomes one of Washington's most paradisiacal playgrounds. Native Americans called it Tahoma, or 'Mother of Waters,' while Seattleites refer to it reverently as 'the Mountain.'

USA's Top Itineraries

NYC to Washington, DC Urban Exploring

5 DAYS

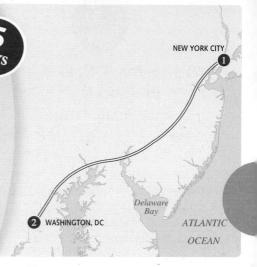

Short visit? Focus on two of the US's most fascinating cities, NYC and Washington, DC, for their world-class museums, iconic buildings and top-notch food and entertainment options.

① New York City (p51)

The great dynamo of art, fashion and culture, New York City is America at its most urbane. Spend three days exploring the metropolis, visiting memorable people-watching 'hoods such as Chinatown, the West and East Villages, the Lower East Side, SoHo, Nolita and the Upper West Side, then museum-hop down the Upper East Side. Have a ramble in Central Park, stroll the High Line and take a detour across the Brooklyn Bridge (go early in the morning to beat the heavy crowds). Prioritize iconic sights, including the Statue of Liberty, Ellis Island and the Metropolitan Museum. Catch a Broadway show or a concert at legendary venues like Carnegie Hall or Lincoln Center. Set aside at least one evening for a big night, taking in Downtown's nightlife. And take a culinary journey around the world: bagels and lox at a Jewish deli, cutting-edge Japanese noodle bars, elegant European bistros on the Upper East Side and sizzling barbecue in Koreatown.

NEW YORK CITY ◯ WASHINGTON, DC

🚆 **Three to four hours** On Amtrak from NYC's Penn Station to Washington's Union Station.

🚌 **Four hours** Numerous inexpensive operators include BoltBus, Megabus and Greyhound.

② Washington, DC (p95)

Take a train or a bus down to Washington, DC, for a look at the nation's capital. With two days here, you can take in the city highlights. Spend a day on the National Mall, taking in major sights like the Washington Monument, the Lincoln Memorial and the Vietnam Veterans Memorial. Visit a few nearby Smithsonian museums, and end the day with dinner and drinks at Dupont Circle. On the next day, head to Georgetown for shopping, cafe-hopping and strolling along atmospheric tree-lined streets. Catch a show at the Kennedy Center, then explore the nightlife on the U Street Corridor. If you have extra time, hop across the Potomac River (via metro) to Virginia for a look at Arlington Cemetery, then take a stroll through old-world Alexandria, and explore George Washington's well-preserved estate at Mount Vernon.

The High Line (p73), New York
GRAHAM CROUCH/GETTY IMAGES ©

Washington, DC, to Provincetown
East Coasting

This exploration along the East Coast takes in three cities with distinct personalities – politically charged Washington, DC, cosmopolitan New York City and historic and heady Boston. Cap it off with a jaunt out to Provincetown for a look at Cape Cod's lovely seaside.

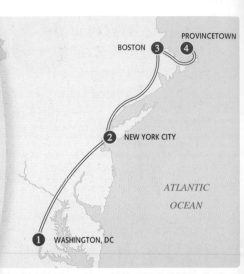

PROVINCETOWN

BOSTON ③ ④

② NEW YORK CITY

ATLANTIC OCEAN

① WASHINGTON, DC

❶ Washington, DC (p95)

Spend the day taking in the grandeur of the Mall. Admire the classical architecture of the Capitol, then head to the nearby National Gallery of Art for a look at the staggering modern-art collection. Afterwards, have lunch at the restaurant inside the National Museum of the American Indian. Visit the rest of the Mall, strolling past the Washington Monument and the somber Vietnam Veterans Memorial, before ending at the Lincoln Memorial. Come evening, have dinner and drinks in one of the lively spots off Dupont Circle.

WASHINGTON, DC ❍ NEW YORK CITY

🚃 **Three to four hours** On Amtrak from Washington's Union Station to NYC's Penn Station. 🚌 **Four hours** By BoltBus, Megabus or Greyhound.

❷ New York City (p51)

After arriving from DC, promenade in lovely Central Park, browse the galleries of the vast Metropolitan Museum, and end the day with ethnic eats and bar-hopping in the East Village. On day two, catch an early-morning subway down to Lower Manhattan for a memorable walk across the Brooklyn Bridge. Afterwards, wander through Chinatown, then go up to SoHo for lunch and more window shopping. In the evening, dine at a cozy, candlelit spot in the West Village, followed by live jazz at the Village Vanguard.

NEW YORK CITY ❍ BOSTON

🚃 **Four hours** On Amtrak from NYC's Penn Station to Boston's South Station. 🚌 **Four hours** By BoltBus, Megabus or Greyhound.

❸ Boston (p166)

Start the day on Boston Common and set off on the brick-lined Freedom Trail, wandering past historic homes and fabled meeting houses. Have lunch at the venerable Union Oyster House and, later, watch the sunset over the city from atop the Prudential Center Skywalk. In the evening feast on old-world cuisine at a charming local haunt in the North End, Boston's 'Little Italy.' End the night at the Warren Tavern, one of the city's most atmospheric old pubs.

BOSTON ❍ PROVINCETOWN

⚓ **One-and-a-half hours** Bay State Cruise Company sails from Boston's World Trade Center Pier. 🚌 **Three-and-a-half hours** Plymouth and Brockton buses connect Boston and Provincetown.

❹ Provincetown (p184)

Hire a bike and ride through forest and along dunes on the Cape Cod National Seashore bike trail. After the ride, refuel on juicy crustaceans at the Lobster Pot. Take a quick stroll through town then head out to Race Point Beach, dramatically set at the northern tip of the Cape. For dinner, feast on yet more seafood, then grab a cocktail at buzzing Patio and watch the night unfold.

Union Oyster House (p176), Boston
MARTIN KREUZER/GETTY IMAGES ©

10 DAYS

New Orleans to Miami
Southern Explorer

Cajun cooking, Southern hospitality and sparkling beaches all play starring roles in this ramble through New Orleans, Nashville, Savannah, Orlando and Miami. You'll also find otherworldly theme parks, antebellum architecture and decadent down-home fare.

NASHVILLE
2

3 SAVANNAH

ATLANTIC OCEAN

1
NEW ORLEANS

4 ORLANDO

Gulf of Mexico

5
MIAMI

❶ New Orleans (p212)

Spend your first day in the Big Easy exploring the French Quarter, taking in Jackson Sq, the scenic riverfront and the history-packed Louisiana State Museum. At night, hear live jazz at a club on French-man St. The next day learn about New Orleans' deep African American roots in the Tremé, then go gallery-hopping in the Warehouse District and have a Cajun feast at Cochon or Coop's.

NEW ORLEANS ◗ NASHVILLE

🚗 **Nine hours** Along 8-59 and 8-65.

❷ Nashville (p232)

It's all about the music when you come to Nashville. Spend two nights drinking up the scene, hitting at least one boot-stompin' honky-tonk and a smokin' blues club. By day, learn more about Nashville's soul at the Country Music Hall of Fame and spend time exploring the District. Make at least one meal Nashville's famous Southern fried chicken.

NASHVILLE ◗ SAVANNAH

🚗 **Eight hours** Along 8-24, 8-75 and 8-16.

❸ Savannah (p242)

After long, music-filled nights in Nashville, recharge in picture-perfect Savannah. Base yourself in one of the city's heritage B&Bs and spend two days taking in the historic district, visiting antebellum man-sions, strolling the riverfront and indulging in rich low-country cooking.

SAVANNAH ◗ ORLANDO

🚗 **Five hours** Along 8-95.

❹ Orlando (p262)

Following the Savannah recharge, it's time for a bit of Walt Disney World–style adventure. With just two days, you'll have to make some tough choices. The safe bet: spend day one in the Magic Kingdom, seeing Cinderella's Castle, Pirates of the Caribbean and nightly fireworks. On day two go on safari at Animal Kingdom and see a show in the Tree of Life. Epcot, with its world showcase of global fare and cul-tural attractions, is another top option.

ORLANDO ◗ MIAMI

🚗 **Four hours** Along Florida's Turnpike (a toll road).

❺ Miami (p270)

End your Southern journey with two days in body-beautiful Miami. Spend time strolling the Technicolor backdrop of the Art Deco Historic District, delving into the contemporary art scene in Wynwood and connecting with Miami's Latin roots in Lit-tle Havana. Set aside plenty of downtime for playing in the waves, and for long walks on Miami Beach, and plan at least one night out in South Beach.

Ocean Drive, Miami Beach (p272)
WITOLD SKRYPCZAK/GETTY IMAGES ©

10 DAYS

Las Vegas to Seattle
Sin City & the Left Coast

The West Coast has an array of mesmerizing attractions: picturesque beaches, verdant scenery and beautifully sited cities with some of the USA's best dining and nightlife. This itinerary starts in Vegas and heads west to five must-see coastal destinations.

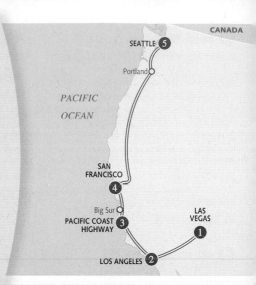

CANADA

SEATTLE **5**

Portland

PACIFIC OCEAN

SAN FRANCISCO **4**

Big Sur
PACIFIC COAST HIGHWAY **3**

LOS ANGELES **2**

LAS VEGAS **1**

❶ Las Vegas (p312)

Spend two days in Sin City, aka Las Vegas, checking out the surreal and over-the-top design of this casino kingdom, where you can travel from ancient Rome to the South Pacific without leaving the Strip. By day bask by lovely pools and visit curiosities like the Atomic Testing Museum. By night, dine at celebrated restaurants such as Sage, see top-notch shows and take in the city's riotous nightlife.

LAS VEGAS ➲ LOS ANGELES

🚗 **Four-and-a-half hours** Along 8-15.

✈ **One hour** Frequent flights.

❷ Los Angeles (p376)

After Las Vegas, spend three days in Los Angeles. Take in the beachside neighborhoods of tony Santa Monica and eccentric Venice. Spend a day wandering around Hollywood and ever-evolving Downtown. Eat your way around the globe in Little Tokyo and other ethnic enclaves. Snap the Hollywood sign from the Griffith Observatory and celebrity-spot, or play in the waves off Malibu.

LOS ANGELES ➲ BIG SUR

🚗 **Five-and-a-half hours** Along Hwy 101 and CA 1.

❸ Pacific Coast Highway (p417)

Although you could fly up to San Francisco in an hour, instead hire a car and take a breathtakingly scenic drive along the Pacific Coast Highway. The long and winding road traverses cliffs with the crashing sea to your left and rolling green hills to your right. Stop at Big Sur to admire the rugged, untrammeled beauty of this coast-line, and pull over again at the Monterey Aquarium for a look at what lies offshore.

BIG SUR ➲ SAN FRANCISCO

🚗 **Three hours** Along CA 1.

❹ San Francisco (p397)

Leave plenty of time for San Francisco. This hilly city has great museums (like the head-turning MH de Young Fine Arts Museum), evocative sites (including the former prison island of Alcatraz) and stunning scenery (from beaches to hilltops and bayside parks). Victorian-lined neighborhoods packed with treasures – of the shopping, eating and drinking variety – are just waiting to be unearthed. San Francisco also makes a fine base for memorable day trips: walking among the towering redwoods at Muir Woods, vineyard-hopping in Napa Valley and gazing at the panorama from the Marin Headlands.

SAN FRANCISCO ➲ SEATTLE

🚗 **14 hours** Along 8-5.

❺ Seattle (p342)

After San Francisco, head up through Portland to Seattle, the gateway to the lush Pacific Northwest. Spend two days here, shopping at Pike Place Market, stepping back in time at Pioneer Sq, and moving into the future via the Space Needle, the monorail and the rock-and-roll sounds of the EMP Museum at the Seattle Center. Don't miss the cafe culture, microbreweries and locavore dining (the seafood is tops).

Alamo Square Park (p402), San Francisco
THOMAS WINZ/GETTY IMAGES ©

Chicago to LA
The Great American Road Trip

Fill the tank, roll down the windows and crank the radio as you drive toward the Southwest's sunbaked landscapes and all the way to California. Beneath great open skies, you'll pass red-rock deserts, Spanish-colonial towns and one awe-inspiring canyon.

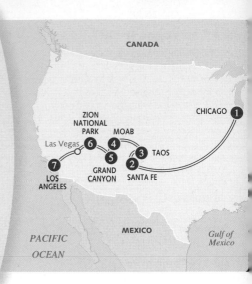

① Chicago (p127)

Start in broad-shouldered Chicago; its sky-scrapers and big-city culture will provide a dramatic contrast to the wild landscapes of the Southwest. Visit the venerable Art Institute of Chicago, eat deep-dish pizza, take an architectural walking tour, stroll through the sculptural wonderland of Millennium Park, visit the ocean-like lakefront and hit a few of Chicago's legendary blues clubs.

CHICAGO ➡ SANTA FE
🚗 **22 hours** Along 8-55, 8-44 and 8-40. ✈ **Three hours** Nonstop to nearby Albuquerque.

② Santa Fe (p324)

The gateway to the Southwest, Santa Fe is an arts-loving city set against the photogenic backdrop of the Sangre de Cristo Mountains. Centuries-old adobe neighborhoods, relic-filled museums and art galleries provide a fine introduction to this culturally rich region. Don't miss tasty Spanish-influenced Southwestern fare, sunset drinks from one of Santa Fe's enticing watering holes and live-music jams at Evangelo's.

SANTA FE ➡ TAOS
🚗 **One-and-a-half hours** Along Hwy 68.

③ Taos (p329)

A short but scenic drive from Santa Fe, Taos boasts a magnificent mountain setting that has long attracted artists, writers and assorted arts-minded bohemians eager to bask in the scenery. You can spend your time browsing art museums or hiking the great outdoors, or checking out the creative restaurants and ecofriendly lodgings. Nearby sights worth a day trip include the ancient clifftop dwellings of Bandelier, and Georgia O'Keeffe's adobe house in Abiquiu.

TAOS ➡ MOAB
🚗 **Seven hours** Along Hwys 64, 160, 184 and 191.

④ Moab (p319)

The drive to Moab is long, but the stunning scenery more than makes up for it. Once there, you can unwind with a microbrew and a first-rate meal, and make plans for the activities ahead: hiking, biking, rafting and horseback riding. Moab is an adventure-

lover's mecca, and well positioned near the spectacular scenery of Arches National Park and Canyonlands National Park.

MOAB ◯ GRAND CANYON, NORTH RIM
🚗 **Seven-and-a-half hours** Along Hwys 191, 8-70, 89 and 67.

⑤ Grand Canyon (p300)

The jewel of the Southwest is the Grand Canyon; its age and vast size simply boggle the imagination. Plan ahead so that you can stay in the lodge at the North Rim. Go for hikes and revel in the experience of standing atop one of Earth's great wonders. The road to the North Rim is often closed in winter so check before you go.

GRAND CANYON ◯ ZION NATIONAL PARK
🚗 **Three hours** Along Hwys 67 and 89.

⑥ Zion National Park (p321)

Although few places can compare with the sheer immensity of the Grand Canyon, Zion National Park will also leave you breathless – particularly if you ascend to the eagles'-nest perch at the end of the Angels Landing Trail. Ideally you should book well in advance at the onsite Zion Lodge, set in the middle of Zion Canyon. There are also decent places to stay in nearby Springdale.

ZION NATIONAL PARK ◯ LOS ANGELES
🚗 **Seven hours** Along 8-15. Detour via Las Vegas.

⑦ Los Angeles (p376)

When you can see the Pacific, your epic road trip has come to an end. Dust off and recharge in palm tree–lined Los Angeles. After days in the wilderness get a dose of culture – high and low – at the Los Angeles County Museum of Art, the Paley Center for Media and the Grammy Museum. Treat yourself to dinner and drinks at a hot spot in West Hollywood, go beachcombing at Santa Monica and tour a few film studios.

Mountain-biking on Porcupine Rim (p467), Moab
ILAN SHACHAM/GETTY IMAGES ©

USA Month by Month

Top Events

⭐ **Mardi Gras**, February or March

⭐ **South by Southwest**, March

⭐ **National Cherry Blossom Festival**, March

⭐ **Chicago Blues Festival**, June

⭐ **Independence Day**, July

 **January**

⭐ **Chinese New Year**

In late January or early February, you'll find colorful celebrations and feasting anywhere there's a Chinatown. NYC throws a festive parade, though San Francisco's is the best, with floats, firecrackers, bands and plenty of merriment.

February

Aside from mountain getaways, many Americans dread February with its long dark nights and frozen days. For foreign visitors, this can be the cheapest time to travel, with ultradiscount rates for flights and hotels.

⭐ **Mardi Gras**

Held in late February or early March, on the day before Ash Wednesday, Mardi Gras (Fat Tuesday) is the finale of Carnival. New Orleans' celebrations (www.mardigras neworleans.com) are legendary as colorful parades, masquerade balls, feasting and plenty of hedonism rule the day.

March

⭐ **National Cherry Blossom Festival**

The brilliant blooms of Japanese cherry blossoms around DC's Tidal Basin are celebrated with concerts, parades, taiko drumming, kite-flying and 90 other events during the five-week fest (www.nationalcherry blossomfestival.org). More than one million go each year, so don't forget to book ahead.

⭐ **South by Southwest**

Each year Austin, TX, becomes ground zero for one of the biggest

(Left) June Gay Pride parade, San Francisco
RICK GERHARTER/GETTY IMAGES ©

music fests in North America. More than 2000 performers play at nearly 100 venues. SXSW (sxsw.com) is also a major film festival and interactive fest – a platform for groundbreaking ideas.

 # April

Jazz Fest

On the last weekend in April, New Orleans hosts the country's best jazz jam (www.nojazzfest.com), with top-notch acts (local resident Harry Connick Jr often headlines) and plenty of good cheer. In addition to world-class jazz, there's also great food and crafts.

Patriots' Day

Massachusetts' big day out falls on the third Monday in April and features Revolutionary War re-enactments and parades in Lexington and Concord, plus the running of the Boston Marathon and a much-watched Red Sox game at home.

 # May

May is true spring and one of the loveliest times to travel, with blooming wildflowers and generally mild sunny weather. Summer crowds and high prices have yet to arrive.

Beale Street Music Festival

Blues lovers descend on Memphis for this venerable music fest (www.memphisinmay.org) held over three days in early May.

Cinco de Mayo

Celebrate Mexico's victory over the French with salsa music and pitchers of margaritas across the country. LA, San Francisco and Denver all throw some of the biggest bashes.

 # June

Summer is here. Americans spend more time at outdoor cafes and restaurants, and head to the shore or to national parks. School is out; vacationers fill the highways and resorts, bringing higher prices.

Gay Pride

In some cities gay-pride celebrations last a week, but in San Francisco it's a month-long party, where the last weekend in June sees giant parades. You'll find other great pride events at major cities across the country.

Chicago Blues Festival

It's the globe's biggest free blues fest (www.chicagobluesfestival.us), with three days of the music that made Chicago famous. More than 640,000 people unfurl blankets by the multiple stages that take over Grant Park in early June.

Mermaid Parade

In Brooklyn, NYC, Coney Island celebrates summer's steamy arrival with a kitsch-loving parade (www.coneyisland.com), complete with skimpily attired mermaids and horn-blowing mermen.

CMA Music Festival

This legendary country-music fest (www.cmaworld.com) is one of Nashville's biggest celebrations. It features more than 400 artists performing at stages on Riverfront Park and LP Field.

 # July

Independence Day

The nation celebrates its birthday on July 4 with a bang, as nearly every town and city stages a massive fireworks show. Quick to the draw, Chicago goes off on the 3rd. Washington, DC, New York, Philadelphia and Boston are all great spots.

Oregon Brewers Festival

The beer-loving city of Portland pulls out the stops and pours a heady array of handcrafted perfection (www.oregon brewfest.com), featuring 80 different beers from around the country. There are plenty of choices, and it's nicely set along the banks of the Willamette River.

August

Expect blasting heat, with temperatures and humidity less bearable the further south you go. You'll find people-packed beaches, high prices and empty cities on weekends, when residents escape to the nearest waterfront.

Lollapalooza

This mondo rock fest (www.lollapalooza. com) sees more than 100 bands spilling off eight stages in Grant Park on the first Friday-to-Sunday in August.

September

Santa Fe Fiesta

Santa Fe hosts the nation's longest-running festival (www.santafefiesta. org), a spirited two-week-long event with parades, concerts and the burning of Old Man Gloom.

Burning Man Festival

Over one week, some 50,000 revelers, artists and assorted free spirits descend on Nevada's Black Rock Desert to create a temporary metropolis of art installations, theme camps and environmental curiosities. It culminates in the burning of a giant stick figure (www.burningman.com).

New York Film Festival

Just one of many big film fests (www.film-linc.com) in NYC – Tribeca Film Fest in late April is another goodie. This one features world premieres from across the globe.

October

Temperatures are falling, as autumn brings fiery colors to northern climes. It's high season where the leaves are most brilliant (New England); elsewhere expect lower prices and fewer crowds.

Fantasy Fest

Key West's answer to Mardi Gras brings more than 100,000 revelers to the subtropical enclave in the week leading up to Halloween. Expect to see parades, colorful floats, costume parties, the selecting of a conch king and queen and plenty of alcohol-fueled merriment (www. fantasyfest.net).

Halloween

In NYC, you can don a costume and join the Halloween

parade up Sixth Ave. West Hollywood in Los Angeles and San Francisco's Castro district are great places to see outrageous outfits. Salem also hosts spirited events throughout October.

November

 Thanksgiving

On the fourth Thursday of November, Americans gather with family and friends over day-long feasts – roast turkey, sweet potatoes, cranberry sauce, wine, pumpkin pie and loads of other dishes. New York City hosts a huge parade, and there's pro football on TV.

December

Winter arrives as ski season kicks off in the Rockies (out east conditions aren't usually ideal until January). Aside from winter sports,

December means heading inside and curling up by the fire.

 Art Basel

This massive arts fest (www.artbasel miamibeach.com) is four days of cutting-edge art, film, architecture and design. More than 250 major galleries from across the globe come to the event, with works by some 2000 artists; plus much hobnobbing with a glitterati crowd in Miami Beach.

 New Year's Eve

Americans are of two minds when it comes to ringing in the New Year. Some join festive crowds to celebrate; others plot a getaway to escape the mayhem. Whichever you choose, plan well in advance. Expect high prices (especially in NYC).

(Far left) May Traditional Mexican dancing at a Cinco de Mayo celebration, Los Angeles **(Left) September** Burning Man Festival, Nevada

(FAR LEFT) LONELY PLANET/GETTY IMAGES ©;
(LEFT) MITCHELL AIDELBAUM/ GETTY IMAGES ©

What's New

For this new edition of Discover USA, we've hunted down the fresh, the transformed, the hot and the happening. Here are a few of our favorites. For up-to-the-minute recommendations, see lonelyplanet.com/usa

1 REINVENTING NYC
As always, the Big Apple is on the cusp of reinvention. The ongoing High Line (now in stage three), plus waterfront parks on Manhattan's west side and in Brooklyn, continue to make the city more appealing than ever. Brooklyn has a new pro basketball team (the Nets) plus a high-tech new arena (Barclays Center) where they play. Hockey lovers will see the Islanders hold court there in 2015. (p73)

2 BIKE-LOVING CITIES
The bicycle is fast becoming the urbanite's best friend. New York City, Chicago, Boston, Denver, Miami and Washington, DC, all have bike-sharing programs, making it easy to grab a bike and go.

3 CHIHULY GARDEN & GLASS
This new museum in the Seattle Center displays the spectacular work of Dale Chihuly, a master of blown-glass art. You'll never again look at glasswork the same way. (p343)

4 SEATTLE'S GREAT WHEEL
Ferris wheels now grace the skylines of many cities, and Seattle has jumped on the bandwagon. Its lofty Great Wheel (www.seattlegreatwheel.com; 1301 Alaskan Way; adult/child $13/8.50; ☺11am-10pm Mon-Thu, to midnight Fri & Sat, 10am-10pm Sun; ☒University St) is designed to lure visitors to Seattle's waterfront.

5 MOB MUSEUM
This stellar Vegas attraction delves deep into the lore of organized crime. Learn how money is laundered, listen in on a wiretap and get your mug shot taken. (p313)

6 SAN FRANCISCO EXPLORATORIUM
California's best-loved science museum has reopened in a splashy waterfront space at Pier 15, with indoor and outdoor galleries packed with award-winning interactive exhibits. (p401)

7 MUSICAL INSTRUMENT MUSEUM
Valhalla for music lovers, this new Phoenix site showcases sounds from more than 200 countries. Music and video performances automatically start as you stop beside individual displays. (p309)

8 BOSTON'S SEAPORT DISTRICT
Formerly fish piers and warehouses, this brand-new district has loads of new restaurants, many with harbor views. It's also home to the new Boston Tea Party Ships & Museum. (p167)

9 NATIONAL MUSEUM OF AFRICAN AMERICAN HISTORY AND CULTURE
Washington, DC's latest work in progress is a $500-million museum that explores the richness of the African American experience. It is scheduled to open in 2015. (p109)

Get Inspired

 ## Books

o **Motherless Brooklyn** (Jonathan Lethem, 1999) Darkly humorous novel with a cast of wild characters.

o **The Amazing Adventures of Kavalier & Clay** (Michael Chabon, 2000) Pulitzer Prize–winning novel of art, adventures, escapism and comic books.

o **Song of Solomon** (Toni Morrison, 1977) Powerful coming-of-age story full of magic and folklore by one of America's finest novelists (and a Nobel Prize winner).

o **On the Road** (Jack Kerouac, 1957) A Beat Generation classic of post-WWII America.

 ## Films

o **The Hangover** (Todd Phillips, 2009) Hilarious tale of things gone horribly wrong at a bachelor party in Vegas.

o **Annie Hall** (Woody Allen, 1977) Funny and poignant tale of love and loss – one of Allen's best.

o **Philadelphia Story** (George Cukor, 1940) Romantic comedy starring Cary Grant and Katherine Hepburn.

o **Easy Rider** (Dennis Hopper, 1969) Bikers on a journey through a nation in turmoil.

 ## Music

o **Mothership Connection** (Parliament, 1975) One of the finest funk albums of all time.

o **Kind of Blue** (Miles Davis, 1959) Beautifully conceived jazz album.

o **Highway 61 Revisited** (Bob Dylan, 1965) The finest of road music by a folk-singing legend.

o **What's Going On** (Marvin Gaye, 1971) Groundbreaking work by one of Motown's native sons.

o **Off the Wall** (Michael Jackson, 1979) MJ's grooviest album still rocks after all these years.

o **Nevermind** (Nirvana, 1991) Launched the grunge movement.

Websites

o **Discover America** (www.discoveramerica .com) Official USA tourism site with loads of trip ideas.

o **Festivals.com** (www. festivals.com) America's best celebrations.

o **New York Times Travel** (http://travel.nytimes. com) Travel news, advice and features.

Short on time?

This list will give you an instant insight into the country.

Read *State by State: a Panoramic Portrait of America* (2008) A collection of 50 essays about the 50 states, many by well-known literary personalities.

Watch *Forrest Gump* (Robert Zemeckis, 1994) Feel-good Oscar-winning film spanning major events of the late 20th century.

Listen *Best of John Lee Hooker* (1962) First-rate blues by an all-time great.

Log on www.away.com has boundless ideas for outdoor and urban adventure travel.

Monument Valley Navajo Tribal Park (p323)
RUTH EASTHAM & MAX PAOLI/GETTY IMAGES ©

Need to Know

Currency
US dollar ($)

Language
English

Visas
Many visitors don't need visas for less than 90-day stays; others do. See http://travel.state.gov for details.

Money
ATMs widely available. Credit cards accepted at most hotels, restaurants and shops.

Cell Phones
Foreign phones that operate on tri- or quad-band frequencies will work in the USA. Or purchase an inexpensive local cell phone with a pay-as-you-go plan.

Wi-Fi
Common in most hotels and cafes and some public squares.

Internet Access
Internet cafes are rare; get online at public libraries and copy centers (like FedEx Offices).

Tipping
Tip restaurant servers 15% to 20%, bartenders 10% to 15% per round (minimum per drink $1) and taxi drivers 10% to 15%.

When to Go

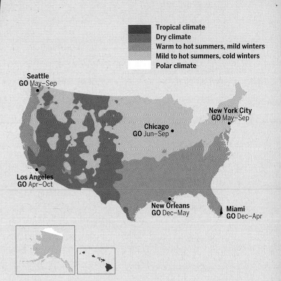

Tropical climate
Dry climate
Warm to hot summers, mild winters
Mild to hot summers, cold winters
Polar climate

Seattle
GO May–Sep

New York City
GO May–Sep

Chicago
GO Jun–Sep

Los Angeles
GO Apr–Oct

New Orleans
GO Dec–May

Miami
GO Dec–Apr

High Season (Jun–Aug)
• Warm to hot days across the country.

• Busiest season, with big crowds and higher prices especially at beach towns and resorts.

• In ski-resort areas, January to March is high season.

Shoulder Season (Oct, Apr & May)
• Milder temps, fewer crowds.

• Spring flowers (April); fiery autumn colors (October) in many parts, especially New England.

Low Season (Nov–Mar)
• Wintery days, with snowfall in the north, and heavier rains in some regions.

• Lowest prices for accommodation (aside from ski resorts and warmer getaway destinations).

Advance Planning

• **Six months before** Reserve accommodation at mega-popular sites like the Grand Canyon and Walt Disney World.

• **Three months before** Reserve internal flights and trains.

• **One month before** Book tickets to must-see Broadway shows and big-name concerts. Reserve at ultra-popular restaurants like Chez Panisse.

• **One week before** Peruse entertainment listings and eating and nightlife reviews. Book walking and outdoor-adventure tours.

Daily Costs

Budget Less than $100

o Dorm beds: $20 to $30; campgrounds: $15 to $30; budget motels: $60

o Local buses, subways and other mass transit: $2 to $3

o Lunch from a cafe or food truck: $5 to $8

Midrange $150–250

o Double room in midrange hotel: $100 to $200

o Dinner at a popular restaurant: $60 to $100 for two

o Car hire: from $30 per day

Top End More than $250

o Lodging in a resort: from $250

o Top restaurants: $60 to $100 per person

o Big nights out (plays, concerts, nightclubs): $60 to $200

Exchange Rates

Australia	A$1	$0.91
Canada	C$1	$0.95
Europe	€1	$1.35
Japan	¥100	$0.99
New Zealand	NZ$1	$0.82
UK	UK£1	$1.62

For current exchange rates see www.xe.com

What to Bring

o **Drivers license** Your home license should be sufficient.

o **Dress clothes** Essential if you go to a top restaurant or have a big night out.

o **A half-empty suitcase** Room for the clothes, jewelry, music, books and other temptations you purchase.

o **Raincoat** Keep it handy for unexpected thunderstorms on the East Coast and the more expected drizzle in the northwest.

o **Binoculars** A must-have for spotting wildlife in national parks.

o **Travel insurance** Check the policy for coverage of adventure sports (skiing, diving, climbing), luggage loss and healthcare.

Arriving in the USA

o **JFK, New York** From JFK take the AirTrain to Jamaica Station and then LIRR to Penn Station, which costs $12 to $15 (45 minutes). A taxi to Manhattan costs $52, plus toll and tip (45 to 90 minutes).

o **Los Angeles International (LAX)** LAX Flyaway Bus to Union Station costs $7 (30 to 50 minutes); door-to-door Prime Time & Supershuttle costs $16 to $28 (35 to 90 minutes). A taxi to Downtown costs $47, to Santa Monica it's about $35.

o **Miami International** SuperShuttle to South Beach is $21 (50 to 90 minutes); taxi to Miami Beach is $34 (40 to 60 minutes); or take the Metrorail to Downtown (Government Center) for $2 (15 minutes).

Getting Around

o **Train** Decent network (on Amtrak) along the East Coast (Miami up to Boston) and West Coast (San Diego to Seattle) and a few spots in between (New Orleans, Chicago).

o **Bus** Private companies cover the whole country. Cheaper and usually faster than trains.

Sleeping

o **National parks** Old-fashioned lodges and rustic inns with simple rooms that often boast fantastic views. Reserving well ahead is essential.

o **B&Bs** Character-filled guesthouses, some set in historic buildings.

o **Hotels** Everything from luxury boutique hotels to soulless (but cheap!) chain hotels along the Interstate.

Be Forewarned

o **Summertime** Big crowds and busy highways wherever you go from June through August.

o **Heat** Can be relentless in the summer. Plan indoor activities (film-going, museums, shopping) for a break from the sun.

o **Crime** Keep your wits about you and avoid deserted urban areas.

New York City

Loud, fast and pulsing with energy, New York City is symphonic, exhausting and always evolving. Coming here is like stepping into a movie, one that contains all imagined possibilities. From the southern reaches of Manhattan to the outer rim of Queens, New York City is a vertiginous mix of beauty and grit, with people from every corner of the globe mixing on the teeming streets. One of the city's greatest attributes is its astounding diversity, which manifests in great ethnic restaurants, music-filled clubs and colorful storefronts.

The New York City experience is about so many things: wandering the people-packed streets of Chinatown, fine dining in the West Village, gallery-hopping in Chelsea, catching an award-winning show off Broadway or sipping cocktails on the Lower East Side. This is just the beginning, and there really is no end.

Interior skylight of the Guggenheim Museum (p92)

51

Central Park (p76)
LISA-BLUE/GETTY IMAGES ©

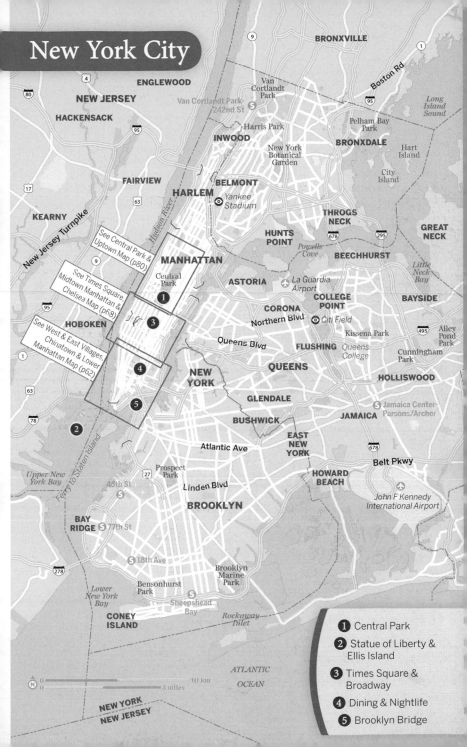

New York City's Highlights

Central Park

This majestic 843-acre wonderland (p76) in the middle of Manhattan offers New Yorkers an oasis from the rigors of urban life, with lush lawns, cool forests, flowering gardens, glassy lakes and meandering, wooded paths. This 'people's park' is one of the city's most popular year-round attractions, with boating and outdoor concerts in summer and sledding and ice-skating in winter.

RICHARD I'ANSON/GETTY IMAGES ©

2 Statue of Liberty & Ellis Island

In a city full of icons, the Statue of Liberty (p66) – gazing majestically from her harbor island perch – is magnificent. Over her left shoulder lies Ellis Island, the fabled gateway to America for millions of immigrants from 1892 to 1954. The interactive Immigration Museum, housed in a beautifully detailed red-brick building, provides a fascinating journey back in time.

Times Square & Broadway

3

Smack in the middle of Midtown Manhattan, the always-crowded and ever-colorful Times Square (p74) is the quintessential stop for first-time visitors who want to take the pulse of the throbbing metropolis. Its glittery marquees and billboards also demarcate the epicenter of NYC's renowned Theater District, where much-loved revivals, over-the-top musicals and critically acclaimed dramas draw big crowds every night of the week.

4

Dining & Nightlife

The range of international cuisine you'll find in NYC is staggering (p82). Get ready to plunge your chopsticks into authentic Cantonese or Korean, slurp down fresh oysters, nibble on Spanish tapas or Turkish mezze, and feast on Indian, Thai, Greek, French or even just classic American fare. Or spend your calories on liquid refreshment, drinking in New York's heady bar scene. The live music and clubs are sustenance enough for some. Above: Bemelmans Bar (p89)

5

Brooklyn Bridge

Walking across this graceful structure (p65) provides inspiration for poets and photographers; go for a stroll there and you'll soon understand why. Just after sunrise is magical – you'll have the bridge mostly to yourself. Or go at sunset for golden-lit views of the skyscrapers of Lower Manhattan and the Statue of Liberty.

New York City's Best...

Neighborhoods

○ **Chinatown** Head here for sensory overload: fragrant markets, overflowing shops and pan-Asian restaurants. (p61)

○ **Tribeca & SoHo** Browse boutiques and eateries in cast-iron buildings along the brick streets in these trendy neighborhoods. (p61)

○ **East Village** Find alternative shops, cafe culture and great nightlife in this bohemian 'hood. (p64)

○ **West (Greenwich) Village** Meandering, tree-lined streets hide an array of intimate dining and drinking spots. (p65)

Museums & Galleries

○ **Metropolitan Museum of Art** The greatest museum of all, with two million objects spread across 17 acres. (p72)

○ **Museum of Modern Art** Features innovative multimedia exhibits, a sculpture garden and film screenings. (p67)

○ **Guggenheim Museum** The architectural icon hosts excellent retrospectives. (p92)

○ **Chelsea Galleries** Dozens of galleries pack the western streets of this once-industrial neighborhood. (p67)

Ethnic Eats

○ **Katz's Delicatessen** A long-popular, old-school deli with much-celebrated pastrami sandwiches. (p83)

○ **Momofuku Noodle Bar** David Chang's brilliantly inventive eatery, with superb ramen and steamed buns. (p84)

○ **Boqueria Soho** Dazzling tapas plates and refreshing Spanish wines at this Iberian star downtown. (p83)

○ **Eataly** Feast on all things Italian at this sprawling food market. (p85)

Need to Know

Night Spots

○ **Village Vanguard** A venerable jazz spot that's hosted legends for 50 years. (p89)

○ **DBA** A beer-lover's Valhalla in the nightlife-loving East Village. (p88)

○ **Top of the Strand** Fantastic views over Manhattan. (p89)

○ **79th Street Boat Basin** Outdoor spot perched over the Hudson River. (p89)

○ **Bemelmans Bar** Uber-classy lounge complete with white-coated waiters and giant *Madeline* murals. (p89)

ADVANCE PLANNING

○ **One month before** Call to book tables at trendy restaurants; reserve seats at popular shows.

○ **One week before** Buy and print tickets to visit the Empire State Building, Top of the Rock and other popular sights.

RESOURCES

○ **New York magazine** (www.nymag.com/visitorsguide) Up-to-date tips for culture-savvy visitors.

○ **NYC** (www.nycgo.com) Comprehensive site run by the city's tourism department.

○ **Gothamist** (www.gothamist.com) Quirky news and NYC gossip.

GETTING AROUND

○ **Airports** (www.panynj.gov/airports) Key airports are JFK and LaGuardia (both in Queens), and Newark in New Jersey. Each has loads of transport links to the city.

○ **Bicycle** Always wear a helmet. Riding on the sidewalk is illegal. If you want to zip across town, there are hundreds of **Citi Bike** (p93) stations for hiring a bike in a hurry. For maps of bike lanes visit www.nycbikemaps.com.

○ **Subway** Purchase MetroCards (usable on local buses too) from station vending machines or subway attendants.

○ **Taxi** Only hail one if the taxi's roof light is on (otherwise it's taken).

○ **Walking** Manhattan is divided into east and west sides; Fifth Ave is the dividing line.

BE FOREWARNED

○ **Public restrooms/toilets** Few and far between; your best bet is to pop into a Starbucks.

○ **Restaurants** Many places don't take reservations; some places only take cash.

○ **Smoking** Banned in all enclosed public places including bars and restaurants, plus most parks.

○ **Subways** Weekend schedule changes (because of constant track work) are confusing. See www.mta.info.

Left: Brownstone buildings, Brooklyn (p93);
Above: Aerial view of Manhattan, New York City

New York City Walking Tour

Manhattan's most unruly maze of streets can be found in Greenwich Village, historically a neighborhood of poets, radicals and bohemians. An afternoon stroll along its cobbled, tree-lined streets is not to be missed.

WALK FACTS
- **Start** Commerce St
- **Finish** Sixth Ave & W 10th St
- **Distance** 1.5 miles
- **Duration** 1½ hours

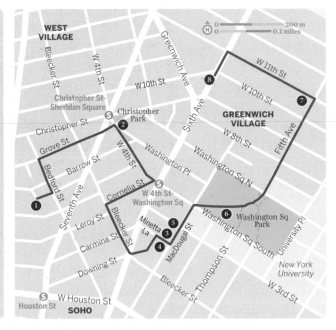

❶ Cherry Lane Theater

Start your walk at the Cherry Lane Theater. Established in 1924, the small playhouse is the city's oldest continuously running off-Broadway theater. Back in the 1940s, this was the epicenter of creativity when it came to the performing arts.

❷ Christopher Park

Walk to Bedford St, turn left, then right on Grove St. After two blocks, stop at tiny Christopher Park, where two white, life-sized statues of same-sex couples (*Gay Liberation*, 1992) stand guard. On the park's north side is the legendary Stonewall Inn, where a clutch of fed-up drag queens rioted

for their civil rights in 1969, signaling the start of the gay revolution.

❸ Cafe Wha?

Head down W 4th St, turn right down restaurant-lined Cornelia St, left on Bleecker then across Sixth Ave. Continue east on the crooked Minetta St, up to Cafe Wha?, the notorious institution where many young musicians and comedians – including Bob Dylan and Richard Pryor – got their start.

❹ Minetta Tavern

Across the street is the historic Minetta Tavern, which opened as a speakeasy in 1922. Its walls are lined with photos of celebs who have visited.

58

⑤ Cafe Reggio

Turn left up MacDougal St to reach the cozy Cafe Reggio at number 119. Its original owners claimed to be the first to bring cappuccino from Italy to the US in 1927.

⑥ Washington Square Park

Keep going up MacDougal St and continue to Washington Square Park, which has a long history as a magnet for radicals hosting anti-war, pro-marijuana and dyke pride demonstrations, among others. It's pure theater on warm days, when the square fills with buskers, chess players, sunbathers and strollers.

⑦ Weatherman House

Exit the park beneath the iconic arch; head up Fifth Ave and turn left on W 11th St, where you'll pass the infamous Weatherman House (18 W 11th St), used in 1970 as a hideout and bomb factory for an anti-government group until an explosion killed three members and destroyed the house. It was rebuilt in its current form in 1978.

⑧ Jefferson Market Library

Make your way up and around the corner to the Jefferson Market Library, straddling a triangular plot of land at the intersection of several roads. The unmissable 'Ruskinian Gothic' spire was once a fire lookout tower. In the 1870s, it was used as a courthouse and today it houses a branch of the public library.

New York City in....

TWO DAYS

Explore Chinatown, SoHo, Nolita and the West and East Villages, and end the day with **Times Square** (p74), a Broadway show and drinks in Midtown. Early on day two, stroll across the **Brooklyn Bridge** (p65) then head uptown to the **Metropolitan Museum of Art** (p72). Stroll through **Central Park** (p76) and lunch at the Boathouse, then head downtown for a ferry ride to the **Statue of Liberty** (p66) and Ellis Island, or visit the **National September 11 Memorial** (p60). Have dinner at a charming spot in the West Village.

FOUR DAYS

On day three, grab a bite at the **Chelsea Market** (p85), then stroll the **High Line** (p73). Stop for lunch in the Meatpacking District before visiting art galleries in Chelsea, and see an evening performance at **Lincoln Center** (p72). On day four, visit Midtown landmarks: the **Empire State Building** (p70), **MoMA** (p67) and **Rockefeller Center** (p70). Go window-shopping up Fifth Ave then catch a live band downtown at **Joe's Pub** (p90) or the **Bowery Ballroom** (p90).

Chelsea Market (p85)
MICHELLE BENNETT/GETTY IMAGES ©

Discover
New York City

At a Glance

View from the Top of the Rock (p70)
RICHARD I'ANSON/GETTY IMAGES ©

Sights

LOWER MANHATTAN

Ellis Island   Landmark, Museum
(☎212-363 3200; www.nps.gov/elis; admission free, ferry incl Statue of Liberty adult/child $17/9; ⊙9:30am-5pm; ⑤1 to South Ferry, 4/5 to Bowling Green) The way-station from 1892 to 1954 for more than 12 million immigrants who were hoping to make new lives in the United States, Ellis Island conjures up the humble and sometimes miserable beginnings of the experience of coming to America – as well as the fulfillment of dreams. Ferries to the Statue of Liberty make a second stop at the immigration station on Ellis Island.

The handsome main building has been restored as the **Immigration Museum**, with fascinating exhibits and a film about immigrant experiences, the processing of immigrants and how the influx changed the USA. As of 2013, Ellis Island remained closed indefinitely following extensive damages from Hurricane Sandy.

National September 11 Memorial   Memorial
(Map p62; ☎212-266-5211; www.911memorial.org; ⑤R to Cortlandt St) **FREE** This moving site honors the memory of the nearly 3000 people killed during the terrorist attacks of September 11, 2001. Its focus is two large pools with cascading waterfalls set in the footprints of the north and south towers of the destroyed World Trade Center. Bronze parapets surrounding the pools are inscribed with the names of those killed in the attacks. Admission is free, but visitor passes are required. They can be reserved through the memorial's website for a $2 service fee. Passes for same-day visits do

not have a service fee and are available on a first come, first served basis.

Nearby is the **9/11 Tribute Center** (Map p62; ☏866-737-1184; www.tributewtc.org; 120 Liberty St; adult/child $17/5; ⊗10am-6pm Mon-Sat, to 5pm Sun; ⑤E to World Trade Center, R/W to Cortland St), which provides exhibits, first-person testimony and walking tours of the site (adult/child $22/7, includes gallery admission, several tours daily). The museum is scheduled to open in spring 2014.

South Street Seaport
Neighborhood

(Map p62; www.southstreetseaport.com; ⑤A/C, J/Z, 2/3, 4/5 to Fulton St) This 11-block enclave of shops, piers and sights combines the best and worst in historic preservation. It's not on the radar for most New Yorkers, but tourists are drawn to the sea air, the nautical feel, the frequent street performers and the mobbed restaurants.

WALL STREET & THE FINANCIAL DISTRICT

Battery Park & Around
Neighborhood

The southwestern tip of Manhattan Island has been extended with landfill over the years to form **Battery Park** (Map p62; www.nycgovparks.org; Broadway at Battery Pl; ⊗sunrise-1am; ⑤4/5 to Bowling Green, 1 to South Ferry), so named for the gun batteries that used to be housed at the bulkheads. **Castle Clinton** (Map p62; www.nps.gov/cacl; Battery Park; ⊗8:30am-5pm; ☎; ⑤1 to South Ferry, 4/5 to Bowling Green), a fortification built in 1811 to protect Manhattan from the British, was originally 900ft offshore but is now at the edge of Battery Park, with only its walls remaining. Battery Place is also the start of the stunning **Hudson River Park** (Map p62; www.hudsonriverpark.org; Manhattan's west side from Battery Park to 59th St; ⑤1 to Franklin St, 1 to Canal St), which incorporates renovated piers, grassy spaces, gardens, basketball courts, a trapeze school, food concessions and, best of all, a ribbon of a bike/skate/running path that stretches 5 miles up to 59th St.

TRIBECA & SOHO

The 'TRIangle BElow CAnal St,' bordered roughly by Broadway to the east and Chambers St to the south, is the more downtown of these two sister 'hoods. It has old warehouses, very expensive loft apartments and chichi restaurants.

SoHo has nothing to do with its London counterpart, but instead, like Tribeca, takes its name from its geographical placement: SOuth of HOuston St. SoHo is filled with block upon block of cast-iron industrial buildings that date to the period just after the Civil War, when this was the city's leading commercial district. It had a bohemian/artsy heyday that had ended by the 1980s, and now this super-gentrified area is a major shopping destination, home to chain stores and boutiques alike and to hordes of consumers, especially on weekends.

Nearby are two small areas, **NoHo** ('north of Houston') and **NoLita** ('north of Little Italy'), respectively, are known for excellent shopping – lots of small, independent and stylish clothing boutiques – and dining.

CHINATOWN & LITTLE ITALY

The best reason to visit Chinatown is to experience a feast for the senses – it's the only spot in the city where you can simultaneously see whole roasted pigs hanging in butcher-shop windows, get whiffs of fresh fish and hear the twangs of Cantonese and Vietnamese rise over the calls of knock-off-Prada-bag hawkers on Canal St.

Little Italy, once a truly authentic pocket of Italian people, culture and eateries, is constantly shrinking as Chinatown expands. Still, loyal Italian Americans, mostly from the suburbs, flock here to gather around red-and-white-checked tablecloths at one of a handful of longtime red-sauce restaurants. Join them for a stroll along Mulberry St, and take a peek at the **Old St Patrick's Cathedral** (263 Mulberry St), which became the city's first Roman Catholic cathedral in 1809.

West & East Villages, Chinatown & Lower Manhattan

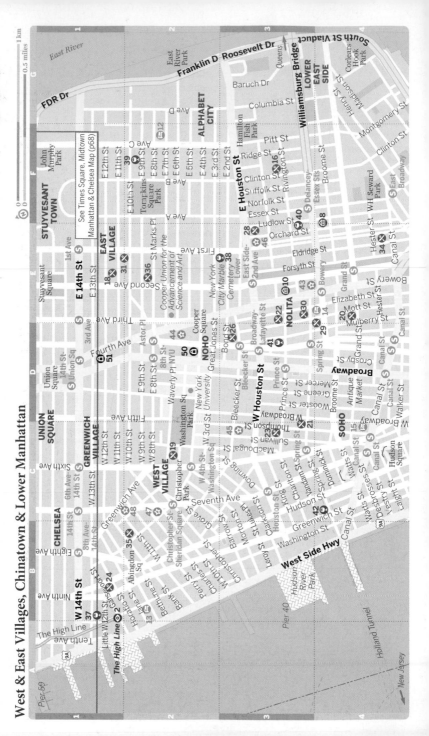

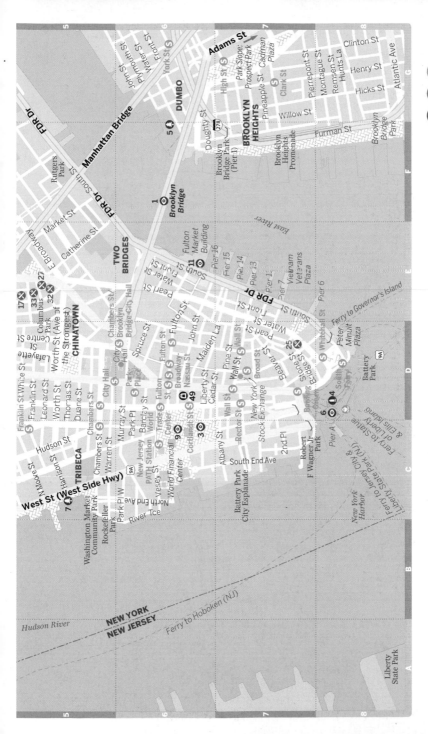

NEW YORK

NEW JERSEY

Hudson River

Ferry to Hoboken (NJ)

Liberty State Park

New York Harbor

Ferry to Jersey City & Liberty State Park (NJ)

Ferry to Statue of Liberty & Ellis Island

Battery Park

FDR Dr

Rutgers Park

Manhattan Bridge

FDR Dr – South St

Market St

Catherine St

E Broadway

DUMBO

John St
Plymouth St
Water St
York St

Adams St

5

Brooklyn Bridge (Pier 1)

Doughty St

High St

Park Slope/Prospect Park

Pineapple St

BROOKLYN HEIGHTS

Cadman Plaza

Willow St

Clark St

Clinton St

Henry St

Hicks St

Atlantic Ave

Pierrepont St
Montague St
Remsen St
Hunts La

Brooklyn Heights Promenade

Furman St

Brooklyn Bridge Park

East River

1
Brooklyn Bridge

TWO BRIDGES

Fulton Market Building

Pier 16
Pier 15
Pier 14
Pier 13
Pier 1
Pier 7
Pier 6

11

South St
Water St
Front St

Vietnam Veterans Plaza

FDR Dr

South St
Water St
Front St
Pearl St

Ferry to Governor's Island

Peter Minuit Plaza

17
33
27
32

Columbus Park

CHINATOWN

Franklin St White St
Franklin St
Leonard St
Worth St
Thomas St
Duane St

Lafayette St
Centre St
Worth St (Ave of the Strongest)

Chambers St

Brooklyn Bridge–City Hall

Spruce St

Fulton St

John St

Maiden La

Pine St

Wall St

Broad St

Beaver St

Whitehall St

Stone St

South Ferry

Hudson St

Moore St

TRIBECA

West St (West Side Hwy)

Harrison St

7

Chambers St
Warren St

Washington Market Community Park

Rockefeller Park

River Tce

Park Pl W

North End Ave

Park Pl

Murray St

Barclay St

Vesey St

New Jersey PATH Station

World Financial Center

Battery Park City Esplanade

South End Ave

2nd Pl

Robert F Wagner Jr Park

Pier A

Chambers St

City Hall

City Hall Park

Park Place

Fulton St

World Trade Center

Cortlandt St

Albany St

Rector St

New York Stock Exchange

Liberty St

Cedar St

Broadway
Nassau St

9

49

3

25

6

1

4

Pearl St

South St

9A

9A

DUMBO

West & East Villages, Chinatown & Lower Manhattan

LOWER EAST SIDE

First came the Jews, then the Latinos, followed by the hipsters and accompanying posers, frat-boy bros and the bridge-and-tunnel contingent. Today, this neighborhood, once the densest in the world, is focused on being cool – offering low-lit lounges, live-music clubs and trendy bistros. Luxury high-rise condominiums and boutique hotels co-exist with public-housing projects (read Richard Price's novel *Lush Life* for entertaining insight into this class conflict). Nevertheless, 40% of residents are still immigrants and two-thirds speak a language other than English at home.

Lower East Side
Tenement Museum   Museum
(Map p62; ☎212-982-8420; www.tenement.org; 103 Orchard St; tours from $22; ⊙visitor center 10am-5:30pm, tours 10:15am-5pm) There's

no museum in New York that humanizes the city's colorful past quite like this one. The neighborhood's heartbreaking but inspiring heritage is on full display in several recreations of turn-of-the-20th-century tenements. Always evolving and expanding, the museum has a variety of tours and talks.

EAST VILLAGE

If you've been dreaming of those quintessential New York City moments – graffiti on crimson brick, punks and grannies walking side by side, and cute cafes with rickety tables spilling out onto the sidewalks – then the East Village is your Holy Grail. Stick to the area around Tompkins Square Park, and the lettered avenues (known as Alphabet City) to its east, for interesting little nooks in which to imbibe and ingest – as well as a collection of great little community gardens that

 Don't Miss
Brooklyn Bridge

Marianne Moore's description of the world's first suspension bridge – which inspired poets from Walt Whitman to Jack Kerouac even before its completion – as a 'climactic ornament, a double rainbow' is perhaps most evocative. Walking across the grand Brooklyn Bridge is a rite of passage for New Yorkers and visitors alike – with this in mind, walk no more than two abreast or else you're in danger of colliding with runners and speeding cyclists. With an unprecedented span of 1596ft, it remains a compelling symbol of US achievement and a superbly graceful structure, despite the fact that its construction was plagued by budget overruns and the deaths of 20 workers. The bridge (see map p62) and the smooth pedestrian/bicyclist path, beginning just east of City Hall, affords wonderful views of Lower Manhattan and Brooklyn. On the Brooklyn side, the ever-expanding Brooklyn Bridge Park is a great place to continue your stroll.

provide leafy respites and sometimes even live performances.

WEST VILLAGE & GREENWICH VILLAGE

Once a symbol for all things artistic, outlandish and bohemian, this storied and popular neighborhood – the birthplace of the gay-rights movement as well as the former home of Beat poets and important artists – feels worlds away from busy Broadway, and in fact feels almost European. Known by most visitors as 'Greenwich Village,' although that term is not used by locals (West Village encompasses Greenwich Village, which is the area immediately around Washington Square Park), it has narrow streets lined with well-groomed and high-priced real estate, as well as cafes and restaurants, making it an ideal place to wander.

AGNIESZKA SZYMCZAK/GETTY IMAGES ©

★ Don't Miss
Statue of Liberty

In a city full of American icons, the Statue of Liberty is perhaps the most famous. Conceived as early as 1865 by French intellectual Edouard Laboulaye as a monument to the republican principals shared by France and the USA, it's still generally recognized as a symbol for the ideals of opportunity and freedom to many. French sculptor Frédéric-Auguste Bartholdi traveled to New York in 1871 to select the site, then spent more than 10 years in Paris designing and making the 151ft-tall figure *Liberty Enlightening the World*. It was then shipped to New York, erected on a small island in the harbor and unveiled in 1886.

The trip to Liberty island, via ferry, is usually made in conjunction with nearby Ellis Island. **Ferries** (Map p62; ☏ 201-604-2800, 877-523-9849; www.statuecruises.com; adult/child $17/9; ⊙ every 30min 9am-5pm, extended summer hours) leave from Battery Park and tickets include admission to both sights, and reservations can be made in advance (additional $3 for crown admission).

NEED TO KNOW

☏ 877-523-9849; www.nps.gov/stli; Liberty Island; adult/child incl Ellis Island $17/9, incl crown & Ellis Island $20/12; ⊙ 9:30am-5pm; Ⓢ 1 to South Ferry, 4/5 to Bowling Green

Washington Square Park   Park
(Map p62; Fifth Ave at Washington Sq N; Ⓢ A/C/E, B/D/F/V to W 4th St-Washington Sq, N/R/W to 8th St-NYU) This park began as a 'potter's field' – a burial ground for the penniless – and its status as a cemetery protected it from development. It is now a completely renovated and incredibly well-used park, especially on the weekend. New York University defines the area around the park and beyond, both architecturally and demographically.

MEATPACKING DISTRICT

The neighborhood was once home to 250 slaughterhouses and was best known for its groups of transsexual prostitutes, S&M sex clubs and, of course, its sides of beef. These days the hugely popular High Line park has only intensified an ever-increasing proliferation of trendy wine bars, eateries, nightclubs, designer clothing stores, chic hotels and high-rent condos.

CHELSEA

This 'hood is popular for two main attractions: one, the parade of gorgeous gay men (known affectionately as 'Chelsea boys') who roam Eighth Ave, darting from gyms to trendy happy hours; and two, it's one of the hubs of the city's art-gallery scene – it's currently home to nearly 200 modern-art exhibition spaces, most of which are clustered west of Tenth Ave.

FLATIRON DISTRICT

The famous 1902 **Flatiron Building** (Map p68; Broadway cnr Fifth Ave & 23rd St; ⑤N/R, 6 to 23rd St) has a distinctive triangular shape to match its site. Its surrounding district is a fashionable area of boutiques, loft apartments and a burgeoning high-tech corridor, the city's answer to Silicon Valley. Peaceful **Madison Square Park**, bordered by 23rd and 26th Sts and Fifth and Madison Aves, has an active dog run, rotating outdoor sculptures, shaded park benches and a popular burger joint.

UNION SQUARE

Like the Noah's Ark of New York, **Union Square** (Map p68; www. unionsquarenyc.org; 17th St btwn Broadway & Park Ave S; ⑤L, N/Q/R, 4/5/6 to 14th St-Union Sq) rescues at least two of every kind from the curling seas of concrete. Here, amid the tapestry

of stone steps and fenced-in foliage, you'll find businessfolk, loiterers, skateboarders, college kids and throngs of protestors chanting fervently for various causes.

Greenmarket Farmers Market
Food Market

(Map p68; ☎212-788-7476; www.grownyc.org; 17th St btwn Broadway & Park Ave S; ⏰8am-6pm Mon, Wed, Fri & Sat) ✐ Four days a week, Union Sq's north end hosts the most popular of the nearly 50 greenmarkets throughout the five boroughs, where even celebrity chefs come for just-picked rarities including fiddlehead ferns, heirloom tomatoes and fresh curry leaves.

MIDTOWN

The classic NYC fantasy – shiny skyscrapers, teeming mobs of worker bees, Fifth Ave store windows, taxi traffic – and some of the city's most popular attractions can be found here.

Museum of Modern Art
Museum

(MoMA; Map p68; www.moma.org; 11 W 53rd St btwn Fifth & Sixth Aves, Midtown West;

Museum of Modern Art
DOSFOTOS/GETTY IMAGES ©

Times Square, Midtown Manhattan & Chelsea

See Central Park & Uptown Map (p80)

Clinton Cove (Pier 96)

Hudson River Park

Dewitt Clinton Park

W 57th St

57th St-7th Ave

30

20

W 55th St

25

W 53rd St

New York City & Company

7th Ave

28

27

W 51st St

Seventh Ave

50th St

49th St

W 49th St

Worldwide Plaza

W 47th St

13

TIMES SQUARE

THEATER DISTRICT

W 45th St

Times Square Museum & Visitor Center

HELL'S KITCHEN

Pier 83

12

W 42nd St

42nd St-Port Authority

Times Square

1

Pier 81

19

Port Authority Bus Terminal

42nd St-Times Sq

Lincoln Tunnel

W 40th St

W 38th St

Jacob Javits Convention Center

W 36th St

GARMENT DISTRICT

Boltbus Bus Stop (Philadelphia & Boston)

34th St-Penn Station

35

Megabus (Departures)

W 34th St

W 33rd St

Boltbus Bus Stop (DC & Baltimore)

34

Penn Station

33

KOREATOWN

W 30th St

Megabus (Arrivals)

Hudson River

W 28th St

Chelsea Park

28th St

W 26th St

Chelsea Waterside Park

W 23rd St

23rd St

23rd St

CHELSEA

W 21st St

Chelsea Piers

W 19th St

15

32

18th St

See West & East Villages, Chinatown & Lower Manhattan Map (p62)

21

8th Ave-14th St

14th St

W 14th St

Twelfth Ave (West Side Hwy)

Eleventh Ave (West Side Hwy)

Eleventh Ave

Tenth Ave

Ninth Ave

Eighth Ave

Seventh Ave

Broadway

The High Line

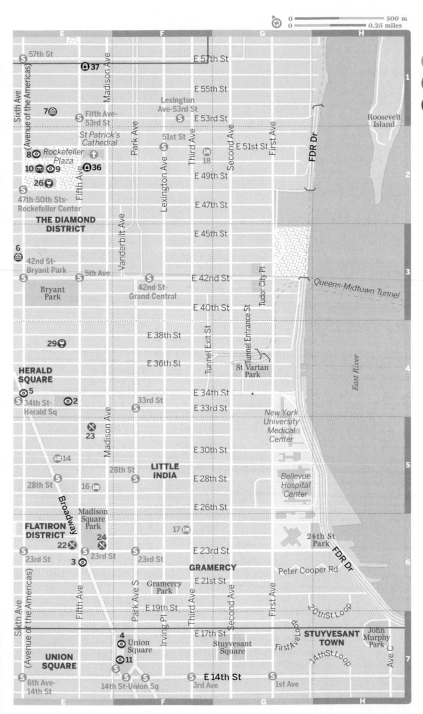

0 — 500 m
0 — 0.25 miles

57th St ⓢ

🔒 **37**

E 57th St

E 55th St

Lexington
Ave-53rd St ⓢ

E 53rd St

Fifth Ave-
53rd St ⓢ

7 🏛

Sixth Ave
(Avenue of the Americas)

Madison Ave

Park Ave

51st St ⓢ

Third Ave

Second Ave

First Ave

Roosevelt
Island

FDR Dr

St Patrick's
Cathedral

8 ◎ *Rockefeller
Plaza* ⓘ

Lexington Ave

E 51st St

ⓘ **18**

10 ◎◎ **9** ⓘ**36**

E 49th St

26 🍴

Fifth Ave

⓪

47th-50th Sts-
Rockefeller Center

E 47th St

**THE DIAMOND
DISTRICT**

Vanderbilt Ave

E 45th St

E 42nd St

6 🏛

42nd St-
Bryant Park ⓢ

5th Ave ⓢ

◎ E 42nd St

Queens-Midtown Tunnel

Bryant
Park

42nd St-
Grand Central

E 40th St

Tudor City Pl

Tunnel Entrance St

29 🍴

E 38th St

Tunnel Exit St

E 36th St

**HERALD
SQUARE**

E 34th St

St Vartan
Park

East River

ⓢ**5**

34th St-
Herald Sq ⓢ

◎**2**

33rd St ⓢ

E 33rd St

New York
University
Medical
Center

Madison Ave

❌
23

E 30th St

🍴**14**

28th St

**LITTLE
INDIA**

E 28th St

Bellevue
Hospital
Center

28th St ⓢ

16 🍴

ⓢ

E 26th St

**FLATIRON
DISTRICT**

Broadway

Madison
Square
Park

17 🍴

E 24th St
Park

FDR Dr

22 ❌

24 ❌

23rd St ⓢ

ⓢ **23rd St**

ⓢ 23rd St

E 23rd St

3 ◎

GRAMERCY

Peter Cooper Rd

Fifth Ave

E 21st St

Gramercy
Park

20thSt Loop

Park Ave S

Irving Pl

E 19th St

Third Ave

Second Ave

First Ave

4 ◎ Union
Square

E 17th St

**STUYVESANT
TOWN**

John
Murphy
Park

FirstAveLoop

11 ◎

Stuyvesant
Square

14thSt Loop

Ave C

**UNION
SQUARE**

Sixth Ave
(Avenue of the Americas)

ⓢ
6th Ave-
14th St

ⓢ ⓢ ⓢ
14th St-Union Sq

ⓢ **E 14th St**
3rd Ave

ⓢ
1st Ave

Times Square, Midtown Manhattan & Chelsea

adult/child $25/free, 4-8pm Fri free; ⏱10:30am-5:30pm Sat-Thu, to 8pm Fri; 🛜; **S** E, M to 5th Ave-53rd St) Since its founding in 1929, MoMA has amassed over 150,000 artworks, documenting the emerging creative ideas and movements of the late 19th century through to those that dominate today. You'll find more A-listers here than at an Oscars after-party: Van Gogh, Matisse, Picasso, Warhol, Lichtenstein, Rothko, Pollock and Bourgeois. For art buffs, it's Valhalla. For the uninitiated, it's a thrilling crash course in all that is beautiful and addictive about art.

Rockefeller Center Notable Building (Map p68; www.rockefellercenter.com; Fifth to Sixth Aves & 48th to 51st Sts; ⏱24hr, times vary for individual businesses; **S** B/D/F/M to 47th-50th Sts-Rockefeller Center) The 360-degree views from the tri-level observation deck of the **Top of the Rock** (Map p68; www.topoftherocknyc.com; 30 Rockefeller Plaza at 49th St, entrance on W 50th St btwn Fifth & Sixth Aves; adult/child $27/17, sunrise/sunset combo $40/22; ⏱8am-midnight, last elevator at 11pm; **S** B/D/F/M to 47th-50th Sts-Rockefeller Center) are absolutely stunning and should not be

missed; on a clear day you can see quite a distance across the river into New Jersey. In winter the ground-floor outdoor space is abuzz with ice-skaters and Christmas-tree gawkers. Within the complex is the 1932, 6000-seat **Radio City Music Hall** (Map p68; www.radiocity.com; 1260 Sixth Ave at 51st St; tours adult/child $19.95/15; ⏱tours 11am-3pm).

Empire State Building
Notable Building, Lookout (Map p68; www.esbnyc.com; 350 Fifth Ave at 34th St; 86th-floor observation deck adult/child $27/21, incl 102nd-floor observation deck $44/38; ⏱8am-2am, last elevators up 1:15am; **S** B/D/F/M, N/Q/R to 34th St-Herald Sq) One of the most famous members of New York's skyline is a limestone classic built in just 410 days, or seven million man-hours, during the depths of the Depression at a cost of $41 million. You can ride the elevator to observatories on the 86th and 102nd floors, but be prepared for crowds; try to come very early or very late (and purchase your tickets ahead of time online, or pony up for $50 'express passes') for an optimal experience.

International Center of Photography
Gallery

(ICP; Map p68; www.icp.org; 1133 Sixth Ave at 43rd St; adult/child $14/free, by donation Fri 5-8pm; ☻10am-6pm Tue-Thu, Sat & Sun, to 8pm Fri; 🛜; ⑤B/D/F/M to 42nd St-Bryant Park) This is the city's most important show-case for major photographers, especially photojournalists. Its past exhibitions have included work by Henri Cartier-Bresson, Matthew Brady and Robert Capa.

Herald Square
Square

(Map p68; cnr Broadway, Sixth Ave & 34th St; ⑤B/D/F/M, N/Q/R to 34th St-Herald Sq) This crowded convergence of Broadway, Sixth Ave and 34th St is best known as the home of **Macy's** department store, where you can still ride some of the remaining original wooden elevators to floors featuring goods ranging from home furnishings to lingerie. The busy square gets its name from a long-defunct newspaper, the *Herald*.

Museum of Arts & Design
Museum

(MAD; Map p80; www.madmuseum.org; 2 Columbus Circle btwn Eighth Ave & Broadway; adult/child $16/free; ☻10am-6pm Tue, Wed, Sat & Sun, to 9pm Thu & Fri; ⑤A/C, B/D, 1 to 59th St-Columbus Circle) On the southern side of the circle, exhibiting a diverse international collection of modern, folk, craft and fine-art pieces. The plush and trippy design of **Robert** (Map p80; www.robertnyc. com; ☻11.30am-10pm Mon, 11.30am-midnight Tue-Fri, 11am-midnight Sat, 11am-10pm Sun), the 9th-floor restaurant, complements fantastic views of Central Park.

UPPER WEST SIDE

Shorthand for liberal, progressive and intellectual New York, this neighborhood comprises the west side of Manhattan from Central Park to the Hudson River, and from Columbus Circle to 110th St. Here you'll still find massive, ornate apartments and a diverse mix of stable, upwardly mobile folks (with many actors and classical musicians sprinkled throughout), and some lovely green spaces – **Riverside Park** stretches for 4 miles between W 72nd St and W 158th St along the Hudson River, and is a great place for strolling, running, cycling or simply gazing over the river.

Radio City Music Hall

Lincoln Center
Cultural Center

(Map p80; ☎212-875-5456; www.lincolncenter.
org; Columbus Ave btwn 62nd & 66th Sts; public
plazas free, tours adult/student $18/15; ♿;
🚇1 to 66th St-Lincoln Center) The $1.2 bil-
lion redevelopment project completed in
2012 brings new life to the world's largest
performing-arts center. The lavishly designed **Metropolitan Opera House** (MET),
the largest opera house in the world, seats
3900 people. Fascinating one-hour **tours**
of the complex leave from the lobby of
Avery Fisher Hall daily; these tours vary
from architectural to backstage tours.

American Museum of
Natural History
Museum

(Map p80; ☎212-769-5100; www.amnh.org;
Central Park West at 79th St; suggested donation
adult/child $22/12.50; ⏰10am-5:45pm, Rose
Center to 8:45pm Fri, Butterfly Conservancy Oct-
May; ♿; 🚇B, C to 81st St-Museum of Natural
History, 1 to 79th St) Founded in 1869, this
museum includes more than 30 million
artifacts, interactive exhibits and loads
of taxidermy. It's most famous for its
three large dinosaur halls, an enormous
(fake) blue whale that hangs from the

ceiling above the Hall of Ocean Life and
the elaborate **Rose Center for Earth &
Space**, with space-show theaters and the
planetarium.

UPPER EAST SIDE

The Upper East Side (UES) is home to
New York's greatest concentration of cultural centers, including the grand dame
that is the Metropolitan Museum of Art,
and many refer to Fifth Ave above 57th
St as Museum Mile. Home to ladies who
lunch as well as frat boys who drink, the
neighborhood becomes decidedly less
chichi the further east you go.

Metropolitan Museum
of Art
Museum

(Map p80; ☎212-535-7710; www.metmuseum.
org; 1000 Fifth Ave at 82nd St; suggested donation adult/child $25/free; ⏰10am-5:30pm
Sun-Thu, to 9pm Fri & Sat; ♿; 🚇4/5/6 to 86th
St) The Metropolitan Museum of Art (aka
'the Met') is a self-contained cultural city-
state, with two million individual objects
in its collection and an annual budget of
over $120 million. With more than five
million visitors a year, it is New York's

Van Gogh paintings at the Metropolitan Museum of Art

GRAHAM CROUCH/GETTY IMAGES ©

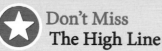

Don't Miss
The High Line

With the completion of the High Line, a 30ft-high abandoned stretch of elevated railroad track transformed into a long ribbon of parkland (from Gansevoort St to W 34th St; entrances are at Gansevoort, 14th, 16th, 18th, 20th and 30th Sts; elevator access at all but 18th St), there's finally some greenery amid the asphalt jungle. Only three stories above the streetscape, this thoughtfully and carefully designed mix of contemporary, industrial and natural elements is nevertheless a refuge and escape from the ordinary. A glass-front amphitheater with bleacher-like seating sits just above 10th Ave – bring some food and join local workers on their lunch break. The third and final phase bends closer to the Hudson at 34th St, and is scheduled to open in 2014. The Whitney Museum of American Art (long located on the Upper East Side), will relocate to its Renzo Piano–designed home situated between the High Line and the Hudson River in 2015.

NEED TO KNOW

Map p62; ☏212-500-6035; www.thehighline.org; Gansevoort St; ⊙7am-7pm; 🚌M11 to Washington St, M11, M14 to 9th Ave, M23, M34 to 10th Ave, Ⓢ L or A/C/E to 14th St-8th Ave, C/E to 23rd St-8th Ave

most popular single-site tourist attraction.

Highlight rooms include Egyptian Art, American Paintings and Sculpture, Arms and Armor, Modern Art, Greek and Roman Art and European Paintings. Its 19th-century European paintings and sculpture galleries have been greatly expanded and refurbished.

Don't miss the gorgeous rooftop, which offers bar service and spectacular views throughout the summer.

JEAN-PIERRE LESCOURRET/GETTY IMAGES ©

 ## Don't Miss
Times Square & Theater District

There are few images more universally iconic than the glittering orb dropping from **Times Square** on New Year's Eve – the first one descended 100 years ago. Near the intersection of Broadway and Seventh Ave, 'the Crossroads of the World' draws 35 million visitors annually.

The Times Square area is at least as famous as New York's official **Theater District**, with dozens of Broadway and off-Broadway theaters located in an area that stretches from 41st to 54th Sts, between Sixth and Ninth Aves.

NEED TO KNOW

Map p68; www.timessquare.com; Broadway at Seventh Ave; S N/Q/R, S, 1/2/3, 7 to Times Sq-42nd St

Frick Collection Gallery

(Map p80; ✆212-288-0700; www.frick.org; 1 E 70th St at Fifth Ave; admission $18, by donation 11am-1pm Sun, children under 10 not admitted; ⏰10am-6pm Tue-Sat, 11am-5pm Sun; S 6 to 68th St-Hunter College) This spectacular art collection sits in a mansion built by Henry Clay Frick in 1914. The 12 richly furnished rooms on the ground floor display paintings by Titian, Vermeer, El Greco, Goya and other masters. It's rarely crowded, providing a welcome break from the swarms of visitors at other museums.

 ## Tours

Big Onion Walking Tours Walking

(✆888-606-9255; www.bigonion.com; tours $20) Popular and quirky guided tours specializing in ethnic and neighborhood tours.

Circle Line Boat

(Map p68; ✆212-563-3200; www.circleline42. com; Pier 83, W 42nd St; tickets from $29; S A/C/E to 42nd St-Port Authority Bus Terminal) Ferry-boat tours, from semicircle to a full island cruise with guided commentary, as well as powerful speedboat trips are available.

Gray Line Sightseeing Bus
(Map p68; www.newyorksightseeing.com; 777 8th Ave; adult/child from $42/$32) Hop-on, hop-off double-decker multilingual guided bus tours.

Sleeping

SOHO

**Soho Grand
Hotel** Boutique Hotel **$$$**
(Map p62; ✆212-965-3000; www.sohogrand. com; 310 W Broadway; d $195-450; ✤@✧✿; ⑤6, N/Q/R, J to Canal St) The original boutique hotel of the 'hood still reigns, with its striking glass-and-cast-iron lobby stairway, and 367 rooms with cool, clean lines plus Frette linens, plasma flat-screen TVs and Kiehl's grooming products. The lobby's Grand Lounge buzzes with action.

LOWER EAST SIDE, EAST VILLAGE & NOLITA

Nolitan Hotel Hotel **$$**
(Map p62; ✆212-925-2555; www.nolitanhotel. com; 30 Kenmare St btwn Elizabeth & Mott Sts; r from $143; ✤✧✿; ⑤J to Bowery, 4/6 to Spring St, B/D to Grand St) Set behind a memorable facade of floating postive-negative Tetris bricks, the Nolitan is a great find. Tuck into a good book in the inviting lobby lounge, or head upstairs to your stylish pad, which feels like it's waiting to be photographed in the next CB2 catalog.

**East Village Bed &
Coffee** B&B **$$**
(Map p62; ✆212-533-4175; www.bedandcoffee. com; 110 Ave C btwn 7th & 8th Sts; s/d with shared bath from $125/130; ✤✧; ⑤F/V to Lower East Side-2nd Ave) This family home has been transformed into a quirky, arty, offbeat B&B with colorful, themed private rooms (one shared bathroom and kitchen per floor) and even free bikes.

New York for Children

Contrary to popular belief, New York can be a pretty child-friendly city. Cutting-edge playgrounds abound, from Union Square to Battery Park, and there's lots of green space on the West Side. Other major attractions include the **Children's Museum of Manhattan** (Map p80; www.cmom.org; 212 W 83rd St btwn Amsterdam Ave & Broadway; admission $11; ◷10am-5pm Tue-Fri & Sun, to 7pm Sat; ⓘ; ⑤B, C to 81st St-Museum of Natural History; 1 to 86th St), the **Brooklyn Children's Museum** (www.brooklynkids. org; 145 Brooklyn Ave at St Marks Ave, Crown Heights; admission $9; ◷10am-5pm Tues-Sun; ⓘ; ⑤C to Kingston-Throop Aves, 3 to Kingston Ave), the Central Park and Bronx zoos and the Coney Island aquarium. Times Square's themed megastores and their neighboring kid-friendly restaurants are good options.

CHELSEA, MEATPACKING DISTRICT & WEST (GREENWICH) VILLAGE

Jane Hotel Hotel **$**
(Map p62; ✆212-924-6700; www.thejanenyc. com; 113 Jane St btwn Washington St & West Side Hwy; r with shared bath from $99; ⓟ✤✧; ⑤L to 8th Ave, A/C/E to 14th St, 1/2 to Christopher St-Sheridan Sq) Originally built for sailors, the Jane became a temporary refuge for survivors of the *Titanic,* then a YMCA and a rock-and-roll venue. The single-bunk rooms feature flat-screen TVs and the communal showers are more than adequate.

Chelsea Lodge Hotel **$$**
(Map p68; ✆212-243-4499; www.chelsealodge. com; 318 W 20th St btwn Eighth & Ninth Aves; s/d from $118/128; ✤; ⑤A/C/E to 14th St, 1 to
Continued on p81

Don't Miss
Central Park

It might be tempting to think that Central Park, over 800 acres of picturesque meadows, ponds and woods, represents Manhattan in its raw state. It doesn't. Designed by Frederick Law Olmsted and Calvert Vaux, the park is the result of serious engineering: thousands of workers shifted 10 million cartloads of soil to transform swamp and rocky outcroppings into the 'people's park.'

Map p80

www.centralparknyc.org

59th & 110th Sts btwn Central Park West & Fifth Ave

6am-1am

Strawberry Fields

This tear-shaped garden serves as a memorial to former Beatle John Lennon. It is composed of a grove of stately elms and a tiled mosaic that reads, simply, 'Imagine.' Find it at the level of 72nd St on the park's west side.

Bethesda Terrace & Mall

The arched walkways of Bethesda Terrace, crowned by the magnificent Bethesda Fountain, have long been a gathering area for New Yorkers of all flavors. To the south is the Mall (featured in countless movies), a promenade shrouded in mature North American elms. The southern stretch, known as Literary Walk, is flanked by statues of famous authors.

Conservatory Water & Around

North of the zoo at the level of 74th St is the Conservatory Water, where model sailboats drift lazily and kids scramble about on a toadstool-studded statue of Alice in Wonderland. There are Saturday story hours at the Hans Christian Andersen statue to the west of the water (at 11am from June to September).

Great Lawn & Around

The Great Lawn is a massive emerald carpet at the center of the park – between 79th and 86th Sts – and is surrounded by ball fields and London plane trees. Immediately to the southeast is the Delacorte Theater, home to the annual Shakespeare in the Park festival, as well as Belvedere Castle, a lookout. Further south, between 72nd and 79th Sts, is the leafy Ramble, a popular birding destination (and legendary gay pick-up spot). On the southeastern end is the Loeb Boathouse, home to a waterside restaurant that offers rowboat and bicycle rentals.

Local Knowledge

Central Park

BY ROBERT REID OF REIDONTRAVEL.COM, THE HOME OF THE PLATE OF FOOD TRAVEL MUSEUM.

1 SHEEP MEADOW
The heart of the park, this 15-acre lawn has the best vantage points of New York's skyline bumping against the world's greatest example of foresight in urban planning. Even if you've not been, you've seen it a lot (perhaps in the iconic scene in *Wall Street* where Michael Douglas bloodies Charlie Sheen). One thing: don't bring a sheep. They've been a no-no since 1934.

2 BOATHOUSE
Every time I make it to the eastern edge of Central Park's lake and stop for a sandwich or drink at the Loeb Boathouse, I realize I don't come enough. It's a superb spot to rest the legs and feel like the park is really the city's backyard. If you do poke your hand in the water, don't worry, it's not as mucky as Woody Allen makes it out to be in *Manhattan*

3 CONCERTS IN CENTRAL PARK
One of my favorite New York moments was when Mayor Rudy Giuliani declared August 7, 1997 'Garth Brooks Day' in New York. Garth Brooks? Here? But that's the power of the Central Park stage.

4 GREAT VIEWS
Central Park is filled with spots where you'll forget you're in the city. But the best vantage point is from above, on the rooftop terrace of the Metropolitan Museum of Art (p72; pictured left). A sea of trees lies just below, lipped in the distance by buildings (like the Dakota, where John Lennon died in 1980).

5 THE ZOO
New York's oldest zoo was created almost by accident – the park builders were given a bear and a few animals in the 1860s (flowers, anyone?), which were caged in the park. From there, it grew into a proper zoo. Simon and Garfunkel wrote a song about it.

Central Park

THE LUNGS OF NEW YORK

The rectangular patch of green that occupies Manhattan's heart began life in the mid-19th century as a swampy piece of land that was carefully bulldozed into the idyllic nature-scape you see today. Since officially becoming Central Park, it has brought New Yorkers of all stripes together in interesting and unexpected ways. The park has served as a place for the rich to show off their fancy carriages (1860s), for the poor to enjoy free Sunday concerts (1880s) and for activists to hold be-ins against the Vietnam War (1960s).

Since then, legions of locals – not to mention travelers from all kinds of faraway places – have poured in to stroll, picnic, sunbathe, play ball and catch free concerts and performances of works by Shakespeare.

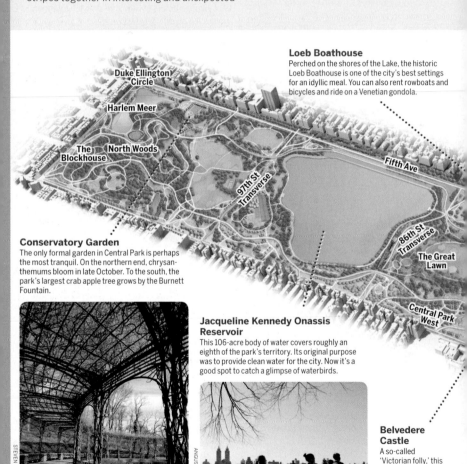

Loeb Boathouse
Perched on the shores of the Lake, the historic Loeb Boathouse is one of the city's best settings for an idyllic meal. You can also rent rowboats and bicycles and ride on a Venetian gondola.

Duke Ellington Circle

Harlem Meer

The Blockhouse

North Woods

97th St Transverse

Fifth Ave

86th St Transverse

The Great Lawn

Central Park West

Conservatory Garden
The only formal garden in Central Park is perhaps the most tranquil. On the northern end, chrysanthemums bloom in late October. To the south, the park's largest crab apple tree grows by the Burnett Fountain.

Jacqueline Kennedy Onassis Reservoir
This 106-acre body of water covers roughly an eighth of the park's territory. Its original purpose was to provide clean water for the city. Now it's a good spot to catch a glimpse of waterbirds.

Belvedere Castle
A so-called 'Victorian folly,' this Gothic-Romanesque castle serves no other purpose than to be a very dramatic lookout point. It was built by Central Park co-designer Calvert Vaux in 1869.

The park's varied terrain offers a wonderland of experiences. There are quiet, woodsy knolls in the north. To the south is the reservoir, crowded with joggers. There are European gardens, a zoo and various bodies of water. For maximum flamboyance, hit the Sheep Meadow on a sunny day, when all of New York shows up to lounge.

Central Park is more than just a green space. It is New York City's backyard.

FACTS & FIGURES

» **Landscape architects** Frederick Law Olmsted and Calvert Vaux

» **Year that construction began** 1858

» **Acres** 843

» **On film** Hundreds of movies have been shot on location, from Depression-era blockbusters such as *Gold Diggers* (1933) to the monster-attack flick *Cloverfield* (2008).

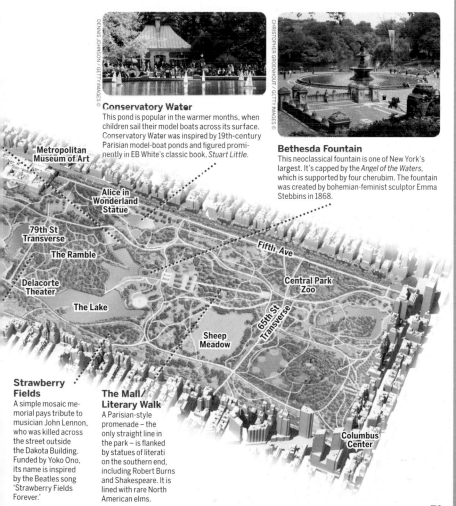

Conservatory Water
This pond is popular in the warmer months, when children sail their model boats across its surface. Conservatory Water was inspired by 19th-century Parisian model-boat ponds and figured prominently in EB White's classic book, *Stuart Little*.

Bethesda Fountain
This neoclassical fountain is one of New York's largest. It's capped by the *Angel of the Waters*, which is supported by four cherubim. The fountain was created by bohemian-feminist sculptor Emma Stebbins in 1868.

Metropolitan Museum of Art

Alice in Wonderland Statue

79th St Transverse

The Ramble

Delacorte Theater

The Lake

Fifth Ave

Central Park Zoo

65th St Transverse

Sheep Meadow

Columbus Center

Strawberry Fields
A simple mosaic memorial pays tribute to musician John Lennon, who was killed across the street outside the Dakota Building. Funded by Yoko Ono, its name is inspired by the Beatles song 'Strawberry Fields Forever.'

The Mall/ Literary Walk
A Parisian-style promenade – the only straight line in the park – is flanked by statues of literati on the southern end, including Robert Burns and Shakespeare. It is lined with rare North American elms.

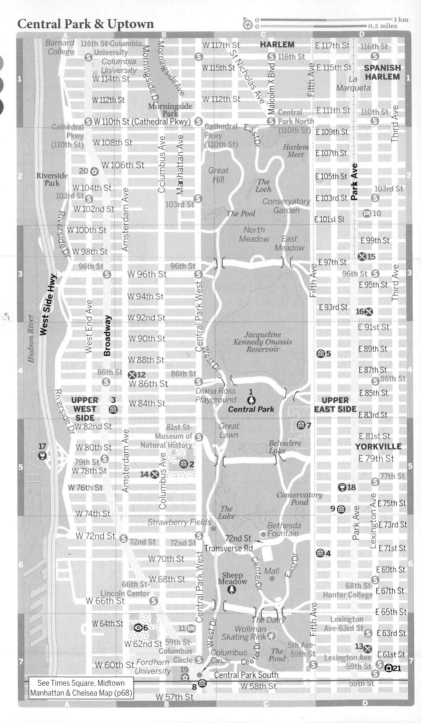

Central Park & Uptown

See Times Square, Midtown
Manhattan & Chelsea Map (p68)

Central Park & Uptown

Continued from p75

18th St) Housed in a landmark brownstone in Chelsea, the European-style, 20-room Chelsea Lodge has well-kept but small rooms.

Ace Hotel
New York City   Boutique Hotel **$$$**
(Map p68; ☎212-679-2222; www.acehotel.com/newyork; 20 W 29th St btwn Broadway & Fifth Ave; r $249-549; ❄🛜🐾; ⓢN/R to 28th St) This outpost of a hip Pacific Northwest chain is on the northern edge of Chelsea. Clever touches such as vintage turntables and handwritten welcome notes elevate the Ace beyond the standard.

UNION SQUARE, FLATIRON DISTRICT & GRAMERCY PARK
Gershwin Hotel   Hotel **$$**
(Map p68; ☎212-545-8000; www.gershwin-hotel.com; 7 E 27th St at Fifth Ave; r from $215; ❄@🛜; ⓢN/R, 6 to 28th St) This popular and funky spot is half youth hostel, half hotel, and buzzes with original pop art, touring bands and a young and artsy European clientele.

Marcel
   Boutique Hotel **$$$**
(Map p68; ☎212-696-3800; www.nychotels.com; 201 E 24th St at Third Ave; d from $210; ❄@🛜; ⓢ6 to 23rd St) Minimalist, with earth-tone touches, this 97-room inn is a poor man's chic boutique and that's not a bad thing.

Modernist rooms on the avenue have great views, and the sleek lounge is a great place to unwind.

MIDTOWN
Yotel   Hotel **$$**
(Map p68; ☎646-449-7700; www.yotel.com; 570 Tenth Ave at 41st St; r from $149; ❄🛜; ⓢA/C/E to 42nd St Port Authority Bus Terminal, 1/2/3, N/Q/R, S, 7 to Times Sq-42nd St) Part futuristic spaceport, part Austin Powers set, this uber-cool 669-room option bases its rooms on airplane classes. All rooms feature floor-to-ceiling windows with great views, slick bathrooms and iPod connectivity.

Pod 51 Hotel
   Hotel **$$**
(Map p68; ☎866-414-4617; www.thepodhotel.com; 230 E 51st St btwn Second & Third Aves; r from $89; ❄🛜; ⓢ6 to 51st St; E, V to Lexington Ave-53rd St) This affordable hot spot has a range of room types, most barely big enough for the bed. 'Pods' have bright bedding, tight workspaces, flat-screen TVs, iPod docking stations and 'rain' showerheads.

UPPER WEST SIDE
YMCA   Hostel **$$**
(Map p80; ☎212-912-2600; www.ymca.com; 5 W 63rd St at Central Park West; r from $100; ❄@; ⓢA/B/C/D to 59th St-Columbus Circle) Just steps from Central Park, this grand

art-deco building has basic, but clean, rooms. Guests have access to extensive, but old-school gym, racquetball courts, pool and sauna.

UPPER EAST SIDE

Bubba & Bean Lodges   B&B $$
(Map p80; ☎917-345-7914; www.bblodges.com; 1598 Lexington Ave btwn 101st & 102nd Sts; r from $180; ❄ 🎧; S 6 to 103rd St) Hardwood floors, crisp white walls and pretty navy bedspreads make the rooms at this nifty B&B feel spacious, modern and youthful.

Eating

LOWER MANHATTAN & TRIBECA

Fraunces Tavern   American $$
(Map p62; ☎212-968-1776; www.fraunces tavern.com; 54 Pearl St; mains $15-24; ⏱noon-5pm; S N/R to Whitehall) Can you really pass up a chance to eat where George Washington supped in 1762? Expect heaping portions of tavern stew, clam chowder and beef Wellington and, for dessert, bread pudding, spiked fig and apple tart or strawberry shortcake.

CHINATOWN, LITTLE ITALY & NOLITA

Lovely Day   Pan-Asian $
(Map p62; ☎212-925-3310; 196 Elizabeth St btwn Prince & Spring Sts; mains $9; ⏱11am-11pm; S J/M/Z to Bowery St, 6 to Spring St) Everything is just precious inside this affordable and funky nook that serves lovingly prepared Thai-inflected food.

Café Gitane   Moroccan $$
(Map p62; ☎212-334-9552; www.cafegitanenyc. com; 242 Mott St at Prince St; mains $14-16; ⏱8:30am-midnight Sun-Thu, to 12:30am Fri & Sat; S N/R to Prince St, 6 to Spring St) Label-conscious shoppers love this authentic bistro, with its dark, aromatic coffee and tempting dishes such as yellowfin tuna ceviche and spicy meatballs in tomato turmeric sauce.

Left: Katz's Delicatessen; **Below:** A cafe in Brooklyn (p93)
(LEFT) HUW JONES/GETTY IMAGES ©; (BELOW) IMAGE SOURCE/GETTY IMAGES ©

Lombardi's   Pizza $$

(Map p62; 🖊 212-941-7994; 32 Spring St btwn Mulberry & Mott Sts; 6-slice pizza $16.50; ⊙11:30am-11pm Mon-Thu & Sun, to midnight Fri & Sat; [S] 6 to Spring St) The first pizzeria in America was Lombardi's, and it still draws crowds for its excellent thin-crust pizza.

LOWER EAST SIDE

Katz's Delicatessen   Deli $

(Map p62; 🖊 212-254-2246; www.katzs delicatessen.com; 205 E Houston St at Ludlow St; pastrami on rye $17; ⊙8am-10:45pm Mon-Wed & Sun, to 2:45am Thu-Sat ; [S] F/V to Lower East Side-2nd Ave) One of the few remaining Jewish delicatessens in the city, Katz's whips up massive pastrami and corned beef sandwiches. Hold on to the ticket you're handed when you walk in to this New York City icon, and pay cash only.

Alias   Modern American $$

(Map p62; 🖊 212-505-5011; 76 Clinton St; ⊙6-11pm Tue-Fri, 11am-11:30pm Sat, 10:30am-10:30pm Sun; [S] F to Delancey St) Alias continues to deliver delicious, fresh food, heavy on seasonal ingredients, with dishes like Wild Alaskan black cod, maple syrup–drenched pears with ricotta and tomato-braised brisket.

SOHO & NOHO

Boqueria Soho   Spanish Tapas $$

(Map p62; 🖊 212-343-4255; 171 Spring St btwn West Broadway & Thompson St; mains $13.50; ⊙lunch & dinner daily, brunch Sat & Sun; [S] C/E to Spring St) This expansive, welcoming tapas joint features classics as well as new twists on the expected, and you can watch them being assembled as you sip your unique beer-and-pear sangria and peer into the open kitchen.

Dutch   Modern American $$

(Map p62; 🖊 212-677-6200; www.thedutchnyc. com; 131 Sullivan St btwn Prince & Houston Sts; mains $19-52; ⊙11:30am-3pm Mon-Fri,

Best Eating in Chinatown

With hundreds of restaurants, from holes-in-the-wall to banquet-sized dining rooms, Chinatown is wonderful for exploring cheap eats on an empty stomach.

Amazing 66 (Map p62; 66 Mott St, at Canal St; mains $7; ☺11am-11pm; ⑤6, J, N/Q to Canal St) Terrific Cantonese lunches.

Prosperity Dumpling (Map p62; ☎212-343-0683; 46 Eldridge St btwn Hester & Canal Sts; dumplings $1-3; ☺7:30am-10pm; ⑤B/D to Grand St; F to East Broadway; J to Bowery) Among the best dumpling joints.

Bánh Mì Saigon Bakery (Map p62; ☎212-941-1514; www.banhmisaigonnyc.com; 198 Grand St btwn Mulberry & Mott Sts, sandwiches $3.50-5.75; ☺8am-6pm; ⑤N/Q/R, J/Z, 6 to Canal St) Some of the best Vietnamese sandwiches in town.

Joe's Shanghai (Map p62; ☎212-233-8888; www.joeshanghairestaurants.com; 9 Pell St btwn Bowery & Doyers St; mains $5-26; ☺11am-11pm; ⑤N/Q/R, J/Z, 6 to Canal St, B/D to Grand St) Always busy and tourist-friendly. Does good noodle and soup dishes.

Nom Wah Tea Parlor (Map p62; 13 Doyers St; mains $4-9; ☺10:30am-9pm; ⑤6, J, N/Q to Canal St) Looks like a well-worn American diner, but is the oldest dim sum place in the city.

Original Chinatown Ice Cream Factory (Map p62; ☎212-608-4170; www.chinatownicecreamfactory.com; 65 Bayard St; scoop $4; ☺11am-10pm; ⦿; ⑤N/Q/R, J/Z, 6 to Canal St) Flavorful scoops of green tea, ginger, passionfruit and lychee sorbets.

5:30pm-midnight Mon-Thu & Sun, 5:30pm-1am Fri & Sat, 10am-3pm Sat & Sun; ⑤C/E to Spring St, N/R to Prince St, 1 to Houston St) Oysters on ice and freshly baked homemade pies are the notable bookends of a meal – in the middle is fresh-from-the-farm cuisine, served in casseroles with the perfect amount of ceremony.

Il Buco
Italian $$$

(Map p62; ☎212-533-1932; www.ilbuco.com; 47 Bond St btwn Bowery & Lafayette St; mains $21-32; ☺noon-11pm Mon-Thu, to midnight Fri & Sat, 5-10:30pm Sun; ⑤B/D/F/V to Broadway-Lafayette St, 6 to Bleecker St) This charming, atmospheric nook features hanging copper pots, kerosene lamps and antique furniture, plus a stunning menu and wine list. Sink your teeth into seasonal and ever-changing highlights like white polenta with braised broccoli rabe and anchovies.

EAST VILLAGE

Veselka
Ukrainian $

(Map p62; ☎212-228-9682; www.veselka.com; 144 Second Ave at 9th St; mains $6-14; ☺24hr; ⑤L to 3rd Ave, 6 to Astor Pl) Generations of East Villagers have been coming to this bustling institution for blintzes and breakfast regardless of the hour.

Angelica Kitchen
Vegan, Cafe $$

(Map p62; ☎212-228-2909; www.angelicakitchen.com; 300 E 12th St btwn First & Second Aves; dishes $14-20; ☺11:30am-10:30pm; ⦿; ⑤L to 1st Ave) This enduring herbivore classic has a calming vibe and enough creative options to make your head spin.

Momofuku Noodle Bar
Noodles $$

(Map p62; ☎212-777-7773; www.momofuku.com/noodle-bar/; 171 First Ave btwn 10th & 11th Sts; mains $16-25; ☺noon-11pm Sun-Thu, to 2am Fri & Sat; ⑤L to 1st Ave, 6 to Astor Pl) Ramen and steamed buns are the name of the game at this infinitely creative Japanese eatery, part of the growing David Chang empire. Seating is on stools at a long bar or at communal tables.

CHELSEA, MEATPACKING DISTRICT & WEST (GREENWICH) VILLAGE

Chelsea Market   Market $
(Map p68; www.chelseamarket.com; 75 9th Ave; ☺7am-9pm Mon-Sat, 8am-8pm Sun; ⑤A/C/E to 14th St) This former factory has an 800ft-long shopping concourse lined with bakeries, cafes, food stalls, gourmet shops and eateries.

Fatty Crab   Pan-Asian $$
(Map p62; ☏212-352-3590; www.fattycrab.com; 643 Hudson St btwn Gansevoort & Horatio Sts; mains $16-28; ☺noon-midnight Mon-Wed, to 2am Thu & Fri, 11am-2am Sat, 11am-midnight Sun; ⑤L to 8th Ave; A/C/E, 1/2/3 to 14th St) This small Malaysian-inspired joint is always teeming with locals who swing by in droves to devour fish curries and pork belly accompanied by a signature selection of cocktails.

Tartine   French $$
(Map p62; ☏212-229-2611; www.tartinecafenyc.com; 253 W 11th St btwn 4th St & Waverly Pl; mains $10-24; ☺9am-10:30pm Mon-Sat, to 10pm Sun; ⑤1/2/3 to 14th St, 1/2 to Christopher St-Sheridan Sq, L to 8th Ave) Tartine is the corner bistro of your Frenchified dreams: wobbly stacks of chairs and tables, pink steaks and escargot, set in a teeny-tiny room. It's BYOB.

Babbo   Italian $$$
(Map p62; ☏212-777-0303; www.babbonyc.com; 110 Waverly Pl; mains $19-29; ☺11:30am-11:15pm, from 5pm Sun; ⑤C/E, B/D/F to W 4th St, 1 to Christopher St-Sheridan Sq) This two-level split townhouse might be

the best in celebrity chef Mario Batali's empire. Reserve ahead.

UNION SQUARE & FLATIRON DISTRICT & GRAMERCY PARK

Shake Shack   Burgers $
(Map p68; ☏212-989-6600; www.shakeshack.com; cnr 23rd St & Madison Ave; burgers from $3.60; ☺11am-11pm; ⑤R/W to 23rd St) Tourists line up in droves for the hamburgers and shakes at this Madison Square Park counter-window institution.

Eataly   Italian $$
(Map p68; www.eatalyny.com; 200 Fifth Ave at 23rd St; ☺8am-11pm; ⑤F, N/R, 6 to 23rd St) Across from Madison Square Park, Eataly features specialty dining halls, all with a different focus (pizza, fish, vegetables, meat, pasta). There's also a gelateria, a grocery and the *pièce de résistance,* a rooftop beer garden restaurant.

A hot dog stand on Broadway
MERTEN SNIJDERS/GETTY IMAGES ©

MIDTOWN

Burger Joint
Burgers **$**

(Map p68; www.burgerjointny.com; Le Parker Meridien, 119 W 56th St btwn Sixth & Seventh Aves; burgers from $7.80; ⊗11am-11:30pm Sun-Thu, to midnight Fri & Sat; ⑤F to 57th St) This speakeasy burger hut loiters behind the curtain in the lobby of the Le Parker Meridien hotel. You'll find graffiti-strewn walls, retro booths and attitude-loaded staff slapping up beef-n-patty brilliance.

Hangawi
Korean **$$**

(Map p68; ☏212-213-0077; www.hangawi restaurant.com; 12 E 32nd St btwn Fifth & Madison Aves; lunch dishes $10-16, dinner mains $16-26; ⊗noon-2:45pm & 5-10:15pm Mon-Thu, to 10.30pm Fri, 1-10.30pm Sat, 5-9:30pm Sun; ⍝; ⑤B/D/F/M, N/Q/R to 34th St-Herald Sq) Leave your shoes at the entrance and slip into a soothing, zenlike space at this sublime restaurant serving meat-free Korean fare.

Taboon
Mediterranean **$$$**

(Map p68; ☏212-713-0271; 773 Tenth Ave; mains $25-32; ⊗5-11pm Mon-Sat, 11am-10pm Sun; ⑤C/E to 50th St) A white-domed oven grabs the eye as you enter this airy, stone-floored and brick-walled eatery.

The food is a fusion from both sides of the Mediterranean.

UPPER WEST SIDE

Barney Greengrass
Deli **$$**

(Map p80; www.barneygreengrass.com; 541 Amsterdam Ave at 86th St; mains $9-20, bagel with cream cheese $5; ⊗8:30am-6pm Tue-Sun; ⍗; ⑤1 to 86th St) Old-school Upper Westsiders and pilgrims from other neighborhoods crowd this century-old 'sturgeon king.' It serves a long list of traditional if pricey Jewish delicacies, from bagels and lox to sturgeon scrambled with eggs and onions.

Dovetail
Modern American **$$$**

(Map p80; ☏212-362-3800; www.dovetailnyc. com; 103 W 77th St at Columbus Ave; tasting menu $88, mains $36-58; ⊗5:30-10pm Mon-Sat, 11:30am-10pm Sun; ⍝; ⑤A/C, B to 81st St-Museum of Natural History, 1 to 79th St) Everything about this Michelin-starred restaurant is simple, from the decor (exposed brick, bare tables) to the uncomplicated seasonal menus focused on bracingly fresh produce and quality meats.

A display of pretzels

Detour:
Queens

Of the city's five boroughs, Queens is top dog in size and runner-up in head count. So where to begin? Start your explorations in Long Island City (LIC). It's packed with contemporary-art musts like **MoMA PS1** (www.momaps1.org ; 22-25 Jackson Ave at 46th Ave, Long Island City; adult/child $10/free, admission for MoMA ticketholders free, Warm Up party admission online/at venue $15/18; ☺noon-6pm Thu-Mon, Warm Up parties 3-9pm Sat Jul-early Sep; ⓢE, M to 23rd St-Ely Ave, G to 21st, 7 to 45th Rd-Court House Sq) and the lesser-known **Fisher Landau Center for Art** (www.flcart.org; 38-27 30th St, Long Island City; admission free; ☺noon-5pm Thu-Mon; ⓢN/Q to 39th Ave). Watch the sun set over Manhattan from **Gantry Plaza State Park** (www.nysparks.com/parks/149; 4-09 47th Rd, Long Island City; ⓢ7 to Vernon Blvd-Jackson Ave), and sip and sup in the locally loved restaurants lining Vernon Blvd.

You could also spend the day exploring neighboring Astoria, taste-testing its ethnic nosh spots; the Greek restaurant **Taverna Kyclades** (☎718-545-8666; www. tavernakyclades.com; 33-07 Ditmars Ave at 33rd St, Astoria; mains $11.50-35; ☺noon-11pm Mon-Sat, to 10pm Sun; ⓢN/Q to Astoria-Ditmars Blvd) is a favorite. Down Czech beers at the **Bohemian Hall & Beer Garden** (www.bohemianhall.com; 29-19 24th Ave btwn 29th & 31st Sts, Astoria; ☺5pm-1am Mon-Thu, to 3am Fri, noon-3am Sat, noon-1am Sun ; ⓢN/Q to Astoria Blvd), and get a cultural fix at the brilliant **Noguchi Museum** (www.noguchi.org; 9-01 33rd Rd at Vernon Blvd, Long Island City; adult/child $10/free, by donation 1st Fri of the month; ☺10am-5pm Wed-Fri, 11am-6pm Sat & Sun; ⓢN/Q to Broadway).

Further out, Flushing (home to NYC's biggest Chinatown) also merits a full-day adventure, with hawker-style food stands and restaurants – such as the superb **Hunan Kitchen of Grand Sichuan** (www.thegrandsichuan.com; 42-47 Main St, Flushing; mains $9.50-23; ☺11am-12.30am; ⓢ7 to Flushing-Main St) – plus exotic grocery stores, kitschy malls and reflexology therapists.

UPPER EAST SIDE

Earl's Beer & Cheese   American $
(Map p80; www.earlsny.com; 1259 Park Ave btwn 97th & 98th Sts; grilled cheese $6-8, mains $8-17; ☺4pm-midnight Tue-Fri, 11am-midnight Sat & Sun; ⓢ6 to 96th St) Chef Corey Cova's comfort-food outpost channels a hipster hunting vibe. Basic grilled cheese is a paradigm shifter, served with pork belly, fried egg and kimchi. There is also mac 'n' cheese and waffles (with foie gras), none of it like anything you've ever eaten.

Sfoglia   Italian $$$
(Map p80; ☎212-831-1402; 1402 Lexington Ave at E 92nd St; mains $26; ☺noon-10pm Mon-Sat, from 5:30pm Sun; ⓢ6 to 96th St) A darling of the critics, Sfoglia brought its winning combo of fresh seafood and homemade Italian from Nantucket to New York.

David Burke
Townhouse   Modern American $$$
(Map p80; ☎212-813-2121; www.david burketownhouse.com; 133 E 61st; mains $20-55; ☺11:45am-10:30pm Mon-Sat, 10:30am-9pm Sun; ⓢF to Lexington Ave-63rd St, N/R, W to Lexington Ave-59th St) Despite the stylish trappings, food is the focus in this converted Upper East Side townhouse. Standouts include salmon with warm potato knish, pretzel-crusted crabcake and yellowfin tuna on saltrock.

 Drinking & Nightlife

DOWNTOWN

Birreria   Beer Garden
(Map p68; www.eatalyny.com; 200 Fifth Ave at 23rd St; mains $17-26; ☺11:30am-midnight Sun-Wed, to 1am Thu-Sat ; ⓢF/M, N/R, 6 to 23rd St)

Atop Eataly is this rooftop garden, with an encyclopedic beer menu and tasty fare (try the signature pork shoulder).

Pravda
Cocktail Bar

(Map p62; ☎212-226-4944; 281 Lafayette St btwn Prince & Houston Sts; ⑤B/D/F/V to Broadway-Lafayette St) This subterranean bar heavy with Soviet-era nostalgia has red-leather banquettes and inviting armchairs. Enjoy blinis and handsomely made cocktails.

DBA
Bar

(Map p62; ☎212-475-5097; www.drinkgoodstuff. com; 41 First Ave btwn 2nd & 3rd Sts; ⊙1pm-4am; ⑤F/V to Lower East Side-2nd Ave) There are more than 200 beers here, plus 130 single-malt scotches and a few dozen tequilas. There's a tiny plastic-chair patio out the back, but most of the action is near the taps.

Louis 649
Bar

(Map p62; ☎212-673-1190; www.louis649.com; 649 E 9th St, near Ave C; ⊙6pm-4am; ⑤L to 1st Ave) Beloved by its patrons for the affordable prices and down-home, no-frills decor.

Sway Lounge
Club

(Map p62; ☎212-620-5220; www.swaylounge. com; 305 Spring St; ⊙10pm-3am Thu-Sun; ⑤C/E to Spring St) Small, seductive and sleek with an elegant Moroccan decor, Sway's got a tough door policy, but there's room to dance to '80s on Thursday nights, rock and hip-hop Fridays, and DJs like Mark Ronson and DJ Herschel other nights.

Mehanata
Club

(Map p62; ☎212-625-0981; www.mehanata.com; 113 Ludlow St; ⑤F, J/M/Z to Delancey St-Essex St) The 'Bulgarian Bar' is still gypsy heaven for East Euro chic and indie popsters. East Euro DJs spin some nights, and belly dancers and 'gypsy bands' take the small stage for jumping-in-place dancers.

Cielo
Club

(Map p62; ☎212-645-5700; www.cieloclub. com; 18 Little W 12th St; cover charge $15-25; ⊙10:30pm-5am Mon-Sat; ⑤A/C/E, L to 8th Ave-14th St) Known for its intimate space and kick-ass sound system, this space age–looking Meatpacking District staple packs in a fashionable, multiculti crowd

Jazz at Lincoln Center (p89)

Jazz

From bebop to free improvisation, in classic art-deco clubs and at intimate jam sessions, you'll find a stunning array of talent in NYC.

Smalls (Map p62; ☏212-252-5091; www.smallsjazzclub.com; 183 W 4th St; cover $20) is a subterranean jazz dungeon that rivals the world-famous **Village Vanguard** (Map p62; ☏212-255-4037; www.villagevanguard.com; 178 Seventh Ave at 11th St; ⓢ1/2/3 to 14th St) in terms of sheer talent.

Heading uptown, Dizzy's Club Coca-Cola, at **Jazz at Lincoln Center** (Map p80; ☏tickets to Dizzy's Club Coca-Cola 212-258-9595, tickets to Rose Theater & Allen Room 212-721-6500; www.jazzatlincolncenter.org; Time Warner Center, Broadway at 60th St; ⓢA/C, B/D, 1 to 59th St-Columbus Circle) – one of Lincoln Center's three jazz venues – has stunning views overlooking Central Park and nightly shows featuring top line-ups. Further north on the Upper West Side, check out the **Smoke Jazz & Supper Club-Lounge** (Map p80; ☏212-864-6662; www.smokejazz.com; 2751 Broadway btwn W 105th & 106th Sts), which gets crowded on weekends.

nightly for its blend of tribal, old-school house and soulful grooves.

MIDTOWN

Russian Vodka Room   Bar
(Map p68; ☏212-307-5835; 265 W 52nd St btwn Eighth Ave & Broadway; ⓢC/E to 50th St) Actual Russians aren't uncommon at this swanky and welcoming bar. The lighting is dark and the corner booths intimate, but more importantly the dozens of flavored vodkas, from cranberry to horseradish, are fun to experiment with.

Top of the Strand   Cocktail Bar
(Map p68; www.topofthestrand.com; Strand Hotel, 33 W 37th St btwn Fifth & Sixth Aves; ⊙5pm-midnight Mon & Sun, to 1am Tue-Sat; ♿; ⓢB/D/F/M to 34th St) For that 'Oh my God, I'm in New York' feeling, head to the Strand Hotel's rooftop bar, order a martini and take in the staggering view of the Empire State Building.

Morrell Wine Bar & Café   Bar, Cafe
(Map p68; ☏212-262-7700; 1 Rockefeller Plaza, W 48th St btwn Fifth & Sixth Aves; ⊙11:30am-11pm Mon-Sat, noon-6pm Sun; ⓢB/D/F/M to 47th-50th Sts-Rockefeller Center) The list of vinos at this pioneering wine bar is over 2000 long, with a whopping 150 available by the glass. And the airy, split-level room, right

across from the famous skating rink, is equally as intoxicating.

Therapy   Gay
(Map p68; www.therapy-nyc.com; 348 W 52nd St btwn Eighth & Ninth Aves; ⊙5pm-2am Sun-Thu, to 4am Fri & Sat; ⓢC/E, 1 to 50th St) Multi-leveled, airy and sleekly contemporary, Therapy is a longstanding gay Hell's Kitchen hot spot.

UPTOWN

79th Street Boat Basin   Bar
(Map p80; W 79th St, in Riverside Park; ⊙noon-11pm) A covered, open-sided party spot under the ancient arches of a park over-pass, this is an Upper West Side favorite once spring hits. Order a pitcher and some snacks and enjoy the sunset view over the Hudson River.

Bemelmans Bar   Lounge
(Map p80; www.thecarlyle.com/dining/bemelmans_bar; Carlyle Hotel, 35 E 76th St at Madison Ave; ⊙noon-2am Mon-Sat, to 12:30am Sun; ⓢ6 to 77th St) Waiters wear white jack-ets, a baby grand piano is always being played and Ludwig Bemelman's *Madeline* murals surround you. It's a classic spot for a serious cocktail.

⭐ Entertainment

New York magazine, *Time Out New York* and the weekend editions of the *New York Times* are great guides for what's on once you arrive.

LIVE MUSIC

Joe's Pub   Live Music

(Map p62; 📞212-539-8778; www.joespub.com; Public Theater, 425 Lafayette St btwn Astor Pl & 4th St; 🚇R/W to 8th St-NYU, 6 to Astor Pl) Part cabaret theater, part rock and new-indie venue, this small and lovely supper club hosts a wonderful variety of styles, voices and talent.

Rockwood Music Hall   Live Music

(Map p62; 📞212-477-4155; www.rockwood musichall.com; 196 Allen St btwn Houston & Stanton Sts; 🚇F/V to Lower East Side-2nd Ave) This breadbox-sized two-room concert space features a rapid-fire flow of bands and singer-songwriters, no cover, and a max of one hour per band.

Bowery Ballroom   Live Music

(Map p62; 📞212-533-2111; www.boweryballroom. com; 6 Delancey St at Bowery St; 🕐performance times vary; 🚇J/M/Z to Bowery St) This terrific, medium-sized venue has the perfect sound and feel for more blown-up indie-rock acts (The Shins, Stephen Malkmus, Patti Smith).

Le Poisson Rouge   Live Music

(Map p62; 📞212-505-3474; www.lepoissonrouge. com; 158 Bleecker St; 🚇A/C/E, B/D/F/V to W 4th St-Washington Sq) This Bleecker St basement club is one of the premier venues for experimental contemporary, from classical to indie rock to electro-acoustic.

THEATER

Choose from current shows by checking print publications, or a website such as **Theater Mania** (📞212-352-3101; www. theatermania.com). You can purchase tickets through **Telecharge** (📞212-239-6200; www. telecharge.com) and **Ticketmaster** (📞800-745-3000, 800-448-7849; www.ticketmaster. com) for standard ticket sales, or **TKTS ticket booths** (www.tdf.org/tkts; cnr Front & John Sts; 🕐11am-6pm Mon-Sat, to 4pm Sun; 🚇A/C to Broadway-Nassau, 2/3, 4/5, J/Z to Fulton St) for same-day tickets to a selection of Broadway and off-Broadway musicals at up to 50% off regular prices.

SPORTS

The uber-successful **New York Yankees** (📞718-293-6000, tickets 877-469-9849) play at **Yankee Stadium** (📞718-293-4300, tickets 212-926-5337; www.yankees.com; E 161st St at River Ave, the Bronx; tours $20, tickets $20-235; 🚇B/D, 4 to 161st St-Yankee Stadium), while the more historically beleaguered **New York Mets** (📞718-507-8499; www.mets.com; tickets $19-130) play at **Citi**

Carnegie Hall

Field (126th St at Roosevelt Ave, Flushing, Queens; **S** 7 to Mets-Willets Pt).

For basketball, you can get courtside with the NBA's **New York Knicks** (Map p68; www.nyknicks.com; tickets from $109) at **Madison Square Garden** (Map p68; www.thegarden.com; Seventh Ave btwn 31st & 33rd Sts, Midtown West; **S** A/C/E, 1/2/3 to 34th St-Penn Station), called the 'mecca of basketball,' and the rejuvenated franchise of the **Brooklyn Nets** (www.nba.com/nets; tickets from $15), previously the New Jersey Nets, who played their inaugural season at the **Barclays Center** (www.barclayscenter.com; cnr Flatbush & Atlantic Aves, Prospect Heights; **S** B/D, N/Q/R, 2/3, 4/5 to Atlantic Ave) in downtown Brooklyn in 2012.

New York City's NFL (pro-football) teams, the **Giants** (www.giants.com) and **Jets** (www.newyorkjets.com), share **MetLife Stadium** in East Rutherford, New Jersey.

 Shopping

While chain stores have proliferated, NYC is still the best American city for shopping. It's not unusual for shops – especially downtown boutiques – to stay open until 10pm or 11pm.

DOWNTOWN

Strand Book Store
Books

(Map p62; ☎212-473-1452; www.strandbooks.com; 828 Broadway at 12th St; ☺9:30am-10:30pm Mon-Sat, 11am-10:30pm Sun; **S** L, N/Q/R/W, 4/5/6 to 14th St-Union Sq) The city's preeminent bibliophile warehouse, selling new and used books.

Century 21
Fashion

(Map p62; www.c21stores.com; 22 Cortlandt St btwn Church St & Broadway; ☺7:45am-9pm Mon-Wed, to 9:30pm Thu & Fri, 10am-9pm Sat, 11am-8pm Sun; **S** A/C, J/Z, 2/3, 4/5 to Fulton St, N/R to Cortlandt St) A four-level department store loved by New Yorkers of every income. It's shorthand for designer bargains.

♥ If You Like...
Performing Arts

If you like the Lincoln Center (p72), don't pass up an opportunity to see a great show at one of these celebrated venues.

1 BROOKLYN ACADEMY OF MUSIC
(BAM; ☎718-636-4139; www.bam.org; 30 Lafayette Ave at Ashland Pl, Fort Greene; **S** 2/3, 4/5, B, Q to Atlantic Ave) Like an edgier version of Lincoln Center, BAM hosts everything from modern dance to opera, cutting-edge theater and music concerts.

2 CARNEGIE HALL
(Map p68; ☎212-247-7800; www.carnegiehall.org; W 57th St & Seventh Ave; tours adult/child $15/5; ☺tours 11.30am, 12.30pm, 2pm & 3pm Mon-Fri, 11.30am & 12.30pm Sat, 12.30pm Sun Oct-May; **S** N/Q/R to 57th St-7th Ave) Since 1891, the historic Carnegie Hall has hosted performances by the likes of Tchaikovsky, Mahler and Prokofiev, and more recently Stevie Wonder, Sting and Tony Bennett.

3 JOYCE THEATER
(Map p68; ☎212-242-0800; www.joyce.org; 175 Eighth Ave; **S** C/E to 23rd St; A/C/E to 8th Ave-14th St; 1 to 18th St) A favorite among dance junkies because of its excellent sight lines and offbeat offerings.

Other Music
Music

(Map p62; ☎212-477-8150; www.othermusic.com; 15 E 4th St; ☺11am-9pm Mon-Fri, noon-8pm Sat, noon-7pm Sun; **S** 6 to Bleecker St) This indie-run music has won over a loyal fan base with its informed selection of new and used CDs and vinyl.

MIDTOWN & UPTOWN

Tiffany & Co
Jewelry, Homewares

(Map p68; www.tiffany.com; 727 Fifth Ave; ☺10am-7pm Mon-Sat, noon-6pm Sun; **S** F to 57th St, N/Q/R to 5th Ave-59th St) This famous jeweler, with the trademark clock-hoisting Atlas over the door, carries fine

If You Like...
Cutting-Edge Art Exhibitions

If you like the Museum of Modern Art (p67), pay a visit to New York's other three world-class contemporary art galleries.

1 NEW MUSEUM OF CONTEMPORARY ART
(Map p62; ☏212-219-1222; www.newmuseum.org; 235 Bowery btwn Stanton & Rivington Sts; adult/child $16/free, 7-9pm Thu free; ☺11am-6pm Wed & Fri-Sun, to 9pm Thu; ⓢN/R to Prince St, F to 2nd Ave, J/Z to Bowery, 6 to Spring St) Housed in an architecturally ambitious building on a formerly gritty Bowery strip, the stellar New Museum is dedicated solely to contemporary art.

2 GUGGENHEIM MUSEUM
(Map p80; ☏212-423-3500; www.guggenheim.org; 1071 Fifth Ave at 89th St; adult/child $22/free, by donation 5:45-7:45pm Sat; ☺10am-5:45pm Sun-Wed & Fri, to 7:45pm Sat; ⓓ; ⓢ4/5/6 to 86th St) This inspired work of Frank Lloyd Wright, and its sweeping spiral of a staircase, is a superb sculpture, holding 20th-century paintings by Picasso, Pollock, Chagall and Kandinsky.

3 WHITNEY MUSEUM OF AMERICAN ART
(Map p80; ☏212-570-3600; www.whitney.org; 945 Madison Ave at 75th St; adult/child $20/free; ☺11am-6pm Wed, Thu, Sat & Sun, 1-9pm Fri; ⓢ6 to 77th St) One of the few museums that concentrates on American works of art, specializing in 20th-century and contemporary art, with works by Hopper, Pollock and Rothko, as well as special shows, such as the much-ballyhooed Biennial. Currently uptown, the Whitney will move to a new Renzo Piano–designed building in the Meatpacking District in 2015.

diamond rings, watches, necklaces and other accessories, as well as crystal and glassware.

Saks Fifth Ave Department Store
(Map p68; www.saksfifthavenue.com; 611 Fifth Ave at 50th St; ☺10am-8pm Mon-Sat, 11am-7pm Sun; ⓢB/D/F/M to 47th-50th Sts-Rockefeller Center, E/M to 5th Ave-53rd St) Complete with beautiful vintage elevators, Saks' 10-floor flagship store fuses old-world glamour with solid service and must-have labels.

Macy's Department Store
(Map p68; www.macys.com; 151 W 34th St at Broadway; ☺9am-9.30pm Mon-Fri, 10am-9.30pm Sat, 11am-8.30pm Sun; ⓢB/D/F/M, N/Q/R to 34th St-Herald Sq) The grande dame of Midtown department stores sells everything from jeans to kitchen appliances.

Bloomingdale's Department Store
(Map p80; www.bloomingdales.com; 1000 Third Ave at E 59th St; ☺10am-8:30pm Mon-Sat, 11am-7pm Sun; ☏; ⓢ4/5/6 to 59th St, N/Q/R to Lexington Ave-59th St) Uptown, the sprawling, overwhelming Bloomingdale's is akin to the Metro-politan Museum of Art for shoppers.

ⓘ Information

New York City & Company (Map p68; ☏212-484-1222; www.nycgo.com; 810 Seventh Ave at 53rd St; ☺8:30am-6pm Mon-Fri, 9am-5pm Sat & Sun; ⓢB/D/E to 7th Ave) The official information service of the Convention & Visitors Bureau has helpful multilingual staff and various branches around town.

ⓘ Getting Around

To/from the Airport

Taxis charge a $52 flat rate (plus toll and tip) from JFK to anywhere in Manhattan. Fares are metered from Newark (approximately $55 to $75) and LaGuardia ($40 to $50).

A cheaper and pretty easy option to or from JFK is the AirTrain ($5 one way), which connects to subway lines into the city ($2.50; coming from the city, take the Far Rockaway–bound A train) or to the LIRR ($7 to $10 one way) at Jamaica Station in Queens (this is probably the quickest route to Penn Station in the city).

To or from Newark, the AirTrain links all terminals to a New Jersey Transit train station, which connects to Penn Station in NYC ($12.50 one way combined NJ Transit/Airtrain ticket).

All three airports are also served by express buses ($16) and shuttle vans ($23); such

Detour:
Brooklyn

Brooklyn is a world in and of itself. With 2.5 million people and growing, from well-to-do new parents seeking stately brownstones in Park Slope to young band members wanting cheap rents near gigs in Williamsburg, this borough has long succeeded Manhattan in the cool and livability factors in many people's minds. With sandy beaches and breezy boardwalks at one end, foodie destinations at the other, and a massive range of ethnic enclaves, world-class entertainment, stately architecture and endless shopping strips in between, Brooklyn is a rival to Manhattan's attractions.

Here's a quick rundown of top neighborhoods for exploring:

Williamsburg Young alternative scene with loads of art galleries, record stores, bars and eateries.

Brooklyn Heights Gorgeous tree-lined streets and a promenade with stellar Lower Manhattan views (at the end of Montague St).

Dumbo Atmospheric brick streets on the waterfront; art galleries, shops, cafes and picture-postcard Manhattan views.

Fort Greene Pretty and racially diverse 'hood; home of famed Brooklyn Academy of Music (p91), a highly respected performing-arts complex and cinema.

Boerum Hill, Cobble Hill & Carroll Gardens Tree-lined streets, attractive brownstones, and restaurant-lined Smith and Court Sts.

Park Slope Classic brownstones, loads of great eateries and boutiques (along Fifth Ave and Seventh Ave), and lush 585-acre **Prospect Park** (☎718-965-8951; www.prospectpark.org; Grand Army Plaza; ⏰5am-1am; S2/3 to Grand Army Plaza, F to 15th St-Prospect Park) and the **Brooklyn Botanic Garden** (www.bbg.org; 1000 Washington Ave at Crown St; adult/child $10/free, Tue & 10am-noon Sat free; ⏰8am-6pm Tue-Fri, 10am-6pm Sat & Sun mid-March–Oct, 8am-4:30pm Tue-Fri, 10am-4:30pm Sat & Sun Nov–Mar; ♿; S2/3 to Eastern Pkwy-Brooklyn Museum).

Coney Island Old-fashioned boardwalk, amusement park and **aquarium** (www.nyaquarium.com; Surf Ave & W 8th St; adult/child $15/11, with 4-D theater show $19/15; ⏰10am-6pm Mon-Fri, to 7pm Sat & Sun May-Sep; ♿; SF, Q to W 8th St-NY Aquarium).

companies include the New York Airport Service Express Bus (☎718-560-3915; www.nyairportservice.com; ⏰ approx every 20 min), which leaves every 20 or so minutes for Port Authority, Penn Station (NYC) and Grand Central Station; and Super Shuttle Manhattan (www.supershuttle.com), which picks you (and others) up anywhere, on demand, with a reservation.

Bicycle

Launched in 2013, Citi Bike (www.citibikenyc.com; 24hr/7 days $11/27) is NYC's new bike-sharing program.

Public Transportation

The Metropolitan Transport Authority (MTA; ☎718-330-1234; www.mta.info) runs both the subway and bus systems (per ride $2.50). To board, you must purchase a MetroCard, available at subway windows and self-serve machines, which accept change, dollars or credit/debit cards; purchasing many rides at once works out cheaper per trip.

Washington, DC

No matter your politics, it's hard to not fall for the nation's capital.

Washington, DC, is a proud and complicated city of grand boulevards, iconic monuments, and idyllic vistas over the Potomac River. Its museums and historic sites bear tribute to both the beauty and the horrors of years past. Even on a short visit you can delve into the world of Americana – from moving artworks by Native American painters to memorable moonwalks from the likes of Neil Armstrong and Michael Jackson.

Of course DC is much more than a mere museum piece or marble backdrop to nightly news reports. It is a city of tree-lined neighborhoods and a vibrant theater scene, with ethnically diverse restaurants and a dynamism percolating just beneath the surface. It has a number of markets, historic cobblestone streets and a rich African-American heritage.

Lincoln Memorial (p108)

The Capitol (p112) and Washington Monument (p105)

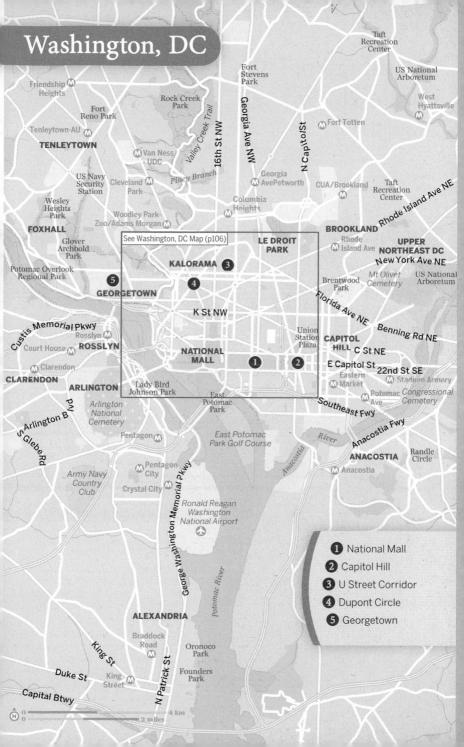

Washington, DC's Highlights

National Mall

Marble buildings that resemble Greek temples, Abe Lincoln and a reflecting pool, hallowed memorials and staggering museums – the Mall (p104 and p110) is all this and more. It is America's great public space, where citizens come to visit iconic sights, protest their government, go for scenic runs and commune with the country's most revered icons. Below: *The Three Soliders* bronze statue by Frederick Hart, Vietnam Veterans Memorial, National Mall

Capitol Hill

Looming large over DC and America's political landscape, the magnificent Capitol (p112) building, with its massive 285ft cast-iron dome, is both the geographic heart of the city and the political center of the US government. It is also the nexus of the fascinating Capitol Hill neighborhood, home to a vibrant restaurant scene, streets lined with elegant townhouses, and a fabulous food market. Left: Interior of the Capitol's dome

U Street Corridor

3

Home to eclectic galleries, boutiques and cafes, the U Street Corridor (p123) has seen dramatic changes since its days of urban decay in the late 20th century. By night, live music spills out of clubs and bars, while restaurant-goers pack stylish, low-lit dining rooms. This is Washington at its most diverse – whether black, white, straight or gay – and an obligatory stop when exploring the capital. Right: Mural at Bohemian Caverns jazz club, U Street

JASON COLSTON/GETTY IMAGES ©

4

5

Dupont Circle

A well-heeled splice of gay community and DC diplomatic scene, this is city life at its best. Great restaurants, bars, bookstores, cafes, captivating architecture and the electric energy of a lived-in, happening neighborhood make Dupont (p121) worth a linger. The local historic mansions have largely been converted into embassies, and Embassy Row (on Massachusetts Ave) runs through DC's thumping gay heart.

Georgetown

Historic buildings are thick on the ground and dripping antebellum charm in Washington's most aristocratic neighborhood. Leafy Georgetown (p113) is older than the city itself and home to the prestigious university that fuels the neighborhood's intellectual and nocturnal excesses. Great shopping and top-notch dining, plus scenic walks along the Potomac River and the picturesque C&O Canal begin here. Above: Bridge over the C&O Canal

Washington, DC's Best...

Activities for Kids

○ **National Zoo** Home to 2000 animals, including gorillas, cheetahs and pandas. (p113)

○ **National Museum of Natural History** Woolly mammoths, dinosaur bones and prehistoric sea creatures. (p104)

○ **National Mall** Run free on the grassy expanse, ride a carousel and go paddle-boating on the nearby Tidal Basin. (p104)

○ **International Spy Museum** Indulge budding spymasters at this fun, gadget-filled showcase. (p109)

Restaurants

○ **Ethiopic** Serves some of the city's best Ethiopian fare. (p118)

○ **Central Michel Richard** Celebrated bistro that blends gourmet ingredients with comfort-fare recipes. (p118)

○ **Eastern Market** Sumptuous food market with legendary crab cakes. (p117)

○ **Zaytinya** Delicious Mediterranean small plates by Spanish superstar José Andrés. (p118)

Museums

○ **National Museum of American History** A treasure chest of glorious Americana. (p104)

○ **National Museum of the American Indian** Fascinating overview of America's great indigenous cultures. (p105)

○ **Newseum** Delve into the momentous events that have shaped our times. (p112)

○ **US Holocaust Memorial Museum** A moving journey into some of the darkest days of the 20th century. (p105)

Need to Know

Architectural Gems

Jefferson Memorial
Thoughtful quotes by the great president, plus sublime views over the Tidal Basin. (p105)

Union Station A magnificent beaux-arts building. (p125)

Washington National Cathedral A Gothic masterpiece that seems straight out of medieval Europe. (p113)

Library of Congress
An inspiring monument to human knowledge, including a grand reading room with a 160ft-high dome. (p108)

Left: National Museum of the American Indian (p105); **Above:** Jefferson Memorial (p105)

ADVANCE PLANNING

Three to six months before Book a tour of the Capitol and try to book a visit to the White House.

One month before Reserve at popular restaurants and book concerts and plays.

One week before Purchase online tickets to get guaranteed line-free admission to popular sights including the Washington Monument, Ford's Theatre and the US Holocaust Memorial Museum.

RESOURCES

Washington, DC (www.washington.org) Official tourism site with useful links.

Washingtonian (www.washingtonian.com) Excellent insight into dining, shopping, entertainment and local luminaries.

Washington City Paper (www.washingtoncitypaper.com) Edgy weekly with handy listings.

DCist (www.dcist.com) Insider look at all things DC.

GETTING AROUND

Airports Key airports: Ronald Reagan Washington National (www.metwashairports.com), by metro; Washington Dulles International (www.metwashairports.com), by shuttle or taxi; and BWI (www.bwiairport.com), by shuttle, train or taxi.

Bicycle Capital Bikeshare (www.capitalbikeshare) has over 200 quick-hire stations.

Metro (www.wmata.com) Fast, safe and convenient; buy cards from self-service machines.

Taxi Widely available.

Walking Washington is divided into northeast, northwest, southeast and southwest, with the Capitol at the center. Letters go east–west, numbers north–south.

BE FOREWARNED

Museum entry Security checks (through metal detectors) are common. Arrive early to beat queues.

Crime Be cautious late at night, particularly in nightlife hot spots such as U St and Adams Morgan; muggings on lonely side streets can occur.

Georgetown Walking Tour

Founded in 1751, this neighborhood is older than Washington, DC, itself. It's home to a world-class university, garden-lined streets, fantastic shopping and dining, and idyllic scenery along the Potomac River and old C&O Canal.

WALK FACTS

- **Start** 37th & O Sts NW
- **End** Washington Harbor
- **Distance** 2.7 miles
- **Duration** 2½ hours

❶ Georgetown University

Begin at stately Georgetown University (founded 1789). Enter the campus through the iron gates at 37th and O Sts NW to admire the Gothic spires of the Healy Building.

❷ Exorcist Stairs

From the gates, walk one block east on O St and turn right on 36th St. Two blocks on, you'll pass the spot where demonically possessed Regan of *The Exorcist* sent victims to their screaming deaths.

❸ Halcyon House

Turn left and walk two blocks east on Prospect St. The private Halcyon House (3400

Prospect St) dates back to 1786; in 1900 the eccentric Albert Clemens (nephew of Mark Twain) purchased the property and, believing constant renovation would extend his life, added countless rooms.

❹ Cox's Row

Turn left on 34th St and right on N St. On the left, the five Federal houses from 3327 to 3339 are known as Cox's Row, built by the fashionable Georgetown mayor John Cox (served 1823–45).

❺ Marbury House

Further down the block, the formal, red-brick Marbury House (3307 N St) was the home of John and Jacqueline Kennedy before John became president and they moved into the White House.

⑥ Tudor Place

Continue along N St and turn left on 31st St. Five blocks up you'll find Tudor Place, the gracious urban estate of the prominent Custis Peter clan (descendants of George Washington).

⑦ Dumbarton Oaks

Continue further up 31st St to one of Georgetown's hidden highlights, the eclectic museum and gorgeous gardens of Dumbarton Oaks.

⑧ Montrose Park

Turn right and walk east on R St. The cobblestone trail on the left was years ago dubbed Lovers' Lane. It leads down into lush Dumbarton Oaks Park. Further along R St, tamer Montrose Park hosts the requisite dogs chasing balls and kids on swings.

⑨ Old Stone House

Continue on R St, turn right on 28th St and right again on M St. After two blocks, you'll pass the Old Stone House. It was built in 1765, making it the oldest standing building in Washington.

⑩ C&O Canal

Turn left onto Jefferson St and cross the C&O Canal, a bucolic waterway with a picturesque cobbled lane running alongside it. The canal, one of the civil engineering feats of the 19th century, runs 185 miles from here to Cumberland, MD.

⑪ Washington Harbor

End your saunter at Washington Harbor, a riverside complex with loads of outdoor restaurants and bars. There are great views over the Potomac River, with Roosevelt Island in front and the Kennedy Center to the left.

Washington, DC in...

TWO DAYS

Start at the **Air & Space Museum** (p104), followed by the **Museum of Natural History** (p104). Visit the **Museum of the American Indian** (p105) for aboriginal lore. Wander to the **Lincoln Memorial** (p108) and **Vietnam Veterans Memorial** (p108), then to U Street for dinner. The next day head to the **US Holocaust Memorial Museum** (p105); stroll alongside the Tidal Basin and see the **Martin Luther King Jr National Memorial** (p105). At twilight pass the **White House** (p120), then have dinner around Capitol Hill.

FOUR DAYS

On day three, take our walking tour, followed by lunch at **Martin's Tavern** (p122). Hike in **Rock Creek Park** (p114) then head to Dupont Circle for dinner, followed by drinks at **18th Street Lounge** (p123). On the last day visit the **Newseum** (p112), **Capitol** (p112) and **Library of Congress** (p108), then walk to **Eastern Market** (p117) for a meal. That evening, go to bohemian H Street NE; **Granville Moore's** (p117) is a good place to start the night.

Jefferson Building, Library of Congress (p108)

Discover
Washington, DC

At a Glance

- **National Mall** (p104) Iconic museums and monuments, sparse eating options.

- **Capitol Hill** (p108) Architectural gems and a foodie-loving market.

- **Tidal Basin** (p109) Cherry blossoms, picturesque memorials.

- **Downtown** (p109) People-packed streets, shopping, dining.

- **Adams Morgan, Shaw & U Street** (p123) Washington's best nightlife.

- **Dupont Circle** (p121) Trendy eating and drinking spots.

- **Georgetown** (p113) Historic university district with diverse shops and eateries.

 Sights

NATIONAL MALL & AROUND

The 1.9-mile-long lawn is anchored at one end by the Lincoln Memorial, at the other by Capitol Hill, intersected by the reflecting pool and WWII memorial, and centered by the Washington Monument. For more, see p110.

National Air & Space Museum — Museum
(✆202-633-1000; http://airandspace.si.edu; cnr 6th St & Independence Ave SW; ◷10am-5:30pm, to 7:30pm mid-Mar–early Sep; ⓜL'Enfant Plaza) **FREE** The National Air & Space Museum is the most popular Smithsonian museum; everyone flocks to see the Wright brothers' flyer, Chuck Yeager's *Bell X-1*, Charles Lindbergh's *Spirit of St Louis* and the *Apollo 11* command module. There's also an IMAX theater, planetarium and ride simulator (adult/child $9/7.50 each).

National Museum of Natural History — Museum
(www.mnh.si.edu; cnr 10th St & Constitution Ave NW; ◷10am-5:30pm, to 7:30pm Jun-Aug; ⚄; ⓜSmithsonian, Federal Triangle) **FREE** A favorite with the kids, the Museum of Natural History showcases dinosaur skeletons, an archaeology/anthropology collection, wonders from the ocean, and unusual gems and minerals, including the 45-carat Hope Diamond.

National Museum of American History — Museum
(www.americanhistory.si.edu; cnr 14th St & Constitution Ave NW; ◷10am-5:30pm, to 7:30pm Jun-Aug; ⚄; ⓜSmithsonian, Federal Triangle) **FREE** The Museum of American History is

Georgetown (p113)
NINO H PHOTOGRAPHY/GETTY IMAGES ©

accented with the daily bric-a-brac of the American experience – synagogue shawls, protest signs and cotton gins – plus an enormous display of the original Star-Spangled Banner and icons such as Dorothy's slippers and Kermit the Frog.

National Museum of the American Indian
Museum

(www.americanindian.si.edu; cnr 4th St & Independence Ave SW; ⊙10am-5:30pm; ♿; Ⓜ L'Enfant Plaza) FREE The Museum of the American Indian provides a fine introduction to the indigenous people of the Americas, with an array of costumes, video and audio recordings, and cultural artifacts. Don't miss the regionally specialized menu of Native-inspired dishes at **Mitsitam Native Foods Cafe** (www.mitsitamcafe.com; mains $8-18; ⊙11am-5pm) on the ground floor.

Hirshhorn Museum & Sculpture Garden
Museum

(www.hirshhorn.si.edu; cnr 7th St & Independence Ave SW; ⊙10am-5:30pm, sculpture garden 7:30am-dusk; ♿; Ⓜ Smithsonian) FREE The doughnut-shaped Hirshhorn Museum & Sculpture Garden houses a huge collection of modern art, including pieces by Rodin, O'Keeffe, Warhol, Man Ray and de Kooning.

National Gallery of Art
Museum

(☏202-737-4215; www.nga.gov; Constitution Ave NW btwn 3rd & 7th Sts; ⊙10am-5pm Mon-Sat, 11am-6pm Sun; Ⓜ Archives-Navy Memorial) FREE Set in two massive buildings, the National Gallery of Art houses a staggering art collection (more than 100,000 objects), spanning the Middle Ages to the present.

US Holocaust Memorial Museum
Museum

(☏202-488-0400; www.ushmm.org; 100 Raoul Wallenberg Pl SW; ⊙10am-5:20pm, to 6:20pm Mon-Fri Apr & May; Ⓜ Smithsonian) FREE For a deep understanding of the Holocaust – its victims, perpetrators and bystanders – this harrowing museum is a must-see. Only a limited number of visitors are admitted each day; go early.

If You Like...
Evocative Memorials

If you like the Lincoln Memorial (p108), visit Washington's other awe-inspiring memorials, which celebrate visionaries, statesmen and courageous commoners alike.

1 MARTIN LUTHER KING JR NATIONAL MEMORIAL
(www.mlkmemorial.org) Featuring quotes taken from a dozen speeches, this memorial is a moving tribute to one of the world's great peace advocates.

2 JEFFERSON MEMORIAL
(900 Ohio Dr SW) The domed memorial is etched with the Founding Father's most famous writings, plus you'll find wonderful views across the Tidal Basin onto the Mall.

3 FDR MEMORIAL
(Memorial Park) A 7.5-acre tribute to Franklin D. Roosevelt, the longest-serving president in US history, and the era in which he governed.

4 NATIONAL WWII MEMORIAL
(www.wwiimemorial.com; 17th St; Ⓜ Smithsonian) Occupying one end of the reflecting pool, the National WWII Memorial honors the 400,000 Americans who died in the war, along with the 16 million US soldiers who served.

Washington Monument
Monument

(☏202-233-3520; www.nps.gov/wamo; 2 15th St NW; ⊙9am-5pm, to 10pm Jun-Aug; Ⓜ Smithsonian) FREE Peaking at 555ft (and 5in), the Washington Monument is the tallest building in the district, and provides stellar views from the top. Tickets are free but must be reserved from the **kiosk** (15th St btwn Madison Dr NW & Jefferson Dr SW; ⊙8:30am-4:30pm), or you can order them in advance by calling the **National Park Service** (☏877-444-6777; www.recreation.gov; tickets $1.50).

Washington, DC

Washington National Cathedral (0.8mi)

National Zoo (0.5mi)

United States Naval Observatory

Whitehaven St NW

Duke Ellington Memorial Bridge

Kalorama Park

40 ✕

18th St NW

42 ✕

Rock Creek Pkwy NW

Rock Creek

Connecticut Ave NW

Columbia Rd NW

Belmont Rd NW

Kalorama Circle

Wyoming Ave NW

29

California St NW

Dumbarton Oaks Park

Massachusetts Ave NW

Waterside Dr NW

California St NW

Wyoming Ave NW

Vernon St NW

Willard Pl NW

17th St NW

16th St NW

T St NW

S St NW

Montrose Park

4 🏛

Avon Pl NW

Oak Hill Cemetery

Decatur Pl NW

Sheridan Circle

38

Florida Ave NW

Swann St NW

S St NW

Swann St NW

32

30

R St NW

S St NW

32nd St NW

Wisconsin Ave NW

33rd St NW

Q St NW

30th St NW

29th St NW

28th St NW

Mill Rd

20 🏛

36 ✕

New Hampshire Ave NW

R St NW

Corcoran St NW

Q St NW

P St NW

O St NW

Dumbarton St NW

27th St NW

Rock Creek

N St NW

DC2NY

33

Dupont Circle Ⓜ

46 ✕

O St NW

Scott Circle

N St NW

Tombs (0.1mi)

48 ✕

Capital Crescent Trail (0.1mi)

28

39 ✕

22nd St NW

21st St NW

New Hampshire Ave NW

53

Connecticut Ave NW

Pennsylvania Ave NW

23rd St NW

M St NW

M St NW

M St NW

21st St NW

20th St NW

19th St NW

18th St NW

L St NW

17th St NW

16th St NW

Whitehurst Fwy

Juarez Circle

25th St NW

24th St NW

23rd St NW

22nd St NW

Pennsylvania Ave NW

K St NW

I St NW

Farragut North Ⓜ

Farragut West Ⓜ

Foggy Bottom-GWU Ⓜ

23 ♿

Theodore Roosevelt Island

F St NW

59 ✪

H St NW

G St NW

F St NW

20th St NW

19th St NW

18th St NW

H St NW

P

Lafayette Sq

3 ◉

White House

E St NW

E St NW

Rawlins Park

17th St NW

E St NW

United States Navy Bureau of Medicine & Surgery

Virginia Ave NW

D St NW

C St NW

C St NW

The Ellipse

Mount Vernon Trail

Constitution Ave NW

Rock Creek Pkwy

26 ❶

Constitution Gardens

11 ❶

Reflecting Pool

West Potomac Park

19 ❶

27 ❶

Independence Ave SW

George Washington Memorial Pkwy

Boundary Dr

Arlington Cemetery Ⓜ

Women in Military Service for America Memorial (0.1mi)

Arlington National Cemetery

Lady Bird Johnson Park

Potomac River

W Basin Dr SW

Ohio Dr SW

5 ❶

Memorial Park

Tidal Basin

9 ❶

East Potomac Park

106

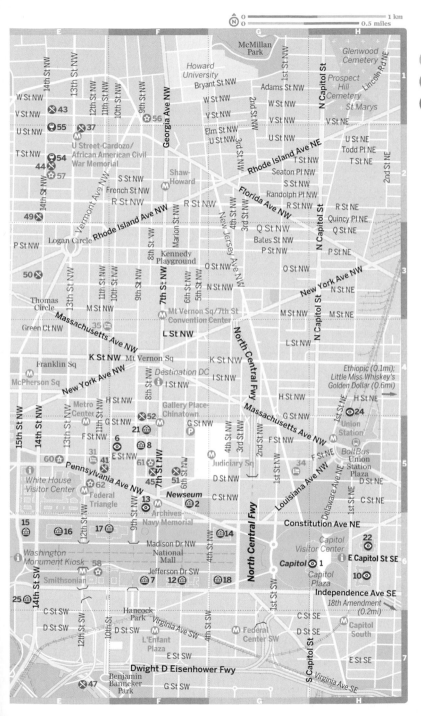

McMillan Park

Glenwood Cemetery

Howard University
Bryant St NW

Prospect Hill Cemetery

St Marys

W St NW
V St NW
U St NW
T St NW

43
55
37
56
54
44
57

U Street-Cardozo/ African American Civil War Memorial

Shaw-Howard

French St NW

49

Logan Circle

Rhode Island Ave NW

Kennedy Playground

50

Thomas Circle

Green Ct NW

Massachusetts Ave NW

35

Mt Vernon Sq/7th St Convention Center

K St NW Mt Vernon Sq

Franklin Sq

McPherson Sq

New York Ave NW

Destination DC
I St NW

Gallery Place-Chinatown

Metro Center

52
21
6
8
31
41
61
60
62

White House Visitor Center

Pennsylvania Ave NW

Federal Triangle

13

Newseum
2

Archives-Navy Memorial

45
51

Judiciary Sq

34

Ethiopic (0.1mi);
Little Miss Whiskey's Golden Dollar (0.6mi)

24

Union Station

BoltBus Union Station Plaza

15
16
17
14

Washington Monument Kiosk
58

Smithsonian

Madison Dr NW
National Mall

Jefferson Dr SW

7
12
18

25

Constitution Ave NE

Capitol Visitor Center

22

Capitol
1

E Capitol St SE

10

Capitol Plaza

Independence Ave SE

18th Amendment (0.2mi)

Hancock Park

Virginia Ave SW

L'Enfant Plaza

Federal Center SW

Capitol South

Dwight D Eisenhower Fwy

47

Benjamin Banneker Park

G St SW

North Central Fwy

Massachusetts Ave NW

Louisiana Ave NW

Delaware Ave NE

Washington, DC

Lincoln Memorial   Monument

(📞202-426-6841; www.nps.gov/linc; west end of Mall, at 23rd St; ⏰24 hr; Ⓜ Foggy Bottom-GWU) FREE Anchoring the Mall's west end is the hallowed shrine to Abraham Lincoln, who gazes peacefully across the reflecting pool beneath his neoclassical Doric-columned abode.

Vietnam Veterans Memorial   Monument

(📞202-426-6841; www.nps.gov/vive; west end of Mall, at 22nd St; ⏰24 hr; Ⓜ Foggy Bottom-GWU) FREE The opposite of DC's white, gleaming marble is this black, low-lying 'V,' an expression of the psychic scar that was wrought by the Vietnam War. The monument follows a descent deeper into the earth, with the names of the 58,267 dead soldiers – listed in the order in which they died – chiseled into the dark wall.

CAPITOL HILL

Library of Congress   Landmark

(www.loc.gov; 1st St SE; ⏰8:30am-4:30pm Mon-Sat) FREE To prove to Europeans that America is cultured, John Adams plunked the world's largest library on Capitol Hill. The visitor center and departure point for tours of the reading rooms are located in the **Jefferson Building**, just behind the Capitol building.

Supreme Court Landmark

(☎202-479-3030; www.supremecourt.gov; 1 1st St NE; ⊗9am-4:30pm Mon-Fri; Ⓜ Capitol South) FREE Even non-law students are impressed by the highest court in America. Arrive early to watch arguments (periodic Mondays through Wednesdays October to April). You can visit the permanent exhibits and the building's seven-spiral staircase year-round.

TIDAL BASIN

It's magnificent to stroll around this constructed inlet and watch the monument lights wink across the Potomac. The blooms here are loveliest during the Cherry Blossom Festival, the city's annual spring rejuvenation, when the basin bursts into a pink and white floral collage. **Paddleboat rentals** (☎202-479-2426; www. tidalbasinpaddleboats.com/; 1501 Maine Ave SW; 2-person boat per hr $12) are available at the boathouse.

DOWNTOWN

Reynolds Center for American Art Museum

(☎202-275-1500; www.americanart.si.edu; cnr 8th & F Sts NW; ⊗11:30am-7pm; Ⓜ Gallery Pl-Chinatown) FREE Don't miss the Reynolds Center for American Art, which combines the **National Portrait Gallery** (www.npg. si.edu) with the **American Art Museum** (http://americanart.si.edu). Works here are outstanding and range from haunting depictions of both the inner city and rural heartland to the self-taught visions of itinerant wanderers.

National Archives Landmark

(☎866-272-6272; www.archives.gov; 700 Pennsylvania Ave NW; ⊗10am-5:30pm Sep–mid-Mar, to 7pm mid-March–Aug; Ⓜ Archives-Navy Memorial) FREE It's hard not to feel a little in awe of the big three documents in the National Archives. The Declaration of Independence, the Constitution and the Bill of Rights, plus one of four copies of the Magna Carta: taken together, it becomes

clear just how radical the American experiment was for its time.

International Spy Museum Museum

(☎202-393-7798; www.spymuseum.org; 800 F St NW; adult/child $20/15; ⊗9am-7pm; ♿; Ⓜ Gallery Place-Chinatown) You like those bits in the Bond movies with Q? Then you'll like the immensely popular International Spy Museum. All the undercover tools of the trade on display make this place great for (secret) history buffs. Get there early.

Ford's Theatre Historic Site

(☎202-426-6924; www.fords.org; 511 10th St NW; tours $2.50; ⊗9am-4:30pm; Ⓜ Metro Center, Ⓜ Gallery Place-Chinatown) FREE On April 14, 1865, John Wilkes Booth assassinated Abraham Lincoln in his box seat here. The theater still operates today; you can also take a tour of the theater, and learn about the events that transpired on that fateful April night. There's a small

Smithsonian

Massive in size and ambition, the 19 Smithsonian museums, galleries and zoo comprise the world's largest museum and research complex. Massive dinosaur skeletons, lunar modules and artworks from every corner of the globe are all part of the Smithsonian largesse.

All of the museums are free and most are open daily (except Christmas Day) from 10am to 5:30pm. Some have extended hours in summer.

The Smithsonian's latest work-in-progress is the $500-million **National Museum of African American History and Culture** (www.nmaahc.si.edu; cnr Constitution Ave & 14th St NW), scheduled to open in 2015. Until then, you can peruse its temporary galleries on the 2nd floor of the National Museum of American History.

National Mall

Folks often call the Mall 'America's Front Yard,' and that's a pretty good analogy. It is indeed a lawn, unfurling scrubby green grass from the Capitol west to the Lincoln Memorial. It's also America's great public space, where citizens come to protest their government, go for scenic runs and connect with the nation's most cherished ideals writ large in stone, landscaping, monuments and memorials.

You can sample quite a bit in a day, though it'll be a full one that requires roughly 4 miles of walking. Start at the **Vietnam Veterans Memorial** ❶, then head counterclockwise around the Mall, swooping in on the **Lincoln Memorial** ❷, **Martin Luther King Jr Memorial** ❸ and **Washington Monument** ❹. You can also pause for the cause of the Korean War and WWII, among other monuments that dot the Mall's western portion.

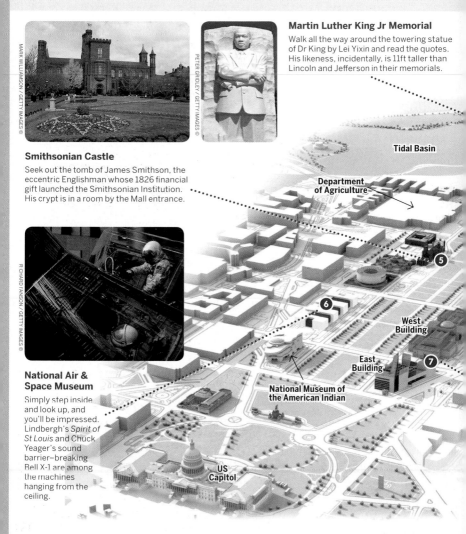

Martin Luther King Jr Memorial

Walk all the way around the towering statue of Dr King by Lei Yixin and read the quotes. His likeness, incidentally, is 11ft taller than Lincoln and Jefferson in their memorials.

Smithsonian Castle

Seek out the tomb of James Smithson, the eccentric Englishman whose 1826 financial gift launched the Smithsonian Institution. His crypt is in a room by the Mall entrance.

Tidal Basin

Department of Agriculture

❺

❻

West Building

East Building

❼

National Air & Space Museum

Simply step inside and look up, and you'll be impressed. Lindbergh's *Spirit of St Louis* and Chuck Yeager's sound barrier–breaking Bell X-1 are among the machines hanging from the ceiling.

National Museum of the American Indian

US Capitol

MARK WILLIAMSON / GETTY IMAGES ©

PETER GRIDLEY / GETTY IMAGES ©

RICHARD I'ANSON / GETTY IMAGES ©

Then it's onward to the museums, all fabulous and all free. Begin at the **Smithsonian Castle ⑤** to get your bearings – and to say thanks to the guy making all this awesomeness possible – and commence browsing through the **National Air & Space Museum ⑥**, **National Gallery of Art & National Sculpture Garden ⑦** and **National Museum of Natural History ⑧**.

TOP TIPS

Start early, especially in summer. You'll avoid the crowds, but more importantly you'll avoid the blazing heat. Try to finish with the monuments and be in the air-conditioned museums by 10:30am. Also, consider bringing snacks, since the only food available is from scattered cart vendors and museum cafes.

Lincoln Memorial

Commune with Abe in his chair, then head down the steps to the marker where Martin Luther King Jr gave his 'Dream' speech. The view of the Reflecting Pool and Washington Monument is one of DC's best.

STEVEN GREAVES / GETTY IMAGES ©

Korean War Veterans Memorial

National WWII Memorial

National Museum of American History

National Sculpture Garden

Vietnam Veterans Memorial

Check the symbol that's beside each name. A diamond indicates 'killed, body recovered.' A plus sign indicates 'missing and unaccounted for.' There are approximately 1200 of the latter.

Washington Monument

As you approach the obelisk, look a third of the way up. See how it's slightly lighter in color at the bottom? Builders had to use different marble after the first source dried up.

National Museum of Natural History

Wave to Henry, the elephant who guards the rotunda, then zip to the 2nd floor's Hope Diamond. The 45.52-carat bauble has cursed its owners, including Marie Antoinette, or so the story goes.

National Gallery of Art & National Sculpture Garden

Beeline to Gallery 6 (West Building) and ogle the Western Hemisphere's only Leonardo da Vinci painting. Outdoors, amble amid whimsical sculptures by Miró, Calder and Lichtenstein. Also check out IM Pei's design of the East Building.

EDDIE BRADY / GETTY IMAGES ©

DAVID A. DOBBS/GETTY IMAGES ©

Don't Miss
The Capitol

Since 1800, this is where the legislative branch of American government – ie Congress – has met to write the country's laws. The lower House of Representatives (435 members) and upper Senate (100) meet respectively in the south and north wings of the building.

A **visitor center** showcases the exhaustive background of a building that fairly sweats history. If you book in advance (through http://tours.visitthecapitol.gov) you can go on a free tour of the building, which is as daunting as the exterior, if a little cluttered with the busts, statues and personal mementos of generations of Congress members.

To watch Congress in action, US citizens can request visitor passes from their representatives or senators (📞202-224-3121); foreign visitors should show their passports at the House gallery. Congressional committee hearings are actually more interesting (and substantive) if you care about what's being debated; check for a schedule, locations and to see if they're open to the public (they often are) at www.house.gov and www.senate.gov.

NEED TO KNOW
📞202-225-6827; www.visitthecapitol.gov; 1st St NE & East Capitol St; admission free; 🕗8:30am-4:30pm Mon-Sat; Ⓜ Capitol South

Lincoln Museum devoted to Lincoln's presidency that you can see as part of the tour. Arrive early to get a ticket, as limited numbers are admitted each day. You can also use your ticket to explore the nearby **Petersen House** (516 10th St), where Lincoln eventually gave up the ghost.

DUPONT CIRCLE

Phillips Collection — Museum
(www.phillipscollection.org; 1600 21st St NW; admission Mon-Fri free, Sat & Sun $10, ticketed exhibitions $12, chamber-music series per ticket $20; ⏲10am-5pm Tue,Wed, Fri & Sat, to 8:30pm Thu, 11am-6pm Sun, chamber-music series 4pm Sun Oct-May; ⓜDupont Circle) The first modern-art museum in the country (opened in 1921) houses a small but exquisite collection of European and American works – including pieces by Gauguin, van Gogh, Matisse, Picasso, O'Keeffe, Hopper and many other greats. It's partially set in a beautifully restored Georgian Revival mansion.

GEORGETOWN

Thousands of the bright and beautiful, from Georgetown students to ivory-tower academics and diplomats, call this leafy, aristocratic neighborhood home. At night, shop-a-block M St becomes congested with traffic, turning into a weird mix of high-school cruising and high-street boutique.

Dumbarton Oaks — Museum, Gardens
(www.doaks.org; 1703 32nd St NW; museum free, gardens adult/child $8/5; ⏲museum 2-5pm Tue-Sun, gardens 2-6pm Tue-Sun) A museum featuring exquisite Byzantine and pre-Columbian art is housed within this historic mansion. More impressive are the 10 acres of beautifully designed formal gardens, which are simply stunning during the springtime blooms. Visit on weekdays to beat the crowds.

UPPER NORTHWEST DC

National Zoo — Zoo
(www.nationalzoo.si.edu; 3001 Connecticut Ave NW; ⏲10am-6pm Apr-Oct, to 4:30pm Nov-Mar; ⓜCleveland Park, Woodley Park-Zoo/Adams Morgan) FREE Home to more than 2000 individual animals (400 different species) in natural habitats, this 163-acre zoo is famed for giant pandas Mei Xiang and Tian Tian.

Washington National Cathedral — Church
(☎202-537-6200; www.nationalcathedral.org; 3101 Wisconsin Ave NW; suggested donation adult/child $10/$5; ⏲10am-5:30pm Mon-Fri, to 8pm some days May-Sep, 10am-4pm Sat,

Street scene, Georgetown

113

8am-4pm Sun; M Tenleytown-AU to southbound bus 31, 32, 36, 37) This Gothic cathedral, as dramatic as its European counterparts, blends both the spiritual and the profane in its architectural treasures.

 **Activities**

The 1754 acres of **Rock Creek Park** (www. nps.gov/rocr; ☉sunrise-sunset; M Cleveland Park, Woodley Park-Zoo/Adams Morgan) follow Rock Creek as it winds through the northwest of the city. There are miles of bicycling, hiking and horseback-riding trails, and even a few coyotes. The C&O Canal offers bicycling and hiking trails in canalside parks, and the lovely 11-mile **Capital Crescent Trail** (www.cctrail.org; **Water St**) connects Georgetown north to Silver Spring, MD, via splendid Potomac River views.

Thompson Boat Center   Kayaking, Bike Rental
(www.thompsonboatcenter.com; 2900 Virginia Ave NW; water craft per hr/day from $14/35, bikes

per hr/day from $10/30; ☉8am-5pm Mar-Oct) At the Potomac River end of Rock Creek Park, it rents canoes, kayaks and bicycles.

Big Wheel Bikes   Bike Rental
(www.bigwheelbikes.com; 1034 33rd St NW; per 3hr/day $21/35; ☉11am-7pm Tue-Fri, 10am-6pm Sat & Sun) A good bike-rental outfit. Three-hour minimum rentals.

 Tours

DC Metro Food Tours   Food Tour
(☎800-979-3370; www.dcmetrofoodtours.com; per person $30-65) These walking tours take in the culinary riches of DC, exploring various neighborhoods and stopping for bites along the way.

DC by Foot   Walking Tour
(www.dcbyfoot.com) Guides for this free, tip-based walking tour dispense intriguing stories and historical details during different walks covering the National Mall, Arlington Cemetery and Lincoln's assassination.

🛏 Sleeping

CAPITOL HILL

Liaison Hotel **$$**
(☎202-638-1616; www.affinia.com; 415 New Jersey Ave NW; r from $200; P@🛜≋; MUnion Station) The Liaison has jazzed up the accommodation options in Capitol Hill. You'll find stylish modernist rooms and a festive rooftop pool.

DOWNTOWN & WHITE HOUSE AREA

Hotel Harrington Hotel **$$**
(☎800-424-8532, 202-628-8140; www.hotel-harrington.com; 436 11th St NW; r $130-200; P❄🛜🚻; MFederal Triangle) One of the most affordable options near the Mall, this aging, family-run hotel has small, basic rooms that are clean but in definite need of an update.

Morrison-Clark Inn Historic Hotel **$$**
(☎202-898-1200; www.morrisonclark.com; 1015 L St NW; r $200-350; P❄@🛜; MMt Vernon Sq/7th St Convention Center) Listed on the Register of Historic Places, this elegant inn comprises two 1864 residences filled with fine antiques, chandeliers, richly hued drapes and other features evocative of the antebellum South.

ADAMS MORGAN

American Guest House B&B **$$**
(☎202-588-1180; www.americanguesthouse. com; 2005 Columbia Rd NW; r incl breakfast $160-220; ❄@🛜; MDupont Circle) This 12-room bed-and-breakfast earns high marks for its warm, friendly service, good breakfasts and elegantly furnished rooms.

DUPONT CIRCLE

Dupont Collection B&B **$$**
(☎202-467-6777; http://thedupontcollection. com; r $120-260; P❄🛜) If you're craving a good range of B&B coziness in the heart of the capital, check out these excellent heritage properties. Most centrally

115

JEAN-PIERRE LESCOURRET/GETTY IMAGES ©

Don't Miss
White House

The White House has survived both fire and insults (Jefferson groused that it was 'big enough for two emperors, one Pope and the grand Lama'). Although its facade has changed little since 1924, its interior has seen frequent renovations. Franklin Roosevelt added a pool; Truman gutted the whole place (and simply discarded many of its historical features – today's rooms are historical replicas); Jacqueline Kennedy brought back antique furnishings and historic details; Nixon added a bowling alley; Carter installed solar roof panels, which Reagan then removed; Clinton added a jogging track; and George W Bush included a T-ball field. Cars can no longer pass the White House on Pennsylvania Ave, clearing the area for posing school groups and round-the-clock peace activists.

Unfortunately, getting inside is nearly impossible. Tours must be arranged (up to six months) in advance. US citizens must apply via one of their state's members of Congress, and others must apply through either the US consulate in their home country or their country's consulate in DC. If that sounds like too much work, pop into the **White House visitor center** (www.whitehouse.gov; cnr 15th & E Sts NW; ⊙7:30am-4pm); it's not the real deal but, hey, there's executive paraphernalia scattered about.

NEED TO KNOW
☏tours 202-456-7041; www.whitehouse.gov; ⊙tours 7:30am-11am Tue-Sat; Ⓜ Farragut West, Farragut North, McPherson Square, Metro Center

located are the inns at **Dupont North** (📞202-467-6777; www.thedupontcollection.com; 1620 T St NW; r incl breakfast $115-270; ❄️📶; Ⓜ️Dupont Circle) and **Dupont South** (📞202-467-6777; www.thedupontcollection.com; 1312 19th St NW; r incl breakfast $115-230; ❄️📶; Ⓜ️Dupont Circle); the former feels like the modern home of a wealthy friend, while the latter evokes much more of a chintz-and-lacy-linen sensibility.

Carlyle Suites
Apartment **$$$**

(📞202-234-3200; www.carlylesuites.com; 1731 New Hampshire Ave NW; apt $180-320; 🅿️❄️@📶♿; Ⓜ️Dupont Circle) Inside this all-suites art-deco gem, you'll find sizeable, handsomely furnished rooms with crisp white linens, luxury mattresses, 37in flat-screen TVs and full kitchens.

🍴 Eating

CAPITOL HILL

Eastern Market
Market **$**

(225 7th St SE; 🕐7am-7pm Tue-Fri, to 6pm Sat, 9am-5pm Sun) One of the icons of Capitol Hill, this covered arcade sprawls with delectable produce and good cheer on the weekends. The crab cakes at the Market Lunch stall are divine.

Toki Underground
Asian **$**

(📞202-388-3086; www.tokiunderground.com; 1234 H St NE; mains $10; 🕐5-10pm Mon-Wed, to 11pm Thu, to midnight Fri & Sat; 🚌H Street shuttle) Spicy, belly-warming ramen noodles and dumplings sum up the menu in wee Toki. Despite the name, Toki Underground is on the 2nd floor. It's not marked; look for the Pug bar sign.

Maine Avenue Fish Market
Seafood **$**

(1100 Maine Ave SW; meals from $7; 🕐8am-9pm; Ⓜ️L'Enfant Plaza) If you're a seafood lover, this sprawling and bustling fish market should take high priority on your itinerary. Plump oysters, crab cakes, soft-shell crabs, steamed crabs and peel-and-eat shrimp are just the beginning...

Granville Moore's
Belgian **$$**

(📞202-399-2546; www.granvillemoores.com; 1238 H St NE; mains $11-16; 🕐5pm-midnight Sun-Thu, to 3am Fri & Sat; 🚌H Street shuttle) One of the anchors of the bohemian Atlas District (which runs along H St NE), Granville Moore's bills itself as a gastropub with

Eastern Market

a Belgian fetish. Indeed you'll find more than 70 Belgian beers, good pub fare and fun crowds most nights.

Ethiopic
Ethiopian $$

(☏202-675-2066; 401 H St NE ; mains $12-17; ⏰5-10pm Tue-Thu, from noon Fri & Sun; 🚍H Street shuttle) In a city with no shortage of Ethiopian joints, Ethiopic stands above the rest. We're big fans of the signature hot *wat* (stews) and *tibs* (sauteed meat and veg), derived from tender lamb that's sat in a bath of herbs and satisfyingly hot spices.

DOWNTOWN & WHITE HOUSE AREA

Rasika
Indian $$

(☏202-637-1222; www.rasikarestaurant.com; 633 D St NW; mains $17-26; ⏰lunch Mon-Fri, dinner daily; 🍷; Ⓜ Archives-Navy Memorial) Decorated like a Jaipur palace, Rasika serves delicious, innovative Indian dishes. Don't miss Narangi duck and perfectly prepared *dal* (lentils).

Hill Country Barbecue
Barbecue $$

(☏202-556-2050; 410 7th St NW; mains $13-22; ⏰11:30am-2am; Ⓜ Archives-Navy Memorial, Gallery Place-Chinatown) This Texas-themed joint serves magnificent barbecue. Downstairs you'll find bands playing fun Texas honky-tonk shows.

Zaytinya
Mediterranean $$

(☏202-638-0800; 701 9th St NW; mezze $7-13; ⏰11:30am-11:30pm Tue-Sat, to 10pm Sun & Mon) One of the culinary crown jewels of chef José Andrés, ever-popular Zaytinya serves superb Greek, Turkish and Lebanese mezze (small plates) in a long, narrow dining room with soaring ceilings and all-glass walls.

Central Michel Richard
Fusion $$$

(☏202-626-0015; 1001 Pennsylvania Ave NW; mains $19-34; ⏰11:30am-2:30pm Mon-Fri, 5-10:30pm Mon-Thu, to 11pm Fri & Sat; 🍷; Ⓜ Federal Triangle, Archives-Navy Memorial) This renowned bistro serves old-school favorites with a twist: lobster burgers, a sinfully complex meatloaf, and fried chicken that redefines what fried chicken can be.

U STREET, SHAW & LOGAN CIRCLE

Ben's Chili Bowl
American $

(www.benschilibowl.com; 1213 U St; mains $5-9; ⏰11am-2am Mon-Thu, to 4am Fri & Sat, to midnight Sun; Ⓜ U St-Cardozo) One of DC's landmarks, Ben's has been going strong for over 50 years, doling out burgers, fries and the well-loved chili-smothered half-smokes (pork and beef sausages –DC's smokier version of the hot dog) from this old-school U St storefront.

Jefferson Memorial (p105)
TETRA IMAGES/GETTY IMAGES ©

BARRY WINIKER/GETTY IMAGES ©

Don't Miss
Newseum

Although you'll have to pay up, this massive, highly interactive news museum is well worth the admission price. You can delve inside the major events of recent years (the fall of the Berlin Wall, September 11, Hurricane Katrina), and spend hours watching moving film footage, perusing Pulitzer Prize–winning photographs and reading works by journalists killed in the line of duty.

Unaffiliated with the Smithsonian (ergo the cost of admission), the 'most interactive museum in the world' is dedicated to the craft of news gathering and dissemination. There's a ton to see here, and it's spread over six levels.

The concourse level displays FBI artifacts from prominent news stories, such as the Unabomber's cabin and John Dillinger's death mask. Level 3 holds a memorial to journalists killed in pursuit of the truth. Level 4 has twisted wreckage from the September 11, 2001, attacks and haunting final images from Bill Biggart's camera (Biggart was the only journalist to be killed that day). Level 6 offers a terrace with awesome views of Pennsylvania Ave up to the Capitol.

Tickets are usable for two consecutive days, so you don't have to view it all at once.

NEED TO KNOW

www.newseum.org; 555 Pennsylvania Ave NW; adult/child $22/13; ⏱9am-5pm; 🚻; Ⓜ Archives-Navy Memorial, Judiciary Sq

---

El Centro   Mexican **$$**
(📞202-328-3131; 1819 14th St NW; mains $9-20; ⏱11am-11pm daily, brunch 10:30am-3pm Sat & Sun; 🍴; Ⓜ U St-Cardozo) El Centro offers excellent noveau-Mexican cuisine with unforgettable duck tacos and the best slow-roasted carnitas in town. It also has a great rooftop deck and attracts a

DOUG STEAKLEY/GETTY IMAGES ©

★ Don't Miss
Arlington National Cemetery

Arlington County, just across the Potomac River from DC, was part of Washington until it was returned to Virginia in 1847. Today it's best known as the somber final resting place of more than 300,000 military personnel and their dependents, with veterans of every US war from the Revolution to Iraq.

Spread over 612 hilly acres, much of the cemetery was built on the grounds of **Arlington House**, the former home of Robert E Lee and his wife, Mary Anna Custis Lee, a descendant of Martha Washington. When Lee left to lead Virginia's army in the Civil War, Union troops confiscated the property to bury their dead.

The **Tomb of the Unknowns** contains the remains of unidentified American servicemen from both world wars and the Korean War. Military guards retain a round-the-clock vigil, and the changing of the guard (every half hour from March to September, every hour from October to February) is one of Arlington's most moving sights.

An eternal flame marks the **grave of John F Kennedy**, next to those of Jacqueline Kennedy Onassis and two of her infant children.

Tourmobiles (☎202-554-5100; www.tourmobile.com; adult/child $8.50/4.25) are a handy way to visit the cemetery's memorials.

NEED TO KNOW
☎877-907-8585; www.arlingtoncemetery.mil; tour bus adult/child $8.75/4.50; ☺8am-7pm Apr-Sep, to 5pm Oct-Mar

Washington, DC, for Children

The top destination for families is undoubtedly the (free!) National Zoo (p113), and museums around the city will entertain and educate children of all ages. But if you – or they – tire of indoor attractions, there are plenty of enticing green spaces, such as the excellent **Yards Park** (www.yardspark.org; 355 Water St SE; ⏰7am to 2 hours past sunset; Ⓜ Navy Yard).

The **National Theatre** (☎202-628-6161; www.nationaltheatre.org; 1321 Pennsylvania Ave NW; ⏰box office 10am-9pm Mon-Sat, noon-8pm Sun; Ⓜ Federal Triangle) offers free Saturday-morning performances, from puppet shows to tap dancers (reservations required); the **Discovery Theater** (www.discoverytheater.org; 1100 Jefferson Dr SW; 🚻; Ⓜ Smithsonian) stages entertaining shows for young audiences.

Eight-to-12-year-olds can spend the night inside the National Museum of Natural History during **Smithsonian Sleepovers** (☎202-633-3030; smithsoniansleepovers.org), held approximately every two weeks.

nightlife-loving crowd on weekends (the bar is open till 2am).

Pig
American $$

(☎202-290-2821; 1320 14th St NW; mains $12-21; ⏰noon-10:30pm Mon & Tue, to 11pm Wed & Thu, to 11:30pm Fri, 11am-11:30pm Sat, to 10pm Sun; Ⓜ U St-Cardozo) The Pig lives up to its name, offering plenty of porcine-inspired treats from crispy shank to a decadent cutlet-and-gruyere sandwich that will leave you lost for words.

Eatonville
Southern $$

(☎202-332-9672; www.eatonvillerestaurant. com; 2121 U St NW; mains $9-21; ⏰11am-11pm Mon-Thu, to midnight Fri, 3pm-midnight Sat, 3-11pm Sun; Ⓜ U St-Cardozo) Serving stellar Southern cuisine, Eatonville whips up scrumptious plates of catfish with cheese grits, and andouille-and-sweet-potato hash.

Pearl Dive Oyster Palace
Seafood $$

(www.pearldivedc.com; 1612 14th St NW; mains $19-25; ⏰noon-3pm Fri & Sat, 11am-3pm Sun, 5-10pm daily; Ⓜ U St-Cardozo) 🌿 Flashy Pearl Dive serves exceptional sustainable oysters from both coasts, along with braised duck and oyster gumbo, crab cakes, and insanely rich peanut-butter chocolate

pie. No reservations; you'll need to pull a number (like at a deli).

ADAMS MORGAN

Diner
American $$

(www.dinerdc.com; 2453 18th St NW; mains $8-16; ⏰24hr; 🚻; Ⓜ Woodley Park Zoo/Adams Morgan) The Diner is the ideal spot for late-night breakfast, (crowded) weekend Bloody Mary brunches or anytime you want unfussy, well-prepared American fare. It's a good spot for kids, too (they'll even hang their Diner-made colorings on the wall).

Cashion's Eat Place
American $$$

(☎202-797-1819; www.cashionseatplace.com; 1819 Columbia Rd NW; mains $17-34; ⏰5:30-11pm Tue-Sun; Ⓜ Woodley Park-Zoo/Adams Morgan) With an original menu and inviting decor, this little bistro is lauded as one of the city's very best. The bar serves fancy late-night fare, such as pork cheek and goat's cheese quesadillas, till 2am on Friday and Saturday.

DUPONT CIRCLE

Afterwords Cafe
American $$

(☎202-387-3825; www.kramers.com; 1517 Connecticut Ave; mains $15-24; ⏰7:30am-1:30am Sun-Thu, 24hr Fri & Sat; Ⓜ Dupont Circle) Not your average bookstore cafe, this buzzing

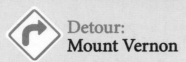

Detour:
Mount Vernon

One of the most visited historic shrines in the nation, **Mount Vernon** (☎703-780-2000, 800-429-1520; www.mountvernon.org; 3200 Mount Vernon Memorial Hwy, Mt Vernon; adult/child $17/8; ⏰8am-5pm Apr-Aug, 9am-4pm Nov-Feb, 9am-5pm Mar, Sep & Oct) was the beloved home of George and Martha Washington, who lived here from their marriage, in 1759, until his death, in 1799. Now owned and operated by the Mount Vernon Ladies Association, the estate offers glimpses of 18th-century farm life and the first president's life as a country planter.

Mount Vernon is 16 miles south of DC off the Mount Vernon Memorial Hwy. **Grayline** (☎202-289-1995; www.grayline.com; adult/child incl Mt Vernon admission from $55/20) offers tours departing DC's Union Station daily and year-round. For DIY travel, take Metro Rail's Yellow Line to Huntington Station in Virginia. Exit at the lower level (Huntington Ave) of the station and take the Fairfax Connector Bus 101 to Mount Vernon's entrance gate.

Several companies offer seasonal boat trips from DC and Alexandria; the best value is **Potomac Riverboat Company** (☎703-684-0580; www.potomacriverboatco.com; adult/child incl Mt Vernon admission $40/20). A healthy alternative is to take a lovely bike ride along the Potomac River from DC (18 miles from Roosevelt Island). During warmer months, you can take a 40-minute **Sightseeing Cruise** (www.potomacriverboatco.com; round trip including Mt Vernon access adult/child $40/20; ⏰Tue-Sun May-Aug, Sat & Sun Apr & Sep) from Mount Vernon.

---

spot overflows with good cheer at its packed cafe tables and outdoor patio. The menu features tasty bistro fare and an ample beer selection.

Bistrot du Coin   French $$
(☎202-234-6969; www.bistrotducoin.com; 1738 Connecticut Ave; mains $14-24; ⏰11:30am-11pm, to 1am Thu-Sat; ⓂDupont Circle) At this classic French bistro, you'll find consistently good onion soup, classic *steak-frites* (grilled steak and French fries) and nine varieties of its famous *moules* (mussels).

Little Serow   Thai $$$
(1511 17th St NW; fixed menu per person $45; ⏰5:30-10pm Tue-Thu, to 10:30pm Fri & Sat) Little Serrow serves superlative Northern Thai cuisine. The single-option menu changes by the week, and every dish comes with mountains of heaping fresh herbs. Arrive early to score a table (no reservations).

GEORGETOWN

Martin's Tavern   American $$
(☎202-333-7370; www.martins-tavern.com; 1264 Wisconsin Ave NW; mains $12-25; ⏰11am-1:30am Mon-Thu, to 2:30am Fri, 9am-2:30am Sat, 8am-1:30am Sun) Martin's is a favorite with Georgetown students and US presidents, who all enjoy the tavern's old-fashioned dining room and unfussy classics such as thick burgers, crab cakes and prime rib.

🍸 Drinking & Nightlife

Little Miss Whiskey's
Golden Dollar   Bar
(www.littlemisswhiskeys.com; 1104 H St NE; ⏰from 5pm; 🚌H Street shuttle) The decor at this multi-level space hovers between whimsical and baroque, but the vibe is fun and easy-going and the drinks are strong. Club kids pack the dance floor on weekends.

18th Amendment
Bar

(www.18thdc.com; 613 Pennsylvania Ave SE; Eastern Market, Capitol South) The Amendment embraces a speakeasy theme – hence the name.

Marvin
Bar

(www.marvindc.com; 2007 14th St NW; MU St-Cardozo) Stylish Marvin has a low-lit lounge with vaulted ceilings where DJs spin soul and rare grooves to a mixed 14th St crowd. The upstairs roof deck is a draw all year round.

Bar Pilar
Bar

(www.barpilar.com; 1833 14th St NW; MU St-Cardozo) Friendly neighborhood favorite Bar Pilar serves seasonal organic tapas dishes and excellent cocktails in a small, nicely designed space.

18th Street Lounge
Lounge

(www.eighteenthstreetlounge.com; 1212 18th St NW; ☺from 5:30pm Tue-Fri, from 9:30pm Sat & Sun; MDupont Circle) Chandeliers, velvet sofas, antique wallpaper and an attractive dance-loving crowd adorn this multi-floored mansion

Tombs
Bar

(www.tombs.com; 1226 36th St NW; ☺from 11:30am Mon-Sat, from 9:30am Sun) If it looks familiar, think back to the '80s; this was the setting for St Elmo's Fire. Today this cozy windowless bar is a favorite with Georgetown students and teaching assistants boozing under crew regalia.

⭐ Entertainment

See the weekly **Washington City Paper** (www.washingtoncitypaper.com) or **Washington Post** (www.washingtonpost.com) weekend section for comprehensive listings. **Ticketplace** (http://culturecapital.tix.com; 407 7th St NW; ☺11am-6pm Wed-Fri, 10am-5pm Sat) sells same-day concert and show tickets at half price (no phone sales).

LIVE MUSIC
Black Cat
Live Music

(www.blackcatdc.com; 1811 14th St NW, U St; admission $5-15; MU St-Cardozo) A pillar of DC's music scene since the 1990s, the battered Black Cat has hosted all the greats of years past (White Stripes, the Strokes and Arcade Fire, among others).

Mount Vernon

Detour:
Alexandria

The charming colonial village of Alexandria is just 5 miles and 250 years away from Washington. Once a salty port town, 'Old Town' (as it is known to locals) is today a posh collection of red-brick colonial homes, cobblestone streets, flickering gas lamps and a waterfront promenade. King St is packed with boutiques, outdoor cafes and neighborhood bars and restaurants.

Gadsby's Tavern Museum (www.gadsbystavern.org; 134 N Royal St; adult/child $5/2; ⏱10am-5pm Tue-Sat, 1-5pm Sun & Mon; Ⓜ King St then trolley) has exhibits on colonial life and is still a working pub and restaurant; past guests include George Washington and Thomas Jefferson. Near the waterfront the **Torpedo Factory Art Center** (www.torpedofactory.org; 105 N Union St; ⏱10am-6pm, to 7pm Thu; Ⓜ King St then trolley) FREE is a former munitions factory that houses dozens of galleries and studios.

To get to Alexandria from downtown DC, take the yellow or blue metro line to King St Metro station. A free trolley makes the 1-mile journey between the metro station and the waterfront (11:30am to 10pm daily, every 20 minutes).

9:30 Club — Live Music
(www.930.com; 815 V St NW, U St; admission from $10; Ⓜ U St-Cardozo) The 9:30, which can pack 1200 people into a surprisingly intimate venue, is the granddaddy of the live-music scene in DC.

PERFORMING ARTS

Kennedy Center — Performing Arts
(☎202-467-4600; www.kennedy-center.org; 2700 F St NW, Georgetown; Ⓜ Foggy Bottom-GWU) Perched on 17 acres along the Potomac, the magnificent Kennedy Center hosts a staggering array of performances. The Millennium Stage puts on free performances at 6pm daily.

Shakespeare Theatre — Theater
(☎202-547-1122; www.shakespearetheatre.org; 450 7th St NW; tickets from $30; ⏱box office 10am-6pm Mon-Sat, noon-6pm Sun; Ⓜ Archives-Navy Memorial) The nation's foremost Shakespeare company presents masterfully staged pieces by the Bard as well as works by George Bernard Shaw, Oscar Wilde, Henrik Ibsen, Eugene O'Neill and other greats.

SPORTS

Washington Redskins — Football
(☎301-276-6800; www.redskins.com; 1600 Fedex Way, Landover, MD; tickets from $65) The city's football team plays at FedEx Field, east of DC in Maryland. The season runs from September to February.

Washington Nationals — Baseball
(www.nationals.com; 1500 S Capitol St SE; Ⓜ Navy Yard) DC's baseball team plays at Nationals Park, along the Anacostia riverfront in southeast DC. The season runs from April through October.

Washington Wizards — Basketball
(www.nba.com/wizards; 601 F St NW; ⏱box office 10am-5:30pm Mon-Sat; Ⓜ Gallery Pl-Chinatown) NBA season runs from October through April, with home games played at the Verizon Center.

❶ Information

Destination DC (☎202-789-7000; www.washington.org; 4th fl, 901 7th St NW) DC's official tourism site.

Getting There & Away

Bus

There are numerous cheap bus services to New York (four to five hours). Most charge around $20 one way.

BoltBus ([📞]877-265-8287; www.boltbus.com; [📶]) Leaves from the upper level of Union Station.

DC2NY ([📞]202-332-2691; www.dc2ny.com; 20th St & Massachusetts Ave NW; [📶]) Leaves from near Dupont Circle.

Greyhound ([📞]202-589-5141; www.greyhound. com; 1005 1st St NE) Provides nationwide service. The terminal is a few blocks north of Union Station; take a cab after dark.

Megabus ([📞]877-462-6342; us.megabus.com; [📶]) Leaves from Union Station.

Train

Amtrak ([📞]800-872-7245; www.amtrak. com) Set inside the magnificent beaux-arts Union Station (www.unionstationdc.com; 50 Massachusetts Ave NE; [M]Union Station). Trains depart for nationwide destinations, including New York City (3½ hours), Chicago (18 hours) and Miami (24 hours).

Getting Around

To/from the Airport

Metrobus 5A (www.wmata.com) Runs from Dulles to Rosslyn Metro station (35 minutes) and central DC (L'Enfant Plaza, 48 minutes); it departs every 30 to 40 minutes. The combo bus/ Metro fare is about $8.

Metrorail (www.wmata. com) National airport has its own Metro rail station, which is fast and cheap.

Washington Flyer (www. washfly.com) Runs every 30 minutes from Dulles to West Falls Church Metro ($10).

Public Transportation

Metrorail ([📞]202-637-7000; www.wmata.com) The metro will get you to most sights, hotels and business districts, and the Maryland and Virginia suburbs. Machines inside stations sell computerized fare cards based on distance traveled. Unlimited travel passes are also available.

Circulator (www.dccirculator.com) Buses run along handy routes – including Union Station to and from Georgetown. One-way fare costs $1.

Taxi

For a cab, try Capitol Cab ([📞]202-636-1600), Diamond ([📞]202-387-6200) or Yellow Cab ([📞]202-544-1212).

Memorial Day parade in front of Washington Monument (p105)
STEPHEN J BOITANO/GETTY IMAGES ©

Chicago

There's something about this cloud-scraping city that bewitches. Well, maybe not during the six-month winter, when the 'Windy City' gets slapped by snowy blasts. But come May – when the weather warms and everyone dashes for the outdoor festivals, ballparks, lakefront beaches and beer gardens – nowhere tops Chicago (and we also mean this literally, as the skyscrapers here are among the nation's tallest).

Beyond its mighty architecture, Chicago is a city of Mexican, Polish, Vietnamese and other ethnic neighborhoods, great for wandering through. It's a city of blues, jazz and rock clubs, with music on every night of the week. And it's a chowhound's town, where diners queue for everything from down-home hot dogs to some of North America's top restaurants.

Forgive us, but it has to be said: the Windy City will blow you away with its low-key, cultured awesomeness.

Crown Fountain, Millennium Park (p143)   **127**

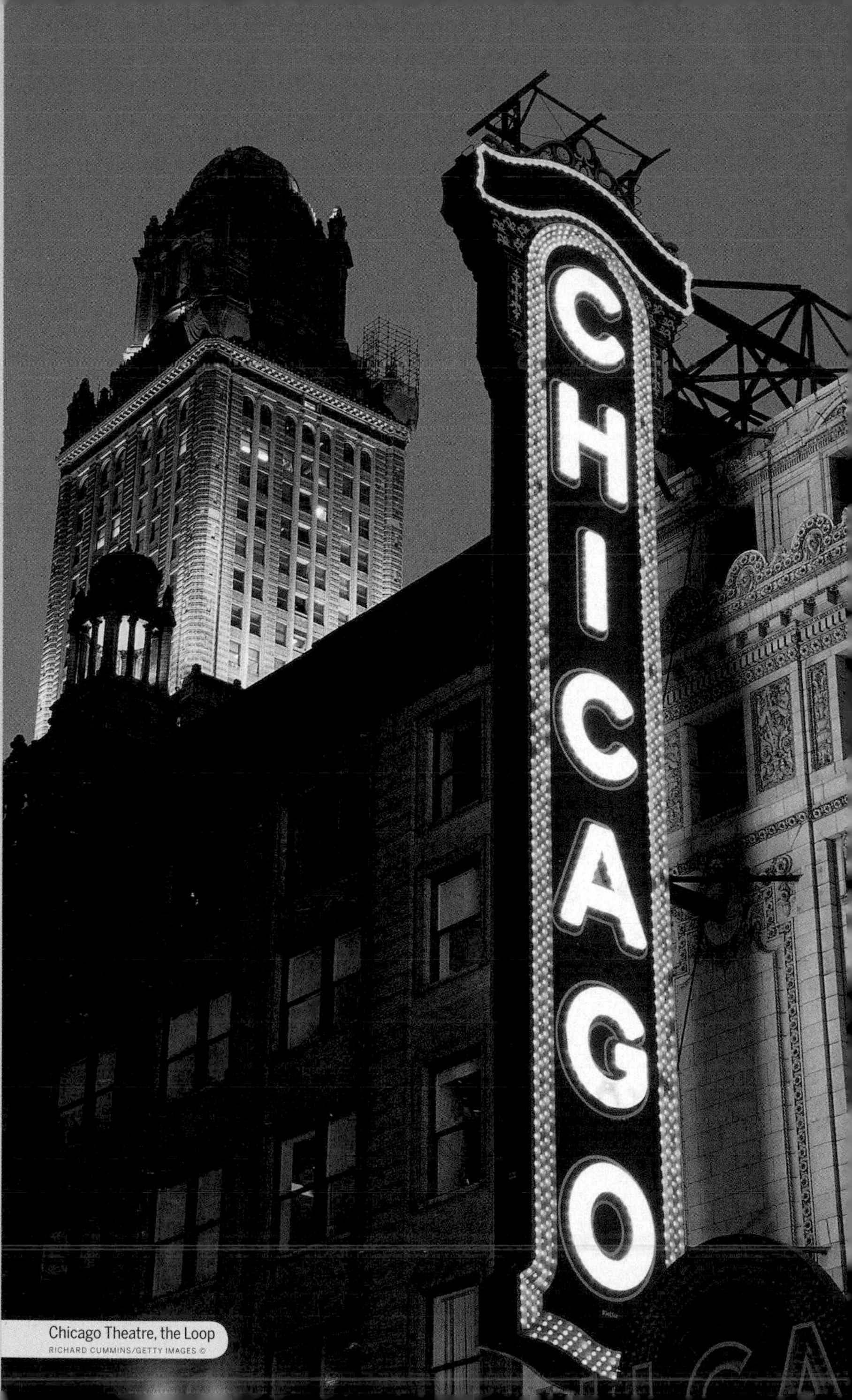

Chicago Theatre, the Loop
RICHARD CUMMINS/GETTY IMAGES ©

Chicago

1 Millennium Park

2 Art Institute of Chicago

3 Lincoln Park

4 Deep-Dish Pizza

5 John Hancock Center

Morse Ⓜ
Ⓜ Loyola
Granville
EDGEWATER Ⓜ
Thorndale
W Peterson Ave
Bryn Ⓜ
Mawr
Rosehill
Cemetery
East
River **LINCOLN** **ANDERSONVILLE**
Park **SQUARE** W Foster Ave
North Branch
Chicago River **UPTOWN**
Kedzie Western Waveland
Ⓜ Ⓜ Ⓜ Park
Kimball Francisco Rockwell Damen
O'Hare International *Graceland*
(10mi) Horner *Cemetery*
Irving Park
Park Ⓜ W Irving Park Rd
Addison Ⓜ **LAKEVIEW**
Ⓜ W Addison St
Belmont
Ⓜ W Belmont Ave
N Western Ave
N Milwaukee Ave
John F Kennedy Expwy
Logan **LINCOLN**
Ⓜ Square **PARK**
W Fullerton Ave North
LOGAN Ave
SQUARE California Beach
Ⓜ **BUCKTOWN** Clybourn
Western Station *Lake Michigan*
Ⓜ (Metra) 3
OLD TOWN Lincoln
Damen Park
W North Ave Ⓜ W North Ave
W North Ave **HUMBOLDT** Division
PARK **WICKER** Goose
PARK Island
UKRAINIAN Chicago Ⓜ
VILLAGE Ⓜ Ⓜ 5
W Grand Ave 4
Cicero Garfield Grand Ⓜ Ⓜ Grand
Ⓜ Park Ashland
Pulaski California **GREEKTOWN** 1 Millennium
Ⓜ Kedzie Ⓜ **THE LOOP** Park
Pulaski Kedzie- Medical Racine 2
Ⓜ Homan Center Ⓜ **LITTLE**
Eisenhower Expwy Western Ⓜ Polk **ITALY**
W Roosevelt Rd
See Downtown Chicago Map (p138)
Central Douglas
Park Kedzie California 12th St
Kildare Ⓜ Ⓜ Ⓜ 18th St Beach
Pulaski Western Cermak-
Ⓜ W Cermak Rd Ⓜ Hoyne Chinatown
Halsted **CHINATOWN** 27th St Station
Ⓜ (Metra)
Ashland McGuane 31st St
Park Beach
Sanitary Drainage & Ship Canal Sox-35th St **BRONZEVILLE**
35th St/Archer Ⓜ Woodland
Ⓜ 35th St- Park
McKinley **BRIDGEPORT** Bronzeville-IIT
Park W Pershing Rd Ⓜ Indiana
Adlai Stevenson Expwy 43rd St
Ⓜ
4 km **KENWOOD**
0 Ⓜ 47th St Station
S Cicero Ave 2 miles 47th St Ⓜ (Metra)
51st St 51st-53rd St
Ⓜ 55th-56th-57th Station (Metra)
S Archer Ave Kedzie Western St Station (Metra)
Pulaski Ⓜ Ⓜ **HYDE**
W 55th St W Garfield Blvd Sherman Garfield Garfield **PARK** 57th St
Park Ⓜ Beach

Chicago's Highlights

Millennium Park

Chicago's showpiece (p142) shines with whimsical public art. Where to start amid the mod designs? Pritzker Pavilion, Frank Gehry's swooping silver band shell? Jaume Plensa's *Crown Fountain*, with its human gargoyles? Anish Kapoor's silvery sculpture *Cloud Gate* (aka 'The Bean')? Or maybe someplace away from the crowds, like the veiled Lurie Garden, abloom with prairie flowers. Summer concerts and winter ice-skating add to the fun. Below: *Cloud Gate* by Anish Kapoor

Art Institute of Chicago

The second-largest art museum in the country, the Art Institute (p137) houses treasures and masterpieces from around the globe, including a fabulous selection of Impressionist and post-Impressionist paintings. The Modern Wing, dazzling with natural light, hangs Picassos and Mirós on its 3rd floor. An added bonus is the mod, pedestrian Nichols Bridgeway arching into Millennium Park.

Lincoln Park

Lincoln Park (p141) is Chicago's largest green space, an urban oasis spanning 1200 leafy acres along the lakefront. Lincoln Park is also the name for the abutting neighborhood. Both are alive day and night with people jogging, walking dogs, pushing strollers and driving in circles looking for a place to park. Highlights include a zoo, a conservatory filled with exotic blooms and the Southern California–style North Avenue Beach. Right: Lincoln Park Conservatory

Deep-Dish Pizza

Chicago's iconic dish boasts a thick, buttery crust that rises two or three inches above the plate and cradles a molten pile of toppings. One gooey piece is practically a meal. It was invented back in 1943 at Pizzeria Uno, and is required eating for any self-respecting pizza lover visiting the Windy City. Top contenders for Chicago's best pizza are Gino's East, Giordano's and, of course, the deep-dish birthplace, Uno's. For details, see p147.

John Hancock Center

The 100-story John Hancock Center (p141) has unrivaled views over the lake and the city beside it. Those needing a city history lesson should ascend to the 94th-floor observatory and listen to the edifying audio tour that comes with admission. Those secure in their knowledge should shoot up to the 96th-floor Signature Lounge for a drink.

Chicago's Best...

Museums

o **Field Museum of Natural History** Delve far into the past while exploring the eye-opening collections. (p137)

o **Shedd Aquarium** Whales, dolphins, sharks and other fascinating creatures from the deep. (p137)

o **Adler Planetarium & Astronomy Museum** Journey to the nether regions of outer space at this lakeside gem. (p137)

o **Museum of Science & Industry** Geek out at the largest science museum in the western hemisphere. (p144)

Architecture

o **Willis Tower** Breathtaking views from the 103rd-floor Skydeck. (p136)

o **Rookery** Floating staircases feature in Frank Lloyd Wright's light-filled atrium. (p144)

o **Chicago Board of Trade** An art-deco, photogenic classic. (p144)

o **Robie House** Frank Lloyd Wright's masterpiece in Hyde Park. (p144)

Dining

o **Longman & Eagle** Logan Sq favorite with an inventive (Michelin-starred) American menu. (p150)

o **Alinea** New American cooking reaches high art at this futuristic restaurant. (p148)

o **Hopleaf** A charming bistro with delectable fare and a wide selection of Belgian beer. (p149)

o **Purple Pig** Buzzing Michigan Ave eatery serving mouthwatering tapas. (p148)

Need to Know

Live Music

o **Buddy Guy's Legends** Top music club where you can catch some of the world's best blues players. (p153)

o **Grant Park Orchestra** Catch free summer concerts in Millennium Park. (p154)

o **Kingston Mines** A Lincoln Park favorite with smokin'-hot blues. (p151)

o **Green Mill** Al Capone's former hang-out is a great spot to hear top-notch jazz (p151)

o **Hideout** A rambling indie-rock club near Bucktown. (p153)

ADVANCE PLANNING

o **Two months before** Chowhounds who crave dinner at top-end restaurants such as Alinea, Next or Topolobampo should make reservations.

o **One month before** Browse www.goldstar.com for half-price tickets to theater, sports events and concerts.

o **One week before** Buy online discount cards (try www.gochicagocard.com or www.citypass.com) if you're planning to do a lot of sightseeing.

RESOURCES

o **Explore Chicago** (www.explorechicago.org) The city's official tourism site.

o **Chicagoist** (www.chicagoist.com) Quirky take on news, food, arts and events.

o **Gapers Block** (www.gapersblock.com) News and events with Chicago attitude.

o **Chicago Gluttons** (www.chicagogluttons.com) Entertaining, unvarnished restaurant reviews by a group of foul-mouthed 'regular Joes.'

GETTING AROUND

o **Airport** O'Hare International Airport (ORD; www.ohare.com) is the main airport; the CTA Blue Line offers a quick trip to downtown ($5). Airport shuttles are $32 per person, cabs about $50. From Midway Airport (www.flychicago.com) take the CTA Orange Line.

o **Public transport** The CTA offers an extensive network of elevated/subway train cars (aka the El). Purchase a Transit Card from station vending machines. Rides cost about $3.

o **Taxi** Cabs are plentiful in the Loop, north to Andersonville and west to Wicker Park/Bucktown.

o **Train** Amtrak trains depart at least once daily for San Francisco, Seattle, New York City and New Orleans.

BE FOREWARNED

o **Planning** Pre-booking accommodation during summer is a good idea, especially when festivals are on.

o **Weather** Winter (late November into April) can be long and brutal.

Left: Chicago Board of Trade (p144);
Above: A performance at Hideout (p133)

(LEFT) ANN CECIL/GETTY IMAGES ©;
(ABOVE) CHARLES COOK/GETTY IMAGES ©

133

Chicago Walking Tour

This tour swoops through the Loop, highlighting Chicago's revered art and architecture, with a visit to Al Capone's dentist thrown in for good measure.

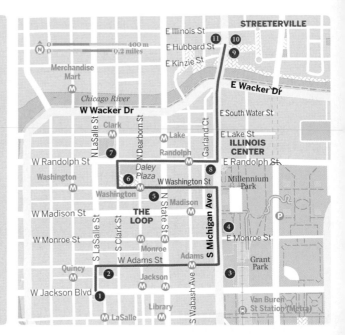

WALK FACTS

- **Start** Chicago Board of Trade
- **Finish** Billy Goat Tavern
- **Distance** 3 miles
- **Duration** 2 hours

❶ Chicago Board of Trade

Start at the Chicago Board of Trade (p144), where fast-talking guys in Technicolor coats traffic futures and options inside a stunning art-deco building.

❷ Rookery

A few blocks north, step into the Rookery (p144) – a historic 1888 landmark building with a lobby remodeled by Frank Lloyd Wright in 1905. Pigeons used to roost here, hence the name.

❸ Art Institute of Chicago

Head east on Adams St to the Art Institute of Chicago (p137), one of the city's most-

visited attractions. The lion statues out front make for a classic, keepsake photo.

❹ Millennium Park

Walk a few blocks north to avant-garde Millennium Park and saunter in to explore the famous *Cloud Gate* (aka 'the Bean'), human-gargoyle fountains and other contemporary designs.

❺ Hotel Burnham

When you depart Millennium Park, head west on Washington St to Hotel Burnham (p146). It's housed in the Reliance Building, which was the precursor to modern skyscraper design; Capone's dentist drilled teeth in what's now room 809.

6 Untitled

Just west, *Untitled*, created by Pablo Picasso, is ensconced in Daley Plaza. Bird/dog/woman? You decide.

7 Monument with Standing Beast

Head north on Clark St to Jean Dubuffet's *Monument with Standing Beast*, another head-scratching sculpture.

8 Cultural Center

Walk east on Randolph St through the theater district. Pop into the Cultural Center (p136) and have a look at its exquisite interior; its rooms are modeled on the Doge's Palace in Venice and Palazzo Vecchio in Florence.

9 Wrigley Building

Walk north on Michigan Ave and cross the Chicago River. Just north of the bridge you'll pass the Wrigley Building, a 1920s construction that ranks among one of Chicago's finest architectural works.

10 Tribune Tower

Nearby is the Gothic, eye-popping Tribune Tower. Have a close look when passing to see chunks of the Taj Mahal, Parthenon and other famous structures embedded in the lower walls.

11 Billy Goat Tavern

To finish your tour, visit Billy Goat Tavern (p147), a vintage Chicago dive that spawned the Curse of the Cubs. Just look around at the walls and you'll get the details; here it is in short. The tavern's owner, Billy Sianis, once tried to enter Wrigley Field with his pet goat. The smelly creature was denied entry, so Sianis called down a mighty curse on the baseball team in retaliation. They've stunk ever since.

Chicago in...

TWO DAYS

Take our walking tour through the Loop, then stop for a deep-dish pizza at **Giordano's** (p147). Catch the sunset from the **John Hancock Center** (p141). On day two explore the **Art Institute of Chicago** (p137) or the **Field Museum of Natural History** (p137). Browse boutiques and grab a stylish dinner in Wicker Park before heading to the **Green Mill** (p151) for late-night jazz.

FOUR DAYS

On your third day, rent a bicycle, dip your toes in Lake Michigan at **North Ave Beach** (p145) and cruise through **Lincoln Park** (p141), stopping at the zoo and conservatory. If it's baseball season, head to **Wrigley Field** (p144) for a Cubs game. A blues club, such as **Buddy Guy's Legends** (p153), is a fine way to finish the day. Pick a neighborhood on your fourth day to eat, shop and soak up the culture: murals and mole sauce in Pilsen, pagodas and Vietnamese sandwiches in Uptown, or Frank Lloyd Wright architecture in Hyde Park. Then see a play at one of Chicago's 200 theaters, or comedy at **Second City** (p154).

Field Museum of Natural History (p137)

Discover Chicago

At a Glance

- **The Loop** (p136) City center, with great architecture and museums.

- **South Loop** (p137) Home to the lakefront park-and-museum district, aka Museum Campus.

- **Near North** (p140) Shopping on the Magnificent Mile and amusement on Navy Pier.

- **Lincoln Park** (p141) Lush park and adjoining 'hood with a zoo, conservatory and popular beach.

- **Uptown** (p149) 'Little Saigon' with Vietnamese, Thai and Chinese restaurants and shops.

- **Wicker Park, Bucktown & Ukrainian Village** (p150) Packed with galleries, boutiques, music clubs and lounges.

Cyclists on Oak St Beach (p145)
PETER PTSCHELINZEW/GETTY IMAGES ©

◉ Sights

THE LOOP

Willis Tower   Tower
(☏312-875-9696; www.the-skydeck.com; 233 S Wacker Dr; adult/child $18/12; ⊙9am-10pm Apr-Sep, 10am-8pm Oct-Mar; ⓜBrown, Orange, Purple, Pink Line to Quincy) It's Chicago's tallest building, and the 103rd-floor Skydeck puts you 1454ft into the heavens. Take the ear-popping, 70-second elevator ride to the top, then step onto one of the glass-floored ledges jutting in mid-air for a knee-buckling perspective straight down. The entrance is on Jackson Blvd.

Chicago Cultural Center   Cultural Building
(☏312-744-6630; www.chicagocultural-center.org; 78 E Washington St; ⊙8am-7pm Mon-Thu, to 6pm Fri, 9am-6pm Sat, 10am-6pm Sun; 🛜; ⓜBrown, Orange, Green, Purple, Pink Line to Randolph) **FREE** The block-long building houses ongoing art exhibitions and foreign films, as well as jazz, classical and electronic dance-music concerts at lunchtime (12:15pm Monday to Friday). It also contains the world's largest Tiffany stained-glass dome and Chicago's main visitor center.

Grant Park   Park
(Michigan Ave btwn 12th & Randolph Sts; ⊙6am-11pm) Grant Park hosts the city's mega-events, such as Taste of Chicago, Blues Fest and Lollapalooza. **Buckingham Fountain** (cnr E Congress Pkwy & S Columbus Dr; ⓜRed Line to Harrison) is Grant's centerpiece. It lets loose on the hour every hour between 9am and 11pm mid-April to mid-October, accompanied at night by multicolored lights and music.

JOHN ROGER PALMOUR/GETTY IMAGES ©

Don't Miss
Art Institute of Chicago

This is the second-largest art museum in the country. The collection of Impressionist and post-Impressionist paintings is second only to those in France, and the number of surrealist works is tremendous. Download the free app for DIY tours: it offers 50 jaunts, everything from highlights (Grant Wood's *American Gothic*, Edward Hopper's *Nighthawks*) to a 'birthday-suit tour' of naked works.

NEED TO KNOW

(☎312-443-3600; www.artic.edu; 111 S Michigan Ave; adult/child $23/free; ☺10:30am-5pm, to 8pm Thu; 🖥 ♿; Ⓜ Brown, Orange, Green, Purple, Pink Line to Adams

SOUTH LOOP

Field Museum of Natural History — Museum

(☎312-922-9410; www.fieldmuseum.org; 1400 S Lake Shore Dr; adult/child $15/10; ☺9am-5pm; ♿; 🚌146, 130) Houses everything but the kitchen sink – beetles, mummies, gemstones, Bushman the stuffed ape. The collection's rockstar is Sue, the largest *Tyrannosaurus rex* yet discovered. Special exhibits, such as the 3D movie, cost extra.

Shedd Aquarium — Aquarium

(☎312-939-2438; www.sheddaquarium.org; 1200 S Lake Shore Dr; adult/child $29/20; ☺9am-6pm Jun-Aug, to 5pm Sep-May; ♿; 🚌146, 130) Top draws at the kiddie-mobbed Shedd Aquarium include the Oceanarium, with its beluga whales and frolicking white-sided dolphins, and the shark exhibit, where there's just 5in of Plexiglas between you and two dozen fierce-looking swimmers.

Adler Planetarium & Astronomy Museum — Museum

(☎312-922-7827; www.adlerplanetarium. org; 1300 S Lake Shore Dr; adult/child $12/8;

Downtown Chicago

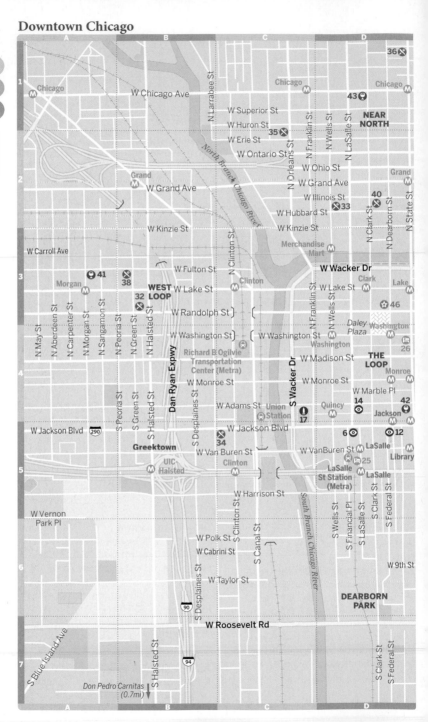

CHICAGO

NEAR NORTH

WEST LOOP

THE LOOP

Greektown

DEARBORN PARK

Don Pedro Carnitas
(0.7mi)

0   1 km
0   0.5 miles

E Pearson St

2 ⊙ *John Hancock Center*

🔒 **51**

ⓘ

30

❌ **31**

E Superior St

Water Works Visitors Center

N Michigan Ave (Magnificent Mile)

Lake Shore Park

E Chicago Ave

STREETERVILLE

E Ontario St

E Ohio St

E Grand Ave

E Illinois St

11 ⊙

❌ **37**

24

❌ **39**

❌ **27**

20 ✦

E North Water St

E Kinzie St

River Esplanade

E Wacker Dr

ILLINOIS CENTER

E Wacker Pl

E Lake St

Randolph Ⓜ

❌ **18**

Chicago Cultural Center Visitors Center

E Randolph St

44 🚇   ⓘ

8 ⊙ **22**

49 ✦

19 ✦

47 ✦

Madison Ⓜ

23

3 ⊙ *Millennium Park*

❌ **29**

E Monroe St

Adams Ⓜ

1 🏛 *Art Institute of Chicago*

21

28 ❌

Van Buren St Station (Metra)

10 ⊙ **5**

Lakefront Path

Harrison Ⓜ

✦ **50**

✦ **45**

E Balbo Ave

PRINTER'S ROW

Grant Park Tennis Courts

Grant Park

Hutchinson Field

E 9th St

E 11th St

Roosevelt Ⓜ

E Roosevelt Rd

Grant Park

Roosevelt Rd/ Museum Campus Station

MUSEUM CAMPUS

15 ⊙

CENTRAL STATION

9 🏛

E Solidarity Dr

4 🏛

E 13th St

E 14th St

Burnham Park

Burnham Harbor

18 ✦

LAKE MICHIGAN

Water Filtration Plant

Olive Park

Ohio Street Beach

🅿

13 ⊙ 🏛 **7**

🏛 **16**

Oak St Beach (0.3mi)

Lakefront Path

N Lake Shore Dr

S Lake Shore Dr

S Columbus Dr

Butler Field

🅿

S Holden Ct

S Michigan Ave

S State St

S Wabash Ave

S Lynn White Dr

Downtown Chicago

⊙ 9:30am-6pm Jun-Aug, 10am-4pm Sep-May; 🚻; ☐146, 130) Space enthusiasts will get a big bang (pun!) out of the Adler. There are public telescopes from which to view the stars, 3D lectures where you can learn about supernovas, and the Planet Explorers exhibit where kids can 'launch' a rocket.

NEAR NORTH

Navy Pier
Waterfront

(🕾312-595-7437; www.navypier.com; 600 E Grand Ave; ⊙10am-10pm Sun-Thu, to midnight Fri & Sat; 🚻; Ⓜ Red Line to Grand, then trolley) FREE Half-mile-long Navy Pier is Chicago's most-visited attraction, sporting a 150ft Ferris wheel and other carnival rides ($5 to $6 each), an IMAX theater, a beer garden and gimmicky chain restaurants. The fireworks displays on summer Wednesdays (9:30pm) and Saturdays (10:15pm) are a treat.

The Chicago Children's Museum (p148) and **Smith Museum of Stained Glass Windows** (🕾312-595-5024; 600 E Grand Ave; ⊙10am-10pm Sun-Thu, to midnight Fri & Sat; Ⓜ Red Line to Grand, then trolley) FREE are also on the pier, as are several boat-cruise operators. Try the **Shoreline water taxi** (www.shorelinesightseeing.com; one way adult/child $8/5; ⊙10am-6:30pm late May-early Sep) for a fun ride to the Museum Campus (adult/child $8/5).

Magnificent Mile
Street

(www.themagnificentmile.com; N Michigan Ave) Spanning Michigan Ave between the river and Oak St, the Mag Mile is the much-touted upscale shopping strip, where Bloomingdales, Neiman's and Saks will lighten your wallet.

PETER PTSCHELINZEW/GETTY IMAGES ©

Don't Miss
John Hancock Center

Get high in Chicago's third-tallest skyscraper. In many ways this view surpasses the one at Willis Tower. Ascend to the 94th-floor observatory for the 'skywalk' (a screened-in porch that lets you feel the wind) and informative displays about the surrounding buildings. Or bypass the education and head to the 96th-floor Signature Lounge, where the view (pictured above) is free if you buy a drink.

NEED TO KNOW
☏888-875-8439; www.jhochicago.com; 875 N Michigan Ave; adult/child $18/12; ⏱9am-11pm; Ⓜ Red Line to Chicago

LINCOLN PARK & OLD TOWN

Lincoln Park Zoo   Zoo
(☏312-742-2000; www.lpzoo.org; 2200 N Cannon Dr; ⏱10am-4:30pm Nov-Mar, to 5pm Apr-Oct, to 6:30pm Sat & Sun Jun-Aug; ♿; 🚌151) FREE
A local family favorite, filled with gorillas, lions, tigers and other exotic creatures in the shadow of downtown.

Lincoln Park
Conservatory   Gardens
(☏312-742-7736; www.lincolnparkconservancy.org; 2391 N Stockton Dr; ⏱9am-5pm; 🚌151) FREE Near the zoo's north entrance, the

magnificent 1891 hothouse coaxes palms, ferns and orchids to flourish.

Chicago History Museum   Museum
(☏312-642-4600; www.chicagohistory.org; 1601 N Clark St; adult/child $14/free; ⏱9:30am-4:30pm Mon-Sat, noon-5pm Sun; ♿; 🚌22) Multimedia displays cover it all, from the Great Fire to the 1968 Democratic Convention.

LAKE VIEW & WRIGLEYVILLE

North of Lincoln Park, these neighborhoods can be enjoyed by ambling along Halsted St, Clark St, Belmont Ave or

Don't Miss
Millennium Park

One of Chicago's most important new projects in the past 100 years is this stunning art-filled green space in the heart of the Loop. Lovely views, daring works of sculpture, high-tech fountains, hidden gardens, free summer concerts and a winter skating rink are all part of the allure at this much-loved park.

☎ 312-742-1168

www.millenniumpark.org

201 E Randolph St

 6am-11pm

Ⓜ Brown, Orange, Green, Purple, Pink Line to Randolph

The Park that Almost Wasn't

The park was slated to open in 2000 (hence the name) but construction delays pushed it back. The whole thing seemed headed for disaster, with costs rising far in excess of the original budget of $150 million. The final bill came to $475 million; private donors such as the Pritzker and Crown families and Boeing ended up paying $200 million to complete the project.

The Magic Bean

The biggest draw is 'the Bean' – officially *Cloud Gate* – Anish Kapoor's 110-ton, silver-drop sculpture. The Bean wasn't always so well loved. Kapoor was still polishing and grinding the 168 stainless steel plates when the city first showed it to the public in 2004. The surface was supposed to be seamless but it wasn't yet, and soon after its debut it went back under wraps and didn't re-emerge until 2006.

Splashy Fountain

Jaume Plensa's *Crown Fountain* is another crowd pleaser. Its two 50ft-high glass-block towers contain video displays that flash the faces of Chicagoans who agreed to strap into Plensa's special dental chair, where he immobilized their heads for filming. Each mug puckers up and spurts water, just like the gargoyles atop Notre Dame Cathedral. A set of non-puckering faces appears in winter, when the fountain is dry.

Pritzker Pavilion

Pritzker Pavilion (pictured left) is Millennium Park's acoustically awesome band shell. Architect Frank Gehry designed it, with his trademark swooping exterior. Supposedly it's modeled on gefilte fish: as a child, Gehry watched his grandma make the dish, and he was struck by the fish's shape and movement before she hacked it to death. The pipes that criss-cross over the lawn are threaded with speakers.

Millennium Park

BY KATIE LAW, MANAGER OF CHICAGO GREETER AND VOLUNTEER SERVICES

1 THE MAGIC BEAN

It's a mirror reflecting the city. Everyone wants to take a picture. Most people stand in the front courtyard, but there are good vantage points at the sculpture's north and south ends, too. For great people watching, go up the stairs on Washington St, on the Park Grill's north side, where there are shady benches.

2 SPLASHY CROWN FOUNTAIN

One thousand faces appear on the two towers' video displays to blow out water. Kids love it, it's like a water park for them.

3 THE SECRET GARDEN

People often overlook the Lurie Garden, because it's hidden behind a big hedge. It's planted with all native Midwest grasses, trees and flowers, and there's a little river to dangle your feet in. On weekends volunteers give free tours of the grounds. Another thing visitors miss is walking all the way across the snaky BP Bridge to the Maggie Daley Park, which is being revamped to have ice skating, rock climbing and gardens.

4 MUSICAL VIEWS

Sitting in the evening at a concert at Pritzker Pavilion, on the lawn looking up through the grid Frank Gehry put up, and seeing all the architecture at the corner of Randolph and Michigan – there's nothing like it. When summer hits, there are free concerts almost every night – with indie rock and new music on Mondays.

5 CYCLING & ICE SKATING

Renting bikes at the McDonald's Cycle Center is popular. In winter you can go ice-skating at the McCormick Tribune Rink. In summer, the rink converts into a beer garden operated by the Park Grill – a great place to take a break.

Famous Loop Architecture

Ever since it presented the world with the first skyscraper, Chicago has thought big with its architecture and pushed the envelope of modern design. The Loop is a fantastic place to roam and gawk at these ambitious structures.

The Chicago Architecture Foundation (p145) runs tours that explain the following buildings and more:

Chicago Board of Trade (141 W Jackson Blvd; M Brown, Orange, Purple, Pink Line to LaSalle) A 1930 art-deco gem. Inside, manic traders swap futures and options. Outside, check out the giant statue of Ceres, the goddess of agriculture, that tops the building.

Rookery (www.gowright.org/rookery; 209 S LaSalle St; ⏰9:30am-5:30pm Mon-Fri; M Brown, Orange, Purple, Pink Line to Quincy) The 1888 Rookery looks fortresslike outside, but the inside is light and airy thanks to Frank Lloyd Wright's atrium overhaul. Tours ($5 to $10) are available at noon on weekdays.

Monadnock Building (www.monadnockbuilding.com; 53 W Jackson Blvd; M Blue Line to Jackson) Architectural pilgrims get weak-kneed when they see the Monadnock Building, which is two buildings in one. The north is the older, traditional design from 1891, while the south is the newer, mod half from 1893.

Southport Ave, which are well supplied with restaurants, bars and shops. The only real sight is ivy-covered **Wrigley Field** (www.cubs.com; 1060 W Addison St; M Red Line to Addison), named after the chewing-gum guy and home to the much-loved but perpetually losing Chicago Cubs.

HYDE PARK & SOUTH SIDE

Museum of Science & Industry   Museum
(☎773-684-1414; www.msichicago.org; 5700 S Lake Shore Dr; adult/child $18/11; ⏰9:30am-5:30pm Jun-Aug, reduced hours Sep-May; 👶; 🚌6, M Metra to 55th-56th-57th) Geek out at the largest science museum in the western hemisphere. Highlights include a WWII German U-boat nestled in an underground display ($8 extra to tour it) and the 'Science Storms' exhibit with a mock tornado and tsunami.

Robie House   Architecture
(☎312-994-4000; www.gowright.org; 5757 S Woodlawn Ave; adult/child $15/12; ⏰11am-3pm Thu-Mon; 🚌6, M Metra to 55th-56th-57th) Of the numerous buildings that Frank Lloyd

Wright designed around Chicago, none is more famous or influential than Robie House. The resemblance of its horizontal lines to the flat landscape of the Midwestern prairie became known as the Prairie style. Inside are 174 stained-glass windows and doors, which you'll see on the hour-long tours (frequency varies by season).

🤸 Activities

Riding along the 18-mile lakefront path is a fantastic way to see the city. Bike-rental companies listed here also offer two- to four-hour tours ($35 to $60, including bikes) that cover themes like the lakefront, beer and pizza munching, or South Side sights (highly recommended).

Millennium Park's **McCormick Tribune Ice Rink** (www.millenniumpark.org; 55 N Michigan Ave; skate rental $10; ⏰late Nov-late Feb) heats up when the temperature plummets.

Bike Chicago   Cycling
(☎312-729-1000; www.bikechicago.com; 239 E Randolph St; bikes per hr/day from $10/35, tour

adult/child from $39/25; ⏱6:30am-8pm Mon-Fri, from 8am Sat & Sun, closed Sat & Sun Nov-Mar; Ⓜ Brown, Orange, Green, Purple, Pink Line to Randolph) Multiple locations, including Millennium Park and Navy Pier.

Bobby's Bike Hike   Cycling
(☎312-915-0995; www.bobbysbikehike.com; 465 N McClurg Ct; half/full day from $23/32; ⏱8am-8pm Jun-Aug, 8:30am-7pm Sep-Nov & Mar-May; Ⓜ Red Line to Grand) At the River East Docks' Ogden Slip.

North Ave Beach   Beach
(www.cpdbeaches.com; 1600 N Lake Shore Dr; ⚐; 🚍151) Chicago's most popular and amenity-laden stretch of sand wafts a southern California vibe. You can rent kayaks, jet skis, stand-up paddleboards and lounge chairs, as well as eat and drink at the party-orientated beach house. It's 2 miles north of the Loop.

Oak St Beach   Beach
(www.cpdbeaches.com; 1000 N Lake Shore Dr; Ⓜ Red Line to Chicago) Packs in bodies beautiful at the edge of downtown.

12th Street Beach   Beach
(www.cpdbeaches.com; 1200 S Linn White Dr; 🚍146, 130) A path runs from the Adler Planetarium to this handsome, secluded crescent of sand.

Tours

Chicago Architecture
Foundation   Boat, Walking Tours
(CAF; ☎312-922-3432; www.architecture.org; 224 S Michigan Ave; tours $10-40; Ⓜ Brown, Orange, Green, Purple, Pink Line to Adams) The gold-standard boat tours ($40) sail from Michigan Ave's river dock. The popular Rise of the Skyscraper walking tours ($17) leave from the downtown Michigan Ave address.

InstaGreeter   Walking Tour
(www.chicagogreeter.com/instagreeter; 77 E Randolph St; ⏱10am-3pm Fri-Sun; Ⓜ Brown, Orange, Green, Purple, Pink Line to Randolph) FREE Offers one-hour Loop tours on the spot from the Chicago Cultural Center visitor center.

Spiral staircase inside the Rookery

145

Sleeping

LOOP & NEAR NORTH

Buckingham Athletic
Club Hotel   Boutique Hotel $$

(☎312-663-8910; www.bac-chicago.com;
440 S LaSalle St; r incl breakfast $169-209;
P ❄ 🛜 🌊; M Brown, Orange, Purple, Pink Line
to LaSalle) Tucked into the 40th floor of the
Chicago Stock Exchange building, this 21-
room hotel is not easy to find. The benefit
if you do? Elegant rooms so spacious
they'd be considered suites elsewhere.
There's also free access to the namesake
gym with lap pool.

Acme Hotel   Boutique Hotel $$$

(☎312-894-0800; www.acmehotelcompany.
com; 15 E Ohio St; r $179-309; P ❄ @ 🛜;
M Red Line to Grand) Urban bohemians are
loving the Acme for its indie-cool style at
(usually) affordable rates. The 130 rooms
mix industrial fixtures with retro lamps,
mid-century furniture and funky modern
art. Graffiti, neon and lava lights decorate
the common areas.

Hotel Burnham   Boutique Hotel $$$

(☎312-782-1111; www.burnhamhotel.com; 1 W
Washington St; r $269-399; P ❄ @ 🛜 🏃 🐾;
M Blue Line to Washington) Housed in the
landmark 1890s Reliance Building, Hotel
Burnham's super-slick decor woos architecture buffs. Mahogany writing desks
and chaise lounges furnish the bright,
butter-colored rooms.

LAKE VIEW & WICKER PARK/
BUCKTOWN

Willows Hotel   Boutique Hotel $$

(☎773-528-8400; www.willowshotelchicago.
com; 555 W Surf St; r incl breakfast $149-265;
P ❄ 🛜; 🚌22) Small and stylish, the Willows wins an architectural gold star. The
chic little lobby provides a swell refuge
of overstuffed chairs by the fireplace,
while the 55 rooms, done up in shades
of peach, cream and soft green, evoke a
19th-century French countryside feel.

Wicker Park Inn   B&B $$

(☎773-486-2743; www.wickerparkinn.com; 1329
N Wicker Park Ave; r incl breakfast $149-199;
❄ 🛜 🏃; M Blue Line to Damen) This brick
row house is steps away from rockin' restaurants and nightlife. The sunny rooms
aren't huge, but have hardwood floors,
pastel colors and small desk spaces.

Longman & Eagle   Inn $$

(☎773-276-7110; www.longmanand
eagle.com; 2657 N Kedzie Ave; r
$85-200; ❄ 🛜; M Blue Line to
Logan Sq) Check in at the
Michelin-starred gastropub
downstairs, then head
to your wood-floored,
vintage-stylish accom-
modation on the floor
above. The six rooms
aren't particularly
soundproofed, but after
using your whiskey
tokens in the bar, you
probably won't care.

Adler Planetarium & Astronomy
Museum (p137)
BRUCE LEIGHTY/GETTY IMAGES ©

Eating

THE LOOP & SOUTH LOOP

Lou Mitchell's   Breakfast **$**
(www.loumitchellsrestaurant.com; 565 W Jackson Blvd; mains $6-11; ⏱5:30am-3pm Mon-Sat, 7am-3pm Sun; 🚻; Ⓜ Blue Line to Clinton)
A relic of Route 66; Lou's old-school waiters deliver double-yolked eggs and thick-cut French toast just west of the Loop by Union Station.

Cafecito   Cuban **$**
(www.cafecitochicago.com; 26 E Congress Pkwy; sandwiches $5-7; ⏱7am-9pm Mon-Fri, 10am-6pm Sat & Sun; 🛜; Ⓜ Brown, Orange, Purple, Pink Line to Library) Cafecito serves killer Cuban sandwiches layered with citrus-garlic-marinated roasted pork and ham. Strong coffee and hearty egg sandwiches make a fine breakfast.

Pizzeria Uno   Pizzeria **$$**
(www.unos.com; 29 E Ohio St; small pizzas from $13; ⏱11am-1am Mon-Fri, to 2am Sat, to 11pm Sun; Ⓜ Red Line to Grand) One of Chicago's great culinary gifts to the world, the deep-dish pizza has been served with panache since its inception here in 1943.

Gage   Pub **$$$**
(📞 312-372-4243; www.thegagechicago.com; 24 S Michigan Ave; mains $17-36; ⏱11am-11pm, to midnight Fri; Ⓜ Brown, Orange, Green, Purple, Pink Line to Madison) This gastropub serves Irish-tinged grub with a fanciful twist, such as Guinness-battered fish and chips, and fries smothered in curry gravy. The booze rocks, too, including a solid whiskey list and small-batch beers that pair with the food.

NEAR NORTH

This is where you'll find Chicago's mother lode of restaurants.

Billy Goat Tavern   Burgers **$**
(www.billygoattavern.com; lower level, 430 N Michigan Ave; burgers $4-6; ⏱6am-2am Mon-Fri, 10am-2am Sat & Sun; Ⓜ Red Line to Grand) *Tribune* and *Sun-Times* reporters have guz-

If You Like...
Deep-Dish Pizza

If you like the classic deep-dished decadence served at Pizzeria Uno (left), don't miss these places, all of which have their own die-hard fan base.

1 GINO'S EAST
(www.ginoseast.com; 162 E Superior St; small pizzas from $15; ⏱11am-9:30pm Mon-Sat, from noon Sun; Ⓜ Red Line to Chicago) Write on the walls while you wait for your pie.

2 LOU MALNATI'S
(www.loumalnatis.com; 439 N Wells St; small pizzas from $7; ⏱11am-11pm Mon-Thu, 11am-midnight Fri & Sat, noon-11pm Sun; Ⓜ Brown, Purple Line to Merchandise Mart) Famous for its butter crust.

3 GIORDANO'S
(www.giordanos.com; 730 N Rush St; small pizzas from $15; ⏱11am-10:30pm Sun-Thu, to 11:30pm Fri & Sat; Ⓜ Red Line to Chicago) Perfectly tangy tomato sauce.

4 PIZANO'S
(www.pizanoschicago.com; 864 N State St; 10-in pizzas from $14; ⏱11am-2am Sun-Fri, to 3am Sat; Ⓜ Red Line to Chicago) Oprah's favorite.

zled in the subterranean Billy Goat Tavern for decades. Order a 'cheezborger' and Schlitz, then look around at the newspapered walls to get the scoop on infamous local stories, such as the Cubs Curse.

Mr Beef   Sandwiches **$**
(www.mrbeefonorleans.com; 666 N Orleans St; sandwiches $4-7; ⏱9am-5pm Mon-Fri, 10am-3pm Sat, plus 10:30pm-4am Fri & Sat; Ⓜ Brown, Purple Line to Chicago) A Chicago specialty, the Italian beef sandwich stacks up like this: thin-sliced, slow-cooked roast beef that's sopped in natural gravy and *giardiniera* (spicy, pickled vegetables), and then heaped on a hoagie roll.

Chicago for Children

Chicago is a kid's kind of town. Top choices for toddlin' times include the following:

Chicago Children's Museum (📞312-527-1000; www.chicagochildrensmuseum.org; 700 E Grand Ave; admission $14; 🕐10am-6pm Sun-Wed, to 8pm Thu-Sat; 🚻; MRed Line to Grand, then trolley) Climb, dig and splash in this educational playland on Navy Pier; follow with an expedition down the carnival-like wharf itself, including spins on the Ferris wheel and carousel.

Chicago Children's Theatre (📞773-227-0180; www.chicagochildrenstheatre.org) See a show by one of the best kids' theater troupes in the country. Performances take place at venues around town.

American Girl Place (www.americangirl.com; 835 N Michigan Ave; 🕐10am-8pm Mon-Thu, 9am-9pm Fri & Sat, 9am-6pm Sun; 🚻; MRed Line to Chicago) Young ladies sip tea and get new hair-dos with their dolls at this multistory, girl-power palace.

Chic-A-Go-Go (www.roctober.com/chicagogo) Groove at a taping of this cable-access TV show that's like a kiddie version of 'Soul Train.'

Look up **Chicago Parent** (www.chicagoparent.com), a dandy resource. Other kid-friendly offerings include North Ave Beach (p145), Field Museum of Natural History (p137), Shedd Aquarium (p137), Lincoln Park Zoo (p141), Art Institute of Chicago (p137) and Museum of Science & Industry (p144).

Xoco
Mexican $$
(www.rickbayless.com; 449 N Clark St; mains $9-13; 🕐8am-9pm Tue-Thu, to 10pm Fri & Sat; MRed Line to Grand) 🍴 Crunch into warm *churros* (spiraled dough fritters) for breakfast, meaty *tortas* (sandwiches) for lunch and rich *caldos* (soups) for dinner at celeb chef Rick Bayless' Mexican street-food joint.

Purple Pig
Mediterranean $$
(📞312-464-1744; www.thepurplepigchicago.com; 500 N Michigan Ave; small plates $8-16; 🕐11:30am-midnight Sun-Thu, 1am Fri & Sat; 🍴; MRed Line to Grand) The Pig's Magnificent Mile location, wide-ranging meat and veggie menu, long list of affordable vinos and late-night serving hours make it a crowd pleaser. Milk-braised pork shoulder is the hamtastic specialty.

LINCOLN PARK & OLD TOWN

Halsted, Lincoln and Clark Sts are the main veins teeming with restaurants and bars.

Wiener's Circle
American $
(📞773-477-7444; 2622 N Clark St; hot dogs $3-6; 🕐10:30am-4am Sun-Thu, to 5am Fri & Sat; MBrown, Purple Line to Diversey) As famous for its unruly, foul-mouthed ambiance as for its char-dogs and cheddar fries, the Wiener Circle is *the* place for drunken, late-night munchies.

Alinea
Modern American $$$
(📞312-867-0110; www.alinearestaurant.com; 1723 N Halsted St; multicourse menu $210-265; 🕐5:30-9:30pm Wed-Sun; MRed Line to North/Clybourn) Widely regarded as North America's best restaurant, Alinea brings on 20 courses of mind-bending molecular gastronomy. Dishes may emanate from a centrifuge or be pressed into a capsule, a la duck served with a 'pillow of lavender air.' There are no reservations. Instead Alinea sells tickets two to three months in advance. Sign up at the website for details.

LAKE VIEW & WRIGLEYVILLE

Clark, Halsted, Belmont and Southport are fertile grazing streets.

Crisp
Asian **$**

(www.crisponline.com; 2940 N Broadway; mains $7-12; ⏱11:30am-9pm; M Brown Line to Wellington) Music pours from the stereo, and cheap, delicious Korean fusions arrive from the kitchen at this cheerful cafe. The 'Bad Boy Buddha' bowl, a variation on *bi bim bop* (mixed vegetables with rice), is one of the best cheap lunches in town.

Mia Francesca
Italian **$$**

(☎773-281-3310; www.miafrancesca.com; 3311 N Clark St; mains $13-25; ⏱5-10pm Mon-Thu, 5-11pm Fri, 10am-11pm Sat, 10am-10pm Sun; M Red, Brown, Purple Line to Belmont) Local chain Mia's buzzes with regulars who come for the trattoria's Italian standards, such as seafood linguine, spinach ravioli and mushroom-sauced veal medallions, all prepared with simple flair.

ANDERSONVILLE & UPTOWN

For 'Little Saigon' take the CTA Red Line to Argyle. For the European cafes in Andersonville, go one stop further to Berwyn. Whichever you choose, take an empty stomach!

Hopleaf
European **$$**

(☎773-334-9851; www.hopleaf.com; 5148 N Clark St; mains $11-26; ⏱noon-11pm Mon-Thu, to midnight Fri & Sat, to 10pm Sun; M Red Line to Berwyn) A cozy, European-style tavern, Hopleaf draws crowds for its Montréal-style smoked brisket, cashew-butter-and-fig-jam sandwich and the house specialty – *frites* (fries) and ale-soaked mussels. It also pours 200 types of brew, heavy on the Belgian ales.

Tank Noodle
Vietnamese **$$**

(☎773-878-2253; www.tank-noodle.com; 4953 N Broadway; mains $8-14; ⏱8:30am-10pm Mon, Tue & Thu-Sat, to 9pm Sun; M Red Line to Argyle) The official name is of this popular restaurant is Pho Xe Tang, but everyone just calls it Tank Noodle. The crowds come for *banh mi* (Vietnamese sandwiches), served on crunchy fresh baguette rolls, and the *pho* (rice noodle soup), which is widely regarded as the city's best.

A giant hot dog at the Chicago History Museum (p141)

WICKER PARK, BUCKTOWN & UKRAINIAN VILLAGE

Trendy restaurants open almost every day in these 'hoods.

Big Star Taqueria
Mexican $

(www.bigstarchicago.com; 1531 N Damen Ave; tacos $3-4; ⊙11:30am-2am; Ⓜ Blue Line to Damen) This honky-tonk gets packed, but damn, the tacos are worth the wait – pork belly in tomato-*guajillo* (chili) sauce and lamb shoulder with *queso fresco* (white cheese) accompany the specialty whiskey list. Cash only.

Ruxbin
Modern American $$$

(☎312-624-8509; www.ruxbinchicago.com; 851 N Ashland Ave; mains $25-30; ⊙5:30-10pm Tue-Sat, to 9pm Sun; Ⓜ Blue Line to Division) The passion of the brother-sister team who run Ruxbin is evident in everything from the warm decor made of found items to the artfully prepared flavors in dishes like the pork-belly salad with grapefruit, corn-bread and blue cheese. It's a wee place of just 32 seats, and BYO.

LOGAN SQUARE & HUMBOLDT PARK

Logan Sq has become a mecca for inventive, no-pretense chefs. Eats and drinks ring the intersection of Milwaukee, Logan and Kedzie Blvds.

Hot Doug's
American $

(☎773-279-9550; www.hotdougs.com; 3324 N California Ave; mains $3-9; ⊙10:30am-4pm Mon-Sat; Ⓜ Blue Line to California to bus 52) Doug is the most famous weenie maker in town, and deservedly so. He serves multiple dog styles (Polish, bratwursts, Chicago) cooked multiple dog ways (char-grilled, deep-fried, steamed). Doug also makes gourmet 'haute dogs,' such as blue-cheese pork with cherry cream sauce. Cash only.

Longman & Eagle
American $$$

(☎773-276-7110; www.longmanandeagle.com; 2657 N Kedzie Ave; mains $17-29; ⊙9am-2am; Ⓜ Blue Line to Logan Sq) This shabby-chic tavern is great for both eating and drinking. It even earned a Michelin star for its beautifully cooked comfort foods like vanilla brioche French toast for breakfast, wild-boar sloppy joes for lunch and maple-braised pork shank for dinner. Reservations not accepted.

NEAR WEST SIDE & PILSEN

The West Loop booms with hot-chef restaurants. Stroll along Randolph and Fulton Market Sts and take your pick. Greektown extends along S Halsted St (take the Blue Line to UIC-Halsted). The Mexican Pilsen enclave has loads of eateries around W 18th St.

Don Pedro Carnitas
Mexican $

(1113 W 18th St; tacos $1.50-2; ⊙6am-6pm Mon-Fri, 5am-5pm Sat, 5am-3pm Sun; Ⓜ Pink Line to 18th) At this

Buddy Guy's Legends (p153)
CHARLES COOK/GETTY IMAGES ©

no-frills Pilsen meat hive, a man with a machete salutes you at the front counter. He awaits your command to hack off pork pieces, and then wraps the thick chunks with onion and cilantro in a fresh tortilla. Cash only.

Little Goat
Diner **$$**

(www.littlegoatchicago.com; 820 W Randolph St; mains $8-12; ⏲7am-2am; 📶🖊; Ⓜ Green, Pink Line to Morgan) Sit on a vintage twirly stool and order off the all-day breakfast menu. Better yet, try lunchtime favorites like the goat sloppy joe with mashed potato tempura or the pork belly on scallion pancakes.

Publican
American **$$$**

(📞312-733-9555; www.thepublican restaurant.com; 837 W Fulton Market; mains $19-25; ⏲3:30-10:30pm Mon-Thu, 3:30-11:30pm Fri, 10am-11:30pm Sat & Sun; Ⓜ Green, Pink Line to Morgan) 🖊 Set up like a swanky beer hall, Publican specializes in oysters, hams and fine suds – all from small family farms and microbreweries.

🍷 Drinking & Nightlife

THE LOOP & NEAR NORTH

Signature Lounge
Lounge

(www.signatureroom.com; 875 N Michigan Ave; drinks $6-16; ⏲from 11am; Ⓜ Red Line to Chicago) Have the Hancock Observatory view without the Hancock Observatory admission price. Grab the elevator up to the 96th floor and order a beverage while looking out over the city. Women: don't miss the bathroom view.

Berghoff
Bar

(www.theberghoff.com; 17 W Adams St; ⏲11am-9pm Mon-Sat; Ⓜ Blue, Red Line to Jackson) The Berghoff was the first spot in town to serve a legal drink after Prohibition (ask to see the liquor license stamped '#1'). Little has changed around the antique wood bar since then.

Clark Street Ale House
Bar

(www.clarkstreetalehouse.com; 742 N Clark St; ⏲from 4pm; Ⓜ Red Line to Chicago) Do as the

 If You Like…
Blues & Jazz

If you like blues, hit Buddy Guy's Legends (p153), then check out some of these other venerable spots. Blues and jazz have deep roots in Chicago, and indie rock clubs slouch on almost every corner. Cover charges range from $5 to $20.

1 KINGSTON MINES
(www.kingstonmines.com; 2548 N Halsted St; tickets $12-15; ⏲8pm-4am Mon-Thu, from 7pm Fri & Sat, from 6pm Sun; Ⓜ Brown, Purple, Red Line to Fullerton) Two stages running seven nights a week ensure somebody's always on. It's noisy, hot, sweaty, crowded and conveniently located in Lincoln Park.

2 GREEN MILL
(www.greenmilljazz.com; 4802 N Broadway; cover charge $5-15; ⏲noon-4am Mon-Sat, from 11am Sun; Ⓜ Red Line to Lawrence) The timeless Green Mill earned its notoriety as Al Capone's favorite speakeasy (the tunnels where he hid the booze are still underneath the bar). Local and national jazz artists perform nightly; Green Mill also hosts the nationally acclaimed poetry slam on Sundays.

3 BLUES
(www.chicagobluesbar.com; 2519 N Halsted St; tickets $7-10; ⏲from 8pm; Ⓜ Brown, Purple, Red Line to Fullerton) Long, narrow and high-volume, this veteran blues club draws a slightly older crowd that soaks up every crackling, electrified moment.

retro sign advises and 'Stop & Drink Liquor.' Midwestern microbrews are the main draw; order a three-beer sampler for $6.

Intelligentsia Coffee
Cafe

(www.intelligentsiacoffee.com; 53 E Randolph St; ⏲6:30am-8pm Mon-Fri, 7am-9pm Sat, 7am-7pm Sun; Ⓜ Brown, Orange, Green, Purple, Pink Line to Randolph) The local chain roasts its own beans and percolates strong stuff. Staff recently won the US Barista Championship.

OLD TOWN & WRIGLEYVILLE

Old Town Ale House   Bar
(www.theoldtownalehouse.com; 219 W North Ave; ⏰3pm-4am Mon-Fri, from noon Sat & Sun; Ⓜ Brown, Purple Line to Sedgwick) This unpretentious favorite lets you mingle with beautiful people and grizzled regulars, seated pint by pint under the nude-politician paintings. It's across the street from Second City.

Gingerman Tavern   Bar
(3740 N Clark St; ⏰from 3pm Mon-Fri, from noon Sat & Sun; Ⓜ Red Line to Addison) The pool tables, good beer selection and pierced-and-tattooed patrons make Gingerman wonderfully different from the surrounding Wrigleyville sports bars.

Smart Bar   Club
(www.smartbarchicago.com; 3730 N Clark St; ⏰10pm-4am Wed-Sat; Ⓜ Red Line to Addison) A long-standing, unpretentious favorite for dancing, attached to the Metro rock club.

WICKER PARK, BUCKTOWN & UKRAINIAN VILLAGE

Map Room   Bar
(www.maproom.com; 1949 N Hoyne Ave; ⏰from 6:30am Mon-Fri, from 7:30am Sat, from 11am Sun; 📶) At this map-and-globe-filled 'traveler tavern' artsy types sip coffee by day and suds from the 200-strong beer list by night.

Danny's   Bar
(1951 W Dickens Ave; ⏰from 7pm; Ⓜ Blue Line to Damen) Danny's comfortably dim and dog-eared ambience is perfect for conversations over a pint. A poetry-reading series and occasional DJs add to the scruffy artiness.

LOGAN SQUARE

Late Bar   Club
(www.latebarchicago.com; 3534 W Belmont Ave; ⏰from 10pm Tue-Sat; Ⓜ Blue Line to Belmont) Owned by a couple of DJs, Late Bar has a weird, New Wave vibe that attracts fans of all stripes. It's off the beaten path in a rather forlorn stretch of Logan Sq, though it is easily reachable via the Blue Line train.

WEST LOOP

Aviary   Cocktail Bar
(www.theaviary.com; 955 W Fulton Market; ⏰from 6pm Tue-Sat; Ⓜ Green, Pink Line to Morgan) The Aviary won the James Beard Award for best cocktails in the nation. The ethereal drinks are like nothing you've laid lips on before. Some arrive with Bunsen burners, others with a slingshot you use to break the ice. It's wise to make reservations online.

Entertainment

For same-day theater seats at half price, try **Hot Tix** (www.hottix.org; 72 E Randolph St; ⏰10am-6pm Tue-Sat, 11am-4pm Sun). You can buy them online, or in person at booths in the **Chicago Tourism Center** (72 E Randolph St) and Water Works Visitor Center (p155). Check the **Reader** (www.chicagoreader.com) for listings.

Blues Fans' Pilgrimage

From 1957 to 1967, the humble building at 2120 S Michigan Ave was Chess Records, the seminal electric blues label. Muddy Waters, Howlin' Wolf and Bo Diddley cut tracks here, and paved the way for rock 'n' roll with their sick licks and amped-up sound. The studio is now called **Willie Dixon's Blues Heaven** (☎312-808-1286; www.bluesheaven.com; 2120 S Michigan Ave; tours $5-10; ⏰11am-4pm Mon-Fri, noon-2pm Sat; 🚌1), named for the bassist who wrote most of the Chess hits. Staff give tours of the premises, and free blues concerts rock the side garden on summer Thursdays at 6pm. The building is near Chinatown, about a mile south of the Museum Campus.

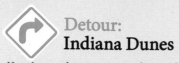

Detour:
Indiana Dunes

Hugely popular on summer days with sunbathers from Chicago and South Bend, Indiana Dunes National Lakeshore stretches along 21 miles of Lake Michigan's shoreline. In addition to its beaches, the area is noted for its plant variety: everything from cacti to pine trees sprouts here. Hiking trails crisscross the dunes and woodlands, winding by a peat bog, a still-operating 1870s farm and a blue heron rookery, among other payoffs. Stop at the **Dorothy Buell Visitor Center** (☏219-926-7561; Hwy 49; ⊙8:30am-6:30pm Jun-Aug, to 4:30pm Sep-May) for beach details, a schedule of ranger-guided walks and activities, and to pick up hiking, biking and birding maps.

Indiana Dunes State Park (☏219-926-1952; www.dnr.in.gov/parklake; per car $10) is a 2100-acre, shoreside pocket within the national lakeshore; it's located at the end of Hwy 49, near Chesterton. It has more amenities but also more regulation and more crowds (plus the vehicle entry fee). Winter brings out cross-country skiers; summer brings out hikers. Seven trails zigzag over the landscape; No 4 up Mt Tom rewards with Chicago skyline views.

The Dunes are an easy day trip from Chicago. Driving there takes one hour. The South Shore Metra train (www.nictd.com) makes the journey from Millennium Station downtown, and it's about 1¼ hours to the Dune Park or Beverly Shores stops (note both stations are a 1.5-mile walk from the beach).

LIVE MUSIC

Buddy Guy's Legends   Blues
(www.buddyguys.com; 700 S Wabash Ave; tickets Sun-Thu $10, Fri & Sat $20; ⊙from 5pm Mon & Tue, from 11am Wed-Fri, from noon Sat & Sun; Ⓜ Red Line to Harrison) Top local and national acts wail on the stage of local icon Buddy Guy. The man himself usually plugs in his axe for a series of shows in January.

SummerDance   Music
(☏312-742-4007; www.chicagosummerdance. org; 601 S Michigan Ave; ⊙6pm Thu-Sat, 4pm Sun late Jun–mid-Sep; Ⓜ Red Line to Harrison) **FREE** Boogie at the Spirit of Music Garden in Grant Park with a multi-ethnic mash-up of locals. Bands play rumba, samba and other world beats preceded by fun dance lessons – all free.

Whistler   Live Music
(☏773-227-3530; www.whistlerchicago.com; 2421 N Milwaukee Ave; ⊙from 6pm Mon-Thu, from 5pm Fri-Sun; Ⓜ Blue Line to California) **FREE** Indie bands and jazz trios brood at this artsy little club in Logan Sq. There's never a cover charge.

Hideout   Live Music
(www.hideoutchicago.com; 1354 W Wabansia Ave; ⊙7pm-late Tue & Sat, from 4pm Wed-Fri, varies Sun & Mon; 🚌72) Hidden behind a factory at the edge of Bucktown, this two-room lodge of indie rock and alt-country is well worth seeking out. Music and other events (bingo, literary readings etc) take place nightly.

THEATER & COMEDY

The Theater District is a cluster of big, neon-lit venues at State and Randolph Sts. **Broadway in Chicago** (☏800-775-2000; www.broadwayinchicago.com) handles tickets for most.

Goodman Theatre   Theater
(☏312-443-3800; www.goodmantheatre.org; 170 N Dearborn St; Ⓜ Brown, Orange, Green, Purple, Pink, Blue Line to Clark/Lake) This is one of Chicago's top drama houses and its Theater District facility is gorgeous. It

Detour:
Oak Park

Located 10 miles west of the Loop, and easily reached via CTA train, is Oak Park, home of two famous sons: novelist Ernest Hemingway, who was born here, and architect Frank Lloyd Wright, who lived and worked here from 1889 to 1909.

During Wright's 20 years in Oak Park, he designed many houses. Stop at the **visitor center** (📞888-625-7275; www.visitoakpark.com; 1010 W Lake St; 🕙10am-5pm) and buy an architectural site map ($4.25), which gives their locations. To actually get inside a Wright-designed dwelling, you'll need to visit the **Frank Lloyd Wright Home & Studio** (📞312-994-4000; www.gowright.org; 951 Chicago Ave; adult/child/camera $15/12/5; 🕙11am-4pm). Tour frequency varies, from every 20 minutes on summer weekends to every hour in winter. The studio also offers guided neighborhood walking tours, as well as a self-guided audio version.

Though Hemingway called Oak Park a 'village of wide lawns and narrow minds,' the town still pays homage to him at the **Ernest Hemingway Museum** (📞708-848-2222; www.ehfop.org; 200 N Oak Park Ave; adult/child $10/8; 🕙1-5pm Sun-Fri, from 10am Sat). Admission includes access to **Hemingway's Birthplace** (339 N Oak Park Ave; 🕙1-5pm Sun-Fri, from 10am Sat) across the street.

From downtown Chicago, take the CTA Green Line to its terminus at the Harlem stop, which lands you a quarter-mile from the visitor center. The train traverses some bleak neighborhoods before emerging into Oak Park's wide-lawn splendor.

---

specializes in new and classic American productions.

Second City
Comedy

(📞312-337-3992; www.secondcity.com; 1616 N Wells St; Ⓜ Brown, Purple Line to Sedgwick) It's the cream of the crop, where Bill Murray, Stephen Colbert, Tina Fey and many more honed their wit.

PERFORMING ARTS
Grant Park Orchestra
Classical Music

(📞312-742-7638; www.grantparkmusic festival.com; Pritzker Pavilion, Millennium Park; 🕙6:30pm Wed & Fri, 7:30pm Sat mid-Jun–mid-Aug; Ⓜ Brown, Orange, Green, Purple, Pink Line to Randolph) **FREE** The beloved group puts on free classical concerts in Millennium Park throughout the summer.

Hubbard Street Dance Chicago
Dance

(📞312-850-9744; www.hubbardstreetdance. com; 205 E Randolph St; Ⓜ Brown, Orange, Green, Purple, Pink Line to Randolph) Chicago's preeminent dance company performs at the Harris Theater for Music and Dance.

🔒 Shopping

A siren song for shoppers emanates from N Michigan Ave, along the Magnificent Mile. **Water Tower Place** (www.shopwatertow-er.com; 835 N Michigan Ave; 🕙10am-9pm Mon-Sat, 11am-6pm Sun; Ⓜ Red Line to Chicago) is among the large vertical malls here. Moving onward, boutiques fill Wicker Park/ Bucktown (indie and vintage), Lincoln Park (posh), Lake View (countercultural) and Andersonville (all of the above).

ℹ️ Information

Choose Chicago (www.choosechicago.com) is the city's tourism bureau. It operates the following two visitor centers, each with a staffed information desk, CTA transit-card kiosk and free wi-fi.

Chicago Cultural Center Visitors Center (77 E Randolph St; 🕙9am-7pm Mon-Thu, 9am-6pm Fri & Sat, 10am-6pm Sun; 📶; Ⓜ Brown, Orange, Green, Purple, Pink Line to Randolph) Offers brochures, staffed information desk, transit cards, free wi-fi and InstaGreeter tours of the Loop (Friday through Sunday).

Water Works Visitors Center (163 E Pearson St; ⓒ9am-7pm Mon-Thu, 9am-6pm Fri & Sat, 10am-6pm Sun; 🛜; MRed Line to Chicago) There's a staffed information desk and a Hot Tix booth inside selling discounted theater tickets.

ⓘ Getting There & Around

To/from the Airport

Chicago Midway Airport Eleven miles southwest of the Loop, connected via the CTA Orange Line ($3). Shuttle vans cost $27, taxis cost $30 to $40.

O'Hare International Airport Seventeen miles northwest of the Loop. The CTA Blue Line train ($5) runs 24/7. Trains depart every 10 minutes or so; they reach downtown in 40 minutes. Airport Express shuttle vans cost $32, taxis around $50. They can take as long as the train, depending on traffic.

Public Transportation

The Chicago Transit Authority (CTA; www. transitchicago.com) operates the city's buses and the elevated/subway train system (aka the El). Standard fare per train is $3 (except from O'Hare, where it costs $5) and includes two transfers. Unlimited ride passes (one-/three-day pass $10/20) are also available. Get them at rail stations and drug stores.

Train

Chicago's classic Union Station (www. chicagounionstation.com; 225 S Canal St) is the hub for Amtrak (☏800-872-7245; www.amtrak. com) national and regional services.

Bicycle

Chicago is a cycling-savvy city with 200 miles of bike lanes and a bike-share program called Divvy (www.divvybikes.com). The Department of Transportation (www.chicagocompletestreets. org) provides free maps.

Taxi

Recommended companies:

Flash Cab (☏773-561-1444; www.flashcab.com)

Yellow Cab (☏312-829-4222; www. yellowcabchicago.com)

BP Bridge, Millennium Park (p142)

RICK GERHARTER/GETTY IMAGES ©; BP BRIDGE ARCHITECT: FRANK GEHRY

Boston & New England

New England may look small on a map, but don't let that fool you. From big-city Boston – the cradle of the American experiment – to the rugged shores of Maine, New England packs a dazzling array of attractions. Historical sites, world-class restaurants and age-old fishing villages are all part of the vibrant mix.

On the coast you'll find sandy beaches begging for a dip and pristine harbor towns sprinkled with old mansions, wide lawns and quaint antique shops and galleries. The joys here are simple but amply rewarding – from cracking open a lobster at a weathered seafood shack by the water, to hiking a coastal trail past tranquil ponds and along seacliffs. And if you're lucky enough to be here in autumn, you'll be rewarded with the most brilliant fall foliage you'll ever see.

Frenchman Bay, Bar Harbor (p199)

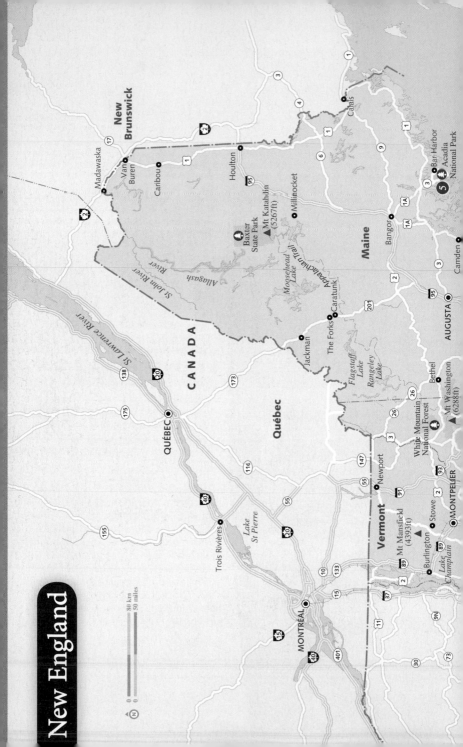

New England

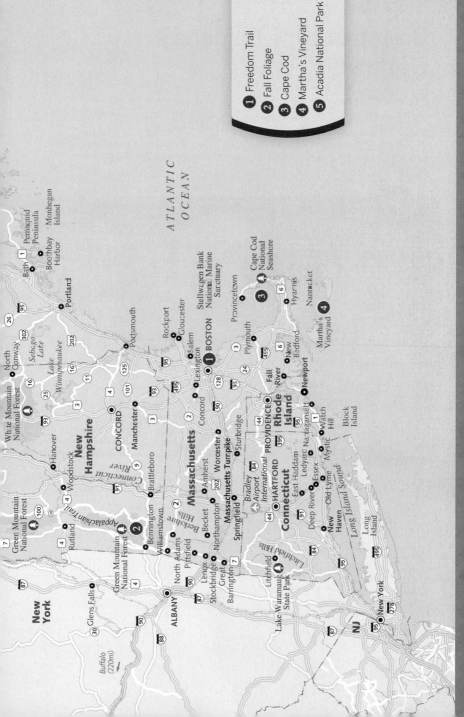

1 Freedom Trail

2 Fall Foliage

3 Cape Cod

4 Martha's Vineyard

5 Acadia National Park

ATLANTIC OCEAN

Monhegan Island

Pemaquid Peninsula

Boothbay Harbor

Bath **1**

Portland

95

26

302

North Conway

Sebago Lake

Lake Winnipesaukee

16

25

16

11

125

White Mountain National Forest **4**

93

Hanover

Woodstock

4

New Hampshire

Connecticut River

Brattleboro

101

CONCORD

Manchester

3

93

3

Portsmouth

Rockport

Gloucester

Salem

95

Lexington

1 BOSTON

Concord

2

495

128

90

Stellwagen Bank National Marine Sanctuary

Provincetown

Cape Cod National Seashore

3

4

Hyannis **6**

Nantucket

3

Plymouth

24

95

Massachusetts

Amherst

Worcester **202**

Sturbridge

Massachusetts Turnpike

90

Springfield

Bradley International Airport

91

HARTFORD

44

Connecticut

84

Fall River

195

New Bedford **6**

6

Rhode Island

PROVIDENCE **395**

144

95

1

Newport **4** Martha's Vineyard

Narragansett

Watch Hill

Mystic

Block Island

Green Mountain National Forest

100

7

4

Rutland

Bennington

Williamstown

2

Berkshire Hills

Becket

Northampton

North Adams

Pittsfield

Lenox

Stockbridge

Great Barrington

7

90

87

Appalachian Trail **2**

Green Mountain National Forest

4

New York

Glens Falls

30

Buffalo (220mi)

ALBANY

87

88

90

Ledyard

East Haddam

Essex

Deep River

New Haven

Old Lyme

91

Litchfield Hills

Litchfield

Lake Waramaug State Park **1**

84

95

Long Island Sound

Long Island

495

New York

95

278

NJ

87

Boston & New England's Highlights

Freedom Trail

Following in the footsteps of Colonial rebels, Boston's Freedom Trail (p170) takes in pivotal sights that give an insight into the birth of the USA. Along the red bricks, you'll visit burial grounds, chapels, secret meeting houses, a wooden warship and battle sites. While the main landmarks are easy to find, an insider's perspective will help you break from the crowds and dig deeper. Below: Memorial Hall, Massachusetts State House (p167)

1

2 Fall Foliage

From late September to mid-October, New England becomes a fiery blaze of color, with leaves of red, orange, yellow and gold covering the rolling forests and hillsides. A well-planned road trip beneath crisp autumn skies is the best way to take in the cinematic beauty – stopping for fresh cranberries, hot apple cider and other goodies at orchards and farmers markets along the way.

Cape Cod

Clamber across the National Seashore dunes, cycle the Cape Cod Rail Trail or eat oysters at Wellfleet Harbor – this sandy peninsula (p179) serves up a bounty of local flavor. Fringed with 400 miles of sparkling shoreline, the cape rates as New England's top beach destination. When you've had your fill of sun and sand, get out and explore artist enclaves, take a cruise or join the free-spirited street scene in Provincetown. Right: Commercial St, Provincetown (p184)

Martha's Vineyard

New England's biggest island (p187) is also one of its premier vacation destinations, with picture-perfect harbor towns, decadent restaurants and wildlife-filled reserves. Days can be spent beachcombing, wave-frolicking, bike riding, gallery hopping and exploring the island's fascinating maritime history. Kayaking, windsurfing and drinking wine at the Vineyard's own vineyard are other fine ways to spend a sun-drenched afternoon.

Acadia National Park

The jewel of Maine's jagged seashore, Acadia National Park (p198) is set with forest-covered mountains, placid lakes and dramatic coastline. This 108-sq-mile island is New England's most biodiverse setting and home to an abundance of outdoor adventures, including hiking, mountain biking, camping, birdwatching and kayaking. The gateway to it all is Bar Harbor, an elegant town with wide lawns, delectable restaurants and heritage inns.

Boston & New England's Best...

Lobster

o **Brewster Fish House** A humble spot serving some of the cape's best seafood and lobster bisque. (p182)

o **Lobster Pot** Fantastic place in Provincetown for chowing on lobster. (p185)

o **Lobster Dock** Succulent, butter-dripping lobster served in a wooden-shack setting on Boothbay Harbor. (p198)

o **Trenton Bridge Lobster Pound** Pull up a picnic table and crack open a lobster at this buzzing eatery near Acadia National Park. (p201)

Historic Sites

o **Beacon Hill** This leafy Boston neighborhood, complete with gold-domed 18th-century State House, is packed with history. (p167)

o **North End** Littered with picturesque narrow streets and colonial buildings. (p167)

o **Strawbery Banke Museum** Portsmouth's sprawling living-history museum is a great spot to delve into the past. (p194)

o **Edgartown** Grand homes (some dating back to the 1600s) line the streets of this maritime-rich town on Martha's Vineyard. (p189)

Coastal Resorts

o **Provincetown** Heritage inns and a lively atmosphere at the cape's northern tip. (p184)

o **Nantucket** Picturesque and landmark village with gorgeous beaches nearby. (p186)

o **Oak Bluffs** Sunny summertime fun at the gateway to Martha's Vineyard. (p188)

o **Bar Harbor** A coastal gem in Maine with elegant homes and inns, good restaurants and plenty of waterside adventures. (p199)

Outdoor Activities

○ **Hiking** Hike and bike the trails of the awe-inspiring Acadia National Park. (p198)

○ **Cycling** Cycle the scenic 22-mile Cape Cod Rail Trail. (p182)

○ **Whale watching** Go eye-to-eye with giants of the deep off Provincetown. (p185)

○ **Boating** Take a scenic cruise on lovely Lake Champlain in upstate Vermont. (p193)

○ **Kayaking** Paddle around the islands of Casco Bay, near Portland. (p197)

t: Coopering demonstration, Strawberry Banke seum (p194); **Above:** Kayaking, Vermont (p190)

Need to Know

ADVANCE PLANNING

○ **Six months before** Reserve accommodation if traveling during busy times, including summer and peak leaf season in autumn.

○ **One month before** Browse online for tickets to theater, sporting events and concerts.

○ **One week before** Book walking tours, cruises and other activities.

RESOURCES

○ **Discover New England** (www.discovernewengland.org) Official tourism site with info on destinations throughout New England.

○ **Boston.com** (www.boston.com/travel/explorene) Listings of travel tips and itineraries.

○ **Yankee** (www.yankeemagazine.com) Excellent general-interest site with classic things to see, destination profiles and events.

○ **Visit New England.com** (www.visitnewengland.com) One of many online travel resources, with a comprehensive listing of hotels and attractions.

GETTING AROUND

○ **Airport** Boston's Logan International Airport (BOS) is New England's main hub. From the airport, take the 'T' (subway) downtown (30 minutes).

○ **Bike** Boston's bike-sharing scheme (www.thehubway.com) allows quick and inexpensive rides across the city.

○ **Bus** Greyhound (www.greyhound.com) runs between major towns.

○ **Hire car** You'll need a car to explore the region thoroughly, though in Boston it's easier to rely on public transport.

○ **Train** Amtrak (www.amtrak.com) connects Boston with New York City.

BE FOREWARNED

○ **Opening days** Some museums are closed on Monday.

○ **Crowds** Traffic can be hellish during summer; if possible, avoid traveling on weekends to popular destinations like Cape Cod, Martha's Vineyard and Bar Harbor.

○ **Cold** Prepare for brisk ocean temperatures, even during summer. In winter, brace yourself for snow and icy winds.

Boston & New England Itineraries

Stunning coastline, historic towns, outdoor adventures –
New England has all this and more. Its relatively compact
size means you can cram a lot into a short trip and take
in more than a few of the region's many highlights.

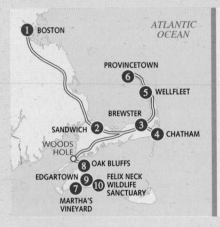

5 DAYS

BOSTON TO CAPE COD

A Captivating Threesome: City, Cape & Island

Spend a day exploring **❶ Boston** (p166). Stroll through Boston Common, visit the historic sites of Beacon Hill and enjoy a first-rate meal in a North End trattoria.

On day two, rise early for the drive east. First stop: **❷ Sandwich** (p179), Cape Cod's oldest village. Take in the historic center with its swan pond and colorful museums, then stroll along Sandy Neck Beach. Next, head to **❸ Brewster** (p181) for a lobster feast and a visit to the idyllic Nickerson State Park. Wander through **❹ Chatham** (p182) and have a splash on Lighthouse Beach then check out **❺ Wellfleet** (p183), with its lovely beaches, tony art galleries

and famous oysters. In **❻ Provincetown** (p184), book a whale-watching cruise, enjoy a seafood feast and take in the riotous cabaret scene.

On day four, head to Woods Hole for the vehicle ferry to **❼ Martha's Vineyard** (p187). Check out the pretty cottages of **❽ Oak Bluffs** (p188), take a scenic bike trail along the coast, get out on the water at Vineyard Haven, explore historic **❾ Edgartown** (p189), and stroll among the birdlife-filled marshes and ponds of **❿ Felix Neck Wildlife Sanctuary** (p190). From here, head back to the mainland for a final night in Boston.

BOSTON TO BAR HARBOR

Cruising up the Coast

Start in ❶ **Boston** (p166), taking in the scenic waterfront, heady Cambridge and the historic Freedom Trail walk. Go north to ❷ **Salem** (p179), rich in maritime history and the infamous site of the Witch Trials. The New Hampshire coast is tiny, but don't miss ❸ **Portsmouth** (p194), an old shipbuilding center with heritage homes and a lively foodie scene, before crossing into Maine. In the vibrant waterside city of ❹ **Portland** (p196), explore the lamplit lanes of the Old Port, take in the art-gallery scene, and dine at one of the city's award-winning restaurants. Continue north to ❺ **Boothbay Harbor** (p198) for fresh-off-the-boat lobster and scenic harbor cruises. To get away from it all, take a boat out to ❻ **Monhegan Island** (p201) for walks along the seacliffs and an overnight stay in an ocean-front guesthouse. Near the trip's end, book a night at a historic B&B in ❼ **Bar Harbor** (p199). Rise early the next day to take in the natural splendor of inspiring ❽ **Acadia National Park** (p198). You can go for a hike up Cadillac Mountain, cycle along miles of former carriage roads and explore the surf-pounded beaches and dramatic cliffs of the island.

Man with lobster buoys, Cape Cod (p179)

165

Discover Boston & New England

BOSTON

One of America's oldest cities is also one of its youngest. A score of colleges and universities add a fresh face to this historic capital and feed a thriving arts and entertainment scene. But don't think for a minute that Boston is all about the literati. Grab a seat in the bleachers at Fenway Park and join the fanatical fans cheering on the Red Sox.

◉ Sights

BOSTON COMMON & PUBLIC GARDEN

Boston Common Park
(btwn Tremont, Charles, Beacon & Park Sts; ⊘6am-midnight; ▥; Ⓣ Park St) The Boston Common has served many purposes over the years, including as a campground for British troops during the Revolutionary War and as green grass for cattle grazing until 1830. Although there is still a grazing ordinance on the books, the Common today serves picnickers, sunbathers and people-watchers.

Public Garden Gardens
(www.friendsofthepublicgarden. org; btwn Charles, Beacon, Boylston & Arlington Sts; ⊘6am-midnight; ▥; Ⓣ Arlington) Adjoining Boston Common, the 24-acre Public Garden provides an inviting oasis of bountiful flowers and shady trees. Its centerpiece, a tranquil lagoon with old-fashioned pedal-powered **Swan Boats** (www.swanboats.com; adult/child/senior $2.75/1.50/2; ⊘10am-4pm, to 5pm mid-Jun–Aug; Ⓣ Arlington), has been delighting children for generations.

Charles River, Boston
JEAN-PIERRE LESCOURRET/GETTY IMAGES ©

BEACON HILL & DOWNTOWN

Rising above Boston Common is Beacon Hill, one of the city's most historic and affluent neighborhoods.

Massachusetts State House
Notable Building

(www.sec.state.ma.us; cnr Beacon & Bowdoin Sts; ☉9am-5pm, tours 10am-3:30pm Mon-Fri; [T]Park St) **FREE** Crowning Beacon Hill is the golden-domed capitol building, the seat of Massachusetts' government since 1798. Volunteers lead free 40-minute tours.

Faneuil Hall
Historic Building

(www.faneuilhall.com; Congress St; ☉9am-5pm; [T]Haymarket or Aquarium) **FREE** This landmark red-brick hall, topped with its famed grasshopper weathervane, has been a market and public meeting place since 1742. Today the hall, Quincy Market and North and South Market buildings make up the Faneuil Hall Marketplace, chockfull of small shops and eateries.

New England Aquarium
Aquarium

(www.neaq.org; Central Wharf; adult/child/senior $23/16/21; ☉9am-5pm Mon-Fri, to 6pm Sat & Sun, 1hr later Jul & Aug; [P][♿]; [T]Aquarium) 🖉 The aquarium's main attraction is the newly renovated three-story cylindrical saltwater tank, which swirls with more than 600 creatures great and small, including turtles, sharks and eels. Other attractions include the penguin pool, the marine mammal exhibit and the shark-and-ray touch tank. The aquarium also organizes **whale-watching cruises** (www.neaq.org; Central Wharf; adult/child/infant $40/32/15; ☉10am Apr-Oct, additional cruises May-Sep; [♿]; [T]Aquarium).

NORTH END & CHARLESTOWN

An old-world warren of narrow streets, the Italian North End offers visitors an irresistible mix of colorful period buildings and mouthwatering eateries. Colonial sights spill across the river into Charlestown, home to America's oldest battleship.

Paul Revere House
Historic House

(☎617-523-2338; www.paulreverehouse. org; 19 North Sq; adult/child/senior & student $3.50/1/3; ☉9:30am-5:15pm, shorter hours Nov-Apr; [♿]; [T]Haymarket) This original 17th-century building was the home of famed patriot Paul Revere. A self-guided tour through the house and courtyard gives a glimpse of what life was like for the Revere family (which included 16 children!).

Old North Church
Church

(www.oldnorth.com; 193 Salem St; donation $1, tour adult/child $5/4; ☉9am-5pm Mar-Oct, 10am-4pm Tue-Sun Nov-Feb; [T]Haymarket or North Station) Every American knows the line from Longfellow's poem 'Paul Revere's Ride': 'One if by land, Two if by sea...' It was here, on the night of April 18, 1775, that the sexton hung two lanterns from the steeple, as a signal that the British would march on Lexington and Concord via the sea route.

USS Constitution
Historic Site

(www.oldironsides.com; Charlestown Navy Yard; ☉10am-6pm Tue-Sun Apr-Oct, to 4pm Thu-Sun Nov-Mar; [♿]; [🚌]93 from Haymarket, [⛴]F4 from Long Wharf) **FREE** Clamber the decks of this legendary warship, built in 1797. Its oak-timbered hull is so thick that cannonballs literally bounced off it, earning it the nickname 'Old Ironsides.'

SEAPORT DISTRICT

Following the HarborWalk, it's a pleasant stroll across the Northern Ave Bridge and into the up-and-coming Seaport District.

Boston Tea Party Ships & Museum
Museum

(www.bostonteapartyship.com; Congress St Bridge; [♿]; [T]South Station) After years of restoration, the Tea Party Ships are now moored at the reconstructed Griffin's Wharf, alongside a new museum dedicated to the Revolution's most catalytic event. Interactive exhibits allows visitors to meet re-enactors in period costume, explore the ships and even participate in the protest.

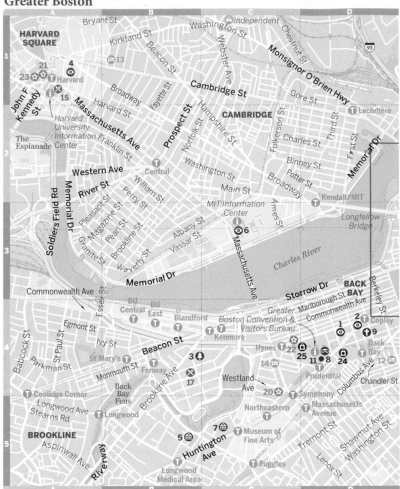

CHINATOWN, THEATER DISTRICT & SOUTH END

Compact Chinatown offers enticing Asian eateries cheek-by-jowl, while the overlapping Theater District is clustered with performing-arts venues. To the west, the sprawling South End boasts one of America's largest concentrations of Victorian row houses, a burgeoning art community and a terrific restaurant scene.

BACK BAY

Extending west from Boston Common, this well-groomed neighborhood boasts graceful brownstone residences, grand edifices and the tony shopping mecca of Newbury St.

Copley Square   Plaza
(T Copley) Here you'll find a cluster of handsome historic buildings, including the ornate neo-Romanesque **Trinity Church** (www.trinitychurchboston.org; 206 Clarendon St; adult/child/senior & student

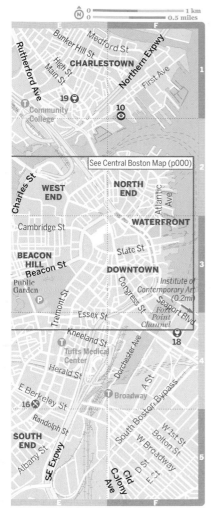

Greater Boston

◎ Sights
1	Boston Public Library	D4
2	Copley Square	D4
3	Fenway Park	B4
4	Harvard University	A1
5	Isabella Stewart Gardner Museum	B5
6	Massachusetts Institute of Technology	C3
7	Museum of Fine Arts	C5
8	Prudential Center Skywalk Observatory	D4
9	Trinity Church	D4
10	USS Constitution	F1

◎ Activities, Courses & Tours
11	Boston Duck Tours	D4

◎ Sleeping
12	Chandler Inn	D4
13	Irving House	B1
14	Oasis Guest House	C4

◎ Eating
15	Clover Food Lab	A1
16	Myers & Chang	E4
17	Tasty Burger	B4

◎ Drinking & Nightlife
18	Drink	F4
19	Warren Tavern	E1

◎ Entertainment
20	Boston Symphony Orchestra	C4
21	Club Passim	A1
22	Red Room @ Café 939	C4
23	Sinclair	A1

◎ Shopping
24	Copley Place	D4
25	Prudential Center	D4

Prudential Center Skywalk Observatory   Lookout

(www.prudentialcenter.com; 800 Boylston St; adult/child/senior & student $15/10/13; ◷10am-10pm Mar-Oct, to 8pm Nov-Feb; ℗ 🚻; ⓣPrudential) From the 50th floor, take in spectacular 360-degree views of Boston and Cambridge.

FENWAY & KENMORE SQUARE

Kenmore Sq is best for baseball and beer, while the southern part of the Fenway is dedicated to higher-minded cultural pursuits.

Museum of Fine Arts   Museum

(MFA; www.mfa.org; 465 Huntington Ave; adult/child/senior & student $22/10/20; ◷10am-5pm

$7/free/5; ◷10am-3:30pm Mon-Fri, 9am-4pm Sat, 1-5pm Sun; ⓣCopley). Across the street, the Renaissance Revival **Boston Public Library** (www.bpl.org; 700 Boylston St; ◷9am-9pm Mon-Thu & 9am-5pm Fri & Sat year-round, 1-5pm Sun Oct-May; 🛜; ⓣCopley) `FREE` is America's first municipal library. Pick up a self-guided tour brochure and wander around, noting murals by John Singer Sargent and sculpture by Augustus Saint-Gaudens.

Don't Miss
Freedom Trail

The best introduction to revolutionary Boston, the Freedom Trail is a red-brick path that winds past 16 sites that were pivotal to America's independence. The 2.5-mile trail follows the course of the conflict, starting at the Boston Common, the nation's oldest public park. It ends at Bunker Hill Monument, site of the devastating American Revolution battle.

Site of the Boston Massacre

Encircled by cobblestones, this site marks the spot where the first blood was shed for the American independence movement. On March 5, 1770, an angry mob of colonists swarmed the British soldiers guarding the State House. Sam Adams, John Hancock and about 40 other protestors hurled snowballs, rocks and insults. Thus provoked, the

soldiers fired into the crowd and killed five townspeople, including Crispus Attucks, a former slave. The incident sparked enormous anti-British sentiment in the lead-up to the revolution.

Paul Revere House

On the night of April 18, 1775, silversmith Paul Revere set out from his home on North Sq. He was one of three horseback messengers on this night who carried advance warning of the British march into Concord and Lexington. The small clapboard house is the original 1680 structure, Boston's oldest building still standing.

Bunker Hill Monument

'Don't fire until you see the whites of their eyes!' came the order from Colonel Prescott to revolutionary troops on June 17, 1775. Considering the ill-preparedness of the revolutionary soldiers, the bloody battle that followed resulted in a surprising number of casualties. Ultimately, the Redcoats prevailed. The fame of the so-called Battle of Bunker Hill is ironic, since most of the fighting actually took place on Breed's Hill, where the Bunker Hill Monument stands today. The 220ft granite hilltop obelisk rewards physically fit visitors with fine Boston views at the top of 295 steps.

Local Knowledge

Freedom Trail

BY GRETCHEN GROZIER,
BOSTON BY FOOT TOUR
LEADER

1 MASSACHUSETTS STATE HOUSE
A lot of people see the outside of the State House, but never enter. Inside is magnificent, with artwork and historic treasures. The Civil War collection includes the tattered flag of the 54th Massachusetts, the African American regiment featured in the movie *Glory*. Don't miss the Robert Gould Shaw Memorial, opposite the State House, honoring the regiment.

2 KING'S CHAPEL
Colonists were not thrilled with the building of the king's Anglican church on the edge of the Puritan burying ground, so the exterior was purposely plain. But inside it's very elaborate, with a wine glass pulpit, a fantastic organ and a canopy over the royal governor's pew. Paul Revere called the church bell, which he cast, 'the sweetest bell I ever made.'

3 FANEUIL HALL
Most people walk through Faneuil Hall's ground-floor shops and wonder what the building is. You have to go upstairs. The 2nd floor held Colonial town meetings, including pivotal debates that led to the American Revolution. The first utterance about separating from England occurred here. In later years, abolitionists took the floor and JFK made speeches here.

4 OLD NORTH CHURCH
History students offer behind-the-scenes church tours (pictured left) during summer. There's a fee but it's worth it. They go into the crypt, where a thousand people are buried, and up into the tower whose eight bells are pealed so mathematically that the bell ringers' guild is staffed by MIT students.

5 USS CONSTITUTION
The oldest commissioned warship in the US Navy is definitely worth a visit. It's a great kid stop. You can go on the ship and see the cannon, then into the museum which has fake swords, props and sailor uniforms kids can dress up in.

Central Boston

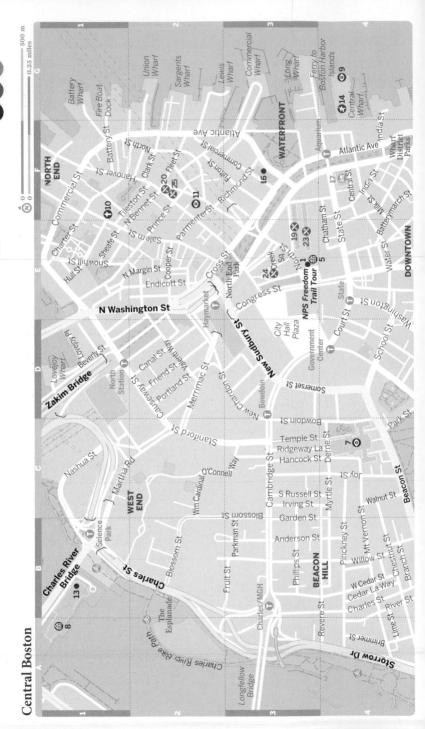

500 m
0.25 miles

NORTH END

WATERFRONT

Union Wharf
Sargents Wharf
Lewis Wharf
Commercial Wharf
Long Wharf
Ferry to Boston Harbor Islands
Central Wharf

Battery Wharf
Fire Boat Dock

Commercial St
Battery St
North St
Hanover St
Clark St
Fleet St
Tileston St
N Bennet St
Prince St
Charter St
Sheafe St
Salem St
Hull St
Snowhill St
N Margin St
Cooper St
Endicott St
Parmenter St
Cross St
Richmond St
Fulton St
Commercial St
Atlantic Ave

North End Park

Atlantic Ave
Aquarium

Wharf District Parks
India St
Central St
Chatham St
Milk St
Batterymarch St
State St
Water St
Washington St

DOWNTOWN

N Washington St

Haymarket

New Sudbury St
Congress St
Union St
Creek Sq

NPS Freedom Trail Tour

City Hall Plaza

Government Center
Court St
State
School St

Somerset St
Bowdoin St
Bowdoin

Temple St
Ridgeway La
Hancock St
Derne St
Joy St

Zakim Bridge

North Station

Lovejoy Wharf
Lovejoy Pl
Beverly St
Canal St
Friend St
Valenti Way
Portland St
Merrimac St
Stanford St
Causeway St
New Chardon St

WEST END

Nashua St
Martha Rd
Wm Cardinal O'Connell Way
Blossom St

Cambridge St
S Russell St
Irving St
Garden St
Anderson St

Phillips St
Parkman St
Fruit St

BEACON HILL

Pinckney St
Myrtle St
Mt Vernon St
Willow St
W Cedar St
Cedar La Way
Chestnut St
Branch St
Charles St
River St
Walnut St
Beacon St

Charles River Bridge

Science Park
Charles St

The Esplanade
Charles River Bike Path
Longfellow Bridge

Charles/MGH

Revere St
Lime St
Brimmer St

Storrow Dr

8
13

9
14

10
20
5
11
16

19
23
24
1
5
17

7

Central Boston

Sat-Tue, to 10pm Wed-Fri; 🚻; T Museum of Fine Arts or Ruggles) One of the country's finest art museums just got better with the opening of its spectacular new Art of the Americas wing; its 53 galleries showcase everything from pre-Columbian art to Paul Revere silver and Winslow Homer paintings.

CAMBRIDGE

On the north side of the Charles River lies politically progressive Cambridge, home to academic heavyweights Harvard University and Massachusetts Institute of Technology (MIT). At its hub, **Harvard Square** overflows with cafes, bookstores and street performers.

Boston for Children

Boston's small scale makes it easy for families to explore. A good place to start is the Public Garden (p166), where swan boats ply the lagoon and tiny tots climb on the bronze **statues** from Robert McCloskey's classic Boston tale *Make Way for Ducklings*. Across the street at the Boston Common (p166), kids can cool their toes in the Frog Pond, ride the carousel and romp at the playground. At the New England Aquarium (p167), kids of all ages will enjoy face-to-face encounters with underwater creatures.

Great tours for kids:

Boston for Little Feet (see below) The only Freedom Trail walking tour designed especially for children aged six to 12.

Urban AdvenTours (p179) Rents kids' bikes and helmets, as well as bike trailers for toddlers.

Boston Duck Tours (see below) Quirky quackiness is always a hit.

Recommended museums for kids are **Boston Children's Museum** (www.bostonchildrensmuseum.org; 300 Congress St; admission $14, Fri evening $1; ⊙10am-5pm Sat-Thu, 10am-9pm Fri; 👶; T South Station) 🖉 and the **Museum of Science** (www.mos.org; Charles River Dam; adult/child/senior $22/19/20, theater & planetarium $10/8/9; ⊙9am-5pm Sat-Thu Sep-Jun, to 7pm Jul & Aug, to 9pm Fri year-round; P 👶; T Science Park) 🖉.

Harvard University   University

(www.harvard.edu; Massachusetts Ave; tours free; ⊙tours 10am, noon & 2pm Mon-Fri, 2pm Sat; T Harvard) Along Massachusetts Ave, opposite the Harvard T station, lies the leafy campus of Harvard University. Dozens of Nobel laureates and eight US presidents are among its graduates – for other chewy tidbits join a free student-led campus tour at the **Harvard University Information Center** (📞617-495-1573; www.harvard.edu/visitors; 1350 Massachusetts Ave).

Massachusetts Institute of Technology   University

(MIT; www.mit.edu; 77 Massachusetts Ave; T Kendall/MIT) Nerds rule ever so proudly at America's foremost tech campus. Stop at the **MIT Information Center** (www.mit.edu; 77 Massachusetts Ave; ⊙tours 11am & 3pm Mon-Fri; T Central) for the scoop on where to see campus art, including Henry Moore bronzes and cutting-edge architecture by the likes of Frank Gehry.

Tours

Boston Duck Tours   Boat Tour

(📞617-267-3825; www.bostonducktours.com; adult/child/senior $34/23/28; 👶) These ridiculously popular tours use WWII amphibious vehicles that cruise the downtown streets before splashing into the Charles River. Tours depart from the **Museum of Science** (1 Science Park; 🀄; T Aquarium, Science Park or Prudential) or from behind the Prudential Center.

Boston by Foot   Walking Tour

(www.bostonbyfoot.com; adult/child $12/8; 👶) This fantastic nonprofit offers 90-minute walking tours, with specialty themes like Literary Landmarks, Boston Underfoot (with highlights from the Big Dig and the T) and **Boston for Little Feet** – a child-friendly version of the Freedom Trail.

NPS Freedom Trail Tour
Walking Tour

(www.nps.gov/bost; Faneuil Hall; ⊙10am & 2pm Apr-Nov; ; T State) FREE Guides dressed in Colonial garb lead free 90-minute walking tours along part of the Freedom Trail, departing from the visitor center in Faneuil Hall. Show up at least 30 minutes early to snag a spot.

Sleeping

Oasis Guest House Guesthouse $$

(☎617-230-0105, 617-267-2262; www.oasisgh. com; 22 Edgerly Rd; r $136-228, without bath $114-148; P ✳ 🛜; T Hynes or Symphony) True to its name, this homey guesthouse is a peaceful, pleasant oasis in the midst of Boston's chaotic city streets. Thirty-odd guest rooms occupy four attractive, brick, bow-front town houses on this tree-lined lane.

Harborside Inn Boutique Hotel $$

(☎617-723-7500; www.harborsideinnboston. com; 185 State St; r from $169; P ✳ @ 🛜; T Aquarium) In a respectfully renovated 19th-century warehouse, this waterfront hostelry has guestrooms with original exposed brick-and-granite walls and hardwood floors. They're offset perfectly by Oriental area carpets, sleigh beds and reproduction Federal-era furnishings.

Irving House Guesthouse $$

(☎617-547-4600; www. irvinghouse.com; 24 Irving St; r $165-270, s/d with shared bath $135-60/ $165-205; P ✳ @ 🛜 ♿; T Harvard) 🌿 Call it a big inn or a homey hotel, this property welcomes the world-weariest travelers. The 44 rooms range in size, but every bed is covered with a quilt and big windows let in plenty of light.

Chandler Inn Hotel $$

(☎617-482-3450, 800-842-3450; www.chandler inn.com; 26 Chandler St; r from $170; ✳ 🛜 ♿; T Back Bay) The Chandler Inn is looking fine, after a complete overhaul. Small but sleek rooms have benefited from a designer's touch, giving them a sophisticated, urban glow. On site is the South End drinking institution, Fritz.

❌ Eating

Indulge in affordable Asian fare in Chinatown and Italian feasts in the North End; or head to the South End for the city's trendiest foodie scene.

BEACON HILL & DOWNTOWN

Quincy Market Food Court $

(Congress St; ⊙10am-9pm Mon-Sat, noon-6pm Sun; 🥢 ♿; T Haymarket) This food hall packs variety with some 20 restaurants and more than 40 food stalls.

Acorn St, Beacon Hill (p167)
JEAN-PIERRE LESCOURRET/GETTY IMAGES ©

Durgin Park
American $$

(www.durgin-park.com; North Market, Faneuil Hall; lunch mains $9-15, dinner $15-30; ⏱11:30am-9pm; 👶; Ⓣ Haymarket) Durgin Park's been dishing out New England staples like Yankee pot roast, Indian pudding and slow-cooked Boston baked beans since 1827.

Union Oyster House
Seafood $$

(www.unionoysterhouse.com; 41 Union St; mains $15-25; ⏱11am-9:30pm; Ⓣ Haymarket) Slurp up fresh-shucked oysters and a heaping of history at Boston's oldest (1826) restaurant.

NORTH END

Volle Nolle
Sandwiches $

(351 Hanover St; sandwiches $8-12; ⏱11am-11pm; 🍴👶; Ⓣ Haymarket) Amid black-slate tables and pressed-tin walls, you'll find a chalkboard menu of fresh salads, delicious flatbread sandwiches and dark rich coffee.

Giacomo's Ristorante
Italian $$

(www.giacomosblog-boston.blogspot.com; 355 Hanover St; mains $14-19; ⏱4:30-10pm Mon-Sat, 4-9:30pm Sun; 🍴; Ⓣ Haymarket) Arrive early to get a table at this small, extremely convivial spot serving huge plates of southern Italian fare. Cash only.

SEAPORT DISTRICT

Barking Crab
Seafood $$

(www.barkingcrab.com; 88 Sleeper St; mains $12-30; ⏱11:30am-10pm Sun-Wed, to 11pm Thu-Sat; 🚌SL1 or SL2, Ⓣ South Station) Big buckets of crabs, steamers dripping in lemon and butter, paper plates piled high with all things fried... The food is plentiful and cheap, best enjoyed at communal picnic tables overlooking the water.

CHINATOWN, THEATER DISTRICT & SOUTH END

Gourmet Dumpling House
Chinese, Taiwanese $

(www.gourmetdumpling.com; 52 Beach St; lunch $8, dinner mains $10-15; ⏱11am-1am; 🍴; Ⓣ Chinatown) Shanghai soup dumplings are fresh, doughy and delicious, though the menu offers plenty of other options, including scrumptious crispy scallion pancakes.

Shops along Newbury St (p178), Boston

Myers & Chang
Asian $$$

(📞617-542-5200; www.myersandchang. com; 1145 Washington St; small plates $10-18; ⏰11:30am-11pm Fri & Sat, to 10pm Sun-Thu; 🍴; 🚇SL4 or SL5, ⟙Tufts Medical Center) This super-hip Asian spot blends Thai, Chinese and Vietnamese cuisines, which means delicious dumplings, spicy stir-fries and oodles of noodles.

BACK BAY & FENWAY

Tasty Burger
Burgers $

(www.tastyburger.com; 1301 Boylston St; burgers $4-6; ⏰11am-2am; 📶; ⟙Fenway) Once a Mobile station, it's now a retro burger joint, with picnic tables outside and a pool table inside.

Parish Café
Sandwiches $$

(www.parishcafe.com; 361 Boylston St; sandwiches $12-15; ⏰noon-2am; 🍴; ⟙Arlington) The menu at Parish features a rotating roster of salads and sandwiches, each designed by a local celebrity chef, including Lydia Shire, Ken Oringer and Barbara Lynch.

CAMBRIDGE

Clover Food Lab
Vegetarian $

(www.cloverfoodlab.com; 7 Holyoke St; mains $6-7; ⏰7am-midnight; 🍴📶; ⟙Harvard) 🌱 Clover is on the cutting edge. It's all high-tech with its 'live' menu updates and electronic ordering system. But it's really about the food – local, seasonal, vegetarian food – which is cheap, delicious and fast.

🍷 Drinking & Nightlife

Drink
Cocktail Bar

(www.drinkfortpoint.com; 348 Congress St S; ⏰4pm-1am; 🚇SL1 or SL2, ⟙South Station) The bar takes seriously the art of drink mixology – and you will too, after you sample one of its concoctions at this atmospheric, subterranean space.

Warren Tavern
Historic Pub

(www.warrentavern.com; 2 Pleasant St; ⏰11am-1am; ⟙Community College) One of the oldest pubs in Boston, the Warren Tavern has been pouring pints for its customers since George Washington and Paul Revere drank here.

Cheap Seats

Half-price tickets to same-day theater and concerts in Boston are sold at **BosTix** (www.bostix.org; ⏰10am-6pm Tue-Sat, 11am-4pm Sun) at Faneuil Hall and Copley Sq. No plastic – these deals are cash only.

⭐ Entertainment

For up-to-the-minute listings, grab a copy of the free *Boston Phoenix*.

From April to September, join the fans cheering on the **Boston Red Sox** (www. redsox.com) at **Fenway Park** (4 Yawkey Way; adult/child/senior $12/10/11; ⏰9am-4pm Apr-Oct, 10am-2pm Nov-Mar; 📶; ⟙Kenmore), major-league baseball's oldest (1912) and most storied ballpark.

Club Passim
Folk Music

(📞617-492-7679; www.clubpassim.org; 47 Palmer St, tickets $15-30; ⟙Harvard) Folkies flock to this venerable Cambridge club, which has been a haunt of up-and-coming folk singers since the days of Dylan and Baez.

Red Room @ Café 939
Live Music

(www.cafe939.com; 939 Boylston St; ⟙Hynes) Run by Berklee students, the Red Room is emerging as one of Boston's best music venues.

Sinclair
Live Music

(www.sinclaircambridge.com; 52 Church St; tickets $15-18; ⏰11am-1am Tue-Sun, 5pm-1am Mon; ⟙Harvard) A great new small venue to catch live music, Sinclair attracts a good range of local and regional bands and DJs.

Boston Symphony Orchestra
Classical Music

(BSO; 📞617-266-1200; www.bso.org; Symphony Hall, 301 Massachusetts Ave; tickets $30-115; ⟙Symphony) From September to April, the celebrated Boston Symphony Orchestra performs in this gorgeous venue.

Boston Ballet
Dance

(☎617-695-6950; www.bostonballet.org; tickets $15-100) Boston's skillful ballet troupe performs both modern and classic works at the **Opera House** (www.bostonoperahouse.com; 539 Washington St; T Downtown Crossing).

🔒 Shopping

Newbury St in the Back Bay and Charles St on Beacon Hill are Boston's best shopping destinations for the traditional and trendy. Harvard Sq is famous for bookstores and the South End is the city's up-and-coming art district. **Copley Place** (www.simon.com; 100 Huntington Ave; ☺10am-8pm Mon-Sat, noon-6pm Sun; T Back Bay) and the **Prudential Center** (www.prudential-center.com; 800 Boylston St; ☺10am-9pm; 🛜; T Prudential), both in Back Bay, are big indoor malls.

ℹ️ Information

Greater Boston Convention & Visitors Bureau (GBCVB; www.bostonusa.com) Boston Common (☎617-426-3115; 148 Tremont St, Boston Common; ☺8:30am-5pm Mon-Fri, 9am-5pm Sat & Sun; T Park St); Prudential Center (www.bostonusa.com; 800 Boylston St, Prudential Center; ☺9am-6pm; T Prudential)

ℹ️ Getting There & Away

The train and bus stations are conveniently side by side, and the airport is a short subway ride away.

Air

Logan International Airport (☎800-235-6426; www.massport.com/logan) is just across Boston Harbor from the city center.

Bus

South Station (700 Atlantic Ave) is the terminal for an extensive network of long-distance buses operated by Greyhound and regional bus companies. To NYC, **Yo! Bus** (www.yobus.com; one way $12-28; 🛜; T South Station) runs six buses a day from South Station, while **Go Buses** (www.gobuses.com; one way from $15; 🛜; T Alewife) depart from Cambridge.

Train

The **Amtrak** (☎800-872-7245; www.amtrak.com; South Station) terminal is at South Station.

ℹ️ Getting Around

To/from the Airport

Logan International Airport is just a few miles from downtown Boston: take the blue-line subway or the silver-line bus.

Subway

The **MBTA** (☎800-392-6100, 617-222-3200; www.mbta.com; per ride $2-2.50; ☺5:30am-12:30am) operates the 'T'. Five color-coded lines radiate 'outbound' from the downtown stations of Park St, Downtown Crossing and Government Center.

Taxi

Flag taxis on the street, find them at major hotels or call **Metro Cab** (☎617-242-8000) or **Independent** (☎617-426-8700).

Museum of Fine Arts (p169), Boston
KIM GRANT/GETTY IMAGES ©

Bicycle

Boston's bike-share program is the Hubway (www.thehubway.com; 30 min free, 60/90/120 min $2/6/14; ⏱24hr), with 60 Hubway stations around town. For leisurely riding or long trips, rent a bike from Urban AdvenTours (☏617-670-0637; www.urbanadventours.com; 103 Atlantic Ave; tours $50; ♿; Ⓣ Aquarium).

SALEM

Salem is renowned for the witch hysteria of 1692, when innocent folks were put to death for practicing witchcraft. Nowadays, the town embraces its role as 'Witch City' with witchy museums, spooky tours and Halloween madness.

These incidents obscure the city's true claim to fame: its glory days as a center for clipper-ship trade with the Far East. The **Salem Maritime National Historic Site** (www.nps.gov/sama; 193 Derby St; ⏱9am-5pm) **FREE** tells the story. Stroll out to the end of **Derby Wharf** and peek inside the 1871 **lighthouse** or climb aboard the tall ship **Friendship**. Get complete information from the **NPS Regional Visitor Center** (www.nps.gov/sama; 2 New Liberty St; ⏱9am-5pm).

The exceptional **Peabody Essex Museum** (www.pem.org; 161 Essex St; adult/child $15/free; ⏱10am-5pm Tue-Sun; ♿) was founded upon the art, artifacts and curios collected by Salem traders during their early expeditions to the Far East.

The most poignant site in Salem is the **Witch Trials Memorial** (Charter St), which honors the innocent victims.

CAPE COD

Clambering across the National Seashore dunes, cycling the Cape Cod Rail Trail, eating oysters at Wellfleet Harbor – this sandy peninsula serves up a bounty of local flavor. Fringed with 400 miles of sparkling shoreline, 'the Cape,' as it's called by Cape Codders, rates as New England's top beach destination. But there's a lot more than just beaches here.

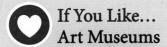

If You Like...
Art Museums

If you like Boston's celebrated Museum of Fine Arts (p169), it's well worthwhile visiting these other captivating galleries:

1 INSTITUTE OF CONTEMPORARY ART
(ICA; www.icaboston.org; 100 Northern Ave; adult/child/student/senior $15/free/10/13; ⏱10am-5pm Tue, Wed, Sat & Sun, to 9pm Thu & Fri; Ⓟ♿; 🚌SL1 or SL2, Ⓣ South Station) This dazzling museum snags rave exhibits by the likes of street artist Shepard Fairey. The building's striking cantilevered architecture defines modern, and its floor-to-ceiling glass walls pop with Boston's most dramatic harbor view.

2 ISABELLA STEWART GARDNER MUSEUM
(www.gardnermuseum.org; 280 The Fenway; adult/child/student/senior $15/free/5/12; ⏱11am-5pm Wed-Mon, to 9pm Thu; ♿; Ⓣ Museum of Fine Arts) Gardner assembled her vast collection – which ranges from Rembrandts to portraits by Bostonian John Singer Sargent – a century ago and lived in the magnificent Venetian-style palazzo that houses it all. Seeing the mansion itself, with its garden courtyard, is alone worth the price of admission.

When you've had your fill of sun and sand, get out and explore artist enclaves, take a cruise, or join the free-spirited street scene in Provincetown.

Sandwich

The cape's oldest village wraps its historic center around a picturesque swan pond with a gristmill (c 1654) and several small museums.

If you're ready for salt spray, head to **Sandy Neck Beach** (Sandy Neck Rd, West Barnstable), off MA 6A, a 6-mile dune-backed strand (parking $15 to $20) that's ideal for beachcombing and a bracing swim.

Cape Cod, Martha's Vineyard & Nantucket

0 — 10 km
0 — 5 miles

Hingham
Cohasset

Boston (25mi)

Hanover

Pembroke
14
Marshfield
53
3
3A

Plympton
106

Plymouth Bay
Plymouth

44
Manomet
58
3
3A

Rochester
South Middleboro
495
Myles Standish State Forest
Cape Cod Canal
25
Sagamore
6
Buzzards Bay
28
Bourne
North Falmouth
130
Old Silver Beach
Falmouth
East Falmouth
Mashpee
Falmouth Heights
Woods Hole

Buzzards Bay
195

Cedarville
Shawme-Crowell State Forest
Sandwich
West Barnstable
Marstons Mills
28
Hyannis
Hyannisport
South Yarmouth

Mid-Cape Hwy
Dennis
East Dennis
Brewster
137
Harwich Port
134
6

Stellwagen Bank National Marine Sanctuary

ATLANTIC OCEAN

Race Point Beach
Herring Cove Beach
Provincetown
North Truro
Truro
6
Wellfleet

Cape Cod National Seashore

Cape Cod Bay

Wellfleet Harbor
Wellfleet Beaches

Eastham
Rock Harbor
Orleans
Nickerson State Park

Pleasant Bay
28
Chatham
Lighthouse Beach

Yarmouth
6A

Monomoy National Wildlife Refuge

MONOMOY ISLAND

Vineyard Sound

Vineyard Haven
Oak Bluffs
Tisbury

Menemsha
West Tisbury
Chilmark
Aquinnah
MARTHA'S VINEYARD
Katama Beach

Edgartown
Chappaquiddick Island
Muskeget Island

Nantucket Sound

Great Point Light
Coskata
Wauwinet

Madaket
Cisco
Surfside
Nantucket
Siasconset
NANTUCKET

ATLANTIC OCEAN

Elizabeth Islands

Ferry to Boston (seasonal)

Heritage Museums & Gardens

Museum (508-888-3300; www.heritagemuseumsand-gardens.org; 67 Grove St; adult/child $15/7; 10am-5pm;) The 76-acre Heritage Museums & Gardens sports a superb vintage automobile collection, an authentic **1912 carousel** (rides free with admission), unusual folk-art collections and one of the finest **rhododendron gardens** in America.

Belfry Inne & Bistro B&B $$$

(☎508-888-8550; www.belfryinn.com; 8 Jarves St; r incl breakfast $149-299; ❄🛜) Ever fall asleep in church? Then you'll love the rooms, some with stained-glass windows, in this creatively restored former church, now an upmarket B&B.

Seafood Sam's Seafood $$

(www.seafoodsams.com; 6 Coast Guard Rd; mains $8-20; ⏲11am-9pm; 👪) Sam's is a good family choice for fish and chips, fried clams and lobster rolls. Dine at outdoor picnic tables overlooking Cape Cod Canal and watch the fishing boats sail by.

Falmouth

Fantastic beaches and a scenic seaside bike trail highlight the cape's second-largest town.

Old Silver Beach Beach

(off MA 28A; 👪) Deeply indented Falmouth has 70 miles of coastline, none of it finer than this long, sandy stretch of beach. A rock jetty, sandbars and tidal pools provide fun diversions for kids. Parking costs $20.

Shining Sea Bikeway Cycling

(👪) A bright star among the cape's stellar bike trails, this 10.7-mile beauty runs along the entire west coast of Falmouth, offering unspoiled views of salt ponds, marsh and seascapes. Bike rentals are available at the north end of the trail.

Falmouth Heights Motor Lodge Motel $$

(☎508-548-3623; www.falmouthheightsresort.com; 146 Falmouth Heights Rd; r incl breakfast $129-259; ❄🛜🏊👪) All 28 rooms are a cut above the competition. The beach and Vineyard ferry are minutes away.

Clam Shack Seafood $

(☎508-540-7758; 227 Clinton Ave; light meals $6-15; ⏲11:30am-7:30pm) A classic, right on Falmouth Harbor.

Maison Villatte Cafe $

(☎774-255-1855; 267 Main St; snacks $3-10; ⏲7am-7pm Wed-Sat, to 5pm Sun) Head here for flaky croissants, sinful pastries and hearty sandwiches.

Hyannis

Cape Cod's commercial hub, Hyannis is best known to visitors as the summer home of the Kennedy clan and a jumping-off point for ferries to Nantucket and Martha's Vineyard.

The town's mile-long Main St is fun to stroll and is the place for dining, drinking and shopping. **Kalmus Beach** (Ocean St) is popular for windsurfing, while **Craigville Beach** (Craigville Beach Rd, Centerville) is where the college set goes; parking at either costs $15 to $20.

John F Kennedy Hyannis Museum Museum

(☎508-790-3077; http://jfkhyannismuseum.org; 397 Main St; adult/child $8/3; ⏲9am-5pm Mon-Sat, noon-5pm Sun) Celebrates America's 35th president with photographs, videos and mementos.

SeaCoast Inn Motel $$

(☎508-775-3828; www.seacoastcapecod.com; 33 Ocean St; r incl breakfast $128-168; ❄@🛜) There's no view or pool, but the rooms are thoroughly comfy, most have kitchenettes and the price is a deal for Hyannis.

Bistrot de Soleil Mediterranean $$

(www.bistrotdesoleil.com; 350 Stevens St at Main St; mains $10-25; ⏲11:30am-9pm) Mediterranean influences meet fresh local ingredients in a menu that ranges from gourmet wood-fired pizzas to filet mignon.

Raw Bar Seafood $$

(www.therawbar.com; 230 Ocean St; lobster rolls $26; ⏲11am-7pm) Come here for the mother of all lobster rolls, rivalled only by the view of Hyannis Harbor.

Brewster

Woodsy Brewster, on the cape's bay side, makes a good base for outdoorsy types, with biking, hiking and water activities.

Nickerson State Park · Park
(☎508-896-3491; 3488 MA 6A; per car $5; ⊙dawn-dusk; 🅿) Miles of cycling and walking trails and eight ponds with sandy beaches highlight this 2000-acre oasis.

Jack's Boat Rental · Boating
(☎508-349-9808; www.jacksboatrental.com; rentals per hr $25-45; ⊙10am-6pm) This operation, within Nickerson State Park, rents canoes, kayaks and sailboats.

Barb's Bike Rental · Cycling
(☎508-896-7231; www.barbsbikeshop.com; bicycles per half/full day $18/24; ⊙9am-6pm) Rents bicycles by the park entrance.

Old Sea Pines Inn · B&B $$
(☎508-896-6114; www.oldseapinesinn.com; 2553 MA 6A; r incl breakfast $85-195; @🛜🅿) A former girls' boarding school dating to 1840, this inn retains an engaging yesteryear look: antique fittings, sepia photographs and claw-foot bathtubs, plus rocking chairs on the porch.

Cycling the Rail Trail

A poster child for the rails-to-trail movement, the **Cape Cod Rail Trail** follows a former railroad track for 22 glorious miles past cranberry bogs and along sandy ponds ideal for a dip. It's one of the finest cycling trails in all New England. There's a hefty dose of Olde Cape Cod scenery en route and you can detour into quiet villages for lunch or sightseeing. The path begins in Dennis on MA 134 and continues all the way to Wellfleet. If you have time to do only part of the trail, begin at Nickerson State Park in Brewster and head for the Cape Cod National Seashore in Eastham.

Bicycle rentals are available at the trailhead in Dennis, at Nickerson State Park and opposite the National Seashore's Salt Pond Visitor Center (p183).

Brewster Fish House · Seafood $$
(www.brewsterfish.com; 2208 MA 6A; mains $14-32; ⊙11:30am-3pm & 5-9:30pm) A favorite of seafood lovers. Start with the lobster bisque, naturally sweet with chunks of fresh lobster. Just 11 tables, and no reservations, so think lunch or early dinner to avoid long waits.

Chatham

Upscale inns and tony shops are a hallmark of the cape's most genteel town. Start your exploring on Main St, with its old sea captains' houses and cool art galleries.

At **Chatham Fish Pier** (Shore Rd) watch fishermen unload their catch and spot seals basking on nearby shoals. A mile south on Shore Rd is **Lighthouse Beach**, an endless expanse of sea and sandbars that offers some of the finest beach strolling on Cape Cod. The 7600-acre **Monomoy National Wildlife Refuge** (www.fws.gov/northeast/monomoy) 🍃 covers two uninhabited islands thick with shorebirds; to see it up close take a boat tour with **Monomoy Island Excursions** (☎508-430-7772; www.monomoysealcruise.com; 702 MA 28, Harwich Port; 1½hr boat tours adult/child $35/30).

Bow Roof House · B&B $$
(☎508-945-1346; 59 Queen Anne Rd; r incl breakfast $115) This homey, six-room, c 1780 house is delightfully old-fashioned in price and offerings, and within easy walking distance of the town center and beach.

Chatham Cookware Café · Cafe $
(☎508-945-1250; 524 Main St; sandwiches $8; ⊙6:30am-4pm) The downtown spot for a coffee fix, homemade muffins and sandwiches.

Chatham Fish Pier Market · Seafood $$
(www.chathamfishpiermarket.com; 45 Barcliff Ave; mains $12-25; ⊙10am-7pm Mon-Thu, to 8pm Fri-Sun) If you like it fresh and local to the core, this salt-sprayed fish shack, with its

KIM GRANT/GETTY IMAGES ©

 ### Don't Miss
Cape Cod National Seashore

Cape Cod National Seashore extends some 40 miles around the curve of the Outer Cape and encompasses most of the shoreline from Eastham to Provincetown. It's a treasure trove of unspoiled beaches, dunes, salt marshes and forests. The **Salt Pond Visitor Center** (📞508-255-3421; 50 Doane Rd, cnr US 6 & Nauset Rd, Eastham; ⊙9am-5pm) `FREE` is the place to start, with exhibits and films about the area's ecology and the scoop on the park's numerous cycling and hiking trails, some of which begin right at the center.

Coast Guard Beach, just down the road from the visitor center, is a stunner that attracts everyone from surfers to beachcombers. Summertime beach parking passes cost $15/45 per day/season and are valid at all Cape Cod National Seashore beaches including Provincetown.

NEED TO KNOW
www.nps.gov/caco

own sushi chef and day boats, is for you. The chowder's incredible.

Wellfleet

Art galleries, primo beaches and those famous Wellfleet oysters lure visitors to this little seaside town.

 ## Sights

Wellfleet Beaches   Beaches
Marconi Beach has a monument to Guglielmo Marconi, who sent the first wireless transmission across the Atlantic from this site, and a beach backed by undulating dunes. The adjacent **White Crest Beach** and **Cahoon Hollow Beach**

183

offer high-octane surfing. **SickDay Surf Shop** (📞508-214-4158; www.sickdaysurf.com; 361 Main St; surfboards per day $25-30; ⏰9am-9pm Mon-Sat) rents surfboards.

Wellfleet Bay Wildlife Sanctuary   Nature Reserve
(📞508-349-2615; www.massaudubon.org; West Rd, off US 6; adult/child $5/3; ⏰8:30am-dusk; 🌿 Birders flock to Mass Audubon's 1100-acre sanctuary, where trails cross tidal creeks, salt marshes and beaches.

🛏 Sleeping & Eating

Even'Tide Motel   Motel $$
(📞508-349-3410; www.eventidemotel.com; 650 US 6; r from $135, cottages per week $1100-2800; ❄🏊🚻) This 31-room motel, set back from the highway in a grove of pine trees, also has nine cottages. Pluses include a large indoor pool, picnic facilities and a playground.

PB Boulangerie & Bistro   Bakery $
(www.pbboulangeriebistro.com; 15 Lecount Hollow Rd; pastries from $3; ⏰7am-7pm Tue-Sun) Incredible pastries, artisan breads and delicious sandwiches.

Mac's Seafood Market   Seafood $$
(www.macsseafood.com; 265 Commercial St, Wellfleet Town Pier; mains $7-20; ⏰11am-3pm Mon-Fri, to 8pm Sat & Sun; 🍴) Head here for market-fresh seafood at bargain prices.

⭐ Entertainment

Beachcomber   Live Music
(📞508-349-6055; www.thebeachcomber.com; 1120 Cahoon Hollow Rd; ⏰5pm-1am) 'Da Coma' is a great summertime hang-out. It's set in a former lifesaving station right on Cahoon Hollow Beach, so you can watch the surf action till the sun goes down. After dark bands take the stage.

Wellfleet Drive-In   Cinema
(📞508-349-7176; www.wellfleetcinemas.com; US 6; adult/child $9/6; 🚻) Enjoy an evening of nostalgia at this old-fashioned drive-in theater.

Provincetown

This is it: as far as you can go on the cape, and more than just geographically. The draw is irresistible. Fringe writers and artists began making a summer haven

Art installation, *They Also Faced the Sea*, by Ewa Nogiec and Norma Holt, Provincetown

in Provincetown a century ago. Today this sandy outpost has morphed into the hottest gay and lesbian destination in the Northeast. Flamboyant street scenes, brilliant art galleries and unbridled night-life paint the town center. Provincetown's untamed coastline and vast beaches beg to be explored.

 Sights & Activities

Province Lands Visitor Center
Beach

(☎508-487-1256; www.nps.gov/caco; Race Point Rd; ⏰9am-5pm; P) 🅿 FREE Overlooking Race Point Beach, this Cape Cod National Seashore visitor center has displays on dune ecology and a rooftop observation deck with an eye-popping 360-degree view of the outermost reaches of Cape Cod.

Race Point Beach
Beach

(Race Point Rd) On the wild tip of the cape, Race Point is a breathtaking stretch of sand, with crashing surf and undulating dunes as far as the eye can see.

Herring Cove Beach
Beach

(Province Lands Rd) This popular swimming beach faces west, making it a spectacular place to be at sunset.

Provincetown Art Association & Museum
Museum

(PAAM; www.paam.org; 460 Commercial St; adult/child $7/free; ⏰11am-8pm Mon-Thu, to 10pm Fri, to 5pm Sat & Sun) This vibrant museum showcases the works of artists who have found their inspiration in Provincetown.

Dolphin Fleet Whale Watch
Whale-Watching

(☎508-240-3636; www.whalewatch.com; MacMillan Wharf; adult/child $44/29; ⏰Apr-Oct; 👪) 🅿 Offers up to 12 whale-watch tours daily. Expect splashy fun, watching breaching humpback whales.

Sleeping

Moffett House
Guesthouse $$

(☎508-487-6615; www.moffetthouse.com; 296a Commercial St; r with shared bath $90-159; ❄🛜🐾) Set back in a quiet alleyway, this guesthouse has a bonus: free bicycles. Rooms are basic, but there are lots of opportunities to meet fellow travelers.

Race Point Lighthouse
Inn $$

(☎508-487-9930; www.racepointlighthouse.net; Race Point; r $155-185) 🅿 If unspoiled sand dunes and a 19th-century lighthouse sound like good company, book one of the three bedrooms in the old lighthouse-keeper's house.

 Eating

Cafe Heaven
Cafe $

(☎508-487-9639; 199 Commercial St; mains $7-12; ⏰8am-3pm) An art-filled storefront with decadent French toast and healthy salads.

Fanizzi's by the Sea
Seafood $$

(☎508-487-1964; www.fanizzisrestaurant.com; 539 Commercial St; mains $10-25; ⏰11:30am-9:30pm; 👪) An amazing water view and reasonable prices make Fanizzi's a local favorite.

Mews Restaurant & Cafe
Modern American $$$

(☎508-487-1500; www.mews.com; 429 Commercial St; mains $14-35; ⏰5:30-10pm) Want affordable gourmet? Skip the excellent but pricey restaurant and go upstairs to the bar for a fab view, great martinis and scrumptious bistro fare.

Lobster Pot
Seafood $$$

(☎508-487-0842; www.ptownlobsterpot.com; 321 Commercial St; mains $22-37; ⏰11:30am-9pm) True to its name, this bustling fish house is a top place for lobster. Best way to beat the crowd is to come mid-afternoon.

🍷 Drinking & Nightlife

Patio
Cafe

(www.ptownpatio.com; 328 Commercial St; ⏱11am-11pm) Grab yourself a sidewalk table and order up a ginger mojito at this umbrella-shaded cafe hugging the pulsating center of Commercial St.

Ross' Grill
Bar

(www.rossgrille.com; 237 Commercial St; ⏱11:30am-10pm) A romantic place to have a drink with a water view.

Pied Bar
Gay & Lesbian

(www.piedbar.com; 193 Commercial St) An iconic drinking spot, particularly around sunset, for the gay crowd.

Crown & Anchor
Gay & Lesbian

(www.onlyatthecrown.com; 247 Commercial St) The queen of the scene, this multiwing complex has a nightclub, a leather bar and a steamy cabaret.

ℹ️ Getting There & Away

Plymouth & Brockton buses (www.p-b.com) connect Boston and Provincetown ($35, 3½ hours). From mid-May to mid-October, **Bay State Cruise Company** (📞877-783-3799; www.boston-ptown.com; 200 Seaport Blvd, Boston; round trip adult/child fast ferry $85/62, slow ferry $46/free; ⏱mid-May–mid-Oct) runs a ferry between Boston's World Trade Center Pier and MacMillan Wharf. A round trip takes about 1½ hours.

NANTUCKET

Once home port to the world's largest whaling fleet, Nantucket has a storied past that is reflected in its period homes and cobbled streets. When whaling went bust in the mid-19th century the town plunged from riches to rags. The population dwindled, and its grand old houses sat idle until wealthy urbanites discovered Nantucket made a fine place to summer. High-end tourism has been Nantucket's mainstay ever since.

👁️ Sights & Activities

Step off the boat and you're in the only place in the USA where the entire town is a National Historic Landmark. It's a bit like stepping into a museum – wander around and soak up the atmosphere. Start your explorations by strolling up Main St, where you'll find the grandest whaling-era mansions lined up in a row.

Nantucket Whaling Museum
Museum

(13 Broad St; adult/child $20/5; ⏱10am-5pm mid-May–Oct, 11am-4pm Nov–mid-May) A top sight is this evocative museum in a former spermaceti (whale-oil) candle factory.

A Nantucket street
BARRETT & MACKAY/GETTY IMAGES ©

Nantucket Beaches
Beaches

If you have kids, head to **Children's Beach**, right in Nantucket town, where the water's calm and there's a playground. **Surfside Beach**, 2 miles to the south, is where the college crowd heads for an active scene and bodysurfing waves. The best place to catch the sunset is **Madaket Beach**, 5.5 miles west of town.

Cycling
Cycling

No destination on the island is more than 8 miles from town and thanks to Nantucket's relatively flat terrain and dedicated bike trails, cycling is an easy way to explore. For a fun outing, cycle to the picturesque village of **Siasconset** ('Sconset), known for its rose-covered cottages. A couple of companies rent bikes ($30 a day) right at the ferry docks.

 ## Sleeping

Centerboard Inn
B&B $$$

(✆508-228-2811; www.centerboardinn.com; 8 Chestnut St; r incl breakfast $249-419; ✷ @ 🛜) At this pampering inn, rooms sport an upscale island decor, breakfast includes savory treats and the location is perfect for sightseeing.

Barnacle Inn
B&B $$$

(✆508-228-0332; www.thebarnacleinn.com; 11 Fair St; r incl breakfast from $200, with shared bath from $140) Folksy owners and simple, quaint accommodations that hearken to earlier times are in store at this turn-of-the-19th-century inn.

 ## Eating

Centre Street Bistro
Cafe $$

(www.nantucketbistro.com; 29 Centre St; mains $8-30; ⏱11:30am-9:30pm Wed-Sat; 🛜 🍴) Settle in at a parasol-shaded sidewalk table and watch the traffic trickle by at this relaxed cafe. The chef-owners make everything from scratch, including delicious warm goat-cheese tarts.

Club Car
Pub $$

(www.theclubcar.com; 1 Main St; mains $12-30; ⏱11:30am-1am) This converted railroad car, a vestige of the actual railroad that sank in the sands of Nantucket, dishes up consistently good food, including the best lobster roll in town.

Black-Eyed Susan's
Cafe $$

(www.black-eyedsusans.com; 10 India St; mains $9-30; ⏱7am-1pm daily, 6-10pm Mon-Sat) Snag a seat on the back patio and try the sourdough French toast topped with caramelized pecans and Jack Daniel's butter. At dinner the fish of the day with black-eyed peas takes top honors. BYO alcohol.

ℹ Getting There & Around

Boat

The Steamship Authority (✆508-477-8600; www.steamshipauthority.com) runs ferries throughout the day between Hyannis and Nantucket. The fast ferry (round trip adult/child $69/35) takes an hour; the slow ferry (round trip adult/child $35/18) takes 2¼ hours.

Bus

Getting around Nantucket is a snap. The NRTA Shuttle (www.shuttlenantucket.com; rides $1-2, day pass $7; ⏱late May-Sep) operates buses around town and to 'Sconset, Madaket and the beaches. Buses have bike racks, so cyclists can bus one way and pedal back.

MARTHA'S VINEYARD

New England's largest island is a world unto itself. Home to 15,500 year-round residents, its population swells to 100,000 in summer. The towns are charming, the beaches good, the restaurants chef-driven. And there's something for every mood here – fine-dine in gentrified Edgartown one day and hit the cotton-candy and carousel scene in Oak Bluffs the next.

ℹ Getting There & Around

Boat

Frequent ferries operated by the Steamship Authority link Woods Hole to both Vineyard Haven and Oak Bluffs, a 45-minute voyage. If you're bringing a car, book well in advance.

Below: Heirloom tomatoes, Martha's Vineyard; **Right:** An Oak Bluffs house
(BELOW) REGGIE CASAGRANDE/GETTY IMAGES ©; (RIGHT) GLENN VAN DER KNIJFF/GETTY IMAGES ©

From Hyannis, Hy-Line Cruises (☏508-778-2600; www.hylinecruises.com; Ocean St Dock; round trip adult/child slow ferry $45/free, fast ferry $72/48) operates a slow ferry (1½ hours) once daily to Oak Bluffs and a high-speed ferry (55 minutes) five times daily.

Bus

Martha's Vineyard Regional Transit Authority (www.vineyardtransit.com; 1-/3-day pass $7/15) operates a bus network with frequent service between towns.

Oak Bluffs

Odds are this ferry-port town, where the lion's share of boats arrive, will be your introduction to the island. Welcome to the Vineyard's summer fun mecca – a place to wander with an ice-cream cone in hand, poke around honky-tonk sights and go clubbing into the night.

Bike Trail   Cycling

A scenic bike trail runs along the coast connecting Oak Bluffs, Vineyard Haven and Edgartown – it's largely flat so makes a good pedal for families. Rent bicycles at **Anderson's Bike Rental** (☏508-693-9346; www.andersonsbikerentals.com; 1 Circuit Ave Extension; bicycles per day adult/child $18/10; ⊙9am-6pm) near the ferry terminal.

Nashua House   Inn **$$**

(☏508-693-0043; www.nashuahouse.com; 30 Kennebec Ave; r with shared bath $99-219; ❄️🛜♿) You'll find suitably simple and spotlessly clean accommodations at this small inn right in the center of town.

Narragansett House   B&B **$$**

(☏508-693-3627; www.narragansetthouse.com; 46 Narragansett Ave; r incl breakfast $150-300; ❄️🛜) On a quiet residential street, this B&B occupies two adjacent Victorian gingerbread-trimmed houses just a stroll from the town center.

Linda Jean's   Diner $
(www.lindajeansrestaurant.com; 25 Circuit Ave; mains $5-15; ⊙6am-10:30pm) The town's best all-around inexpensive eatery rakes in the locals with unbeatable blueberry pancakes, juicy burgers and simple but filling dinners.

Slice of Life   Cafe $$
(www.sliceoflifemv.com; 50 Circuit Ave; mains $8-24; ⊙8am-9pm; ⁂) At breakfast, there's good coffee, portobello omelets and potato pancakes. At dinner the roasted cod with sun-dried tomatoes is a savory favorite.

....

Edgartown

Perched on a fine natural harbor, Edgartown has a rich maritime history and a patrician air. At the height of the whaling era it was home to more than 100 sea captains whose fortunes built the grand old homes that line the streets today.

Katama Beach   Beach
(Katama Rd) The Vineyard's best beach lies 4 miles south of Edgartown center. Also called South Beach, Katama stretches for three magnificent miles. Rugged surf will please surfers on the ocean side. Some swimmers prefer the protected salt ponds on the inland side.

Edgartown Inn   Guesthouse $$
(☎508-627-4794; www.edgartowninn.com; 56 N Water St; r from $175, with shared bath from $125; ⁂) The best bargain in town, with 20 straightforward rooms spread across three adjacent buildings. The oldest dates to 1798 and claims Nathaniel Hawthorne and Daniel Webster among its earliest guests!

Among the Flowers Café   Cafe $$
(☎508-627-3233; 17 Mayhew Lane; mains $8-20; ⊙8am-3:30pm; ⁂) Join the in-the-know crowd on the garden patio for homemade soups, waffles, sandwiches, crepes and even lobster rolls. In July and August, they add dinner as well.

⭐ Don't Miss
Up-Island

Known as Up-Island, the rural western half of Martha's Vineyard is a patchwork of rolling hills, small farms and open fields frequented by wild turkey and deer. Feast your eyes and your belly at the picturesque fishing village of **Menemsha**, where you'll find seafood shacks with food so fresh the boats unload their catch at the back door. They'll shuck you an oyster and steam you a lobster while you watch and you can eat al fresco on a harborside bench.

The coastal **Aquinnah Cliffs**, also known as the Gay Head Cliffs, are so special they're a National Natural Landmark. These 150ft-high cliffs glow with an amazing array of colors that can be best appreciated in the late-afternoon light. You can hang out at **Aquinnah Public Beach** (parking $15), just below the multihued cliffs, or walk a mile north along the shore to an area that's popular with nude sunbathers.

Cedar Tree Neck Sanctuary (www.sheriffsmeadow.org; Indian Hill Rd; ⏱8:30am-5:30pm) **FREE**, off State Rd, has an inviting 2.5-mile hike across native bogs and forest to a coastal bluff with views of Cape Cod. The Massachusetts Audubon Society's **Felix Neck Wildlife Sanctuary** (www.massaudubon.org; Edgartown–Vineyard Haven Rd; adult/child $4/3; ⏱dawn-dusk; 🚻) is a birder's paradise with 4 miles of trails skirting marshes and ponds.

VERMONT

Whether seen under blankets of snow, patchworks of blazing fall leaves or the exuberant greens of spring and summer, Vermont's blend of bucolic farmland, mountains and picturesque small villages make it one of America's most appealing states. Hikers, bikers, skiers and kayakers will find four-season bliss here. Foodies will love it here too: small farmers have made Vermont a locavore paradise, complemented by America's densest collection of craft brewers.

Brattleboro

Perched at the confluence of the Connecticut and West Rivers, Brattleboro is a little gem that reveals its facets to those who stroll the streets and prowl the dozens of independent shops and eateries.

Begin at Main St, which is lined with period buildings, including the handsome art-deco Latchis Building, which houses a hotel and theater. Windham County, surrounding Brattleboro, boasts several covered bridges. Pick up a driving guide to them at the **Brattleboro Chamber of Commerce** (☏877-254-4565, 802-254-4565; www.brattleborochamber.org; 180 Main St; ⊙9am-5pm Mon-Fri).

Forty Putney Road B&B
B&B $$$
(☏800-941-2413, 802-254-6268; www.forty-putneyroad.com; 192 Putney Rd; r incl breakfast $159-329; @ 🛜) This 1930 B&B with a small cheery pub is a sweet spot just north of town. It has a glorious backyard, four rooms and a separate, self-contained cottage. Overlooking the West River estuary, it also offers boat and bike rentals that are just a five-minute walk away.

Riverview Café
Cafe $
(☏802-254-9841; 36 Bridge St; mains $6-18; ⊙8am-8pm) Enjoy alfresco dining smack on the Connecticut River at this celebrated restaurant emphasizing fresh regional ingredients.

Bennington

Bennington is a mix of historic Vermont village (Old Bennington),

workaday town (Bennington proper) and college town (North Bennington). It is also home to the famous Bennington Monument, which commemorates the crucial Battle of Bennington during the American Revolution.

As Bennington is within the bounds of the Green Mountain National Forest, there are many hiking trails nearby, including the granddaddies of them all: the Appalachian and Long Trails.

Bennington Battle Monument
Historic Site
(www.benningtonbattlemonument.com; 15 Monument Circle; adult/child $3/1; ⊙9am-5pm mid-Apr–Oct) Vermont's loftiest structure offers an unbeatable 360-degree view of the countryside with peeks at covered bridges and across to New York. An elevator whisks you painlessly to the top.

Robert Frost Stone House Museum
Museum
(☏802-447-6200; www.frostfriends.org; 121 VT 7A, Shaftsbury; adult/under 18yr $5/2.50; ⊙10am-5pm Wed-Sun May-Oct) This modest

Fall in Vermont
RON AND PATTY THOMAS PHOTOGRAPHY/GETTY IMAGES ©

Detour:
Scenic Drive: VT 100

Running up the rugged backbone of Vermont, VT 100 meanders through the rural heart of the state. This quintessential country road rambles past rolling pastures speckled with cows, through tiny villages with white-steepled churches and along green mountains crossed with hiking trails and ski slopes. It's the perfect side trip for those who want to slow down, inhale pine-scented air and soak up the bucolic country life that forms the very soul of Vermont. Think farm stands, century-old farmhouses converted to small inns, pottery shops, country stores and home-style cafes. The road runs north to south all the way from Massachusetts to Canada. It has some tranquil moments but never a dull one – jump on at any point for a taste of it.

museum opens a window into the poet's life, with one entire room dedicated to his most famous work, 'Stopping by Woods on a Snowy Evening,' which he penned here in the 1920s.

Greenwood Lodge
& Campsites   Hostel, Campground $
(☏802-442-2547; www.campvermont.com/greenwood; VT 9, Prospect Mountain; 2-person tent/RV site $27/35, dm/d from $29/70; ☺mid-May–late Oct) Nestled in the Green Mountains in Woodford, this 120-acre space with three ponds is home to one of Vermont's best-sited hostels. Accommodations include 17 budget beds and 40 campsites. You'll find it easily, 8 miles east of Bennington on VT 9 at the Prospect Mountain ski area. Facilities include hot showers and a game room.

Henry House   B&B $$
(☏802-442-7045; www.thehenryhouseinn.com; 1338 Murphy Rd, North Bennington; r incl breakfast $100-155; ☎) Sit on the rocking chair and watch the traffic trickle across a covered bridge at this Colonial home built in 1769 by American Revolution hero William Henry. This is the real deal on 25 peaceful acres and dripping with so much original character you might expect long-gone Lieutenant Henry to walk down the hall.

Blue Benn Diner   Diner $
(☏802-442-5140; 314 North St; mains $5-12; ☺6am-4:45pm Mon Fri, 7am-3:45pm Sat & Sun; ☑) This classic 1950s-era diner serves breakfast all day and a healthy mix of American, Asian and Mexican fare – including vegetarian options. Tabletop jukeboxes add to the charm.

Burlington

This hip college town on the shores of scenic Lake Champlain is one of those places that makes you think, wouldn't it be great to live here? The cafe and club scene is on par with a much bigger city, while the slow, friendly pace is pure small town.

◉ Sights

Vermont's largest city is a manageable place with most of its cafes and pubs on or near Church St Marketplace, a brick-lined pedestrian mall, where half of Burlington hangs on a sunny day. The mall sits midway between the University of Vermont and Lake Champlain.

Shelburne Museum   Museum
(☏802-985-3346; www.shelburnemuseum.org; US 7, Shelburne; adult/child $22/11, after 3pm $15/7; ☺10am-5pm mid-May–Oct; ⛟) This extraordinary 45-acre museum, 9 miles south of Burlington in Shelburne, boasts a stellar collection of American folk art, New England architecture and, well, just about everything. The wildly eclectic collection ranges from an early American

sawmill to the Lake Champlain side-wheeler steamship *Ticonderoga*.

Shelburne Farms
Farm

(☏802-985-8686; www.shelburnefarms.org; 1611 Harbor Rd, Shelburne; adult/child $8/5; ⏱9am-5:30pm mid-May–mid-Oct, 10am-5pm mid-Oct–mid-May; 👪) 🌿 You can get a taste of Vermont farm life at this classic 1400-acre farm laid out by Frederick Law Olmsted, America's premier 19th-century landscape architect. Try your hand at milking a cow, feed the chickens, or hike the extensive nature trails through pastures and along Lake Champlain. The farm is 8 miles south of Burlington, off US 7.

Magic Hat Brewery
Brewery

(☏802-658-2739; www.magichat.net; 5 Bartlett Bay Rd, South Burlington; ⏱10am-6pm Mon-Sat, noon-5pm Sun) Drink in the history of one of Vermont's most dynamic microbreweries on a fun, free, self-guided tour. Afterwards, sample a few experimental brews from the four dozen taps in the on-site Growler Bar. The brewery is located 3.5 miles south of downtown Burlington, on the west side of US 7.

Activities

Ready for outdoor adventures? Head to the waterfront, where options include boating on Lake Champlain and cycling, jogging and walking on the 9-mile shorefront Burlington Bike Path. Jump-off points and equipment rentals for all these activities are within a block of each other near the waterfront end of Main St.

Local Motion
Bicycle Rental

(☏802-652-2453; www.localmotion.org; 1 Steele St; bicycles per day $30; ⏱10am-6pm; 👪) 🌿 Rents quality bikes.

Lake Champlain Cruises
Cruise

(☏802-864-7669; www.lakechamplaincruises.com; 1 King St; 1½ hr trip adult/child $15/6) For an inexpensive cruise of the lake, hop aboard the 115ft *Northern Lights,* a replicated 19th-century steamboat.

Sleeping

Lang House
B&B $$

(☏802-652-2500; www.langhouse.com; 360 Main St; r incl breakfast $145-245; ❄🛜) Burlington's most elegant B&B occupies

Portsmouth (p194)

DENIS JR. TANGNEY/GETTY IMAGES ©

a centrally located, tastefully restored 19th-century Victorian home and carriage house with 11 spacious rooms, some with fireplaces. Pampering touches include wine glasses and robes in each room, and sumptuous breakfasts served in an alcove-laden room decorated with old photographs of the city. Reserve ahead for one of the 3rd-floor rooms with lake views.

Willard Street Inn   Inn $$
(☏802-651-8710; www.willardstreetinn.com; 349 S Willard St; r incl breakfast $150-265; 📶) Perched on a hill within easy walking distance of UVM and the Church St Marketplace, this mansion, fusing Queen Anne and Georgian Revival styles, was built in the late 1880s. It has a fine-wood and cut-glass elegance, yet radiates a welcoming warmth. Many of the guest rooms overlook Lake Champlain.

Eating & Drinking

Penny Cluse Cafe   Cafe $
(www.pennycluse.com; 169 Cherry St; mains $7-11; ☺6:45am-3pm Mon-Fri, 8am-3pm Sat & Sun) 🍃 In the heart of downtown, one of Burlington's most popular breakfast spots whips up pancakes, breakfast burritos, omelets and tofu scrambles along with sandwiches, fish tacos, salads and the best chile relleno you'll find east of the Mississippi.

American Flatbread   Pizzeria $$
(www.americanflatbread.com/restaurants/burlington-vt; 115 St Paul St; flatbreads $14-23; ☺restaurant 11:30am-2:30pm & 5-10pm, taproom 11:30am-late) 🍃 Central downtown location, bustling atmosphere, great microbrews on tap, and some of the best flatbread (thin-crust pizza) you'll find anywhere in the world are reason enough to make this one of your first lunch or dinner stops in Burlington.

Vermont Pub & Brewery   Microbrewery
(www.vermontbrewery.com; 144 College St; mains $6-16; ☺11:30am-1am Sun-Wed, to 2am Thu-Sat) This large pub's specialty seasonal brews are made on the premises, including weekly limited releases. There's also

plenty of British pub fare to accompany the pints.

Splash at the Boathouse   Bar
(☏802-658-2244; www.splashattheboathouse.com; 0 College St; ☺11:30am-2am) Perched atop Burlington's floating boathouse, this restaurant-bar has stellar views over Lake Champlain. It's great for a sunset cocktail.

PORTSMOUTH

America's third-oldest city (1623), Portsmouth wears its history on its sleeve. Its roots are in shipbuilding, but New Hampshire's sole coastal city also has a hip, youthful energy. The old maritime warehouses along the harbor now house cafes and boutiques. Elegant period homes built by shipbuilding tycoons have been converted into B&Bs.

🎯 Sights & Activities

Strawbery Banke Museum   Museum
(☏603-433-1100; www.strawberybanke.org; cnr Hancock & Marcy Sts; adult/child $17.50/10; ☺10am-5pm May-Oct) Spread across a 10-acre site, the Strawbery Banke Museum is an eclectic blend of period homes that date back to the 1690s. Costumed guides recount tales that took place among the 40 buildings (10 furnished).

USS Albacore   Museum
(☏603-436-3680; http://ussalbacore.org; 600 Market St; adult/child $6/3; ☺9:30am-5pm Jun–mid-Oct, to 4pm Thu-Mon mid-Oct–May) Like a fish out of water, this 205ft-long submarine is now a beached museum on a grassy lawn.

Isles of Shoals Steamship Co   Cruise
(☏603-431-5500; www.islesofshoals.com; 315 Market St; adult/child $28/18; 👪) From mid-June to October the company runs an excellent tour of the harbor and the historic Isles of Shoals aboard a replica 1900s ferry.

Sleeping

Ale House Inn
Inn **$$**

(☏603-431-7760; www.alehouseinn.com; 121 Bow St; r $150-280; P 🛜) This brick warehouse for the Portsmouth Brewing Company is now Portsmouth's snazziest boutique, fusing contemporary design with comfort.

Inn at Strawbery Banke
B&B **$$**

(☏603-436-7242; www.innatstrawberybanke. com; 314 Court St; r incl breakfast $170-190; P 🛜) Set amid the historic buildings of Strawbery Banke, this Colonial charmer has seven small but attractive rooms, each uniquely set with quilted bedspreads and brass or canopy beds.

Eating & Drinking

Head to the intersection of Market and Congress Sts, where restaurants and cafes are thick on the ground.

Friendly Toast
Diner **$**

(113 Congress St; mains $7-12; ⏲7am-10pm Sun-Thu, to 2am Fri & Sat; 🛜 🍴) Fun, whimsical furnishings set the scene for filling sandwiches, omelets, Tex-Mex and vegetarian fare at this retro diner.

Black Trumpet Bistro
International **$$$**

(☏603-431-0887; www.blacktrumpetbistro.com; 29 Ceres St; mains $17-38; ⏲5:30-9pm) Oozing sophistication, this chef-driven bistro serves unique combinations (like house-made sausages infused with cocoa beans or seared haddock with yuzu and miso).

Jumpin' Jays Fish Cafe
Seafood **$$$**

(☏603-766-3474; www.jumpinjays.com; 150 Congress St; mains $20-28; ⏲5:30-10pm) This exceptional seafood cafe offers fresh catches of the day, plus a raw bar and a huge appetizer menu.

Portsmouth Brewery
Microbrewery

(www.portsmouthbrewery.com; 56 Market St; ⏲11:30am-12:30am; 🛜) Classically set with tin ceilings and exposed brick walls, this airy brewpub serves excellent home-grown pilsners, porters and ales.

Thirsty Moose Taphouse
Pub

(www.thirstymoosetaphouse.com; 21 Congress St; snacks $3-11, brunch $10-17; ⏲11:30am-1am

Fall in Maine

GARETH MCCORMACK/GETTY IMAGES ©

Mon-Sat, 10:30am-1pm Sun) Pours more than 100 beers on tap, leaning heavily on New England brews.

COASTAL MAINE

Maine is New England's frontier – a land so vast it could swallow the region's five other states with scarcely a gulp. The sea looms large with mile after mile of sandy beaches, craggy sea cliffs and quiet harbors. Time-honored fishing villages and seaside lobster joints are the fame of Maine.

Portland

The 18th-century poet Henry Wadsworth Longfellow referred to his childhood city as the 'jewel by the sea,' and thanks to a hefty revitalization effort, Portland once again sparkles. Its lively waterfront, burgeoning gallery scene and manageable size add up to great exploring. Foodies, rev up your taste buds: cutting-edge cafes

and chef-driven restaurants have turned Portland into the hottest dining scene north of Boston.

◉ Sights

Old Port   Neighborhood
Handsome 19th-century brick buildings line the streets of the Old Port, with Portland's most enticing shops, pubs and restaurants located within this five-square-block district. By night, flickering gas lanterns add to the atmosphere. What to do here? Eat some wicked fresh seafood, down a local microbrew, buy a nautical-themed T-shirt from an up-and-coming designer, and peruse the many tiny local art galleries.

Portland Museum of Art   Museum
(☎207-775-6148; www.portlandmuseum.org; 7 Congress Sq; adult/child $12/6, 5-9pm Fri free; ⊙10am-5pm Sat-Thu, to 9pm Fri, closed Mon mid-Oct–May) Showcasing works of American legends like Winslow Homer, Edward Hopper and Andrew Wyeth, Maine's finest art museum also boasts a few works by European masters like Degas, Picasso and Renoir.

Fort Williams Park   Lighthouse
(⊙sunrise-sunset) 🅿 FREE Four miles southeast of Portland on Cape Elizabeth, 90-acre Fort Williams Park is worth visiting simply for the panoramas and picnic possibilities. Adjacent to the fort stands the **Portland Head Light**, the oldest of Maine's 52 functioning lighthouses.

Longfellow House
Historic Building
(☎207-879-0427; www.mainehistory.org; 489 Congress St; adult/child $12/3; ⊙10am-5pm Mon-Sat, noon-5pm Sun May-Oct) This impeccably restored 19th-century house is

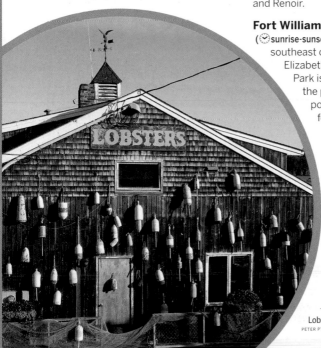

Lobster restaurant, Bar Harbor (p199)
PETER PTSCHELINZEW/GETTY IMAGES ©

where revered American poet Henry Wadsworth Longfellow grew.

Children's Museum of Maine
Museum

(☏207-828-1234; www.childrensmuseumofme.org; 142 Free St; admission $9; ◷10am-5pm Mon-Sat, noon-5pm Sun, closed Mon Sep-May; ♿) Kids ages zero to 10 shriek and squeal as they haul traps aboard a replica lobster boat, milk a fake cow on a model farm, or monkey around on an indoor rock-climbing wall.

Activities

For a whole different angle on Portland and Casco Bay, hop one of the boats offering narrated scenic cruises out of Portland Harbor.

Casco Bay Lines
Cruise

(☏207-774-7871; www.cascobaylines.com; 56 Commercial St; adult $13-24, child $7-11) This outfit cruises the Casco Bay islands delivering mail, freight and visitors. It also offers cruises to Bailey Island (adult/child $25/12).

Maine Island Kayak Company
Kayaking

(☏207-766-2373; www.maineislandkayak.com; 70 Luther St, Peak Island; tour $70; ◷May-Nov) On Peak Island, a 15-minute cruise from downtown on the Casco Bay Lines, this well-run outfitter offers fun day and overnight trips exploring the islands of Casco Bay.

Maine Narrow Gauge Railroad Co & Museum
Railroad

(☏207-828-0814; www.mngrr.org; 58 Fore St; adult/child $10/6; ◷10am-4pm mid-May–Oct, shorter hours off-season; ♿) Ride antique steam trains along Casco Bay; journeys depart on the hour.

Sleeping

Inn at St John
Inn $

(☏207-773-6481; www.innatstjohn.com; 939 Congress St; r incl breakfast $79-169; P 🛜) This turn-of-the-century hotel has a stuck-in-time feel, from the old-fashioned pigeon-hole mailboxes behind the lobby desk to the narrow, sweetly floral rooms. Ask for a room away from noisy Congress St.

Morrill Mansion
B&B $$

(☏207-774-6900; www.morrillmansion.com; 249 Vaughan St; r incl breakfast $149-239; 🛜) The handsome B&B has seven guest rooms furnished in a trim, classic style. Think hardwood floors and lots of tasteful khaki and taupe shades.

Portland Harbor Hotel
Hotel $$$

(☏207-775-9090; www.portlandharborhotel.com; 468 Fore St; r from $269; P 🛜) This independent hotel has a classically coiffed lobby, where guests relax on upholstered leather chairs surrounding the glowing fireplace. The rooms carry on the classicism, with sunny gold walls and pert blue toile bedspreads.

Eating

Two Fat Cats Bakery
Bakery $

(☏207-347-5144; www.twofatcatsbakery.com; 47 India St; treats $3-7; ◷8am-6pm Mon-Fri, to 5pm Sat, 10am-4pm Sun) Tiny bakery serving pastries, pies, melt-in-your-mouth chocolate-chip cookies and fabulous Whoopie Pies.

Green Elephant
Vegetarian $$

(☏207-347-3111; www.greenelephantmaine.com; 608 Congress St; mains $9-13; ◷11:30am-2:30pm Tue-Sat & 5-9:30pm Tue-Sun; 🍴) Even carnivores shouldn't miss the brilliant vegetarian fare at this Zen-chic, Thai-inspired cafe.

J's Oyster
Seafood $$

(www.jsoyster.com; 5 Portland Pier; mains $6-24; ◷11:30am-11:30pm Mon-Sat, noon-10:30pm Sun) This well-loved dive has the cheapest raw oysters in town. Eat 'em on the deck overlooking the pier.

Fore Street
New American $$$

(☏207-775-2717; www.forestreet.biz; 288 Fore St; mains $20-31; ◷5:30-11pm) Chef-owner Sam Hayward has turned roasting into a high art at Fore Street, one of Maine's most lauded restaurants. Local, seasonal eating is taken very seriously here and the menu changes daily to offer what's freshest.

Hugo's

Fusion $$$

(207-774-8538; www.hugos.net; 88 Middle St; mains $24-30; 5:30-9pm Tue-Sat) James Beard Award–winning chef Rob Evans presides over this temple of molecular gastronomy.

 Drinking & Entertainment

Gritty McDuff's Brew Pub

Brewpub

(www.grittys.com; 396 Fore St; 11am-1am) You'll find a generally raucous crowd drinking excellent beers – Gritty brews its own award-winning ales downstairs.

Big Easy Blues Club

Club

(www.bigeasyportland.com; 55 Market St; 9pm-1am Tue-Sat, 4-9pm Sun, 6-10pm Mon) This small music club features a mostly local lineup of rock, jazz and blues bands.

Information

Greater Portland Convention & Visitors Bureau (www.visitportland.com; Ocean Gateway Bldg, 239 Park Ave; 8am-5pm Mon-Fri, 10am-5pm Sat)

Getting There & Around

Portland International Jetport (PWM; 207-874-8877; www.portlandjetport.org) has nonstop flights to cities in the eastern US.

Greyhound (www.greyhound.com) buses and **Amtrak** (800-872-7245; www.amtrak.com) trains connect Portland and Boston; both take about 2½ hours and charge $20 to $24 one way.

The local bus **Metro** (www.gpmetrobus.com; fares $1.50), which runs throughout the city, has its main terminus at Monument Sq, the intersection of Elm and Congress Sts.

BOOTHBAY HARBOR

On a fjord-like harbor, this achingly picturesque fishing village with narrow, winding streets is thick with tourists in the summer. Other than eating lobster, the main activity here is hopping on boats. **Balmy**

Days Cruises (207-633-2284; www.balmydayscruises.com; Pier 8; harbor tour adult/child $15/8, day-trip cruise to Monhegan $32/18, sailing tour $24/18) runs one-hour harbor-tour cruises, day trips to Monhegan Island and 1½-hour sailing trips around the scenic islands near Boothbay.

Topside Inn

B&B $$

(207-633-5404; www.topsideinn.com; 60 McKown St; r incl breakfast $165-275;) Atop McKown Hill, this grand gray mansion has Boothbay's best harbor views. Rooms are elegantly turned out in crisp nautical prints and beachy shades of sage, sea glass and khaki.

Lobster Dock

Seafood $$

(www.thelobsterdock.com; 49 Atlantic Ave; mains $10-26; 11:30am-8:30pm) Of all the lobster joints in Boothbay Harbor, this sprawling wooden waterfront shack is one of the best and cheapest. The whole, butter-dripping lobster is superb.

ACADIA NATIONAL PARK

The only national park in New England, **Acadia** (www.nps.gov/acad) encompasses an unspoiled wilderness of undulating coastal mountains, towering sea cliffs, surf-pounded beaches and quiet ponds. The dramatic landscape offers a plethora of activities for both leisurely hikers and adrenaline junkies.

The park covers over 62 sq miles, including most of mountainous Mt Desert Island, and holds diverse wildlife including moose, puffins and bald eagles.

Sights & Activities

CADILLAC MOUNTAIN

The majestic centerpiece of Acadia National Park is Cadillac Mountain (1530ft), reached by a 3.5-mile spur road off Park Loop Rd. Four **trails** lead to the summit from four directions should you prefer hiking to driving.

OTHER ACTIVITIES

Some 125 miles of **hiking trails** criss-cross Acadia National Park, from easy half-mile nature walks and level rambles to mountain treks up steep and rocky terrain. A standout is the 3-mile round-trip **Ocean Trail**, which runs between Sand Beach and Otter Cliffs and takes in the most interesting coastal scenery in the park. Pick up a guide describing all the trails at the visitor center.

The park's 45 miles of carriage roads are the prime attraction for **cycling**. You can rent mountain bikes at **Acadia Bike** (📞207-288-9605; www.acadiabike.com; 48 Cottage St; per day $22; ⏰8am-8pm).

Information

The park is open year-round, though Park Loop Rd and most facilities are closed in winter. An admission fee is charged from May 1 to October 31. The fee, which is valid for seven consecutive days, is $22 per vehicle between mid-June and early October ($10 at other times) and $12 on bike or foot.

Start your exploration at Hulls Cove Visitor Center (📞207-288-3338; ME 3; 7-day park admission per vehicle $22, walkers & cyclists $12; ⏰8am-4:30pm mid-Apr–mid-Jun & Oct, to 6pm

mid-Jun–Aug, to 5pm Sep), from where the 20-mile Park Loop Rd circumnavigates the eastern portion of the park.

Getting Around

The convenient Island Explorer (www.exploreacadia.com; ⏰late Jun–early Oct) runs eight shuttle bus routes throughout Acadia National Park and to adjacent Bar Harbor, linking trailheads, campgrounds and accommodations.

BAR HARBOR

Set on the doorstep of Acadia National Park, this alluring coastal town once rivaled Newport, RI, as a trendy summer destination for wealthy Americans. Today many of the old mansions have been turned into inviting inns and the town has become a magnet for outdoor enthusiasts.

Activities

Bar Harbor Whale Watch Co   Cruise (📞207-288-2386; www.barharborwhales.com; 1 West St; adult $34-64, child $22-34; ⏰mid-May–Oct) Operates four-hour whale-watching

Acadia National Park

FRANK WING/GETTY IMAGES ©

WWW.CFWPHOTOGRAPHY.COM/GETTY IMAGES ©

⭐ Don't Miss
Park Loop Road

Park Loop Rd, the main sightseeing jaunt through Acadia, takes you to several of the park's highlights. If you're up for a bracing swim or just want to stroll Acadia's longest beach, stop at **Sand Beach**. About a mile beyond Sand Beach you'll come to **Thunder Hole**, where wild Atlantic waves crash into a deep, narrow chasm with such force that a thundering boom is created, loudest during incoming tides. Look to the south to see **Otter Cliffs**, a favorite rock-climbing spot that rises vertically from the sea. At **Jordan Pond** (pictured above) choose from a 1-mile nature trail loop around the south side of the pond or a 3.5-mile trail that skirts the entire pond. After you've worked up an appetite, reward yourself with a relaxing afternoon tea on the lawn of **Jordan Pond House** (📞207-276-3316; www.thejordanpondhouse.com; afternoon tea $9.50, mains $10-28; ⊙11:30am-9pm mid-May–Oct). Near the end of Park Loop Rd a side road leads up to Cadillac Mountain.

and puffin-watching cruises, among other options.

Downeast Windjammer Cruises
Cruise
(📞207-288-4585; www.downeastwindjammer.com; 27 Main St; adult/child $40/30) Offers two-hour cruises on the majestic 151ft, four-masted schooner *Margaret Todd*.

Acadian Nature Cruises
Cruise
(📞207-288-2386; www.acadiannaturecruises.com; 1 West St; adult/child $28/17; ⊙mid-May–Oct) See whales, porpoises, bald eagles, seals and more on these narrated two-hour nature cruises.

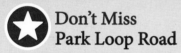 Sleeping

Holland Inn
B&B **$$**
(📞207-288-4804; www.hollandinn.com; 35 Holland Ave; r incl breakfast $95-185; 🛜) In a

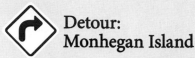

Detour: Monhegan Island

This small granite island with high cliffs and crashing surf 9 miles off the Maine coast attracts summer day-trippers, artists and nature-lovers who find inspiration in the dramatic views and agreeable isolation. Tidy and manageable, Monhegan is just 1.5 miles long and a half-mile wide. The online **Monhegan Island Visitor's Guide** (www.monheganwelcome.com) has information and accommodation links. Rooms typically book out in summer, so plan ahead if you're not just visiting on a day trip.

In addition to its 17 miles of walking trails, there's an 1824 **lighthouse** with a small museum in the former keeper's house and several **artists' studios** that you can poke your head into.

Departing Port Clyde, the **Monhegan Boat Line** (207-372-8848; www.monheganboat.com; round trip adult/child $32/18) runs three trips daily to Monhegan from late May to mid-October, and once a day for the rest of the year. The **MV Hardy III** (800-278-3346; www.hardyboat.com; round trip adult/child $32/18; mid-Jun–Sep) departs for Monhegan twice daily from New Harbor, on the east side of the Pemaquid Peninsula. Both boats take approximately one hour and both have early-morning departures and late-afternoon returns, perfect for day-tripping.

quiet residential neighborhood walking distance from downtown, this restored 1895 house and adjacent cottage has nine homey, unfrilly rooms.

Aysgarth Station Inn   B&B $$

(207-288-9655; www.aysgarth.com; 20 Roberts Ave; r incl breakfast $115-165; ❄) On a quiet side street, this 1895 B&B has six cozy rooms with homey touches. Request the Tan Hill room, which is on the 3rd floor, for a view of Cadillac Mountain.

Eating

Cafe This Way   American $$

(207-288-4483; www.cafethisway.com; 14½ Mount Desert St; mains breakfast $6-9, dinner $15-25; ⏱7-11:30am Mon-Sat, 8am-1pm Sun, 5:30-9pm nightly; ✈) In a sprawling white cottage, this quirky eatery serves the best breakfast in town, with plump Maine blueberry pancakes and eggs Benedict with smoked salmon. It also serves eclectic, sophisticated dinners. Sit in the garden.

2 Cats   Cafe $$

(207-288-2808; www.2catsbarharbor.com; 130 Cottage St; mains $8-19; ⏱7am-1pm; ✈) On weekends crowds line up for smoked-trout omelets and homemade muffins at this sunny, arty little cafe. Lunch offerings include slightly heartier fare, like burritos and seafood dishes.

Trenton Bridge Lobster Pound   Seafood $$

(ME 3, Ellsworth; lobsters $10-15; ⏱10:30am-8pm Mon-Sat) Sit at a picnic table and crack open a boiled lobster at this traditional lobster pound bordering the causeway that connects Mount Desert Island to mainland Maine.

Mâche Bistro   French $$$

(207-288-0447; www.machebistro.com; 135 Cottage St; mains $18-28; ⏱5-10:30pm Mon-Sat) Almost certainly Bar Harbor's best midrange restaurant, Mâche serves contemporary French-inflected fare in a stylishly renovated cottage. Reservations are crucial.

New Orleans & the South

More than any other part of the country, the South has an identity all its own: a musical way of speaking, a complicated political history and pride in a shared culture that cuts across state lines.

Nurtured by deep roots yet shaped by hardship, the South has produced some of the US's most important culture, from novelists such as William Faulkner and Flannery O'Connor, to foodstuffs like barbecue, bourbon and Coca-Cola, to music like blues and rock and roll. The cities of the South are some of the country's most fascinating, with antebellum beauties like New Orleans and Savannah, and musical legends including Nashville and Memphis.

But it's the legendary Southern hospitality that makes travel in the region such a pleasure. People round here love to talk. Stay long enough and you'll no doubt be invited for dinner.

Performers at Preservation Hall (p223)

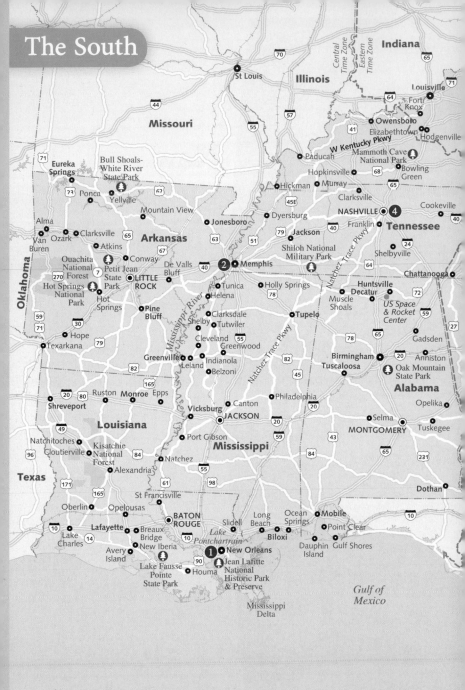

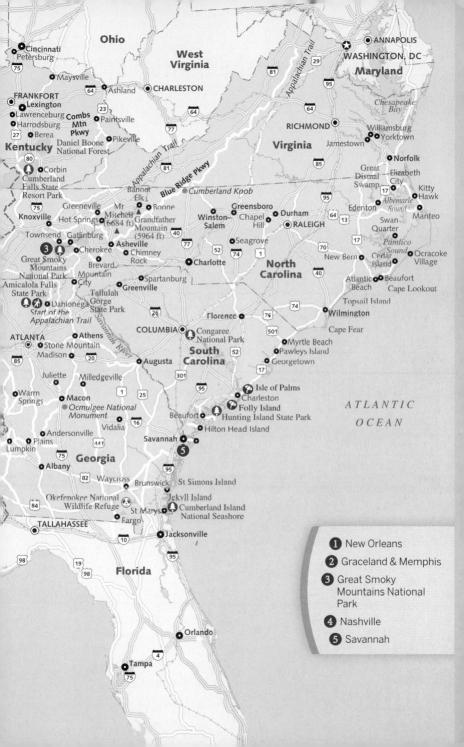

Ohio

Cincinnati
Petersburg
75

West Virginia

Maysville

FRANKFORT
Lexington
Lawrenceburg
Harrodsburg
27 Berea
Kentucky
80
Corbin
Cumberland
Falls State
Resort Park

Ashland
CHARLESTON
64
77
Paintsville
Pikeville
Daniel Boone
National Forest

23
Combs
Mtn
Pkwy

Appalachian Trail
29
ANNAPOLIS
WASHINGTON, DC
Maryland
81
95
64
64
RICHMOND
85
Virginia
Jamestown

Chesapeake Bay

Williamsburg
Yorktown
Norfolk
Great
Dismal
Swamp
Elizabeth
City
17
Edenton
Albemarle Sound
Kitty Hawk
Manteo

Banner
Elk
Blue Ridge Pkwy
Cumberland Knob
Greeneville
Mt
Mitchell
(6684 ft)
Boone
Grandfather
Mountain
(5964 ft)
Hot Springs
Townsend
Knoxville
Gatlinburg
Cherokee
Asheville
Chimney
Rock
3
Great Smoky
Mountains
National Park
Amicalola Falls
State Park
Brevard
Mountain
City
Greenville
Spartanburg
Tallulah
Gorge
State Park
Dahlonega
Start of the
Appalachian Trail
Appalachian Trail
81
Greensboro
Winston–
Salem
Chapel
Hill
Durham
RALEIGH
64
13
Swan
Quarter
New Bern
Pamlico Sound
Cedar
Island
Ocracoke
Village
Atlantic
Beach
Beaufort
Cape Lookout
Seagrove
40
77
52
74
North Carolina
40
70
17
95
Charlotte

Topsail Island
Florence
76
74
Wilmington
Cape Fear
26
COLUMBIA
Congaree
National Park
South Carolina
501
Myrtle Beach
Pawleys Island
Georgetown
17

ATLANTIC
OCEAN

ATLANTA
Athens
Stone Mountain
Madison
85
20
Juliette
Milledgeville
Warm
Springs
Macon
Ocmulgee National
Monument
1
25
Vidalia
Andersonville
Plains
Lumpkin
441
75
Albany
82
Waycross
16
301
95
Augusta
Savannah Rivers
Isle of Palms
7
Charleston
7
Folly Island
Beaufort
Hunting Island State Park
Hilton Head Island
Savannah
5

Brunswick
St Simons Island
Okefenokee National
Wildlife Refuge
St Marys
Jekyll Island
Cumberland Island
National Seashore
Fargo
TALLAHASSEE
84
10
Jacksonville
98
19
98
95
Florida

Orlando

4
Tampa
75

1 New Orleans
2 Graceland & Memphis
3 Great Smoky
  Mountains National
  Park
4 Nashville
5 Savannah

New Orleans & the South's Highlights

New Orleans

A clash of cultures and storied history makes New Orleans (p212) what it is today: the most culturally rich, gastronomically delectable, inherently beautiful city in America. History, cuisine, music and architecture combine seamlessly in the Big Easy, weaving a unique kaleidoscopic web of tradition that's so very, very easy to love. Below: House in French Quarter, New Orleans

1

2 ## Graceland & Memphis

Memphis has a wild spirit fueled by its burgeoning music scene. Roll along the streets of downtown – a jumble of Victorian mansions and eerie abandoned factories – to Beale St, birthplace of the blues and home to smokin'-hot music joints. Then pay your respects to the king at the palatial wonderland of kitsch, Graceland (p229). Left: Blues Club on Beale St, Memphis

STEPHEN SAKS/GETTY IMAGES ©

Great Smoky Mountains National Park

3

Called 'land of the blue smoke' by the Cherokee, this territory (p237) is in the Appalachians, the world's oldest mountain range, featuring miles of cool, humid deciduous forest. There's superb hiking throughout the park, intriguing relics left by early settlers and magnificent vistas that seem to lurk around every bend.

4

Nashville

For country-music fans, there's no place like Nashville (p232). Since the 1920s the city has been attracting musicians who have taken the country genre from the 'hillbilly music' of the early 20th century to the slick 'Nashville sound' of the 1960s, and to the punk-tinged alt-country of the 1990s. Boot-stompin' live-music bars, historic sites, theme parks and a big friendly welcome are all part of the Nashville experience.

5

Savannah

With its gorgeous mansions, cotton warehouses, beautiful squares and Colonial public buildings, Savannah (p242) preserves its past with pride and grace. However, unlike its sister city of Charleston, SC, which retains its reputation as a dignified and refined cultural center, Savannah isn't clean-cut – the town has been described as 'a beautiful lady with a dirty face.'

New Orleans & the South's Best...

Southern Cookin'

○ **Cochon** Award-winning brasserie serving heavenly pulled pork, best washed down with moonshine. (p221)

○ **Wilkes' House** A Southern feast with all the fixings served family-style in lovely Savannah. (p243)

○ **City House** Inventive fusion fare that melds Italian and New South cooking, plus great cocktails, at a hidden Nashville gem. (p235)

○ **Cozy Corner** The humble plate of barbecue becomes high art at this classic Memphis spot. (p231)

Live Music

○ **Wild Bill's** Smokin'-hot blues in a well-worn Memphis juke joint. (p231)

○ **Station Inn** Hit this Nashville classic for some of the best bluegrass jams in the South. (p236)

○ **Preservation Hall** Legendary New Orleans club that's a mecca for lovers of traditional and Dixieland jazz. (p223)

○ **Blue Moon Saloon** In the heart of Cajun country, don't miss this riotous backyard venue. (p225)

Historic Sites

○ **National Civil Rights Museum** Located on the site of Martin Luther King Jr's tragic assassination is this tribute to his enduring legacy. (p227)

○ **Charleston Historic District** This beautifully preserved center is sprinkled with antebellum mansions. (p238)

○ **Louisiana State Museum** Delve into the past with fascinating exhibits set in heritage buildings (the oldest dating to 1813). (p213)

○ **Hermitage** See what 19th-century life was like for folks working on this 1000-acre plantation. (p234)

Need to Know

Scenery

○ **Swamp tours** Take a ride into the bayou on a swamp tour just outside of New Orleans. (p224)

○ **Cumberland Island** Picturesque island with wetland vegetation, plus wild turkeys, feral horses and pristine beaches. (p244)

○ **Natchez Trace Parkway** A lush roadway near Nashville, lined with historic sites. (p237)

○ **Blue Ridge Parkway** Travel the spine of the southern Appalachians, with stunning views on either side. (p239)

Left: Mansion in Charleston Historic District (p238); **Above:** Blue Ridge Parkway (p239)

ADVANCE PLANNING

○ **Six months before** Book accommodation well in advance if you're going to Mardi Gras or Jazzfest.

○ **Two months before** Browse upcoming shows and festivals in New Orleans and Nashville; snag tickets to big events.

○ **Two weeks before** Reserve a table at top restaurants.

○ **One week before** Book tours, river cruises and other activities.

RESOURCES

○ **Gambit** (www.bestofneworleans. com) Free weekly hot sheet of music, culture, politics and classifieds.

○ **Arts Council of New Orleans** (www. artsneworleans.org) Great site for up-to-date info on gigs, gallery openings and other happenings.

○ **Off Beat** (www.offbeat. com) Free monthly specializing in New Orleans' music scene.

○ **Metromix** (www. nashville.metromix. com) Handy music and entertainment listings for Nashville.

○ **Memphis Flyer** (www. memphisflyer.com) Free Memphis entertainment weekly.

○ **Visit Savannah** (www. savannahvisit.com) Handy reference, including upcoming events.

GETTING AROUND

○ **Airports** Nashville Airport (www.nashintl.com) is a $25 to $27 taxi ride from downtown; New Orleans (www.flymsy.com) is a $34 taxi ride to its central district. Savannah (www. savannahairport.com), Memphis (www.mscaa. com) and Charleston (www. chs-airport.com) are other options.

○ **Bus** Greyhound (www. greyhound.com) operates between major towns.

○ **Hire car** Essential for exploring beyond big cities.

○ **Train** Routes include New Orleans–Chicago via Memphis, New Orleans– LA, and Miami–NYC via Savannah and Charleston.

BE FOREWARNED

○ **Crime** New Orleans and Memphis have high crime rates; neighborhoods go from good to ghetto very quickly.

○ **Museums** Some are closed on Mondays.

New Orleans & the South Itineraries

Great music, mouthwatering feasts and eye-popping scenery are yours for the taking on these memorable journeys. Revel in the cultural riches of New Orleans; if time allows, tack on a grand tour around the South.

NEW ORLEANS TO LAFAYETTE

5 DAYS
The Big Easy & Cajun Country

Explore the picturesque streets of the French Quarter in ❶ **New Orleans** (p212). That night, have a bang-up meal at Bayona (p220), followed by live jazz at Preservation Hall (p223). On day two explore the historic mansions of the Garden District and browse the boutiques and galleries along Magazine St. Catch the St Charles Ave streetcar back to the Warehouse District and go museum-hopping in the afternoon. Have dinner at fabulous Cochon (p221).

The next day, head out on a morning swamp tour (p224) to spy alligators, birds and other creatures amid the bio-rich wetlands. In the afternoon catch the Canal St streetcar out to lush City Park and the New Orleans Museum of Art (p218). That evening drink in the music joints along Frenchmen St in Faubourg Marigny. On your fourth day, take a road trip to ❷ **Lafayette** (p224) in the heart of Cajun Country, and browse exhibits at Vermilionville (p224). That night, hit one of Lafayette's jumpin' dance halls.

On the final day, explore the Cajun Wetlands near Lafayette. Take in the swampy scenery of the ❸ **Atchafalaya Basin** (p226), then chow down on crawfish in ❹ **Breaux Bridge** (p226) before heading back to New Orleans.

NEW ORLEANS TO SAVANNAH

Greatest Hits of the South

Start in ❶**New Orleans** (p212). Explore the French Quarter, take a riverfront stroll and drink in the fantastic live music scene along Faubourg Marigny's Frenchmen St. Next up is ❷**Memphis**, a 6½ hour drive north. Visit the National Civil Rights Museum (p227), Sun Studio (p228) and Graceland (p229); in the evening, stroll along carnivalesque Beale St before hitting a Memphis blues joint.

After Memphis, go 3½ hours east to ❸**Nashville**. Check out the Country Music Hall of Fame & Museum (p232), the state capitol, and leafy Vanderbilt University. That night join the fray at a country-music-

loving honky-tonk. From Nashville drive four hours' east to the ❹**Great Smoky Mountains National Park** (p237) to hike amid craggy peaks and waterfalls.

Drive southeast 350 miles (six hours) to ❺**Charleston** (p238). Its historic district has beautifully preserved antebellum mansions, Lowcountry cuisine and antique-filled B&Bs. Last stop is ❻**Savannah** (p242), a 2¼ hour drive southwest. Take in the pretty parks and riverfront, browse historic 19th-century homes and feast at a farm-to-table gem.

Historic house, Cades Cove (p238)
RICHARD CUMMINS/GETTY IMAGES ©

Discover New Orleans & the South

Musicians, New Orleans
LONELY PLANET/GETTY IMAGES ©

NEW ORLEANS

New Orleans is very much of America, and extraordinarily removed from it as well. 'Nola' is something, and somewhere, else. Founded by the French and administered by the Spanish (and then the French again), she is, with her sidewalk cafes and iron balconies, one of America's most European cities. But she is also, with her *vodoun* (voo-doo), weekly secondline parades (essentially, neigborhood parades), Mardi Gras Indians, jazz and brass and gumbo, the most African and Caribbean city in the country as well. New Orleans celebrates; while America is on deadline, this city is getting a cocktail after a long lunch. But after seeing how people here rebuilt their homes after floods and storms, it would be foolish to call the locals lazy.

◉ Sights

FRENCH QUARTER

Elegant, Caribbean-colonial architecture, lush gardens and wrought-iron accents are the visual norm in the French Quarter. But this is also the heart of New Orleans' tourism scene. Bourbon St generates a loutish membrane that sometimes makes the rest of the Quarter difficult to appreciate. Look past this. The Vieux Carré (Old Quarter; first laid out in 1722) is the focal point of much of this city's culture and in the quieter back lanes and alleyways there's a sense of faded time shaken and stirred with joie de vivre.

Jackson Square   Square, Plaza
(☎504-568-6968; www.jackson-square.com; Decatur & St Peter Sts) Jackson Sq is the heart of the Quarter. Sprinkled with lazing

loungers, surrounded by fortune-tellers, sketch artists and traveling showfolk and overlooked by cathedrals, offices and shops plucked from a fairy tale, this is one of America's great green spaces.

St Louis Cathedral
Cathedral

(📞504 525-9585; Jackson Sq; donations accepted; 🕙9am-5pm Mon-Sat, 1-5pm Sun) St Louis Cathedral is Jackson Sq's masterpiece. Designed by Gilberto Guillemard, this is one of the finest examples of French ecumenical (church) architecture in America.

Louisiana State Museum
Museum

(http://lsm.crt.state.la.us; adult/child per bldg $6/free; 🕙10am-4:30pm Tue-Sun) This institution operates several buildings across the state. The standouts here include the 1911 **Cabildo (701 Chartres St)**, on the left of the cathedral, a Louisiana history museum located in the old city hall where Plessy vs Ferguson (which legalized segregation) was argued. The huge number of exhibits inside can easily eat up half a day, the remainder of which can be spent in the Cabildo's sister building, on the right of the church, the 1813 **Presbytère (751 Chartres St; 👪)**. Inside is an excellent **Mardi Gras museum**, with displays of costumes, parade floats and royal jewelry; and a poignant **Katrina & Beyond** exhibit, chronicling this devastating storm.

Historic New Orleans Collection
Museum

(HNOC; www.hnoc.org; 533 Royal St; tours $5; 🕙9:30am-4:30pm Tue-Sat, from 10:30am Sun) **FREE** In several exquisitely restored buildings are thoughtfully curated exhibits with an emphasis on archival materials, such as the original transfer documents of the Louisiana Purchase. Separate home, architecture/courtyard and history tours also run at 10am, 11am, 2pm and 3pm.

Old Ursuline Convent
Historic Building

(1112 Chartres St; adult/child $5/3; 🕙tours 10am-4pm Mon-Sat) In 1727, 12 Ursuline nuns arrived in New Orleans to care for the French garrison's 'miserable little hospi-

tal' and to educate the young girls of the colony. Between 1745 and 1752 the French colonial army built what is now the oldest structure in the Mississippi River Valley and the only remaining French building in the Quarter.

THE TREMÉ

The oldest African American neighborhood in the city is steeped in a lot of history. Leafy **Esplanade Ave**, which borders the neighborhood, is full of Creole mansions, and is one of the prettiest streets in the city.

Backstreet Cultural Museum
Museum

(www.backstreetmuseum.org; 1116 St Claude Ave; admission $8; 🕙10am-5pm Tue-Sat) This is the place to see one facet of this town's distinctive customs – its African American side – and how they're expressed in daily life. If you have any interest in Mardi Gras Indian suits (African Americans who dress up in Carnivalesque Native American costume), second lines and the activities of social aid and pleasure clubs (the local African American community version of civic associations), you need to stop by.

Le Musée de FPC
Museum

(Free People of Color Museum; www.lemusee defpc.com; 2336 Esplanade Ave; adult/child $10/5; 🕙11am-4pm Wed-Sat) Inside a lovely 1859 Greek Revival mansion in the Upper Tremé, this museum showcases a 30-year collection of artifacts, documents, furniture and art, telling the story of a forgotten subculture: the 'free people of color' before the Civil War.

St Louis Cemetery No 1
Cemetery

(Basin St; 🕙9am-3pm Mon-Sat, to noon Sun; 👪) This cemetery received the remains of most early Creoles. The shallow water table necessitated above-ground burials, with bodies placed in the family tombs you see to this day.

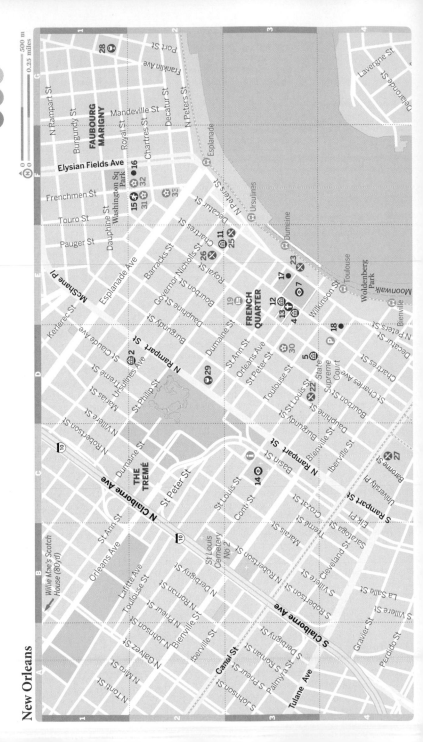

500 m
0.25 miles

Willie Mae's Scotch House (80yd)

FAUBOURG MARIGNY

Elysian Fields Ave

THE TREMÉ

FRENCH QUARTER

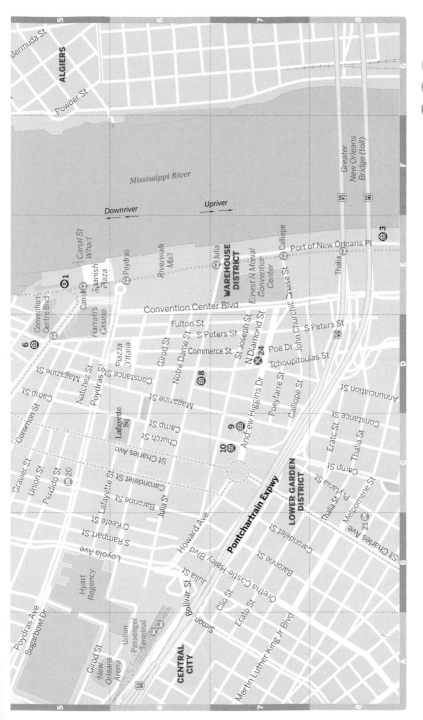

ALGIERS

Bermuda St

Powder St

Mississippi River

Downriver

Upriver

Canal St Wharf

Greater New Orleans Bridge (toll)

Riverwalk Mall

Poydras

Julia

Calliope

Thalia

Port of New Orleans Pl

WAREHOUSE DISTRICT

Ernest N Morial Convention Center

Chase St

◉1

Convention Centre Blvd

Canal

Spanish Plaza

Harrah's Casino

Convention Center Blvd

Fulton St

S Peters St

St Joseph St

N Diamond St

Poe Dr

John Churchill Chase St

S Peters St

Piazza D'Italia

Girod St

Notre Dame St

Commerce St

✕24

Tchoupitoulas St

Poeyfarre St

Calliope St

Annunciation St

Magazine St

Natchez St

Poydras St

Constance St

🏛8

Magazine St

Camp St

Common St

Gravier St

Union St

Perdido St

🏛20

Lafayette Sq

Church St

Camp St

Andrew Higgins Dr

🏛9

St Charles Ave

🏛10

Carondelet St

Lafayette St

Baronne St

Julia St

Poydras Ave

Sugarbowl Dr

Girod St

New Orleans Arena

Union Passenger Terminal

Hyatt Regency

Loyola Ave

S Rampart St

O'Keefe St

Howard Ave

Bolivar St

Julia St

Simon

Clio St

Erato St

Oretha Castle-Haley Blvd

Martin Luther King Jr Blvd

Pontchartrain Expwy

LOWER GARDEN DISTRICT

Carondelet St

Baronne St

St Charles Ave

Erato St

Eratc St

Camp St

Constance St

Thalia St

Prytania St

Melpomene St

Thalia St

🏛21

CENTRAL CITY

❸3

215

New Orleans

FAUBOURG MARIGNY, THE BYWATER & THE NINTH WARD

North of the French Quarter are the Creole suburbs (*faubourgs*, which more accurately means 'neighborhoods') of the Marigny and the Bywater. The Marigny is the heart of the local gay scene. **Frenchmen St**, which runs through the center of the 'hood, is a fantastic strip of live-music goodness. Nearby **St Claude Ave** now boasts a collection of good live-music venues, which is less Dixie-style jazz and more punk and bounce (a local style of frenetic dance music).

The Bywater is a collection of candy-colored shotgun houses and Creole cottages. It has the heaviest concentration of transplants in the city and an ever-expanding number of hip new restaurant and bars.

CBD & WAREHOUSE DISTRICT

National World War II Museum
Museum

(☏504-528-1944; www.ddaymuseum.org; 945 Magazine St; adult/child $22/13, with 1/2 films add $5/10, ◷9am-5pm) The museum presents an admirably nuanced and thorough analysis of the biggest war of the 20th century. Of particular note is the **D-Day exhibition**, arguably the most in-depth of its type in the country. *Beyond All Boundaries*, a film narrated by Tom Hanks and shown on a 120ft-wide immersive screen in the new **Solomon Victory Theater**, is a loud, proud and awesome extravaganza.

Ogden Museum of Southern Art
Museum

(☏504-539-9600; www.ogdenmuseum.org; 925 Camp St; adult/student/child $10/8/5; ◷10am-5pm Wed-Mon, 10am-5pm & 6-8pm Thu) New Orleans entrepreneur Roger Houston Ogden has assembled one of the finest collections of Southern art anywhere, which includes huge galleries ranging from Impressionist landscapes to outsider folk-art quirkiness. There's live music from 6pm to 8pm Thursday.

Blaine Kern's Mardi Gras World
Museum

(☏504-655-9586; www.mardigrasworld. com; 1380 Port of New Orleans Pl; adult/child $19.95/12.95; ◷tours 9:30am-4:30pm; ♿) This garish and good-fun spot houses (and constructs) many of the greatest floats used in Mardi Gras parades.

Aquarium of the Americas
Aquarium

(☏504-581-4629; www.auduboninstitute.org; 1 Canal St; adult/child $22.50/16, with IMAX $29/23, with Audubon Zoo $36/25; ◷10am-5pm; ♿) Simulates an eclectic selection of watery habitats – look for the rare white alligator. You can buy combination tickets to the IMAX theater next door, the nearby Insectarium, the Audubon Zoo in Uptown or all of the above (adult/child $44.50/27.50).

Insectarium Museum, Garden
(📞504-581-4629; www.auduboninstitute.org; 423 Canal St; adult/child $16.50/12; ⏰10am-5pm; 👫) A supremely kid-friendly learning center that's a joy for budding entomologists. The Japanese garden dotted with whispering butterflies is particularly beautiful.

GARDEN DISTRICT & UPTOWN

The main architectural division in New Orleans is between the elegant townhouses of the Creole and French northeast and the magnificent mansions of the American district, settled after the Louisiana Purchase. These huge structures, plantation-esque in their appearance, are most commonly found in the Garden District and Uptown. Magnificent oak trees arch over St Charles Ave, which cuts through the heart of this sector and where the supremely pictur-esque **St Charles Avenue streetcar** (per ride $1.25; 👫) runs. The boutiques and galleries of **Magazine St** form the best shopping strip in the city.

Audubon Zoological Gardens Zoo
(www.auduboninstitute.org; 6500 Magazine St; adult/child $17.50/12; ⏰10am-5pm Mon-Fri, to 6pm Sat & Sun; 👫) This wonderful zoo is great for kids and adults. It contains the ultracool **Louisiana Swamp** exhibit, full of alligators, bobcats, foxes, bears and snapping turtles.

CITY PARK & MID-CITY
City Park Park
(www.neworleanscitypark.com; City Park Ave) The Canal streetcar makes the run from the CBD to City Park. Three miles long, 1 mile wide, stroked by weeping willows and Spanish moss and dotted with museums,

Local Knowledge

New Orleans: Don't Miss

BY GRACE WILSON,
COMMUNITY ENGAGEMENT SPECIALIST FOR
ENTERTAINMENT, NOLA.COM; *THE TIMES-PICAYUNE*

1 PRESERVATION HALL
What sets this city apart is that it is the birthplace of America's truest art form: jazz. Hear authentic, traditional jazz every night at Preservation Hall (p223). No food. No frills. Just jazz.

2 CITY PARK
City Park remains one of the largest city parks in the US. Near the New Orleans Museum of Art, around Big Lake, rent a bike or a paddleboat. Gondolas venture into the park's lagoons and NOMA's Besthoff Sculpture Garden (free and open daily).

3 ARNAUD'S FRENCH 75 BAR
At 813 Rue Bienville is a bastion of authentic, historic New Orleans. Of course, it's famous for its French 75s, but mixologist Chris Hannah will make you the best Ramos Gin Fizz or Sazerac – or any other libation.

4 ST CHARLES STREETCAR
Hop on the St Charles Streetcar at Bourbon and Canal Sts. As you chug under the canopy of oaks, snap pictures of the mansions of St Charles Ave. Hop off for easy walks to shop-lined Magazine St, Audubon Zoo and trendy Oak St.

5 BACKSTREET MUSEUM AND SECONDLINE PARADES
'Secondline' comes from the second line of paraders that follow a jazz funeral, behind the family and friends. They generally happen every Sunday; the Backstreet Cultural Museum (p213) in the Tremé neighborhood has all the information.

gardens, waterways, bridges, birds and the occasional alligator, City Park is the nation's fifth-largest urban park (bigger than Central Park in NYC) and New Orleans' prettiest.

New Orleans Museum of Art
Museum

(www.noma.org; 1 Collins Diboll Circle; adult/child $10/6; ⊙10am-6pm Tue-Thu, to 9pm Fri, 11am-5pm Sat & Sun) Inside City Park, this elegant museum was opened in 1911 and is well worth a visit both for its special exhibitions and top-floor galleries of African, Native American, Oceanic and Asian art. Don't miss the **sculpture garden** (⊙10am-4:30pm Sat-Thu, to 8:45pm Fri) **FREE** with a cutting-edge collection in lush, meticulously planned grounds.

Courses

New Orleans School of Cooking
Cooking

(☎800-237-4841; www.neworleansschoolof cooking.com; 524 St Louis St; courses $24-29)

Most open courses are food demonstrations. Menus rotate daily, but rest assured you'll be snacking on creations such as gumbo, jambalaya and pralines at the end of class, all the while learning about the history of the city as told by the charismatic chefs. A hands-on class in cooking Creole cuisine is offered as well ($125).

Tours

The **Jean Lafitte National Historic Park and Preserve** (☎504-589-2133, 504-589-3822; www.nps.gov/jela; 419 Decatur St, French Quarter; ⊙9am-5pm) visitor center leads free walking tours of the French Quarter at 9:30am (get tickets at 9am).

Confederacy of Cruisers
Cycling

(☎504-400-5468; www.confederacyofcruisers. com; tours from $49) Get yourself out of the Quarter and on two wheels – this super informative, laid-back bike tour takes you through Nola's non-Disneyland neighborhoods – Faubourg Marigny, Esplanade Ridge, the Tremé – often with a bar stop

Left: Preservation Hall (p223); **Below:** Mardi Gras float, New Orleans

(LEFT) JUDY BELLAH/GETTY IMAGES ©; (BELOW) WITOLD SKRYPCZAK/GETTY IMAGES ©

and the occasional jazz funeral pop-in along the way.

Friends of the Cabildo

Walking Tour

(☏524-9118, 523-3939; www.friendsofthe cabildo.org; 523 St Ann St; adult/student/child $15/12/free; ☉10am & 1:30pm Tue-Sun) Volunteers lead the best available walking tours of the Quarter.

Sleeping

Prytania Park Hotel

Hotel $

(☏504-524-0427; www.prytaniaparkhotel.com; 1525 Prytania St, Garden District; r from $75, ste from $100; P✻🛜) This complex of three separate hotels in the Garden District offers friendly, well-located bang for the buck. It's a perfect spot for folks of all budgets bouncing between the Quarter and the Garden District and/or Uptown.

Bywater Bed & Breakfast

B&B $

(☏504-944-8438; www.bywaterbnb.com; 1026 Clouet St, Bywater; r without bath $100) An artsy B&B, Bywater is particularly popular with the LGBT crowd, and is about as homey and laid-back as it gets. The walls double as gallery space, showcasing a collection of vibrant outsider and folk art. The four guest rooms are simple and comfortable with more cheery paint and art.

Columns

Historic Hotel $$

(☏504-899-9308; www.thecolumns.com; 3811 St Charles Ave, Garden District; r incl breakfast from $170 Sat & Sun, from $134 Mon-Fri; ✻🛜) This stately 1883 Italianate mansion in the Garden District is both elegant and relaxed, boasting a stained glass–topped staircase, elaborate marble fireplaces, richly carved woodwork and other original features. There's also a lovely 2nd-floor porch overlooking oak-draped St Charles Ave and an inviting bar.

New Orleans for Children

Many of New Orleans' daytime attractions are well suited for kids, including the Audubon Zoo (p217), Aquarium of the Americas (p216) and Insectarium (p217).

Carousel Gardens (📞504-483-9402; www.neworleanscitypark.com; 7 Victory Ave, City Park; admission $3; 🕐10am-3pm Tue-Fri, 11am-6pm Sat & Sun, extended hours summer) The 1906 carousel is a gem of vintage carny-ride happiness.

Louisiana Children's Museum (📞504-523-1357; www.lcm.org; 420 Julia St; admission $8; 🕐9:30am-4:30pm Tue-Sat, from noon Sun, to 5pm summer) Great hands-on exploratory exhibits and toddler area.

Cornstalk Hotel   B&B **$$$**
(📞504-523-1515; www.cornstalkhotel.com; 915 Royal St, French Quarter; r $125-250; ✳🛜) Pass through the famous cast-iron fence and into a plush, antiqued B&B where the serenity sweeps away the whirl of the busy streets outside.

Le Pavillon   Historic Hotel **$$$**
(📞504-581-3111; www.lepavillon.com; 833 Poydras Ave, French Quarter; r $160-299, ste $199-499; P✳🛜🏊) Built in 1907, this elegant European-style hotel's opulent marble lobby, plush, classic rooms and rooftop pool are a steal.

Degas House   Historic Hotel **$$$**
(📞504-821-5009; www.degashouse.com; 2306 Esplanade Ave; r incl breakfast from $199; P✳🛜) Edgar Degas, the famed French Impressionist, lived in this 1852 Italianate house in Tremé when visiting his mother's family in the early 1870s. Arty rooms recall the painter's stay with reproductions of his work and period furnishings.

 # Eating

FRENCH QUARTER

Croissant D'Or Patisserie   Cafe **$**
(617 Ursulines Ave; items $1.50-5.75; 🕐6:30am-3pm Wed-Mon) This wonderful pastry shop is where many Quarter residents start their day.

Café du Monde   Cafe **$**
(800 Decatur St; beignets $2.14; 🕐24hr; 👪) It's touristy, but a requisite stop for the beignets (square, sugar-coated fritters).

Coop's Place   Cajun **$**
(📞525-9053; 1109 Decatur St; mains $8-17.50; 🕐11am-3am) For a cheap but thoroughly satisfying meal in the Quarter, this Cajun country shack disguised as a divey bar is as good as it gets: try the rabbit and sausage jambalaya or the red beans and rice for a taste of Cajun heaven.

Bayona   Modern American **$$$**
(📞504-525-4455; www.bayona.com; 430 Dauphine St; mains $27-32; 🕐11:30am-2pm Mon-Fri, plus 6-10pm Mon-Thu, to 11pm Fri & Sat) Bayona is a great splurge in the Quarter. Expect fish, fowl and game on the daily-changing menu divided between long-time classics and daily specials.

THE TREMÉ

Willie Mae's Scotch House   Southern **$$**
(2401 St Ann St; fried chicken $10; 🕐11am-7pm Mon-Sat) Whips up some of the best fried chicken in the south.

BYWATER

The Joint   Barbecue **$**
(📞504-949-3232; 701 Mazant St; mains $7-17; 🕐11:30am-10pm Mon-Sat) The Joint's barbecue is world-class. Knock some ribs or pulled pork or brisket back with some sweet tea in the backyard garden and learn to love life.

Satsuma   Health Food **$**
(📞504-304-5962; 3218 Dauphine St; breakfast & lunch under $10, dinner mains $8-16; 🕐7am-7pm)

Amid pop art–decorated walls, Satsuma has a chalkboard menu of organic sandwiches, Mediterranean-inspired salads, seafood and ginger limeade (pure ambrosia on a hot day).

Bacchanal
Cafe **$$**
(www.bacchanalwine.com; 600 Poland Ave; mains $8-16, cheese from $5; ⊙11am-midnight) Order some wine and cheese, then kick back in an overgrown garden to whoever showed up to play live music that day. Or order from the inventive full menu cooked out of the kitchen in the back (cash only).

Elizabeth's
Cajun, Creole **$$$**
(www.elizabeths-restaurant.com; 601 Gallier St; mains $16-26; ⊙8am-2:30pm & 6-10pm Tue-Sat, 8am-2:30pm Sun) Elizabeth's is deceptively divey, mixing corner-shack ambiance, folk-art music gallery and excellent food.

CBD & WAREHOUSE DISTRICT

Domenica
Italian **$$**
(☏504-648-6020; 123 Baronne St; mains $13-30; ⊙11am-11pm; ✈) Domenica's excellent rustic pizzas are loaded with nontraditional but savory toppings – spicy lamb meatballs, roast pork shoulder – and served amid wooden refectory tables and a soaring ceiling.

Cochon
Contemporary Cajun **$$$**
(☏504-588-2123; www.cochonrestaurant.com; 930 Tchoupitoulas St; mains $19-25; ⊙11am-10pm Mon-Fri, 5:30-10pm Sat) James Beard Award–winning chef Donald Link heads this fabulous brasserie that serves up gourmet Southern comfort food. The housemade Louisiana *cochon* – moist pulled pork – is outstanding. Reservations are essential.

GARDEN DISTRICT & UPTOWN

Boucherie
New Southern **$$**
(☏504-862-5514; www.boucherie-nola.com; 8115 Jeannette St, Uptown; large plates $13-18; ⊙11am-3pm & 5:30-9pm Tue-Sat) For dinner, blackened shrimp-and-grits cakes are darkly sweet and savory, garlic Parmesan fries are gloriously gooey and the smoked Wagyu beef brisket melts in your mouth. Just amazing.

Domilise's Po-Boys
Creole **$$**
(5240 Annunciation St, Uptown; po'boys $9-15; ⊙10am-7pm Mon-Wed & Fri, 10:30am-7pm Sat) This dilapidated white shack by the river serves legendary po'boys (traditional Louisiana submarine sandwich). Cash only.

Mat and Naddie's
Contemporary Creole **$$$**
(☏504-861-9600; 937 Leonidas St, Uptown; mains $22-29; ⊙5:30-9:30pm Thu-Sat, Mon & Tue) Set in a beautiful riverfront house with a Christmas light–bedecked patio in the back, M&N's has rich, innovative dishes (sherry-marinated grilled quail

Chicken and sausage jambalaya
LAURI PATTERSON/GETTY IMAGES ©

with waffles, for instance). All are quite delicious.

 Drinking

Skip loutish Bourbon St and get into the neighborhoods, where you can experience some of the best bars in America.

Tonique   Bar
(www.bartonique.com; 820 Rampart St, French Quarter) If you're going to drink in the Quarter (on the edge of it, anyway), this serious cocktail bar is the place, where cool folks who appreciate an excellent concoction gather over the best Sazerac in town.

Mimi's in the Marigny   Bar
(2601 Royal St, Faubourg Marigny; ⏱to 5am) This great bi-level bar (pool table downstairs, music upstairs) serves up excellent Spanish tapas and has a casual neighborhood vibe.

St Joe's   Bar
(5535 Magazine St, Uptown) Good-time Uptown pious-themed bar with great blueberry mojitos, a cool back courtyard and friendly ambiance.

 Entertainment

Check *Gambit* (www.bestofneworleans.com), *Offbeat* (www.offbeat.com) or www.nolafunguide.com to see what's on.

Spotted Cat   Live Music
(www.spottedcatmusicclub.com; 623 Frenchmen St, Faubourg Marigny) A throwback retro cool permeates through this excellent Frenchmen staple you might recognize from numerous episodes of *Tremé*. Jazz is on nightly and there's rarely a cover charge.

Three Muses   Jazz
(www.thethreemuses.com; 536 Frenchmen St, Marigny; ⏱4-10pm Wed, Thu, Sun & Mon, to 2am Fri & Sat) A great place to start the night, Three Muses marries excellent bands with gourmet cuisine.

Rock & Bowl   Live Music
(☎504-861-1700; www.rockandbowl.com; 3000 S Carrollton Ave, Mid-City; ⏱5pm-late, live music Wed-Sat; 👫) Come see a strange, wonderful combination of bowling alley, deli, and a huge live music and dance venue. Thursday night's zydeco shows are fabulous.

Sazerac cocktail

KEVIN O'MARA/GETTY IMAGES ©

Preservation Hall   Jazz

(www.preservationhall.com; 726 St Peter St,
French Quarter; cover $15; ⊘8-11pm) A verita-
ble museum of traditional and Dixieland
jazz, Preservation Hall is a pilgrimage.
The downside: no air-conditioning,
limited seating and no booze.

ℹ Information

The city's official visitor website is www.
neworleansonline.com.

Basin St Visitor's Center (☏504-293-
2600; www.neworleanscvb.com; 501 Basin St,
French Quarter; ⊘9am-5pm) This interactive
tourist info center has loads of helpful info.

ℹ Getting There & Away

Louis Armstrong New Orleans International
Airport (MSY; www.flymsy.com; 900 Airline
Hwy), 11 miles west of the city, handles
primarily domestic flights.

The Union Passenger Terminal (☏504-
299-1880; 1001 Loyola Ave) is home to
Greyhound (☏504-525-6075; ⊘5:15am-1pm
& 2:30-6pm) bus services and Amtrak (☏504-
528-1610; ⊘ticketing 5:45am-10pm) train
services.

ℹ Getting Around

To/from the Airport

The Airport Shuttle (☏866-596-2699; www.
airportshuttleneworleans.com; one way $20) runs
to downtown hotels.

Taxis downtown cost $34 for one or two people,
$14 more for each additional passenger.

Public Transportation

The Regional Transit Authority (RTA; www.norta.
com) runs the local bus service. Bus and streetcar
fares are $1.25, plus 25¢ for transfers. RTA Visitor
Passes for one/three days cost $5/12.

Taxi

For a taxi, call United Cabs (☏504-522-9771;
www.unitedcabs.com).

Bicycle

Rent bicycles at Bicycle Michael's (☏504-945-
9505; www.bicyclemichaels.com; 622 Frenchmen
St, Faubourg Marigny; rentals per day $35;
⊘10am-7pm Mon, Tue & Thu-Sat, to 5pm Sun).

♥ If You Like…
Live Music

If you like Preservation Hall and Three
Muses, check out these other top music
spots.

1 TIPITINA'S
(www.tipitinas.com; 501 Napoleon Ave, Uptown)
Legendary Uptown club hosting local jazz, blues,
soul and funk.

2 SNUG HARBOR
(www.snugjazz.com; 626 Frenchmen
St, Marigny) In the Marigny, the city's best
contemporary jazz venue is all about world-class
music and a good variety of acts.

3 CHICKIE WAH WAH
(☏504-304-4714; www.chickiewahwah.com;
2828 Canal St, Mid-City; ⊘shows around 8pm)
This great jazz club hosts top names such as John
Mooney and Papa Mali in a cozy setting where
the French Quarter seems light years away.

BARATARIA PRESERVE

This section of the **Jean Lafitte National
Historical Park & Preserve**, south of
New Orleans near the town of Marrero,
provides the easiest access to the dense
swamplands that ring New Orleans. The
8 miles of platform trails are a stunning
way to tread lightly through the fecund,
thriving swamp where you can check out
gators and other fascinating plant life and
creatures. The preserve is home to alligators, nutrias (read: big invasive rats), tree
frogs and hundreds of species of birds. It
is well worth taking a ranger-led walk to
learn about the many ecosystems that
make up what are often lumped together
as 'wetlands.'

Start at the **NPS Visitors Center**
(☏504-589-2330; www.nps.gov/jela; Hwy 3134;
⊘9am-5pm; 🚻) FREE, 1 mile west of Hwy
45 off the Barataria Blvd exit, where you
can pick up a map or join a guided walk
or canoe trip (most Saturday mornings

Swamp Tours

You haven't experienced Louisiana unless you've been out on its waterways, and the easiest way is to join a swamp tour. Arrange tours in New Orleans or go on your own and contract directly with a bayou-side company.

Louisiana Lost Land Tours (☑504-400-5920; http://lostlandstours.org) Wonderful tours that include kayak paddles into the wetlands and a motorboat tour of Barataria Bay.

Annie Miller's Son's Swamp & Marsh Tours (☑985-868-4758; www.annie-miller.com; 3718 Southdown Mandalay Rd, Houma; adult/child $15/10; ⊞) The son of legendary swamp guide Annie Miller has taken up his mom's tracks.

Cajun Encounters (☑504-834-1770; www.cajunencounters.com; without/with pick-up from $25/50, night tours $40/70) Popular, well run and offering a wide variety of options, including night tours.

and monthly on full-moon nights; call to reserve a spot). To rent canoes or kayaks for a tour or an independent paddle, go to **Bayou Barn** (☑504-689-2663; http://bayoubarn.com; 7145 Barataria Blvd; canoes per person $20, 1-person kayak per day $25; ⊙10am-6pm Thu-Sun) about 3 miles from the park entrance.

CAJUN COUNTRY

When people think of 'Louisiana,' this (and New Orleans) is the image that comes to mind: miles of bayou, sawdust-strewn shacks, a unique take on French and lots of good food. Welcome to Cajun Country, also called Acadiana for French settlers exiled from L'Acadie (now Nova Scotia, Canada) by the British in 1755.

Cajuns are the largest French-speaking minority in the US – prepare to hear it on radios, in church services and in the sing-song lilt of local English accents.

···

Lafayette

The term 'undiscovered gem' gets thrown around too much in travel writing, but Lafayette really fits the bill. There's an entirely fantastic amount of good eating and lots of music venues here, plus one of the best free music festivals in the country – **Festival International de Louisiane** (www.festivalinternational.com; ⊙last weekend Apr). This is a university town; bands are rocking almost every night. Sundays are quiet, though there are some delicious brunch options.

◉ Sights

Vermilionville Village (☑337-233-4077; www.vermilionville.org; 300 Fisher Rd; adult/student $8/6; ⊙10am-4pm Tue-Sun; ⊞) A tranquil restored/re-created 19th-century Cajun village wends along the bayou near the airport. Friendly, enthusiastic costumed docents explain Cajun, Creole and Native American history, and local bands perform on Sundays. Also offers guided **boat tours** (☑337-233-4077; adult/student $12/8; ⊙10:30am Tue-Sat Mar-May & Sep-Nov) of Bayou Vermilion.

🛏 Sleeping & Eating

Blue Moon Guest House Guesthouse $ (☑337-234-2422, 877-766-2583; www.bluemoonguesthouse.com; 215 E Convent St; dm $18, r $73-94; P ❄ @ 📶) This tidy old home is an upscale hostel-like hang-out that's walking distance from downtown. Snag a bed and you'll be on the guest list for Lafayette's most popular down-home music venue, located in the backyard.

Buchanan Lofts Boutique Apartments $$ (☑337-534-4922; www.buchananlofts.com; 403 S Buchanan; r per night/week from $110/600; P ❄ @ 📶) These über-hip lofts could be in New York City if they weren't so big; they're doused in contemporary-cool art and design, all fruits of the friendly owner's globetrotting.

Johnson's Boucanière   Cajun **$**
(1111 St John St; mains under $10; ☺10am-6pm Tue-Thu, to 9pm Fri, 7am-9pm Sat) This resurrected 70-year-old family prairie smoker business turns out detour-worthy *boudin* (Cajun-style pork and rice sausage) and an unbeatable smoked pork-brisket sandwich.

Artmosphere   American **$**
(☏337-233-3331; 902 Johnston St; mains under $10; ☺11am-2am Mon-Sat, to midnight Sun; 🎵) At this student favorite, you'll find good vegan/vegetarian food and a decent beer selection, pus live music most nights.

French Press   Breakfast **$$$**
(www.thefrenchpresslafayette.com; 214 E Vermillion; breakfast $6-$10.50, dinner mains $29-38; ☺7am-2pm Tue-Thu, 7am-2pm & 5:30-9pm Fri, 9am-2pm & 5:30-9pm Sat, 9am-2pm Sun; 🛜) This French-Cajun hybrid is the best culinary thing going in Lafayette. Breakfast features a sinful Cajun benedict, while at dinner the rack of lamb with truffled gratin steals the show.

Entertainment

Cajun restaurants like **Randol's** (☏337-981-7080; www.randols.com; 2320 Kaliste Saloom Rd; ☺5-10pm Sun-Thu, to 11pm Fri & Sat) and **Prejean's** (☏337-896-3247; www.prejeans.com; 3480 NE Evangeline Thruway/I-49) feature live music on weekends nights.

Blue Moon Saloon   Live Music
(www.bluemoonpresents.com; 215 E Convent St; cover $5-8) This intimate venue on the back porch of the accompanying guesthouse has good music, good people and good beer.

Information

Visitor Center (☏800-346-1958, 337-232-3737; www.lafayettetravel.com; 1400 NW Evangeline Thruway; ☺8:30am-5pm Mon-Fri, 9am-5pm Sat & Sun)

Getting There & Away

Greyhound (☏337-235-1541; 100 Lee Ave) operates from a hub beside the central

Bayou, Louisiana

commercial district, making several runs daily to New Orleans (3½ hours). The **Amtrak (100 Lee Ave)** train *Sunset Limited* goes to New Orleans three times a week.

Cajun Wetlands

In 1755, the Grand Dérangement, the British expulsion of rural French settlers from Acadiana (now Nova Scotia, Canada), created a homeless population of Acadians who searched for decades for a place to settle. In 1785, seven boatloads of exiles arrived in New Orleans. By the early 19th century, 3000 to 4000 Acadians occupied the swamplands southwest of New Orleans. Native American tribes such as the Attakapas helped them learn to eke out a living based upon fishing and trapping, and the aquatic way of life is still the backdrop to modern living.

East and south of Lafayette, the **Atchafalaya Basin** is the preternatural heart of the Cajun wetlands. Stop in to the **Atchafalaya Welcome Center** (☎337-228-1094; www.louisianatravel.com/atchafalaya-welcome-center; I-10, exit 121; ☺8:30am-5pm) to learn how to penetrate the dense jungle protecting these swamps, lakes and bayous from the casual visitor (incidentally, it also screens one of the most gloriously cheesy nature films in existence). They'll fill you in on camping in **Indian Bayou** and exploring the **Sherburne Wildlife Management Area**, as well as the exquisitely situated **Lake Fausse Pointe State Park**.

Eleven miles east of Lafayette in the compact, crawfish-lovin' town of **Breaux Bridge**, you'll find the utterly unexpected **Café des Amis** (www.cafedesamis.com; 140 E Bridge St; mains $17-26; ☺11am-2pm Tue, to 9pm Wed & Thu, 7:30am-9:30pm Fri & Sat, 8am-2pm Sun), where you can relax amid funky local art as waiters trot out sumptuous weekend breakfasts, sometimes set to a zydeco jam. Just 3.5 miles south of Breaux Bridge, **Lake Martin** (Lake Martin Rd) is a wonderful introduction to bayou landscapes. This bird sanctuary hosts thousands of great and cattle egrets, blue heron and more than a few gators.

Check out the friendly **Tourist Center** (☎337-332-8500; www.breauxbridgelive.com; 318 E Bridge St; ☺8am-4pm Mon-Fri, to noon Sat), which can hook you up with one of numerous B&Bs in town, or the wonderful **Bayou Cabins** (☎337-332-6158; www.bayoucabins.com; 100 W Mills Ave; cabins $60-125): 14 completely individualized cabins situated on Bayou Teche, some with 1950s retro furnishings, others decked out in regional folk art.

MEMPHIS

Memphis, Tennessee, doesn't just attract tourists. It draws pilgrims. Music-lovers lose themselves to the throb of blues guitar on Beale St. Barbecue connoisseurs descend to stuff themselves psychotic on smoky pulled pork and dry-rubbed ribs. Elvis fanatics fly in to worship at the altar of the King at Graceland. You could spend days hopping from one museum or historic site to another, stopping only for barbecue, and leave happy.

Sights

DOWNTOWN

The pedestrian-only stretch of Beale St is a 24-hour carnival zone, where you'll find deep-fried funnel cakes, to-go beer counters, and music, music, music.

Memphis Rock 'n' Soul Museum
Museum

(☎901-205-2533; www.memphisrocknsoul.org; cnr Lt George W Lee Ave & 3rd St; adult/child $11/8; ☺10am-7pm) The Smithsonian's museum, next to FedEx Forum, examines how African American and white music mingled in the Mississippi Delta to create the modern rock and soul sound.

Gibson Beale Street Showcase
Factory Tour

(www.gibson.com; 145 Lt George W Lee Ave; admission $10, no children under 5; ☺tours 11am-4pm Mon-Sat, noon-4pm Sun) Take the fascinating 45-minute tour of this enormous place to see master craftspeople

RAY LASKOWITZ/GETTY IMAGES ©

 Don't Miss
National Civil Rights Museum

Housed across the street from the Lorraine Motel (pictured above), where the Reverend Dr Martin Luther King Jr was fatally shot on April 4, 1968, is this gut-wrenching museum. The museum's extensive exhibits and detailed timeline chronicle the struggle for African American freedom and equality. Both Dr King's cultural contribution and his assassination serve as prisms for looking at the Civil Rights movement, its precursors and its continuing impact on American life. The turquoise exterior of the 1950s motel and two preserved interior rooms remain much as they were at the time of King's death, and serve as pilgrimage points in their own right. The museum is five blocks south of Beale St.

NEED TO KNOW

www.civilrightsmuseum.org; 450 Mulberry St; adult/student & senior/ child $10/9/8; ⊙9am-5pm Mon & Wed-Sat, 1-5pm Sun Sep-May, to 6pm Jun-Aug

transform solid blocks of wood into Stratocasters. Tours leave on the hour.

Peabody Ducks   Marching Ducks
(www.peabodymemphis.com; 149 Union Ave; ⊙11am & 5pm; 👪) FREE Every day at 11am sharp, five ducks file from the Peabody Hotel's gilded elevator, waddle across the red-carpeted lobby, and decamp in the marble lobby fountain for a day of happy splashing. The ducks make the reverse

march at 5pm, when they retire to their penthouse accompanied by their red-coated Duckmaster.

NORTH OF DOWNTOWN

Mud Island   Park
(www.mudisland.com; 125 N Front St; ⊙10am-5pm Tue-Sun Apr-Oct, later Jun-Aug; 👪)
FREE A small peninsula jutting into the Mississippi, Mud Island is downtown

Memphis' best-loved green space. Hop the monorail ($4, or free with Mississippi River Museum admission) or walk across the bridge to the park, where you can jog and rent bikes.

Mississippi River Museum   Museum

(www.mudisland.com/c-3-mississippi-river-museum.aspx; 350 East 3rd Street; adult/child $15/10; ⏱10am-5pm Apr-Oct) Located on Mud Island, this place is part Aquarium, part geological and historical examination of America's greatest river.

EAST OF DOWNTOWN

Sun Studio   Studio Tour

(📞800-441-6249; www.sunstudio.com; 706 Union Ave; adult/child $12/free; ⏱10:30am-5:30pm) It doesn't look like much from outside, but this dusty storefront is ground zero for American rock 'n' roll music. Starting in the early 1950s, Sun's Sam Phillips recorded blues artists such as Howlin' Wolf, BB King and Ike Turner, followed by the rockabilly dynasty of Jerry Lee Lewis, Johnny Cash, Roy Orbison and, of course, the King himself (who started here in 1953).

Children's Museum of Memphis   Museum

(www.cmom.com; 2525 Central Ave; admission $12; ⏱9am-5pm; 👶) Gives the kids a chance to let loose and play in, on and with exhibits such as an airplane cockpit, tornado generator and waterwheel. For $5 extra you can maraud through the fun **Splash Park**, a plaza with over 40 spouts and sprayers that will keep the kids cool and smiling.

OVERTON PARK

Off Poplar Ave in Midtown, stately homes surround this 342-acre rolling green oasis in the middle of this often gritty city. If Beale St is Memphis' heart, then Overton Park is its lungs.

Memphis Zoo   Zoo

(www.memphiszoo.org; 2000 Prentiss Pl; adult/child $15/10; ⏱9am-5pm Mar-Oct, to 4pm Nov-Feb; @👶) At the park's northwestern

corner, this world-class zoo hosts two giant panda stars in a $16-million exhibit on native Chinese habitat. Other residents include the full gamut of monkeys, polar bears, penguins, eagles and sea lions.

Levitt Shell   Architecture

(www.levittshell.org) A historic band shell and the site of Elvis' first concert, in 1954. Today the mod-looking white shell hosts free concerts all summer.

SOUTH OF DOWNTOWN

Stax Museum of American Soul Music   Museum

(📞901-942-7685; www.staxmuseum.com; 926 E McLemore Ave; adult/child $12/9; ⏱10am-5pm Tue-Sat, 1-5pm Sun Mar-Oct, closed Mon Nov-Mar) Wanna get funky? Head directly to Soulsville USA, where this 17,000-sq-ft museum sits on the site of the old Stax recording studio. This venerable spot was soul music's epicenter in the 1960s, when Otis Redding, Booker T and the MGs and Wilson Pickett recorded here. Dive into soul music history with photos, displays of '60s and '70s peacock clothing and, above all, Isaac Hayes' 1972 Superfly Cadillac outfitted with shag fur and 24-carat-gold exterior trim.

Full Gospel Tabernacle Church   Church

(www.algreenmusic.com; 787 Hale Rd; ⏱services 11:30am & 4pm Sun) If you're in town on a Sunday, put on your Sunday best and head to services in South Memphis, where soul-music legend turned reverend Al Green presides over a powerful choir. Visitors are welcome, and usually take up about half the pews. Join in the whooping 'hallelujahs,' but don't forget the tithe (a few bucks is fine). Green is not around every weekend, but services are a fascinating cultural experience nonetheless.

🖐 Tours

American Dream Safari   Culture

(📞901-527-8870; www.americandreamsafari. com; walking tour per person $15, driving tours per vehicle from $200) Southern culture junkie Tad Pierson shows you the quirky, personal side of Memphis – juke joints,

RAY LASKOWITZ/GETTY IMAGES ©

Don't Miss
Graceland

If you only make one stop in Memphis, it ought to be here: the sublimely kitschy, gloriously bizarre home of the King of Rock and Roll. Though born in Mississippi, Elvis Presley was a true son of Memphis, raised in the Lauderdale Courts public housing projects, inspired by blues clubs on Beale St, and discovered at Sun Studio. In the spring of 1957, the already-famous 22-year-old spent $100,000 on a Colonial-style mansion, named Graceland by its previous owners.

The King himself had the place, ahem, redecorated in 1974. With a 15ft couch, fake waterfall, yellow vinyl walls and green shag-carpet ceiling, it's a virtual textbook of ostentatious '70s style. You'll begin your tour at the visitor plaza on the other side of Elvis Presley Blvd. Book ahead in the busy season to ensure a prompt tour time. The basic self-guided mansion tour comes with an engaging headset audio narration. Pay $4 extra to see the car museum, and two custom planes (check out the blue-and-gold private bathroom on the *Lisa Marie*, a Convair 880 Jet).

Priscilla Presley (who divorced Elvis in 1973) opened Graceland to tours in 1982, and now millions come to pay homage to the King, who died here (in the upstairs bathroom) from heart failure in 1977. Throngs of fans still weep at his grave, next to the swimming pool out the back. Graceland is 9 miles south of Downtown on US 51 (Elvis Presley Blvd). You can also hop on the free shuttle from Sun Studio. Parking costs $10.

NEED TO KNOW

☏ 901-332-3322; www.elvis.com; Elvis Presley Blvd/US 51; tours house only adult/child $33/30, full tour $37/33; ⊙ 9am-5pm Mon-Sat, to 4pm Sun, shorter hours & closed Tue winter; P

gospel churches, decaying buildings – on foot or in his pink Cadillac.

Blues City Tours
Bus Tour

(☏901-522-9229; www.bluescitytours.com; adult/child from $24/19) A variety of themed bus tours, including an Elvis tour and a Memphis music tour.

 ## Sleeping

Talbot Heirs
Guesthouse $$

(☏901-527-9772, 800-955-3956; www.talbot-house.com; 99 S 2nd St; ste from $130; ❄️🛜) Inconspicuously located on the 2nd floor of a busy Downtown street, this cheerful guesthouse is one of Memphis' best-kept secrets. Spacious suites are more like hip studio apartments than hotel rooms, with Asian rugs and funky local artwork, and kitchens are stocked with snacks.

Sleep Inn at Court Square
Hotel $$

(☏901-522-9700; www.sleepinn.com; 400 N Front St; r from $114; P❄️🛜) Our pick of the cheaper Downtown digs, this stubby stucco box, part of a jumble of corporate sleeps, has pleasant, airy rooms with flatscreen TVs.

Heartbreak Hotel
Hotel $$

(☏877-777-0606, 901-332-1000; www.elvis.com/epheartbreakhotel/; 3677 Elvis Presley Blvd; d from $120; ❄️@🛜🏊) At the end of Lonely St (seriously) across from Graceland, this basic hotel is tarted up with all things Elvis.

 ## Eating

Gus's World Famous Fried Chicken
Chicken $

(☏901-527-4877; 310 S Front St; mains $6-9; ◷11am-9pm Sun-Thu, to 10pm Fri & Sat) Fried-chicken connisseurs across the globe dream about the gossamer-light fried chicken at this neon-lit eatery. On busy nights, waits can top an hour.

Alcenia's
Southern $

(www.alcenias.com; 317 N Main St; mains $6-9; ◷11am-5pm Tue-Fri, 9am-3pm Sat) The lunch menu at this funky little gold- and purple-painted cafe rotates daily – look for fried chicken and catfish, melt-in-your-mouth spiced cabbage and an eggy custard pie.

Sun Studio (p228)

Charlie Vergos' Rendezvous
Barbecue **$$**

(☎901-523-2746; www.hogsfly.com; 52 S 2nd St; mains $10-20; ⏰4:30-10:30pm Tue-Thu, 11am-11pm Fri, from 11:30am Sat) Tucked in an alleyway off Union Ave, this subterranean institution sells delicious barbecue. With a superb, no-nonsense wait staff, and walls plastered with historic memorabilia, eating here is an event. Expect a wait.

Majestic Grille
Continental **$$$**

(☎901-522-8555; www.majesticgrille.com; 145 S Main St; mains $17-36; ⏰11am-10pm Mon-Thu, to 11pm Fri & Sat, to 9pm Sun) Set in an old silent-movie theater, with a handsome dark-wood dining room, the Majestic cooks up classic continental fare, including seared tuna and grilled pork tenderloin, and four varieties of hand-cut filet mignon. It's near Beale St.

Bar DKDC
Gastropub **$**

(www.facebook.com/BARDKDC; 964 S Cooper St; dishes $3-8; ⏰5pm-3am Wed-Sun) It's all tapas here, and the food is cheap and flavorful. Try the sugarcane shrimp, the island jerk fish club sandwich or guava glazed pork chop.

Cozy Corner
Barbecue **$$**

(www.cozycornerbbq.com; 745 N Pkwy; mains $7-12; ⏰11am-9pm Tue-Sat) Slouch in a torn vinyl booth and devour an entire barbecued Cornish game hen, the house specialty at this cult favorite. Save room for sweet-potato pie.

Soul Fish Cafe
Seafood **$$**

(☎901-755-6988; www.soulfishcafe.com; 862 S Cooper St; mains $10-13; ⏰11am-10pm Mon-Sat, to 9pm Sun) A cute cinderblock cafe in the Cooper-Young neighborhood, known for delectable po'boys, fried fish plates and, in a departure, some rather indulgent cakes.

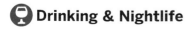 Drinking & Nightlife

Beale St is the obvious spot for live blues, rock and jazz. For a more local crowd head to the hip Cooper-Young neighborhood. For live music, check the **Mem-phis Flyer** (www.memphisflyer.com) online calendar.

Detour:
Jack Daniel's Distillery

The irony of this **distillery** (www.jackdaniels.com; 182 Lynchburg Hwy; ⏰9am-4:30pm) **FREE** being in a 'dry county' is lost on no one – though local liquor laws dictate that no hard stuff can be sold within county lines, the distillery does give small samples on its free hour-long tours. For $10 you can take a two-hour Distillery Tour (book in advance), where you'll get a more generous sample. This is the oldest registered distillery in the US – the folks at Jack Daniels have been dripping whiskey through layers of charcoal then aging it in oak barrels since 1866. It's located off Hwy 55 in tiny Lynchburg.

Earnestine & Hazel's
Bar

(531 S Main St) One of the great dive bars in Memphis has a 2nd floor full of rusty bedsprings and claw-foot tubs, remnants of its brothel past. The Soul Burger, the bar's only food, is the stuff of legend.

Cove
Bar

(www.thecovememphis.com; 2559 Broad Ave) This hipsterish dive rocks a nautical theme while serving retro cocktails and upscale bar snacks (oysters on the half shell, chips with fresh anchovies).

⭐ Entertainment

Wild Bill's
Blues

(1580 Vollentine Ave; ⏰10pm-late Fri & Sat) Order a 40oz beer and a basket of wings then sit back to watch some of the greatest blues acts in Memphis.

Hi-Tone Cafe
Live Music

(www.hitonememphis.com; 1913 Poplar Ave) Near Overton Park, this unassuming little dive is one of the city's best places to hear live local bands and touring indie acts.

Rum Boogie
Blues

(912-528-0150; www.rumboogie.com; 182 Beale St) Huge, popular and loud, this Cajun-themed Beale club hops every night to the tunes of a tight house blues band.

Information

Tennessee State Visitor Center (☎888-633-9099, 901-543-5333; www.memphistravel.com; 119 N Riverside Dr; ⏱9am-5pm Nov-Mar, to 6pm Apr-Oct) Brochures for the whole state.

❶ Getting There & Around

Memphis International Airport (MEM; ☎901-922-8000; www.memphisairport.org; 2491 Winchester Rd) is 12 miles southeast of Downtown via I-55; taxis to Downtown cost about $30. **Memphis Area Transit Authority** (MATA; www.matatransit.com; 444 N Main St; fares $1.75)

operates local buses; buses 2 and 32 go to the airport.

MATA's vintage **trolleys** ($1, every 12 minutes) ply Main St and Front St downtown. Greyhound (www.greyhound.com; 203 Union Ave) is right Downtown, as is Central Station (www.amtrak.com; 545 S Main St), the Amtrak terminal.

NASHVILLE

For country-music fans and wannabe songwriters all over the world, a trip to Nashville is the ultimate pilgrimage. Its many musical attractions range from the Country Music Hall of Fame to the revered Grand Ole Opry to Jack White's niche of a record label. It also has a lively university community, some excellent down-home grub, and some seriously kitschy souvenirs.

Sights

DOWNTOWN

The historic 2nd Ave N business area is the heart of the **District**, with shops, restaurants, underground saloons and nightclubs. It's a bit like the French Quarter meets Hollywood Boulevard drenched in bourbon and country twang. Two blocks west, **Printers Alley** is a narrow cobblestoned lane known for its nightlife since the 1940s. Along the Cumberland River, **Riverfront Park** is a landscaped promenade, featuring **Fort Nashborough** (1st Ave), a replica of the city's original outpost.

Country Music Hall of Fame & Museum
Museum

(www.countrymusichalloffame.com; 222 5th Ave S; adult/child $22/14, audio tour additional $2, Studio B 1hr tour adult/child $13/11; ⏱9am-5pm) 'Honor Thy Music' is the catchphrase

Cumberland River, Nashville
RICHARD CUMMINS/GETTY IMAGES ©

Detour:
Clarksdale

If you come here for anything, come for the love of music. Clarksdale is the real deal. It hosts a healthy blues-lovin' tourist industry, but what keeps it genuine is its residents: they adore music. It's no surprise that big-name blues bands still honor Clarksdale on the weekends and that music museums sprinkle the area.

For a primer on all things blues-worthy, visit the **Delta Blues Museum** (www.deltabluesmuseum.org; 1 Blues Alley; adult/senior & student $7/5; ◷9am-5pm Mon-Sat), which displays a small but well-presented collection of memorabilia. The shrine to delta legend Muddy Waters includes the actual cabin where he grew up.

Clarksdale's best place to see blues singers howl is **Red's** (☏662-627-3166; 395 Sunflower Ave; cover $10; ◷live music 9pm Fri & Sat), a juke joint, with neon-red mood lighting and general soulful disintegration. For blues in more polished evirons, we recommend Morgan Freeman's **Ground Zero** (www.groundzerobluesclub.com; 0 Blues Alley; ◷11am-2pm Mon & Tue, to 11pm Wed & Thu, to 1am Fri & Sat). Bands take the stage Wednesday to Saturday.

Rust (www.rustclarksdale.com; 218 Delta Ave; mains $12-36; ◷6-9pm Tue-Thu, to 10pm Fri & Sat) serves Southern comfort food amid junkyard-chic decor – a good place for a bite before a show. The **Shack Up Inn** (☏662-624-8329; www.shackupinn.com; Hwy 49; d $75-165; P ❄ ☎) evokes the blues like no other: guests stay in refurbished sharecropper cabins or the creatively renovated cotton gin.

Two big music fests are worth planning a trip around. The **Juke Joint Festival** (www.jukejointfestival.com; tickets $15; ◷Apr) features more than 100 music events spread over three days, and the **Sunflower River Blues and Gospel Festival** (www.sunflowerfest.org; ◷Aug) draws big names and good cheer to the delta.

---

of this monumental museum, reflecting the near-biblical importance of country music to Nashville's soul. Gaze at Patsy Cline's cocktail gown, Hank Williams' guitar, Elvis' gold Cadillac and Conway Twitty's yearbook picture (back when he was Harold Jenkins).

Ryman Auditorium
Historic Building

(www.ryman.com; 116 5th Ave N; self-guided tour adult/child $13/6.50, backstage tour $17/10.50; ◷9am-4pm) The so-called 'Mother Church of Country Music' has hosted a laundry list of 20th-century performers, from Martha Graham to Elvis to Katherine Hepburn to Bob Dylan. The soaring brick tabernacle was built in 1890 by wealthy riverboat captain Thomas Ryman to house religious revivals, and watching a show from one of its 2000 seats can still be described as a spiritual experience.

WEST END

Along West End Ave, starting at 21st Ave, sits prestigious **Vanderbilt University**, founded in 1883 by railway magnate Cornelius Vanderbilt. The 330-acre campus buzzes with some 12,000 students, and student culture influences much of Midtown's vibe.

Parthenon
Park, Gallery

(www.parthenon.org; 2600 West End Ave; adult/child $6/4; ◷9am-4:30pm Tue-Sat, plus Sun summer) Yes, that is indeed a reproduction Athenian Parthenon sitting in **Centennial Park**. Originally built in 1897 for Tennessee's Centennial Exposition and rebuilt in 1930 due to popular demand, the full-scale plaster copy of the 438 BC original now houses an art museum with a collection of American paintings and a 42ft statue of the Greek goddess Athena.

Detour:
Plantations near Nashville

The former home of seventh president Andrew Jackson, **Hermitage** (☏615-889-2941; www.thehermitage.com; 4580 Rachel's Lane; adult/child $19/14; ☺8:30am-5pm Apr-Oct, 9am-4:30pm Oct-Mar), lies 15 miles east of downtown. The 1000-acre plantation is a peek into what life was like for a mid-South gentleman farmer in the 19th century. Tour the Federal-style brick mansion, now a furnished house museum with costumed interpreters, and see Jackson's original 1804 log cabin and the old slave quarters (Jackson was a lifelong supporter of slavery, at times owning up to 150 slaves; a special exhibit tells their stories).

The Harding-Jackson family began raising thoroughbreds at **Belle Meade Plantation** (☏615-356-0501; www.bellemeadeplantation.com; 5025 Harding Pike; adult/student 13-18 yr/child under 13 yr $16/10/8; ☺9am-5pm Mon-Sat, 11am-5pm Sun), 6 miles west of Nashville, in the early 1800s. Nearly every horse entered in the Kentucky Derby in the past six years is a descendant of Belle Meade's studly sire, Bonnie Scotland, who died in 1880. Yes, Bonnie can be a boy's name! The 1853 mansion is open to visitors, as are various interesting outbuildings, including a model slave cabin.

MUSIC VALLEY

This suburban tourist zone is about 10 miles northeast of downtown at Hwy 155/Briley Pkwy, exits 11 and 12B, and reachable by bus.

Grand Ole Opry House　Museum
(☏615-871-6779; www.opry.com; 2802 Opryland Dr; tours adult/child $18.50/13.50; ☺museum 10:30am-6pm Mar-Dec) This unassuming modern brick building seats 4400 for the **Grand Ole Opry (tickets adult $28-88, child $18-53)** on Friday and Saturday from March to November. Guided backstage tours are offered daily by reservation – book online up to two weeks ahead. Across the plaza, a small, free **museum** tells the story of the Opry with wax characters, colorful costumes and dioramas.

🕐 Tours

NashTrash　Bus Tour
(☏615-226-7300; www.nashtrash.com; 900 8th Ave N; 1½hr tours $35) The big-haired 'Jugg Sisters' lead a campy frolic through the risqué side of Nashville history while guests sip BYO booze on the big pink bus. Buy well ahead.

General Jackson Showboat　Boat Tour
(☏615-458-3900; www.generaljackson.com; tours from $45) Paddleboat sightseeing cruises of varying length on the Cumberland River, some with music and food.

Sleeping

Nashville Downtown Hostel　Hostel $
(☏615-497-1208; www.nashvillehostel.com; 177 1st Ave N; dm/r $28/85; P) Well located and up to the minute in style and function, this place is set with wood-floored rooms with timber columns and beamed ceilings. The lively basement lounge is a great spot to meet other travelers.

Gaylord Opryland Hotel　Resort $$
(☏866-972-6779, 615-889-1000; www.gaylordhotels.com; 2800 Opryland Dr; r from $149; P✳@☎☝) This whopping 2881-room hotel is a universe unto itself. Why set foot outdoors when you could ride a paddleboat along an artificial river, eat sushi beneath a faux waterfall in an indoor garden, shop for bolo ties in a model 19th-century town, or sip scotch in an antebellum-style

mansion, all *inside* the hotel's three massive glass atriums.

Eating

Prince's Hot Chicken
Fried Chicken **$**

(123 Ewing Dr; quarter/half/whole chicken $5/9/18; ⏱noon-10pm Tue-Thu, to 4am Fri, 2pm-4am Sat; **P**) Cayenne-rubbed 'hot chicken,' fried to succulent perfection and served on a piece of white bread with a side of pickles, is Nashville's unique contribution to the culinary universe.

Marché Artisan Foods
Bistro **$$**

(www.marcheartisanfoods.com; 1000 Main St; mains $9-16; ⏱8am-9pm Tue-Sat, to 4pm Sun) In rapidly gentrifying Five Points, this lovely and bright glass box serves up farm-to-table plates like a corned-beef Ruben on marble rye, a lamb burger and a warm broccoli salad with brown rice.

Monell's
Southern **$$**

(📞615-248-4747; www.monellstn.com; 1235 6th Ave N; all you can eat $13-19; ⏱10:30am-2pm Mon, 10:30am-2pm & 5-8:30pm Tue-Fri, 8:30am-3pm & 5-8:30pm Sat, 8:30am-4pm Sun) In an old brick house just north of the District, Monell's is beloved for down-home Southern food served family style.

Tavern
Gastropub **$$**

(www.mstreetnashville.com; 1904 Broadway; mains $9-22; ⏱11am-1am Mon-Thu, to 3am Fri, 10am-3am Sat, to 1am Sun) This Music Row gastropub does everything from a Thai Cobb salad to wood-grilled artichokes to Aussie-style meat pies to steak and seafood. All affordably priced.

City House
New Southern **$$$**

(📞615-736-5838; www.cityhousenashville.com; 1222 4th Ave N; mains

$15-24; ⏱5-10pm Mon & Wed-Sat, to 9pm Sun) This signless brick building in Nashville's gentrifying Germantown hides one of the city's best restaurants. The food, cooked in an open kitchen in the warehouse-like space, is a crackling bang-up of Italy meets New South.

Southern
Bar & Grill **$$$**

(www.thesouthernnashville.com; 150 3rd Ave; lunch mains $11-15, dinner mains $14-48; ⏱7:30am-10pm Mon-Thu, to midnight Fri, 10am-midnight Sat, 10am-10pm Sun) A brand-new eatery in the heart of downtown, Southern has a wide and enticing menu of oysters, craft beers, gourmet burgers, fish tacos and double-smoked pork chops, plus a plethora of steaks.

Drinking & Nightlife

3 Crow Bar
Bar

(www.3crowbar.com; 1024 Woodland St; ⏱11am-3am; 📶) Garage-door windows roll open onto this truly divey cinderblock cavern with ample table and bar space in Five Points. This is the kinda joint you can lay

Shop sign, Nashville
PETER PTSCHELINZEW/GETTY IMAGES ©

back and enjoy not for a few minutes, but a few hours. Great back patio.

Whiskey Kitchen   Pub
(www.whiskeykitchen.com; 118 12th Ave S) In the Gulch, an up-and-coming patch of rehabbed warehouses adjacent to downtown, this neo-Southern gastropub with a mile-long whiskey menu attracts an upmarket crowd.

Soulshine   Pub
(www.soulshinepizza.com; 1907 Division St; ☉11am-1am Sun-Thu, to 2am Fri & Sat) A two-story, concrete-floor, brickhouse pub and pizzeria in Midtown. Bands rock the wide rooftop patio on weekend nights.

⭐ Entertainment

Station Inn   Bluegrass
(📞615-255-3307; www.stationinn.com; 402 12th Ave S; ☉open mic 7pm, live bands 9pm) Sit at one of the small cocktail tables, squeezed together on the worn-wood floor in this beer-only dive, illuminated with stage

lights, and neon signs, and behold the lightning fingers of bluegrass savants.

Bluebird Cafe   Club
(📞615-383-1461; www.bluebirdcafe.com; 4104 Hillsboro Rd; cover free-$15; ☉shows 6:30pm & 9:30pm) It's in a strip mall in suburban South Nashville, but don't let that fool you: some of the best original singer-songwriters in country music have graced this tiny stage.

Tootsie's Orchid Lounge   Honky-Tonk
(📞615-726-7937; www.tootsies.net; 422 Broadway; ☉10am-late) FREE The most venerated of the downtown honky-tonks, Tootsie's is a blessed dive oozing boot-stomping, hillbilly, beer-soaked grace.

Robert's Western World   Honky-Tonk
(www.robertswesternworld.com; 416 Broadway; ☉11am-2am) FREE Buy a pair of boots, a beer or a burger at Robert's, a longtime favorite on the strip. Music starts at 11am and goes all night.

ℹ️ Information

Nashville Visitors Information Center
(📞800-657-6910, 615-259-4747; www.visitmusiccity.com; 501 Broadway, Sommet Center; ☉8:30am-5:30pm) Pick up free city maps here at the glass tower. Great online resource.

ℹ️ Getting There & Around

Nashville International Airport (BNS; 📞615-275-1675; www.nashintl.com) is 8 miles east of town. Taxis charge a flat rate of $25 to $27 to downtown or Opryland.

Greyhound (www.greyhound.com; 709 5th Ave S) is downtown.

Country Music Hall of Fame (p232)
DANITA DELIMONT/GETTY IMAGES ©

Scenic Drive: Nashville's Country Tracks

About 25 miles southwest of Nashville off Hwy 100, drivers pick up the **Natchez Trace Pkwy**, which leads 444 miles southwest to Natchez, MS. This northern section is one of its most attractive stretches, with broad-leafed trees leaning together to form an arch over the winding road. There are three primitive campsites along the way, free and available on a first-come, first-served basis. Near the parkway entrance, stop at the landmark **Loveless Cafe** (📞 615-646-9700; www.lovelesscafe. com; 8400 Hwy 100 , Nashville, TN 37221), a 1950s roadhouse famous for its biscuits with homemade preserves, country ham and ample portions of Southern fried chicken.

GREAT SMOKY MOUNTAINS NATIONAL PARK

Spread across Tennessee and North Carolina, the Great Smoky Mountains National Park is a moody, magical place. Covering 815 square miles, it is one of the world's most diverse areas. Landscapes range from deep, dim spruce forest to sunny meadows carpeted with daisies and Queen Anne's lace to wide, coffee-brown rivers. There's ample hiking and camping, and opportunities for horseback riding, bike rental and fly-fishing.

Although it attracts some 10 million annual visitors, 95% of visitors never venture further than 100 yards from their cars, so it's easy to leave the teeming masses behind.

ℹ️ Information

Stop by a visitor center to pick up a park map and the free *Smokies Guide*. The park's three interior visitor centers are Sugarlands Visitor Center (📞 865-436-1291; www.nps.gov/grsm; 🕑 8am-7pm Jun-Aug, hours vary Sep-May), at the park's northern entrance near Gatlinburg; Cades Cove Visitor Center (📞 877-444-6777; 🕑 9am-7pm Apr-Aug, earlier Sep-Mar), halfway up Cades Cove Loop Rd, off Hwy 441 near the Gatlinburg entrance; and Oconaluftee Visitor Center (📞 general information 865-436-1200, visitor center 865-436-1200; Hwy 441; 🕑 8am-7pm Jun-Aug, hours vary Sep-May), at the park's southern entrance near Cherokee in North Carolina.

👁️ Sights & Activities

Newfound Gap Rd/Hwy 441 is the only thoroughfare that crosses Great Smoky Mountains National Park, winding through the mountains from Gatlinburg, TN, to the town of Cherokee, NC, in the southeast.

NORTH CAROLINA SIDE

Near the town of Cherokee, the **Mountain Farm Museum** (📞 423-436-1200; www. nps.gov/grsm; 🕑 dawn-dusk) is a restored 19th-century farmstead, complete with barn, blacksmith shop and smokehouse, assembled from original buildings from different parts of the park. Just north is the 1886 **Mingus Mill** (self-guided tours free; 🕑 9am-5pm daily mid-Mar–mid-Nov, plus 9am-5pm Thanksgiving weekend), a turbine-powered mill that still grinds wheat and corn much as it always has.

To the east, remote **Cataloochee Valley** has several historic buildings to wander through and is a prime location for elk and black bears.

Right on the Tennessee–North Carolina border, you can drive right up to the dizzying heights of **Clingmans Dome**, the third-highest mountain east of the Mississippi, with futuristic observation tower.

There are some great hikes, including the following:

○ **Big Creek Trail** Hike an easy 2 miles to Mouse Creek Falls; the trailhead's near I-40 on the park's northeastern edge.

○ **Boogerman Trail** Moderate 7-mile loop passing old farmsteads; accessible via Cove Creek Rd.

○ **Shuckstack Tower** Starting at massive Fontana Dam, climb 3.5 miles for stunning views from an old fire tower.

TENNESSEE SIDE

The remains of the 19th-century settlement at **Cades Cove** are some of the park's most popular sights, as evidenced by the teeth-grinding summer traffic jams on the loop road

Mt LeConte offers terrific hiking, as well as the only non-camping accommodations, **LeConte Lodge** (☎ 865-429-5704; www.lecontelodge.com; cabins per person adult/4-12yr $126/85). The only way to get to the lodge's rustic, electricity-free cabins is via an 8-mile uphill slog. It's so popular you need to reserve up to a year in advance.

CHARLESTON

This lovely city will embrace you with the warmth and hospitality of an old and dear friend – who died in the 1700s. We jest, but the cannons, cemeteries and carriage rides do conjure an earlier era. And that historic romanticism, along with the food and Southern graciousness, is what makes Charleston one of the world's favorite cities and one of the most popular tourist destinations in the South.

◉ Sights

HISTORIC DISTRICT

The quarter south of Beaufain and Hasell Sts has the bulk of the antebellum mansions, shops, bars and cafes. At the southernmost tip of the peninsula are the antebellum mansions of the Battery.

Gateway Walk Churches
Long a culturally diverse city, Charleston gave refuge to persecuted French Protestants, Baptists and Jews over the years and earned the nickname the 'Holy City' for its abundance of houses of worship. The Gateway Walk, a little-known garden path between Archdale St and Philadelphia Alley, connects four of the city's most beautiful historic churches: the white-columned **St John's Lutheran Church** (5 Clifford St); the Gothic Revival

Horse-drawn wagon tour of Charleston

DENNIS K JOHNSON/GETTY IMAGES ©

Scenic Drive: Blue Ridge Parkway

Commissioned by President Franklin D Roosevelt as a Depression-era public-works project, the Blue Ridge Parkway traverses the southern Appalachians from Virginia's Shenandoah National Park at Mile 0 to the Great Smoky Mountains National Park at Mile 469.

North Carolina's piece of the parkway twists and turns for 262 miles of killer alpine vistas. The **National Park Service** (NPS; www.nps.gov/blri; ☾May-Oct) runs campgrounds and visitor centers but note that restrooms and gas stations are few and far between.

Parkway highlights and campgrounds include the following, from the Virginia border south:

Cumberland Knob (Mile 217.5) NPS visitor center; easy walk to the knob.

Doughton Park (Mile 241.1) Trails and camping.

Blowing Rock (Mile 291.8) Small town named for a craggy, commercialized cliff that offers great views.

Moses H Cone Memorial Park (Mile 294.1) A lovely old estate with carriage trails and a craft shop.

Julian Price Memorial Park (Mile 296.9) Camping.

Grandfather Mountain (Mile 305.1) Hugely popular for its mile-high pedestrian 'swinging bridge.'

Linville Falls (Mile 316.4) Short hiking trails to the falls; campsites.

Little Switzerland (Mile 334) Old-style mountain resort.

Mt Mitchell State Park (Mile 355.5) Highest peak east of the Mississippi (6684ft); hiking and camping.

Craggy Gardens (Mile 364) Hiking trails exploding with rhododendron blossoms in summer.

Folk Art Center (Mile 382) High-end Appalachian crafts for sale.

Blue Ridge Parkway Visitor Center (Mile 384) Inspiring film, interactive map, trail information.

Mt Pisgah (Mile 408.8) Hiking, camping, restaurant, inn.

Graveyard Fields (Mile 418) Short hiking trails to waterfalls.

Unitarian Church (4 Archdale St); the striking Romanesque **Circular Congregational Church** (150 Meeting St), originally founded in 1681; and **St Philip's Church** (146 Church St), with its picturesque steeple and 17th-century graveyard, parts of which were once reserved for 'strangers and transient white persons.'

Old Slave Mart Museum   Museum (www.nps.gov/nr/travel/charleston/osm.htm; 6 Chalmers St; adult/child $7/5; ☾9am-5pm Mon-Sat) African men, women and children were once auctioned off here; it's now a museum of South Carolina's shameful past. Text-heavy exhibits illuminate the slave experience; the few artifacts, such as leg shackles, are especially chilling.

Aiken-Rhett House   Historic Building (www.historiccharleston.org; 48 Elizabeth St; admission $10; ☾10am-5pm Mon-Sat, 2-5pm Sun) The only surviving urban plantation, this house gives a fascinating glimpse into antebellum life. The role of slaves is also presented, and you can wander into their dorm-style quarters behind the main house.

Old Exchange & Provost Dungeon   Historic Building
(www.oldexchange.org; 122 E Bay St; adult/child $8/4; 9am-5pm;) Kids love the dungeon, used as a prison for pirates and for American patriots held by the British during the Revolutionary War. Costumed guides lead the dungeon tours.

The Battery & White Point Gardens   Garden
Stroll past cannons and statues of military heroes in the gardens, then walk the promenade and look for Fort Sumter.

Rainbow Row   Neighborhood
Around the corner from White Point Gardens, this stretch of lower E Bay St is one of the most photographed areas of town for its candy-colored houses.

MARION SQUARE

Formerly home to the state weapons arsenal, this pleasant 10-acre park has various monuments and an excellent Saturday farmers market.

AQUARIUM WHARF

Aquarium Wharf surrounds pretty Liberty Sq and is a great place to stroll and watch the tugboats guiding ships into the fourth-largest container port in the US. The wharf is the main embarkation point for tours to Fort Sumter.

Fort Sumter   Historic Site
The first shots of the Civil War rang out at Fort Sumter, on a pentagon-shaped island in the harbor. A Confederate stronghold, the fort was shelled to bits by Union forces from 1863 to 1865. A few original guns and fortifications give a feel for the momentous history. The only way to get here is by **boat tours** (boat tour 843-722-2628, park 843-883-3123; www.nps.gov/fosu; adult/child $18/11), which depart from 340 Concord St and from Patriot's Point in Mt Pleasant.

South Carolina Aquarium   Aquarium
(www.scaquarium.org; 100 Aquarium Wharf; adult/child $25/15; 9am-5pm Mar-Aug, to 4pm Sep-Feb;) Ticket prices are steep, so this riverside aquarium is best for a rainy day. Exhibits showcase the state's diverse aquatic life. The highlight is the 42ft Great Ocean Tank, which teems with sharks and alien-looking puffer fish.

 Tours

Culinary Tours of Charleston   Culinary
(843-722-8687; www.culinarytoursof charleston.com; 2½hr tour $42) You'll likely sample grits, pralines, barbecue and more on this walking tour of Charleston's restaurants and markets.

Adventure Harbor Tours   Boat
(843-442-9455; www.adventureharbortours. com; adult/child $55/30) Runs fun trips to uninhabited Morris Island, great for shelling.

Charleston Footprints   Walking
(843-478-4718; www.charlestonfootprints. com; 2hr tour $20) A highly rated walking tour of historical Charleston sights.

Sleeping

B&Bs fill up quickly, so try using a local agency such as **Historic Charleston B&B** (843-722-6606; www.historiccharlestonbed andbreakfast.com; 57 Broad St).

Indigo Inn   Boutique $$
(843-577-5900; www.indigoinn.com; 1 Maiden Ln; r $171) This place has a prime location in the middle of the historic district and an oasis-like private courtyard, where guests can enjoy free wine and cheese by the fountain. Decor gives a nod to the 18th century, and the beds are quite comfy.

1837 Bed & Breakfast   B&B $$
(877-723-1837, 843-723-7166; www.1837bb. com; 126 Wentworth St; r incl breakfast $129-169;) Close to the College of Charleston, this B&B may bring to mind

the home of your eccentric, antique-loving aunt. The 1837 has nine charmingly overdecorated rooms, including three in the old brick carriage house.

Anchorage Inn
Inn **$$**

(☏843-723-8300; www.anchoragecharleston.com; 26 Vendue Range; r from $159; ❄❀) One of the best-value examples of Charleston's intimate Historic District inns. Its rooms have the dark and small feel of ship's quarters but they're plenty plush.

Ansonborough Inn
Hotel **$$$**

(☏800-522-2073; www.ansonboroughinn.com; 21 Hasell St; r incl breakfast $209-259; P❄@❀) A central atrium done up with burnished pine, exposed beams and nautical-themed oil paintings makes this intimate Historic District hotel feel like an antique sailing ship. Huge guest rooms mix old and new, with worn leather couches, high ceilings and flatscreen TVs. Complimentary wine and cheese social from 5pm to 6pm.

Eating

The Ordinary
Seafood **$$**

(☏843-414-7060; www.eattheordinary.com; 544 King St; small plates $5-25, large $24-28; ◷from 3pm Tue-Sun) The Ordinary is a buzzy seafood hall and oyster bar inside a cavernous 1927 bank building.

Hominy Grill
New Southern **$$**

(www.hominygrill.com; 207 Rutledge Ave; mains $8-18; ◷7:30am-9pm Mon-Fri, 9am-9pm Sat, to 3pm Sun; ✒) Slightly off the beaten path, this neighborhood cafe serves modern, vegetarian-friendly Lowcountry cuisine in an old barbershop. The shady patio is tops for brunch.

Husk
New Southern **$$$**

(☏843-577-2500; www.huskrestaurant.com; 76 Queen St; brunch & lunch $10-16, dinner $27-30; ◷11:30am-2:30pm Mon-Sat, 5:30-10pm Sun-Thu, 5:30-11pm Fri & Sat, brunch 10am-2:30pm Sun) Everything – *everything* – on the menu at this buzzed-about restaurant is grown or raised in the South, from the jalapeño marmalade-topped Georgia corn soup to the yuzu-scented Cooper River oysters, to the local lard featured in the 'pork butter'

Linn Cove viaduct, Blue Ridge Parkway (p239)

If You Like...
Southern Cooking

If you like the celebrated New South cuisine at Husk (p241), make time to dine at these other great Charleston restaurants.

1 FIG

(☎843-805-5900; www.eatatfig.com; 232 Meeting St; mains $28-31; ⏰5:30-10:30pm Mon-Thu, to 11pm Fri & Sat) Foodies swoon over inspired nouvelle-Southern fare like crispy pig's trotters (that means 'feet' – local and hormone-free, of course) with celery-root remoulade in this rustic-chic dining room.

2 S.N.O.B.

(☎843-723-3424; www.mavericksouthernkitchens.com; 192 E Bay St; lunch $10-14, dinner $18-34; ⏰11:30am-3pm Mon-Fri, 5:30pm-late nightly) The cheeky name (it stands for 'slightly north of Broad,' as in Broad St) reflects the anything-goes spirit of this upscale-casual spot. It draws raves for its eclectic menu, filled with treats such as barbecue tuna with fried oysters and sautéed squab breast over South Carolina rice.

brought out with the restaurant's addictive sesame-seed rolls.

ⓘ Information

Visitor Center (☎843-853-8000; www.charlestoncvb.com; 375 Meeting St; ⏰8:30am-5pm) Find help with accommodations and tours or watch a half-hour video on Charleston history in this spacious renovated warehouse.

ⓘ Getting There & Around

Charleston International Airport (CHS; ☎843-767-7000; www.chs-airport.com; 5500 International Blvd) is 12 miles outside of town in North Charleston, with 124 daily flights to 17 destinations.

The Greyhound station (3610 Dorchester Rd) and the Amtrak train station (4565 Gaynor Ave) are both in North Charleston.

CARTA (www.ridecarta.com; fare $1.75) runs city-wide buses; the free DASH streetcars do three loop routes from the visitor center.

SAVANNAH

Like a Southern belle with an electric blue streak in her hair, this grand historic town revolves around formal antebellum architecture and the revelry of local students from Savannah College of Art & Design (SCAD). It sits alongside the Savannah River, about 18 miles from the coast, amid Lowcountry swamps and mammoth live oak trees dripping with Spanish moss. With its colonial mansions, and beautiful squares, Savannah preserves its past with pride and grace. However, unlike its sister city of Charleston, SC, which retains its reputation as a dignified and refined cultural center, Savannah is a little gritty, lived in, and real.

◉ Sights & Activities

The Central Park of Savannah is a sprawling rectangular green space called **Forsyth Park**. The park's beautiful fountain is a quintessential photo op. Savannah's **riverfront** is mostly populated with forgettable shops and cafes, but it's worth a short stroll, as is **Jones St**, among Savannah's prettiest thanks to the mossy oaks that hold hands from either side.

Wormsloe Plantation Historic Site   Plantation
(www.gastateparks.org; 7601 Skidaway Rd; adult/senior/6-17yr/1-5yr $10/9/4.50/1; ⏰9am-5pm Tue-Sun) A short drive from downtown, on the beautiful **Isle of Hope**, this is one of the most photographed sites in town. The real draw is the dreamy entrance through a corridor of mossy, ancient oaks that runs for 1.5 miles, known as the **Avenue of the Oaks**.

Owens-Thomas House   Historic Building
(www.telfair.org; 124 Abercorn St; adult/child $15/5; ⏰noon-5pm Mon, 10am-5pm Tue-Sat, 1-5pm Sun) Completed in 1819 by British architect William Jay, this gorgeous villa exemplifies English Regency-style architecture, which is known for its symmetry. The guided tour is fussy, but it delivers interesting trivia about the mansion.

Jepson Center for the Arts
Gallery

(JCA; www.telfair.org; 207 W York St; adult/child $12/5; ☺10am-5pm Mon, Wed, Fri & Sat, to 8pm Thu, noon-5pm Sun; 🚻) Looking pretty darn space-age by Savannah's standards, the JCA focuses on 20th- and 21st-century art. Its contents are modest in size but intriguing. There's also a neat interactive area for kids.

Ralph Mark Gilbert Civil Rights Museum
Museum

(460 Martin Luther King Jr Blvd; adult/senior/child $8/6/4; ☺9am-5pm Tue-Sat) Set in what was once the most successful black-owned bank in America, this private museum focuses on the local history of segregated schools, hotels, hospitals, jobs and lunch counters. Push the buttons at Levy's lunch counter for a stinging dramatization.

Savannah Bike Tours
Cycling

(📞912-704-4043; www.savannahbiketours.com; 41 Habersham St) This outfit offers two-hour bike tours on its fleet of cruisers.

🛌 Sleeping

Azalea Inn
Inn $$

(📞912-236-2707; www.azaleainn.com; 217 E Huntingdon St; r from $199; P ❄ 🛜 🏊) A humble stunner on a quiet street; we love this sweet canary-yellow historic inn near Forsyth Park. The 10 rooms aren't huge, but are well done with varnished dark-wood floors, crown mouldings, four-post beds and a small dipping pool out back.

Bed & Breakfast Inn
B&B $$

(📞912-238-0518; www.savannahbnb.com; 117 W Gordon St; r $179-229; P ❄ 🛜) Spittin' distance from Savan-

nah's most architecturally diverse square (Monterrey), this is a well-loved, well-worn establishment (meaning it does show its age). Easy to walk right by on a uniform street of 1850 row houses, its location is ideal.

Mansion on Forsyth Park
Hotel $$$

(📞912-238-5158; www.mansiononforsythpark.com; 700 Drayton St; r Sat & Sun $249, Mon–Fri $199; P ❄ @ 🛜 🏊) A choice location and chic design highlight the luxe accommodations on offer at the 18,000-sq-ft Mansion. The best part of the hotel-spa is the amazing local and international art that crowds its walls and hallways, with over 400 pieces in all.

Eating

Wilkes' House
Southern $$

(www.mrswilkes.com; 107 W Jones St; lunch $16; ☺11am-2pm Mon-Fri) The line outside can begin as early as 8am at this first-come, first-served, Southern comfort-food institution. Once the lunch bell rings and

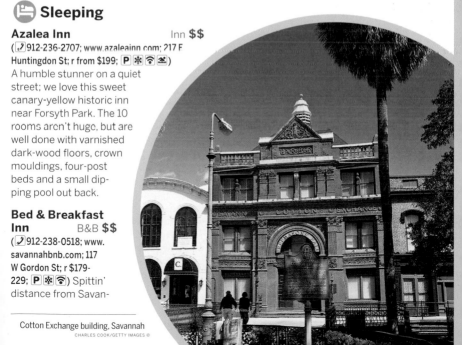

Cotton Exchange building, Savannah
CHARLES COOK/GETTY IMAGES ©

you are seated family-style, the kitchen unloads on you: fried chicken, beef stew, meatloaf, cheese potatoes, collard greens, black-eyed peas, mac 'n' cheese, rutabaga, candied yams, squash casserole, creamed corn *and* biscuits.

Papillote   Cafe $$

(www.papillote-savannah.com; 218 W Broughton St; mains $9-14; ☺10:30am-7pm Wed-Fri, 9:30am-5pm Sat & Sun) One of our favorite new spots in town serves creative yet simple delights, like a chicken curry pot pie, and a baguette stuffed with braised pork, roasted red peppers and melted Swiss. The omelets and brioche French toast for brunch are popular too.

Circa 1875   Bistro $$

(☏912-443-1875; www.circa1875.com; 48 Whitaker St; mains $12-28; ☺bar 5pm-2am, dinner 6-11pm) A gorgeous little bistro downtown with high tin ceilings, turn-of-the-century tiled floors, and a dynamite burger drenched in peppercorn sauce and served with truffle fries. They also do frog legs, escargot, pâté, steak tartare and steak frites, of course.

11 Ten Local   New American $$$

(☏912-790-9000; www.local11ten.com; 1110 Bull St; mains $24-32; ☺6-10pm Mon-Sat) Upscale, sustainable, local, fresh: these elements help create an elegant, well-run restaurant that's – hands down – the best in Savannah.

Olde Pink House   New Southern $$$

(☏912-232-4286; www.plantersinnsavannah. com/savannah-dining.htm; 23 Abercorn St; mains $25-31; ☺11am-10:30pm) This is the place for classic Southern food done upscale. Dine in the slender digs upstairs, or go underground to the fabulous tavern where the piano player rumbles and the room is cozy, funky and perfect.

🍷 Drinking & Nightlife

Rocks on the Roof   Bar

(www.bohemianhotelsavannah.com/dining/ lounge; 102 West Bay St; ☺from 11am; 🛜) The expansive rooftop bar at the Bohemian Hotel is breezy, fun and best when the weather is nice and the firepit is glowing. The views are sensational.

Abe's on Lincoln   Bar

(17 Lincoln St) Ditch the tourists – drink with the locals in dark, dank, all-wood environs. It hosts open-mic nights and occasional live performances.

ℹ️ Information

Visitor Center (☏912-944-0455; www. savannahvisit.com; 301 Martin Luther King Jr Blvd; ☺8:30am–5pm Mon-Fri, 9am-5pm Sat & Sun) Excellent resources and services, plus many privately operated city tours start here. There is also a small tourist-info kiosk at Forsyth Park.

ℹ️ Getting There & Around

The **Savannah/Hilton Head International Airport** (SAV; www.savannahairport.com) is about 5 miles west of downtown off I-16. Taxis from the airport to the Historic District cost a standard $28. The **Amtrak station** (www.amtrak.com; 2611 Seaboard Coastline Dr) is just a few miles west of the Historic District.

CUMBERLAND ISLAND & ST MARYS

An unspoiled paradise, a backpacker's fantasy, a site for day trips or extended stays – it's clear why the family of 19th-century industrialist and philanthropist Andrew Carnegie used Cumberland as a retreat long ago. Most of this southernmost barrier island is now occupied by the **Cumberland Island National Seashore** (www.nps.gov/cuis; admission $4). Almost half of its 36,415 acres consists of marsh, mudflats and tidal creeks. On the ocean side are 16 miles of wide, sandy beach that you might have all to yourself. The island's interior is characterized by maritime forest. Ruins from the Carnegie estate **Dungeness** are astounding, as are the wild turkeys, tiny fiddler crabs and beautiful butterflies. Feral horses roam the island and are a common sight.

The only public access to the island is via boat to/from the quirky, lazy town of **St Marys** (www.stmaryswelcome.com). Convenient and pleasant **ferries** (☎912-882-4335; www.nps.gov/cuis; round trip adult/senior/child $20/18/14) leave from the mainland at the St Marys dock at 9am and 11:45am and return at 10:15am and 4:45pm. Reservations are staunchly recommended well before you arrive, and visitors are required to check in at the **Visitor's Center** (☎912-882-4336; www.nps.gov/cuis; ⊙8am-4:30pm) at the dock at least 30 minutes prior to departure. December through February, the ferry does not operate on Tuesday or Wednesday.

St Marys caters to tourists visiting Cumberland. This tiny, lush one-horse town has a number of comfortable B&Bs, including the lovely **Spencer House Inn** (☎912-882-1872; www.spencerhouseinn.com; 200 Osborne St; r $135-245), circa 1872. When you're hungry, find **Riverside Cafe** (www.riversidecafesaintmarys.com; 106 St Marys Rd; mains $8-18; ⊙11am-9pm Mon-Fri, from 8:30am Sat & Sun), a wonderful Greek diner with sea views.

OUTER BANKS

These fragile ribbons of sand trace the coastline for 100 miles, cut off from the mainland by various sounds and waterways. From north to south, the barrier islands of **Bodie** (pronounced 'Body'), **Roanoke**, **Hatteras** and **Ocracoke**, essentially large sandbars, are linked by bridges and ferries. The far-northern communities of **Corolla** (pronounced kur-*all*-ah, not like the car), **Duck** and **Southern Shores** are former duck-hunting grounds for the northeastern rich, and are quiet and upscale. The nearly contiguous Bodie Island towns of **Kitty Hawk**, **Kill Devil Hills** and **Nags Head** are heavily developed and more populist in nature, with fried-fish joints, drive-thru beer shops, motels and dozens of sandals 'n' sunblock shops. **Roanoke Island**, west of Bodie Island, offers Colonial history and the quaint waterfront town of **Manteo**. Further south, **Hatteras Island** is a protected national seashore with a few teeny villages and a wild, windswept beauty. At the southern end of Outer Banks (aka OBX), wild ponies run free and old salts shuck oysters and weave hammocks

Forsyth Park (p242), Savannah

on **Ocracoke Island**, accessible only by ferry.

A meandering drive down Hwy 12, which connects much of the Outer Banks, is one of the truly great American road trips, whether you come during the stunningly desolate winter months or the sunny summer.

Sights

Corolla, the northernmost town on US 158, is famed for its wild horses. Descendants of Colonial Spanish mustangs, the horses roam the northern dunes, and numerous commercial outfitters go in search of them. The nonprofit **Corolla Wild Horse Fund** (www.corollawildhorses.com; 1129 Corolla Village Rd; 9:30am-5pm Mon-Fri, 10am-4pm Sat Jun-Aug, 10am-4pm Mon-Fri Sep-May) FREE runs a small museum and leads tours.

Currituck Heritage Park
Historic Buildings

(Corolla; dawn-dusk) The sunflower-yellow, art nouveau–style **Whalehead Club** (www.whaleheadclub.org; tours $10; tours 10am-5pm Mon-Sat mid-Mar–Dec, 11am-4pm Dec–mid-Mar),

built in the 1920s as a hunting 'cottage' for a Philadelphia industrialist, is the centerpiece of this manicured park in the village of Corolla. You can also climb the **Currituck Beach Lighthouse** (www.currituckbeachlight.com; adult/child $7/free; 9am-5pm Mar 23-Nov 23), or check out the modern **Outer Banks Center for Wildlife Education** (www.ncwildlife.org/obx; 1160 Village Ln; 9am-4:30pm Mon-Sat) FREE for an interesting film about area history, info on local hiking trails and a life-size marsh diorama.

Wright Brothers National Memorial
Park, Museum

(www.nps.gov/wrbr; Mile 7.5, US 158 Bypass; adult/child $4/free; 9am-5pm, to 6pm summer) Self-taught engineers Wilbur and Orville Wright launched the world's first successful airplane flight on December 17, 1903 (it lasted 12 seconds). Climb a nearby hill, where the brothers conducted earlier glider experiments, for fantastic views of sea and sound. The on-site **Wright Brothers Visitor Center** has a reproduction of the 1903 flyer and exhibits.

Statue of Orville Wright by Stephen Smith, Wright Brothers National Memorial

ANNE RIPPY/GETTY IMAGES ©

Detour:
Ocracoke Island

Crowded in summer and desolate in winter, **Ocracoke Village** (www.ocracokevillage.com) is a funky little community that moves at a slower pace. The village is at the southern end of 14-mile-long Ocracoke Island and is accessed from Hatteras via the free Hatteras–Ocracoke ferry (p249), which lands at the northeastern end of the island.

The older residents still speak in the 17th-century British dialect known as 'Hoi Toide' (their pronunciation of 'high tide') and refer to non-islanders as 'dingbatters.' You can camp by the beach where wild ponies run, have a fish sandwich in a local pub, bike around the village's narrow streets or visit the 1823 **Ocracoke Lighthouse**, the oldest one still operating in North Carolina.

The island makes a terrific day trip from Hatteras Island. You can also stay the night at one of a handful of B&Bs.

For good eats, try the shrimp-basket special on the patio of **Dajio** (dajiorestaurant.com; 305 Irvin Garrish Hwy) from 3pm to 5pm, followed by the lemon berry marscapone. For drinks, savor a Grasshopper latte with chocolate mint and toffee at **Ocracoke Coffee** (www.ocracokecoffee.com; 226 Back Rd) or quaff a beer at **Howard's Pub** (mains $8-23; ⏰11am-10pm early Mar-late Nov, may stay open later on Fri & Sat), a big old wooden pub that's been an island tradition for beer and fried seafood since the 1850s.

Want to get on the water? Take a kayaking tour with **Ride the Wind** (☎252-928-6311; www.surfocracoke.com; 2-2½hr tours adult/child $35/15).

Fort Raleigh National Historic Site
Historic Buildings

In the late 1580s, three decades before the Pilgrims landed at Plymouth Rock, a group of 116 British colonists disappeared without a trace from their Roanoke Island settlement. The fate of the 'Lost Colony' remains one of America's greatest mysteries, and one of the site's star attractions is the beloved musical the **Lost Colony Outdoor Drama** (www.thelostcolony.org; 1409 National Park Dr; adult/child $26.50/9.50; ⏰8pm Mon-Sat Jun-late Aug).

Cape Hatteras National Seashore
Islands

(www.nps.gov/caha) Extending some 70 miles from south of Nags Head to the south end of Ocracoke Island, this fragile necklace of islands remains blissfully free of overdevelopment. Natural attractions include local and migratory water birds, marshes, woodlands, dunes and miles of empty beaches.

Bodie Island Lighthouse
Lighthouse

(☎252-441-5711, ticket reservations 255-475-9417; Bodie Island Lighthouse Rd, Bodie Island; museum free, tours adult/child $8/4; ⏰museum 9am-6pm Jun-Aug, to 5pm Sep-May, tours 9am-5:45pm late Apr-early Oct; 👪) This photogenic lighthouse opened its doors to visitors in 2013. The 156ft-high structure still has its original Fresnel lens, a rarity. Entry is by guided tour.

Pea Island National Wildlife Refuge
Preserve

(☎252-987-2394; www.fws.gov/peaisland; Hwy 12; ⏰visitor center 9am-4pm, trails dawn-dusk) At the northern end of Hatteras Island, this 5834-acre preserve is a birdwatcher's heaven, with two nature trails (one fully disabled-accessible) and 13 miles of unspoiled beach.

Cape Hatteras Lighthouse — Lighthouse

(www.nps.gov/caha; climbing tours adult/child $8/4; ☉visitor center 9am-5pm Sep-May, to 6pm Jun-Aug; lighthouse late Apr-early Oct) At 208ft, this striking black-and-white-striped edifice is the tallest brick lighthouse in the US and is one of North Carolina's most iconic images. Climb the 248 steps and check out the visitor center.

Graveyard of the Atlantic Museum — Museum

(☎252-986-2995; www.graveyardoftheatlantic. com; 59200 Museum Dr; donations appreciated; ☉10am-4pm Mon-Sat Apr-Oct, Mon-Fri Nov-Mar) **FREE** Exhibits about shipwrecks, piracy and salvaged cargo are highlights at this maritime museum at the end of the road.

 Activities

Kitty Hawk Kites — Adventure Sports

(☎877-359-2447, 252-441-2426; www.kittyhawk. com; 3933 S Croatan Hwy; hang gliding $99; bike rental per day $25, kayaks $39-49, stand-up paddleboards $59) Has locations all over OBX offering beginners' kiteboarding lessons (two hours $300) and hang-gliding lessons at Jockey's Ridge State Park (from $99). It also rents kayaks, sailboats, stand-up paddleboards, bikes and inline skates.

Corolla Outback Adventures — Driving Tours

(☎252-453-4484; www.corollaoutback.com; 1150 Ocean Trail, Corolla; 2hr tour adult/child $50/25) Tours bounce you down the beach and through the dunes to see the wild mustangs that roam the northern Outer Banks.

Outer Banks Dive Center — Diving

(☎252-449-8349; www.obxdive.com; 3917 S Croatan Hwy; wreck dives $120) Has NAUI-certified instructors who run everything from basic classes to guided dives of the shipwrecks of the Graveyard of the Atlantic.

Sleeping

Breakwater Inn — Motel $$

(☎252-986-2565; www.breakwaterhatteras. com; 57896 Hwy 12; r/ste inn $159/189, motel $104/134; P ❋ ☎ ☒) The end of the road doesn't look so bad at this three-story inn. Rooms come with kitchenettes and private decks that have views of the sound. Breakwater Inn is near the Hatteras–Ocracoke ferry landing.

Shutters on the Banks — Hotel $$

(☎800-848-3728; www. shuttersonthebanks.com; 405 S Virginia Dare Trail; r $149-289; P ❋ ☎ ☒) This welcoming beachfront hotel exudes a sassy, colorful style. The inviting rooms come with plantation windows and colorful bedspreads as

Ocracoke Lighthouse (p247)
STEVE DUNWELL/GETTY IMAGES ©

well as a flatscreen TV, refrigerator and microwave.

 Eating

The main tourist strip on Bodie Island has the most restaurants and nightlife, but many are only open Memorial Day (last Monday in May) through early fall.

John's Drive-In
Seafood **$**

(www.johnsdrivein.com; 3716 N Virginia Dare Trail; mains $2-13; ⏱11am-5pm Mon, Tue & Thu, to 6pm Fri-Sun May-Sep) A Kitty Hawk institution for perfectly fried baskets of 'dolphin' (mahimahi) and rockfish, to be eaten at outdoor picnic tables and washed down with one of hundreds of possible milkshake varieties.

Kill Devil Grill
Seafood**$$**

(☎252-449-8181; www.thekilldevilgrill.com; Beach Rd, Mile 9¾; lunch $7-11, dinner $9-20; ⏱11:30am-10pm Tue-Sat) Set inside a 1939 diner, this place whips up good pub grub and mouthwatering seafood, and portions are generous.

Mama Quan's OBX Grill & Tiki Bar
Californian, Seafood **$$**

(www.mamakwans.com; 1701 S Virginia Dare Trail; lunch $9-15, dinner $10-25; ⏱11:30am-2am Mon-Sat, to midnight Sat) Don't miss Mama Quan's phenomenal fish tacos.

ℹ Getting There & Away

No public transportation exists to or on the Outer Banks. However, the North Carolina Ferry System (☎800-293-3779; www.ncdot.gov/ferry) operates several routes, including the free 40-minute Hatteras–Ocracoke car ferry, which runs at least hourly from 5:15am to 11:45pm from Hatteras in high season; reservations aren't accepted. North Carolina ferries also run between Ocracoke and Cedar Island (one way $15, 2¼ hours) and Ocracoke and Swan Quarter on the mainland ($15, 2½ hours) every two hours or so; reservations are recommended in summer for these two routes.

WILLIAMSBURG

If you visit only one historical town in Virginia, make it Williamsburg, home to Colonial Williamsburg, one of the largest, most comprehensive living-history museums in the world. If any place is going to get kids into history, this is it, but it's plenty of fun for adults too.

The actual town of Williamsburg, Virginia's capital from 1699 to 1780, is a stately place. The prestigious campus of the College of William & Mary adds a decent dash of youth culture, with coffee shops, cheap pubs and fashion boutiques.

The **Williamsburg Hotel & Motel Association** (☎800-446-9244; www.gowilliamsburg.com) at the visitor center will help find and book accommodations at no cost. If you stay in Colonial Williamsburg, guesthouses can provide discount admission tickets (adult/child $30/15).

College of William & Mary
Historic Building

(www.wm.edu; 200 Stadium Dr) Chartered in 1693, the College of William & Mary is the second-oldest college in the country and retains the oldest academic building in continued use in the USA, the Sir Christopher Wren Building.

Williamsburg White House
B&B **$$**

(☎757-229-8580; www.awilliamsburgwhitehouse.com; 718 Jamestown Rd; r $160-200, ste $375; P 🛜) This romantic, beautifully furnished B&B is located across the campus of William & Mary, just a few blocks' walk from Colonial Williamsburg. It's a favorite spot of visiting politicos, but the atmosphere and amicable management exudes more stateliness than stuffiness.

Colonial Williamsburg Historic Lodging
Guesthouse **$$$**

(☎757-253-2277; www.history.org; r $150-270) For true 18th-century immersion, guests can stay in one of 26 original colonial houses inside the historic district. Accommodations range in size and style, though the best have period furnishings, canopy beds and wood-burning fireplaces.

BOB STEFKO/GETTY IMAGES ©

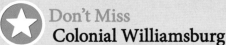

Don't Miss

Colonial Williamsburg

The restored capital of England's largest colony in the New World is a must-see for visitors of all ages. This is not some cheesy theme park; Colonial Williamsburg is a living, breathing, working history museum that transports visitors to the 1700s.

The 301-acre historic area contains 88 original 18th-century buildings and several hundred faithful reproductions. Costumed townsfolk and 'interpreters' in period dress go about their colonial jobs as blacksmiths, apothecaries, printers, bartenders, soldiers and patriots, breaking character only long enough to pose for a snapshot.

Costumed patriots such as Patrick Henry and Thomas Jefferson still deliver impassioned speeches for freedom but, to its credit, Colonial Williamsburg has grown up a little. Where once it was all about projecting a rah-rah version of American-heck-yeah in a powdered wig, today re-enactors debate and question slavery, women's suffrage, the rights of indigenous Americans and the very moral right of revolution.

Walking around the historic district and patronizing the shops and taverns is free, but entry to building tours and most exhibits is restricted to ticket holders. Expect crowds, lines and petulant children, especially in summer.

To park and to purchase tickets, follow the signs to the visitor center, north of the historic district between Hwy 132 and Colonial Pkwy, where kids can hire period costumes for $25 per day. Start with a 30-minute film about Williamsburg, and peruse *Williamsburg This Week*, listing programs and events.

Parking is free; shuttle buses run frequently to and from the historic district, or you can walk along the tree-lined footpath. You can also buy tickets at the Merchants Sq information booth.

NEED TO KNOW

www.colonialwilliamsburg.org; adult/child $42/21; ⊙9am-5pm

King's Arms Tavern
Modern American **$$**

(☏757-229-2141; 416 E Duke of Gloucester St; lunch mains $13-15, dinner $31-37; ⏱11:30am-2:30pm & 5-9pm) Of the four restaurants located within Colonial Williamsburg, this is the most elegant, serving early-American cuisine such as game pie – venison, rabbit and duck braised in port-wine sauce.

Fat Canary
American **$$$**

(☏757-229-3333; 410 Duke of Gloucester St, Merchants Sq; mains $28-39; ⏱5-10pm) Top-notch service, excellent wines and heavenly desserts are only slightly upstaged by the magnificent seasonal cuisine at this Williamsburg gem (recent favorites: pan-seared sea scallops with oyster pork belly; and wild rice–stuffed quail).

JAMESTOWN

On May 14, 1607, a group of 104 English men and boys settled on this swampy island with a charter from the Virginia Company of London to search for gold and other riches. Instead, they found starvation and disease. By January of 1608, only about 40 colonists were still alive, and these had resorted to cannibalism to survive. The colony survived the 'Starving Time' with the leadership of Captain James Smith and help from Powhatan, a local king. In 1619 the elected House of Burgesses convened, forming the first democratic government in the Americas.

Historic Jamestowne (☏757-856-1200; www.historicjamestowne.org; 1368 Colonial Pkwy; adult/child $14/free; ⏱8:30am-4:30pm), run by the NPS, is the original Jamestown site. Start your visit at the on-site museum and check out the statues of John Smith and Pocahontas. The original Jamestown ruins were rediscovered in 1994; visitors can watch the ongoing archaeological work at the site.

More child-friendly, the state-run **Jamestown Settlement** (☏757-253-4838; www.historyisfun.org; 2110 Jamestown Rd; adult/child $16/7.50, incl Yorktown Victory Center $20.50/10.25; ⏱9am-5pm; P♿) reconstructs the 1607 James Fort, a Native American village and full-scale replicas of the first ships that brought the settlers to Jamestown, along with multimedia exhibits and costumed interpreters portraying life in the 17th century.

YORKTOWN

On October 19, 1781, British General Cornwallis surrendered to George Washington here, effectively ending the American Revolution. Overpowered by massive American guns on land and cut off from the sea by the French, the British were in a hopeless position. Although Washington anticipated a much longer siege, the devastating barrage quickly overwhelmed Cornwallis, who surrendered within days.

Yorktown Battlefield (☏757-898-3400; 1000 Colonial Pkwy; incl Historic Jamestowne adult/child $10/free; ⏱9am-5pm, P♿) ✎, run by the NPS, is the site of the last major battle of the American Revolution. Start your tour at the visitor center and check out the orientation film and the display of Washington's original tent. The 7-mile Battlefield Rd tour takes you past the major highlights. Don't miss a walk through the last British defensive sites, Redoubts 9 and 10.

The state-run **Yorktown Victory Center** (☏757-887-1776; www.historyisfun.org; 200 Water St; adult/child $9.75/5.50; ⏱9am-5pm; P♿) ✎ is an interactive, living-history museum that focuses on reconstruction, reenactment and the Revolution's impact on the people who lived through it. At the re-created encampment, costumed Continental soldiers fire cannons and discuss food preparation and field medicine of the day.

The actual town of Yorktown is a pleasant waterfront village overlooking the York River with a nice range of shops, restaurants and pubs. Set in an atmospheric 1720 house, the **Carrot Tree** (☏757-988-1999; 411 Main St; mains $10-16; ⏱11am-3:30pm daily, 5-8:30pm Thu-Sat) is a good, affordable spot serving playfully named dishes such as Lord Nelson's BBQ and Battlefield beef stroganoff.

Florida

Blessed with almost year-round sunshine, Florida is a captivating subtropical peninsula famed for its white-sand beaches, aquamarine waters and fiery red sunsets. Surreal, garish and perpetually self amused, Florida is a fantasy-filled swampy wonderland of giddy delights, from alligators, mermaids and Mickey Mouse to Miami's hedonistic, art-fueled, celebrity playground.

Florida's gorgeous beaches are its calling card, and you could visit one every day of the year and still not see them all. But the state offers much more: the prehistoric Everglades with its dizzying plant and animal life, Orlando's phantasmagorical theme parks, the art-deco eye-candy of South Beach, Key West's nightly carnival, and Key Largo's Technicolored coral reefs. Given its wide-ranging offerings, diversity thrives in Florida: Cubans, retirees, fishing folk, environmentalists, Christian fundamentalists and circus performers all contribute to the ever-mutable social landscape.

Ocean Dr (p272), Miami Beach

Florida

Dothan

Alabama

Georgia

Lake Seminole

Mobile

TALLAHASSEE

Pensacola

Fort Walton Beach

Destin

Edward Ball Wakulla Springs State Park

Perdido Key

Gulf Islands National Seashore

Pensacola Beach

Grayton Beach State Park

Seaside

Panama City

St Marks

Panama City Beach

St Andrews State Park

Apalachicola River

Apalachee Bay

St Vincent Island

Apalachicola

St George Island

Steinhatchee

Gulf of Mexico

N

0   100 km
0   60 miles

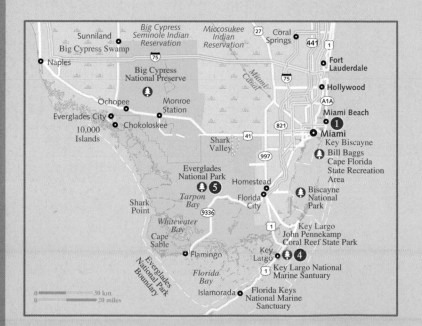

Sunniland

Big Cypress Seminole Indian Reservation

Miccosukee Indian Reservation

Coral Springs

Big Cypress Swamp

Naples

Fort Lauderdale

Big Cypress National Preserve

Miami Canal

Hollywood

Ochopee

Monroe Station

Miami Beach

Everglades City

1 Miami

Chokoloskee

Key Biscayne

10,000 Islands

Shark Valley

Bill Baggs Cape Florida State Recreation Area

Everglades National Park

5

Tarpon Bay

Homestead

Florida City

Biscayne National Park

Shark Point

Whitewater Bay

Cape Sable

Flamingo

Key Largo
John Pennekamp Coral Reef State Park

Florida Bay

Key Largo

4

Key Largo National Marine Sanctuary

Islamorada

Everglades National Park Boundary

Florida Keys National Marine Sanctuary

0   30 km
0   20 miles

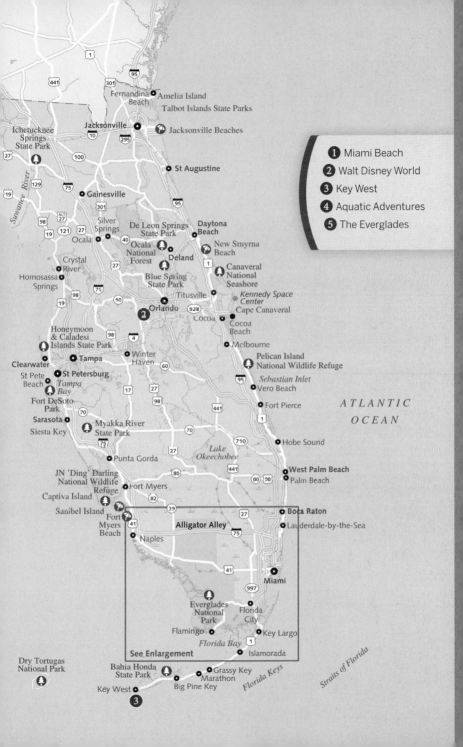

Florida's Highlights

Miami Beach

White sand, deep-blue Atlantic water and sun worshippers from every corner of the globe are all part of the enchanting scenery on lovely Miami Beach (p270). Frolicking in the waves by day, strolling the restaurant-lined Española Way by night, then wandering through its stunning Art Deco Historic District are good introductions to the Miami lifestyle. Cocktails, seafood feasts, steamy salsa: it's all part of quintessential Miami. Below: Art Deco Historic District (p270)

1

2 Walt Disney World

Walt Disney World (p266) stretches superlatives (and, admittedly, queues) like few other places. While the rides are good, when it comes to the sheer variety of parades, light displays and dance shows, it sets the bar in the theme-park world. Left: Cinderella Castle, Magic Kingdom

Key West

At the end of the road in the continental US, the eccentric-loving island of Key West (p285) has a long, colorful past of pirates, sunken treasures, literary legends and plenty of ghosts.

Today, local residents celebrate their free-spirited ethos, while visitors soak up the mellow vibe, share drinks and swap stories with local characters, snorkel the crystal-clear waters and reset their internal clocks to 'island time.' Right: Sunhat weaver

3

4

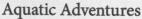

5

Aquatic Adventures

No matter where you are in Florida, you're never more than 60 miles from the shoreline, and there are boundless adventures beyond the beaches. Head to the Keys (p281) for snorkeling in crystal-clear water that's home to a vibrant coral reef, or book a boat tour or fishing expedition along the coast. There's also kayaking, windsurfing and a host of other waterside adventures – Miami (p270) is a good place to start.

The Everglades

With a geological history dating to prehistoric times, the Everglades (p279) cover more than 1.5 million acres and are home to a staggering variety of plant and animal life, including 69 species on America's endangered list. Manatees, alligators, Florida panthers, bottlenose dolphins and some 350 bird species inhabit this vast wetland ecosystem. There are many ways to experience it, including by canoe, kayak, bike or on foot. Above: Great blue heron, the Everglades

Florida's Best...

Beaches

○ **South Beach, Miami**
Home to lovely sands and the eye-candy that saunters here. (p272)

○ **Fort Zachary Taylor** Key West's prettiest beach, with swaying pines and calm waters. (p287)

○ **Bahia Honda State Park** One of Florida's most beautiful beaches lies some 45 minutes east of Key West. (p285)

○ **Sanibel Island** The idyllic beaches on this barrier island are a beachcomber's paradise. (p282)

Activities for Families

○ **Universal Orlando Resort** Entertainment galore, including Universal Studios and the Wizarding World of Harry Potter. (p262)

○ **Animal Kingdom** Take an African safari then check out the staggering Tree of Life. (p265)

○ **Watson Island** Home to the Miami Children's Museum and the wildlife-packed Jungle Island. (p278)

○ **Everglades by tram** This tour reveals loads of wildlife, including ibis, herons and alligators. (p280)

Wildlife Spotting

○ **10,000 Islands** Spy wondrous wildlife, including dolphins and manatees, on an Everglades cruise. (p280)

○ **John Pennekamp Coral Reef State Park** Go eye-to-eye with iridescent tropical fish and coral blooms in this vibrant underwater world. (p281)

○ **Grassy Key** At the Dolphin Research Center, you can learn all about our aquatic cousins. (p284)

○ **JN 'Ding' Darling National Wildlife Refuge** A first-rate birdwatching site on peaceful Sanibel Island. (p282)

Bars & Nightlife

○ **Room** A hip and sexy bar in hedonistic South Beach. (p276)

○ **Green Parrot** A fabulous Key West dive that's been going strong for over a century. (p289)

○ **House of Blues** For a break from the Big Mouse, head to this live-music spot in downtown Disney. (p269)

○ **Tobacco Road** Ramshackle old roadhouse in Miami with a celebrated indie-rock scene. (p277)

ADVANCE PLANNING

○ **Six months before** Disney-goers should book accommodation and special dining (ie Cinderella's Royal Table). Purchase theme-park tickets to safeguard against future price increases.

○ **Two months before** Book attractions that can sell out (like Discovery Cove), and pro sports and concerts in Miami.

○ **One week before** Book walking and Everglades tours.

RESOURCES

○ **Cool Junkie** (www.cooljunkie.com) Nightlife and other goings-on in Miami.

○ **Beached Miami** (www. beachedmiami.com) Arts, nightlife, music and other happenings.

○ **Greater Miami & the Beaches** (www. miamiandbeaches.com) Official Miami site with events listings.

○ **EvergladesOnline.com** (www.evergladesonline. com) Handy info for the Everglades and nearby gateways.

○ **Visit Orlando** (www. visitorlando.com) Good resource for trip planning.

○ **Florida Keys & Key West** (www.fla-keys.com) Useful for Keys-bound travelers.

GETTING AROUND

○ **Airports** Miami International Airport (p278), Orlando (MCO; www. orlandoairports.net) and Key West (p289) are gateways.

○ **Boat** Key West Express (p289) runs fast catamarans from Miami to Key West.

○ **Train** Amtrak (p278) has daily trains between Miami and New York City via Orlando.

BE FOREWARNED

○ **Hurricanes** Official season: June 1 to November 30.

○ **Traffic** A major headache in Miami and other large cities.

○ **Crime** In Miami, be cautious in Little Haiti, stretches of the Miami riverfront and Biscayne Blvd, and deserted South Beach areas below 5th St.

eft: Roseate spoonbills, Sanibel Island (p282);
Above: Sanibel Island
(LEFT) PREMIUM UIG/GETTY IMAGES ©;
(ABOVE) NICHOLAS REUSS/GETTY IMAGES ©

Florida Itineraries

In two weeks, you can visit the world's finest theme parks in Orlando, then head south for rewarding exploration in Miami, the Everglades and the Florida Keys. Great beaches, seafood feasts, wildlife watching and aquatic adventures are all essential experiences.

5 DAYS

DISNEY WORLD, UNIVERSAL STUDIOS & ORLANDO
Magical Journeys

Spend your first day at the ❶ **Magic Kingdom** (p266), Walt Disney World's most famous attraction. Visit Cinderella's Castle, get a dose of yo-ho-ho at Pirates of the Caribbean and take a thrilling ride on Space Mountain. Dine with princesses at Cinderella's Royal Table, then catch the nightly fireworks show. On day two, head to ❷ **Epcot** (p265). At the World Showcase, 'travel' through 11 countries, catch live shows, browse native arts and crafts, and feast on global fare. Stick around for the brilliant Illuminations light show.

Rise early for the ❸ **Animal Kingdom** (p265). Go on the Kilimanjaro Safari

to see elephants, giraffes and other African wildlife. Catch a show inside the 14-story Tree of Life, then have dinner at African-inspired Boma. On day four, enter Universal Studio's ❹ **Islands of Adventure** (p262), with its dazzling rides, shows and interactive amusement. Delve into the worlds of Marvel Super Heroes, Jurassic Park, Doctor Seuss and Harry Potter.

On your last day, take it easy basking on the beach, snorkeling the reefs and frolicking with dolphins in the tropical-style setting of ❺ **Discovery Cove** (p264). That evening, have a memorable meal at the celebrated Ravenous Pig (p264).

7 DAYS

Beaches, Wetlands & Coral Reefs

In **1 Miami**, explore the Art Deco Historic District (p270) and people-watch on South Beach, then go for Haitian cuisine at Tap Tap (p276) and cocktails at Skybar (p277). On day two, visit Little Havana, gallery-filled Wynwood and the Design District, and Little Haiti. Catch a show at Tobacco Road (p277). The next day stop at the **2 Ernest Coe Visitor Center** for hiking and wildlife-watching; it's a good spot to begin exploring **3 Everglades National Park** (p279). Go deeper to **4 Flamingo Marina** (p280) for a wetlands boat ride, then spend the night in **5 Key Largo** (p281). In the morning, dive the underwater splendors of **6 John**

Pennekamp Coral Reef State Park (p281), then take a glass-bottom boat tour.

On day five, enjoy the scenic drive along the Overseas Hwy before a seafood feast at Morada Bay on **7 Islamorada** (p283). Swim off Marathon's **8 Sombrero Beach** (p284) then walk in **9 Bahia Honda State Park** (p285). Spend your last two days in **10 Key West** (p285): visit Hemingway House, watch the sunset from Mallory Sq, take a catamaran trip, bar-hop on Duval St, and get your fill of key lime pie, conch fritters and margaritas.

Art Deco Historic District (p270), Miami Beach
STEVE ALLEN/GETTY IMAGES ©

Discover Florida

ORLANDO

Like Las Vegas, Orlando is almost entirely given over to fantasy. It's a place to come when you want to imagine you're somewhere else: Hogwarts, perhaps, or Cinderella's Castle, or Dr Seuss' world, or an African safari.

Yet there is, in fact, a real city to explore, one with tree-shaded parks of the natural variety, art museums, orchestras, and dinners that don't involve high-fiving Goofy.

◉ Sights & Activities

Fashionable Thornton Park has several good restaurants and bars, while Loch Haven Park is home to a cluster of cultural institutions.

Like a theme park itself, International Dr (I-Dr) has shoulder-to-shoulder high-energy amusements. Sprinkled among the major theme, wildlife and water parks, smaller attractions shout for attention: Ripley's Believe It or Not, the upside-down WonderWorks and an indoor skydiving experience. Chain restaurants and hotels also crowd the thoroughfare.

Universal Orlando Resort Theme Park
(☎407-363-8000; www.universal
orlando.com; 1000 Universal Studios
Plaza; single/both parks $92/128, dis-
counts on multi-day passes; ◷daily, hours
vary) Universal is giving Disney a run for
its money with this mega-complex that
features two theme parks, a water park,
three hotels and Universal CityWalk, an
entertainment district that connects the
two parks. But where Disney World is all
happy and magical, Universal Orlando gets

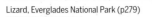

Lizard, Everglades National Park (p279)
MARK NEWMAN/GETTY IMAGES ©

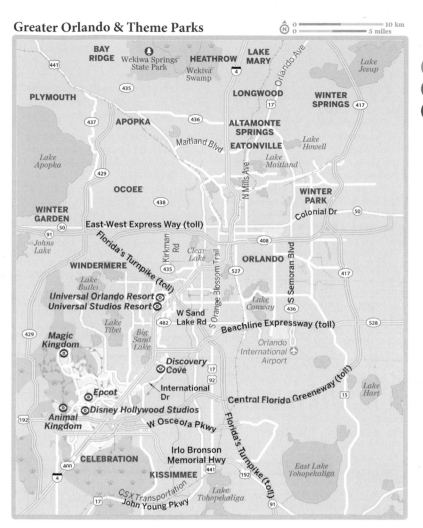

your adrenaline pumping with revved-up rides and entertaining shows. The first of the two parks, **Universal Studios**, has a Hollywood backlot feel and simulation-heavy rides dedicated to television and the silver screen, from *The Simpsons* and *Shrek* to *Revenge of the Mummy* and *Twister*. Universal's **Islands of Adventure** is tops with coaster-lovers but also has plenty for the little ones in Toon Lagoon and Seuss Landing.

But the absolute highlight – and the hottest thing to hit Orlando since Cinderella's Castle – is the **Wizarding World of Harry Potter**. Located within Islands of Adventure, it's easily the most fantastically realized themed experience in Florida. Muggles are invited to poke along the cobbled streets and impossibly crooked buildings of Hogsmeade, sip frothy Butter Beer and mail a card via Owl Post, all in the shadow of Hogwarts Caste. The detail and authenticity tickle the fancy at every turn, from the screeches of the mandrakes in the shop windows to the groans of Moaning Myrtle in the bathroom; keep your eyes peeled for magical happenings.

Review multiple ticket options online, which can include add-ons like Express Plus line skipping and a dining plan; resort hotel guests also get nice park perks.

Discovery Cove — Water Park

(☏877-557-7404; www.discoverycove.com; 6000 Discovery Cove Way; admission $169-269, incl dolphin swim $229-379; ☺8am-5:30pm) Attendance is limited, ensuring Discovery Cove retains the feel of an exclusive tropical resort, complete with beaches, a fish-filled reef and an aviary. No high-speed thrills or frantic screaming, just blessed relaxation and the chance to swim with dolphins. The price is steep, but everything is included: buffet lunch, beer, towels, parking, even a day pass to SeaWorld.

Sleeping

In addition to the Walt Disney World resorts, Orlando has countless lodging options.

EO Inn & Spa — Boutique Hotel $$

(☏407-481-8485; www.eoinn.com; 227 N Eola Dr; r $129-229; P ✴ 🛜 🛝) Sleek and understated, this downtown boutique inn overlooks Lake Eola near Thornton Park, with neutral-toned rooms that are elegant in their simplicity.

Barefoot'n in the Keys — Motel $$

(☏877-978-3314; www.barefootn.com; 2754 Florida Plaza Blvd; ste $89-199; @ 🛝 🛗) Clean, bright and spacious suites in a yellow six-story building. Low-key, friendly and close to Disney, this makes an excellent alternative to generic chains.

Eating

Dandelion Communitea Café — Vegetarian $

(http://dandelioncommunitea.com; 618 N Thornton Ave; mains $6-10; ☺11am-10pm Mon-Sat, to 5pm Sun; 🅿 🛗) 🌱 This pillar of creative, sustainable, locavore vegetarianism is genuinely delicious, with tons of community spirit.

Graffiti Junktion American Burger Bar — Burgers $

(www.graffitijunktion.com; 900 E Washington St, Thornton Park; mains $6-13; ☺11pm-2am) This neon graffiti–covered happenin' hang-out is all about massive burgers with attitude. Top yours with a fried egg, artichoke hearts, chili, avocado and more.

Ravenous Pig — American $$$

(☏407-628-2333; www.theravenouspig.com; 1234 Orange Ave, Winter Park; mains $13-33; ☺11:30am-2pm & 5:30-9:30pm Tue-Sat) One of Orlando's most talked-about foodie destinations, this bustling hot spot serves designer cocktails and creative, delicious versions of shrimp and grits, and lobster tacos. Reservations recommended.

ℹ Information

For city information, discount tickets to attractions, and good multilingual guides and maps, visit Orlando's **Official Visitor Center** (☏407-363-5872; www.visitorlando.com; 8723 International Dr; ☺8:30am-6pm).

ℹ Getting There & Around

Orlando International Airport (MCO; www.orlandoairports.net) has buses and taxis to major tourist areas. **Amtrak** (www.amtrak.com; 1400 Sligh Blvd) has daily trains south to Miami and north to New York City.

I-Ride Trolley (www.iridetrolley.com; rides adult/under 12yr $1.50/free) buses run along I-Dr.

WALT DISNEY WORLD RESORT

This is a self-contained city. Apart from the four main parks (Magic Kingdom, Epcot, Disney Hollywood Studios and Animal Kingdom), there are loads of other attractions, including top restaurants and some truly plush hotels.

◎ Sights & Activities

Anytime schools are out – during summer and holidays – WDW will be the most crowded. The least crowded times are January to February, mid-September through October and early December.

Animal Kingdom   Theme Park

This sometimes surreal blend of African safari, zoo, rides, costumed characters, shows and dinosaurs establishes its own distinct tone. It's best at animal encounters and shows, with the 110-acre **Kilimanjaro Safaris** as its centerpiece. The iconic **Tree of Life** houses the fun It's Tough to Be a Bug! show, and **Expedition Everest** and **Kali River Rapids** are the top thrill rides.

Disney Hollywood Studios   Theme Park

Formerly Disney-MGM Studios, this is the least charming of Disney's parks. However, it does have two of WDW's most exciting rides: the unpredictable elevator in the **Twilight Zone Tower of Terror** and the Aerosmith-themed **Rock 'n' Roller Coaster**. Wannabe singers can audition for the American Idol Experience, kids can join the Jedi Training Academy, and various programs present Walt Disney himself and how Disney's movies are made.

Epcot   Theme Park

An acronym for 'Experimental Prototype Community of Tomorrow,' Epcot was Disney's vision of a high-tech city when it opened in 1982. It's divided into halves: **Future World**, with rides and corporate-sponsored interactive exhibits, and **World Showcase**, providing an interesting toe-dip into the cultures of 11 countries. Epcot is much more soothingly low-key than other parks, and it has some of the best food and shopping.

Sleeping

WDW has 24 family-friendly sleeping options, from camping to deluxe resorts, and Disney guests receive great perks (extended park hours, discount dining plans, free transportation, airport shuttles).

One of our favorite deluxe resorts is the Yosemite-style **Wilderness Lodge** (40/-824-3200; 901 Timberline Dr; r from $319; P ❄ 🛜 ⧖ 👫; 🛏); the 'rustic opulence' theme includes erupting geysers, a lakelike swimming area and bunk beds for the kids. And for wilderness on a budget, we love the **Fort Wilderness Resort &**

The Wizarding World of Harry Potter (p263), Universal Orlando Resort

Don't Miss
Walt Disney World

Covering 40 sq miles, Walt Disney World is the largest theme-park resort in the world. It includes four theme parks, two water parks, two dozen hotels, 100 restaurants and two shopping and nightlife districts – proving that it's not such a small world, after all. With or without kids, you won't be able to resist Disney's infectious enthusiasm and warm-hearted nostalgia.

WDW

📞 407-939-5277

http://disneyworld.disney.go.com

When most people think of WDW – especially kids – it's the Magic Kingdom they're picturing. This is where you'll find all the classic Disney experiences, such as the iconic Cinderella's Castle, Space Mountain and other rides, and the nighttime fireworks and light parade illuminating Main Street, USA. For Disney mythology, it doesn't get better.

Cinderella's Castle is at the center of the park, and from there paths lead to the different 'lands': Tomorrowland, Fantasyland, Adventureland and Liberty Square.

Tomorrowland

Tomorrowland is where Space Mountain hurtles you through the darkness of outer space. This indoor roller-coaster is the most popular ride in the Magic Kingdom, so come first thing, and if the line is already excruciating get a FastPass.

Fantasyland

Fantasyland is the highlight of any Disney trip for the eight-and-under crowd. This is the land of Mickey and Minnie, Goofy and Donald Duck, Snow White and the Seven Dwarves, and many more big names.

Adventureland

Adventureland features pirates and jungles, magic carpets and tree houses, and other whimsical and silly representations of the exotic locales from storybooks and imagination.

Liberty Square

Liberty Square is the home of the Haunted Mansion, a rambling, 19th-century mansion that's a Disney favorite, and Frontierland is Disney's answer to the Wild West.

Walt Disney World

REPORTER DEWAYNE BEVIL COVERS THEME PARKS AND ATTRACTIONS FOR THE *ORLANDO SENTINEL*.

1 **MAGIC KINGDOM**
No first-time visitor to Walt Disney World should miss Magic Kingdom, the theme park that changed the Florida tourism landscape. Nostalgia and classic attractions dominate, and Disney has upgraded favorites such as Haunted Mansion and the Enchanted Tiki Room, even using interactive features to make the standing-in-line routine less tedious. Magic Kingdom is a winner with little princesses, and that is unlikely to change with New Fantasyland, the largest expansion in the theme park's history.

2 **TOY STORY MIDWAY MANIA**
The long, long line leading into this ride is testimony to its extreme popularity. Once aboard, guests are effectively shrunk into a video game with characters from the Pixar movies.

3 **WILD AFRICA TREK**
A behind-the-scenes tour at Disney's Animal Kingdom takes guests off the beaten track with unique angles on rhinos and crocodiles, rope bridges and extended quality time on the theme park's Kilimanjaro Safaris. Only a few dozen folks are allowed each day, and it's $189 per person on top of regular admission.

4 **EPCOT INTERNATIONAL FOOD & WINE FESTIVAL**
This seasonal event, which kicks off in September, spotlights global cuisine throughout the park's World Showcase. Food is served tapas-style during the festival, which lasts six weeks and is a local favorite.

5 **FIREWORKS**
Major pyrotechnics are a nightly event at WDW. The 'Wishes' show, complete with real-life Tinker Bell flying out of Cinderella Castle, caps off the day at Magic Kingdom (arrive early for the clever 'Celebrate the Magic' castle-projection show). 'IllumiNations' is the impressive finale at Epcot. Boat excursions linked with the fireworks shows are available on selected nights.

Campground (☎407-824-2900; campsites $54-120, cabins from $325; ❄🛜🏊🚻🐾;🍴) with tent sites and cabins that sleep up to six people.

Disney's Value Resorts (https:// disneyworld.disney.go.com; r $90-150) are the least expensive option (besides camping); quality is equivalent to basic chain hotels, and (fair warning) they are favored by school groups.

Eating

Theme-park food ranges from OK to awful; the most interesting is served in Epcot's World Showcase. Sit-down meals are best, but *always* make reservations; seats can be impossible to get without one. For any dining, you can call **central reservations** (☎407-939-3463) up to 180 days in advance.

Disney has three dinner shows (a luau, country-style BBQ and vaudeville show) and about 15 character meals, and these are insanely popular (see website for details). Book them the minute your 180-day window opens. The most sought-after meal is **Cinderella's Royal Table** (adult $43-54, child $28-33) inside the Magic Kingdom's castle, where you dine with Disney princesses.

Sci-Fi Dine-In Theater
American **$$**
(Hollywood Studios; mains $13-30; ⏱11am-10:30pm; 🚹) Dine in Cadillacs and watch classic sci-fi flicks.

O'Hana
Hawaiian **$$$**
(Polynesian Resort; adult $36-43, child $18-20; ⏱7:30-11am, 5-10pm) Great South Pacific decor and interactive Polynesian-themed luau shenanigans with all-you-care-to-eat meals served family style.

California Grill
American **$$$**
(Disney's Contemporary Resort; mains $32-49; ⏱5-10pm; 🚹) Coveted seats with great views of the Magic Kingdom fireworks.

Boma
Buffet **$$$**
(Animal Kingdom Lodge; adult/child breakfast $23/13, dinner $40/19 ; ⏱7:30-11am, 4:30-

Left: Domino players in Máximo Gómez Park (p270);
Below: Bengal tiger, Zoo Miami (p278)

(LEFT) MAXIMO GOMEZ PARK MURAL BY OSCAR THOMAS, RICHARD I'ANSON/GETTY IMAGES © ;
(BELOW) MARK NEWMAN/GETTY IMAGES ©

9:30pm;) African-inspired eatery with pleasant surroundings and a buffet several notches above the rest.

Victoria and Albert   American $$$
(Grand Floridian; prix fixe $135) A true jacket-and-tie, crystal-goblet romantic gourmet restaurant – no kidding, and no kids under 10.

⭐ Entertainment

In addition to theme-park events like Magic Kingdom parades and fireworks and Epcot's Illuminations, Disney has two entertainment districts – Downtown Disney and Disney's Boardwalk – with eats, bars, music, movies, shops and shows.

Cirque du Soleil
La Nouba   Performing Arts
(☎407-939-7600; www.cirquedusoleil.com; Downtown Disney's West Side; adult $61-144, 3-9yr $49-117; ☺6pm & 9pm Tue-Sat) This

mind-blowing acrobatic extravaganza is one of the best shows at Disney.

House of Blues   Live Music
(☎407-934-2583; www.houseofblues.com; 1490 E Buena Vista Dr) Top acts visit this national chain; Sunday's Gospel Brunch truly rocks.

ℹ️ Information

You can buy tickets for one park per day, or a Park Hopper passes that allow entrance to all four parks. Check online for packages, and buy in advance to avoid lines at the gate. For discounts, check out www.mousesavers.com and www.undercovertourist.com.

ℹ️ Getting There & Around

Most hotels in Kissimmee and Orlando – and all Disney properties – offer free transportation to Walt Disney World. Disney-owned resorts also offer free transportation from the airport. Drivers can reach all four parks via I-4 and park for $14.

The Magic Kingdom lot is huge; trams get you to the entrance.

Within Walt Disney World, a complex network of monorails, boats and buses get you between the parks, resorts and entertainment districts.

MIAMI

Miami moves to a different rhythm from anywhere else in the USA. Pastel-hued, subtropical beauty and Latin sexiness are everywhere: from the cigar-filled dance halls where Havana expats dance to *son* and *boleros* to the exclusive nightclubs where stiletto-heeled Brazilian models shake to Latin hip-hop. Whether you're meeting avant-garde gallery hipsters or passing the buffed, perfect bodies recumbent along South Beach, everyone can seem oh-so-artfully posed. Meanwhile, street vendors and restaurants dish out flavors of the Caribbean, Cuba, Argentina and Haiti. For travelers, the city can be as intoxicating as a sweaty-glassed *mojito*.

Sights

MIAMI BEACH

Art Deco Historic District　Neighborhood
The well-preserved, pastel-hued Art Deco Historic District verily screams 'Miami.' It's the largest concentration of deco anywhere in the world, with approximately 1200 buildings lining the streets around Ocean Dr and Collins Ave. For tours and info, make your first stop the **Art Deco Welcome Center** (☑ 305-531-3484; 1001 Ocean Dr, South Beach; guided tour per adult/child/senior $20/free/15; ☺ tours 10:30am Fri-Wed, 6:30pm Thu).

World Erotic Art Museum　Museum
(www.weam.com; 1205 Washington Ave; over 18yr $15; ☺ 11am-10pm Mon-Thu, to midnight Fri-Sun) Unfazed by SoBe's bare flesh? Something will get your attention here, with an amazingly extensive collection of naughty and erotic art, and even furniture depicting all sorts of parts and acts.

LITTLE HAVANA

As SW 8th St heads away from downtown, it becomes **Calle Ocho** (pronounced *kah*-yeh *oh*-cho, Spanish for 'Eighth Street'). That's when you know you've arrived in Little Havana, the most prominent community of Cuban Americans in the US. Despite the cultural monuments, this is no Cuban theme park. The district remains a living, breathing immigrant enclave, though one whose residents have become, admittedly, more broadly Central American. One of the best times to come is the last Friday of the month during **Viernes Culturales** (www.viernesculturales.org), or 'Cultural Fridays,' a street fair showcasing Latino artists and musicians.

Máximo Gómez Park　Park
(SW 8th St at SW 15th Ave; ☺ 9am-6pm) Get a sensory-filled taste of old Cuba. It's also known as 'Domino Park,' and you'll

Miami Beach

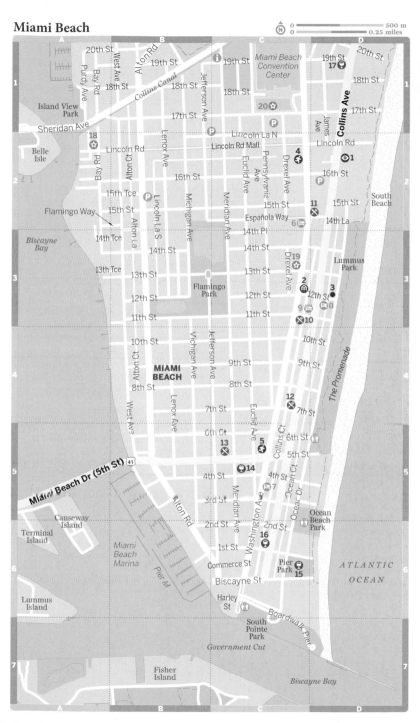

Miami Beach

Miami Beach has some of the best beaches in the country, with white sand and warm aquamarine water that rivals the Bahamas. That movie in your head of art-deco hotels, in-line-skating models, preening young studs and cruising cars? That's **Ocean Dr** (from 1st to 11th Sts), where the beach is merely a backdrop for strutting peacocks. This confluence of waves, sunshine and exhibitionist beauty is what made **South Beach** (or 'SoBe') world famous.

Just a few blocks north, **Lincoln Rd** (between Alton Rd and Washington Ave) becomes a pedestrian mall, or outdoor fashion runway, so all may admire SoBe's fabulously gorgeous creatures.

understand why when you see the old-timers throwing bones.

El Crédito Cigars Cigars
(☏305-858-4162; 1106 SW 8th St) One of Miami's most popular cigar stores; watch *tabaqueros* hand-roll them.

DESIGN DISTRICT, WYNWOOD & LITTLE HAITI

Proving that SoBe doesn't hold the lease on hip, these two trendy areas north of downtown – which were all but deserted 25 years ago – have ensconced themselves as bastions of art and design. The **Design District** (www.miamidesigndistrict.net) is a mecca for interior designers, home to dozens of galleries and contemporary furniture, fixture and design showrooms.

Just south of the Design District, **Wynwood** is a notable arts district, with myriad galleries and art studios housed in abandoned factories and warehouses. The second Saturday of the month features the **Wynwood and Design**

District Arts Walks (www.artcircuits.com; ◷7-10pm 2nd Saturday of the month) FREE, with music, food and wine from 7pm to 10pm.

The home of Miami's Haitian refugees, **Little Haiti** is defined by brightly painted homes, markets and *botanicas* (voodoo shops).

Wynwood Walls Public Art
(www.thewynwoodwalls.com; NW 2nd Ave btwn 25th & 26th Sts; ◷noon-8pm Wed-Sat) Not a gallery per se, Wynwood Walls is a collection of murals and paintings laid out over an open courtyard in the heart of Wynwood. What's on offer tends to change with the coming and going of major arts events like Art Basel.

CORAL GABLES & COCONUT GROVE

For a slower pace and a more European feel, head inland. Designed as a 'model suburb' by George Merrick in the early 1920s, Coral Gables is a Mediterranean-style village that's centered around the shops and restaurants of the **Miracle Mile**, a four-block section of Coral Way between Douglas and LeJeune Rds.

**Vizcaya Museum
& Gardens** Historic Building
(www.vizcayamuseum.org; 3251 S Miami Ave; adult/6-12yr $15/6; ◷9:30am-4:30pm Wed-Mon) In Coconut Grove, this Italian Renaissance–style villa, the housing equivalent of a Fabergé egg, is Miami's most fairytale residence. The 70 rooms are stuffed with centuries-old furnishings and art, and the 30-acre grounds contain splendid formal gardens and Florentine gazebos.

Biltmore Hotel Historic Building
(☏855-311-6903; www.biltmorehotel.com; 1200 Anastasia Ave) Architecturally speaking, the crown jewel of Coral Gables is this magnificent edifice that once housed a speakeasy run by Al Capone. Even if you don't stay, drop by for a drink at the bar and gawk at the pool, or catch a free tour on Sunday afternoon.

Venetian Pool
Swimming

(www.coralgablesvenetianpool.com; 2701 De Soto Blvd; adult/child $11/7.35; ⊘hours vary; ⏢) 'Swimming pool' doesn't even begin to describe it: with waterfalls, grottos and an Italianate feel, this spring-fed pool made by filling in the limestone quarry used to build Coral Gables looks like a vacation home for rich mermaids.

GREATER MIAMI
Ancient Spanish Monastery
Church

(☏305-945-1461; www.spanishmonastery. com; 16711 W Dixie Hwy; adult/child $8/4; ⊘10am-4:30pm Mon-Sat, from 11am Sun) Said to be the oldest building in the Western Hemisphere, this monastery was built in Segovia, Spain, in 1141 and shipped here by William Randolph Hearst. Call to confirm hours.

 **Activities**

Skating or cycling the strip along Ocean Dr in South Beach is pure Miami; also try the Rickenbacker Causeway to Key Biscayne.

Fritz's Skate, Bike & Surf
Sports Rentals

(☏305-532-1954; www.fritzsmiamibeach.com; 1620 Washington Ave; bike & skate rentals per hour/day/week $10/24/69; ⊘10am-9pm Mon-Sat, to 8pm Sun) Sports-equipment rentals and free in-line skate lessons (10:30am Sunday).

Miami Beach Bicycle Center
Cycling

(www.bikemiamibeach.com; 601 5th St; per hr/day from $5/14; ⊘10am-7pm Mon-Sat, to 5pm Sun) Convenient bike rentals in the heart of SoBe.

Boucher Brothers Watersports
Water Sports

(☏305-535-8177; www.boucherbrothers.com; ⊘10:30am-4:30pm) Rentals and lessons for all sorts of water-related activities: kayaking, waterskiing, windsurfing, parasailing, waverunners and boats. You can find locations up and down the beach.

Sailboards Miami
Water Sports

(☏305-892-8992; www.sailboardsmiami.com; 1 Rickenbacker Causeway; ⊘10am-6pm Fri-Tue) The waters off Key Biscayne are perfect

Vintage car, South Beach, Miami

Map showing the Greater Miami area, including neighborhoods such as Carol City, North Beach, Opa-Locka, Hialeah, Liberty City, Little Haiti, Design District, Wynwood, Little Havana, Coconut Grove, Miami Beach, Key Biscayne, Kendall, and Pinecrest, with the Atlantic Ocean and Biscayne Bay.

Greater Miami

for windsurfing, kayaking and kiteboarding; get your gear and lessons here.

Sleeping

Clay Hotel
Hotel **$**

(☏305-534-2988, 800-379-2529; www.clayhotel.com; 1438 Washington Ave; r $88-190; ❄@🌐) Located in a 100-year-old Spanish-style villa – legend has it that Al Capone once slept here – the Clay has clean and comfortable rooms and is located right on Espanola Way.

Hotel St Augustine
Boutique Hotel **$$**

(☏305-532-0570; www.hotelstaugustine.com; 347 Washington Ave; r $126-289; P❄🌐) Wood that's blonder than Barbie and a crisp-and-clean deco theme combine to

create one of South Beach's most elegant yet stunningly modern sleeps. A hip-and-homey standout.

Lords Hotel
Boutique Hotel **$$**

(☏877-448-4754; www.lordssouthbeach.com; 1120 Collins Ave; r $120-240, ste $330-540; P❄🌐⊠) The epicenter of South Beach's gay scene is this 'appropriately oriented' hotel, with rooms decked out in lemony yellow and offset by pop art. Lords is hip, yet doesn't affect an attitude.

Kent Hotel
Boutique Hotel **$$**

(☏305-604-5068; www.thekenthotel.com; 1131 Collins Ave; r $69-199; P❄🌐) The lobby is a kick, filled with fuchsia and electric-orange geometric furniture plus bright Lucite toy blocks. Rooms continue the playfulness. One of South Beach's better deals.

Circa 39
Boutique Hotel **$$**

(☏305-538-4900; www.circa39.com; 3900 Collins Ave; r $85-144; P❄@⊠) If you love South Beach style but loathe South Beach attitude, Circa has got your back. Combines one of the funkiest lobbies in Miami, hip icy-blue-and-white rooms and a welcoming attitude. Web rates are phenomenal.

Hotel St Michel
Hotel **$$**

(☏305-444-1666; www.hotelstmichel.com; 162 Alcazar Ave; r $85-225; P❄🌐♟) You could conceivably think you're in Europe in this vaulted place at Coral Gables, with inlaid floors, old-world charm and just 28 rooms.

Biltmore Hotel
Historic Hotel **$$$**

(☏855-311-6903; www.biltmorehotel.com; 1200 Anastasia Ave; r from $209; P❄🌐⊠♟) This 1926 hotel is a National Historic Landmark and an icon of luxury. Standard rooms may be small, but public spaces are palatial; its fabulous pool is the largest hotel pool in the country.

Eating

Puerto Sagua
Cuban **$**

(☏305-673-1115; 700 Collins Ave; most mains $6-20; ⊙7:30am-2am) Pull up to the counter

Latin American Spice in Miami

Thanks to its immigrant heritage, Miami is legendary for its authentic Cuban, Haitian, Brazilian and other Latin American cuisines. For a good introduction to Cuban food, sidle up to a Cuban *loncheria* (snack bar) and order a *pan cubano:* a buttered, grilled baguette stuffed with ham, roast pork, cheese, mustard and pickles. For dinner, order the classic *ropa vieja:* shredded flank steak cooked in tomatoes and peppers, and accompanied by fried plantains, black beans and yellow rice.

Other treats to look for include Haitian *griots* (marinated fried pork), Jamaican jerk chicken, Brazilian barbecue, Central American *gallo pinto* (red beans and rice) and *batidos,* a milky, refreshing Latin American fruit smoothie.

for authentic, tasty and inexpensive *ropa vieja* (shredded beef), black beans and *arroz con pollo* (rice with chicken) – plus some of the best Cuban coffee in town – at this beloved Cuban diner.

11th St Diner
Diner $

(www.eleventhstreetdiner.com; 1065 Washington Ave; mains $9-18; ⏰24hr except midnight-7am Wed) This deco diner housed inside a gleaming Pullman train car sees round-the-clock activity and is especially popular with people staggering home from clubs.

Tap Tap
Haitian $$

(☎305-672-2898; www.taptaprestaurant.com; 819 5th St; mains $9-20; ⏰noon-11:30pm) In this tropi-psychedelic Haitian eatery, you dine under bright murals of Papa Legba, enjoying cuisine that's a happy marriage of West Africa, France and the Caribbean: try spicy pumpkin soup, curried goat

and *mayi moulen,* a signature side of cornmeal.

Versailles
Cuban $$

(☎305-444-0240; www.versaillesrestaurant.com; 3555 SW 8th St; mains $5-26; ⏰8am-1am) *The* Cuban restaurant in town is not to be missed. It finds room for everybody in the large, cafeteria-style dining rooms.

Osteria del Teatro
Italian $$$

(☎305-538-7850; http://osteriadelteatro miami.com; 1443 Washington Ave; mains $17-38; ⏰6-11pm Mon-Thu, to 1am Fri-Sun) Stick to the specials of one of Miami's oldest and best Italian restaurants, and you can't go wrong. Better yet, let the gracious Italian waiters coddle and order for you. They never pick wrong.

Michy's
Fusion $$$

(☎305-759-2001; http://michysmiami.com; 6927 Biscayne Blvd; meals $29-38; ⏰6-10:30pm Tue-Thu, to 11pm Fri & Sat, to 10pm Sun; 🖬) Organic, locally sourced ingredients and a stylish, fantastical decor are what you'll find at Michelle 'Michy' Bernstein's place. It's one of the brightest stars in Miami's culinary constellation.

🍷 Drinking & Nightlife

There are tons of bars along Ocean Dr; a meander at happy hour will get you half-price drinks. To increase your chances of getting into the major nightclubs, call ahead to get on the guest list. In South Beach clubs and live-music venues, cover charges range from $20 to $25; elsewhere you'll get in for around half that. For events calendars and gallery, bar and club reviews, check out www.cooljunkie.com and www.beachedmiami.com.

Room
Bar

(www.theotheroom.com; 100 Collins Ave; ⏰7pm-5am) This dark, atmospheric, boutique-beer bar in SoBe is a gem: hip and sexy as hell but with a low-key attitude. Per the name, it's small and gets crowded.

Abraxas
Bar

(407 Meridian Ave; ⏰7pm-3am Sun & Mon, 5pm-5am Tue-Sat) In a classic deco building,

Abraxas couldn't be friendlier. Uncrowded and serving fantastic beer from around the world, it's tucked away in a residential part of South Beach.

Electric Pickle   Bar
(www.electricpicklemiami.com; 2826 N Miami Ave; ⏰10pm-5am Wed-Sat) In Wynwood, arty hipsters become glamorous club kids in this two-story hepcat hot spot. The Pickle is sexy, gorgeous and literate.

Skybar   Club
(☏305-695-3100; Shore Club, 1901 Collins Ave; 4pm-2am Mon-Wed, to 3am Thu-Sat) Sip chic cocktails on the alfresco terrace. Or, if you're 'somebody,' head for the indoor A-list Red Room. Both have a luxurious Moroccan theme and beautiful people-watching.

Twist   Club
(☏305-538-9478; www.twistsobe.com; 1057 Washington Ave; ⏰1pm-5am) This gay hangout has serious staying power and a little bit of something for everyone, including dancing, drag shows and go-go dancers.

Nikki Beach Club   Club
(☏305-538-1111; www.nikkibeach.com; 1 Ocean Dr; cover from $25; ⏰11am-6pm Mon-Tue, to 11pm Wed-Sat, to 5pm Sun) Lounge on beds or inside your own tipi in this beach-chic outdoor space that's right on the sand.

Mansion   Club
(☏305-532-1525; www.mansionmiami.com; 1235 Washington Ave; cover from $20; ⏰11pm-5am Wed-Sat) Prepare for some quality time with the velvet rope and wear something head-turning to enter this grandiose, exclusive megaclub.

Entertainment

LIVE MUSIC

Hoy Como Ayer   Live Music
(☏305-541-2631; www.hoycomoayer.us; 2212 SW 8th St; ⏰from 9pm Thu-Sat) Authentic Cuban music.

Tobacco Road   Live Music
(☏305-374-1198; www.tobacco-road.com; 626 S Miami Ave; ⏰11:30am-5am) Old-school

roadhouse around since 1912; blues, jazz and occasional impromptu jams by well-known rockers.

Jazid   Lounge
(☏305-673-9372; www.jazid.net; 1342 Washington Ave; ⏰10pm-5am) Jazz in a candlelit lounge; upstairs, DJ-fueled soul and hip-hop.

THEATER & CULTURE

Adrienne Arsht Center for the
Performing Arts   Performing Arts
(www.arshtcenter.org; 1300 Biscayne Blvd) Showcases jazz from around the world, as well as theater, dance, music, comedy and more.

New World Center   Classical Music
(www.newworldcenter.com; 500 17th St) The new home of the acclaimed New World Symphony is one of the most beautiful buildings in Miami.

Colony Theater   Performing Arts
(www.mbculture.com; 1040 Lincoln Rd) Everything – from off-Broadway productions to ballet and movies – plays in this renovated 1934 art-deco showpiece.

SPORTS

Miami Dolphins   Football
(☏305-943-8000, www.miamidolphins.com, Sun Life Stadium, 2269 Dan Marino Blvd; tickets from $35) NFL football season runs from August to December.

Florida Marlins   Baseball
(http://miami.marlins.mlb.com; Marlins Park, 501 Marlins Way; tickets from $15) MLB baseball season is May to September.

Miami Heat   Basketball
(☏786-777-1000; www.nba.com/heat; American Airlines Arena, 601 Biscayne Blvd; tickets from $20) NBA basketball season is November to April.

Florida Panthers   Hockey
(☏954-835-7825; http://panthers.nhl.com; BB&T Center, 1 Panther Pkwy, Sunrise; tickets from $15) NHL hockey season runs mid-October to mid-April.

Miami for Children

The best beaches for kids are in Miami Beach north of 21st St (especially at 53rd St, which has a playground and public toilets) and the dune-packed beach around 73rd St. Also head south to Matheson Hammock Park, which has calm artificial lagoons.

Miami Seaquarium (www.miamiseaquarium.com; 4400 Rickenbacker Causeway; adult/child $40/30; ☺9:30am-6pm, last entry 4:30pm) On the way to Key Biscayne, this 38-acre marine-life park is more extensive than the usual aquarium; it also rehabilitates dolphins, manatees and sea turtles, and presents great animal shows.

Miami Children's Museum (www.miamichildrensmuseum.org; 980 MacArthur Causeway; admission $16; ☺10am-6pm) On Watson Island, between downtown Miami and Miami Beach, this hands-on museum has fun music and art studios.

Jungle Island (www.jungleisland.com; 1111 Parrot Jungle Trail, off MacArthur Causeway; adult/child $35/27; ☺10am-5pm) Jungle Island is packed with tropical birds, alligators, orangutans, chimps and (to the delight of *Napoleon Dynamite* fans) a liger, a cross between a lion and a tiger.

Zoo Miami (Metrozoo; www.miamimetrozoo.com; 12400 SW 152nd St; adult/child $16/12; ☺9:30am-5:30pm, last admission 4pm) Miami's tropical weather makes strolling around Zoo Miami almost feel like a day in the wild. Highlights include riding the Safari Monorail and feeding the Samburu giraffes ($2).

Monkey Jungle (www.monkeyjungle.com; 14805 SW 216th St; adult/child $30/24; ☺9:30am-5pm, last entry 4pm) The tagline, 'Where humans are caged and monkeys run wild,' tells you all you need to know – except for the fact that it's in far south Miami.

🛍 Shopping

Browse for one-of-a-kind and designer items at the South Beach boutiques around Collins Ave between 6th and 9th Sts and along Lincoln Rd mall. For unique items, try Little Havana and the Design District.

ℹ Information

Greater Miami & the Beaches Convention & Visitors Bureau (☏305-539-3000; www.miamiandbeaches.com; 701 Brickell Ave, 27th fl; ☺8:30am-5pm Mon-Fri) Located in an oddly intimidating high-rise building.

Miami Beach Chamber of Commerce (☏305-674-1300; www.miamibeachchamber.com; 1920 Meridian Ave; ☺9am-5pm Mon-Fri) You can purchase a Meter Card here. Denominations come in $10, $20 and $25 (and meters cost $1 per hour).

ℹ Getting There & Away

Miami International Airport (MIA; www.miami-airport.com) is about 6 miles west of downtown, and is accessible by SuperShuttle (☏305-871-8210; www.supershuttle.com) as well as by Tri-Rail (☏800-874-7245; www.tri-rail.com), a rail link that connects MIA with downtown.

Amtrak (☏800-872-7245, 305-835-1222; www.amtrak.com; 8303 NW 37th Ave) has a main Miami terminal.

ℹ Getting Around

Metro-Dade Transit (☏305-891-3131; www.miamidade.gov/transit/routes.asp) runs the local Metrobus and Metrorail ($2), as well as the free Metromover monorail serving downtown.

THE EVERGLADES

Contrary to what you may have heard, the Everglades isn't a swamp. Or at least, it's not *only* a swamp. It's most accurately characterized as a wet prairie – grasslands that happen to be flooded most of the year. Nor is it stagnant. In the wet season, a horizon-wide river creeps ever-so-slowly beneath the rustling saw grass and around the subtly raised cypress and hardwood hammocks toward the ocean. The Everglades are indeed filled with alligators – and perhaps a few dead bodies, as *CSI: Miami* would have it. Yet its beauty is not measured in fear or geological drama, but in the timeless, slow Jurassic flap of a great blue heron as it glides over its vast and shockingly gentle domain.

Which is one reason that exploring the Everglades by foot, bicycle, canoe and kayak (or camping) is so much more satisfying than by noisy, vibrating airboat. There is an incredible variety of wonderful creatures to see within this unique, subtropical wilderness, and there are accessible entrances that, at the cost of a few hours, get you easily into the Everglades' soft heart.

The Everglades has two seasons: the summer wet season and the winter dry season. Winter – from December to April – is the prime time to visit: the weather is mild and pleasant, and the wildlife is out in abundance. In summer (May through October) it's stiflingly hot, humid and buggy, with frequent afternoon thunderstorms. In addition, as water sources spread out, so the animals disperse.

Everglades National Park

The park has three main entrances and areas: in the south along Rte 9336 through Homestead and Florida City to Ernest Coe Visitor Center and, at road's end, Flamingo; along the Tamiami Trail/Hwy 41 in the north to Shark Valley; and on the Gulf Coast near Everglades City.

The main park entry points have visitor centers where you can get maps, camping permits and ranger information. You only need to pay the entrance fee (per car/pedestrian $10/5 for seven days) once to access all points.

Red-bellied woodpecker, Everglades National Park

Even in winter it's almost impossible to avoid mosquitoes, but they're ferocious in summer: bring *strong* repellent.

Shark Valley — Park

(☏305-221-8776; www.nps.gov/ever/planyourvisit/svdirections.htm; 36000 SW 8th St; car/cyclist $10/5; ⊙9:15am-5:15pm) For a quick Everglades overview, start at Shark Valley. Here you can take an excellent two-hour **tram tour** (☏305-221-8455; www.sharkvalleytramtours.com; adult/child $20/12.75) along a 15-mile asphalt trail and see copious amounts of alligators in the winter months. The pancake-flat trail is perfect for bicycles, which can be rented at the entrance for $7.50 per hour. Bring water with you.

Ernest Coe Visitor Center — Park

(☏305-242-7700; www.nps.gov/ever; Hwy 9336; ⊙9am-5pm) Those with a day to give the Glades could start with this visitor center in the south. It has excellent, museum-quality exhibits and tons of activity info: the road accesses numerous short trails and lots of top-drawer canoeing opportunities. At the nearby **Royal Palm Area** (☏305-242-7700; Hwy 9336), you can catch two short trails: the **Anhinga Trail** is great for wildlife spotting, especially alligators in winter; and the **Gumbo-Limbo Trail** showcases plants and trees.

Flamingo Visitor Center — Park

(☏239-695-2945; ⊙8am-4:30pm) From Royal Palm, Hwy 9336 cuts through the belly of the park for 38 miles until it reaches the isolated Flamingo Visitor Center, which has maps of canoeing and hiking trails. **Flamingo Marina** (☏239-695-3101; ⊙store hours 7am-5:30pm Mon-Fri, from 6am Sat & Sun) offers backcountry boat tours and kayak/canoe rentals for self-guided trips along the coast.

Gulf Coast Visitor Center — Park

(☏239-695-3311; 815 Oyster Bar Lane, off Hwy 29, Everglades City; ⊙9am-4:30pm) Those with time should consider visiting the northwestern edge of the Everglades, where the mangroves and waterways of the **10,000 Islands** offer incredible canoeing and kayaking opportunities, and great boat tours with a chance to spot dolphins. The visitor center is next to the marina, with rentals (from $13 per hour) and various guided boat trips (from $25).

Sanibel Island (p282)

FLORIDA KEYS

Before 1912, when Henry Flagler completed his railroad that connected the Keys to the mainland, this 126-mile string of islands was just a series of untethered bumps of land accessible only by boat. Flagler's railroad was destroyed by a hurricane in 1935, but what remained of its bridges allowed the Overseas Hwy to be completed in 1938. Now, streams of travelers swarm down from the mainland to indulge in the alluring jade-green waters, laid-back island lifestyle, great fishing, and idyllic snorkeling and diving.

Upper Keys

Stretching from Key Largo to Islamorada, the Upper Keys are cluttered with touristy shops and motels. At first you can't even see the water from the highway, then – bam – you're in Islamorada and water is everywhere.

KEY LARGO

Key Largo has long been romanticized in movies and song, so it can be a shock to arrive and find...no Bogart, no Bacall, no love-sick Sade. On the side roads you can find some of those legendary island idiosyncracies, and dive underwater for the most amazing coral reef in the continental US.

 ## Activities

John Pennekamp Coral Reef State Park
Park

(📞305-451-6300; www.pennekamppark.com; MM 102.6 oceanside; car/motorcycle/cyclist or pedestrian $8/4/2; ⏰8am-sunset, aquarium 8am-5pm; 👪) The USA's first underwater park, Pennekamp contains the third-largest coral barrier reef in the world – the only one in the US – and is home to a panoply of sea life and the oft-photographed statue *Christ of the Deep*. Your options for seeing the reef are many: take a 2½-hour **glass-bottom boat tour** (📞305-451-6300; adult/child $24/17; ⏰9:15am, 12:15pm & 3:15pm) on a thoroughly modern 65ft catamaran. Dive in with a **snorkeling trip** (📞305-451-

Detour: Key Biscayne

If you don't make it to the Florida Keys, come to the **Bill Baggs Cape Florida State Park** (www.floridastateparks.org/capeflorida; 1200 S Crandon Blvd; per car $8, pedestrian $2; ⏰8am-sunset) for a taste of their unique island ecosystems. The 494-acre space is a tangled clot of tropical fauna and dark mangroves, all interconnected by sandy trails and wooden boardwalks, and surrounded by miles of pale ocean. A concession shack rents kayaks, bikes, in-line skates, beach chairs and umbrellas. At the southernmost tip, the 1825 brick Cape Florida Lighthouse offers free tours at 10am and 1pm Thursday through Monday.

6300; adult/child $30/25) or two-tank **diving trip** (📞305-451-6322; $55); half-day trips leave twice daily, usually around 9am and 1pm. Or go DIY and rent a canoe or kayak (per hour single/double $12/17) and journey through a 3-mile network of water trails. Call the park for boat-rental information.

African Queen
Boat Tour

(📞305-451-8080; www.africanqueenflkeys.com; Mile 100 oceanside at the Holiday Inn Marina; canal cruise $49, dinner cruise $89) The steamboat used in the 1951 movie starring Humphrey Bogart and Katherine Hepburn has been restored, and you can now climb aboard on a canal or dinner cruise. Canal cruises are held every two hours from 10am to 6pm. It's best to call for reservations as the tiny vessel only accommodates six.

Florida Bay Outfitters
Kayaking

(📞305-451-3018; www.kayakfloridakeys.com; Mile 104 bayside; kayak rental per half-day $40)

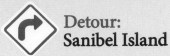

Detour:
Sanibel Island

Shaped like a fish hook trying to lure Fort Myers, these two slivers of barrier island lie across a 2-mile causeway (toll $6). Upscale but unpretentious, with a carefully managed shoreline that feels remarkably lush and undeveloped, the islands are idyllic, cushy getaways, where bikes are the preferred mode of travel, the shelling is legendary and romantic meals are a reservation away. The **Sanibel & Captiva Islands Chamber of Commerce** (📞239-472-1080; www.sanibel-captiva.org; 1159 Causeway Rd; ⏰9am-5pm; 📶) is one of the most helpful visitor centers around and can help with accommodations.

In addition to its fabulous beaches, Sanibel's 6300-acre **JN 'Ding' Darling National Wildlife Refuge** (📞239-472-1100; www.fws.gov/dingdarling; 1 Wildlife Dr; per car/cyclist $5/1; ⏰Wildlife Drive from 7am, closed Fri, visitor center 9am-5pm) is a splendid refuge that's home to an abundance of seabirds and wildlife. It has an excellent nature center, a 5-mile Wildlife Drive, narrated tram tours and easy kayaking in Tarpon Bay. For tours and boat rentals, contact **Tarpon Bay Explorers** (📞239-472-8900; www.tarponbayexplorers.com; 900 Tarpon Bay Rd; ⏰8am-6pm).

Like a mermaid's jewel box, the **Bailey-Matthews Shell Museum** (📞239-395-2233; www.shellmuseum.org; 3075 Sanibel-Captiva Rd; adult/5-16yr $9/5; ⏰10am-5pm) is a natural history of the sea, with displays of shells from worldwide. To rent bikes or any other pedalled vehicle, visit **Billy's Rentals** (📞239-472-5248; www.billysrentals.com; 1470 Periwinkle Way; bikes per 2hr/day from $5/15; ⏰8:30am-5pm).

The five-room **Tarpon Tale Inn** (📞239-472-0939; www.tarpontale.com; 367 Periwinkle Way; r $80-219; ❄@📶♿🐕) does a nice imitation of a charming, hammock-strung B&B, but without breakfast. For romantic gourmet food, **Sweet Melissa's Cafe** (📞239-472-1956; www.sweetmelissascafe.net; 1625 Periwinkle Way; tapas $9-16, mains $26-34; ⏰11:30am-2:30pm Mon-Fri, from 5pm Mon-Sat) offers creative, relaxed refinement.

See the keys from the water: rent a kayak or canoe or catch a guided trip.

Horizon Divers · Diving
(📞305-453-3535; www.horizondivers.com; 100 Ocean Dr, off Mile 100 oceanside; snorkel/scuba trips $50/80) Get beneath the surface on a scuba or snorkel trip with Horizon's friendly crew.

Sleeping

Largo Lodge · Hotel $$
(📞305-451-0424; www.largolodge.com; Mile 102 bayside; cottages $150-265; Ⓟ) These six charming, sunny cottages with their own private beach are surrounded by palm trees, tropical flowers and lots of roaming birds, for a taste of Florida in the good old days.

Key Largo House Boatel · Hotel $$
(📞305-766-0871; www.keylargohouseboatel.com; Shoreland Dr, Mile 103.5 oceanside; houseboat small/medium/large from $75/100/150) These five houseboats are a steal. The largest is incredibly spacious, sleeping six people comfortably. The boats are right on the docks, so no possibility of being isolated from land (or booze). Call for directions.

Eating & Drinking

Mrs Mac's Kitchen · American $
(📞305-451-3722; www.mrsmacskitchen.com; Mile 99.4 bayside; breakfast & lunch $8-12, dinner $9-22; ⏰7am-9:30pm Mon-Sat) This cute roadside diner bedecked with rusty license plates serves classic highway food such as burgers and fish baskets.

Alabama Jack's
Seafood, Bar $

(http://alabamajacks.com; 58000 Card Sound Rd; mains $7-14; ☉11am-7pm) On the back road between Key Largo and Florida City (about 15 miles north of Key Largo), this funky open-air joint draws an eclectic booze-hungry crowd of genuine Keys characters. Try the rave-worthy conch fritters.

Key Largo Conch House
Fusion $$

(🕿305-453-4844; www.keylargocoffeehouse. com; Mile 100.2 oceanside; mains $8-26; ☉8am-10pm) Now *this* feels like the islands: conch architecture, tropical foliage, and crab and conch dishes that ease you off the mainland.

Fish House
Seafood $$

(🕿305-451-4665; www.fishhouse.com; Mile 102.4 oceanside; mains $9-24; ☉11:30am-10pm; 🚼) Delivers on its name, serving fish, fish and more fish that's as fresh as it gets. Your main decision: fried, broiled, jerked, blackened or grilled?

ISLAMORADA

It sounds like an island, but Islamorada is actually a string of several islands, the epicenter of which is Upper Matecumbe Key. It's right around here that the view starts to open up, allowing you to fully appreciate the fact that you're surrounded by water. Several little nooks of beach are easily accessible, providing scenic rest stops.

🔘 Sights & Activities

Billed as the 'Sportfishing Capital of the World,' Islamorada is an angler's paradise.

Indian Key
Historic State Park
Island

(🕿305-664-2540; www.floridastateparks. org/indiankey; Mile 78.5 oceanside; per person $2.50; ☉8am-sunset) A few hundred yards offshore, this peaceful little island contains the derelict, crumbling foundations of a 19th-century settlement that was wiped out by Native Americans during the Second Seminole War. It's a moody ramble, accessible only by kayak or boat,

which you can rent from Robbie's Marina (see below).

Lignumvitae Key
Botanical State Park
Island

(🕿305-664-2540; www.floridastateparks. org/lignumvitaekey; admission $2.50, tour $2; ☉tours 10am & 2pm Fri-Sun) It'll feel like just you and about a jillion mosquitoes on this bayside island park, with virgin tropical forests and the 1919 Matheson House. Come for the shipwrecked isolation. Robbie's Marina offers boat rentals and tours.

Anne's Beach
Beach

(Mile 73.5 oceanside) The area's best public beach; shaded picnic tables and a ribbon of sand.

Robbie's Marina
Marina

(🕿305-664-8070; www.robbies.com; Mile 77.5 bayside; half-day kayak & canoe rentals $40-75; ☉9am-8pm) This marina/roadside attraction offers the buffet of boating options: fishing charters, jet skiing, party boats, ecotours, snorkeling trips, kayak rentals and more (come here to visit the area's island parks).

🛏 Sleeping & Eating

Lime Tree Bay
Resort Motel
Motel $$

(🕿800-723-4519, 305-664-4740; www.lime-treebayresort.com; Mile 68.5 bayside; r $135-175, ste $185-395) A plethora of hammocks and lawn chairs provide front-row seats for the spectacular sunsets at this 2.5-acre waterfront hideaway.

Ragged Edge Resort
Resort $$

(🕿305-852-5389; www.ragged-edge.com; 243 Treasure Harbor Rd; apt $69-259; P ❄ ☲) You can swim off the docks at this happily unpretentious oceanfront complex off Mile 86.5. It has 10 spotless and popular studios and apartments, and a happily comatose vibe.

Morada Bay
American $$$

(🕿305-664-0604; www.moradabay-restaurant. com; Mile 81.6 bayside; mains $14-33; ☉11:30am-10pm) Grab a table under a palm tree on the white-sand beach and sip a rum drink with your fresh seafood for a lovely, easy-going Caribbean experience. Don't miss the monthly full-moon party.

Middle Keys

GRASSY KEY

To reach Grassy Key in the Middle Keys, you enjoy a vivid sensation of island-hopping, ending with the biggest hop, the **Seven Mile Bridge**, one of the world's longest causeways.

Dolphin Research Center
Wildlife Reserve

(📞 305-289-1121; www.dolphins.org; Mile 59 bayside; adult/under 4yr/4-12yr/senior $20/free/15/17.50, swim program $180-650; ⏰ 9am-4pm) By far the most popular activity on Grassy Key is swimming with the descendants of Flipper. Of all the dolphin swimming spots in the Keys, we prefer this one; the dolphins are free to leave the grounds and a lot of marine-biology research goes on behind the scenes.

MARATHON

Halfway between Key Largo and Key West, Marathon is the most sizable town; it's a good base and a hub for commercial fishing and lobster boats.

Sights & Activities

Crane Point Museum
Museum

(www.cranepoint.net; Mile 50.5 bayside; adult/child $12.50/8.50; ⏰ 9am-5pm Mon-Sat, from noon Sun; 👶) Escape all the development at this 63-acre reserve, where you'll find a vast system of nature trails and mangroves, a raised boardwalk and a rare early-20th-century Bahamian-style house. Kids will enjoy pirate and wreck exhibits, a walk-through coral reef tunnel and the bird hospital.

Pigeon Key National Historic District
Island

(📞 305-743-5999; www.pigeonkey.net; tours leave from Mile 47 oceanside; adult/child/under 5yr $12/9/free; ⏰ tours 10am, noon & 2pm) On the Marathon side of Seven Mile Bridge,

this tiny key served as a camp for the workers who toiled to build the Overseas Hwy in the 1930s. You can tour the historic structures or just sun and snorkel on the beach. Reach it by ferry, included in admission, or walk or bike your way there on the **Old Seven Mile Bridge**, which is closed to traffic but serves as the 'World's Longest Fishing Bridge.'

Sombrero Beach
Beach

(Sombrero Beach Rd, off Mile 50 oceanside) This beautiful little white-sand beach has a playscape, shady picnic spots and big clean bathrooms.

Marathon Kayak
Kayaking

(📞 305-395-0355; www.marathonkayak.com; 3hr tours $60) Kayak Dave is a reliable source for kayak instruction and excellent guided tours.

🛏 Sleeping & Eating

Seascape Motel & Marina
Motel $$

(📞 305-743-6212; www.seascapemoteland marina.com; 1275 76th St Ocean E, btwn Miles 51 & 52; r from $99; P ❄ 🛜 ♨ 👶) Choose one of the nine crisp, clean rooms or an apartment that sleeps six at this oceanfront hideaway with a waterfront pool, boat dock and barbecue area.

Keys Fisheries
Seafood $

(www.keysfisheries.com; 3502 Gulfview Ave; mains $7-16; ⏰ 11am-9pm) Shoo the seagulls from your picnic table on the deck and dig in to fresh seafood in a down-and-dirty dockside atmosphere. The lobster reuben is the stuff of legend.

Hurricane
American $$

(📞 305-743-2200; Mile 49.5 bayside; mains $9-19; ⏰ 11am-midnight) As well as being a favorite Marathon bar, the Hurricane also serves an excellent menu of creative South Florida–inspired goodness, like snapper stuffed with crabmeat and conch sliders jerked in Caribbean seasoning.

Island Fish Co
Seafood $$

(📞 305-743-4191; www.islandfishco.com; Mile 54 bayside; mains $8-22; ⏰ 8am-11pm) Grab a spicy bowl of conch chowder and a seat overlooking the water at this huge, open-air tiki hut that has a raw bar and copious fish specialties.

Lower Keys

The Lower Keys (Miles 46 to 0) are fierce bastions of conch culture in all its variety.

One of Florida's most acclaimed beaches – and certainly the best in the Keys for its shallow, warm water – is at **Bahia Honda State Park** (☏305-872-3210; www.bahiahondapark.com; Mile 36.8; per car/motorcycle/cyclist $5/4/2; ⊙8am-sunset; [♿]), a 524-acre park with nature trails, ranger-led programs, water-sports rentals and some of the best coral reefs outside Key Largo.

Offshore from **Looe Key** is a marine sanctuary teeming with colorful tropical fish and coral; try **Looe Key Dive Center** (☏305-872-2215; www.diveflakeys.com; snorkel/dive $44/84) on Ramrod Key for snorkeling and diving day trips, including wreck dives.

Overnight camping at **Bahia Honda State Park** (☏305-872-2353; www.reserveamerica.com; sites $36, cabins $160; [P]) is sublime; it'd be perfect except for the sandflies. There are six popular waterfront cabins. Reserve far ahead for all. For a completely different experience, book one of the four cozily scrumptious rooms at **Deer Run Bed & Breakfast** (☏305-872-2015; www.deerrunfloridabb.com; 1997 Long Beach Dr, Big Pine Key, off Mile 33 oceanside; r $235-355; [P][♨]). This state-certified green lodge and vegetarian B&B is a garden of quirky delights, and the owners are extremely helpful.

On Big Pine Key, stop in for a pizza, beer and ambience at **No Name Pub** (☏305-872-9115; N Watson Blvd, Big Pine Key, off Mile 30.5 bayside; mains $7-18; ⊙11am-11pm) – if you can find it. The quirky hideout is right before the causeway that gets you to **No Name Key**. While you're there, staple a dollar bill to the wall to contribute to the collection of approximately $60,000 wallpapering the room.

Key West

Key West's funky, laid-back vibe has long attracted artists, renegades and free spirits. In the words of one local: 'It's like they shook the United States and all the nuts fell to the bottom.' Part of that independent streak is rooted in Key West's geography: it's barely connected to the USA, and it's closer to Cuba than to the rest of the States. There's only one road in, and it's not on the way to anywhere. In other words, it's an easy place to do your own thing.

The island has a long and colorful history that includes pirates, sunken

Cyclist in Key West
COREY RICH/GETTY IMAGES ©

treasures, literary legends and lots of ghosts. These days though, people flock to Key West to soak up the sun, the mellow atmosphere and more than a little booze. They listen to tales of the past. They snorkel the crystal clear water. And they find their internal clocks set to 'island time.'

◎ Sights

Key West has more than its fair share of historic homes, buildings and districts (like the colorful Bahama Village); it's a walkable town that rewards exploring.

Mallory Square   Square

Sunset at Mallory Sq, at the end of Duval St, is a bizzaro attraction of the highest order. It takes all those energies, subcultures and oddities of Keys life – the hippies, the rednecks, the foreigners and the tourists – and focuses them into one torchlit, playfully edgy (but family-friendly) street party.

Duval Street   Street

Key West locals have a love-hate relationship with their island's most famous road.

Duval, Old Town Key West's main drag, is a miracle mile of booze, tacky everything and awful behavior that still manages, somehow, to be fun.

Hemingway House   House

(✆305-294-1136; www.hemingwayhome. com; 907 Whitehead St; adult/child $13/6; ◷9am-5pm) Ernest Hemingway lived in this Spanish-Colonial house from 1931 to 1940 – to write, drink and fish, if not always in that order. Tours run every half-hour, and as you listen to docent-spun yarns of Papa, you'll see his studio, his unusual pool, and the descendents of his six-toed cats languishing in the sun, on furniture and pretty much wherever they feel like.

Florida Keys Eco-Discovery Center   Museum

(✆305-809-4750; http://eco-discovery.com/ ecokw.html; 35 East Quay Rd; ◷9am-4pm Tue-Sat; P ♿) FREE This excellent nature center pulls together all the plants, animals and habitats that make up the Keys' unique ecosystem and presents them in fresh, accessible ways.

Old Bahia Honda rail bridge, Bahia Honda State Park (p285)

Key West Butterfly & Nature Conservatory
Animal Sanctuary

(☎305-296-2988; www.keywestbutterfly.com; 1316 Duval St; adult/4-12yr $12/8.50; ⊙9am-5pm; ⊞) Even if you have only the faintest interest in butterflies, you'll find yourself entranced by the sheer quantity flittering around you here.

Fort East Martello Museum & Gardens
Museum

(☎305-296-3913; www.kwahs.com/martello.htm; 3501 S Roosevelt Blvd; adult/child $7/5; ⊙9:30am-4:30pm) This fortress preserves interesting historical artifacts and some fabulous folk art by Mario Sanchez and 'junk' sculptures by Stanley Papio. But Martello's most famous resident is Robert the Doll – a genuinely creepy, supposedly haunted, 19th-century doll that's kept in a glass case to keep him from making mischief.

Activities

Getting out on or in the water is one of the top activities. Charters abound for everything from fishing to snorkeling to scuba diving, including dive trips to the **USS Vandenberg**, a 522ft transport ship sunk off the coast to create the world's second-largest artificial reef.

Fort Zachary Taylor
Beach

(www.floridastateparks.org/forttaylor; 601 Howard England Way; per car/pedestrian $6/2; ⊙8am-sunset) Key West has three city beaches, but they aren't special; most people head to Bahia Honda. That said, Fort Zachary Taylor has the best beach on Key West, with white sand, decent swimming and some near-shore snorkeling; it's great for sunsets and picnics.

Dive Key West
Diving

(☎305-296-3823; www.divekeywest.com) Has everything you need for wreck-diving trips, from equipment to charters.

Jolly Rover
Cruise

(☎305-304-2235; www.schoonerjollyrover.com; cnr Greene & Elizabeth Sts, Schooner Wharf; cruise $45) Set sail on a pirate-esque

---

---

schooner offering daytime and sunset cruises.

Reelax Charters
Kayaking

(☎305-304-1392; www.keyskayaking.com; Mile 17 Sugarloaf Key Marina; kayak trips $240) Take a guided kayak tour from nearby Sugarloaf Key.

Sunny Days Catamaran
Snorkeling

(☎866-878-2223; www.sunnydayskeywest.com; 201 Elizabeth St; adult/child $35/22) Our favorite for snorkel trips, water sports and other aquatic adventures.

Clearly Unique
Kayaking

(☎877-282-5327; www.clearlyuniquecharters.com) Rents out glass-bottomed kayaks, providing a unique view of the water.

Sleeping

Caribbean House
Guesthouse $

(☎305-296-0999; www.caribbeanhousekw.com; 226 Petronia St; summer $89, winter $119-139; P ❄ @) In the heart of Bahama Village, rooms are tiny, but they're clean, cozy and cheery. Add free breakfast and

If You Like...
Nightlife

If you like the Green Parrot (p289) and the nightly revelry that is Key West's biggest drawcard, check out these other great nightspots.

1 CAPTAIN TONY'S SALOON
(www.capttonyssaloon.com; 428 Greene St)
This former icehouse, morgue and Hemingway haunt is built around the town's old hanging tree. The eclectic decor includes emancipated bras and signed dollar bills.

2 GARDEN OF EDEN
(224 Duval St) You can make like Adam and Eve at this clothing-optional rooftop bar; the fig leaf is also optional.

3 LA TE DA
(www.lateda.com; 1125 Duval St) The outside bar is where locals gather for mellow chats over beer, and you can catch high-quality drag acts upstairs at the fabulous Crystal Room on weekends.

4 PORCH
(www.theporchkw.com; 429 Caroline St; ⊙10am-2am Mon-Sat, noon-2am Sun) Escape the Duval St frat-boy bars at the Porch, where knowledgeable bartenders dispense artisan beers.

welcoming hosts and you get a rare find in Key West: a bargain.

Key West Bed & Breakfast
B&B **$$**
(☎800-438-6155, 305-296-7274; www.keywestbandb.com; 415 William St; r winter $89-265, summer $79-155; ❄️🛜) Sunny, airy and full of artistic touches: hand-painted pottery here, a working loom there – is that a ship's masthead in the corner? There are also a range of rooms to fit every budget.

L'Habitation
Guesthouse **$$**
(☎305-293-9203; www.lhabitation.com; 408 Eaton St; r $119-189; ❄️🛜) At this beautiful classic Keys cottage, the friendly, bilingual

owners welcome guests in English or French. The cute rooms come kitted out in light tropical shades, with lamps that look like contemporary art pieces and Skittles-bright quilts.

Key Lime Inn
Hotel **$$**
(☎800-549-4430; www.historickeywestinns.com; 725 Truman Ave; r $99-229; P🛜♿)
These cozy cottages are scattered around a tropical hardwood backdrop. Inside, the blissfully cool rooms are greener than a jade mine, with wicker furniture and tiny flat-screens to keep you from ever leaving.

Eating

Don't leave the island without sampling conch fritters – like hushpuppies, but made with conch – or key lime pie, made with key limes, sweetened condensed milk, eggs and sugar on a Graham-cracker crust.

Help Yourself Organic Foods
Vegetarian **$**
(☎315-296-7766; www.helpyourselfcafe.com; 829 Fleming St; dishes $5-12; ⊙8am-6pm; 🍴) Vegetarian, vegan and gluten-free options abound in this cute, colorful cafe.

El Siboney
Cuban **$$**
(900 Catherine St; mains $8-16; ⊙11am-9:30pm) Key West is only 90 miles from Cuba, so this awesome rough-and-ready corner establishment is quite literally the closest you can get to real Cuban food in the US. Cash only.

Blue Heaven
American **$$$**
(☎305-296-8666; http://blueheavenkw.homestead.com; 729 Thomas St; dinner $17-35; ⊙8am-4pm, until 2pm Sun & 5-10:30pm daily) One of the island's quirkiest venues (and it's a high bar), where you dine in an outdoor courtyard with a flock of chickens. Customers gladly wait, bemusedly, for Blue Heaven's well-executed, Southern-fried interpretation of Keys cuisine.

Café Solé
French **$$$**

(📞305-294-0230; www.cafesole.com; 1029 Southard St; dinner $20-34; 🕐5:30-10pm) Conch carpaccio with capers? Yellowtail fillet and foie gras? Oh yes. This locally and critically acclaimed venue is known for its cozy back-porch ambience and innovative menus, the result of a French-trained chef exploring island ingredients.

🍷 Drinking & Entertainment

Hopping (or staggering) from one bar to the next – also known as the 'Duval Crawl' – is a favorite pastime here in the Conch Republic, and there are plenty of options for your drinking pleasure.

Green Parrot
Bar

(www.greenparrot.com; 601 Whitehead St; 🕐10am-4am) This rogue's cantina has the longest tenure of any bar on the island (since 1890). It's a fabulous dive drawing a lively mix of locals and out-of-towners, with a century's worth of strange decor. Men, don't miss the urinal.

Virgilio's
Jazz

(www.virgilioskeywest.com; 524 Duval St) For a little variety, head to this candlelit martini lounge where you can chill to jazz and salsa. Enter on Appelrouth Lane.

ℹ Information

A great trip-planning resource is www.fla-keys.com/keywest. In town, get maps and brochures at Key West Chamber of Commerce (📞305-294-2587; www.keywestchamber.org; 510 Greene St; 🕐8:30am-6:30pm Mon-Sat, to 6pm Sun).

ℹ Getting There & Around

You can fly into Key West International Airport (EYW; www.keywestinternationalairport.com) with frequent flights from major cities, most going through Miami. Or take a fast catamaran from Fort Myers or Miami; call the Key West Express (📞888-539-2628; www.seakeywestexpress.com; adult/child round trip $146/81, one way $86/58) for schedules and fares; discounts apply for advance booking.

Within Key West, bicycles are the preferred mode of travel (rentals along Duval St run $10 to $25 per day).

Shop selling key lime pies, Key West

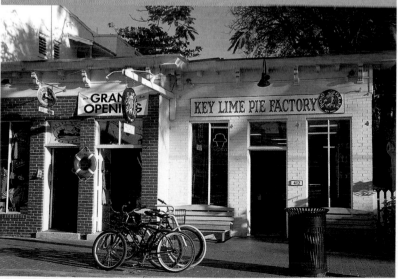

The Grand Canyon & the Southwest

Breathtaking beauty and the allure of adventure merge seamlessly in the Southwest. It's a captivating mix that has drawn dreamers and explorers for centuries. Pioneers staked their claims beside lush riverbanks, prospectors dug into mountains for untold riches, and religious refugees built cities across empty deserts, while astronomers and rocket builders peered into star-filled skies.

For travelers, beauty and adventure still loom large in this land of mountains, deserts and wide-open spaces that sprawl across Arizona, Nevada, Utah and New Mexico. You can hike past red rocks, mountain-bike over wild landscapes, raft through canyons and roll the dice under the mesmerizing lights of Vegas. But remember, beauty and adventure here can also loom small. Study that saguaro up close. Ask Hopi artists about their craft. Savor some green chile stew. It's the tap-you-on-the-shoulder moments you may just cherish the most.

Grand Canyon National Park (p300)

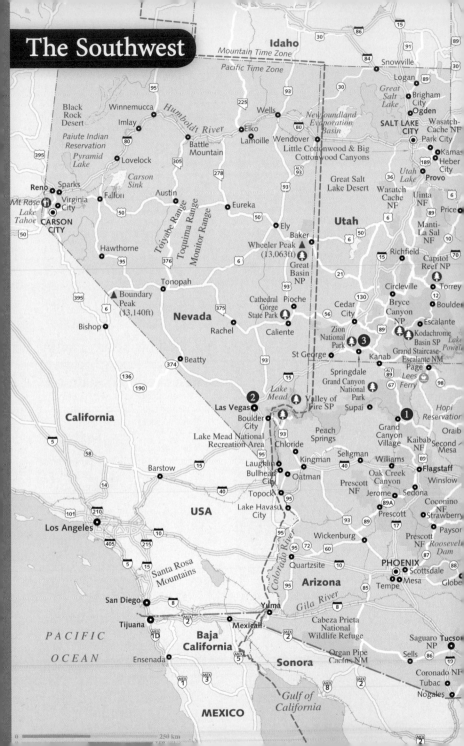

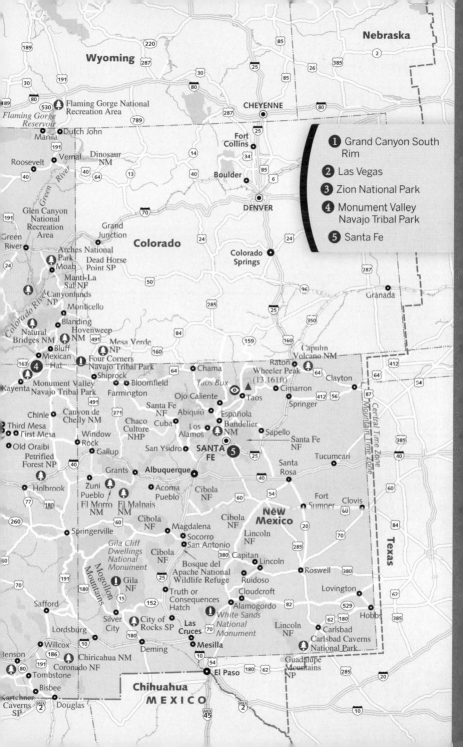

Nebraska

Wyoming

CHEYENNE

Flaming Gorge National
Recreation Area

*Flaming Gorge
Reservoir*

Dutch John

Manila

Fort
Collins

Roosevelt

Vernal

Dinosaur
NM

Boulder

Green River

DENVER

Green
River

Glen Canyon
National
Recreation
Area

Grand
Junction

Colorado

Colorado
Springs

Arches National
Park
Moab

Dead Horse
Point SP

Manti-La
Sal NF

Granada

Canyonlands
NP

Monticello

Natural
Bridges NM

Blanding
Hovenweep
NM

Mesa Verde

Capulin
Volcano NM

Bluff

Mexican
Hat

NP

Four Corners

Raton
Wheeler Peak
(13,161ft)

Clayton

❹ Navajo Tribal Park

Kayenta

Monument Valley
Navajo Tribal Park

Shiprock

Bloomfield

Farmington

Taos Box

Cimarron

Taos

Springer

Chinle

Canyon de
Chelly NM

Santa Fe
NF

Ojo Caliente

Abiquiú

Española

Third Mesa
First Mesa

Chaco
Culture
NHP

Cuba

Los
Alamos

Bandelier
NM

Sapello

Santa Fe
NF

Old Oraibi

Window
Rock

San Ysidro

**SANTA
FE**

❺

Petrified
Forest NP

Gallup

Grants

Albuquerque

Santa
Rosa

Tucumcari

Zuni
Pueblo

Acoma
Pueblo

Cibola
NF

Fort
Sumner

Clovis

El Morro
NM

El Malpais
NM

**New
Mexico**

Springerville

Cibola
NF

Magdalena

Cibola
NF

*Gila Cliff
Dwellings
National
Monument*

Socorro

San Antonio

Cibola
NF

Lincoln
NF

*Mogollon
Mountains*

Cibola
NF

Bosque del
Apache National
Wildlife Refuge

Capitan

Lincoln

Roswell

Gila
NF

Truth or
Consequences
Hatch

Ruidoso

Lovington

Safford

Silver
City

City of
Rocks SP

Cloudcroft

Alamogordo

Lincoln
NF

Carlsbad

Lordsburg

*White Sands
National
Monument*

Hobbs

Holbrook

Las
Cruces

Willcox

Deming

Mesilla

Carlsbad Caverns
National Park

Benson

Chiricahua NM
Coronado NF

Texas

Tombstone

Bisbee

El Paso

Guadalupe
Mountains
NP

Kartchner
Caverns
SP

Douglas

Chihuahua

M E X I C O

Central Time Zone
Mountain Time Zone

❶ Grand Canyon South
Rim

❷ Las Vegas

❸ Zion National Park

❹ Monument Valley
Navajo Tribal Park

❺ Santa Fe

The Grand Canyon & the Southwest's Highlights

Grand Canyon South Rim

It took two billion years to create the canyon, but change is afoot on the South Rim (p301), with new exhibits opening at lightning speed. But don't worry. Beyond the rim, the view remains the same: an immense, mesmerizing tableau that shares the earth's geologic treasures layer by dramatic layer.

Las Vegas

Vegas (p312) is Hollywood for the rest of us, where you get to play the leading role instead of watching someone else do it. It's the only place you can see ancient hieroglyphics, the Eiffel Tower and the canals of Venice all in a few short hours. Sure, they're reproductions, but in a slice of desert that's transformed into one of the most lavish places on earth, nothing is done halfway – not even the illusions. Left: Neon signs, downtown Las Vegas

B. TANAKA/GETTY IMAGES ©

Zion National Park

3

This spectacular red-rock canyon (p321) offers some of the Southwest's most breathtaking scenery, with stunning clifftop panoramas, and soaring massifs that look like ancient carved cathedrals. Over 100 miles of trails take you through dramatic canyons and to vertiginous heights. Those seeking to revel in the experience can book a night at the beautifully sited Zion Lodge. Right: Canyoneering in Zion National Park

4

Monument Valley Navajo Tribal Park

Towering sandstone monoliths rise like ancient sentinels over an endless expanse of desert. The stark beauty of Monument Valley (p323) has been immortalized in road movies and old Westerns, and remains a deep source of pride for the Navajo Nation, who have lived here for generations. Taking a scenic drive is the best way to see the fiery beauty of this unchanged landscape.

5

Santa Fe

Sitting at the base of the Sangre de Cristo range, Santa Fe (p324), at 7000ft, is the highest state capital in the US. It's also one of America's oldest cities, with roots dating to the early 17th century. It's home to fascinating pueblo architecture, a burgeoning gallery scene and excellent restaurants and farmers markets, while outdoor adventures – such as hiking, mountain biking and skiing – are available in its backyard. Above: Santa Fe doorway

The Southwest's Best...

Geologic Wonders

○ **Arches National Park** Photogenic sandstone arches and curiosities such as Balanced Rock. (p322)

○ **Canyonlands National Park** Gallery of ancient wonders – arches, buttes, mesas, spires and canyons. (p322)

○ **Bryce Canyon National Park** Fantastic red-rock park famed for its hoodoos (spire-like rock formations). (p319)

Hiking

○ **Santa Fe** Near town, there's superb hiking in the Pecos Wilderness and Santa Fe National Forest. (p324)

○ **Moab** Outdoors-loving town that's a gateway to adventure. (p319)

○ **South Kaibab** Spectacular scenery along one of the Grand Canyon's loveliest trails. (p301)

○ **Angels Landing Trail** Gasp your way to the top of Zion National Park for awe-inspiring views. (p321)

Museums & Galleries

○ **Heard Museum** Home to one of the nation's finest Native American art collections. (p309)

○ **Georgia O'Keeffe Museum** Santa Fe has a fabulous collection of the Southwest's most famous painter. (p324)

○ **Atomic Testing Museum** Decode the mysteries and horrors of the atomic age at this fascinating Las Vegas attraction. (p313)

○ **Canyon Rd** Scores of art galleries and studios line this vibrant stretch of Santa Fe. (p324)

Left: Petroglyphs, Canyon de Chelly National Park (p322);
Above: Mesa Arch, Canyonlands National Park (p322)
(LEFT) JOHN ELK/GETTY IMAGES ©; (ABOVE) WITOLD SKRYPCZAK/GETTY IMAGES ©

Need to Know

Native American Sites

○ **Acoma Pueblo** One of the oldest continuously inhabited settlements in North America. (p329)

○ **Canyon de Chelly National Monument** Home to ancient clifftop dwellings on Navajo lands. (p322)

○ **Wheelwright Museum of the American Indian** Fantastic collection of Navajo works in Santa Fe. (p324)

○ **Bandelier National Monument** Haunting site of Ancestral Puebloans who lived among the cliffs. (p328)

ADVANCE PLANNING

○ **Nine months before** If you're planning on lodging inside the Grand Canyon, reserve well ahead. Also reserve in advance for Zion and other national park accommodation.

○ **One month before** Buy tickets for festivals and events.

○ **Two weeks before** Reserve at top restaurants in Santa Fe and Taos. Book tours and outdoor excursions.

RESOURCES

○ **American Southwest** (www.americansouthwest.net) Covers parks and natural landscapes.

○ **National Park Service** (www.nps.gov/grca) Has a downloadable trip planner, maps and seasonal guides.

○ **Visit Las Vegas** (www.lasvegas.com) Official city tourism site.

○ **Las Vegas Weekly** (www.lasvegasweekly.com) Vegas food and entertainment.

○ **Santa Fe Reporter** (www.sfreporter.com) Santa Fe dining, arts and entertainment.

GETTING AROUND

○ **Airports** Phoenix (PHX; www.skyharbor.com) has free bus transport to/from downtown; Las Vegas (LAS; www.mccarran.com), has a $7.50 shuttle to hotels on the Strip.

○ **Bus** Greyhound (www.greyhound.com) provides service between major towns.

○ **Hire car** Essential for exploring the Southwest on your own.

○ **Train** Amtrak stops in Flagstaff, Arizona, and Lamy, New Mexico (20 miles south of Santa Fe), on its Chicago–LA run.

BE FOREWARNED

○ **Crowds** Expect big crowds (and debilitating heat) if visiting the Grand Canyon in summer. For a more sedate experience, visit the North Rim rather than the South Rim.

○ **Heat** Temperatures soar in summer (climbing regularly above 90 degrees). Whether hiking or driving, be prepared and take plenty of water.

○ **Respect** Be respectful when interacting with Native Americans; ask permission before taking photos and don't pry about cultural practices.

The Grand Canyon & the Southwest Itineraries

Few places on earth rival the dramatic beauty of the American Southwest. These two itineraries take in canyons, red-rock deserts and alpine scenery, as well as more urbane diversions in Las Vegas and Santa Fe.

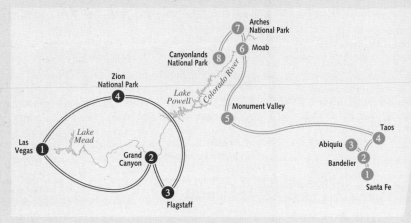

LAS VEGAS & THE GRAND CANYON

Sin City & Wondrous Canyons

Starting in ❶**Las Vegas**, take a surreal trip around the world without leaving the Strip, hopping between the Bellagio (p312), Venetian (p312) and Caesars Palace (p312). Catch a show (perhaps Cirque du Soleil), followed by cocktails at sky-high Mix (p317).

On day two, make the five-hour drive east to Grand Canyon Village, on the South Rim of the ❷**Grand Canyon** (p300). Gaze at the mesmerizing abyss from the Rim Trail, then enjoy more great vistas over dinner at El Tovar (p305). Spend the night and rise early for a scenic day-hike along the Bright Angel Trail. Afterwards, head 80 miles south to ❸**Flagstaff**. Go stargazing at the

Lowell Observatory (p308), then kick up your heels at the honky-tonk Museum Club (p308).

On day four, drive five hours northwest to ❹**Zion National Park** (p321). Gear up for a magnificent hike on Angels Landing Trail, with dramatic views over the red-rock landscape. Spend the night in perfectly sited Zion Lodge. On your last day, make the three-hour drive back to Vegas. Celebrate the big journey over a memorable meal at Sage (p316) then try to win back your travel expenses at the Cosmopolitan (p312).

SANTA FE TO MOAB

Trip Around the Southwest

Spend two days in ❶ **Santa Fe**, taking in the artful vibe of this history-rich town – visit the shops and galleries of Canyon Rd (p324), the stellar Georgia O'Keeffe Museum (p324) and the fascinating Wheelwright Museum (p324).

On day three, explore the ancient clifftop dwellings of ❷ **Bandelier** (p328) and the scenery that inspired O'Keeffe in ❸ **Abiquiu** (p328). The next day, in nearby ❹ **Taos**, visit the photogenic Taos Pueblo (p330), hike amid mountain scenery and overnight in an ecofriendly Earthship (p331).

On day five, drive seven hours west beneath the big skies of Native American country to ❺ **Monument Valley** (p323). Catch the flaming red buttes at sunset, and stay in the Navajo-run View Hotel (p323).

In the morning, head three hours northeast to ❻ **Moab** (p319), an adventure-loving town ringed by mountains. Explore the sandstone formations of ❼ **Arches National Park** (p322) and the awe-inspiring ❽ **Canyonlands National Park** (p322). By evening, refuel at Moab's good restaurants and microbreweries. On your last day, go kayaking, rafting or horseback riding with one of Moab's many outfitters.

Arches National Park (p322)
ROVINGMAGPIE@FLICKR.COM/GETTY IMAGES ©

Discover the Grand Canyon & the Southwest

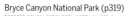

Bryce Canyon National Park (p319)
ROBERTO SONCIN GEROMETTA/GETTY IMAGES ©

GRAND CANYON NATIONAL PARK

Why do folks become giddy when describing the Grand Canyon? One peek over the edge makes it clear. The canyon captivates travelers because of its sheer immensity; it's a tableau that reveals the earth's history layer by dramatic layer. Mother Nature adds artistic details – rugged plateaus, crumbly spires, shadowed ridges – that flirt and catch your eye as the sun crosses the sky.

Snaking along its floor are 277 miles of the Colorado River, which has carved the canyon over the past six million years and exposed rocks up to two billion years old – half the age of the earth.

The two rims of the Grand Canyon offer quite different experiences; they lie more than 200 miles apart by road and are rarely visited on the same trip. Most visitors choose the South Rim with its easy access, wealth of services and vistas that don't disappoint. The quieter North Rim has its own charms; at 8200ft elevation (1000ft higher than the South Rim), its cooler temperatures support wildflower meadows and tall, thick stands of aspen and spruce.

ℹ Information

The most developed area in the Grand Canyon National Park (☏ 928-638-7888; www.nps.gov/grca; entrance ticket vehicles/cyclists & pedestrians $25/12) is Grand Canyon Village, 6 miles north of the South Rim Entrance Station. The North Rim has one entrance, which is 30 miles south of Jacob Lake on Hwy 67; continue another 14 miles south to the actual rim. The North Rim and South Rim are 215 miles apart by car, 21 miles on foot through the canyon, or 10 miles as the condor flies.

June is the driest month, July and August the wettest. January has average overnight lows of 13°F (-11°C) to 20°F (-7°C) and daytime highs around 40°F (4°C). Summer temperatures inside the canyon regularly soar above 100°F (38°C). While the South Rim is open year-round, most visitors come between late May and early September. The North Rim is open from mid-May to mid-October.

The park entrance ticket is valid for seven days and can be used at both rims.

All overnight hikes and backcountry camping in the park require a permit. The Backcountry Information Center (☏928-638-7875, fax 928-638-2125; ⏱8am-noon & 1-5pm, phone staffed 1-5pm Mon-Fri) accepts applications for backpacking permits ($10, plus $5 per person per night) starting four months before the proposed month. Your chances are decent if you apply early (four months in advance for spring and fall) and provide alternative hiking itineraries. Reservations are accepted in person or by mail or fax. For more information see www.nps.gov/grca/planyourvisit/backcountry-permit.htm.

If you arrive without a permit, head to the backcountry office, by Maswik Lodge on the South Rim, to join the waiting list.

As a conservation measure, note that the park no longer sells bottled water. Instead, fill your thermos at water filling stations along the rim or at Canyon View Marketplace. Water bottles constituted 20% of the waste generated in the park.

In addition to the visitor centers listed here, information is available inside the park at Yavapai Museum of Geology (⏱8am-7pm Mar-Nov, to 6pm Dec-Feb), Verkamp's Visitor Center (⏱8am-7pm Mar-Nov, to 6pm Dec-Feb), Kolb Studio (☏928-638-2771; Grand Canyon Village; ⏱8am-7pm Mar-Nov, to 6pm Dec-Feb), Tusayan Ruin & Museum (☏928-638-2305; ⏱9am-5pm) and Desert View Information Center (☏928-638-7893; ⏱9am-5pm).

Grand Canyon Visitor Center (www.nps.gov/grca; South Rim; ⏱8am-5pm Mar-Nov, from 9am Dec-Feb) is 300 yards behind Mather Point; a large plaza holds the visitor center and the Books & More Store. Outdoor bulletin boards display information about trails, tours, ranger programs and the weather.

National Geographic Visitor Center (☏928-638-2468; www.explorethecanyon.com; 450 Hwy 64, Tusayan; adult/child $14/11; ⏱8am-10pm Mar-Oct, 10am-8pm Nov-Feb) is in Tusayan, 7 miles south of Grand Canyon Village; pay your $25 vehicle entrance fee here and spare yourself a potentially long wait at the park entrance, especially in summer. The IMAX theater screens the terrific 34-minute film *Grand Canyon – The Hidden Secrets*.

The North Rim Visitor Center (p307) is adjacent to the Grand Canyon Lodge, with maps, books, trail guides and current conditions.

South Rim

To escape the throngs, visit during fall or winter, especially on weekdays. You'll also gain some solitude by walking a short distance away from the viewpoints on the Rim Trail or by heading into the canyon itself.

⊙ Sights & Activities

A **scenic route** follows the rim on the west side of Grand Canyon Village along Hermit Rd. Closed to private vehicles March through November, the 7-mile road is serviced by the free park shuttle bus; cycling is encouraged because of the relatively light traffic. Stops offer spectacular views, and interpretive signs explain canyon features.

Hiking along the South Rim is among park visitors' favorite pastimes, with options for every skill level. The **Rim Trail** is the most popular, and easiest, walk in the park. It dips in and out of the scrubby pines of Kaibab National Forest and connects a series of scenic points and historical sights over 13 miles. Portions are paved, and every viewpoint is accessed by one of the three shuttle routes. The **Trail of Time** exhibit borders the Rim Trail just west of Yavapai Geology Museum. Here, every meter along the trail represents one million years of geologic history, with exhibits providing the details.

Desert View Drive starts to the east of Grand Canyon Village and follows the canyon rim for 26 miles to Desert View, the east entrance of the park. Pullouts offer spectacular views, and interpretive signs explain canyon features and geology.

Grand Canyon National Park

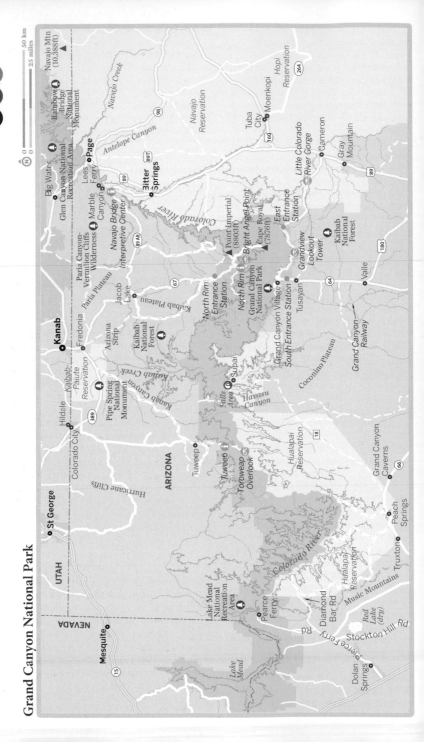

The most popular of the corridor trails is the beautiful **Bright Angel Trail**. The steep and scenic 8-mile descent to the Colorado River is punctuated with four logical turnaround spots. Summer heat can be crippling; day hikers should either turn around at one of the two resthouses (a 3- to 6-mile round trip) or hit the trail at dawn to safely make the longer hikes to Indian Garden and Plateau Point (9.2 and 12.2 miles round trip respectively). Hiking to the river in one day should not be attempted. The trailhead is just west of Bright Angel Lodge.

The **South Kaibab** is arguably one of the park's prettiest trails, combining stunning scenery and unobstructed 360-degree views with every step. Steep, rough and wholly exposed, summer ascents can be dangerous, and during this season rangers discourage all but the shortest day hikes – otherwise it's a grueling 12.6-mile round trip to the river and back. Turn around at **Cedar Ridge**, (about 3 miles round trip), perhaps the park's finest short day hike.

Bright Angel Bicycles
Bicycle Rental

(928-638-3055; www.bikegrandcanyon.com; 10 S Entrance Rd, Grand Canyon Visitor Center; full day adult/child $40/30; 8am-5pm Apr, 8am-6pm May–mid-Sep, 10am-5pm mid-Sep–Oct, 10am-4pm Nov–Mar) Bright Angel rents 'comfort cruiser' bikes. The friendly staff custom-fit each bike to the individual. Also rents wheelchairs ($10 per day).

Tours

Xanterra
Horseback Riding

(303-297-2757; www.grandcanyonlodges.com/mule-rides-716.html) Park tours are run by Xanterra, which has information desks at Bright Angel (p304), Maswik (p305) and **Yavapai** (Grand Canyon Village; Apr-Oct;) lodges. Various daily bus tours (tickets from $22) are offered.

Due to erosion concerns, half-day mule rides into the canyon from the South Rim are not offered and the NP has limited inner-canyon mule rides to

---

those traveling all the way to Phantom Ranch. Rather than going below the rim, three-hour day trips ($123) now take riders along the rim, through the ponderosa, piñon and juniper forest to the Abyss overlook. Overnight trips (one/two people $507/895, year-round) and two-night trips (one/two people $714/1192, November to March) follow the Bright Angel Trail to the river, travel east on the River Trail and cross the river on the Kaibab Suspension Bridge. Riders spend the night at Phantom Ranch.

Sleeping

Advance or same-day reservations are required for the South Rim's six lodges, which are operated by **Xanterra** (📞303-297-2757, 888-297-2757; www.grandcanyonlodges.com). Use this phone number to make advance reservations (highly recommended) at any of the places (although it's best to call Phantom Ranch directly) listed here. For same-day reservations or to reach a guest, call the **South Rim switchboard** (📞928-638-2631). If you can't find accommodations in the national

park, try Tusayan (at South Rim Entrance Station), Valle (31 miles south), Cameron (53 miles east) or Williams (about 60 miles south).

All campgrounds and lodges are open year-round except Desert View.

Phantom Ranch   Cabin $
(📞reservations 888-297-2727; dm $46, cabin $148; ❄) It's not the Four Seasons, but this summer-campy complex has undeniable charm. Perched beside Phantom Creek at the bottom of the canyon, the ranch has basic cabins sleeping four to 10 people and segregated dorms. Call at the first of the month for reservations 13 months ahead. The canteen serves family-style meals (breakfast from $21, dinner $29 to $44).

Bright Angel Lodge   Lodge $$
(www.grandcanyonlodges.com; Grand Canyon Village; r with/without private bath $94/83, suites $185-362, cabins $120-340; ❄ @ 🛜) The log-and-stone Bright Angel offers historic charm and refurbished rooms, the cheapest of which have shared bathrooms.

Rafting the Colorado River

A boat trip down the Colorado is an epic, adrenaline-pumping adventure. The biggest single drop at Lava Falls plummets 37ft. But the true highlight is experiencing the Grand Canyon by looking up, not down from the rim. Its human history comes alive in ruins, wrecks and rock art. Commercial trips run from three days to three weeks and vary in the type of watercraft used. At night you camp under stars on sandy beaches (gear provided). It takes about two or three weeks to run the entire 279 miles of river through the canyon. Shorter sections of around 100 miles take four to nine days. Space is limited and the trips are popular, so book as far in advance as possible – although you might luck out and find a last-minute bargain on a rafting company Facebook page.

Arizona Raft Adventures (📞928-526-8200, 800-786-7238; www.azraft.com; 6-day Upper Canyon hybrid/paddle trips $2025/2125, 10-day Full Canyon motor trips $2965) This multigenerational family-run outfit offers paddle, oar, hybrid (with opportunities for both paddling and floating) and motor trips.

Arizona River Runners (📞800-477-7238, 602-867-4866; www.raftarizona.com; 6-day Upper Canyon oar trip $1925, 8-day Full Canyon motor trip $2650) Have been at their game since 1970, offering oar-powered and motorized trips.

Maswik Lodge
Lodge **$$**

(Grand Canyon Village; r south/north $92/176, cabins $94; ❄ @ 🛜) Set away from the rim, Maswik comprises 16 modern, two-story buildings. Rooms at Maswik North have private patios, air-con, cable TV and forest views; those at Maswik South are smaller with fewer amenities and more forgettable views. Cabins are available in summer only.

El Tovar Hotel
Lodge **$$$**

(Grand Canyon Village; r $183-281, ste $348-440; ❄ 🛜) Open since 1905, this dark-timbered lodge encourages lingering, even if you're not a guest. Inviting porches wrap around the rambling structure and the lobby has plenty of comfy seats – better for gazing at the impressive collection of animal mounts. These public spaces show the lodgelike, genteel elegance of the park's heyday.

Eating & Drinking

El Tovar
Dining Room
International **$$$**

(El Tovar; 📞928-638-2631, ext 6432; breakfast $9-13, lunch $10.25-16, dinner $17.25-33; ⏰6:30-10:45am, 11:15am-2pm & 4:30-10pm) A stone's throw from the canyon's edge, it has the best views of any restaurant in the state, if not the country. The grand stone and dark-oak dining room warms the soul like an upscale lodge of yore, and the food, especially the steaks, makes the trip worthwhile

Arizona Room
American **$$$**

(Bright Angel Lodge; lunch $8-12, dinner $8-28; ⏰11:30am-3pm Mar-Oct & 4:30-10pm Mar-Dec) 🍴 Antler chandeliers hang from the ceiling and picture windows overlook the canyon. Mains include steak, chicken and fish dishes. No reservations; there's often a wait.

Bright Angel Bar
Bar

(Bright Angel Lodge; mains $4-9; ⏰11:30am-10pm) Come here for your post-hike beer and burger. It's a fun place to relax at night when the lack of windows and dark decor aren't such a big deal.

Under the Park-n-Ride program, summer visitors can buy a park ticket at the National Geographic Visitor Center, park their vehicle at a designated lot, then hop aboard a free park shuttle (⏰8am-9:30pm mid-May–early Sep) that follows the Tusayan Route to the Grand Canyon Visitor Center inside the park.

Inside the park, free park shuttles operate along three routes: around Grand Canyon Village, west along Hermits Rest Route and east along Kaibab Trail Route. Buses typically run at least twice per hour, from one hour before sunset to one hour afterward.

North Rim

Head here for blessed solitude; of the park's 4.4 million annual visitors, only 400,000 make the trek to the North Rim. Meadows are thick with wildflowers and dense clusters of willowy aspen and spruce trees, and the air is often crisp, the skies big and blue.

Facilities on the North Rim are closed from mid-October to mid-May.

Call the **North Rim Switchboard** (📞928-638-2612) to reach facilities on the North Rim.

◎ Sights & Activities

The short and easy paved trail (0.5 miles) to **Bright Angel Point** is a canyon must. Beginning from the back porch of Grand Canyon Lodge, it goes to a narrow finger of an overlook with fabulous views.

The **North Kaibab Trail** is the North Rim's only maintained rim-to-river trail and connects with trails to the South Rim. The first 4.7 miles are the steepest, dropping 3050ft to **Roaring Springs** – a popular all-day hike. If you prefer a shorter day hike below the rim, walk just 0.75 miles down to **Coconino Overlook** or 2 miles to the **Supai Tunnel** to get a taste of steep inner-canyon hiking. The 28-mile round trip to the Colorado River is a multiday affair. For a ranger-recommended short hike that works well for families, try the 4-mile round-trip **Cape Final** trail, which leads through

ponderosa pines to sweeping views of the eastern Grand Canyon area.

Canyon Trail Rides (435-679-8665; www.canyonrides.com; mid-May–mid-Oct) offers one-hour ($40) and half-day ($80, minimum age 10 years) mule trips. Of the half-day trips, one is along the rim and the other drops into the Canyon on the North Kaibab Trail.

Sleeping

Accommodations are limited to one lodge and one campground. If these are booked, try your luck 80 miles north in Kanab, UT, or 84 miles northeast in Lees Ferry.

Grand Canyon Lodge Lodge **$$**
(advance reservations 877-386-4383, reservations outside USA 480-337-1320, same-day reservations 928-638-2611; www.grandcanyonlodgenorth.com; r $124, 2-person cabins $124-192, extra guest over 15yr $10; mid-May–mid-Oct;) Made of wood, stone and glass, the lodge enjoys a lofty perch beside the rim. Rustic yet modern cabins make up the majority of accommodations. The most expensive cabins offer two rooms, a porch and beautiful rim views. Reserve far in advance.

Eating & Drinking

The lodge will prepare sack lunches ($12), ready for pickup as early as 5:30am, for those wanting to picnic on the trail. Place your order the day before. For sandwiches, pizza and breakfast burritos, try **Deli in the Pines** (mains $4-8; 7am-9pm, mid-May–mid-Oct), also at the Lodge.

Grand Canyon Lodge Dining Room American **$$**
(928-645-6865 call Jan 1-Apr 15 for next season, 928-638-2611; www.grandcanyonlodgenorth.com; breakfast $7-12, lunch & dinner $12-30; 6:30-10am, 11:30am-2:30pm, 4:45-9:45pm mid-May–mid-Oct) The windows are so huge that you can sit anywhere and get a good view. The menu includes rainbow trout, bison flank steak, several vegetarian

Left: Grand Canyon Lodge; **Below:** Agave plant, Grand Canyon National Park

dishes and Arizona-crafted microbrews. Dinner reservations are required. Next door is the atmospheric **Rough Rider Saloon** (snacks $2-5; ⊙ breakfast 5:30-10:30am, drinks & snacks 11:30am-10:30pm), full of memorabilia from Teddy Roosevelt, the country's most adventurous president.

Grand Canyon Cookout Experience American $$ (adult/child/under 6yr $30/$15/free; ⊙ 6:15pm Jun-Sep; 🖐) This chuck wagon–style cookout featuring barbecue and cornbread is more of an event than a meal. Kids love it. Make arrangements at the Grand Canyon Lodge.

ⓘ Information

North Rim Visitor Center (📞 928-638-7864; www.nps.gov/grca; North Rim; ⊙ 8am-6pm mid-May–mid-Oct, 9am-4pm Oct 16-31) Sitting beside Grand Canyon Lodge, this is the place to get information about the park.

ⓘ Getting There & Around

The Transcanyon Shuttle (📞 928-638-2820, 877-638-2820; www.trans-canyonshuttle.com; one way/round trip $85/160; ⊙ May 15-Oct 31) departs daily from Grand Canyon Lodge for the South Rim (five hours) and is perfect for rim-to-rim hikers. Reserve at least one or two weeks in advance.

FLAGSTAFF

Flagstaff's laid-back charms are myriad, from its pedestrian-friendly historic downtown crammed with eclectic vernacular architecture and vintage neon to its high-altitude pursuits such as skiing and hiking.

Throw in a healthy appreciation for craft beer, freshly roasted coffee beans and an all-round good time and you have the makings of a town you want to slow down and savor.

 Sights

Museum of
Northern Arizona
Museum

(📞928-774-5213; www.musnaz.org; 3101 N
Fort Valley Rd; adult/child/senior $10/6/9;
🕐9am-5pm) For a helpful primer about the
region, stop here. Three miles north of
downtown, the museum spotlights local
geology, biology and arts as well as Native
American anthropology, with exhibits
spotlighting archaeology, history and
customs of local tribes.

Lowell Observatory
Observatory

(📞928-233-3212; www.lowell.edu; 1400 W Mars
Hill Rd; adult/child $12/5; 🕐9am-10pm Jun-Aug,
shorter hours Sep-May) This observatory
witnessed the first sighting of Pluto in
1920. Weather permitting, there's nightly
stargazing, helped by the fact that Flagstaff is the first International Dark Sky
city in the world. Day tours are offered
from 1pm to 4pm.

Activities

Humphreys Peak
Hiking

The state's highest mountain (12,663ft)
is a reasonably straightforward, though
strenuous, hike in summer. The trail,
which begins in the Arizona Snowbowl,
winds through forest, eventually coming
out above the beautifully barren tree line.
The distance is 4.5 miles one way; allow
six to eight hours round trip.

Arizona Snowbowl
Skiing

(📞928-779-1951; www.arizonasnowbowl.com;
Hwy 180 & Snowbowl Rd; lift ticket adult/child
$55/15; 🕐9am-4pm) Six lifts service 40
runs and a snowboarding park at eleva-
tions between 9200ft and 11,500ft. You
can ride the chairlift (adult/child $15/10)
in summer.

Sleeping

Hotel Monte Vista
Hotel $$

(📞928-779-6971; www.hotelmontevista.com; 100
N San Francisco St; d $65-110, ste $120-140; 🛜)
Feather lampshades, vintage furniture,
bold colors and old-fashioned layouts –
things are historically frisky in the 50

rooms and suites here, which are named
for the film stars who slept in them.

Drury Inn & Suites
Hotel $$

(📞928-773-4900; www.druryhotels.com; 300
S Milton Rd; r incl breakfast $155-165, ste $200;
🅿️❄️@🛜🛅🐾) The stone columns in
the lobby set an adventurous mood at
this six-story, LEED-certified property, but
the deal clincher is the hearty Kickback
happy hour which serves up complimen-
tary beer and wine (with a limit) and a
hearty spread of appetizers.

Eating

Beaver Street
Brewery
Brewpub $$

(www.beaverstreetbrewery.com; 11 S Beaver St;
lunch $8-13, dinner $10-20; 🕐11am-11pm Sun-
Thu, to midnight Fri & Sat; 👪) This bustling
brewpub does bar food right, offering
delicious pizzas, burgers and salads. It
usually has five handmade beers on tap
and some seasonal brews.

Criollo Latin Kitchen
Fusion $$

(📞928-774-0541; www.criollolatinkitchen.com;
16 N San Francisco St; lunch $8-17, dinner $10-22,
brunch $8-10; 🕐11am-9pm Mon-Thu, 11am-10pm
Fri, 9am-10pm Sat, 9am-9pm Sun) This Latin
fusion spot has a romantic, industrial setting for cozy cocktail dates and delectable
late-night small plates.

Drinking &
Entertainment

Follow the 1-mile Flagstaff Ale Trail (www.
flagstaffaletrail.com) to sample craft beer
at downtown breweries and a pub or two.

Museum Club
Bar

(📞928-526-9434; www.themuseumclub.com;
3404 E Rte 66; 🕐11am-2am) This honky-tonk
roadhouse has been kickin' up its boot
heels since 1936. Inside what looks like a
huge log cabin you'll find a wooden dance
floor, animals mounted on the walls and a
sumptuous elixir-filled mahogany bar.

Charly's Pub & Grill
Live Music

(📞928-779-1919; www.weatherfordhotel.com; 23
N Leroux St; 🕐8am-10pm) This restaurant at

the Weatherford Hotel has live music on the weekends.

ℹ Information

Visitor Center (📞928-774-9541, 800-842-7293; www.flagstaffarizona.org; 1 E Rte 66; ⏱8am-5pm Mon-Sat, 9am-4pm Sun) Inside the historic Amtrak train station.

ℹ Getting There & Around

Arizona Shuttle (📞928-226-8060, 800-888-2749; www.arizonashuttle.com) has shuttles that run to the south rim of the Grand Canyon ($29 one way), Sedona ($25 one way) and Phoenix Sky Harbor Airport ($45 one way).

Operated by **Amtrak** (📞928-774-8679, 800-872-7245; www.amtrak.com; 1 E Rte 66; ⏱3am-10:45pm), the *Southwest Chief* stops at Flagstaff on its daily run between Chicago and Los Angeles.

PHOENIX

Several 'towns' make up the region known as Greater Phoenix, which is the largest urban area in the Southwest. The City of Phoenix, with its downtown high-rises and top-notch museums, is the patriarch of the bunch.

◎ Sights

Heard Museum Museum
(📞602-252-8848; www.heard.org; 2301 N Central Ave; adult/6-12yr & student/senior $18/7.50/13.50; ⏱9:30am-5pm Mon-Sat, 11am-5pm Sun; ♿) Across 10 galleries, the museum displays Native American art, textiles, and ceramics, and spotlights Native American history and traditions.

Musical Instrument Museum Museum
(📞480-478-6000; www.themim.org; 4725 E Mayo Blvd; adult/13-19yr/child $18/$14/$10; ⏱9am-5pm Mon-Sat, 10am-5pm Sun, to 9pm first Fri of the month) From Ugandan thumb pianos to Hawaiian ukuleles to an Indonesian gong, the ears have it at this new museum that celebrates the world's musical instruments.

♥ If You Like... Scenic Drives

If you like the magnificent Desert View Drive along the Grand Canyon's South Rim, don't miss these other scenic drives.

1 OAK CREEK CANYON
A thrilling plunge past swimming holes, rock slides and crimson canyon walls on Hwy 89A between Flagstaff and Sedona.

2 KAYENTA-MONUMENT VALLEY
(Arizona) Become the star of your own Western on an iconic loop past cinematic red rocks in Navajo Country just off Hwy 163.

3 HIGHWAY 12 SCENIC BYWAY
(http://scenicbyway12.com) Arguably Utah's most diverse and stunning route, Hwy 12 Scenic Byway winds through rugged canyon land on a 124-mile journey west of Bryce Canyon to near Capitol Reef. The section between Escalante and Torrey traverses a moonscape of sculpted slickrock, crosses narrow ridgebacks and climbs over an 11,000ft-tall mountain.

4 BILLY THE KID SCENIC BYWAY
(www.billybyway.com) This mountain-and-valley loop in southeastern New Mexico swoops past Billy the Kid's stomping grounds, Smokey Bear's grave site and the orchard-lined Hondo Valley. From Roswell, take Hwy 380 west.

5 HIGH ROAD TO TAOS
The back road between Santa Fe and Taos passes through sculpted sandstone desert, fresh pine forests and rural villages with historic adobe churches and horse-filled pastures. The 13,000ft Truchas Peaks soar above. From Santa Fe, take Hwy 84/285 to Hwy 513 then follow the signs.

Desert Botanical Garden Gardens
(📞480-941-1225; www.dbg.org; 1201 N Galvin Pkwy; adult/child/student/senior $18/8/10/15; ⏱8am-8pm Oct-Apr, 7am-8pm May-Sep) On 145 acres, this inspirational garden is a refreshing place to reconnect with nature and offers a great introduction to desert plant life.

Phoenix Art Museum   Museum

(📞602-257-1222; www.phxart.org; 1625 N Central Ave; adult/6-17yr/student/senior $15/6/10/12, free Wed 3-9pm & 1st Fri of the month 6-10pm; ⏰10am-9pm Wed, 10am-5pm Thu-Sat, noon-5pm Sun; ♿) The Phoenix Art Museum is Arizona's premier repository of fine art. The collection includes works by Claude Monet, Diego Rivera and Georgia O'Keeffe.

 Activities

Piestewa Peak/Dreamy Draw Recreation Area   Hiking

(📞602-261-8318; www.phoenix.gov/parks; Squaw Peak Dr; ⏰trails 5am-11pm, last entry 6:59pm) The trek to the 2608ft summit is hugely popular and the saguaro-dotted park can get jammed on winter weekends. Dogs are allowed on some trails.

South Mountain Park   Hiking

(📞602-262-7393; 10919 S Central Ave; ⏰5am-11pm, last entry 6:59pm) The 51-mile trail network (leashed dogs allowed) dips through canyons, over grassy hills and past granite walls, offering city views and access to Native American petroglyphs.

Ponderosa Stables   Horseback Riding

(📞602-268-1261; www.arizona-horses.com; 10215 S Central Ave; 1/2hr rides $33/55; ⏰6am-5pm Jun-Sep, 8am-5pm Oct-May) This outfitter leads rides through South Mountain Park. Reservations required for most trips.

Sleeping

Budget Lodge Downtown   Motel $

(📞602-254-7247; www.blphx.com; 402 W Van Buren St; r incl breakfast $60-67; 🅿❄🛜) In the heart of downtown, this simple, two-story motel is a clean, low-cost place to lay your head.

Aloft Phoenix-Airport   Hotel $$

(📞602-275-6300; www.aloftphoenixairport.com; 4450 E Washington St; r $109-149; 🅿@🛜♨🐾) Rooms blend a pop-art sensibility with the cleanest edges of modern design.

Eating & Drinking

Matt's Big Breakfast   Breakfast $

(📞602-254-1074; www.mattsbigbreakfast.com; 825 N 1st St at Garfield St; breakfast $5-10, lunch $7-10; ⏰6:30am-2:30pm) Matt re-opened

Native American handicrafts, Santa Fe (p324)

Verde Valley Wine Trail

Vineyards, wineries and tasting rooms have opened their doors along Hwy 89A and I-17, bringing a dash of style and energy to Cottonwood, Jerome and Cornville.

In Cottonwood, you can float to the Verde River–adjacent **Alcantara Vineyards** (www.alcantaravineyard.com; 3445 S Grapevine Way) then stroll through Old Town where two new tasting rooms, **Arizona Stronghold** (www.azstronghold.com; 1023 N Main St; tastings $9; ⊙noon-7pm Sun-Thu, to 9pm Fri & Sat; 🕿) and **Pillsbury Wine Company** (www.pillsburywine.com; 1012 N Main St; ⊙11am-6pm Sun-Thu, to 8pm Fri), sit across from each other on Main St. Art, views and wine-sipping converge in Jerome, where there's a tasting room on every level of town, starting with **Cellar 433** (www.bittercreekwinery.com; 240 Hull Ave; ⊙11am-5pm Mon-Wed, to 6pm Thu-Sun) near the chamber of commerce visitor center. From there, stroll up to **Caduceus Cellars** (www.caduceus.org; 158 Main St; ⊙11am-6pm Sun-Thu, to 8pm Sun) then end with a final climb to **Jerome Winery** (☏928-639-9067; 403 Clark St; ⊙11am-5pm Mon-Thu, to 8pm Sat, 11am-4pm Sun Jun-Aug, shorter hours Sep-May) with its inviting patio.

Three wineries with tasting rooms hug a short stretch of Page Springs Rd east of Cornville: bistro-housing **Page Springs Cellars** (www.pagespringscellars.com; 1500 N Page Springs Rd; wine tasting $10 ; ⊙11am-7pm Mon-Wed, to 9pm Thu-Sun), welcoming **Oak Creek Vineyards** (www.oakcreekvineyards.net; 1555 N Page Springs Rd; wine tasting $5; ⊙10am-6pm) and mellow-rock-playing **Javelina Leap Vineyard** (www.javelinaleapwinery.com; 1565 Page Springs Rd; wine tasting $8 ; ⊙11am-5pm).

his legendary breakfast joint in a bigger location down the block from its old digs, but folks still cluster on the sidewalk to wait for a table.

Dick's Hideaway　New Mexican **$$**
(☏602-241-1881; http://richardsonsnm.com; 6008 N 16th St; breakfast $5-20, lunch $12-16, dinner $12-35; ⊙7am-midnight Sun-Wed, to 1am Thu-Sat) Grab a table beside the bar or join the communal table in the side room and settle in for hearty servings of savory, chile-slathered enchiladas, tamales and other New Mexican cuisine.

Postino Winecafé Arcadia　Wine Bar
(www.postinowinecafe.com; 3939 E Campbell Ave at 40th St; ⊙11am-11pm Mon-Thu, 11am-midnight Fri, 9am-midnight Sat, 9am-10pm Sun) This convivial, indoor-outdoor wine bar is a perfect gathering spot for a few friends ready to enjoy the good life, but solos will do fine too.

Four Peaks Brewing Company　Brewery
(☏480-303-9967; www.fourpeaks.com; 1340 E 8th St, Tempe; ⊙11am-2am Mon-Sat, 10am-2am Sun) So this is where everybody is. Beer-lovers are in for a treat at this quintessential neighborhood brewpub in a cool Mission Revival–style building.

❶ Information

Downtown Phoenix Visitor Information Center (☏877-225-5749; www.visitphoenix.com; 125 N 2nd St, Suite 120; ⊙8am-5pm Mon-Fri) The Valley's most complete source of tourist information.

❶ Getting There & Around

Sky Harbor International Airport (☏602-273-3300; http://skyharbor.com; 3400 E Sky Harbor Blvd; 🕿) is 3 miles southeast of downtown Phoenix. The free **Phoenix Sky Train**, which began operating in 2013, currently runs between Terminal 4 and the METRO light-rail station at 44th St and E Washington St.

LAS VEGAS

Ah, Vegas. A dazzling rhinestone of a city where you can sip Champagne inside a three-story chandelier. You can also travel the world in a day, gliding through the canals of Venice, climbing the Eiffel Tower and crossing the Brooklyn Bridge. It's a slice of desert that's transformed itself into one of the most lavish places on earth, and nothing is halfway – even the illusions.

Sights

Roughly 4 miles long, the Strip, aka Las Vegas Blvd, is the center of gravity in Sin City. Whether you're walking or driving, distances on the Strip are deceiving; a walk to what looks like a nearby casino usually takes longer than expected.

Downtown Las Vegas is the original town center and home to the city's oldest hotels and casinos: expect a retro feel, cheaper drinks and lower table limits. Its main drag is fun-loving Fremont St, a four-block stretch of casinos and restaurants covered by a dazzling canopy that runs a groovy light show every evening.

THE STRIP

Cosmopolitan Casino
(www.cosmopolitanlasvegas.com; 3708 Las Vegas Blvd S; ☉24hr) The twinkling three-story chandelier inside this sleek addition to the Strip isn't a piece of contemporary art only to be ogled. It's a step-inside, sip-a-swanky-cocktail and survey-your-domain kind of place, worthy of your wildest fairy tale. It's all pure fun, and the Cosmopolitan manages to avoid utter pretension, despite the near-constant wink-wink moments, from the Art-o-Matics (vintage cigarette machines hawking local art, not nicotine) to the hidden pizza joint.

Hard Rock Casino
(www.hardrockhotel.com; 4455 Paradise Rd; ☉24hr) Fresh off a $750 million expansion that added two new towers, the trés-hip Hard Rock is still luring them in with concerts, attitude and a very impressive collection of rock 'n' roll memorabilia. The Joint concert hall, Vanity Nightclub and 'Rehab' summer pool parties at Paradise Beach attract a pimped-out, sex-charged crowd flush with celebrities.

Bellagio Casino
(www.bellagio.com; 3600 Las Vegas Blvd S; ☉24hr) The Bellagio dazzles with Tuscan architecture and an 8.5-acre artificial lake, complete with not-to-be-missed choreographed dancing fountains. The **Bellagio Gallery of Fine Art** (adult/student/child $16/11/free; ☉10am-8pm) showcases temporary exhibits by top-notch artists. The **Bellagio Conservatory & Botanical Gardens** (☉24hr) FREE features changing exhibits throughout the year.

Caesars Palace Casino
(www.caesarspalace.com; 3570 Las Vegas Blvd S; ☉24hr) Forget Caesar. It's King Minos who springs to mind at this sprawling, labyrinth-like Greco-Roman fantasyland where maps are few (and not oriented to the outside). The interior is captivating, however, with marble reproductions of classical statuary, including a not-to-be-missed 4-ton Brahma shrine near the front entrance.

Venetian Casino
(www.venetian.com; 3355 Las Vegas Blvd S; gondola ride adult/private $19/76; ☉24hr) Hand-painted ceiling frescoes, roaming mimes, gondola rides and full-scale reproductions of famous Venice landmarks are found at the romantic Venetian.

Mirage Casino
(www.mirage.com; 3400 Las Vegas Blvd S; ☉24hr) A domed atrium filled with jungle foliage and soothing cascades captures the imagination at this tropically themed wonderland. Circling the atrium is a vast Polynesian-themed casino. Pause by the front desk for the 20,000-gallon saltwater aquarium, featuring 60 species of critters hailing from Fiji to the Red Sea. Out front in the lagoon, a fiery faux volcano erupts hourly after dark until midnight.

DOWNTOWN & OFF THE STRIP

Mob Museum   Museum

(☎702-229-2734; www.themobmuseum.org; 300 Stewart Ave; adult/child $20/14; ☺10am-7pm Sun-Thu, to 8pm Fri & Sat) Bugs. Lucky. Whitey. Yeah goombah, all the boys are hanging out at downtown's new mob museum, which fills three floors in the old federal building. The fascinating, often lurid, exhibits trace the development of organized crime in America and look at the mob's connection to Las Vegas.

Neon Museum   Museum

(☎702-387-6366; www.neonmuseum.org; 770 Las Vegas Blvd N; day tour adult/child $18/12, night tour $25/22; ☺9-10am & 7:30-9pm Jun-Aug, extended daytime hours from 10am Sep-May) A tour of the neon boneyard here is a fun stroll through Sin City's 'electrifying' past. Guides share stories about the city's former bigwigs as you walk past the gaudy signs that fronted their casinos, from Binion's to the Stardust. All tours are guided, and they sell out quickly, so reserve beforehand online.

Atomic Testing Museum   Museum

(www.atomictestingmuseum.org; 755 E Flamingo Rd; adult/child $14/11; ☺10am-5pm Mon-Sat, noon-5pm Sun) Recalling an era when the word 'atomic' conjured modernity and mystery, the Smithsonian-run Atomic Testing Museum remains an intriguing testament to the period when the fantastical – and destructive – power of nuclear energy was tested just outside Las Vegas.

Fremont Street Experience   Plaza

(www.vegasexperience.com; Fremont St, btwn Main St & Las Vegas Blvd; ☺hourly 7pm-midnight) A four-block pedestrian mall topped by an arched steel canopy and filled with computer-controlled lights, the multi-sensory Fremont Street Experience has re-energized downtown. Every evening, the canopy transforms into a six-minute light and sound show enhanced by 550,000 watts of wraparound sound. Bands play on several stages and zipliners whizz past overhead after stepping off Slotzilla, a 12-story slot machine.

Atomic Testing Museum, Las Vegas

RICHARD CUMMINS/GETTY IMAGES ©

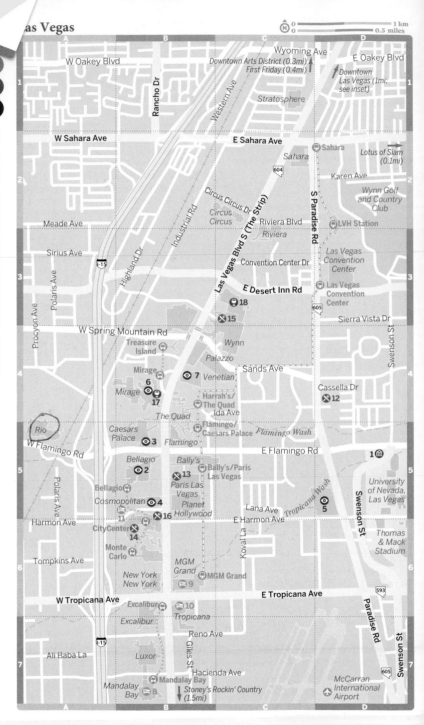

N
0 — 1 km
0 — 0.5 miles

W Oakey Blvd

E Oakey Blvd

Wyoming Ave

Downtown Arts District (0.3mi);
First Friday (0.4mi)

Downtown
Las Vegas (1mi;
see inset)

Stratosphere

Rancho Dr

Western Ave

W Sahara Ave

E Sahara Ave

Sahara

Lotus of Siam
(0.1mi)

Sahara

Karen Ave

604

S Paradise Rd

Wynn Golf
and Country
Club

Circus Circus Dr (The Strip)

Meade Ave

Circus
Circus

Riviera Blvd

Industrial Rd

Highland Dr

Riviera

LVH Station

Sirius Ave

Las Vegas
Convention
Center

I-15

Polaris Ave

Convention Center Dr

Procyon Ave

Las Vegas
Convention
Center

E Desert Inn Rd

605

18

Sierra Vista Dr

15

W Spring Mountain Rd

Wynn

Swenson St

Treasure
Island

Palazzo

Mirage

7 Venetian

Sands Ave

Cassella Dr

Mirage

6

17

Harrah's/
The Quad

12

The Quad

Ida Ave

Rio

Caesars
Palace

3

Flamingo/
Caesars Palace

Flamingo Wash

W Flamingo Rd

Flamingo

E Flamingo Rd

1

Bellagio

2

Bally's

Bally's/Paris
Las Vegas

University
of Nevada,
Las Vegas

Polaris Ave

Bellagio

13

Cosmopolitan

4

Paris Las
Vegas

Swenson St

Harmon Ave

11

16

Planet
Hollywood

Lana Ave

5

Tropicana Wash

CityCenter

14

E Harmon Ave

Koval La

Thomas
& Mack
Stadium

Monte
Carlo

Tompkins Ave

New York
New York

MGM
Grand

9 MGM Grand

E Tropicana Ave

593

W Tropicana Ave

Excalibur

10

Paradise Rd

Excalibur

Tropicana

Reno Ave

Swenson St

I-15

Giles St

Ali Baba La

Luxor

Hacienda Ave

Mandalay
Bay

8 Mandalay Bay

Stoney's Rockin' Country
(1.5mi)

McCarran
International
Airport

605

Las Vegas

Golden Nugget
Casino

(www.goldennugget.com; 129 E Fremont St; ⊙24hr) This casino hotel has set the downtown benchmark for extravagance since opening in 1946. It's currently earning wows for its three-story waterslide, which drops through a 200,000-gallon shark tank.

Downtown Arts District
Arts

On the **First Friday** (www.firstfridaylasvegas. com; ⊙5-11pm) of each month, 10,000 art lovers, hipsters, indie musicians and hangers-on descend on Las Vegas' downtown arts district for gallery openings, performance art, live bands and tattoo artists. The action revolves around S Casino Center Blvd between Colorado Ave and California Ave, northwest of the Stratosphere.

 **Activities**

Desert Adventures
Kayaking, Hiking

(☎702-293-5026; www.kayaklasvegas.com; 1647 Nevada Hwy, Suite A, Boulder City; trips from $149) With Lake Mead and Hoover Dam just 30 minutes away, would-be river rats should check out Desert Adventures for guided half-day, full-day and multiday kayaking adventures. Hiking and horseback-riding trips, too.

Escape Adventures
Mountain Biking

(☎800-596-2953; www.escapeadventures.com; 10575 Discovery Dr; trips incl bike from $129) The source for guided mountain-bike tours of Red Rock Canyon State Park.

 Sleeping

THE STRIP

Vdara
Hotel **$$**

(☎702-590-2767; www.vdara.com; 2600 W Harmon Ave; r $159-196; P🐾?) Cool sophistication and warm hospitality merge easily at Vdara, a no-gaming, all-suites hotel in the new CityCenter complex. With earth-toned walls, chocolate-brown furniture and riparian green pillows, the suites have a soothing 'woodland' appeal, apropos for a LEED-certified property.

Tropicana
Casino Hotel **$$**

(☎702-739-2222; www.troplv.com; 3801 Las Vegas Blvd S; r from $129, ste from $229; P🐾@?) The vibe is finger-snappin' hip, but still inviting, with a bright, monochromatic color scheme, lush, relaxing gardens and earth-toned, breezy rooms and bi-level suites.

MGM Grand
Casino Hotel **$$**

(☎800-929-1111, 702-891-7777; www.mgmgrand. com; 3799 Las Vegas Blvd S; r from $122, ste from $150; P🐾@?🐾) With more than 5000 rooms, this green leviathan is one of the world's largest hotels, but is bigger better? That depends, but top-drawer restaurants, a sprawling pool complex and a monorail station always make it a good bet – if you can find your room.

Detour: Route 66

Running for 2400 miles from Chicago to Los Angeles, Route 66 (aka the 'Mother Road') was the first cross-country highway to be paved, in 1937. Families fled west on it during the Dust Bowl; after WWII, they got their kicks road-tripping. The route was bypassed by Interstate 40 in 1985, but some original parts remain, including approximately 875 miles across New Mexico and Arizona. Some highlights: the Grand Canyon, classic diners and kitschy delights like the Wigwam Motel in Holbrook, Arizona. Check www.historic66.com for details.

Caesars Palace Casino Hotel **$$**
(📞866-227-5938; www.caesarspalace.com; 3570 Las Vegas Blvd S; r from $197; P❄@☙) Send away the centurions and decamp in style – Caesars' standard rooms are some of the most luxurious in town.

Mandalay Bay Casino Hotel **$$$**
(📞702-632-7777, 877-632-7800; www.mandalay bay.com; 3950 Las Vegas Blvd S; r $141-291; P❄@☎☙) The ornately appointed rooms here have a South Seas theme, and the amenities include floor-to-ceiling windows and luxurious bathrooms. Swimmers will swoon over the pool complex, with a sand-and-surf beach.

DOWNTOWN & OFF THE STRIP

Main Street Station Casino Hotel **$**
(📞800-713-8933, 702-387-1896; www.main-streetcasino.com; 200 N Main St; r from $50; P❄☎) For one of the best deals out there, try this 17-floor downtown hotel with marble-tiled foyers and Victorian sconces in the hallways.

Hard Rock Casino Hotel **$$$**
(📞800-473-7625, 702-693-5000; www.hardrockhotel.com; 4455 Paradise Rd; r $122-399; P❄@☎☙) Everything about this boutique hotel spells stardom. French doors reveal skyline and palm-tree views, and brightly colored Euro-minimalist rooms feature souped-up stereos and plasma TVs. The hottest action revolves around the lush Beach Club.

 Eating

THE STRIP

Todd English PUB Pub **$$**
(www.toddenglishpub.com; Crystals, 3720 Las Vegas Blvd S; mains $16-24; ⏰11am-2am Mon-Fri, 9:30am-2am Sat & Sun) A rollicking City Center venture from Bostonian chef Todd English, PUB is a strangely fun cross between a British pub and a frat party, with creative sliders and an 80+ beer list.

Society Café Cafe **$$**
(www.wynnlasvegas.com; Encore, 3121 Las Vegas Blvd S; breakfast $14-22, lunch $14-24, dinner $15-39; ⏰7am-11pm Sun-Thu, to 11:30pm Fri & Sat; 🍴) A slice of reasonably priced culinary heaven amid Encore's loveliness.

Gordon Ramsay Steak Steakhouse **$$$**
(📞877-346-4642; www.parislasvegas.com; Paris, 3655 Las Vegas Blvd S; mains $32-63; ⏰4:30-10:30pm, bar to midnight Fri & Sat) Ribboned in red and and domed by a jaunty Union Jack, this is one of the top seats in town. No reservation? Sit at the bar, where the knowledgable bartenders will explain the cuts and their preparations.

Sage American **$$$**
(📞702-590-8690; www.arialasvegas.com; Aria, 3730 Las Vegas Blvd S; mains $35-54; ⏰5-11pm Mon-Sat) Acclaimed chef Shawn McClain meditates on the seasonally sublime with global inspiration and artisanal, farm-to-table ingredients in one of Vegas' most drop-dead-gorgeous dining rooms.

DOWNTOWN & OFF THE STRIP

Lotus of Siam
Thai **$$**

(☎702-735-3033; www.saipinchutima.com; 953 E Sahara Ave; mains $9-30; ☺11:30am-2:30pm Mon-Fri, buffet to 2pm, 5:30-10pm daily) The top Thai restaurant in the US? According to *Gourmet Magazine,* this is it. One bite of simple pad Thai – or any of the exotic northern Thai dishes – nearly proves it.

Firefly
Tapas **$$**

(www.fireflylv.com; 3824 Paradise Rd; small dishes $4-10, large dishes $12-20; ☺11:30am-2am Sun-Thu) Nosh on traditional Spanish tapas, while the bartender pours sangria and flavor-infused *mojitos*.

Drinking

THE STRIP

Chandelier Bar
Bar

(www.cosmopolitanlasvegas.com; Cosmopolitan, 3708 Las Vegas Blvd S; ☺varies by floor, 24hr for 1st fl) Kick back with the Cosmopolitan hipsters and enjoy the curiously thrilling feeling that you're tipsy inside a giant crystal chandelier.

Mix
Lounge

(www.mandalaybay.com; 64th fl, THEhotel at Mandalay Bay, 3950 Las Vegas Blvd S; cover after 10pm $20-25; ☺5pm-1am Sun-Wed, to 2am Thu, to 3am Fri & Sat) The place to grab sunset cocktails.

Rhumbar
Cocktail Bar

(☎702 792-7615; www.mirage.com; Mirage, 3400 Las Vegas Blvd S; ☺1pm-midnight Sun-Thu, to 2am Fri & Sat) Rhumbar is handy to the Mirage's south entrance. Chill at breezy, beachy open-air lounge tables on the chic Strip-view patio.

XS
Club

(www.xslasvegas.com; Encore, 3131 Las Vegas Blvd S; cover $20-50; ☺9:30pm-4am Fri & Sat, 10:30pm-4am Sun & Mon) The only club where we've seen club-goers jump in the pool to dance (and not be thrown out by the bouncers), XS is a Vegas favorite with a more diverse crowd.

Marquee
Club

(www.cosmopolitanlasvegas.com; Cosmopolitan, 3708 Las Vegas Blvd) Celebrities (we spotted Macy Gray as we danced through the crowd), an outdoor beach club, hot DJs

Las Vegas skyline

RICHARD CUMMINS/GETTY IMAGES ©

and that certain *je ne sais quoi* makes Marquee worth the line.

DOWNTOWN & OFF THE STRIP

Want to chill out with the locals? Head to one of their go-to favorites. New bars and and cafes are opening along E Fremont St, making it the number-one alternative to the Strip.

Griffin
Bar

(📞702-382-0577; 511 E Fremont St; cover $5-10; ⏰5pm-3am Mon-Fri, 7pm-3am Sat, 8pm-2am Sun; 🚌Deuce) Crackling fireplaces, leather booths and an almost unbearably cool jukebox make this dark and cozy spot popular with rebels, hipster sweethearts and surely an in-the-know vampire or two.

Commonwealth
Cocktail Bar

(www.commonwealthlv.com; 525 E Fremont St; ⏰6pm-2am Wed-Fri, 8pm-2am Sat & Sun) Softly glowing chandeliers. Saloon-style bar. Victorian-era bric-a-brac. Enjoy your tipple. It also has a rooftop bar and, we hear, a secret bar within the bar.

 **Entertainment**

Stoney's Rockin' Country
Live Music

(www.stoneysrockincountry.com; 6611 Las Vegas Blvd S; cover $free-20; ⏰7pm-2am Sun-Wed, to 3am Thu-Sat) This fun-lovin' country-western bar recently moved closer to the Strip. Dance lessons are offered every night of the week, with two-stepping on Tuesday at 7:30pm.

LOVE
Performing Arts

(📞800-963-9634, 702-792-7777; www.cirquedu-soleil.com; tickets $99-150; ⏰7pm & 9:30pm Thu-Mon; ♿) This show at the Mirage is a popular addition to the Cirque du Soleil lineup; locals who have seen many Cirque productions come and go say it's the best.

La Rêve
Live Performance

(📞888-320-7110; www.wynnlasvegas.com; Wynn, 3131 Las Vegas Blvd S; tickets from $105; ⏰7pm & 9:30pm Fri-Tue; 🚌Deuce) Aquatic acrobatic feats are the centerpiece of La Rêve, which means 'The Dream' in French.

Elvis impersonator, Las Vegas

DOUG MCKINLAY/GETTY IMAGES ©

ℹ️ Getting There & Around

McCarran International Airport (LAS; ☎702-261-5211; www.mccarran.com; 5757 Wayne Newton Blvd; 📶) has direct flights from many US cities, and some from Canada and Europe. **Bell Trans** (☎702-739-7990; www.bell-trans.com) offers a shuttle service ($7) between the airport and the Strip.

Fast, fun and fully wheelchair accessible, the monorail (www.lvmonorail.com; 1 ride $5, 24/72hr pass $12/28, under 6yr free; ⏱7am-midnight Mon, to 2am Tue-Thu, to 3am Fri-Sun) connects the Sahara Station (closest to Circus Circus) to the MGM Grand, stopping at major Strip megaresorts along the way.

ZION & SOUTHERN UTAH

Local tourist boards call it 'color country,' but the cutesy label hardly does justice to the eye-popping hues that saturate the landscape. The deep-crimson canyons of Zion, the delicate pink-and-orange minarets at Bryce Canyon and the soaring sculpture of Arches: these are truly spectacular national parks.

Bryce Canyon National Park

The Grand Staircase, a series of steplike uplifted rock layers elevating north from the Grand Canyon, culminates at this rightly popular **national park** (☎435-834-5322; www.stateparks.utah.gov; Hwy 63; 7-day vehicle pass $25; tent & RV sites without hookups $15; ⏱24hr; visitor center 8am-8pm May-Sep, to 4:30pm Oct-Apr) in the Pink Cliffs formation. It's full of wondrous sorbet-colored pinnacles and points, steeples and spires, and totem pole–shaped 'hoodoo' formations. The 'canyon' is actually an amphitheater eroded from the cliffs. From Hwy 12, turn south on Hwy 63; the park is 50 miles southwest of Escalante.

Rim Road Scenic Drive (8000ft) travels 18 miles, roughly following the canyon rim past the visitor center, the lodge, incredible overlooks (don't miss **Inspiration Point**) and trailheads,

ending at **Rainbow Point** (9115ft). From early May through early October, a free shuttle bus runs (8am until at least 5:30pm) from a staging area just north of the park to as far south as **Bryce Amphitheater**.

The 1920s **Bryce Canyon Lodge** (☎877-386-4383, 435-834-8700; www.brycecanyonforever.com; Hwy 63; r & cabins $175-200; ⏱Apr-Oct; @) exudes rustic mountain charm. Rooms are in modern hotel-style units, with up-to-date furnishings, and thin-walled duplex cabins with gas fireplaces and front porches. No TVs. The lodge **restaurant** (☎435-834-8700; breakfasts $6-12, lunch & dinner mains $18-40; ⏱7-10:30am, 11:30am-3pm & 5:30-10pm Apr-Oct) is excellent, if expensive.

Just north of the park boundaries, **Ruby's Inn** (☎435-834-5341; www.rubysinn.com; 1000 S Hwy 63; r $115-170, tent sites $26-55, RV sites with hookups $35-60; ❄@📶🐾) is a town as much as it is a resort complex.

Eleven miles east of the park on Hwy 12, the small town of **Tropic** (www.brycecanyoncountry.com/tropic.html) has additional food and lodging.

Moab

Southeastern Utah's largest community (population 5093) bills itself as the state's recreation capital, and...oh man, does it deliver. Scads of rafting and riding (mountain bike, horse, 4WD...) outfitters here make forays into surrounding public lands. Make this your base, too, and you can hike Arches or Canyonlands National Parks during the day, then come back to a comfy bed, a hot tub and your selection of surprisingly good restaurants at night.

🏃 Activities

Area outfitters offer half-day to multiday adventures (from $60 for a sunset 4WD tour to $170 for a white-water day on the river) that include transport, the activity and, sometimes, meals. Book ahead.

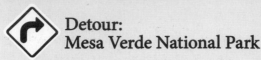

Detour: Mesa Verde National Park

Shrouded in mystery, Mesa Verde, with its cliff dwellings and verdant valley walls, is a fascinating, if slightly eerie, national park to explore. It is here that a civilization of Ancestral Puebloans appears to have vanished in AD 1300, leaving behind a complex civilization of cliff dwellings, some accessed by sheer climbs.

Mesa Verde rewards travelers who set aside a day or more to take the ranger-led tours of Cliff Palace and Balcony House, explore Wetherill Mesa or participate in one of the campfire programs. But if you only have time for a short visit, check out the Chapin Mesa Museum and walk through the Spruce Tree House, where you can climb down a wooden ladder into the cool chamber of a kiva (ceremonial structure, usually partly underground).

The park is in southwestern Colorado, a 2¼-hour drive from Moab.

Sheri Griffith Expeditions   Rafting
(☏800-332-2439; www.griffithexp.com; 2231 S Hwy 191; day trip $170) Highly rated rafting outfitter; some multisport adventures.

Poison Spider Bicycles   Mountain Biking
(☏800-635-1792, 435-259-7882; www.poison-spiderbicycles.com; 497 N Main St; rental per day $45-70) Mountain- and road-bike rentals and tours; superior advice and service.

Moab Desert Adventures   Adventure Sports
(☏877-765-6622, 435-260-2404; www.moab desertadventures.com; 415 N Main St; half/full day $165/285) Top-notch climbing tours scale area towers and walls; canyoneering and multisport packages available.

Red Cliffs Lodge   Horseback Riding
(☏866-812-2002, 435-259-2002; www.redcliffs-lodge.com; Mile 14, Hwy 128; half day $80) Daily half-day trail rides offered; advanced, open-range rides also available.

Sleeping

Adventure Inn   Motel $
(☏866-662-2466, 435-259-6122; www. adventureinnmoab.com; 512 N Main St; r incl breakfast $80-105; ☺Mar-Oct; ✷☎) A great little indie motel, the Adventure Inn has spotless rooms (some with refrigerators) and decent linens, as well as laundry facilities.

Cali Cochitta   B&B $$
(☏888-429-8112, 435-259-4961; www.moab-dreaminn.com; 110 S 200 East; cottages incl breakfast $135-170; ✷☎) Make yourself at home in one of the charming brick cottages a short walk from downtown. A long wooden table on the patio provides a welcome setting for community breakfasts.

Sunflower Hill   Inn $$
(☏800-662-2786, 435-259-2974; www.sunflower hill.com; 185 N 300 East; r incl breakfast $165-225; ✷☎☀) Relax amid the manicured gardens of a rambling 100-year-old farm-house and an early-20th-century home. All 12 guest quarters have a sophisticated country sensibility.

Eating

Love Muffin   Cafe $
(www.lovemuffincafe.com; 139 N Main St; dishes $6-8; ☺7am-2pm; ☎) The largely organic menu at this vibrant cafe includes imaginative sandwiches, breakfast burritos and egg dishes such as 'Verde,' with brisket and slow-roasted salsa.

Miguel's Baja Grill   Mexican $$
(www.miguelsbajagrill.com; 51 N Main St; mains $14-24; ☺5-10pm) Dine on fish tacos or fajitas, and sip margaritas, in the sky-lit breezeway patio lined with brightly painted walls.

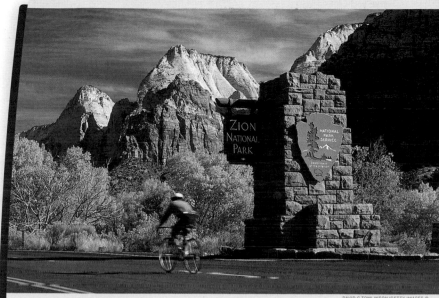

DAVID C TOMLINSON/GETTY IMAGES ©

Don't Miss
Zion National Park

If you enter Zion National Park from the east along Hwy 9, you'll roll past yellow sandstone and **Checkerboard Mesa** before reaching an impressive gallery-dotted tunnel and 3.5 miles of switchbacks going down in red-rock splendor. More than 100 miles of park trails here offer everything from leisurely strolls to wilderness backpacking and camping.

If you've time for only one activity, the 6-mile **scenic drive** that pierces the heart of Zion Canyon is it. From April through October, taking a free shuttle from the visitor center is required, but you can hop off and on at any of the scenic stops and trailheads along the way. The famous **Angels Landing Trail** is a strenuous, 5.4-mile vertigo inducer (1100ft elevation gain, with sheer drop offs), but the views of Zion Canyon are phenomenal. Allow four hours for the round trip.

Smack in the middle of the scenic drive, rustic **Zion Lodge** (📞435-772-7700, 888-297-2757; www.zionlodge.com; Zion Canyon Scenic Dr; r/cabins/ste $185/$195/$225; ✻ @ 🛜) has 81 well-appointed motel rooms and 40 cabins with gas fireplaces. All have wooden porches with stellar red-rock cliff views (and no TVs). The lodge's full-service dining room, **Red Rock Grill** (📞435-772-7760; breakfast & sandwiches $8-14, dinner mains $18-30; 🕐6:30-10:30am, 11:30am-3pm & 5-10pm Mar-Oct, hours vary Nov-Feb), has similarly amazing views. Just outside the park, the town of Springdale offers many more services.

NEED TO KNOW
www.nps.gov/zion; Hwy 9; per vehicle 7 days $25; 🕐24hr; Zion Canyon visitor center Jun-Aug 8am-7:30pm, closes earlier Sep-May

Cowboy Grill
American **$$**

(☑435-259-2002; http://redcliffslodge.com;
Red Cliffs Lodge, Mile 14, Hwy 128; breakfast &
lunch $10-16, dinner mains $14-28; ⊘6:30-10am,
11:30am-2pm & 5-10pm) Incredible Colorado
River sunset views are to be had from the
patio or behind the huge picture windows
here. The hearty meat and seafood dishes
aren't bad either.

ⓘ Information

Moab Information Center (www.discovermoab.
com; cnr Main & Center Sts; ⊘8am-7pm Mon-Sat,
9am-6pm Sun) Excellent source of information
on area parks, trails, activities, camping and
weather; big bookstore, too.

Arches National Park

One of the Southwest's most gorgeous
parks, **Arches** (☑435-719-2299; www.nps.
gov/arch; Hwy 191; per vehicle 7 days $10;
⊘24hr; visitor center 7:30am-6:30pm Mar-
Oct, 9am-4pm Nov-Feb) boasts the world's
greatest concentration of sandstone
arches – more than 2000, ranging from
3ft to 300ft wide at last count. Nearly
one million visitors make the pilgrimage
here, just 5 miles north of Moab, every
year. Many noteworthy arches are easily
reached by paved roads and relatively
short hiking trails; much of the park can
be covered in a day. To avoid crowds,
consider a moonlight exploration, when
it's cooler and the rocks feel ghostly.

Highlights include **Balanced Rock**,
oft-photographed **Delicate Arch**
(best captured in the late afternoon),
spectacularly elongated **Landscape
Arch** and popular **Windows Arches**.
Reservations are necessary for the twice-
daily ranger-led hikes into the maze-like
fins of the **Fiery Furnace**; book at least
a few days in advance either in person or
online at www.recreation.gov.

Canyonlands National Park

Red-rock fins, bridges, needles, spires,
craters, mesas, buttes – **Canyonlands**
(www.nps.gov/cany; per vehicle 7 days $10; tent
& RV sites without hookups $10-15; ⊘24hr) is
a crumbling, decaying beauty, a vision
of ancient earth. Roads and rivers make
inroads into this high-desert wilderness
stretching 527 sq miles, but much of it is
still untamed. You can hike, raft and 4WD
here but be sure that you have plenty of
gas, food and water. **Cataract Canyon**
offers some of the wildest white water
in the West (find outfitters in Moab and
Green River).

The canyons of the Colorado and
Green Rivers divide the park into separate
districts. The **Island in the Sky** district
offers amazing overlooks. The **visitor
center** (☑435-259-4712; Hwy 313, Canyonlands
National Park; ⊘ 8am-6pm Mar-Oct, 9am-
4pm Nov-Feb) is 32 miles northwest of
Moab. Our favorite short hike there is
the half-mile loop to oft-photographed
Mesa Arch, a slender, cliff-hugging span
framing a picturesque view of Washer
Woman Arch and Buck Canyon. Drive
a bit further to reach the **Grand View
Overlook** trail; the path follows the
canyon's edge and ends at a praise-your-
maker precipice.

MONUMENT VALLEY &
NAVAJO NATION

Amid the isolation is some of North Amer-
ica's most spectacular scenery, including
Monument Valley and Canyon de Chelly.
Cultural pride remains strong and many
still speak Navajo as their first language.
The Navajo rely heavily on tourism; visi-
tors can help keep their heritage alive by
staying on reservation land or purchasing
their renowned crafts.

Canyon de Chelly National
Monument

This many-fingered canyon (pronounced
duh-shay) contains several beautiful
Ancestral Puebloan sites important to
Navajo history, including ancient cliff
dwellings. Families still farm the land,
wintering on the rims then moving to hog-
ans (traditional dwellings) on the canyon

 Don't Miss
Monument Valley Navajo Tribal Park

With flaming-red buttes and impossibly slender spires bursting to the heavens, the Monument Valley landscape off Hwy 163 has starred in countless Hollywood Westerns and looms large in many a road-trip daydream.

For up-close views of the towering formations, you'll need to visit the Monument Valley Navajo Tribal Park, where a rough and unpaved scenic driving loop covers 17 miles of stunning valley views. You can drive it in your own vehicle or take a tour (1½ hours $75, 2½ hours $95) organized by one of the kiosks in the parking lot (tours enter areas private vehicles can't).

Inside the tribal park is the **View Hotel** (☏435-727-5555; www.monumentvalleyview.com; Hwy 163; r $209-265, ste $299-329; ❄ ⓤ ☎). Built in harmony with the landscape, the sandstone-colored hotel blends naturally with its surroundings, and most of the 96 rooms have private balconies facing the monuments. The Navajo-based specialties at the adjoining restaurant (mains $10 to $30, no alcohol) are mediocre, but the red-rock panorama is stunning.

The historic **Goulding's Lodge** (☏435-727-3231; www.gouldings.com; r $205-242, tent sites $26, RV sites $5, cabins $92; ❄ ☎ ≈ 👪), just across the border in Utah, offers lodge rooms, camping and small cabins. Book early for summer. In Kayenta, 20 miles south, there are a handful of OK hotels: try the **Wetherill Inn** (☏928-697-3231; www. wetherill-inn.com; 1000 Main St/Hwy 63; r incl breakfast $136; ❄ @ ☎ ≈) if everything in Monument Valley is booked.

NEED TO KNOW

☏435-727-5874; www.navajonationparks.org/htm/monumentvalley.htm; adult/child $5/free; ⊙drive 6am-8:30pm May-Sep, 8am-4:30pm Oct-Apr; visitor center 6am-8pm May-Sep, 8am-5pm Oct-Apr

floor in spring and summer. The canyon is private Navajo property administered by the NPS. Enter hogans only with a guide and don't photograph people without their permission.

The only lodging in the park is **Sacred Canyon Lodge** (📞800-679-2473; www.scacredcanyonlodge.com; r $122-129, ste $178, cafeteria mains $5-17; ⊙cafeteria breakfast, lunch & dinner; ❄@🛜👪), formerly Thunderbird Lodge. It has comfortable rooms and an inexpensive cafeteria serving Navajo and American meals.

The Canyon de Chelly **visitor center** (📞928-674-5500; www.nps.gov/cach; ⊙8am-5pm) is 3 miles from Rte 191 in the small village of Chinle.

SANTA FE

Walking among the historic adobe neighborhoods or even around the tourist-filled plaza, there's no denying that Santa Fe has a timeless, earthy soul. Founded around 1610, Santa Fe is the second-oldest city and oldest state capital in the USA. It's got the oldest public building and throws the oldest annual party in the country (Fiesta). Yet the city is synonymous with contemporary chic, and boasts the second-largest art market in the nation, gourmet restaurants, great museums, spas and a world-class opera.

◎ Sights

Georgia O'Keeffe Museum   Museum

(📞505-946-1000; www.okeeffemuseum.org; 217 Johnson St; adult/child $12/free; ⊙10am-5pm, to 7pm Fri) Possessing the world's largest collection of her work, the Georgia O'Keeffe Museum features the artist's paintings of flowers, bleached skulls and adobe architecture. Tours of O'Keeffe's house in Abiquiu require advance reservations.

Canyon Rd   Galleries

(www.canyonroadarts.com) The epicenter of the city's upscale art scene; more than 100 galleries, studios, shops and restaurants line this narrow historic road.

Wheelwright Museum of the American Indian   Museum

(www.wheelwright.org; 704 Camino Lejo; ⊙10am-5pm Mon-Sat, 1-5pm Sun) FREE In 1937, Mary Cabot established the Wheelwright Museum of the American Indian, part of Museum Hill, to showcase Navajo ceremonial art. While its strength continues to be Navajo exhibits, it now includes contemporary Native American art and historical artifacts as well.

🏃 Activities

The **Pecos Wilderness** and **Santa Fe National Forest**, east of town, have more than 1000 miles of hiking trails, several of which lead to 12,000ft peaks. The popular and scenic **Winsor Trail** starts at the Santa Fe Ski Basin. Summer storms are frequent, so prepare for hikes by checking weather reports. For maps and details, contact the Public Lands Information Center. If mountain biking is your thing, drop into **Mellow Velo** (📞505-995-8356; www.mellowvelo.com; 132 E Marcy St; rentals per day from $35; ⊙9am-5:30pm Mon-Sat), which rents bikes and has loads of information about regional trails.

Busloads of people head up to the Rio Grande and Rio Chama for whitewater river running on day and overnight adventures. Contact **Santa Fe Rafting Co** (📞505-988-4914; www.santaferafting.com; ⊙Apr-Sep) and stay cool on trips through the Rio Grande Gorge (half/full day $65/99), the wild Taos Box (full day $110) or the Rio Chama Wilderness (three days $595).

Ten Thousand Waves   Spa

(📞505-982-9304; www.tenthousandwaves.com; 3451 Hyde Park Rd; communal tubs $24, private tubs per person $31-51; ⊙noon-10:30pm Tue, 9am-10:30pm Wed-Mon Jul-Oct, reduced hours Nov-Jun) The Japanese-style 10,000 Waves, with landscaped grounds concealing eight attractive tubs in a smooth Zen design, offers waterfalls, cold plunges, massage and hot and dry saunas.

ALTRENDO TRAVEL/GETTY IMAGES ©

 ## Don't Miss
Museum of New Mexico

The Museum of New Mexico administers four (or five, depending on how you count them) unique and excellent museums around town. Two (or three) are at the plaza, two are on Museum Hill. Admission is free for children aged 16 and under. Adults can buy a four-day pass with entry into all four (or five) museums for $20.

○ **Museum of International Folk Art** (www.internationalfolkart.org; 706 Camino Lejo; adult/ child $9/free, free 5-8pm Fri summer; ⊙10am-5pm, closed Mon Sep-May) The galleries here, on Museum Hill, are at once whimsical and mind-blowing – featuring the world's largest collection of traditional folk art. Try to hit the incredible folk-art market, held each July.

○ **Museum of Indian Arts & Culture** (www.indianartsandculture.org; 710 Camino Lejo; adult/child $9/free, free Fri 5-8pm summer; ⊙10am-5pm, closed Mon Sep-May) On Museum Hill, this is one of the most complete collections of Native American arts and crafts – and a perfect companion to the nearby Wheelwright Museum (p324).

○ **Palace of the Governors** (📞505-476-5100; www.palaceofthegovernors.org; 105 W Palace Ave; adult/child $9/free; ⊙10am-5pm, closed Mon Oct-May) On the plaza, this 400-year-old abode was once the seat of the Spanish colonial government. It displays a handful of regional relics, but most of its holdings are now shown in an adjacent exhibit space called the **New Mexico History Museum**, a glossy, 96,000-sq-ft expansion.

○ **New Mexico Museum of Art** (www.nmartmuseum.org; 107 W Palace Ave; adult/child $9/free; ⊙10am-5pm, closed Mon Sep-May) Housed in a fine adobe building (pictured above) just off the plaza; there are more than 20,000 pieces of fine art here, mostly by Southwestern artists.

Santa Fe

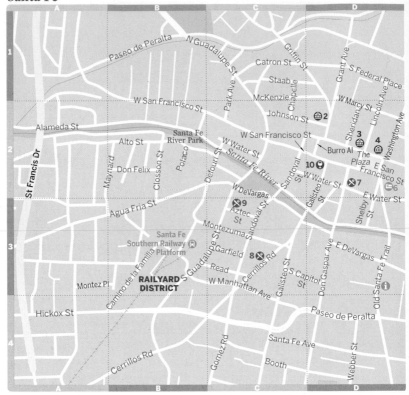

 Sleeping

Silver Saddle Motel
Motel $

(☏505-471-7663; www.santafesilversaddlemotel.com; 2810 Cerrillos Rd; r winter/summer from $45/62; P ❄ @ ☎ 🐾) Shady wooden arcades outside and rustic cowboy-inspired decor inside, including some rooms with attractively tiled kitchenettes. Probably the best value in town.

El Rey Inn
Hotel $$

(☏505-982-1931; www.elreyinnsantafe.com; 1862 Cerrillos Rd; r incl breakfast $105-165, ste from $150; P ❄ @ ☎ ⛵ ♿) A highly recommended classic courtyard hotel, with super rooms, a great pool and hot tub, and even a kids' playground scattered around 5 acres of greenery.

La Fonda
Historic Hotel $$$

(☏800-523-5002; www.lafondasantafe.com; 100 E San Francisco St; r/ste from $140/260; P ❄ @ ☎ ⛵) Claiming to be the original 'Inn at the end of the Santa Fe Trail,' here in one form or another since perhaps 1610, La Fonda has always offered some of the best lodging in town.

Eating

San Marcos Café
New Mexican $

(☏505-471-9298; www.sanmarcosfeed.com; 3877 Hwy 14; mains $7-10; ⏰8am-2pm; ♿) About 10 minutes' drive south on Hwy 14, this spot is well worth the trip. San Marcos has a down-home feeling and the best red chili you'll ever taste. The whole place is connected to a feed store, giving it some genuine Western soul.

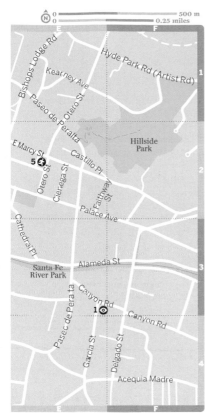

Santa Fe

⊙ Sights
1	Canyon Rd	E3
2	Georgia O'Keeffe Museum	D2
3	New Mexico Museum of Art	D2
4	Palace of the Governors	D2

⊕ Activities, Courses & Tours
5	Mellow Velo	E2

⊜ Sleeping
6	La Fonda	D2

⊗ Eating
7	Cafe Pasqual's	D2
8	Cleopatra's Cafe	C3
9	Cowgirl Hall of Fame	C3

⊙ Drinking & Nightlife
	Bell Tower Bar	(see 6)
10	Evangelo's	D2

and does food right. The chef, from El Salvador, adds a few twists to classic New Mexican and American dishes, while also serving Salvadoran *pupusas* (stuffed corn tortillas), huevos and other specialties.

Cowgirl Hall of Fame Barbecue **$$**
(www.cowgirlsantafe.com; 319 S Guadalupe St; mains $8-18; ⊙11am-11pm Sun-Thu, to midnight Fri & Sat; ) Two-step up to the cobble-stoned courtyard and try the salmon tacos, butternut-squash casserole or the barbecue platter – all served with Western-style feminist flair. There's live music most nights.

Cafe Pasqual's International **$$$**
(☏505-983-9340; www.pasquals.com; 121 Don Gaspar Ave; breakfast & lunch mains $9-17, dinner mains $16-30; ⊙7am-3pm & 5:30-9pm; ☏⊞) Sante Fe's most famous breakfast, for good reason.

⊖ Drinking & Entertainment

Evangelo's Bar
(200 W San Francisco St; noon-1:30am Mon-Sat, to midnight Sun) There's foot-stompin' live music nightly at Evangelo's. The sounds of rock, blues, jazz and Latin combos spill into the street.

Horseman's Haven New Mexican **$**
(4354 Cerrillos Rd; mains $8-12; ⊙8am-8pm Mon-Sat, 8:30am-2pm Sun; ⊞) Hands down the hottest green chili in town! Service is friendly and fast, and the enormous 3-D burrito might be the only thing you need to eat all day.

Cleopatra's Cafe Middle Eastern **$**
(www.cleopatrasantafe.com; Design Center, 418 Cerrillos Rd; mains $6-14; ⊙11am-8pm Mon-Sat; 🛜) Makes up for lack of ambience with taste and value – big platters of delicious kebabs, hummus, falafel and other Middle Eastern favorites. It's inside the Design Center.

Tune-Up Café International **$$**
(www.tuneupsantafe.com; 1115 Hickox St; mains $7-14; ⊙7am-10pm Mon-Fri, from 8am Sat & Sun; ⊞) This local favorite is casual, busy

Detour: Abiquiu

The tiny community of Abiquiu (sounds like 'barbecue'), on Hwy 84 about 45 minutes' drive northwest of Santa Fe, is famous because the renowned artist Georgia O'Keeffe lived and painted here from 1949 until her death in 1986. With the Chama River flowing through farmland and spectacular rock landscape, the ethereal setting continues to attract artists, and many live and work in Abiquiu. O'Keeffe's adobe house is open for limited visits, with one-hour **tours** (☏ 505-685-4539; www.okeeffemuseum.org; $35-45) offered on Tuesday, Thursday and Friday from March to November, and Tuesday through Saturday from June to October – they're often booked months in advance.

A retreat center on 21,000 Technicolor acres that obviously inspired O'Keeffe's work (and was a shooting location for the movie *City Slickers*), **Ghost Ranch** (☏ 505-685-4333; www.ghostranch.org; US Hwy 84; suggested donation $3; 🚹) has hiking trails, a **dinosaur museum** (suggested donation $2; ⊙ 9am-5pm Mon-Sat, 1-5pm Sun) and horseback rides (from $50), including instruction for kids aged four and up ($30). Basic **lodging** (tent sites $19, RV sites $22-29, dm incl breakfast $50, r without/with bath incl breakfast from $70/80) is available, too.

The lovely **Abiquiú Inn** (☏ 505-685-4378, 888-735-2902; www.abiquiuinn.com; US Hwy 84; RV sites $18, r $110-150, casitas from $179; P 🤖 🚹) is a sprawling collection of shaded faux-adobes. Its spacious casitas have kitchenettes, and wi-fi is available in the lobby and the on-site restaurant, **Cafe Abiquiú** (breakfast mains under $10, lunch & dinner mains $10-20; ⊙ 7am-9pm). The lunch and dinner menu includes numerous fish dishes, from chipotle honey-glazed salmon to trout tacos.

Bell Tower Bar
Bar

(100 E San Francisco St; ⊙ 3pm-sunset Mon-Thu, 2pm-sunset Fri-Sun May-Oct, closed Nov-Apr) At La Fonda hotel, ascend five floors to the newly renovated Bell Tower and watch one of those patented New Mexico sunsets.

ⓘ Information

New Mexico Tourism Bureau (☏ 505-827-7440; www.newmexico.org; 491 Old Santa Fe Trail; ⊙ 8am-5pm; @) Has brochures, a hotel reservation line, free coffee and free internet access.

ⓘ Getting There & Around

A few commercial airlines fly daily into Santa Fe Municipal Airport (SAF; ☏ 505-955-2900; wwwsantafenm.gov; 121 Aviation Dr). Many more flights arrive at and depart from Albuquerque (A one-hour drive south of Santa Fe).

Sandia Shuttle Express (☏ 888-775-5696; www.sandiashuttle.com) runs between Santa Fe and the Albuquerque Sunport ($28).

Amtrak (☏ 800-872-7245; www.amtrak.com) stops at Lamy; buses continue 17 miles to Santa Fe.

If you need a taxi, call Capital City Cab (☏ 505-438-0000; www.capitalcitycab.com).

BANDELIER NATIONAL MONUMENT

Ancestral Puebloans dwelt in the cliffsides of beautiful Frijoles Canyon, now preserved within **Bandelier** (www.nps.gov/band; per vehicle $12; ⊙ visitor center 9am-4:30pm, park to dusk; 🚹). The adventurous can climb ladders to reach ancient caves and kivas used until the mid-1500s. There are also almost 50 sq miles of canyon and mesalands offering scenic backpacking trails, plus camping at **Juniper Camp-**

ground (campsites $12), set among the pines near the monument entrance. Note that between 9am and 3pm, from the end of May to mid-October, you need to take a shuttle bus to Bandelier from the White Rock Visitor Center, along Hwy 4.

TAOS

Taos is a place undeniably dominated by the power of its landscape: 12,300ft snowcapped peaks rise behind town; a sage-speckled plateau unrolls to the west before plunging 800ft straight down into the Rio Grande Gorge; the sky can be a searing sapphire blue or an ominous parade of rumbling thunderheads so big they dwarf the mountains. And then there are the sunsets...

 Sights

Millicent Rogers Museum
Museum

(www.millicentrogers.org; 1504 Millicent Rogers Rd; adult/child $10/2; ⊙10am-5pm, closed Mon Nov-Mar) Filled with pottery, jewelry, baskets and textiles, this has one of the best collections of Native American and Spanish Colonial art in the US.

Harwood Foundation Museum
Museum

(www.harwoodmuseum.org; 238 Ledoux St; adult/child $10/free; ⊙10am-5pm Tue-Sat, noon-5pm Sun) Housed in a historic mid-19th-century adobe compound, the Harwood Museum of Art features paintings, drawings, prints, sculpture and photography by northern New Mexico artists, both historical and contemporary.

Taos Historic Museums
Museum

(www.taoshistoricmuseums.org; adult/child each museum $8/4; ⊙10am-5pm Mon-Sat, noon-5pm Sun) Taos Historic Museum runs two houses: **Blumenschein Home** (222 Ledoux St), a trove of art from the 1920s by the Taos Society of Artists, and **Martínez Hacienda** (708 Hacienda Way, off Lower Ranchitos Rd), a 21-room colonial trader's former home from 1804.

If You Like...
Native American
Culture & History

If you like the fascinating clifftop dwellings at Bandelier National Monument outside Santa Fe, don't miss these other spots for Native American culture.

1 WALNUT CANYON NATIONAL MONUMENT
(☏928-526 3367; www.nps.gov/waca; 7-day admission adult/child $5/free; ⊙8am-5pm May-Oct, 9am-5pm Nov-Apr) Sinagua cliff dwellings are set in the nearly vertical walls of a small limestone butte amid a forested canyon at this worth-a-trip monument. A short hiking trail descends past many cliff-dwelling rooms. The monument is 11 miles southeast of Flagstaff off I-40 exit 204.

2 ACOMA PUEBLO
(☏800-747-0181; http://sccc.acomaskycity.org; tours adult/child $20/12; ⊙tours hourly 10am-3pm Fri-Sun mid-Oct–mid-Apr, 9am-3:30pm daily mid-Apr–mid-Oct) The dramatic mesa-top 'Sky City' sits 7000ft above sea level and 367ft above the surrounding plateau. One of the oldest continuously inhabited settlements in North America, this place has been home to pottery-making people since the later part of the 11th century. Guided tours leave from the visitor center at the bottom of the mesa. From I-40, take exit 102, which is about 60 miles west of Albuquerque, then drive 12 miles south.

3 NEWSPAPER ROCK RECREATION AREA
(Utah) This tiny recreation area showcases a single large sandstone rock panel packed with more than 300 petroglyphs attributed to Ute and Ancestral Puebloan groups over a 2000-year period. The many red rock figures etched out of a black 'desert varnish' surface make for great photos. It's located 50 miles south of Moab, east of Canyonlands National Park on Hwy 211.

LEANNE WALKER /GETTY IMAGES ©

Don't Miss
Taos Pueblo

Taos Pueblo is believed to be the oldest continuously inhabited community in the US. Built around AD 1450, the streamside pueblo is the largest existing multistoried pueblo structure in the US and one of the best surviving examples of traditional adobe construction. It roots the town in a long history with a rich cultural legacy – including conquistadors, Catholicism and cowboys.

In the 20th century, Taos became a magnet for artists, writers and creative thinkers, from DH Lawrence to Dennis Hopper. It remains a relaxed and eccentric place, with classic adobe architecture, fine-art galleries, quirky cafes and excellent restaurants. Its 5000 residents include bohemians, alternative-energy aficionados and old-time Hispanic families. It's rural and worldly, and a little bit otherworldly.

Dances held at the pueblo during the Pow-Wow (in July) and San Geronimo Day (September) are open to the public; call or check the website for exact dates. The pueblo closes for 10 weeks around February to March.

NEED TO KNOW

📞505-758-1028; www.taospueblo.com; Taos Pueblo Rd; adult/child $10/free, photo or video permit $6; 🕐8am-4:30pm

San Francisco
de Asís Church   Church

(St Francis Plaza; 🕐9am-4pm Mon-Fri) Four miles south of Taos in Ranchos de Taos, the San Francisco de Asís Church, famed for the angles and curves of its adobe walls, was built in the mid-18th century but didn't open until 1815. It's been memorialized in Georgia O'Keeffe paintings and Ansel Adams photographs.

Rio Grande Gorge Bridge
Bridge, Canyon

At 650ft above the Rio Grande, the steel Rio Grande Gorge Bridge is the second-highest suspension bridge in the US; the view down is eye-popping. For the best pictures of the bridge itself, park at the rest area on the western end of the span.

 **Activities**

During summer, **white-water rafting** is popular in the **Taos Box**, the steep-sided cliffs that frame the Rio Grande. Day-long trips begin at around $100 per person. Contact the visitor center for local outfitters; it also has good info about **hiking** and **mountain-biking** trails.

 **Sleeping**

Sun God Lodge
Motel $

(✆ 575-758-3162; www.sungodlodge.com; 919 Paseo del Pueblo Sur; r from $55; P ❄ 🛜 🐾) The hospitable folks at this well-run two-story motel can fill you in on local history as well as the craziest bar in town. Located 1.5 miles south of the plaza, it's one of the better budget choices in town.

Earthship Rentals
Boutique Hotel $$

(✆ 505-751-0462; www.earthship.com; US Hwy 64; earthship $145-305; 🛜 🛗 🐾) A cross between organic Gaudí architecture and space age fantasy, these sustainable dwellings are put together using recycled tires, aluminum cans and sand, with rain catchment and gray-water systems to minimize their footprint.

Historic Taos Inn
Historic Hotel $$

(✆ 575-758-2233; www.taosinn.com; 125 Paseo del Pueblo Norte; r $75-275; P ❄ 🛜) Even though it's not the plushest place in town, it's still fabulous, with a cozy lobby, a top-notch restaurant, heavy wooden furniture, a sunken fireplace and lots of live local music at its famed Adobe Bar.

 Eating

Taos Diner
Diner $

(www.taosdiner.com; 908 Paseo del Pueblo Norte; mains $4-14; ⊙ 7am-2:30pm; 🛗) It's with some reluctance that we share the existence of this marvelous place, a mountain-town diner with wood-paneled walls, tattooed waitresses, fresh-baked biscuits and coffee cups that are never less than half-full. This is diner grub at its finest, prepared with a Southwestern, organic spin.

Love Apple
Organic $$

(✆ 575-751-0050; www.theloveapple.net; 803 Paseo del Pueblo Norte; mains $13-22; ⊙ 5-9pm Tue-Sun) Housed in the 19th-century adobe Placitas Chapel, the understated rustic-sacred atmosphere is as much a part of this only-in-New-Mexico restaurant as the food is. Make reservations!

❓ Drinking & Entertainment

Adobe Bar
Bar

(Historic Taos Inn, 125 Paseo del Pueblo Norte; ⊙ 11am-11pm) Everybody's welcome in 'the living room of Taos.' There's a streetside patio in summer, an indoor kiva fireplace in winter, plus top-notch margaritas and an eclectic lineup of live music all year round.

ℹ Information

Taos Visitor Center (✆ 575-758-3873; Paseo del Pueblo Sur, Paseo del Cañon; ⊙ 9am-5pm; @ 🛜)

Pacific Northwest

As much a state of mind as a geographic region, the US's northwest corner is a land of subcultures and new trends. It's a place where evergreen trees frame snow-dusted volcanoes, and inspired ideas scribbled on the backs of napkins become tomorrow's business start-ups. You can't peel off history in layers here, but you can gaze wistfully into the future in fast-moving, innovative cities such as Seattle and Portland, both sprinkled with food carts, streetcars, microbrews, green belts, coffee connoisseurs and weird urban sculpture.

Ever since the days of the Oregon Trail, the Northwest has had a hypnotic lure for risk-takers and dreamers, and the metaphoric carrot still dangles. There's the air, so clean they ought to bottle it; the trees, older than many of Rome's Renaissance palaces; and the edge-of-the-continent coastline, holding back the force of the world's largest ocean. Cowboys take note; it doesn't get much more 'wild' or 'west' than this.

Downtown Seattle (p342)
TERENCE LEE/GETTY IMAGES ©

Pacific Northwest

Parksville
Nanaimo
Vancouver Island
VANCOUVER
Strait of Georgia
99
1
1
4
Bellingham
Anacortes
Port Renfrew
Sidney
San Juan Islands
4
Skagit
Cape Flattery
Makah Indian Reservation
Neah Bay
Sooke
17
14
VICTORIA
Port Angeles
Strait of Juan de Fuca
Lake Crescent
Everett
5
Mukilteo
Forks
101
Port Townsend
Puget Sound
405
SEATTLE
1
Mt Olympus (7965ft)
Olympic National Park
5
Bremerton
Hoodsport
Quinault Indian Reservation
Olympic Peninsula
101
Tacoma
Puyallup
Aberdeen
Tumwater
OLYMPIA
3
Grays Harbor
5
Mt Rainier (14,411ft)
Ashford
Willapa Bay
Centralia
Mt St Helens National Volcanic Monument
Packwood
Lewis & Clark National & State Historical Parks
Longview
504
Mt St Helens (8365ft)
Astoria
Seaside
Cannon Beach
26
30
5
Columbia River Gorge
6
Vancouver
Tillamook
Portland
2
Mt Hood (11,239ft)
Dundee
Estacada
McMinnville
211
Bagby Hot Springs
Lincoln City
18
SALEM
Depoe Bay
Newport
99W
22
Breitenbush Hot Springs
101
Corvallis
Albany
20
Mt Jefferson (10,497ft)
Yachats
Cape Perpetua
Willamette R.
McKenzie Bridge
126
Florence
126
Eugene
McKenzie River
Cascade Range
Oregon Dunes National Recreation Area
Reedsport
5
Mt Bachelor (9065ft)
58
Cascade Lakes
Coos Bay
N Umpqua River
Diamond Lake
Bandon
42
Roseburg
Glide
Steamboat
S Umpqua River
Cape Blanco
Port Orford
Wild Rogue Wilderness
Crater Lake National Park
Agness
Gold Beach
Kalmiopsis Wilderness
Galice
Grants Pass
Shady Cove
62
Upper Klamath Lake
Jacksonville
Medford
140
Ashland
Brookings
Cave Junction
Mt Ashland (7533ft)
Klamath Falls
Oregon Caves National Monument
199
Crescent City
5

PACIFIC OCEAN

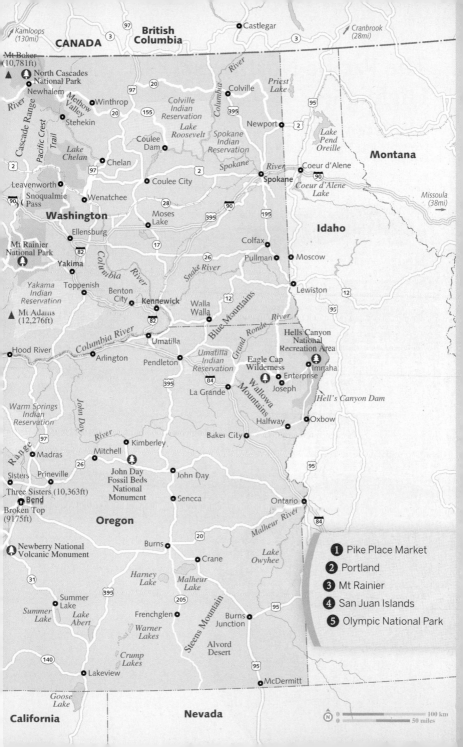

The Pacific Northwest's Highlights

Pike Place Market

Seattle's soul lies not in its sleek downtown skyscrapers, but in charismatic Pike Place Market (p348). Spread over 9 acres, this vivacious 'town within a city' has been exuding its manic energy since 1907. Today, you'll find local farmers, entertaining street theatre, and glimpses of small-town life beneath the urban veneer.

Portland

It's easy to fall for Portland (p358). After all, everyone loves this city. It's as friendly as a big town, and home to a mix of students, artists, cyclists, hipsters, young families, old hippies, ecofreaks and everything in between. There's great food, a relentless music scene and plenty of culture – plus adventures in the great outdoors lie right on Portland's doorstep. Left: Crowdsurfer at a live-music venue, Portland

ANTHONY PIDGEON/GETTY IMAGES ©

Mt Rainier

When the skies are clear, Mt Rainier (p353) looms over Seattle, creating an amazing backdrop to the emerald city. Still very much an active volcano, the 14,411ft peak is the shining centerpiece of a lush national park, which harbors a rare inland temperate rainforest. The hiking here is stunning, whether you opt for a short meander through alpine meadows strewn with wildflowers or the more challenging 93-mile Wonderland Trail.

San Juan Islands

Leafy hedgerows, sleepy settlements and winding lanes jammed with more cyclists than cars – this serene archipelago feels like a world removed from the mainland. Comprising some 450 islands, the San Juan Islands (p356) are a great place to reconnect with nature while cycling, sea kayaking and exploring state parks. There are peaceful island getaways and scenic spots for sea-gazing – keep an eye out for breaching orcas. Above: Orca breaching

Olympic National Park

This vast and pristine wonderland is home to Tolkien-esque valleys, rugged shorelines and misty, old-growth Pacific rainforest. Lakes, hot springs and glacial-capped peaks are a few of the prime attractions of this stellar peninsular park (p355). There's great hiking, kayaking and skiing, and idyllic lodges for relaxing after taking in one of the great wilderness gems of the Northwest. Above: Sol Duc Falls, Olympic National Park

The Pacific Northwest's Best...

Outdoor Activities

○ **Ecola State Park** Surfing, hiking, beachcombing and spectacular sea views from the headlands. (p365)

○ **Olympic National Park** Hike amid pristine beauty in one of the world's only temperate rainforests. (p355)

○ **Mt Rainier National Park** Make the challenging four-day ascent up Mt Rainier. (p353)

○ **Portland** Go kayaking and cycling in this adventure-loving city. (p358)

Wildlife Watching

○ **San Juan Islands** Prime destination for spotting orcas. (p356)

○ **Oregon Coast** Spot migrating gray whales in spring and winter. (p364)

○ **Hoh River Rainforest** Home to Northern Spotted Owls, Roosevelt elk and Olympic black bears. (p355)

○ **Wonderland Trail** The chance to see great herds of elk, mountain goat and deer, plus more than 100 bird species. (p353)

Seafood

○ **Jake's Famous Crawfish** An old-fashioned classic serving some of Portland's best seafood. (p362)

○ **Lowells** Some of the best fish and chips in the Pacific Northwest are served at this spot in Pike Place Market. (p350)

○ **Navarre** This enticing Portland spot serves legendary crab cakes. (p362)

Need to Know

Live Music

- **Crocodile** A reborn Seattle spot that played a major role in the grunge scene. (p352)

- **Doug Fir Lounge** This slick nightspot in South Burnside hosts some of Portland's most promising talent. (p363)

- **Tractor Tavern** Hear a wide mix of folk, honky-tonk and country in this Seattle classic. (p353)

- **Dante's** Bordello-esque Portland space that hosts eclectic concerts and burlesque shows. (p363)

Left: Roosevelt elk, Oregon;
Above: Ecola State Park (p365)

ADVANCE PLANNING

- **Three months before** Book accommodations for June to August.

- **One month before** Browse and buy tickets for upcoming festivals and events.

- **Two weeks before** Reserve at top restaurants in Seattle and Portland. Book tours and outdoor excursions.

RESOURCES

- **Seattle.Gov** (www.seattle.gov) The city's official website.

- **Seattle Weekly** (www.seattleweekly.com) Free weekly with news and entertainment listings.

- **Washington State** (www.experiencewa.com) Washington state's official tourism site.

- **Travel Portland** (www.travelportland.com) Key lowdown on Portland.

- **Willamette Week** (www.wweek.com) Free Portland weekly with loads of entertainment listings.

- **Travel Oregon** (www.traveloregon.com) Lots of tips on Oregon travel, statewide.

GETTING AROUND

- **Airports** Seattle-Tacoma International Airport (www.portseattle.org/seatac), aka 'Sea-Tac,' is linked to downtown by Link Light Rail (30 minutes); taxis are about $35. Portland International Airport (www.flypdx.com) has downtown connections via Max Light Rail (40 minutes); taxis are around $30.

- **Bus** Greyhound (www.greyhound.com) operates between major towns.

- **Hire car** Great for exploring national parks and the coast.

- **Train** Amtrak runs south to California, linking Seattle, Portland and other major urban centers with the Cascades and *Coast Starlight* routes. The famous *Empire Builder* heads east to Chicago from Seattle and Portland (meeting in Spokane, WA).

BE FOREWARNED

- **Weather** Expect cold and plenty of rain between November and March; high passes can be blocked with snow.

- **Hiking** Be prepared when heading into the wilderness: bring warm, weatherproof gear; heed posted warnings about wildlife; be mindful of ticks.

Pacific Northwest Itineraries

Lush forests, snow-capped peaks and wild coastlines are highlights of the Northwest. Eco-conscious Seattle and Portland are famed for global cuisine, coffeehouses, microbreweries and indie culture.

5 DAYS

SEATTLE TO THE SAN JUAN ISLANDS

The Emerald City & Around

Spend the first two days in ❶ **Seattle**. Beat the crowds to the iconic Pike Place Market (p348), where you can sip world-class coffee, shop and snack on diverse temptations. Hit the sprawling galleries of the Seattle Art Museum (p342), then trendy Belltown (p342) for dinner and drinks. On day two, visit the historic district of Pioneer Square, enjoy a sublime view from the Space Needle (p347), ride the futuristic (á la 1962) monorail and rock out at the Experience Music Project (p343).

On day three, drive two hours to ❷ **Mt Rainier National Park** (p353) to hike among glaciers, wildflower-filled alpine meadows and old-growth forests.

On day four, drive the 90 minutes to Anacortes and take a ferry to the lovely ❸ **San Juan Islands**. Spend your last two days exploring idyllic San Juan Island and Orcas Island: go bike riding and sea kayaking, watch whales from Lime Kiln Point State Park, sip wine at San Juan vineyards and take in the views from Mt Constitution.

Above: Totem pole, Pioneer Sq (p343), Seattle;
Top Right: People on a Seattle rooftop

5 DAYS

SEATTLE TO PORTLAND

Pacific Northwest Explorer

Explore downtown ❶ **Seattle**, the waterfront and Seattle Center (p343). On day two, head 90 miles west to the wilderness of ❷ **Olympic National Park** (p355). It's well worth spending two days taking in the rugged coastal scenery, hiking through the unbelievably lush ❸ **Hoh River Rainforest** (p355) and relaxing at one of the park's peaceful inns, like the beautifully set ❹ **Lake Quinault Lodge** (p355).

On day four, drive 240 miles to ❺ **Portland**, known for its roses, bridges, beer and progressive politics. Spend two days visiting downtown landmarks like Pioneer Courthouse Square (p358), wandering through the boutiques and galleries of the Pearl District, and strolling along the Willamette River. Take frequent breaks for coffee and/or microbrews, eat at food trucks and catch a show at Doug Fir Lounge (p363).

On day five, head to the coast. Prepare for jaw-dropping scenery as you pass unspoilt shores along US 101. Base yourself at picturesque ❻ **Cannon Beach**, while exploring the dreamlike scenery of nearby Ecola State Park, with its crashing waves and wild beaches backed by rolling forests. This is a great place for hiking or simply reconnecting with nature.

Discover the Pacific Northwest

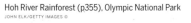

Hoh River Rainforest (p355), Olympic National Park
JOHN ELK/GETTY IMAGES ©

SEATTLE

Surprisingly elegant in places and coolly edgy in others, Seattle is notable for its strong neighborhoods, top-rated university, monstrous traffic jams and proactive city mayors who harbor green credentials. Although it has fermented its own pop culture in recent times, it has yet to create an urban mythology befitting Paris or New York, but it does have 'the Mountain.' Better known as Rainier to its friends, Seattle's unifying symbol is a 14,411ft mass of rock and ice, which acts as a perennial reminder to the city's huddled masses that raw wilderness and potential volcanic catastrophe are never far away.

 Sights

DOWNTOWN

Seattle Art Museum   Museum
(SAM; www.seattleartmuseum.org; 1300 1st Ave; adult/child $17/11; ◷10am-5pm Tue, Wed, Sat & Sun, to 9pm Thu & Fri; 🚇University St) Over the last decade, it has added more than 100,000 sq ft to its gallery space and acquired about $1 billion worth of new art, including works by Zurbarán and Murillo. The museum is known for its extensive Native American artifacts and work from the local Northwest school, in particular by Mark Tobey (1890–1976).

Belltown   Neighborhood
Where industry once fumed, glassy condos now rise in the thin walkable strip of Belltown. The neighborhood gained a reputation for trend-setting nightlife in the 1990s and two of its bar-clubs, the Crocodile (p352) and Shorty's (p352), can still claim

legendary status. Then there are the restaurants – more than 100 of them – and not all are prohibitively expensive. Belltown covers an area of roughly 10 blocks by six blocks, sandwiched in between Downtown and the Seattle Center.

Olympic Sculpture Park
Park, Sculpture

(2901 Western Ave; ☉sunrise-sunset; 🚍13) FREE Worth a visit just for its views of the Olympic Mountains over Elliott Bay, Olympic Sculpture Park has begun to grow into its long-range plan by filling a former brownfield industrial site with vibrant art and plant life.

PIONEER SQUARE

Pioneer Sq is Seattle's oldest quarter, which isn't saying much if you're visiting from Rome or London. Most of the buildings here date from just after the 1889 fire (a devastating inferno that destroyed 25 city blocks, including the entire central business district), and are referred to architecturally as Richardsonian Romanesque, a red-brick revivalist style in vogue at the time.

The quarter today mixes the historic with the seedy, while harboring art galleries, cafes and nightlife.

Klondike Gold Rush National Historical Park
Museum

(www.nps.gov/klse; 117 S Main St; ☉9am-5pm; 🚇International District/Chinatown) FREE This is a shockingly good museum eloquently run by the US National Park Service. It's full of exhibits, photos and news clippings from the 1897 Klondike gold rush, when a Seattle-on-steroids acted as a fueling depot for prospectors bound for the Yukon in Canada.

SEATTLE CENTER

The remnants of the futuristic 1962 World's Fair hosted by Seattle and subtitled Century 21 Exposition are now into their sixth decade at the Seattle Center. And what remnants! The fair was a major success, attracting 10 million visitors, running a profit (rare for the time) and inspiring a skin-crawlingly kitschy Elvis

Higher than the Space Needle

Everyone makes a rush for the iconic Space Needle, but it's neither the tallest nor the cheapest of Seattle's glittering viewpoints. That honor goes to the sleek, tinted-windowed **Columbia Center** (701 5th Ave; adult/concession $9/6; ☉8:30am-4:30pm Mon-Fri), built in 1985. At 932ft high it's the loftiest building in the Pacific Northwest. From the plush observation deck on the 73rd floor you can look down on ferries, cars, islands, roofs and – the Space Needle!

movie, *It Happened at the World's Fair* (1963).

EMP Museum
Museum

(www.empsfm.org; 325 5th Ave N; adult/child $20/14; ☉10am-7pm Jun–mid-Sep, to 5pm mid-Sep–May; 🅼Seattle Center) Recently rebranded as the EMP Museum, this dramatic marriage of supermodern architecture and rock-and-roll history was inaugurated as the Experience Music Project (EMP) in 2000.

Chihuly Garden & Glass
Museum

(🕽206-753-3527; www.chihulygardenandglass.com; 305 W Harrison St; adult/child $19/12; ☉11am-7pm Sun-Thu, to 8pm Fri & Sat; 🅼Seattle Center) Reinforcing the metropolis's position as the Venice of North America, this exquisite exposé of the life and work of dynamic local glass sculptor Dale Chihuly requires a sharp intake of breath on first viewing. It opened in May 2012, and has quickly become a top city icon to rival the Space Needle.

CAPITOL HILL

Millionaires mingle with goth musicians in irreverent Capitol Hill, a well-heeled but liberal neighborhood rightly renowned for its fringe theater, alternative music scene,

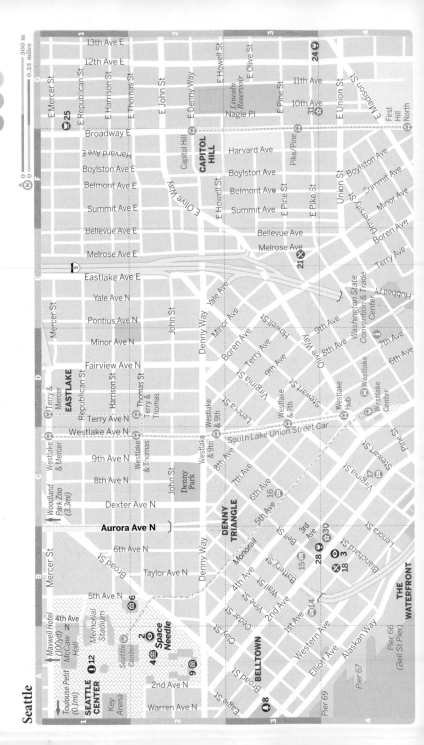

Seattle

500 m
0.25 miles

13th Ave E
12th Ave E
E Mercer St
E Republican St
E Harrison St
E Thomas St
E John St
E Denny Way
E Howell St
E Olive St
24
11th Ave
Lincoln
Reservoir
Nagle Pl
E Pine St
10th Ave
31
E Union St
E Madison St
First
Hill
North

25
Broadway E
Harvard Ave E
Capitol Hill
CAPITOL
HILL
Harvard Ave
Pike/Pine
Union St
Boylston Ave

Boylston Ave E
E Howell St
Boylston Ave
E Pine St
Summit Ave

Belmont Ave E
Belmont Ave
E Pine St
Minor Ave

Summit Ave E
Summit Ave
E Pike St
Boren Ave

Bellevue Ave E
Bellevue Ave
Terry Ave

Melrose Ave E
Melrose Ave
21

Eastlake Ave E
E Olive Way
Washington State
Convention & Trade
Center
Hubbell Pl

Yale Ave N
Yale Ave
9th Ave
7th Ave

Mercer St
Pontius Ave N
Minor Ave N
Denny Way
Minor Ave
Boren Ave
Terry Ave
Howell St
8th Ave
Olive Way
6th Ave

Fairview Ave N
EASTLAKE
Republican St
Harrison St
Thomas St
Virginia St
Stewart St
Westlake Hub
Westlake Center

Terry & Mercer
Terry & Mercer
Westlake & 9th
Lenora St
Westlake & 7th

Westlake & Mercer
Westlake Ave N
South Lake Union Street Car
Pine St

9th Ave N
8th Ave N
Westlake & Thomas
John St
Denny Park
Westlake & 9th
8th Ave
7th Ave
6th Ave
DENNY
TRIANGLE
Virginia St
Stewart St

Dexter Ave N
16

Aurora Ave N
5th Ave
30
28
3

6th Ave N
Taylor Ave N
Denny Way
Monorail
4th Ave
Bell St
3rd Ave
15
18

5th Ave N
6
Wall St
Battery St
Vine St
14
Lenora St
Blanchard St
THE
WATERFRONT

Mercer St
Broad St
Memorial
Stadium
Seattle
Center
2
Space
Needle
4
9
2nd Ave
1st Ave
Cedar St
Clay St
Western Ave
Pier 66
(Bell St Pier)

Maxwell Hotel
(100yd)
4th Ave
Hall
12
SEATTLE
CENTER
Key
Arena
BELLTOWN
8
Elliot Ave
Alaskan Way
Pier 67

Toulouse Petit
(0.1mi)
2nd Ave N
Warren Ave N
Eagle St
Broad St
Pier 69

Woodland
Park Zoo
(3.3mi)

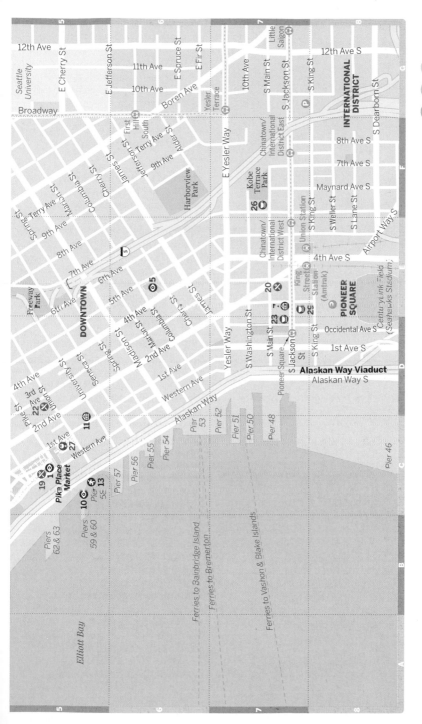

Seattle

indie coffee bars, and vital gay and lesbian culture. The junction of Broadway and E John St is the nexus from which to navigate the quarter's various restaurants, brewpubs, boutiques and dingy – but not dirty – dive bars.

FREMONT

Fremont pitches young hipsters among old hippies in an unlikely urban alliance, and vies with Capitol Hill as Seattle's most irreverent neighborhood. It's full of junk shops, urban sculpture and a healthy sense of its own ludicrousness.

BALLARD

A former seafaring community with a strong Scandinavian heritage, Ballard still feels like a small town engulfed by a bigger city. Traditionally gritty, no-nonsense and uncommercial, it's slowly being condo-ized, but remains a good place to down a microbrew or see a live band.

Hiram M Chittenden Locks   Lock
(3015 NW 54th St; ⊙locks 24hr, ladder & gardens 7am-9pm, visitor center 10am-6pm May-Sep; ☒62) Here, the fresh waters of Lake Washington and Lake Union that flow through the 8-mile-long Lake Washington Ship Canal drop 22ft into saltwater Puget Sound. On the southern side of the locks you can view a fish ladder from underwater glass-sided tanks.

🏃 Activities

A cycling favorite, the 16.5-mile **Burke-Gilman Trail** winds from Ballard to Log Boom Park in Kenmore on Seattle's Eastside. There, it connects with the 11-mile **Sammamish River Trail**, which winds past the Chateau Ste Michelle winery in Woodinville before terminating at Redmond's Marymoor Park.

Get a copy of the *Seattle Bicycling Guide Map,* published by the City of Seattle's **Transportation Bicycle & Pedestrian Program** (www.cityofseattle.net/transportation/bikemaps.htm) online or at bike shops.

For bicycle rentals and tours, try **Recycled Cycles** (www.recycledcycles.com; 1007 NE Boat St; rentals per 6/24hr $20/40; ⊙10am-8pm Mon-Fri, to 6pm Sat & Sun; ☗; ☒66), a friendly U District shop that also rents out chariots and trail-a-bike attachments for kids, or **SBR Seattle Bicycle Rental & Tours** (🕿800-349-0343; www.seattlebicyclerentals.com; Pier 58; rental per hr/day $10/40; ⊙11am-7pm Wed-Mon; ☒University St), which offers reasonable rates and daily tours (book online).

DUANE MILLER/GETTY IMAGES ©

Don't Miss
Space Needle

The needle anchors the World's Fair site, now called the Seattle Center, and, despite its rather steep admission fee, still persuades more than one million annual visitors to ascend to its flying saucer–like observation deck.

NEED TO KNOW
www.spaceneedle.com; 400 Broad St; adult/child $19/12; ⊙10am-11pm Mon-Thu, 9:30am-11:30pm Fri & Sat, 9:30am-11pm Sun; Ⓜ Seattle Center

 Tours

Seattle Free Walking Tours
Walking Tour
(www.seattlefreewalkingtours.org) These intimate two-hour tours meet daily at 11am on the corner of Western Ave and Virginia St. If you have a rip-roaring time (highly likely), there's a suggested $15 donation.

 Sleeping

Moore Hotel
Hotel **$**
(☎206-448-4851; www.moorehotel.com; 1926 2nd Ave; s/d $85/97, with shared bath $68/80; 🛜; 🚊Westlake) Old-world and allegedly haunted, the Moore nonetheless has a

friendly front desk and a prime location. There's a cute little cafe on the premises and the dive-y Nitelite Lounge next door.

Hotel Five
Boutique Hotel **$$**
(☎206-441-9785; www.hotelfiveseattle.com; 2200 5th Ave; r from $165; P❄🛜; 🚊13) This wonderful reincarnation of the old Ramada Inn on Fifth Ave in Belltown mixes retro '70s furniture with sharp color accents to produce something that is dazzlingly modern.

Maxwell Hotel
Boutique Hotel **$$**
(☎206-286-0629; www.themaxwellhotel. com; 300 Roy St; r from $179; P❄@🛜🏊; 🚊Rapid Ride D-Line) A gorgeous boutique

Don't Miss
Pike Place Market

Take a bunch of small businesses and sprinkle them liberally around a spatially challenged waterside strip amid crowds of old-school bohemians, new-wave restaurateurs, tree-huggers, bolshie students, artists, buskers and artisans. The result: Pike Place Market, a cavalcade of noise, smells, personalities, banter and urban theater that's almost London-like in its cosmopolitanism.

www.pikeplacemarket.org

btwn Virginia St & Union St & 1st Ave & Western Ave

⊘9am-6pm Mon-Sat, to 5pm Sun

☒Westlake

History

Pike Place is the oldest continuously operating market in the nation. It was established in 1907 to give local farmers a place to sell their fruit and vegetables and bypass the middlepeople. Soon the greengrocers made room for fishmongers, bakers, ethnic grocers, butchers, cheese sellers and purveyors of the rest of the Northwest's agricultural bounty. The market thrived until the 1960s. Sales began suffering from suburbanization, the growth of supermarkets and the move away from local, small-scale market gardening.

In the wake of the 1962 World's Fair, plans were drawn up to bulldoze the market and build high-rise offices and apartments on this piece of prime downtown real estate. Fortunately, a public outcry prompted an initiative to save the market. The space was cleaned up and restructured, and it has once again become the undeniable heart and soul of downtown. More than 10 million people mill through the market each year.

Layout

Pike Place is made up of several buildings, covering about eight labyrinthine blocks at the top of the bluff overlooking the waterfront. It's easy to get lost – in fact, a slight sense of mayhem and dislocation is part of the market's charm. To help find your way around, pick up a map at the market's information booth on Pike St; it's about 100ft in front of the Public Market clock.

Eating & Drinking

Don't eat before you go. The market is one of the hotbeds of Seattle snacking and dining. You can get everything from a freshly grown Washington apple to steaming bowls of clam chowder. More than 30 restaurants offer a staggering variety of cuisines, including French, Greek, Thai, Japanese and Persian, among others. Some of Seattle's favorite watering holes are also tucked into unlikely corners of the market.

Local Knowledge

Pike Place Market

BY EMILY CRAWFORD,
MARKETING & PR
SPECIALIST

1 FARMERS MARKET
The farmers market is on the cobblestone street of Pike Pl, between Pine and Stewart Sts. Look for a row of white tents on the west side of the street, under which Washington farmers sell their fresh produce (pictured left). Inside the arcade, flower farmers sell colorful, locally grown bouquets.

2 CRAFTS MARKET
In the North Arcade, the daily crafts market provides the opportunity to discover unique, local and handcrafted items and is one of the largest and most diverse in the US. Discover one-of-a-kind accessories and apparel, pottery, glass and metal sculpture, objects of tiles and stone, painting and leather goods.

3 SPECIALTY FOODS
Specialty grocery stores sell pasta, truffle oil, herbed vinegars, olive oils, teas, spices, grains and curries. Shop for cheese, meat, baked goods and products from Bavaria, France, Spain, Italy, Mexico, Africa, India and beyond. Year-round 'high stalls' feature an abundant variety of seasonal fruits and vegetables sourced from around the globe and right here in Washington. Four fish markets provide fresh seafood from Pacific Northwest and Alaskan waters.

4 RACHEL THE PIGGY BANK
Located under the iconic market clock and sign, Rachel the Piggy Bank is the mascot of Pike Place Market and one of our best public fundraisers. She has been 'bringing home the bacon' for the Market Foundation since 1986, raising more than $200,000.

5 ORIGINAL STARBUCKS
The first Starbucks cafe is on Pike Pl in the heart of the market. It keeps to its roots and only serves coffee and espresso, and boasts its original sign and mermaid logo.

Discovery Park

Comprising the largest green space in the city, the park's 534 acres are laced with cliffs, meadows, sand dunes, forest and beaches, all of which provide a welcome breathing space for hemmed-in Seattleites and a vital corridor for wildlife. For a map of the park's trail and road system, stop by the **Discovery Park Environmental Learning Center** (☏206-386-4236; 3801 W Government Way; ☺8:30am-5pm) near the Government Way entrance. The park is located 5 miles northwest of downtown Seattle in the neighborhood of Magnolia. To get there, catch bus 33 from 3rd Ave and Union St downtown.

hotel that graces the Lower Queen Anne neighborhood, the Maxwell's huge designer-chic lobby is enough to make anyone dust off their credit card. Look out for periodic offers online.

Ace Hotel   Hotel **$$**
(☏206-448-4721; www.acehotel.com; 2423 1st Ave; r $199, with shared bath $109; P☎; ☒13) Emulating (almost) its hip Portland cousin, the Ace sports minimal, futuristic decor (everything's white or stainless steel, even the TV), antique French army blankets, condoms instead of pillow mints and a copy of *Kama Sutra* instead of the Bible.

Belltown Inn   Hotel **$$**
(☏206-529-3700; www.belltown-inn.com; 2301 3rd Ave; s/d $159/164; P✳@☎; ☒Rapid Ride D-Line) The Belltown is such a bargain and in such a prime location that it's hard to believe it hasn't accidentally floated over from a smaller, infinitely cheaper city. But no: clean functional rooms, handy kitchenettes, roof terrace, free bikes and – vitally important – borrow-and-return umbrellas are all yours for the price of a posh dinner.

🍴 Eating

Salumi   Sandwiches **$**
(www.salumicuredmeats.com; 309 3rd Ave S; sandwiches $7-10; ☺11am-4pm Tue-Fri; ☒International District/Chinatown) The queue outside Salumi has long been part of the sidewalk furniture. This place has even formed its own community of chatterers, food bloggers, Twitter posters and gourmet-sandwich aficionados who compare notes.

Lowells   Diner **$**
(www.eatatlowells.com; 1519 Pike Pl; mains $6-9; ☺7am-6pm; ☒Westlake) Fish and

Seattle Aquarium (p352)
JOHN ELK/GETTY IMAGES ©

chips is a simple meal often done badly – but not here. Slam down your order for Alaskan cod at the front entry and take it up to the top floor for delicious views over Puget Sound.

Wild Ginger   Asian $$
(www.wildginger.net; 1401 3rd Ave; mains $15-28; ⏰11am-3pm & 5-11pm Mon-Sat, 4-9pm Sun; 🚇University St) Food from around the Pacific Rim – via China, Indonesia, Malaysia, Vietnam and Seattle, of course – is the wide-ranging theme at this highly popular downtown fusion restaurant.

Toulouse Petit   Cajun $$
(📞206-432-9069; 601 Queen Anne Ave N; mains $13-17; ⏰8am-2am; 🚌13) Something of a Seattle phenomenon, Toulouse Petit is hailed for its generous happy hours, cheap brunches and rollicking atmosphere – it's perennially (and boisterously) busy.

360 Local   Northwest $$
(📞206-441-9360; www.local360.org; cnr 1st Ave & Bell St; mains $16-26; ⏰11am-late Mon-Fri, 8am-late Sat & Sun; 🚌13) 🍴 Snaring 90% of its ingredients from within a 360-mile radius, this new restaurant follows its ambitious 'locavore' manifesto pretty rigidly. The farms where your meat was reared are displayed on the daily blackboard menu and the restaurant's wood-finish interior looks like a rustic barn.

Sitka & Spruce   Northwestern $$$
(📞206-324-0662; www.sitkaandspruce.com; 1531 Melrose Ave E; small plates $8-24; ⏰11:30am-2pm & 5:30-10pm; 🚌10) Now in a new location in the Capitol Hill 'hood, this small-plates fine-diner has won acclaim for its casual vibe, constantly changing menu, good wine selection and involved chef-owner (he'll be the guy who brings bread to your table).

🍸 Drinking & Nightlife

You'll find cocktail bars, dance clubs and live music on Capitol Hill. The main drag in Ballard has brick taverns both old and new, filled with the hard-drinking older set in daylight hours and indie rockers at

❤ If You Like...
Cafes

If you like Zeitgeist (below), don't miss these other great Seattle coffeehouses – the perfect retreats when the rain arrives.

1 ESPRESSO VIVACE AT BRIX
(www.espressovivace.com; 532 Broadway E; ⏰6am-11pm; 🚌60) Loved in equal measure for its no-nonsense walk-up stand on Broadway and this newer cafe (a large retro place with a beautiful streamlined modern counter), Vivace is known to have produced some of the Picassos of latte art.

2 PANAMA HOTEL TEA & COFFEE HOUSE
(607 S Main St; ⏰8am-7pm Mon-Sat, from 9am Sun; 🚇Chinatown/International District W) Inside a historic 1910 building, this beautifully relaxed cafe has a wide selection of teas and is one of the few places in Seattle to sell Lavazza Italian coffee.

3 CAFFÈ UMBRIA
(www.caffeumbria.com; 320 Occidental Ave S; ⏰6am-6pm Mon-Fri, 7am-6pm Sat, 8am-5pm Sun; 🚇Pioneer Sq) Umbria has a European flavor with its 8oz cappuccinos, chatty clientele, pretty Italianate tiles and baguettes so fresh they must have been teleported from Milan.

night. Belltown has gone from grungy to shabby chic, and has the advantage of many drinking holes neatly lined up in rows.

Zeitgeist   Cafe
(www.zeitgeistcoffee.com; 171 S Jackson St; ⏰6am-7pm Mon-Fri, from 8am Sat & Sun; 📶; 🚇Pioneer Sq) The comforting buzz of conversation! People actually talk in the attractive exposed-brick confines of Zeitgeist – they're not all glued to their laptops. Bolstered by tongue-loosening doses of caffeine, you can join them discussing the beautiful smoothness of your *doppio macchiato* or the sweet intensity of your to-die-for almond croissant.

THE PACIFIC NORTHWEST SEATTLE

Seattle for Children

Make a beeline for the Seattle Center, preferably on the monorail, where food carts, street entertainers, fountains and green space will make the day fly by. One essential stop is the **Pacific Science Center** (www.pacsci.org; 200 2nd Ave N; adult/child exhibits only $18/13, with Imax $22/17; ⊙10am-5pm Mon-Fri, to 6pm Sat & Sun; ⛹; Ⓜ Seattle Center), which entertains and educates with virtual-reality exhibits, laser shows, holograms, an IMAX theater and a planetarium – parents won't be bored either.

Downtown on Pier 59, **Seattle Aquarium** (www.seattleaquarium.org; 1483 Alaskan Way at Pier 59; adult/child $19/12; ⊙9:30am-5pm; ⛹; 🚇University St) is a fun way to learn about the natural world of the Pacific Northwest. Even better is **Woodland Park Zoo** (📞206-684-4800; www.zoo.org; 5500 Phinney Ave N; adult/child Oct-Apr $12.50/8.75, May-Sep $18.75/11.75; ⊙9:30am-4pm Oct-Apr, to 6pm May-Sep; ⛹; 🚌5) in the Green Lake neighborhood, one of Seattle's greatest tourist attractions and consistently rated as one of the top 10 zoos in the country.

Pike Pub & Brewery   Brewpub
(www.pikebrewing.com; 1415 1st Ave; ⊙11am-midnight; 🚇University St) Leading the way in the microbrewery revolution, this brewpub was an early starter, opening in 1989 underneath Pike Place Market. Today it continues to serve sophisticated pub food and hop-heavy beers in a neo-industrial multilevel space that's a beer nerd's heaven.

Shorty's   Dive Bar
(www.shortydog.com; 2222 2nd Ave; ⊙noon-2am; 🚌13) Shorty's is all about beer, pinball and music, which is mostly punk and metal.

Noble Fir   Bar
(📞206-420-7425; www.thenoblefir.com; 5316 Ballard Ave NW; ⊙4-11pm Mon-Wed, to 1am Thu-Sat, noon-11pm Sun; 🚌17) Possibly the first bar devoted to the theme of wilderness hiking, the Noble Fir is a bright, shiny, new Ballard spot with an epic beer list that might just make you want to abandon all your plans for outdoor adventure.

Elysian Brewing Company   Brewery
(www.elysianbrewing.com; 1221 E Pike St; ⊙11:30am-2am; 🚇Pike-Pine) This is one of Seattle's best brewpubs, and is loved in particular for its spicy pumpkin beers.

Blue Moon   Dive Bar
(712 NE 45th St; ⊙2pm-late; 🚌66) A legendary counterculture dive near the university that first opened in 1934 to celebrate the repeal of the prohibition laws, the Blue Moon makes much of its former literary patrons: doyens Dylan Thomas, Allen Ginsberg and Tom Robbins get mentioned a lot.

⭐ Entertainment

Crocodile   Live Music
(www.thecrocodile.com; 2200 2nd Ave; 🚌13) Everyone who's anyone in Seattle's alt-music scene has since played here, including a famous occasion in 1992 when Nirvana appeared unannounced on a bill supporting Mudhoney.

Neumo's   Live Music
(www.neumos.com; 925 E Pike St; 🚇Pike-Pine) A punk, hip-hop and alternative-music venue that counts Radiohead and Bill Clinton (not together) among its former guests, Neumo's (formerly known as Moe's) fills the big shoes of its original namesake.

JOHN ELK III/GETTY IMAGES ©

Don't Miss
Mt Rainier National Park

The USA's fourth-highest peak outside Alaska, majestic Mt Rainier is also one of its most beguiling. Encased in a 368-sq-mile national park (the world's fifth national park, inaugurated in 1899), the mountain's snowcapped summit and forest-covered foothills harbor numerous hiking trails, huge swaths of flower-carpeted meadows and an alluring conical peak that presents a formidable challenge for aspiring climbers.

The park's official website includes downloadable maps and descriptions of 50 park trails. The most famous is the hardcore, 93-mile **Wonderland Trail**, which circumnavigates Mt Rainier via a well-maintained unbroken route and takes around 10 to 12 days to tackle.

Of the park's four entrances, Nisqually (on Hwy 706 via Ashford, near the park's southwest corner) is the busiest and most convenient and is open year-round. The park's two main nexus points are Longmire and Paradise. Longmire, 7 miles inside the Nisqually entrance, has a **museum** and **information center**, a number of important trailheads and the rustic **National Park Inn**, complete with an excellent restaurant. More hikes and interpretive walks can be found 12 miles further east at loftier Paradise, which is served by the informative **Henry M Jackson Visitor Center** and the vintage **Paradise Inn**.

NEED TO KNOW

www.nps.gov/mora; entry per pedestrian/car $5/15

Tractor Tavern
Live Music

(☎206-789-3599; www.tractortavern.com; 5213 Ballard Ave NW; 🚍17) The premier venue for folk and acoustic music, the elegant Tractor Tavern in Ballard also books local songwriters and regional bands such as Richmond Fontaine, plus touring acts like John Doe and Wayne Hancock.

ℹ️ Information

Seattle Visitor Center & Concierge Services (☎206-461-5840; www.visitseattle.org; Washington State Convention Center, cnr E Pike St & 7th Ave; ⏰9am-5pm)

ℹ️ Getting There & Away

Air

Seattle-Tacoma International Airport (Sea-Tac; ☎206-787-5388; www.portseattle.org/sea-tac; 17801 International Blvd) is 13 miles south of Seattle on I-5.

Boat

Victoria Clipper (www.clippervacations.com) operates several high-speed passenger ferries to Victoria, BC, and to the San Juan Islands.

Train

Amtrak (www.amtrak.com) serves Seattle's **King Street Station** (303 S Jackson St; ⏰6am-10:30pm, ticket counter 6:15am-8pm).

ℹ️ Getting Around

To/from the Airport

There are a number of options for making the 13-mile trek from the airport to downtown Seattle. The most efficient is via the new light-rail service run by **Sound Transit** (www.soundtransit.org).

Public Transportation

The **Seattle Street Car** (www.seattlestreetcar.org) runs from the Westlake Center to Lake Union along a 2.6-mile route. There are 11 stops allowing interconnections with numerous bus routes. A second route from Pioneer Sq via First Hill to Capitol Hill opens in 2014.

Taxi

All Seattle taxi cabs operate at the same rate, set by King County; $2.50 at meter drop, then $2.70 per mile.

Orange Cab Co (☎206-444-0409; www.orangecab.net)

Yellow Cab (☎206-622-6500; www.yellowtaxi.net)

Monorail at EMP Museum (p343)

OLYMPIC NATIONAL PARK

Declared a national monument in 1909 and a national park in 1938, the 1406-sq-mile **Olympic National Park** (www.nps.gov/olym) shelters one of the world's only temperate rainforests and a 57-mile strip of Pacific coastal wilderness that was added in 1953. Opportunities for independent exploration abound, with activities from hiking and fishing to kayaking and skiing.

Eastern Entrances

The graveled Dosewallips River Rd follows the river from US 101 (turn off approximately 1km north of Dosewallips State Park) for 15 miles to **Dosewallips Ranger Station**, where hiking trails begin; call ☎360-565-3130 for road conditions. Even hiking smaller portions of the two long-distance paths, including the 14.9-mile Dosewallips River Trail, with views of glaciated **Mt Anderson**, is reason enough to visit the valley.

Northern Entrances

The park's easiest – and hence most popular – entry point is at **Hurricane Ridge**, 18 miles south of Port Angeles. At the road's end, an interpretive center gives a stupendous view of Mt Olympus (7965ft) and dozens of other peaks. The 5200ft altitude can mean you'll hit inclement weather and the winds here (as the name suggests) can be ferocious. Aside from various summer trekking opportunities, the area maintains one of only two US national park–based ski runs, operated by the small, family-friendly **Hurricane Ridge Ski & Snowboard Area** (www.hurricaneridge.com; 🚠).

Popular for boating and fishing is **Lake Crescent**, the site of the park's oldest and most reasonably priced **lodge** (☎360-928-3211; www.olympicnationalparks.com; 416 Lake Crescent Rd; lodge r $153, cottages $162-300; ☉May-Oct; P❄🛜). Delicious sustainable food is served in the lodge's ecofriendly restaurant. From **Storm King**

Information Station (☎360-928-3380; ☉May-Sep) on the lake's south shore, a 1-mile hike climbs through old-growth forest to Marymere Falls.

Along the Sol Duc River, the **Sol Duc Hot Springs Resort** (☎360-327-3583; www.northolympic.com/solduc; 12076 Sol Duc Hot Springs Rd, Port Angeles; RV sites $36, r $172-210; ☉late Mar-Oct; ❄🛀) 🍴 has lodging, dining, massage and, of course, hot-spring pools (adult/child $10/7.50), as well as great day hikes.

Western Entrances

Isolated by distance and home of one of the country's rainiest microclimates, the Pacific side of the Olympics remains the wildest. Only US 101 offers access to its noted temperate rainforests and untamed coastline. The **Hoh River Rainforest**, at the end of the 19-mile Hoh River Rd, is a Tolkienesque maze of dripping ferns and moss-draped trees. The **Hoh Visitor Center and Campground** (☎360-374-6925; campsites $12; ☉9am-6pm Jul & Aug, to 4:30pm Sep-Jun) has information on guided walks and longer backcountry hikes. There are no hookups or showers; first-come, first-served.

A little to the south lies **Lake Quinault**, a beautiful glacial lake surrounded by forested peaks. It's popular for fishing, boating and swimming, and is punctuated by some of the nation's oldest trees. **Lake Quinault Lodge** (☎360-288-2900; www.olympicnationalparks.com; 345 S Shore Rd; r $202-305; ❄🛜🛀), a luxury classic of 1920s 'parkitecture,' has a heated pool and sauna, a crackling fireplace and a memorable dining room.

ℹ️ Information

The park entry fee is $5/15 per person/vehicle, valid for one week, payable at park entrances.

Olympic National Park Visitor Center (3002 Mt Angeles Rd, Port Angeles; ☉9am-5pm) The best overall center is situated at the Hurricane Ridge gateway, a mile off Hwy 101 in Port Angeles.

ⓘ Getting There & Away

From Seattle, drive to the Seattle Ferry Terminal and cross Puget Sound on the Washington State Ferry System to Bainbridge Island (one hour, car and driver from \$14). Once across, take the 305 N to the 3N to the 104 W to the 101 N, which leads to the northern entrance.

SAN JUAN ISLANDS

Take the ferry west out of Anacortes and you'll feel like you've dropped off the edge of the continent. A thousand metaphoric miles from the urban inquietude of Puget Sound, the nebulous San Juan archipelago conjures up Proustian flashbacks from another era and often feels about as American as – er – Canada (which surrounds it on two sides).

There are 172 landfalls in this expansive archipelago but unless you're rich enough to charter your own yacht or seaplane, you'll be restricted to seeing the big four – San Juan, Orcas, Shaw and Lopez Islands – all served daily by Washington State Ferries. Communally, the islands are famous for their tranquility, whale-watching opportunities, sea kayaking and seditious nonconformity.

A great way to explore the San Juans is by sea kayak or bicycle. Expect a guided half-day trip to cost from \$45 to \$65.

ⓘ Getting There & Around

Washington State Ferries (WSF; www.wsdot. wa.gov/ferries) leave Anacortes for the San Juans. Ferries run to Lopez Island (45 minutes), Orcas Landing (60 minutes) and Friday Harbor on San Juan Island (75 minutes).

Shuttle buses ply Orcas and San Juan Island in the summer months.

San Juan Island

San Juan Island is the archipelago's unofficial capital, a harmonious mix of low forested hills and small rural farms that resonate with a dramatic and unusual 19th-century history.

There are hotels, B&Bs and resorts scattered around the island, but Friday Harbor has the highest concentration.

San Juan Island National Historical Park Historic Site
(www.nps.gov/sajh; ⏱8:30am-4pm, visitor center 8:30am-4:30pm Thu-Sun, daily Jun-Sep) ⚑ **FREE** San Juan Island hides one of the 19th century's oddest political confrontations, the so-called 'Pig War' between the USA and Britain. This curious Cold War standoff is showcased in two historical parks on either end of the island that once housed opposing American and English military encampments.

Lime Kiln Point State Park Park
(⏱8am-5pm mid-Oct–Mar, 6:30am-10pm Apr–mid-Oct) ⚑ Clinging to San Juan Island's rocky west coast, this beautiful park overlooks the deep Haro Strait and is, reputedly, one of the best places in the world to view whales from the shoreline.

Roche Harbor Resort Resort \$\$
(☏800-451-8910; www.rocheharbor.com; Roche Harbor; r with shared bath \$149, 1- to 3-bedroom condos \$275-450, 2-bedroom townhouses \$499; ❄☏⊠♨) Located on the site of the former lime kiln and estate of limestone king John McMillin, this seaside 'village' is a great getaway.

Juniper Lane Guest House Inn \$\$
(☏360-378-7761; www.juniperlaneguesthouse. com; 1312 Beaverton Valley Rd; r \$85-135; ☏) ⚑ The handful of wood-paneled rooms here are decorated with a colorful and eclectic assortment of refurbished or recycled art and furnishings.

Market Chef Deli \$
(225 A St, Friday Harbor; ⏱10am-6pm) ⚑ The Market Chef's specialty is deli sandwiches, and very original ones at that. Join the queue and watch staff prepare the goods with fresh, local ingredients.

Orcas Island

Precipitous, unspoiled and ruggedly beautiful, Orcas Island is the San Juans' emerald icon, excellent for hiking and, more recently, gourmet food. The ferry terminal is at Orcas Landing, 8 miles south of the main village, Eastsound.

On the island's eastern lobe is **Moran State Park** (🕑6:30am-dusk Apr-Sep, from 8am Oct-Mar), dominated by Mt Constitution (2409ft), with 40 miles of trails and an amazing 360-degree mountaintop view.

Kayaking in the calm island waters is a real joy here. **Shearwater** (www.shearwaterkayaks.com; 138 North Beach Rd, Eastsound) has the equipment and know-how. Three-hour guided trips start at $75.

Doe Bay Village Resort & Retreat Hostel, Resort $

(📞360-376-2291; www.doebay.com; dm $55, cabin d from $90, yurts from $120; 🛜) 🍴 Doc Bay has the atmosphere of an artists' commune cum hippie retreat. Accommodations include sea-view campsites, a small hostel with dormitory and private rooms, and various cabins and yurts, most with views of the water.

Outlook Inn Hotel $$

(📞360-376-2200; www.outlookinn.com; 1/1 Main St, Eastsound; r from $119, with shared bath from $79; 🛜) The Outlook Inn (1888) is an island institution that has kept up with the times by expanding into a majestic white (but still quite small) bayside complex. Also on-site is the fancy New Leaf Cafe.

Mijita's
Mexican $$

(310 A St, Eastsound; mains $13-22; 🕑4-9pm Wed-Sun) Ooh and aah over the Mexican native chef's family recipes such as slow-braised short ribs with blackberry mole or the vegetarian quinoa cakes with mushrooms, chevre, almonds and *pipian* (Mexican piquant sauce).

Island Hoppin' Brewery Brewpub

(www.islandhoppinbrewery.com; 33 Hope Lane, Eastsound; 🕑4-9pm Tue-Sun) This is *the* place to go to enjoy six changeable brews on tap while making friends with those islanders who enjoy beer. There's often live music on weekends.

....

Lopez Island

If you're going to Lopez – or 'Slow-pez,' as locals prefer to call it – take a bike. With its undulating terrain and salutation-offering locals (who are famous for their three-fingered 'Lopezian wave'), this is the ideal cycling isle. A leisurely pastoral spin can be tackled in a day, with good overnight digs available next to the marina in the **Lopez Islander Resort** (📞800-736-3434; www.lopezfun.com; Fisherman Bay Rd; r from $139; 🛜🏊🚲), which has a restaurant, gym and pool and offers free parking in Anacortes (another incentive to dump the car). If you arrive cycleless, call up **Village Cycles** (📞360-468-4013; www.villagecycles.net; 9 Old Post Rd; rentals per

Kayakers off the San Juan islands
TOM BOYDEN/GETTY IMAGES ©

hour/day from $7/30; ⊙10am-4pm Wed-Sun), which can deliver a bicycle to the ferry terminal for you.

PORTLAND

Call it what you want – PDX, Stumptown, City of Roses, Bridge City, Beervana or Portlandia – Portland positively rocks. It's a city with a vibrant downtown, pretty residential neighborhoods, ultragreen ambitions and zany characters. Here, liberal idealists outnumber conservative stogies, Gortex jackets are acceptable in fine restaurants and everyone supports countless brewpubs, coffeehouses, knitting circles, lesbian potlucks and eclectic book clubs. Portland is an up-and-coming destination that has finally arrived, and makes for an appealing, can't-miss stop on your adventures in the Pacific Northwest.

⊙ Sights

DOWNTOWN

Tom McCall Waterfront Park   Park
This sinuous, 2-mile-long park flanks the west bank of the Willamette River and is both an unofficial training ground for lunchtime runners and a commuter path for the city's avid army of cyclists. It's also a great spot for picnics, and hosts large summertime festivals.

Pioneer Courthouse Square   Landmark
Portland's downtown hub, this people-friendly brick plaza attracts tourists, sunbathers, lunching office workers, buskers and the odd political activist. Across 6th Ave is the Pioneer Courthouse, the oldest federal building in the Pacific Northwest.

Portland Art Museum   Museum
(☎503-226-2811; www.portlandartmuseum.org; 1219 SW Park Ave; adult/child $15/free; ⊙10am-5pm Tue, Wed & Sat, to 8pm Thu & Fri, noon-5pm

Sun) Right on the South Park Blocks, the art museum's excellent exhibits include Native American carvings, Asian and American art, and English silver.

Aerial Tram
Cable Car

(www.gobytram.com; 3303 SW Bond Ave; round trip $4; ⏱5:30am-9:30pm Mon-Fri, 9am-5pm Sat) Portland's aerial tram runs from the south Waterfront (there's a streetcar stop) to Marquam Hill. The tram runs along a 3300ft line up a vertical ascent of 500ft. The ride takes three minutes.

OLD TOWN & CHINATOWN

The core of rambunctious 1890s Portland, the once-notorious Old Town used to be the lurking grounds of unsavory characters, but today disco queens outnumber drug dealers. It's one of the livelier places in town after dark, when nightclubs and bars open their doors and hipsters start showing up.

Shanghai Tunnels
Historic Site

(www.shanghaitunnels.info; adult/child $13/8) Running beneath Old Town's streets is this series of underground corridors through which, in the 1850s, unscrupulous people would kidnap or 'shanghai' drunken men and sell them to sea captains looking for indentured workers. Tours run Fridays and Saturdays at 6:30pm and 8pm.

Chinatown
Neighborhood

The ornate **Chinatown Gates** (cnr W Burnside St & NW 4th Ave) define the southern edge of Portland's Chinatown, which has a few token Chinese restaurants (most are on 82nd Ave over to the east). The main attraction here is the **Classical Chinese Garden** (☎503-228-8131; www.lansugarden.org; 239 NW Everett St; adult/child $8/7; ⏱10am-6pm), a wonderfully tranquil block of reflecting ponds and manicured greenery.

Saturday Market   Market

(☎503-222-6072; www.portlandsaturday-
market.com; cnr SW Ankeny St & Naito Pkwy;
🕙10am-5pm Sat, 11am-4:30pm Sun Mar-Dec)
The best time to hit the river for a walk is
on a weekend to catch this famous market, which showcases handicrafts, street
entertainers and food booths.

THE PEARL DISTRICT & NORTHWEST

The Pearl District   Neighborhood

(www.explorethepearl.com) Northwest of
downtown, the Pearl District is an old
industrial quarter that has transformed
its once grotty warehouses into expensive lofts, upscale boutiques and creative
restaurants. On the first Thursday of
every month, the zone's abundant **art
galleries** extend their evening hours and
the area turns into a fancy street party
of sorts. The **Jamison Square Fountain
(810 NW 11th Ave)** is one of its prettier urban
spaces, and don't miss the **Museum of
Contemporary Craft** (☎503-223-2654;
www.museumofcontemporarycraft.org; 724 NW
Davis St; admission $4; 🕙11am-6pm Tue-Sat, to
8pm 1st Thu of every month), which has many
fine ceramics.

WEST HILLS

Forest Park   Park

(www.forestparkconservancy.org) Not many
cities have more than 5000 acres of
temperate rainforest within their limits,
but then not many cities are like Portland.
Abutting the more manicured Washington Park to the west is the far wilder
Forest Park, where the dense foliage
harbors plants, animals and an avid hiking
fraternity.

Washington Park   Park

(www.washingtonparkpdx.org) West of Forest Park, extensive Washington Park
contains several attractions within its
400 acres of greenery. **Hoyt Arbore-
tum** (☎503-865-8733; www.hoytarboretum.
org; 4000 Fairview Blvd; 🕙trails 6am-10pm,
visitor center 9am-4pm Mon-Fri, 11am-3pm
Sat & Sun) FREE showcases more than
1000 species of native and exotic trees
and has 12 miles of walking trails. It's
prettiest in the fall. The **International
Rose Test Gardens** (☎503-823-3636; www.
rosegardenstore.org/rose-gardens.cfm; 400
SW Kingston Ave; 🕙7:30am-9pm) FREE has
fine city views and is the centerpiece of
Portland's famous rose blooms; there

Cathedral Park Jazz Festival, Portland

are more than 500 types on show here. Further uphill is the **Japanese Garden** (📞503-223-1321; www.japanesegarden.com; 611 SW Kingston Ave; adult/6-17yr $9.50/6.75; ⏲noon-7pm Mon, 9am-7pm Tue-Fri & Sun, 9am-9pm Sat), another oasis of tranquility.

 Activities

For bike rental, try **Waterfront Bicycle Rentals** (📞503-227-1719; www.waterfrontbikes.com; 10 SW Ash St; per day $40). Good cycling maps can be found at the tourist office and any bike store.

Situated close to the confluence of the Columbia and Willamette Rivers, Portland has miles of navigable waterways. **Portland Kayak Company** (📞503-459-4050; www.portlandkayak.com; 6600 SW Macadam Ave) offers kayaking rentals, instruction and tours including a three-hour circumnavigation of Ross Island on the Willamette River.

Sleeping

Reserve ahead in summer.

Ace Hotel　　　Boutique Hotel **$$**
(📞503-228-2277; www.acehotel.com; 1022 SW Stark St; d from $185, with shared bath from $135; ❄@📶) Portland's trendiest place to sleep is this unique hotel fusing classic, industrial, minimalist and retro styles. From the photo booth and sofa lounge in its lobby to the recycled fabrics and furniture in its rooms, the Ace makes the warehouse feel work.

Jupiter Hotel　　Boutique Motel **$$**
(📞503-230-9200; www.jupiterhotel.com; 800 E Burnside St; d from $159; ❄📶📶) The hippest hotel in town, this slick, remodeled motel is within walking distance of downtown and right next to Doug Fir Lounge (p363), a top-notch live-music venue.

**Clinton Street
Guesthouse**　　Guesthouse **$$**
(📞503-234-8752; www.clintonstreetguesthouse.com; 4220 SE Clinton St; d $100-145; ❄📶)
Four simple but beautiful rooms (two

with shared bathroom) are on offer in this lovely arts-and-crafts house in a residential neighborhood.

Kennedy School　　　Hotel **$$**
(📞503-249-3983; www.mcmenamins.com; 5736 NE 33rd Ave; d $115-155; 📶) This Portland institution, a former elementary school, is now home to a hotel (yes, the bedrooms are converted classrooms), a restaurant, several bars, a microbrewery and a movie theater.

Detour:
Mount Hood

The state's highest peak, Mt Hood (11,240ft) pops into view over much of northern Oregon whenever there's a sunny day, exerting an almost magnetic tug on skiers, hikers and sightseers. Hood is rightly revered for its skiing. There are six ski areas on the mountain, including **Timberline** (📞503-272-3158; www.timberlinelodge.com; lift ticket adult/15-17yr/7-14yr $68/56/42), which lures snow-lovers with the only year-round skiing in the US.

The Mt Hood National Forest protects an astounding 1200 miles of trails. A Northwest Forest Pass ($5) is required at most trailheads. For a memorable overnight stay, book at Timberline's lodge. This gorgeous historic wood gem has awesome views of Mt Hood, access to nearby hiking trails, and the use of two bars and a good dining room.

Mt Hood is about a one-hour drive from Portland along Hwy 26.

Eating

Pok Pok
Thai **$$**

(☎503-232-1387; www.pokpokpdx.com; 3226 SE Division St; mains $11-16; ⏰11:30am-10pm) Spicy Thai street food with a twist draws crowds of flavor seekers to this famous eatery; don't miss the renowned chicken wings. To endure the inevitable long wait, try a tastier-than-it-sounds drinking vinegar at the restaurant's nearby bar, Whiskey Soda Lounge.

Navarre
European **$$**

(☎503-232-3555; www.navarreportland. blogspot.com; 10 NE 28th Ave; small plates $4-8, large plates $10-18; ⏰4:30-10:30pm Mon-Thu, to 11:30pm Fri, 9:30am-11:30pm Sat, to 10:30pm Sun) The paper menu at this industrial-elegant restaurant lists various small plates (don't call them tapas), which rotate daily. Expect a simple and truly delicious approach to crab cakes, lamb and roasted veggies.

Piazza Italia
Italian **$$**

(☎503-478-0619; www.piazzaportland.com; 1129 NW Johnson St; pasta $13-17; ⏰11:30am-3pm & 5-9pm Mon-Thu, to 10pm Fri-Sun) Remember that great *ragù* (meat sauce) you last had in Bologna or those memorable *vongole* (clams) you once polished off in Sicily? Well, you'll find them here in this highly authentic restaurant that succeeds where so many fail: replicating the true essence of Italian food in North America.

Pambiche
Cuban **$$**

(☎503-233-0511; www.pambiche.com; 2811 NE Glisan St; mains $12-17; ⏰11am-10pm Mon-Thu, to midnight Fri, 9am-midnight Sat, to 10pm Sun) Portland's best Cuban food served in a riotously colorful atmosphere.

Jake's Famous Crawfish
Seafood **$$$**

(☎503-226-1419; 401 SW 12th Ave; lunch mains $10-16, dinner mains $19-39; ⏰11:30am-10pm Mon-Thu, to midnight Fri & Sat, 3-10pm Sun) Some of Portland's best seafood can be

---

Portland's Food Carts

One of the most fun ways to explore Portland's cuisine is to eat at a food cart. These semi-permanent kitchens on wheels inhabit parking lots around town and are usually clustered in 'pods,' often with their own communal tables, ATMs and portaloos.

Food-cart locations vary, but the most significant cluster is on the corner of SW Alder St and SW 9th Ave. For a current list and some background information, see www.foodcartsportland.com. Here are our highlights from a highly competitive field:

Nong's Khao Man Gai (☎971-255-3480; www.khaomangai.com; SW 10th Ave & SW Alder St; mains $7; ⏰10am-4pm Mon-Fri) Tender poached chicken with rice.

Viking Soul Food (www.vikingsoulfood.com; 4262 SE Belmont Ave; mains $5-6; ⏰noon-8pm Tue-Thu, 11:30am-9:30pm Fri & Sat, 11:30am-8:30pm Sun) Delicious sweet and savory wraps.

Rip City Grill (www.ripcitygrill.com; cnr SW Moody Ave & Abernethy St; sandwiches $5-7; ⏰10am-2pm Mon-Fri) The tri-tip steak sandwich is not to be missed.

Thrive Pacific NW (www.thrivepacificnw.com; mains $5-8) Organic, free-range and gluten-free exotic food bowls.

Pepper Box (www.pepperboxpdx.com; 2737 NE Martin Luther King Jr Blvd; tacos & quesadillas $3.50-4; ⏰9am-2pm Tue-Fri, to 1pm Sat) Awesome breakfast tacos and fancy quesadillas.

found here within an elegant old-time atmosphere.

Drinking & Nightlife

Breakside Brewery
Brewpub

(☑503-719-6475; www.breakside.com; 820 NE Dekum St; ⊘3-10pm Mon-Thu, noon-11pm Fri & Sat, noon-10pm Sun) More than 20 taps of some of the most experimental, tasty beer you'll ever drink, laced with fruits, vegetables and spices. Good food and nice outdoor seating, too.

Barista
Cafe

(☑503-274-1211; www.baristapdx.com; 539 NW 13th Ave; ⊘6am-6pm Mon-Fri, 7am-6pm Sat & Sun) One of Portland's best coffee shops is owned by award-winning barista Billy Wilson and known for its lattes. It sources its beans from specialty roasters.

Stumptown Coffee Roasters
Cafe

(☑503-230-7702; www.stumptowncoffee.com; 4525 SE Division St; ⊘6am-7pm Mon-Fri, 7am-7pm Sat & Sun) The first microroaster to put Portland on the coffee map, and still its most famous coffee shop.

Departure Lounge
Bar

(☑503-802-5370; www.departureportland.com; 525 SW Morrison St; ⊘4pm-midnight Sun-Thu, to 1am Fri & Sat) This rooftop restaurant-bar (atop the 15th floor of the Nines Hotel) fills a deep downtown void: a cool bar with unforgettable views. The vibe is distinctly spaceship LA, with mod couches and sleek lighting.

⭐ Entertainment

Doug Fir Lounge
Live Music

(☑503-231-9663; www.dougfirlounge.com; 830 E Burnside St) Paul Bunyan meets the Jetsons at this ultratrendy venue. Doug Fir books edgy, hard-to-get talent, drawing crowds from tattooed youth to suburban yuppies. The decent restaurant has long hours; it's located next to the rock star–quality Jupiter Hotel.

 If You Like…
Microbreweries

It's enough to make a native Brit jealous. Portland has about 30 brewpubs within its borders – more than any other city on earth. If you like Breakside Brewery, try some of these other renowned spots.

1 HOPWORKS URBAN BREWERY
(☑503-232-4677; www.hopworksbeer.com; 2944 SE Powell Blvd; ⊘11am-11pm Sun-Thu, to midnight Fri & Sat; 🚲) Organic beers made with local ingredients, served in an ecobuilding with bicycle frames above the bar.

2 GREEN DRAGON
(☑503-517-0660; www.pdxgreendragon. com; 928 SE 9th Ave; ⊘11am-11pm Sun-Wed, to 1am Thu-Sat) Although it is owned by Rogue Breweries, Green Dragon serves a whopping 62 guest taps – and it's an eclectic mix to boot.

3 BELMONT STATION
(☑503-232-8538; www.belmont-station. com; 4500 SE Stark St; ⊘noon-11pm) More than 20 excellent rotating taps in a simple 'biercafé' with sidewalk seating.

Dante's
Live Music

(☑503-345-7892; www.danteslive.com; 350 W Burnside St) This steamy red bar books vaudeville shows along with national acts such as the Dandy Warhols and Concrete Blonde.

Information

Portland Oregon Visitors Association (www. travelportland.com; 701 SW 6th Ave; ⊘8:30am-5:30pm Mon-Fri, 10am-4pm Sat, to 2pm Sun) In Pioneer Courthouse Sq.

🛈 Getting There & Away
Air

Portland International Airport (PDX; ☑503-460-4234; www.flypdx.com; 7000 NE Airport Way) Portland International Airport has daily

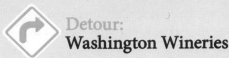

Detour:
Washington Wineries

The fertile land that borders the Nile-like Yakima and Columbia River valleys is awash with enterprising new wineries producing quality grapes that now vie with the Napa and Sonoma Valleys for national recognition. Yakima and its more attractive cousin Ellensburg once held the edge, but nowadays the real star is Walla Walla, where talented restaurateurs and a proactive local council are crafting a wine destination par excellence.

Here are a few of our favorites (www.wineyakimavalley.org is another good resource):

Bonair Winery (www.bonairwine.com; 500 S Bonair Rd, Zillah; ⊙10am-5pm) In the Rattlesnake Hills near Zillah; has lovely gardens and is a laid-back place to sample luscious reds.

Terra Blanca (www.terrablanca.com; 34715 N DeMoss Rd, Benton City; ⊙11am-6pm) Majestically located on Red Mountain, this is one of the fanciest vineyards in the region, and perfect for sipping dessert wines while admiring views over the valley.

Waterbrook Wine (www.waterbrook.com; 10518 W US 12; ⊙11am-6pm Mon-Thu, till 8pm Fri & Sat) The pondside patio of this large winery situated about 10 miles west of Walla Walla is a great place to imbibe a long selection of wines on a sunny day.

Amavi Cellars (3796 Peppers Bridge Rd; ⊙10am-4pm) South of Walla Walla amid a scenic spread of grape and apple orchards, you can sample some of the most talked-about wines in the valley (try the Syrah and Cabernet Sauvignon). The classy yet comfortable outdoor patio has views of the Blue Mountains.

flights all over the US, as well as to several international destinations.

Train

Amtrak (☎503-273-4865; www.amtrak.com; 800 NW 6th Ave) Amtrak offers services up and down the West Coast.

🛈 Getting Around

To/from the Airport

Tri-Met's light-rail MAX line takes about 40 minutes to get from downtown to the airport.

Taxis charge around $34 from the airport to downtown (not including tip).

Public Transportation

Portland has a good public-transportation system, which consists of local buses, streetcars and the MAX light-rail. All are run by **TriMet** (☎503-238-7433; www.trimet.org; 701 SW 6th Ave), which has an information center at Pioneer Courthouse Sq.

Taxi

Try **Broadway Cab** (☎503-333-3333; www.broadwaycab.com) or **Radio Cab** (☎503-227-1212; www.radiocab.net).

OREGON COAST

Thanks to a far-sighted government in the 1910s, Oregon's 363-mile Pacific Coast was set aside as public land. This magnificent littoral is paralleled by US 101, a scenic highway that winds its way through towns, resorts, state parks (more than 70 of them) and wilderness areas. Everyone from campers to gourmet-lovers will find a plethora of ways to enjoy this exceptional region.

Cannon Beach

Charming Cannon Beach is one of the most popular and upscale beach resorts on the Oregon coast. The streets are full of boutiques and art galleries, and lined with colorful flowers.

The coast to the north, protected inside **Ecola State Park**, is the Oregon you may have already visited in your dreams: sea stacks, crashing surf, hidden beaches and gorgeous pristine forest. The park is 1.5 miles from town and is crisscrossed by paths, including part of the Oregon Coast Trail, which leads over Tillamook Head to the town of Seaside.

The **Cannon Beach Hotel** (☎503-436-1392; www.cannonbeachhotellodgings.com; 1116 S Hemlock St; d incl breakfast $139-269; 🛜) is a classy, centrally located hotel with just 10 rooms.

Oregon Dunes National Recreation Area

Stretching for 50 miles between Florence and Coos Bay, the Oregon Dunes form the largest expanse of coastal dunes in the USA. They tower up to 500ft and undulate inland as far as 3 miles to meet coastal forests, harboring curious ecosystems that sustain an abundance of wildlife. Hiking trails, bridle paths, and boating and swimming areas are available, but avoid the stretch south of Reedsport as noisy dune buggies dominate. Inform yourself at the Oregon Dunes National Recreation Area's **headquarters** (☎541-271-3495; www.fs.fed/us/r6/sius law; 855 Highway Ave; ⊙8am-4:30pm Mon-Fri, to 4pm Sat & Sun) in Reedsport.

Crater Lake National Park

It's no exaggeration: Crater Lake is so blue, you'll catch your breath. And if you get to see it on a calm day, the surrounding cliffs are reflected in those deep waters like a mirror. It's a stunningly beautiful sight. Crater Lake is Oregon's only national park (entry costs $10 per vehicle).

The secret lies in the water's purity. No rivers or streams feed the lake, meaning its content is made up entirely of rain and melted snow. It is also exceptionally deep – at 1949ft, it's the deepest lake in the US. The classic tour is the 33-mile rim drive (open from approximately June to mid-October), but there are also exceptional hiking and cross-country skiing opportunities. Note that because the area receives some of the highest snowfalls in North America, the rim drive and north entrance are sometimes closed up until early July.

You can stay from late May to mid-October at the **Cabins at Mazama Village** (☎541-830-8700; www.craterlakelodges.com; d $140) or the majestic and historic **Crater Lake Lodge** (☎888-774-2728; www.craterlakelodges.com; d $165-292; 🛜), opened in 1915.

For more information, head to **Steel Visitor Center** (☎541-594-3100; ⊙9am-5pm May-Oct, 10am-4pm Nov-Apr).

California

With its dramatic coastline, sun-dappled vineyards and snow-covered peaks, California soars beyond even the expectations it sells on Hollywood's silver screens.

More than anything, California is iconic. It was here where the hurly-burly gold rush kicked off in the mid-19th century, where naturalist John Muir rhapsodized about the Sierra Nevada's 'range of light,' and Jack Kerouac and the Beat Generation defined what it really means to hit the road.

California's multicultural melting pot has been cookin' since this bountiful, promised land was staked out by Spain and Mexico. Waves of immigrants still search for their own American dream on these palm tree–studded Pacific shores. It's time for you to join them.

Hikers in a redwood forest, California
JORDAN SIEMENS/GETTY IMAGES ©

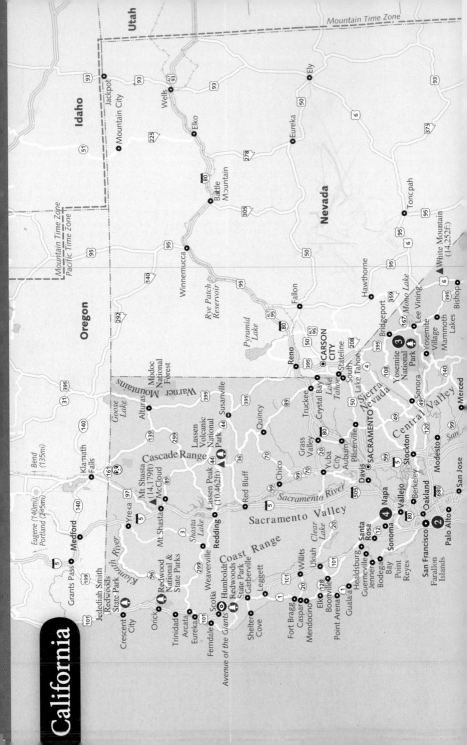

California

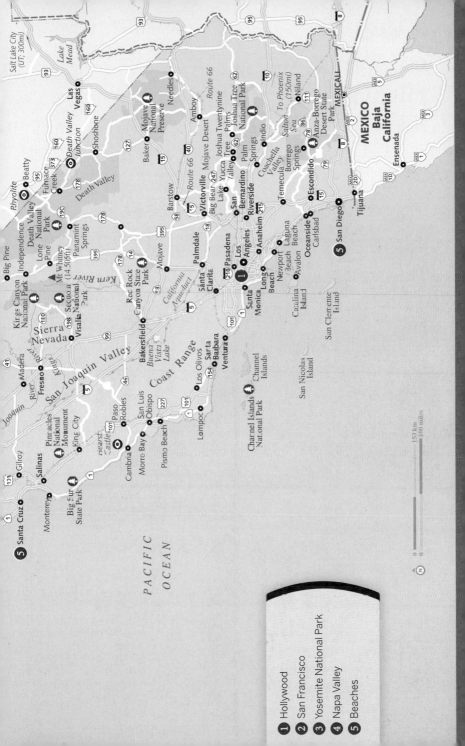

California's Highlights

Hollywood

Hollywood (p381) has been synonymous with motion pictures since Cecil B DeMille shot one of the world's first full-length feature films in a 'Hollywoodland' barn in 1914. LA took center stage in the world of popular culture and has been there ever since. Below: Hollywood Walk of Fame

San Francisco

Rattling cable cars, fog-draped hillsides, picture-book Victorians and stunning views are all part of this captivating city by the bay. Alternately elegant and bohemian, San Francisco (p397) has fascinatingly diverse neighborhoods lined with eclectic shops and boutiques, old-world cafes, hipster-filled nightspots and amber-lit restaurants. Walkable, green and utterly disarming, San Francisco is an easy city to love.

MITCHELL FUNK/GETTY IMAGES ©

Yosemite National Park

The head-turner of America's national parks, Yosemite (p415) garners the devotion of all who enter. From the waterfall-striped granite walls buttressing emerald-green Yosemite Valley to the towering giant sequoias standing like ancient sentinels at Mariposa Grove, you'll feel a sense of awe and reverence that so much natural beauty exists in one place. This paradise for hikers, landscape artists and photographers should not be missed.

Napa Valley

Vineyards litter this scenic, fertile state, and you won't have to travel far for a memorable quaff. One of the finest wine-growing regions lies just north of San Francisco. Amid rolling verdure (with more than a passing resemblance to Tuscany), you'll find the sun-dappled vineyards of the Napa Valley (p413). Tour the fields, sample spicy Zinfandels and refreshing Sauvignon Blancs and drink up the pastoral beauty.

Beaches

Crashing waves, endless stretches of sand and fun along the boardwalk – when it comes to beaches, California's got it covered. Surfers can hang ten at Santa Cruz (p420) or Huntington Beach (p391) – also known as 'Surf City, USA' – while sunbathers can catch some rays along San Diego's boundless Silver Strand (p391). Should you tire of sand and surf, hit the Venice Boardwalk (p386) for some fascinating people-watching. Above: Huntington Beach (p391)

California's Best...

Beaches

○ **Malibu** Spectacular SoCal beauty with great surfing and celebrity appeal. (p382)

○ **Santa Monica** LA's hippest beach, within strolling distance of galleries and great restaurants. (p382)

○ **Huntington Beach** Bonfires, beach volleyball and rolling waves in 'Surf City USA.' (p391)

○ **Coronado Island** Hop on the ferry to reach this head-turner in ever-sunny San Diego. (p391)

Activities for Kids

○ **Disneyland** Journey into imaginary worlds and give Mickey a high five at this famed theme park. (p389)

○ **San Diego Zoo** Budding wildlife lovers will love this sprawling zoo, home to more than 800 animal species. (p392)

○ **Alcatraz** Enjoy the scenic boat ride, then wander the spooky cells of this former island prison. (p404)

Restaurants

○ **Chez Panisse** Legendary birthplace of California cuisine. (p408)

○ **Commonwealth** Deliciously inventive cuisine in an equally avant-garde setting in San Francisco. (p408)

○ **Paradise Cove Beach Cafe** Scrumptious fish tacos and leisurely brunches on a gorgeous beach in Malibu. (p387)

○ **Ad Hoc** Superb farm-to-table cooking – and a menu that changes daily – in the food- and wine-loving Napa Valley. (p414)

Need to Know

Architecture

- **California Academy of Sciences** A $500 million San Francisco masterpiece with LEED platinum credentials (including a 'living roof') designed by Renzo Piano. (p403)

- **Walt Disney Concert Hall** Frank Gehry's surreal and futuristic hall that has become an LA icon. (p377)

- **Old Town** Adobe buildings showcase San Diego's early Spanish settlement. (p392)

- **Golden Gate Bridge** Run it, bike it or just sit on San Francisco's Crissy Field gazing at this captivating icon. (p406)

ADVANCE PLANNING

- **Two months before** Book tickets to big-name concerts, pro games and shows. Reserve accommodations, transportation and/or rental car.

- **One month before** Reserve at top restaurants like Chez Panisse.

- **One week before** Browse entertainment listings.

RESOURCES

- **San Francisco Bay Guardian** (www.sfbg.com) Free weekly covering entertainment listings, reviews and gossip.

- **San Francisco Chronicle** (www.sfgate.com) News, entertainment and event listings from Northern California's largest daily.

- **Napa Valley.com** (www.napavalley.org) Overview of wineries, restaurants, spas, shops and lodgings.

- **ExperienceLA.com** (www.experiencela.com) Cultural calendar packed with LA goings-on.

- **Los Angeles Times** (www.latimes.com) Arts, dining and entertainment.

GETTING AROUND

- **Airports** Los Angeles (LAX) and San Francisco (SFO) are major international airports. Transport to/from LAX to Downtown or West Hollywood is via shuttle ($16 to $25) or taxi ($30 to $50). SFO has fast BART trains to Downtown San Francisco.

- **Bus** Greyhound (www.greyhound.com) provides service between major towns.

- **Hire car** Essential for taking the epic coastal road trip.

- **Train** Amtrak can take you from Seattle to San Francisco and LA, then on to San Diego. Other routes link Chicago with either SF or LA, and New Orleans with LA.

BE FOREWARNED

- **Traffic** Prepare for mind-numbing traffic in LA, San Diego or the San Francisco area. Avoid peak times, including popular getaways (Marin County, wine country, Lake Tahoe), on weekends.

- **Cold summer** Expect foggy, chilly days in San Francisco in summer. Wear layers and save the shorts for Southern California.

ft: Wildflowers, Mailbu (p382); **Above:** Golden Gate Bridge, San Francisco (p406)

California Itineraries

With beaches, vineyards and urban adventures aplenty, you could spend months exploring California. These two itineraries let you delve into two of the US's finest cities, followed by a cinematic drive up the Pacific Coast Hwy.

5 DAYS

LOS ANGELES & SAN FRANCISCO
South vs North

Start in ❶ **Los Angeles** (p376). Go star-searching on the Hollywood Walk of Fame (p381), then drive to the lofty Getty Center (p382) before heading to Venice Board-walk's (p386) seaside sideshow. Watch the sun set over the ocean in Santa Monica. On day two, visit Downtown LA, historic El Pueblo de Los Angeles and futuristic Walt Disney Concert Hall (p377). Grab food in Chinatown and rooftop cocktails at the Standard (p385).

Make your way to ❷ **San Francisco** (p397). Take a bay-front stroll from the Ferry Building (p400) to Fisherman's Wharf, then ferry it to Alcatraz (p404). Hop

a cable car to North Beach (p400) and stroll through Chinatown at dinnertime, followed by a SoMa club. Start day four in the Mission, checking out murals, window-shopping along Valencia, and burrito-feasting at a real-deal taquería. Visit the Haight for vintage boutiques, and Golden Gate Park for the California Academy of Sciences (p403) rainforest dome.

On your last day head across the Golden Gate Bridge for the redwoods of ❸ **Muir Woods** (p412). On the way back stop for a scenic walk at Crissy Field (p401), before dinner at North Beach.

 7 DAYS

SAN DIEGO TO SAN FRANCISCO
Cruising the Pacific Coast Highway

Start in **①San Diego** (p391). Spend the morning exploring Balboa Park and the afternoon basking on Coronado Beach. Have dinner in the Gaslamp Quarter.

On day two, drive north to **②Orange County** (p391) and spend the day hopping between Huntington, Newport and Laguna Beaches. Rise early to beat the traffic up to **③Los Angeles** (p376) for an exploration of Venice, Santa Monica and Malibu. Spend the night in nightlife-loving Hollywood.

On your fourth day take a 90-minute drive to **④Santa Barbara** (p420), a lovely town with a Mediterranean vibe. Continue three hours north to **⑤Hearst** **Castle** (p397) for a glimpse of palatial extravagance, circa 1920s. Another 65 miles north is **⑥Big Sur** (p417), a great spot to break your journey (reserve ahead).

Spend day five exploring the stunning scenery, stopping in Partington Cove, lunching at clifftop Nepenthe and hiking at Andrew Molera State Park. Next up is **⑦Monterey** (p419), known for its excellent aquarium and historic downtown. On your last day, hightail it up to **⑧San Francisco** (p397) and toast the journey's end with a bang-up meal in the city.

Muir Woods National Monument (p412)
CONNOR WALBERG/GETTY IMAGES ©

Discover California

View from the Pacific Coast Highway (p417)
BMINER/GETTY IMAGES ©

LOS ANGELES

If you think you've got LA figured out – celebrities, smog, traffic, bikini babes and pop-star wannabes – think again. Although it's an entertainment capital, the city's truths aren't delivered on movie screens or reality shows; rather, they're seen in bite sized portions of everyday experiences on the streets. The one thing that brings together Angelenos is that they are seekers – or the descendants of seekers – drawn by a dream of fame, fortune or rebirth.

Now is an especially exciting time to visit LA: Hollywood and Downtown are undergoing an urban renaissance, and the art, music, food and fashion scenes are all in high gear. Chances are, the more you explore, the more you'll love 'La-La Land.'

◉ Sights

EL PUEBLO DE LOS ANGELES & AROUND

Compact, colorful and car-free, this historic district is an immersion in LA's Spanish-Mexican roots. Its spine is **Olvera St**, a festive kitsch o rama where you can snap up handmade folkloric trinkets, then chomp on tacos or sugar-sprinkled churros.

La Plaza de Cultura y Artes   Museum
(Map p384; ☎ 213-542-6200; www.lapca.org; 501 N Main St; ☺noon-7pm Wed-Mon) **FREE**
Open since 2010, La Plaza chronicles the Mexican-American experience in LA with exhibits about the city's history from the Zoot Suit Riots to the Chicana movement and Latino art. It adjoins the 1822 church **La Placita** (Map p384; www.laplacita.org; 535 N Main St).

Avila Adobe
Museum

(Map p384; ☎213-628-1274; http://elpueblo.la
city.org; Olvera St; ⊙9am-4pm) FREE Claim-
ing to be LA's oldest building, this 1818
ranch home is decorated with period furniture. A video gives history and highlights
of the neighborhood.

CIVIC CENTER & CULTURAL CORRIDOR

Museum of Contemporary Art
Museum

(MOCA; Map p384; ☎213-626-6222; www.moca.
org; 250 S Grand Ave; adult/child $12/free, free
5-8pm Thu; ⊙11am-5pm Mon & Fri, to 8pm Thu,
to 6pm Sat & Sun) Housed in a building designed by Arata Isozaki, MOCA Grand Ave
stages headline-grabbing special exhibits.
Its permanent collection presents heavy
hitters from the 1940s to the present.

Walt Disney Concert Hall
Cultural Building

(Map p384; ☎info 213-972-7211, tickets 323-850-
2000; www.laphil.org; 111 S Grand Ave; ⊙guided
tours usually 10:30am & 12:30pm Tue-Sat; P)
FREE Architect Frank Gehry's now-iconic
2003 building is a gravity-defying sculpture of curving and billowing stainless-
steel walls that's home base for the Los
Angeles Philharmonic (p388). Free tours
are available subject to concert schedules, and walkways encircle the maze-like
roof and exterior.

Cathedral of Our Lady of the Angels
Church

(Map p384; ☎213-680-5200; www.olacathedral.
org; 555 W Temple St; ⊙6:30am-6pm Mon-Fri,
from 9am Sat, from 7am Sun; P) FREE Architect José Rafael Moneo mixed Gothic
proportions with bold contemporary
design for the main church of LA's
Catholic Archdiocese.

LITTLE TOKYO

Little Tokyo swirls with shopping arcades,
Buddhist temples, public art, traditional
gardens, authentic sushi bars and noodle
shops and a branch of **MOCA** (Map p384;
☎213-626-6222; www.moca.org; 152 N Central
Ave; adult/child $12/free; ⊙11am-5pm Mon & Fri,
to 8pm Thu, to 6pm Sat & Sun).

Japanese American National Museum
Museum

(Map p384; ☎213-625-0414; www.janm.org;
100 N Central Ave; adult/child $9/5; ⊙11am-
5pm Tue-Wed & Fri-Sun, noon-8pm Thu) Get an
in-depth look at the Japanese immigrant
experience, including the painful chapter
of WWII internment camps.

SOUTH PARK

Grammy Museum
Museum

(Map p384; www.grammymuseum.org; 800 W
Olympic Blvd; adult/child $13/11, after 6pm $8;
⊙11:30am-7:30pm Mon-Fri, from 10am Sat &
Sun; ⏶) Music fans of all stripes will get
lost in these mind-expanding interactive
displays about the history of American
music, where interactive sound booths
let you and your entourage try mixing and
remixing pop and rock hits, and singing
and rapping with the stars.

EXPOSITION PARK & AROUND

Just south of the University of Southern
California (USC) campus, this park has a
full day's worth of kid-friendly museums.
Outdoor landmarks include the **Rose Garden** (www.laparks.org; 701 State Dr; admission
free; ⊙9am-sunset Mar 15–Dec 31) and the
1923 **Los Angeles Memorial Coliseum**,
site of the 1932 and 1984 Summer Olympic Games.

Natural History Museum of Los Angeles
Museum

(☎213-763-3466; www.nhm.org; 900 Exposition
Blvd; adult/child $12/5; ⊙9:30am-5pm; ⏶)
Dinos to diamonds, bears to beetles, even
an ultra-rare megamouth shark – this
science museum will take you around the
world and back millions of years in time.

California Science Center
Museum

(☎film schedule 213-744-2109, info 323-724-
3623; www.californiasciencecenter.org; 700
Exposition Park Dr; IMAX movie adult/child
$8.25/5; ⊙10am-5pm; ⏶) FREE A simulated
earthquake, hatching baby chicks and a
giant techno-doll named Tess bring out
the kid in everyone at this great hands-on
science museum.

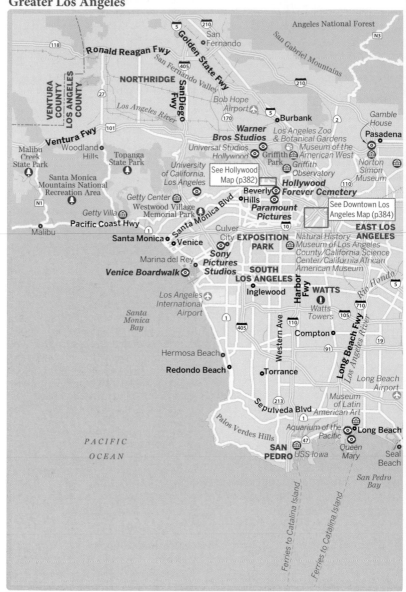

GRIFFITH PARK

America's largest urban **park** (☎323-913-4688; www.laparks.org/dos/parks/griffithpk; 4730 Crystal Springs Dr; ⏰5am-10:30pm, trails sunrise-sunset; P 👫) FREE is five times the size of New York's Central Park, with an outdoor theater, zoo, observatory, museum, merry-go-round, antique and miniature trains, children's playgrounds, golf, tennis and over 50 miles of hiking paths, including to the original *Batman* TV series cave.

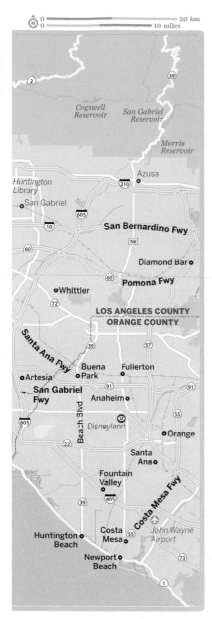

tory are a state-of-the-art planetarium and the Leonard Nimoy Event Horizon multimedia theater.

MID-CITY

Some of LA's best museums line 'Museum Row,' a short stretch of Wilshire Blvd east of Fairfax Ave.

Los Angeles County Museum of Art   Museum

(LACMA; ☎ 323-857-6000; www.lacma. org; 5905 Wilshire Blvd; adult/child $15/free; ⏰ 11am-5pm Mon-Tue & Thu, to 9pm Fri, 10am-7pm Sat & Sun; 🅿) One of the country's top art museums (and the largest in the western US), LACMA has seven buildings brimming with paintings, sculpture and decorative arts: European masters such as Rembrandt, Cézanne and Magritte; ancient pottery from China, Turkey and Iran; photographs by Ansel Adams; and a jewel box of Japanese screen paintings and sculpture.

La Brea Tar Pits   Archaeological Site

Between 11,000 and 40,000 years ago, tarlike bubbling crude oil trapped saber-toothed cats, mammoths and other extinct ice-age critters, which are still being excavated here. Check out their fossilized remains at the **Page Museum** (☎ 323-934-7243, www.tarpits.org; 5801 Wilshire Blvd; adult/child $12/5, free 1st Tue each month Sep-Jun; ⏰ 9:30am-5pm; 🅿 ♿).

BEVERLY HILLS & AROUND

No trip to LA would be complete without a saunter along pricey, pretentious **Rodeo Dr**, a three-block ribbon where sample-size fembots browse for fashions from international houses – from Armani to Zegna – in couture-design stores. If the prices make you gasp, Beverly Dr, one block east, has more down-to-earth boutiques.

Griffith Observatory   Museum

(☎ 213-473-0800; www.griffithobservatory.org; 2800 E Observatory Rd; admission free, planetarium shows adult/child $7/3; ⏰ noon-10pm Tue-Fri, from 10am Sat & Sun; 🅿 ♿) Inside the iconic triple domes of this 1935 observa-

Paley Center for Media   Museum

(☎ 310-786-1000; www.paleycenter.org; 465 N Beverly Dr; suggested donation adult/child $10/5; ⏰ noon-5pm Wed-Sun; 🅿) TV and radio addicts can indulge their passion at this mind-boggling archive of TV and

Don't Miss
Hollywood

Just as an aging movie star gets the occasional facelift, so does Hollywood. While it hasn't recaptured its 'Golden Age' glamour, its modern seediness is disappearing. The Hollywood Walk of Fame honors more than 2000 celebrities with stars embedded in the sidewalk, and multistory mall Hollywood & Highland has nicely framed views of the hillside Hollywood Sign.

TCL Chinese Theatre

Even the most jaded visitor may thrill in the famous forecourt of the **TCL Chinese Theatre** (Map p382; tour info 323-461-3331; 6925 Hollywood Blvd), where generations of screen legends have left their imprints in cement: feet, hands, dreadlocks (Whoopi Goldberg), and even magic wands (young stars of the Harry Potter films).

Dolby Theatre

Real-life celebs sashay along the red carpet of this **theater** (Map p382; ☎323-308-6300; www.dolbytheatre.com; tour adult/child $17/12; ⏰tours usually 10:30am-4pm) for the Academy Awards – columns with names of Oscar-winning films line the entryway. Pricey 30-minute tours take you inside the auditorium, VIP room and past an actual Oscar statuette.

Hollywood Forever Cemetery

Rock 'n' roll faithful flock to the **monument** (☎323-469-1181; www.hollywoodforever.com; 6000 Santa Monica Blvd; ⏰8am-5pm; P) of Johnny Ramone at this historic boneyard, whose other famous residents include Rudolph Valentino, Cecil B DeMille and Bugsy Siegel. Check the online calendar of movie screenings and concerts (yes, really).

Touring Movie & TV Studios

Half the fun of visiting Hollywood is hoping you'll see stars. Up the odds by joining the studio audience of a sitcom or game show, which usually tape between August and March. For free tickets, contact **Audiences Unlimited** (☎818-260-0041; www.tvtickets.com). For an authentic behind-the-scenes look, take a small-group shuttle tour at **Warner Bros Studios** (☎818-972-8687, 877-492-8687; www.wbstudiotour.com; 3400 W Riverside Dr, Burbank; tours from $49; ⏰8:15am-4pm Mon-Sat, hours vary Sun) or **Paramount Pictures** (☎323-956-1777; www.paramount.com; 5555 Melrose Ave; tours from $48; ⏰tours 9:30am-2pm Mon-Fri, hours vary Sat & Sun), or a walking tour of **Sony Pictures Studios** (☎310-244-8687; www.sonypicturesstudiostours.com; 10202 W Washington Blvd; tour $35; ⏰tours usually 9:30am-2:30pm Mon-Fri). All these tours show you around sound stages and backlots (outdoor sets), and inside wardrobe and make-up departments.

Local Knowledge

Hollywood

BY LERON GUBLER,
MASTER OF CEREMONIES,
HOLLYWOOD WALK OF FAME

1 HOLLYWOOD MUSEUM
A great place to spend a few hours looking at costumes, posters, memorabilia, celebrity cars such as Cary Grant's Rolls Royce, and film sets including Hannibal Lecter's cell from *Silence of the Lambs*. It's in the historic Max Factor Building – a former speakeasy.

2 MOVIE PALACES
There are many fantastic restored motion-picture palaces in Hollywood. Disney has its premieres at the El Capitan, which also has a Wurlitzer pipe organ. The Egyptian began the concept of dazzling premieres with klieg lights. The Pantages has a spectacular lobby. And of course there's TCL Chinese Theatre with its famous forecourt and new IMAX screen, the second largest in North America.

3 STUDIO TOURS
For the real flavor of what Hollywood's all about, do a studio tour at Paramount Pictures or Warner Brothers. You get to see working studios in action, and the groups are small. You can watch shows being filmed and tour the backlots and find out about the movies filmed there.

4 HOLLYWOOD WALK OF FAME
It's free! We currently have more than 2500 stars on the **Walk of Fame** (Map p382; www.walkoffame.com; Hollywood Blvd), and average about 24 new ones each year. Besides the stars, 46 buildings along Hollywood Blvd and Vine St have historic markers detailing what happened there.

5 SUNSET RANCH
This stable has been in business for over 70 years – very 'old Hollywood.' Sunset horseback rides through Griffith Park to Burbank are a fun experience because the views are just great: they include the **Hollywood Sign**, the Griffith Observatory and Downtown LA.

Hollywood

radio broadcasts from 1918 through the internet age. Pick your faves, grab a seat at a private console and enjoy. Public programs include lectures and screenings.

WEST LA

Getty Center   Museum
(☎310-440-7300; www.getty.edu; 1200 Getty Center Dr, off I-405; ⊙10am-5:30pm Tue-Sun, to 9pm Sat; P) FREE Triple delights: a stellar art collection from Renaissance masters to David Hockney, with Richard Meier's fabulous architecture and Robert Irwin's ever-changing gardens. On clear days, add breathtaking views of the city and ocean to the list.

MALIBU

Hugging 27 spectacular miles of the Pacific Coast Hwy, Malibu has long been synonymous with surfing and Hollywood stars, but it actually looks far less posh than glossy tabloids make it sound. Still, it has been celebrity central since the 1930s.

One of Malibu's twin natural treasures is mountainous **Malibu Creek State Park** (☎818-880-0367; www.malibucreekstatepark. org; ⊙dawn-dusk), a popular movie and TV filming location with hiking trails galore (parking $12). The other is a string of beaches, including aptly named **Surfrider** west of Malibu Pier, wilder **Point Dume State Beach** and family fave **Zuma Beach** (beach parking $10).

SANTA MONICA

The belle by the beach mixes urban cool with a laid-back vibe. Tourists, teens and street performers make car-free, chain store-lined **Third Street Promenade** the most action-packed zone. For more local flavor, shop celeb-favored **Montana Ave** or eclectic **Main St**, backbone of the neighborhood once nicknamed 'Dogtown,' the birthplace of skateboard culture.

Santa Monica Pier   Amusement Park
(http://santamonicapier.org; all-day ride pass $13-20; P⛲) Kids love the venerable pier, where attractions include a quaint carousel and solar-powered Ferris wheel. Peer under the pier at the tiny **aquarium** (☎310-393-6149; www.healthebay.org; 1600

Ocean Front Walk; adult/child $5/free; ⏰2-5pm Tue-Fri, 12:30-5pm Sat & Sun; 🚻). Parking rates vary seasonally.

Bergamot Station Arts Center

Arts Center

(www.bergamotstation.com; 2525 Michigan Ave; ⏰10am-6pm Tue-Fri, 11am-5:30pm Sat; P) Art fans gravitate inland toward this former trolley stop that houses 35 avant-garde galleries and the progressive **Santa Monica Museum of Art** (www.smmoa.org; 2525 Michigan Ave; donation adult/child $5/3; ⏰11am-6pm Tue-Sat).

🧭 Activities

Get scenic exercise in-line skating or riding along the paved **South Bay Bicycle Trail**, which parallels the beach for most of the 22 miles between Santa Monica and Pacific Palisades. Rental outfits are plentiful in beach towns. Warning: it's crowded on weekends.

Turn on your celeb radar while strutting it with the hot bods along **Runyon Canyon Park** above Hollywood. **Griffith Park** is also laced with trails.

Top beaches for swimming are Malibu's **Zuma Beach**, **Santa Monica State Beach** and the South Bay's **Hermosa Beach.** Malibu's **Surfrider Beach** is a legendary surfing spot. Parking rates vary seasonally.

🛏 Sleeping

For seaside life, base yourself in Santa Monica, Venice or Long Beach. Coolhunters and party people will be happiest in Hollywood or WeHo; culture vultures, in Downtown LA.

Figueroa Hotel Historic Hotel **$$**

(Map p384; 📞800-421-9092, 213-627-8971; www.figueroahotel.com; 939 S Figueroa St; r $148-194, ste $225-265; P❄@🛜≋🐾) A rambling 1920s oasis across from LA Live welcomes travelers with a richly tiled Spanish-style lobby that segues to a sparkling swimming pool. Rooms are furnished in a global mash-up of styles (Morocco, Mexico, Zen), varying in size and configuration.

View of Los Angeles from the Griffith Observatory (p379)

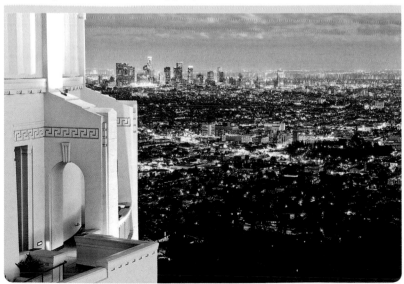

EDDIE BRADY/GETTY IMAGES ©

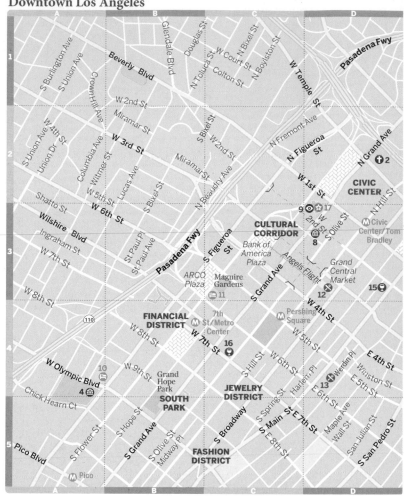

Magic Castle Hotel
Hotel $$

(Map p382; ☎ 323-851-0800; http://magic-castlehotel.com; 7025 Franklin Ave; r incl breakfast from $175; P❄@🤖❄👶) Walls are thin, but renovated apartments in this courtyard building come with contemporary furniture and attractive art, and suites have a separate living room.

Farmer's Daughter Hotel
Motel $$

(☎ 800-334-1658, 323-937-3930; www.farmers daughterhotel.com; 115 S Fairfax Ave; r from $185; P❄@🤖❄) Opposite the Original Farmers Market and CBS Studios, this perennial pleaser gets high marks for its sleek 'urban cowboy' look. Adventurous lovebirds, ask about the No Tell Room.

Sea Shore Motel
Motel $$

(☎ 310-392-2787; www.seashoremotel.com; 2637 Main St; r from $110; P❄🤖) Clean, friendly, family-owned lodgings are two blocks from the beach and right on happening Main St (expect ambient noise). Spanish-tiled rooms are basic but attractive, and

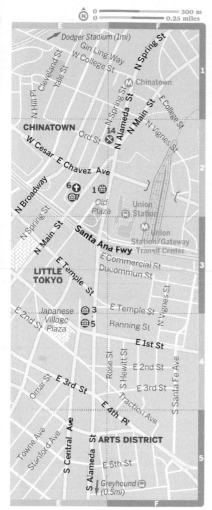

🍴 Eating

LA's culinary scene is California's most vibrant and eclectic, from celebrity chefs whipping up farmers-market menus to down-home authentic global cuisine.

For cheap, fast meals-on-the-go, graze the international food stalls of the historic **Grand Central Market** (Map p384; www.grandcentralsquare.com; 317 S Broadway; ⊙9am-6pm).

Philippe the Original Diner $
(Map p384; ☎213-628-3781; www.philippes. com; 1001 N Alameda St; mains $4-10; ⊙6am-10pm; P 🚻) LAPD hunks, stressed-out attorneys and Midwestern vacationers chow down at this legendary 'home of the French dip sandwich,' dating back to 1908.

Veggie Grill Vegetarian $
(☎323-822-7575; www.veggiegrill.com; 8000 W Sunset Blvd; mains $7-10; ⊙11am-11pm; 🗲 🚻) If crispy chickin' wings or a carne asada sandwich don't sound vegetarian, know that this darn tasty local chain uses

kitchen suites are roomy enough for families.

Standard Downtown LA Boutique Hotel $$$
(Map p384; ☎213-892-8080; http://standardhotels.com/downtown-la; 550 S Flower St; r $245-525, ste $1150-1300; P 🌼 @ 🛜 🐾 🐶) This design-savvy hotel in a former office building goes for a young, hip and shag-happy crowd – the rooftop bar fairly pulses – so don't come here to get a solid night's sleep.

HANAN ISACHAR/GETTY IMAGES ©

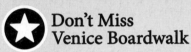

Don't Miss
Venice Boardwalk

The Venice Boardwalk is a freak show, a human zoo, a wacky carnival and an essential LA experience. This cauldron of counterculture is the place to get your hair braided and a *qi gong* back massage, or pick up cheap sunglasses and a Rastafarian knit beret. Encounters with bodybuilders, hoop dreamers, a Speedo-clad snake charmer or a roller-skating Sikh minstrel are almost guaranteed, especially on sunny afternoons. Alas, the vibe gets creepy after dark.

To escape the hubbub, meander inland to the **Venice Canals**, a vestige of Venice's early days when Italian gondoliers poled tourists along artificial waterways. Today locals lollygag in rowboats in this flower-festooned neighborhood. Funky, hipper-than-ever **Abbot Kinney Blvd** (www.abbotkinneyonline.com) is a palm-lined mile of restaurants, cafes, yoga studios, art galleries and eclectic shops selling vintage furniture and handmade fashions.

NEED TO KNOW

Ocean Front Walk; Venice Pier to Rose Ave; ⏱24hr; 🚌MTA 33, 333, BBB 2

seasoned vegetable proteins (mostly tempeh).

Original Farmers Market Market $
(www.farmersmarketla.com; 6333 W 3rd St; most mains $6-12; ⏱9am-9pm Mon-Fri, to 8pm Sat, 10am-7pm Sun; 🅿🚻) Although now heavily commercialized, the market still has a few worthy, budget-friendly eateries,

most *al fresco*. Try Du-Par's classic diner, Cajun-style cooking at the Gumbo Pot or iLoteria! Mexican grill.

Nickel Diner Diner $$
(Map p384; ☎213-623-8301; http://nickeldiner. com; 524 S Main St; mains $7-14; ⏱8am-3:30pm Tue-Sun, 6-10:30pm Tue-Sat) In Downtown's historic theater district, this red-vinyl joint

feels like a 1920s throwback. Ingredients are 21st-century, though: avocados stuffed with quinoa salad, 'lowrider' chili burgers and must-try doughnuts. Expect long waits.

Griddle Café   Breakfast $$
(☎323-874-0377; www.thegriddlecafe.com; 7916 W Sunset Blvd; mains $10-18; ◷7am-4pm Mon-Fri, from 8am Sat & Sun) Whimsically named sugar-bomb pancakes, giant-sized egg scrambles and French-press coffee pots keep the wooden tables and U-shaped counter full all day long at this pit-stop favored by Hollywood's young and tousled.

Lemonade   Californian $$
(http://lemonadela.com; 1661 Abbot Kinney Blvd; small dishes $5-11; ◷11am-9pm) Look for an imaginative seasonal line-up of deli salads, such as butter lettuce with pink grapefruit; seafood plates like seared tuna with watermelon radish; jerk pineapple chicken; custom-made sourdough sandwiches; and lotsa flavored lemonades – blueberry-mint!

Pizzeria & Osteria
Mozza   Italian $$$
(☎323-297-0100; www.mozza-la.com; 6602 Melrose Ave; pizzas $11-20, dinner mains $27-38; ◷pizzeria noon-midnight daily, osteria 5:30-11pm Mon-Fri, 5-11pm Sat & 5-10pm Sun) Reserve weeks ahead for LA's hottest Italian eatery, run by celebrity chefs Mario Batali and Nancy Silverton.

Paradise Cove
Beach Cafe   American $$$
(☎310-457-2503; www.paradisecovemalibu.com; 28128 Pacific Coast Hwy; mains $11-36; ◷8am-10pm; P ♿) It's your movie-perfect image of SoCal: stick your feet in the sand and knock back piña coladas and fish tacos at this California-casual institution on a private beach where *Beach Blanket Bingo* was filmed.

🍷 Drinking

Edison   Bar
(Map p384; ☎213-613-0000; www.edison-downtown.com; 100 W 2nd Ct, off Harlem Pl; ◷5pm-2am Wed-Fri, from 7pm Sat) *Metropolis* meets *Blade Runner* at this industrial-chic basement boîte, where you'll be sipping hand-crafted cocktails surrounded by turbines and other machinery back from its days as a power plant. It's all tarted up with cocoa leather couches, three cavernous bars and a hoity-toity dress code.

Gay & Lesbian LA

'Boystown,' along Santa Monica Blvd in West Hollywood (WeHo), is gay ground zero, where dozens of high-energy bars, cafes, restaurants, gyms and clubs mostly cater to men. Silver Lake, LA's original gay enclave, has evolved from largely leather-and-Levi's to encompass multiethnic, metrosexual hipsters.

Abbey (www.abbeyfoodandbar.com; 692 N Robertson Blvd; mains $9-13; ◷8am-2am) At WeHo's essential gay bar and restaurant, take your pick of preening on a leafy patio, in a slick lounge or on a dance floor, and enjoy flavored martinis and upscale pub grub. A dozen other bars and nightclubs are within walking distance.

Akbar (www.akbarsilverlake.com; 4356 W Sunset Blvd) A killer jukebox and a Los Feliz crowd that's been known to change from hour to hour – gay, straight or just hip, but not too-hip-for-you. Some nights the back room becomes a dance floor.

Roosterfish (www.roosterfishbar.com; 1302 Abbot Kinney Blvd; ◷11am-2am) Venice's oldest gay bar has been serving men for over three decades. Roosterfish is dark and divey yet chill, with a pool table and back patio.

Los Angeles for Children

Keeping kids happy is child's play in LA. The sprawling **Los Angeles Zoo** (☎323-644-4200; www.lazoo.org; 5333 Zoo Dr; adult/child $17/12; ☉10am-5pm; P ♣) in family-friendly Griffith Park (p378) is a sure bet. Dino-fans will dig the La Brea Tar Pits (p379) and the Natural History Museum (p377), while budding scientists crowd the California Science Center (p377). For under-the-sea creatures, head to the **Aquarium of the Pacific** (☎tickets 562-590-3100; www.aquariumofpacific.org; 100 Aquarium Way; adult/child $26/15; ☉9am-6pm; ♣) in Long Beach, where teens might get a kick out of ghost tours of the **Queen Mary** (www.queenmary.com; 1126 Queens Hwy; tours adult/child from $14/7; ☉10am-6:30pm; P). The amusement park at Santa Monica Pier (p382) is fun for all ages. Activities for younger kids are more limited at tween/teen-oriented **Universal Studios Hollywood** (www.universalstudioshollywood.com; 100 Universal City Plaza; admission from $80, under 3yr free; ☉daily, hours vary; P ♣). In neighboring Orange County, Disneyland (p389) and Knott's Berry Farm are ever-popular theme parks.

Copa d'Oro   Bar
(www.copadoro.com; 217 Broadway, Santa Monica; ☉5:30pm-midnight Mon-Wed, to 2am Thu-Sat) A smooth, lamplit ambience will woo your sweetheart at this Santa Monica sanctuary. Artisanal cocktails draw from a well of top-end liquors and a farmers-market's basket of fresh herbs, fruit and even veggies.

Seven Grand   Bar
(Map p384; ☎213-614-0737; http://seven-grandbars.com; 2nd fl, 515 W 7th St; ☉5pm-2am Mon-Wed, from 4pm Thu & Fri, from 7pm Sat) Hipsters have invaded Mummy and Daddy's hunt club, amid tartan-patterned carpeting and deer heads on the walls.

El Carmen   Bar
(8138 W 3rd St; ☉5pm-2am Mon-Fri, from 7pm Sat & Sun) Mounted bull heads and *lucha libre* (Mexican wrestling) masks create an over-the-top 'Tijuana North' look that pulls in an entertainment industry–heavy crowd.

★ Entertainment

Hollywood Bowl   Live Music
(☎323-850-2000; www.hollywoodbowl.com; 2301 N Highland Ave; ☉Jun-Sep; ♣) This historic outdoor amphitheater is the LA Phil's summer home and a stellar place to catch big-name rock, jazz, blues and pop acts. Come early for a preshow picnic (alcohol allowed).

Los Angeles Philharmonic   Orchestra
(Map p384; ☎323-850-2000; www.laphil.org; 111 S Grand Ave) The world-class LA Phil performs classics and cutting-edge works at Walt Disney Concert Hall (p377) under the baton of Venezuelan phenom Gustavo Dudamel.

Hotel Cafe   Live Music
(Map p382; ☎323-461-2040; www.hotelcafe.com; 1623½ N Cahuenga Blvd; tickets $10-20) The 'it' place for handmade music is a so-cial stepping stone for message-minded newbie balladeers. Get there early and enter from the alley.

Dodger Stadium   Baseball
(☎866-363-4377; www.dodgers.com; 1000 Elysian Park Ave; ☉Apr-Sep) LA's Major League Baseball team plays within tobacco-spitting distance of downtown.

❶ Information

Hollywood Visitor Information Center (Map p382; ☎323-467-6412; http://discoverlosangeles.com; Hollywood & Highland complex, 6801 Hollywood Blvd; ⏱10am-10pm Mon-Sat, to 7pm Sun) In the Kodak Theatre walkway.

ℹ Getting There & Away

Air

LA's gateway hub is Los Angeles International Airport (LAX; ☎310-646-5252; www.lawa.org/lax; 1 World Way; 📶), the USA's second busiest.

Bus

Greyhound's main bus terminal (☎213-629-8401; www.greyhound.com; 1716 E 7th St) is in an unsavory part of Downtown LA, so avoid arriving after dark.

Train

Long-distance Amtrak trains roll into Downtown LA's historic Union Station (☎800-872-7245; www.amtrak.com; 800 N Alameda St).

ℹ Getting Around

To/from the Airport

Door-to-door shared-ride vans operated by Prime Time (☎800-733-8267; www.primetimeshuttle.com) and Super Shuttle (☎800-258-3826; www.supershuttle.com) leave from the lower level of LAX terminals; typical destinations include Santa Monica ($19), Hollywood ($25) and Downtown LA ($16).

Curbside dispatchers summon taxis at LAX. A flat fare applies to Downtown LA ($46.50) or Santa Monica ($30 to $35). Otherwise, metered fares (including $4 airport surcharge) average $45 to $55 for Hollywood and up to $95 to Disneyland, excluding tip.

Taxi

Checker (☎800-300-5007; http://ineedtaxi.com)

Independent (☎800-521-8294; http://taxi4u.com/)

DISNEYLAND & ANAHEIM

The mother of all West Coast theme parks, aka the 'Happiest Place on Earth,' Disneyland is a parallel world that's squeaky-clean, enchanting and wacky all at once.

👁 Sights & Activities

Disneyland Park   Theme Park
(♿) Spotless, wholesome Disneyland is still laid out according to Walt's original plans. **Main Street USA**, a pedestrian thoroughfare lined with old-fashioned ice-cream parlors and shops, is the gateway. At its far end is **Sleeping Beauty Castle**, an obligatory photo op and a central landmark worth noting – its towering blue turrets are visible from many areas.

The park's themed sections stuffed with rides and attractions radiate out from Sleeping Beauty Castle like spokes on a wheel.

Your best bet for meeting princesses and other characters in costume is

Walt Disney Concert Hall (p377), designed by Frank Gehry
RICHARD CUMMINS/GETTY IMAGES ©

Fantasyland, home to the spinning teacups of Mad Tea Party, It's a Small World cruise and Peter Pan's Flight. For something a bit more fast-paced, head to the exhilarating Space Mountain roller coaster in **Tomorrowland**, where the Finding Nemo Submarine Voyage and Star Wars' Jedi Training Academy await.

The ever-popular Indiana Jones Adventure ride awaits in **Adventureland**. Nearby **New Orleans Square** offers several worthwhile attractions – the Haunted Mansion (not too scary for older kids) and Pirates of the Caribbean cruise, where cannons shoot across the water, wenches are up for auction and the mechanical Jack Sparrow character is creepily lifelike. Big Thunder Mountain Railroad, another popular roller coaster, is in cowboy-themed **Frontierland**.

If you've got little ones in tow, you'll likely spend time at **Mickey's Toontown** and in **Critter Country**, where families can cool off on Splash Mountain's log-flume ride.

Disney's California Adventure　Theme Park

(DCA;) Disneyland resort's larger but less crowded park, DCA celebrates the natural and pop-cultural glories of the Golden State but lacks the density of attractions and depth of imagination. The best rides are Soarin' Over California, a virtual hang-glide; the famous Twilight Zone Tower of Terror, which drops you down an elevator chute; and Grizzly River Run, a whitewater-rafting ride.

🛏 Sleeping

Alpine Inn　Motel $$

(📞714-772-4422; www.alpineinnanaheim. com; 715 W Katella Ave; r incl breakfast $79-149; ❄@🛜♨🛝) Connoisseurs of kitsch will delight at this alpine chalet covered to the tippy-top of its A-framed rafters with artificial snow and icicles. Compact rooms have mod cons, but it's all about the convenient location outside Disneyland Resort's main gate.

Laguna Beach, Orange County

CALIFORNIA DISNEYLAND & ANAHEIM

ⓘ Getting There & Around

The Disneyland Resort is just off I-5 (Santa Ana Fwy), about 30 miles southeast of Downtown LA.

ORANGE COUNTY BEACHES

If you've seen *The OC* or *Real Housewives*, you'll think you already know what to expect from this giant quilt of suburbia connecting LA and San Diego, lolling beside 42 miles of glorious coastline. In reality, Hummer-driving hunks and Botoxed beauties mix it up with hang-loose surfers and beatnik artists to give each of Orange County's beach towns a distinct vibe.

Just across the LA–OC county line, old-fashioned **Seal Beach** is refreshingly noncommercial, with a quaint walkable downtown. Nine miles further south along the Pacific Coast Hwy (Hwy 1), **Huntington Beach** – aka 'Surf City, USA' – epitomizes SoCal's surfing lifestyle. Fish tacos and happy-hour specials abound at bars and cafes along downtown HB's Main St, not far from a shortboard-sized **surfing museum** (☏714-960-3483; www.surfingmuseum.org; 411 Olive Ave; admission by donation; ⊙noon-5pm Sun & Mon, to 9pm Tue, to 7pm Wed-Fri, 11am-7pm Sat).

Next up is the ritziest of the OC's beach communities: yacht-filled **Newport Beach**. Families and teens steer toward Balboa Peninsula for its beaches, vintage wooden pier and quaint amusement center. From nearby the 1906 Balboa Pavilion, **Balboa Island Ferry** (www.balboaislandferry.com; 410 S Bay Front; adult/child $1/50¢, car incl driver $2; ⊙6:30am-midnight Sun-Thu, to 2am Fri & Sat) shuttles across the bay to Balboa Island for strolls past historic beach cottages and boutiques along Marine Ave.

Continuing south, Hwy 1 zooms past the wild beaches of **Crystal Cove State Park** (☏949-494-3539; www.parks.ca.gov; 8471 N Coast Hwy; per car $15, campsites $25-75) before winding downhill into **Laguna Beach**, the OC's most cultured and charming seaside community. There, secluded beaches, glassy waves and eucalyptus-covered hillsides create a Riviera-like feel.

SAN DIEGO

San Diegans shamelessly promote their hometown as 'America's Finest City.' Smug? Maybe, but it's easy to see why: the weather is practically perfect, with coastal high temperatures hovering around 68°F (20°C) all year, and beaches are rarely more than a quick drive away.

◎ Sights & Activities

DOWNTOWN & EMBARCADERO

The main street, 5th Ave, was once a notorious strip of saloons, gambling joints and bordellos known as Stingaree. These days, Stingaree has been beautifully restored and rechristened the **Gaslamp Quarter**, a heart-thumping playground of restaurants, bars, clubs, boutiques and galleries.

At downtown's northern edge, **Little Italy** (www.littleitalysd.com) has evolved into one of the city's hippest places to live, eat and shop. **India St** is the neighborhood's main drag.

Maritime Museum   Museum
(☏619-234-9153; www.sdmaritime.org; 1492 N Harbor Dr; adult/child $16/8; ⊙9am-9pm late May–early Sep, to 8pm early Sep–late May; 🚼) The 1863 *Star of India* is one of seven historic sailing vessels open to the public at this pirate-worthy museum. A 45-minute historical bay cruise costs just $5 extra.

Gaslamp Museum   Museum
(☏619-233-4692; www.gaslampquarter.org; 410 Island Ave; adult/child $5/4; ⊙10am-5pm Tue-Sat, noon-4pm Sun) Peruse the period exhibits inside this Victorian-era saltbox house that was the one-time home of William Heath Davis, the man credited with founding 'New Town.'

CORONADO

Technically a peninsula, Coronado Island is joined to the mainland by a soaring,

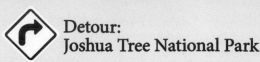

Detour: Joshua Tree National Park

Like figments from a Dr Seuss book, whimsical-looking Joshua trees (actually tree-sized yuccas) welcome visitors to this wilderness park where the Sonora and Mojave Deserts converge. You'll find most of the main attractions, including all of the Joshua trees, in the park's northern half. 'J-Tree' is perennially popular with rock climbers and day hikers, especially in spring when the trees bloom with cream-colored flowers. The mystical quality of this stark, boulder-strewn landscape has inspired countless artists, most famously the rock band U2.

There are no park facilities aside from restrooms. Get gas and stock up on supplies in the three desert communities linked by the Twentynine Palms Hwy (Hwy 62) along the park's northern boundary: down-to-earth Yucca Valley has the most services, while beatnik Joshua Tree has outdoor outfitters and the best eateries.

The park is a little over two hours' drive east of LA.

boomerang-shaped bridge. The main draw here is the **Hotel del Coronado** (**619-435-6611, 800-468-3533; www.hoteldel.com; 1500 Orange Ave**), known for its seaside Victorian architecture and illustrious guest book, which includes Thomas Edison, Brad Pitt and Marilyn Monroe (its exterior stood in for a Miami hotel in the classic flick *Some Like it Hot*).

The hourly **Coronado Ferry** (**619-234-4111; www.sdhe.com; fare $4.25; 9am-10pm**) departs from the Embarcadero's Broadway Pier (990 N Harbor Dr) and from Downtown's San Diego Convention Center. All ferries arrive on Coronado at the foot of 1st St, where **Bikes & Beyond** (**619-435-7180; http://hollandsbicycles.com; 1201 1st St, Coronado; rental per hr/day from $7/25; 9am-sunset**) rents cruisers and tandems, perfect for pedaling past Coronado's beaches sprawled south along the **Silver Strand**.

BALBOA PARK

Balboa Park is an urban oasis brimming with more than a dozen museums, gorgeous gardens and architecture, performance spaces and a zoo. Early 20th-century beaux-arts and Spanish-Colonial buildings (the legacy of world's fairs) are grouped around plazas along east–west El Prado promenade.

San Diego Zoo Zoo

(**619-231-1515; www.sandiegozoo.org; 2920 Zoo Dr; adult/child $44/34; 9am-9pm mid-Jun–early Sep, to 5pm or 6pm early Sep–mid-Jun; P**) If it slithers, crawls, stomps, swims, leaps or flies, chances are you'll find it in this world-famous zoo. It's home to more than 4000 animals representing 800-plus species in a beautifully landscaped setting, including the Australian Outback and Panda Canyon. For a wildlife-viewing experience that's closer to the real thing, get a combo ticket to Escondido's San Diego Zoo Safari Park (p395).

OLD TOWN & MISSION VALLEY

Old Town State Historic Park Historic Site

(**619-220-5422; www.parks.ca.gov; 4002 Wallace St; visitor center & museums 10am-4pm Oct-Apr, to 5pm May-Sep; P**) FREE This open-air park preserves five original adobe buildings and several re-created structures from the first pueblo, including a schoolhouse and newspaper office. Most buildings now contain museums, shops or restaurants. The visitor center offers free guided walking tours at 11am and 2pm daily.

Mission Basilica
San Diego de Alcalá   Church
(📞619-281-8449; www.missionsandiego.com; 10818 San Diego Mission Rd; adult/child $3/1; ⏰9am-4:45pm; 🅿) Secluded in a corner of what's now called Mission Valley, California's 'Mother of the Missions' hides beautifully restored buildings in bougainvillea gardens with views over the valley to the ocean.

MISSION BAY & BEACHES

San Diego's big three beach towns all have ribbons of hedonism where armies of tanned, taut bodies frolic in the sand.

West of amoeba-shaped Mission Bay, surf-friendly **Mission Beach** and its northern neighbor, **Pacific Beach** (aka 'PB'), are connected by car-free **Ocean Front Walk**, which swarms with skaters, joggers and cyclists year-round.

South of Mission Bay, bohemian **Ocean Beach** ('OB') has a fishing pier, beach volleyball and good surf. Its main drag, **Newport Ave**, is chockablock with scruffy bars, flip-flop eateries and shops selling surf gear, tattoos, vintage clothing and antiques.

🛏 Sleeping

Hotel Indigo   Boutique Hotel **$$**
(📞619-727 4000; www.hotelinsd.com; 509 9th Ave; r from $149; 🅿✳@🛜≋👪) 🐾 San Diego's first hotel to be certified by Leadership in Energy & Environmental Design (LEED), this Gaslamp boutique hotel is smartly designed. Popping with vibrant color, room decor is contempo-chic, with huge floor-to-ceiling windows, rain showers and hardwood floors.

Hotel Vyant   B&B **$$**
(📞800-518-9930; www.hotelvyant.com; 505 W Grape St; r from $149, with shared bath from $109; ✳🛜) This pretty Little Italy B&B is a charming place to hang your hat. Two dozen rooms all have inviting beds and bathrobes; deluxe rooms come with a whirlpool tub or kitchenette.

Pearl   Motel **$$**
(📞619-226-6100, 877-732-7574; www.thepearlsd.com; 1410 Rosecrans St; r from $130; 🅿✳🛜≋) A mash-up of a boutique hotel and a 1960s motel, this swingin' crashpad pulls in cool cats. Every sassy room comes with its own pet goldfish, and the tiniest digs have mirrored ceilings. Poolside movie nights and a cocktail bar keep things buzzing.

Inn at Sunset Cliffs   Hotel **$$$**
(📞619-222-7901, 866-786-2453; www.innatsunsetcliffs.com; 1370 Sunset Cliffs Blvd; r/ste from $175/289; 🅿✳@🛜≋👫) Hear the surf crashing onto the rocky shore at this breezy 1960s oceanfront charmer

San Diego's Gaslamp Quarter (p391)
RICHARD CUMMINS/GETTY IMAGES ©

wrapped around a flower-bedecked courtyard.

Eating

Neighborhood
Pub $$

(www.neighborhoodsd.com; 777 G St; mains $7-14; ⏱noon-midnight) More down-to-earth than other trendy gastropubs, this corner joint churns out crowd-pleasers like smoky chipotle burgers, kicky jalapeño mac 'n' cheese and hot dogs with braised pork and fried egg. Order a pint of micro-brewed beer that's hoppy, fruity, malty or sour.

Underbelly
Asian, Fusion $$

(📞619-269-4626; 750 W Fir St; dishes $5-12; ⏱11:30am-midnight) Off Little Italy's bustling strip of pizzerias and wine bars, this sleek noodle shop loads up steaming bowls of ramen with oxtail dumplings, hoisin-glazed short ribs and smoked brisket and bacon (vegetarian versions available). Two dozen craft beers on tap.

Buona Forchetta
Italian $$

(www.buonaforchettasd.com; 3001 Beech St; pizzas $7-15, small plates $5-13; ⏱5-10pm Sun & Tue-Thu, to 11pm Fri & Sat; 🐾) A gold-painted

brick wood-fired oven custom-built in Italy delivers authentic Neapolitan pizzas straight to merrily jammed-together tables at this South Park trattoria with a dog-friendly patio.

Point Loma Seafoods
Seafood $$

(http://pointlomaseafoods.com; 2805 Emerson St; dishes $3-16, mains $9-13; ⏱9am-7pm Mon-Sat, from 10am Sun; P🐾) Stroll up and order right at the counter inside this fish market, grill and deli with a sushi bar, where almost everything is fresh off the boat. It's a briny San Diego institution, with picnic tables outside.

Prado
Californian $$$

(📞619-557-9441; www.pradobalboa.com; House of Hospitality, 1549 El Prado; mains lunch $12-21, dinner $22-35; ⏱11:30am-3pm Mon-Fri, 11am-3pm Sat & Sun, 5-9pm Sun & Tue-Thu, to 10pm Fri & Sat) This sought-after Balboa Park spot spices up fresh Cal-Mediterranean cuisine with Latin and Asian touches, from the seafood paella and chorizo pork burgers to chopped salads. Breezy out-door seating and a colorfully tiled interior are equally inviting. Happy-hour food and drinks are a steal.

La Jolla, San Diego

George's at the Cove
Californian $$$

(📞858-454-4244; www.georgesatthecove.com; 1250 Prospect St, La Jolla; 🕑11am-10pm Mon-Thu, to 11pm Fri-Sun) George's has graced just about every list of top restaurants in California, and chef Trey Foshee's Euro-Cal cuisine is as dramatic as the oceanfront location. Three venues allow you to enjoy it at stratospherically ascending price points: **George's Bar** (lunch mains $10-18), **Ocean Terrace** (dinner mains $18-35) and **California Modern** (dinner mains $30-50).

🍸 Drinking & Entertainment

Prohibition
Lounge

(www.prohibitionsd.com; 548 5th Ave; 🕑7pm-2am Wed-Sat) Sophisticated 1930s-style bar takes music and cocktails seriously. Live jazz, blues, soul sounds or tiki tunes after 9pm.

Tipsy Crow
Bar

(📞619-338-9300; http://thetipsycrow.com; 770 5th Ave; 🕑3pm-2am Mon-Fri, from noon Sat & Sun) In a historic Gaslamp building, this atmospheric watering hole has a lounge-like 'Nest' (rumored to have been a brothel) and brick-walled 'Underground' dance floor with rockin' live bands and comedy acts.

Casbah
Live Music

(📞619-232-4355; www.casbahmusic.com; 2501 Kettner Blvd; tickets $5-45) Catch local bands and indie-rock headliners here and at the legendary **Belly Up** (📞858-481-8140; www.bellyup.com; 143 S Cedros Ave, Solana Beach; tickets $10-45) in Solana Beach.

ⓘ Information

Balboa Park Visitors Center (📞619-239-0512; www.balboapark.org; House of Hospitality, 1549 El Prado; 🕑9:30am-4:30pm) Buy discounted one-day ($39) and seven-day (adult/child $39/27, including zoo $85/49) passports to park museums.

Detour: San Diego Zoo Safari Park

Take a walk on the 'wild' side at this 1800-acre open-range **zoo** (📞760-747-8702; www.sdzsafaripark.org; 15500 San Pasqual Valley Rd; adult/child from $44/34, 2-day ticket incl San Diego Zoo $79/61; 🕑9am-7pm late Jun–mid-Aug, to 5pm or 6pm rest of year; P 🚻). Giraffes graze, lions lounge and rhinos roam more or less freely on the valley floor. For that instant safari feel, board the Africa tram ride, which tours the second-largest continent in just 25 minutes.

The park is in Escondido, about 35 miles northeast of Downtown San Diego. Take the I-15 Fwy to the Via Rancho Pkwy exit, then follow the signs.

San Diego Visitor Information Centers (📞619-236-1212; www.sandiego.org) Downtown (1140 N Harbor Dr; 🕑9am-5pm Jun-Sep, to 4pm Oct-May); La Jolla (📞858-454-5718; 7966 Herschel Ave; 🕑11am-6pm Jun-Sep, to 4pm Oct-May) Downtown's waterfront location sells discounted attraction and tour tickets.

ⓘ Getting There & Away

Served mainly by domestic US and Mexico flights, San Diego International Airport (SAN; 📞619-400-2404; www.san.org; 3325 N Harbor Dr) sits 3 miles northwest of downtown.

Greyhound (📞619-515-1100; www.greyhound.com; 1313 National Ave) has hourly direct buses to Los Angeles ($19, two to three hours).

Amtrak (📞800-872-7245; www.amtrak.com) runs the *Pacific Surfliner* several times daily to Los Angeles ($37, 2¾ hours) and Santa Barbara ($41, 5¾ hours) from downtown's historic Santa Fe Depot (1055 Kettner Blvd).

ⓘ Getting Around

MTS bus 992 ($2.25) runs every 15 to 30 minutes between the airport and downtown from 5am until 11pm daily. Airport shuttles like Super Shuttle charge $8 to $10 to downtown. An airport taxi to downtown averages $10 to $15, plus tip.

DEATH VALLEY NATIONAL PARK

The name itself evokes all that is harsh and hellish – a punishing, barren and lifeless place of Old Testament severity. Yet closer inspection reveals nature puts on a spectacular show here of water-sculpted canyons, windswept sand dunes, palm-shaded oases, jagged mountains and wildlife aplenty. It's also a land of superlatives, holding the US records for hottest temperature (134°F, or 57°C), lowest point (Badwater, 282ft below sea level) and largest national park outside Alaska (more than 5000 sq miles). Peak tourist season is when spring wildflowers bloom.

From **Furnace Creek**, the central hub of the **park** (☎760-786-3200; www.nps.gov/deva; 7-day entry per car $20), drive southeast up to **Zabriskie Point** for spectacular sunset views across the valley and golden badlands eroded into waves, pleats and gullies. Twenty miles southeast at **Dante's View**, you can simultaneously spot the highest (Mt Whitney, 14,505ft) and lowest (Badwater) points in the contiguous USA.

Badwater itself, a timeless landscape of crinkly salt flats, is 17 miles south of Furnace Creek. Along the way, **Golden Canyon** and **Natural Bridge** are easily explored on short hikes from roadside parking lots. A 9-mile detour along **Artists Drive** through a narrow canyon is best in late afternoon when the eroded hillsides erupt in fireworks of color.

Northwest of Furnace Creek, near Stovepipe Wells Village, trek across the Saharan-esque **Mesquite Flat sand dunes** – magical during a full moon – and scramble along the smooth marble walls of **Mosaic Canyon**.

About 35 miles north of Furnace Creek is whimsical **Scotty's Castle** (☎reservations 877-444-6777; www.recreation.gov; tours adult/child from $15/7.50; ☻grounds 7am-5:30pm, tour schedules vary), where tour guides in historical character dress bring to life the Old West tales of con-man 'Death Valley Scotty' (reservations advised).

Activities offered at Furnace Creek Ranch (p397) include horseback riding, golf, mountain biking and hot-springs pool swimming.

Purchase a seven-day entry pass ($20 per car) at self-service pay stations throughout the park. For a free map and newspaper, show your receipt at the **visitor center** (☎760-786-3200; www.nps.gov/deva; ☻8am-5pm) in Furnace Creek,

Hwy 190, Death Valley
WITOLD SKRYPCZAK/GETTY IMAGES ©

where you'll also find a general store, gas station, post office, ATM, laundromat and showers.

Ranch at Furnace Creek
Motel, Cabins **$$**
(☎760-786-2345, 800-236-7916; www. furnacecreekresort.com; Hwy 190; d $139-219; ❄️ 🛜 🏊 👪) Tailor-made for families, this rambling resort offers lodge rooms awash in desert colors with French doors opening onto porches or patios, as well as duplex cabins. The ranch encompasses a natural spring-fed pool, golf course and tennis courts. The **49'er Cafe (mains $10-$25)** cooks up decent American standards, or grab beers and pizza at Corkscrew Saloon.

SAN FRANCISCO & THE BAY AREA

Psychedelic drugs, newfangled technology, gay liberation, green ventures, free speech and culinary experimentation all became mainstream long ago in San Francisco. After 160 years of booms and busts, losing your shirt has become a favorite local pastime at the clothing-optional Bay to Breakers race, Pride Parade and hot Sundays on Baker Beach. So long, inhibitions; hello, San Francisco.

👁 Sights

Let San Francisco's 43 hills and more than 80 arts venues stretch your legs and your imagination, and deliver breathtaking views. Downtown sights are within walking distance of Market St, but keep your city smarts and wits about you, especially around South of Market (SoMa) and the Tenderloin (5th to 9th Sts).

CIVIC CENTER

Asian Art Museum Museum
(☎415-581-3500; www.asianart.org; 200 Larkin St; adult/student/child $12/8/free, 1st Sun of month free; ⏰10am-5pm Tue-Sun, to 9pm Thu Feb-Sep; Ⓜ Civic Center, Ⓑ Civic Center) Imaginations race from ancient Persian miniatures to cutting-edge Japanese

---

♥ If You Like… Offbeat Attractions

If you want to explore California's alternative side, don't miss these spots.

1 HEARST CASTLE
(☎reservations 800-444-4445; www. hearstcastle.org; 750 Hearst Castle Rd; tours adult/child from $25/12; ⏰usually 9am-sunset) Hilltop Hearst Castle is California's most famous monument to wealth and ambition. William Randolph Hearst, the newspaper magnate, entertained Hollywood stars and royalty at this fantasy estate dripping with European antiques, accented by shimmering pools and surrounded by flowering gardens.

2 SALTON SEA
(www.saltonsea.ca.gov) East of Anza-Borrego and south of Joshua Tree awaits a most unexpected sight: the Salton Sea, California's largest lake in the middle of its biggest desert, created in 1905 when the Colorado River breached its banks.

3 SALVATION MOUNTAIN
(www.salvationmountain.us) An unexpected sight is Salvation Mountain, a 100ft-high hill blanketed in colorful paint and found objects and inscribed with religious messages. It's in Niland, about 3 miles off Hwy 111, via Main St

4 RHYOLITE
(www.rhyolitesite.com; off Hwy 374; ⏰sunrise-sunset) Four miles west of Beatty, NV, look for the turn-off to the ghost town of Rhyolite, which epitomizes the hurly-burly, boom-and-bust story of so many Western gold-rush mining towns. Don't overlook the 1906 'bottle house' or the skeletal remains of a three-story bank.

5 ANCIENT BRISTLECONE PINE FOREST
(☎760-873-2500; www.fs.usda.gov/inyo; per car $6; ⏰usually mid-May–Nov) These gnarled, otherworldly-looking trees are found above 10,000ft on the slopes of the White Mountains, where you'd think nothing could grow. The oldest tree – called Methuselah – is estimated to be over 4700 years old.

Downtown San Francisco

0 1 km
0 0.5 miles

San Francisco Bay

Ferries to Larkspur
Ferries to Sausalito
Ferries to Tiburon & Vallejo

Pier 41
Pier 43
Pier 45
Pier 29
Pier 31
Pier 33
Pier 35
Pier 27
Pier 23
Pier 19
Pier 17
Pier 15
Pier 9
Pier 7
Pier 3
Pier 1
Pier 2

The Embarcadero
Embarcadero
California St Cable Car Turnaround
California St
Commercial St

FISHERMAN'S WHARF
NORTH BEACH
CHINATOWN
RUSSIAN HILL
NOB HILL

Aquatic Park
Victoria Park
Fort Mason
Ina Coolbrith Park
Walton Park

Beach St
North Point St
Bay St
Francisco St
Chestnut St
Lombard St
Greenwich St
Filbert St
Union St
Green St
Vallejo St
Broadway
Pacific Ave
Jackson St
Washington St
Clay St
Stone St
Wall Pl
Hyde St
Leavenworth St
Jones St
Taylor St
Stockton St
Powell-Mason Cable Car Turnaround
Powell-Hyde Cable Car Turnaround
Columbus Ave
Valparaiso St
Filbert St
Bergen Pl
Culebra Tce
Polk St
Larkin St
John St
Stone St
Drumm St
Pardee Al
Alta St
Green St
August Al

McDowell Ave
Laguna St
Buchanan St
Octavia Blvd
Gough St
Franklin St
Van Ness Ave
Polk St
Larkin St
Hyde St
Leavenworth St
Jones St
Taylor St
Mason St
Powell St
Stockton St
Pacific Ave
Jackson St
Broadway
Vallejo St
Green St
Union St
Filbert St
Greenwich St
Chestnut St
Francisco St
Bay St
Laguna St
Lombard St

2
4
6
7
8
9
10
11
12
14
17
19
20
22
26
30
36

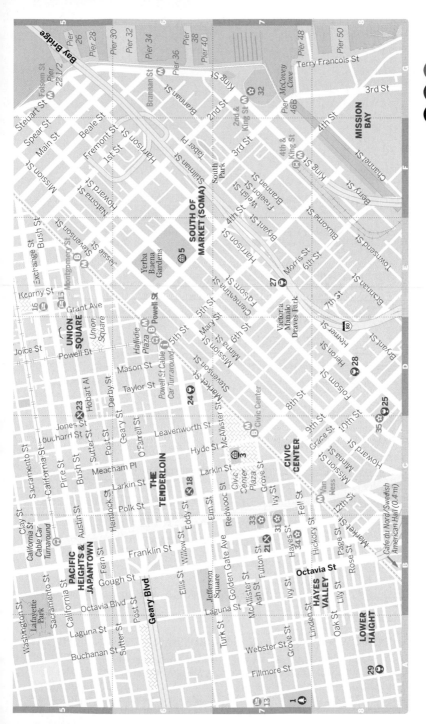

Downtown San Francisco

fashion through three floors spanning 6000 years of Asian arts. Besides the largest collection outside Asia – 18,000 works – the Asian offers excellent programs, from shadow-puppet shows to mixers with cross-cultural DJ mash-ups.

FINANCIAL DISTRICT

Ferry Building　　　　　　　Landmark
(☏415-983-8000; www.ferrybuilding
marketplace.com; Market St & the Embarcadero; ⊙10am-6pm Mon-Fri, 9am-6pm Sat, 11am-5pm Sun; ⊒2, 6, 9, 14, 21, 31, ⓂF, J, K, L, M, N, T) Hedonism thrives at this transit hub turned gourmet emporium, where foodies happily miss their ferries while slurping local oysters and bubbly. Star chefs are spotted at the Tuesday, Thursday and Saturday **farmers market** (☏415-291-3276; www.cuesa.org; ⊙10am-2pm Tue & Thu, from 8am Sat) year-round.

CHINATOWN

Since 1848 this community has survived riots, earthquakes, bootlegging gangsters and politicians' attempts to relocate it down the coast.

Chinese Historical Society of America　　　Museum
(CHSA; ☏415-391-1188; www.chsa.org; 965 Clay St; adult/child $5/2; 1st Thu of month free; ⊙noon-5pm Tue-Fri, 11am-4pm Sat; ⊒1, 30, 45, ⊠California St) Picture what it was like to be Chinese in America during the gold rush, the transcontinental railroad construction or San Francisco's Beat heyday in this 1932 landmark, built as Chinatown's YWCA by Julia Morgan (also chief architect of Hearst Castle).

NORTH BEACH

Beat Museum　　　　　　　Museum
(☏1-800-537-6822; www.kerouac.com; 540 Broadway; adult/student $8/5; ⊙10am-7pm Tue-Sun; ⊒10, 12, 30, 41, 45, ⊠Powell-Hyde, Powell-Mason) The Beat goes on at this obsessive collection of San Francisco literary-scene ephemera c 1950–69.

RUSSIAN HILL & NOB HILL

Lombard Street　　　　　　　Street
(900 block of Lombard St; ⊠Powell-Hyde) In the 1920s, Lombard St's natural 27% grade was too steep for automobiles to

ascend – so local property owners added eight turns to this red-brick street.

FISHERMAN'S WHARF

Exploratorium Museum
(📞415-528-4444; www.exploratorium.edu; Pier 15; adult/child $25/19, Thu evening $15; 🕙10am-5pm Tue-Sun, to 10pm Wed, over-18yr only Thu 6pm-10pm; 🚹; Ⓜ F) 🌿 Hear salt sing, stimulate your appetite with color, and find out what cows see through hands-on exhibits by MacArthur Genius Grant–winners.

Sea Lions at Pier 39 Outdoors
(📞981-1280; www.pier39.com; Beach St & the Embarcadero, Pier 39; 🕙Jan-Jul & whenever else they feel like it; 🚌15, 37, 49, F) Since California law requires boats to make way for marine mammals, yacht owners relinquish valuable slips to hundreds of sea lions who 'haul out' onto the docks from January to July, and whenever else they feel like sunbathing.

THE MARINA & PRESIDIO

Crissy Field Park
(www.crissyfield.org; 1199 East Beach; 🅿; 🚌30, PresidioGo Shuttle) The Presidio's army air-strip has been stripped of asphalt and re-invented as a haven for coastal birds, kite fliers and windsurfers enjoying sweeping views of Golden Gate Bridge.

Baker Beach Beach
(🕙sunrise-sunset; 🅿; 🚌29, PresidioGo Shuttle) Unswimmable waters but unbeatable views of the Golden Gate make this former army beachhead San Francisco's tanning location of choice, especially the clothing-optional north end – at least until the afternoon fog rolls in.

THE MISSION

Balmy Alley Street Art
(📞415-285-2287; www.precitaeyes.org; btwn 24th & 25th Sts; 🚌10, 12, 27, 33, 48, Ⓑ24th St Mission) Inspired by Diego Rivera's 1930s San Francisco murals and outraged by US foreign policy in Central America, Mission artists set out in the 1970s to transform the political landscape, one mural-covered garage door at a time.

Dolores Park Park
(www.doloresparkworks.org; Dolores St, btwn 18th & 20th Sts; 🚹🐾; 🚌14, 33, 49, Ⓑ16th St Mission, Ⓜ J) Semiprofessional tanning,

View of downtown San Francisco from North Beach

THOMAS WINZ/GETTY IMAGES ©

401

taco picnics and a Hunky Jesus Contest every Easter: welcome to San Francisco's sunny side. Dolores Park has something for everyone, from tennis and political protests to the Mayan pyramid playground.

Mission Dolores   Church
(Misión San Francisco de Asís; ☎415-621-8203; www.missiondolores.org; 3321 16th St; adult/child $5/3; ☺9am-4pm Nov-Apr, to 4:30pm May-Oct; 🚌22, 33, Ⓑ16th St Mission, Ⓜ J) The city's oldest building and its namesake, whitewashed adobe Misión San Francisco de Asís was founded in 1776 and rebuilt in 1782 with conscripted Ohlone and Miwok labor – note the ceiling patterned after native baskets.

THE CASTRO

GLBT History Museum   Museum
(☎415-777-5455; www.glbthistory.org/museum; 4127 18th St; admission $5; ☺11am-7pm Mon-Sat, noon-5pm Sun; Ⓜ Castro) America's first gay-history museum showcases Harvey Milk's campaign literature, matchbooks

from long-gone bathhouses, audiovisual interviews with Gore Vidal and pages of the 1950s penal code banning homosexuality.

THE HAIGHT

Alamo Square Park   Park
(Hayes & Scott Sts; 👶; 🚌5, 21, 22, 24) FREE Summit Alamo Sq to see downtown framed by gabled Victorian rooflines and wind-sculpted pines.

Haight & Ashbury   Landmark
(🚌6, 33, 37, 43, 71) The legendary psychedelic '60s intersection remains a counterculture magnet, where you can sign Green Party petitions, commission poems, and hear Hare Krishna on keyboards and Bob Dylan on banjo.

GOLDEN GATE PARK & AROUND

San Francisco was way ahead of its time in 1865, when the city voted to turn 1017 acres of sand dunes into the world's largest city stretch of green, **Golden Gate**

Park. Tenacious park architect William Hammond Hall
ousted hotels and casinos for this
nature preserve. The park ends at **Ocean
Beach** (📞415-561-4323; www.parksconserv-
ancy.org; Great Hwy; ☉sunrise-sunset; 🚌5, 18,
31, Ⓜ︎N), where **Cliff House** restaurant
overlooks the splendid ruin of **Sutro
Baths** (www.nps.gov/goga/historyculture/
sutro baths.htm; Point Lobos Ave; ☉sunrise-
sunset; visitor center 9am-5pm; Ⓟ; 🚌5, 31,
38) 🅿 FREE. Follow the partly paved trail
around **Lands End** for shipwreck sight-
ings and Golden Gate Bridge views.

California Academy of Sciences   Museum

(📞415-379-8000; www.calacademy.org; 55
Music Concourse Dr; adult/child $34.95/24.95,
discount with Muni ticket $3; ☉9:30am-5pm
Mon-Sat, 11am-5pm Sun; 👫; 🚌5, 6, 31, 33, 44,
71, Ⓜ︎N) 🅿 Architect Renzo Piano's LEED-
certified green building houses 38,000
weird and wonderful animals, with a
four-story rainforest and aquarium under
a 'living roof' of California wildflowers.

MH de Young Museum   Museum

(📞415-750-3600; www.famsf.org/deyoung;
50 Hagiwara Tea Garden Dr; adult/child $10/6,
discount with Muni ticket $2, 1st Tue of month
free, online booking fee $1 per ticket; ☉9:30am-
5:15pm Tue-Sun, to 8:45pm Fri mid-Jan–Nov, 🚌5,
44, 71, Ⓜ︎N) Follow sculptor Andy Golds-
worthy's sidewalk fault line into Herzog &
de Meuron's sleek, copper-clad building,
and broaden your artistic horizons with
Oceanic ceremonial masks and sculptor
Al Farrow's cathedrals built from bullets.

Legion of Honor   Museum

(📞415-750-3600; http://legionofhonor.famsf.
org; 100 34th Ave; adult/child $10/6, discount
with Muni ticket $2, 1st Tue of month free;
☉9:30am-5:15pm Tue-Sun; 👫; 🚌1, 18, 38) A
museum as eccentric and illuminating as
San Francisco itself, the Legion showcases a wildly eclectic collection ranging
from Monet water lilies to John Cage
soundscapes, ancient Iraqi ivories to R
Crumb comics.

403

Alcatraz

Book a ferry from Pier 33 and ride 1.5 miles across the bay to explore America's most notorious former prison. The trip itself is worth the money, providing stunning views of the city skyline. Once you've landed at the **Ferry Dock & Pier ❶**, you begin the 580-yard walk to the top of the island and prison; if you're out of shape, there's a twice-hourly tram.

As you climb toward the **Guardhouse ❷**, notice the island's steep slope; before it was a prison, Alcatraz was a fort. In the 1850s, the military quarried the rocky shores into near-vertical cliffs. Ships could then only dock at a single port, separated from the main buildings by a sally port (a drawbridge and moat in what became the guardhouse). Inside, peer through floor grates to see Alcatraz' original prison.

Volunteers tend the brilliant **Officer's Row Gardens ❸** – an orderly counterpoint to the overgrown rose bushes surrounding the burned-out shell of the **Warden's House ❹**. At the top of the hill, by the front door of the **Main Cellhouse ❺**, beauty shots unfurl all around, including a **view of the Golden Gate Bridge ❻**. Above the main door of the administration building, notice the **historic signs & graffiti ❼**, before you step inside the dank, cold prison to find the **Frank Morris cell ❽**, former home to Alcatraz' most notorious jail-breaker.

JOHN A VLAHIDES ©

Historic Signs & Graffiti
During their 1969–71 occupation, Native Americans graffitied the water tower: 'Home of the Free Indian Land.' Above the cellhouse door, examine the eagle-and-flag crest to see how the red-and-white stripes were changed to spell 'Free.'

Warden's House
Fires destroyed the warden's house and other structures during the Indian Occupation. The government blamed the Native Americans; the Native Americans blamed agents provocateurs acting on behalf of the Nixon Administration to undermine public sympathy.

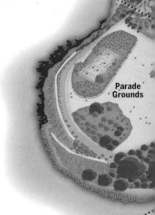

Parade Grounds

TOP TIPS

» Book at least two weeks prior for self-guided daytime visits, longer for ranger-led night tours. For info on garden tours, see www.alcatraz gardens.org.

» Be prepared to hike; a steep path ascends from the ferry landing to the cell block. Most people spend two to three hours on the island. You need only reserve for the outbound ferry; take any ferry back.

» There's no food (just water) but you can bring your own; picnicking is allowed at the ferry dock only. Dress in layers as the weather changes fast and it's usually windy.

DAVID CLAPP / GETTY IMAGES ©

Ferry Dock & Pier
A giant wall map helps you get your bearings. Inside nearby Bldg 64, short films and exhibits provide historical perspective on the prison and details about the Indian Occupation.

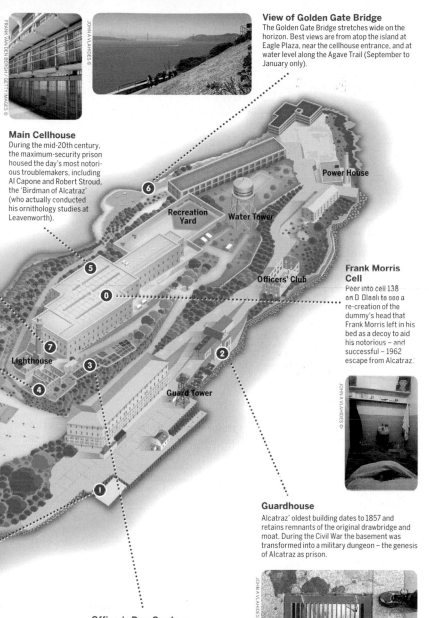

View of Golden Gate Bridge
The Golden Gate Bridge stretches wide on the horizon. Best views are from atop the island at Eagle Plaza, near the cellhouse entrance, and at water level along the Agave Trail (September to January only).

Main Cellhouse
During the mid-20th century, the maximum-security prison housed the day's most notorious troublemakers, including Al Capone and Robert Stroud, the 'Birdman of Alcatraz' (who actually conducted his ornithology studies at Leavenworth).

Power House

Recreation Yard

Water Tower

Officers' Club

Frank Morris Cell
Peer into cell 138 on D Block to see a re-creation of the dummy's head that Frank Morris left in his bed as a decoy to aid his notorious – and successful – 1962 escape from Alcatraz.

Lighthouse

Guard Tower

Guardhouse
Alcatraz' oldest building dates to 1857 and retains remnants of the original drawbridge and moat. During the Civil War the basement was transformed into a military dungeon – the genesis of Alcatraz as prison.

Officer's Row Gardens
In the 19th century soldiers imported topsoil to beautify the island with gardens. Well-trusted prisoners later gardened – Elliott Michener said it kept him sane. Historians, ornithologists and archaeologists choose today's plants.

405

Golden Gate Bridge · Bridge

(www.goldengatebridge.org/visitors; off Lincoln Blvd; northbound free, southbound toll $6; 🚌28, all Golden Gate Transit buses) San Francisco's 1937 suspension bridge was almost nixed by the navy in favor of yellow-striped concrete pylons. Instead, engineer Joseph B Strauss, architects Gertrude and Irving Murrow and daredevil workers created an International Orange deco icon. The southbound toll is billed electronically to your vehicle's license plate; for details, see www.goldengate.org/tolls.

Sleeping

San Remo Hotel · Hotel $

(📞415-776-8688, 800-352-7366; www.sanremo hotel.com; 2237 Mason St; d with shared bath $79-129; @ 🤖 🐾; 🚌30, 47, 🚋Powell-Mason) One of the city's best-value spots, this 1906 inn is an old-fashioned charmer with vintage furnishings. Bargain rooms face the corridor; family suites accommodate up to five.

Orchard Garden Hotel · Boutique Hotel $$

(📞415-399-9807, 888-717-2881; www.the orchardgardenhotel.com; 466 Bush St; r $189-259; ❄@🤖; 🚌2, 3, 30, 45, Ⓑ Montgomery) 🍃 San Francisco's first all-green-practices hotel uses sustainably grown wood, chemical-free cleaning products and luxe recycled fabrics in its soothingly quiet rooms. Don't miss the sunny rooftop terrace.

Hotel Triton · Boutique Hotel $$

(📞415-394-0500, 800-800-1299; www. hoteltriton.com; 342 Grant Ave; r $175-275, ste $350; ❄@🤖🐾; Ⓜ Montgomery, Ⓑ Montgomery) 🍃 Beyond the colorful, comic-bookish lobby are hip rooms with San Francisco–centric details (such as wallpaper of Kerouac's *On the Road*) plus ecofriendly amenities, shag-worthy beds and unlimited ice cream. Don't miss tarot-card readings and chair massages during nightly wine hour.

Hotel Bohème · Boutique Hotel $$

(📞415-433-9111; www.hotelboheme.com; 444 Columbus Ave; r $174-224; @🤖; 🚌10, 12, 30, 41, 45) A love letter to the Beat era, with moody orange, black and sage-green color schemes nodding to the 1950s, and parasol lights and vintage photos.

Marina Motel · Motel $$

(📞415-921-9406, 800-346-6118; www. marinamotel.com; 2576 Lombard St; r $139-199; Ⓟ🤖🐾; 🚌28, 30, 41, 43, 45) The vintage 1939 Marina has a Spanish-Mediterranean look, with a bougainvillea-lined courtyard. Rooms are homey and well maintained, and some have full kitchens (extra $10 to $20).

Inn San Francisco · B&B $$

(📞800-359-0913, 415-641-0188; www.innsf.com;

North Beach (p400), San Francisco
ORIEN HARVEY/GETTY IMAGES ©

943 S Van Ness Ave; r incl breakfast $185-295, with shared bath $135-185, cottage $325-385; P @ 🛜; 🚈14, 49) 🏛 An impeccably maintained 1872 Italianate-Victorian mansion, this inn has period antiques, freshly cut flowers and fluffy feather beds; some have Jacuzzi tubs. Outside there's an English garden and a redwood hot tub.

Parker Guest House   B&B $$
(📞415-621-3222, 888-520-7275; www.parker-guesthouse.com; 520 Church St; r incl breakfast $159-269; @ 🛜; 🚈33, M J) The Castro's stateliest gay digs occupy two side-by-side Edwardian mansions sharing a garden and steam room.

Chateau Tivoli   B&B $$
(📞415-776-5462, 800-228-1647; www.chateau-tivoli.com; 1057 Steiner St; r incl breakfast $170-215, with shared bath $115-135, ste $275 300; 🛜; 🚈5, 22) This glorious chateau off Alamo Sq once hosted Isadora Duncan and Mark Twain, and shows character with turrets, cornices, woodwork and, rumor has it, the ghost of a Victorian opera diva.

Eating

Off the Grid   Food Truck $
(www.offthegridsf.com; dishes $5-10; ⏰5-10pm Fri; 🚈22, 28) Thirty food trucks circle their wagons at Fort Mason for mobile-gourmet feasts. Arrive before 6.30pm or expect 20-minute waits for Chairman Bao's clamshell buns with duck and mango, Roli Roti's free-range herbed roast chicken, and dessert from the Crème Brûlée Man. Cash only.

City View   Chinese $
(📞415-398-2838; 662 Commercial St; dishes $3-8; ⏰11am-2:30pm Mon-Fri, from 10am Sat & Sun; 🚈8X, 10, 12, 30, 45, 🚋California St) Take your seat in the sunny dining room and take your pick from carts loaded with delicate shrimp and leek dumplings, garlicky Chinese broccoli, tangy spare ribs, coconut-dusted custard tarts and other tantalizing dim sum.

Cinecittà   Pizza $
(📞415-291-8830; www.cinecittarestaurant.com; 663 Union St; pizza $12-15; ⏰noon-10pm

San Francisco for Children

The **Children's Creativity Museum** (📞415-820-3320; www.zeum.org; 221 4th St; admission $11; ⏰10am-4pm Wed-Sun Sep-May, Tue-Sun Jun-Aug; 👶; M Powell, B Powell) has technology that's too cool for school: robots, live-action video games, DIY music videos and 3-D animation workshops with Silicon Valley innovators.

At **Aquarium of the Bay** (www.aquariumofthebay.com; Pier 39; adult/child/family $18/10/50; ⏰9am-8pm summer, 10am-6pm winter; 👶; 🚈49, 🚋Powell-Mason, M F), glide through underwater glass tubes on conveyor belts as sharks circle overhead.

Fire Engine Tours (📞415-333-7077; www.fireenginetours.com; departs Beach St, at the Cannery; adult/child $50/30; ⏰tours 9am, 11am, 1pm, 3pm) are hot stuff: take a 75-minute, open-air vintage fire-engine ride over Golden Gate Bridge.

Sun-Thu, to 11pm Fri & Sat; 🍷👶; 🚈8X, 30, 39, 41, 45, 🚋Powell-Mason) Follow tantalizing aromas into this 22-seat eatery for thin-crust Roman pizza, including the classic Travestere (fresh mozzarella, arugula and prosciutto) and Neapolitan Ô Sole Mio (capers, olives, mozzarella and anchovies).

La Taqueria   Mexican $
(📞415-285-7117; 2889 Mission St; burritos $6-8; ⏰11am-9pm Mon-Sat, to 8pm Sun; 🍷; 🚈12, 14, 48, 49, B 24th St Mission) The definitive burrito at La Taqueria has no debatable saffron rice, spinach tortilla or mango salsa, just perfectly grilled meats, slow-cooked beans and classic *tomatillo* or *mesquite* salsa wrapped in a flour tortilla.

Coit Tower

Adding an exclamation mark to San Francisco's landscape, **Coit Tower** (☎415-362-0808; http://sfrecpark.org/ destination/telegraph-hill-pioneer-park/ coit-tower; Telegraph Hill Blvd; elevator entry (nonresident) adult/child $7/5; ⏱10am-5:30pm Mar-Sep, 9am-4:30pm Oct-Feb; ☐39) offers views worth shouting about – especially after you've climbed the giddy, steep **Filbert St steps** to get here.

Brenda's French Soul Food
Creole, Southern **$$**

(☎415-345-8100; www.frenchsoulfood.com; 652 Polk St; mains lunch $9-13, dinner $11-17; ⏱8am-3pm Mon & Tue, to 10pm Wed-Sat, to 8pm Sun; ☐19, 31, 38, 47, 49) Chef-owner Brenda Buenviaje serves Cal-Creole classics, including Hangtown fry (eggs with bacon and fried oysters), shrimp-stuffed po' boys, fried chicken with collard greens, hot-pepper jelly and watermelon sweet tea.

Sweet Woodruff
Cafe, Californian **$$**

(☎415-292-9090; www.sweetwoodruffsf.com; 798 Sutter St; dishes $8-13; ⏱11am-9:45pm; ☐2, 3, 27) 🍃 Little sister to Michelin-starred Sons & Daughters, this storefront cafe uses seasonal-regional ingredients for small plates such as roasted padron peppers with fromage blanc and sea-urchin baked potatoes with bacon.

Starbelly
Californian, Pizza **$$**

(☎415-252-7500; www.starbellysf.com; 3583 16th St; dishes $6-19; ⏱11:30am-11pm Sun-Thu, to midnight Fri & Sat; ⓂCastro) 🍃 Nab a spot on the heated garden patio for *salumi* (Italian cured meat), market-fresh salads, scrumptious pâté, roasted mussels with housemade sausage and thin-crust pizzas.

Magnolia Brewpub
Californian **$$**

(☎415-864-7468; www.magnoliapub.com; 1398 Haight St; mains $11-20; ⏱11am-midnight Mon-Thu, 11am-1am Fri, 10am-1am Sat, 10am-midnight Sun; ☐6, 33, 43, 71) 🍃 Organic pub grub and homebrew samplers keep conversation flowing at communal tables, while grass-fed Prather Ranch burgers satisfy stoner appetites in the booths – it's like the Summer of Love all over again, only with better food.

Jardinière
Californian **$$$**

(☎415-861-5555; www.jardiniere.com; 300 Grove St; mains $19-37; ⏱5-10:30pm Tue-Sat, to 10pm Sun & Mon; ☐5, 21, 47, 49, ⓂVan Ness) 🍃 Iron Chef, Top Chef Master and James Beard Award winner Traci Des Jardins has a particular flair with California's organic vegetables, free-range meats and sustainably caught seafood.

Commonwealth
Californian **$$$**

(☎415-355-1500; www.commonwealthsf.com; 2224 Mission St; small plates $11-16; ⏱5:30-10pm Sun-Thu, to 11pm Fri & Sat; 🍴; ☐14, 22, 33, 49, Ⓑ16th St Mission) California's most imaginative farm-to-table dining isn't in some quaint barn but in a converted cinderblock Mission dive. Here chef Jason Fox serves green strawberries and black radishes with fennel pollen, and poached oysters atop foraged succulents and rhubarb ice.

Chez Panisse
Californian **$$$**

(☎cafe 510-548-5049, restaurant 510-548-5525; 1517 Shattuck Ave; mains $18-29, restaurant prix-fixe dinner $60-95; ⏱cafe 11:30am-2:45pm Mon-Sat, 5-10:30pm Mon-Thu, to 11pm Fri & Sat; restaurant 6-10:30pm Mon-Sat) Genuflect at the culinary temple of Alice Waters: the birthplace of California cuisine remains at the pinnacle of Bay Area dining. Book one month ahead for its seasonally inspired prix-fixe restaurant menu (no substitutions) or upstairs at the à la carte cafe. It's located across the bay in Berkeley.

🍷 Drinking & Nightlife

For a pub crawl, your best bets are North Beach saloons or Mission bars around Valencia and 16th St. Top chefs serve craft cocktails downtown, Hayes Valley has wine bars and the Tenderloin mixes dives with speakeasies. The Castro has historic gay bars and SoMa has leather bars, while Marina bars are preppy and straight, and Haight bars draw mixed alterna-crowds.

Bar Agricole
Bar

(☎ 415-355-9400; www.baragricole.com; 355 11th St; ☺ 6-10pm Sun-Wed, to late Thu-Sat; ☒ 9, 12, 27, 47) Drink your way to a history degree with well-researched cocktails: Bellamy Scotch Sour with egg whites passes the test, but Tequila Fix with lime, pineapple gum and hellfire bitters earns honors.

Comstock Saloon
Bar

(☎ 415-617-0071; www.comstocksaloon.com; 155 Columbus Ave; ☺ 4pm-2am Sat-Thu, from noon Fri; ☒ 8X, 10, 12, 30, 45, ☒ Powell-Mason) Welcome to the Barbary Coast, where cocktails at this Victorian saloon remain period-perfect. Call ahead to claim booths or tufted-velvet parlour seating.

Toronado
Pub

(☎ 415-863-2276; www.toronado.com; 547 Haight St; ☺ 11:30am-2am; ☒ 6, 22, 71, Ⓜ N) Glory hallelujah, beer-lovers: your prayers have been heard with 50-plus beers on tap and hundreds more bottled, including spectacular seasonal microbrews. Bring cash.

Elixir
Bar

(☎ 415-522-1633; www.elixirsf.com; 3200 16th St; ☺ 3pm-2am Mon-Fri, noon-2am Sat & Sun; Ⓑ 16th St Mission) Elixir serves knock-out cocktails made with farm-fresh organic mixers and small-batch spirits that will get you air-guitar-rocking to the killer jukebox.

⭐ Entertainment

LIVE MUSIC

SFJAZZ Center
Jazz

(☎ 866-920-5299; www.sfjazz.org; 201 Franklin St; ☺ showtimes vary; ☒ 5, 7, 21, Ⓜ Van Ness) Jazz greats coast-to-coast and further afield from Argentina to Yemen are showcased at America's newest, largest, LEED-certified green jazz center.

Slim's
Live Music

(☎ 415-255-0333; www.slims-sf.com; 333 11th St; tickets $12-30; ☺ 5pm-2am; ☒ 9, 12, 27, 47) Guaranteed good times by Gogol Bordello, Tenacious D and the Expendables

Coit Tower, with Alcatraz (p404) in the background

LATITUDESTOCK - TTL/GETTY IMAGES ©

fit the bill at this mid-sized club, owned by R&B star Boz Skaggs.

Cafe du Nord/Swedish American Hall
Live Music

(☎415-861-5016; www.cafedunord.com; 2170 Market St; cover varies; Ⓜ Church) Rockers, chanteuses, comedians, raconteurs and burlesque acts perform nightly at this former basement speakeasy with bar and showroom, and the joint still looks like it did in the '30s.

CLASSICAL MUSIC & OPERA

Davies Symphony Hall
Classical Music

(☎415-864-6000; www.sfsymphony.org; 201 Van Ness Ave; Ⓜ Van Ness, Ⓑ Civic Center) Home of nine-time Grammy-winning San Francisco Symphony, conducted with verve by Michael Tilson Thomas. The season runs September to July.

San Francisco Opera
Opera

(☎415-864-3330; www.sfopera.com; War Memorial Opera House, 301 Van Ness Ave; tickets $10-350; Ⓑ Civic Center, Ⓜ Van Ness) San Francisco has been obsessed with opera since the gold rush, and it remains a staple from July to December.

THEATER

Beach Blanket Babylon
Cabaret

(BBB; ☎415-421-4222; www.beachblanketbabylon.com; 678 Green St; admission $25-100; ⊙ shows 8pm Wed, Thu & Fri, 6:30pm & 9:30pm Sat, 2pm & 5pm Sun; ▯8X, ▯Powell-Mason) The Disney-gone-drag musical-comedy cabaret has been running since 1974, but topical jokes keep it outrageous and wigs as big as parade floats are gasp-worthy.

CINEMAS

Castro Theatre
Cinema

(☎415-621-6120; www.thecastrotheatre.com; 429 Castro St; adult/child $11/8.50; ⊙ Tue-Sun; Ⓜ Castro) The Mighty Wurlitzer organ rises from the deco movie palace's orchestra pit before evening shows, ending with (sing along, now): 'San Francisco open your Golden Gate/You let no stranger wait outside your door...'

Musicians jamming in Golden Gate Park (p402)

Gay/Les/Bi/Trans San Francisco

Doesn't matter where you're from, who you love or who's your daddy: if you're here, and queer, welcome home.

Stud (415-252-7883; www.studsf.com; 399 9th St; admission $5-8; ⏱5pm-3am; 🚍12, 19, 27, 47) Join parties-in-progress since 1966: Meow Mix Tuesday drag variety shows; Wednesday raunchy comedy; and Friday 'Some-thing' parties with midnight drag, pool-table crafts and dance beats.

Aunt Charlie's (415-441-2922; www.auntcharlieslounge.com; 133 Turk St; admission $5; MPowell, BPowell) Divey Aunt Charlie's brings vintage pulp-fiction covers to life with drag Hot Boxxx Girls on Friday and Saturday nights (call for reservations), and Thursday's Tubesteak Connection ($5), featuring vintage porn and '80s disco.

EndUp (www.theendup.com; 401 6th St; admission $5-20; ⏱10pm-4am Mon-Thu, 11pm-11am Fri, 10pm Sat-4am Mon; 🚍12, 27, 47) Anyone on the streets after 2am weekends is subject to the magnetic pull of the EndUp's marathon dance sessions and gay Sunday tea dances, in full force since 1973.

Lexington Club (415-863-2052; www.lexingtonclub.com; 3464 19th St; ⏱3pm-2am; 🚍14, 33, 49, B16th St Mission) San Francisco's all-grrrrl bar can be cliquish, so compliment someone on her skirt (she designed it herself) or tattoo (ditto) and mention you're undefeated at pinball, pool or thumb-wrestling.

Cafe Flore (415-621-8579; www.cafeflore.com; 2298 Market St; ⏱7am-midnight Sun-Thu, to 2am Fri & Sat; 📶; MCastro) You haven't done the Castro till you've unwound on Flore's sunny patio.

SPORTS

San Francisco Giants   Baseball
(http://sanfrancisco.giants.mlb.com; AT&T Park; tickets $5-135) Watch and learn how the World Series is won – bushy beards, women's underwear and all.

San Francisco 49ers   Football
(415-656-4900; www.sf49ers.com; Levi's Stadium; tickets $25-100 at www.ticketmaster.com; MT) After decades shivering through games and a fumbled bid for the 2012 Superbowl, the 49ers have a new home in 2014: Santa Clara's brand-new Levi's Stadium.

ℹ Information

San Francisco Visitor Information Center (415-391-2000, events hotline 415-391-2001; www.onlyinsanfrancisco.com; lower level, Hallidie Plaza, Market & Powell Sts; ⏱9am-5pm Mon-Fri, to 3pm Sat & Sun; 🚍Powell-Mason, Powell-Hyde, MPowell St, BPowell St) Provides practical information for tourists, publishes glossy tourist-oriented booklets and runs a 24-hour events hotline.

ℹ Getting There & Away

Air

San Francisco International Airport (SFO; www.flysfo.com) is 14 miles south of downtown off Hwy 101 and accessible by Bay Area Rapid Transit (BART).

Train

Amtrak (800-872-7245; www.amtrakcalifornia.com) *Coast Starlight*'s spectacular 35-hour run from Los Angeles to Seattle stops in Oakland, and *California Zephyr* takes its sweet time (51 hours) from Chicago to Oakland.

Don't Miss Marin County

Majestic redwoods cling to coastal hills just across San Francisco's Golden Gate Bridge in wealthy, laid-back Marin. The windswept, rugged **Marin Headlands** are laced with hiking trails, providing panoramic views of the city and bay. To find the **visitor center** (www.visitmarin.org), take the Alexander Ave exit after crossing north over the Golden Gate Bridge, turn left under the freeway onto Bunker Rd then follow the signs.

Nearby attractions include **Point Bonita Lighthouse**, Rodeo Beach and the educational Marine Mammal Center at Fort Cronkite. Or you can wander among an ancient stand of the world's tallest trees at 520-acre **Muir Woods National Monument** (pictured above), 10 miles northwest of the Golden Gate Bridge. Easy hiking trails loop past thousand-year-old redwoods at Cathedral Grove. By the entrance, a cafe serves light lunches and drinks. Come midweek to avoid crowds; otherwise arrive early morning or late afternoon. Take Hwy 101 to the Hwy 1 exit, then follow the signs.

The southernmost town, **Sausalito**, is a tiny bayside destination for bike trips over the bridge (take the ferry back to San Francisco).

Getting Around

To/from San Francisco International Airport

A taxi to downtown San Francisco costs about $35 to $50.

BART (Bay Area Rapid Transit; www.bart.gov; one way $8.25) Fast 30-minute ride to/from downtown San Francisco from/to SFO BART station of the International Terminal.

SuperShuttle (☎800-258-3826; www.supershuttle.com) Shared van rides to downtown San Francisco for $17.

Public Transportation

MUNI (Municipal Transit Agency; ☎511; www.sfmta.com) operates bus, streetcar and cable-car lines; *MUNI Street & Transit Map* is available free online. Standard fare for buses or streetcars is $2; cable-car fare is $6.

Taxi

Fares run about $2.75 per mile; meters start at $3.50.

DeSoto Cab (☎415-970-1300)

Green Cab (☎415-626-4733; www.626green.com) Fuel-efficient hybrids; worker-owned collective.

Luxor (☎415-282-4141)

Yellow Cab (☎415 333 3333)

WINE COUNTRY

A patchwork of vineyards stretches from sunny inland Napa to windy coastal Sonoma – California's premier wine-growing region. Napa has art-filled tasting rooms by big-name architects, with prices to match. In down-to-earth Sonoma, you may drink in a shed and meet the vintner's dog. Wine Country is at least an hour's drive north of San Francisco via Hwy 101 or I-80.

Napa Valley

More than 200 wineries crowd 30-mile-long Napa Valley along three main routes. Traffic-jammed on weekends, Hwy 29 is lined with blockbuster wineries. Running parallel, Silverado Trail moves faster, passing boutique winemakers, bizarre architecture and cult-hit Cabernet Sauvignon. West toward Sonoma, Hwy 121 (Carneros Hwy) has landmark vineyards specializing in sparkling wines and Pinot Noir.

At the southern end of the valley, **Napa** – the valley's workaday hub – lacks rusticity, but has trendy restaurants and tasting rooms downtown. Stop by the

Napa Valley Welcome Center (☎707-251-5895, 855-333-6272; www.visitnapavalley.com; 600 Main St; ◷9am-5pm daily Sep-Apr, 9am-5pm Mon-Thu, to 6pm Fri-Sun May-Oct) for wine-tasting passes and winery maps.

Heading north on Hwy 29, the former stagecoach stop of tiny **Yountville** has more Michelin-starred eateries per capita than anywhere else in the USA. Another 10 miles north, traffic rolls to a stop in charming **St Helena** – the Beverly Hills of Napa – where there's genteel strolling and shopping (if you can find parking, that is).

At the valley's northern end, folksy **Calistoga** – Napa's least-gentrified town – is home to hot-spring spas and mud-bath emporiums using volcanic ash from nearby Mt St Helena.

◎ Sights & Activities

Frog's Leap   Winery
(☎707-963-4704; www.frogsleap.com; 8815 Conn Creek Rd, Rutherford; tasting $15, incl tour $20; ◷10am-4pm; ⊞⊛) ✿ Meandering paths wind through gardens surrounding an 1884 barn at this LEED-certified winery, pouring stand-out Sauvignon Blanc and Cabernet. Book tours in advance.

Indian Springs Spa   Spa
(☎707-942-4913; www.indianspringscalistoga.com; 1712 Lincoln Ave, Calistoga; ◷by appointment 9am-8pm) Book ahead for a volcanic-mud bath at Calistoga's original 19th century mineral springs resort. Treatments include access to spring-fed pools.

🛏 Sleeping & Eating

Indian Springs Resort   Resort $$$
(☎707-942-4913; www.indianspringscalistoga.com; 1712 Lincoln Ave; motel r $229-299, bungalow $259-349, 2-bedroom bungalow $359-419; ❄⊛⊠⊞) At Calistoga's most harmonious hot-springs resort, charming bungalows (some with kitchens) face a broad lawn with rustling palm trees, shuffleboard and bocce courts, hammocks and barbecue grills.

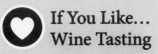

If You Like...
Wine Tasting

If you like sipping the produce of Frog's Leap (p413) in Napa, don't miss these other fine wineries in the area. Keep in mind that most Napa wineries require reservations.

1 HESS COLLECTION
(☎ 707-255-8584; www.hesscollection.com; 4411 Redwood Rd, Napa; tasting $10; ⏰ 10am-5pm) Northwest of downtown Napa, this sustainable winery pairs monster Cabernet with blue-chip modern art by Robert Rauschenberg and others. Reservations suggested.

2 PRIDE MOUNTAIN
(☎ 707-963-4949; www.pridewines.com; 3000 Summit Trail, St Helena; tasting $10, incl tour $15-75; ⏰ by appointment) Cult favorite Pride straddles the Sonoma–Napa border and makes stellar Cabernet, Merlot, Chardonnay and Viognier at an unfussy hilltop estate with spectacular picnicking.

3 CASA NUESTRA
(☎ 866-844-9463; www.casanuestra.com; 3451 Silverado Trail, St Helena; tasting $10; ⏰ by appointment) A peace flag and portrait of Elvis greet you at this tiny solar-powered winery, known for growing unusual varietals. Goats frolic beside the picnic area.

4 CASTELLO DI AMOROSA
(☎ 707-967-6272; www.castellodiamorosa. com; 4045 Hwy 29, Calistoga; admission & tasting $18-28, incl guided tour $33-69; ⏰ 9:30am-6pm, to 5pm Nov-Feb) Tour a recreated 13th-century Tuscan castle, complete with a dungeon tasting room stocked with Italian varietals.

Oxbow Public Market   Market $
(☎ 707-226-6529; www.oxbowpublicmarket.com; 644 1st St, Napa; dishes from $3; ⏰ 9am-7pm Mon-Sat, 10am-5pm Sun) 🌿 Oxbow showcases sustainably produced, artisanal foods by 20-plus vendors. Feast on Hog Island oysters, Model Bakery muffins, Ca' Momi's crispy pizzas or Three Twins organic ice cream.

Gott's Roadside   American $$
(☎ 707-963-3486; http://gotts.com; 933 Main St, St Helena; dishes $3-14; ⏰ 7am-9pm, to 10pm May-Sep; 👶) A 1950s drive-in diner with 21st-century sensibilities: burgers are all-natural beef, organic chicken or sushi-grade tuna, with sides like chili-dusted sweet-potato fries and handmade milkshakes.

Ad Hoc   Californian $$$
(☎ 707-944-2487; www.adhocrestaurant. com; 6476 Washington St, Yountville; prix-fixe dinner from $52; ⏰ 5-10pm Wed-Sun, plus 10am-1pm Sun) Don't ask for a menu at chef Thomas Keller's dressed-down 'experimental' kitchen. Changing daily, a four-course family-style dinner allows no substitutions (except for dietary restrictions), but none are needed – every dish is comforting, fresh and spot-on.

Sonoma Valley

More laid back and less commercial than Napa, Sonoma Valley enfolds over 70 wineries off Hwy 12 – and unlike those in Napa, most welcome picnicking. Note there are actually three Sonomas: the town, the valley and the county.

◉ Sights & Activities

Downtown Sonoma was once the capital of the short-lived Bear Flag Republic. Today **Sonoma Plaza** – the state's largest town square – is bordered by chic boutiques, historical buildings and a **visitor center** (☎ 707-996-1090; www. sonomavalley.com; ⏰ 9am-6pm Jul-Sep, to 5pm Oct-Jun).

Jack London State Historic Park   Park
(☎ 707-938-5216; www.jacklondonpark.com; 2400 London Ranch Rd, Glen Ellen; per car $8, tour adult/child $4/2; ⏰ 9:30am-5pm Thu-Mon) Obey the call of the wild where adventurer-novelist Jack London built his dream house – it burned on the eve of completion in 1913. Tour the writer's

original cottage or browse memorabilia inside the small museum standing in a redwood grove. Twenty miles of hiking and mountain-biking trails weave through the park's 1400 hilltop acres.

Bartholomew Park Winery Winery (☑707-939-3024; www.bartpark.com; 1000 Vineyard Lane, Sonoma; tasting $10, incl tour $20; ☺11am-4:30pm) In a 400-acre nature preserve perfect for picnicking, the family-owned vineyards originally cultivated in 1857 are now organic-certified, yielding citrus-sunshine Sauvignon Blanc and smoky-midnight Merlot.

 ## Sleeping & Eating

Sonoma Hotel Historic Hotel **$$** (☑800-468-6016, 707-996-2996; www.sonomahotel.com; 110 W Spain St, Sonoma; r incl breakfast $115-240) Old-fashioned rooms squeeze inside this 19th-century plaza landmark. Two-night minimum stay most weekends.

Red Grape Italian **$$** (☑707-996-4103; http://theredgrape.com; 529 1st St W, Sonoma; mains $10-20; ☺11:30am-10pm; ⊞) At this sunlight-filled pizzeria, thin-crust pies topped with locally made cheeses, panini sandwiches and pasta shake hands with small-production Sonoma wines.

ℹ **Getting There & Around**

Wine Country begins 75 minutes north of San Francisco, via Hwy 101 or I-80.

YOSEMITE NATIONAL PARK

There's a reason why everybody's heard of it: the granite-peak heights are dizzying, the mist from thunderous waterfalls drenching, the Technicolor wildflower meadows amazing and the majestic silhouettes of El Capitan and Half Dome almost shocking against a crisp blue sky. It's a landscape of dreams, surrounding oh-so-small people on all sides.

Then, alas, the hiss and belch of another tour bus, disgorging dozens, rudely breaks the spell. While staggering crowds can't be ignored, these rules will shake most of 'em:

○ Avoid summer in the valley. Spring's best, especially when waterfalls gush in May. Autumn is blissfully peaceful, and snowy winter days can be magical too.

○ Park your car and leave it – simply by hiking a short distance up almost any trail, you'll lose the car-dependent hordes.

○ Get up early, or go for moonlit hikes with stargazing.

 ## Sights

The main entrances to the **park** (☑209-372-0200; www.nps.gov/yose; 7-day entry per car $20) are at Arch Rock (Hwy 140), Wawona (Hwy 41) and Big Oak Flat (Hwy 120 west). Tioga Pass (Hwy 120 east) is open only seasonally.

YOSEMITE VALLEY

From the ground up, this dramatic valley cut by the meandering Merced River is song-inspiring: rippling green meadow-grass; stately pines; cool, impassive pools reflecting looming granite monoliths; and cascading ribbons of glacially cold white water.

Spring snowmelt turns the valley's famous waterfalls into thunderous cataracts; most are reduced to a mere trickle by late summer. **Yosemite Falls** is North America's tallest, dropping 2425ft in three tiers. A wheelchair-accessible trail leads to the bottom of this cascade or, for solitude and different perspectives, you can trek the grueling switchback trail to the top (7.2 miles round trip). No less impressive are other waterfalls around the valley. A strenuous granite staircase beside **Vernal Fall** leads you, gasping, right to the waterfall's edge for a vertical view – look for rainbows in the clouds of mist.

You can't ignore the valley's monumental **El Capitan** (7569ft), an El Dorado for rock climbers. Toothed **Half**

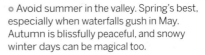

Dome (8842ft) soars above the valley as Yosemite's spiritual centerpiece. The classic panoramic photo op is at **Tunnel View** on Hwy 41 as you drive into the valley. Early or late in the day during spring or early summer, hike 2 miles round trip from the eastern valley floor out to **Mirror Lake** to catch the ever-shifting reflection of Half Dome in the still waters.

GLACIER POINT

Rising 3200ft above the valley floor, dramatic **Glacier Point** (7214ft) practically puts you at eye level with Half Dome. It's about an hour's drive from Yosemite Valley up Glacier Point Rd (usually open from late May into November) off Hwy 41, or a strenuous hike along the **Four Mile Trail** (actually, 4.8 miles one way) or the less-crowded, waterfall-strewn **Panorama Trail** (8.5 miles one way). To hike one-way downhill from Glacier Point, reserve a seat on the hikers' shuttle bus.

TUOLUMNE MEADOWS

A 90-minute drive from Yosemite Valley, high-altitude **Tuolumne Meadows** (pronounced TWOL-uh-mee) draws hikers, backpackers and climbers to the park's northern wilderness. The Sierra Nevada's largest subalpine meadow (8600ft), it's a vivid contrast to the valley, with wildflower fields, azure lakes, ragged granite peaks and polished domes, and cooler temperatures. Hikers and climbers have a paradise of options; swimming and picnicking by lakes are also popular. Access is via scenic Tioga Rd (Hwy 120), which is only open seasonally, following a 19th-century wagon road and older Native American trading route. West of Tuolumne Meadows and **Tenaya Lake**, stop at **Olmsted Point** for epic vistas of Half Dome.

Activities

With over 800 miles of varied hiking trails, you're spoiled for choice. Easy valley-floor routes can get jammed; escape the teeming masses by heading up. The ultimate hike summits **Half Dome** (14 miles round trip), but be warned: it's very strenuous,

and advance **permits** (www.nps.gov/yose/planyourvisit/hdpermits.htm; from $12.50) are required even for day hikes. It's rewarding to hike just as far as the top of Vernal Fall (3 miles round trip) or Nevada Fall (5.8 miles round trip) via the **Mist Trail**. A longer, alternate route to Half Dome follows a more gently graded section of the long-distance **John Muir Trail**.

Yosemite Mountaineering School   Rock Climbing
(☑209-372-8344; www.yosemitemountaineering.com; Curry Village; ☾Apr-Oct) YMS offers topflight instruction for novice to advanced climbers, plus guided climbs and equipment rental.

 Sleeping & Eating

Concessionaire **DNC** (☑801-559-4884; www.yosemitepark.com) has a monopoly on park lodging and eating establishments, including ho-hum food courts and snack bars. Lodging reservations (up to 366 days in advance) are essential during peak season (May through September). During summer, DNC sets up simple canvas-tent cabins at riverside **Housekeeping Camp** (d from $95) in Yosemite Valley; busy **Tuolumne Meadows Lodge** (d from $120), a 90-minute drive from the valley; and quieter **White Wolf Lodge** (d from $120) off Tioga Rd, an hour away from the valley.

Yosemite Lodge at the Falls   Lodge $$$
(r from $220; @ 🛜 🏊 🚻) 🅿 Spacious motel rooms come with eco-friendly upgrades and patios or balconies overlooking Yosemite Falls, meadows or the parking lot. Fork into sustainably caught river trout and organic veggies at the lodge's Mountain Room (dinner mains $18 to $35), open nightly (no reservations).

OUTSIDE YOSEMITE NATIONAL PARK

Yosemite Bug Rustic Mountain Resort   Hostel, Cabins $
(☑209-966-6666, 866-826-7108; www.yosemitebug.com; 6979 Hwy 140, Midpines; dm

$23-26, tent cabins $45-75, r with shared/private bath from $65/75; ⏲cafe 7am-4pm & 6-8:30pm; @📶♿) 🅿 Tucked into the forest about 30 miles west of Yosemite Valley, this mountain hostelry hosts globetrotters who dig the clean rooms, low-key spa, shared kitchen access and laundry. The cafe's fresh, organic and vegetarian-friendly meals (mains $5 to $18) get raves.

ℹ Information

Yosemite Valley Visitor Center (☎209-372-0200; www.nps.gov/yose; ⏲9am-6pm, to 5pm winter) Smaller visitor centers at Wawona, Tuolumne Meadows and Big Oak Flat are open seasonally.

ℹ Getting There & Around

Free shuttle buses loop around Yosemite Valley and, in summer, the Tuolumne Meadows and Wawona/Mariposa Grove areas. **DNC** (☎20 9-372-4386; www.yosemitepark.com) runs hikers' buses from the valley to Tuolumne Meadows (one way/round trip $15/23) and Glacier Point (one way/round trip $25/41). Valley bike rentals (per hour/day $11/32) are available seasonally at Yosemite Lodge and Curry Village.

PACIFIC COAST HIGHWAY

No trip to California would be worth its salt without a jaunt along the surreally scenic Central Coast. Make your escape from those tangled, traffic-jammed freeways and cruise in the slow lane. Snaking for hundreds of miles along dizzying sea cliffs, California's legendary coastal highways connect the dots between star-powered Los Angeles, surfin' San Diego and bohe-

mian San Francisco. In between, you'll uncover hidden beaches and surf breaks, rustic seafood shacks and wooden piers for catching the sunset over boundless Pacific horizons.

....

Big Sur

Much ink has been spilled extolling the raw beauty and energy of this 100-mile stretch of craggy coastline sprawling south of Monterey Bay. More a state of mind than a place you can pinpoint on a map, Big Sur has no traffic lights, banks or strip malls. When the sun goes down, the moon and stars are the only illumination – if summer fog hasn't extinguished them, that is.

Lodging, food and gas are all scarce and pricey in Big Sur. Demand for rooms is high year-round, especially on weekends, so book ahead. The free *Big Sur Guide* (www.bigsurcalifornia.org), an info-packed newspaper, is available everywhere along the way. Note the day-use parking fee ($10) charged at Big Sur's

Hikers on the Mist Trail, Yosemite National Park
JOHN ELK/GETTY IMAGES ©

Detour:
Lake Tahoe

Shimmering in myriad blues and greens, Tahoe is the nation's second-deepest lake. Driving around its spellbinding 72-mile scenic shoreline gives you quite a workout behind the wheel. The north shore is quiet and upscale; the west shore is rugged and old-timey; the east shore is undeveloped; and the south shore is busy with families and flashy casinos. The horned peaks surrounding the lake (elevation 6225ft), which straddles the California–Nevada state line, are four-seasons outdoor playgrounds.

Hwy 89 threads northwest along the thickly forested west shore to **Emerald Bay State Park** (☏530-541-6498; www.parks.ca.gov; per car $8-10; ☉daily late May-Sep), where granite cliffs and pine trees frame a sparkling fjordlike inlet. A 1-mile trail leads steeply downhill to **Vikingsholm Castle** (tours adult/child $10/8; ☉10:30am or 11am-4pm daily late May-Sep). From this 1920s Scandinavian-style mansion, the Rubicon Trail ribbons 4.5 miles north along the lakeshore past petite coves to **DL Bliss State Park** (☏530-525-7277; www.parks.ca.gov; per car $10; ☉usually late May-Sep; ♿), offering sandy beaches. Further north, **Tahoma Meadows B&B Cottages** (☏530-525-1553, 866-525-1533; www.tahomameadows.com; 6821 W Lake Blvd, Homewood; cottages incl breakfast $109-199; 🛜♿🐾) rents darling country cabins.

Tahoe gets packed in summer, on winter weekends and over holidays, when reservations are essential.

state parks is valid for same-day entry to all.

If you're road-tripping from LA to San Francisco, a good place to overnight is at blink-and-you-miss-it Gorda, home of **Treebones Resort** (☏877-424-4787, 805-927-2390; www.treebonesresort.com; 71895 Hwy 1; d with shared bath incl breakfast from $199; 🛜♨♿), which offers back-to-nature clifftop yurts and a small locavarian **restaurant** (dinner mains $24-33; ☉noon-2pm & 5:30pm-8pm) and sushi bar.

Another 3 miles north, **Julia Pfeiffer Burns State Park** hides one of California's only coastal waterfalls, 80ft-high **McWay Falls**; the viewpoint is reached via a quarter-mile stroll. Two more miles north, a steep dirt trail descends from a hairpin turn on Hwy 1 to **Partington Cove**, a raw and breathtaking spot where crashing surf salts your skin – but swimming isn't safe, sorry.

Seven miles further north, nestled among redwoods and wisteria, quaint **Deetjen's Restaurant** (☏831-667-2378; www.deetjens.com; Deetjen's Big Sur Inn, 48865 Hwy 1; dinner mains $24-38; ☉8am-noon Mon-Fri, to 12:30pm Sat & Sun, 6-9pm daily) serves country-style comfort fare. Just north, the beatnik **Henry Miller Memorial Library** (☏831-667-2574; www.henrymiller.org; 48603 Hwy 1; ☉11am-6pm Wed-Mon; @🛜) is the art and soul of Big Sur bohemia, with a jam-packed bookstore, live-music concerts and DJs, open-mic nights and outdoor film screenings. Opposite, food takes a backseat to dramatic ocean views at clifftop **Nepenthe** (☏831-667-2345; www.nepenthebigsur.com; 48510 Hwy 1; mains $15-42; ☉11:30am-4:30pm & 5-10pm), meaning 'island of no sorrow.' Its Ambrosia burger is mighty.

Heading north, **Big Sur Station** (☏831-667-2315; www.fs.usda.gov/lpnf/; ☉8am-4pm, closed Mon & Tue Oct-Apr) can clue you in about hiking trails and camping options. On the opposite side of Hwy 1 just south, turn onto obscurely marked Sycamore Canyon Rd, which drops two narrow, twisting miles to crescent-shaped **Pfeiffer Beach** (per car $5; ☉9am-8pm), with a towering offshore sea arch and strong currents too dangerous for swimming. Dig down into the sand – it's purple!

Next up, **Pfeiffer Big Sur State Park** is crisscrossed by sun-dappled trails through redwood forests, including the 1.4-mile round trip to seasonal Pfeiffer Falls.

Most of Big Sur's commercial activity is concentrated just north along Hwy 1, including private campgrounds with rustic cabins, motels, restaurants, gas stations and shops. **Glen Oaks Motel** (☏831-667-2105; www.glenoaksbigsur.com; 47080 Hwy 1; d from $225; ☎), a redesigned 1950s redwood-and-adobe motor lodge, rents snug rooms and cabins with gas fireplaces. Nearby, the Big Sur River Inn's **general store** (http://bigsurriverinn.com; 46840 Hwy 1; mains $6-9; ☉11am-7pm) hides a burrito and fruit-smoothie bar at the back, while **Maiden Publick House** (☏831-667-2355; Hwy 1; ☉3pm-2am Mon-Fri, from noon Sat & Sun) pulls off an encyclopedic beer menu and live-music jams.

Heading north again, don't skip **Andrew Molera State Park**, a gorgeous trail-laced pastiche of grassy meadows, waterfalls, ocean bluffs and rugged beaches.

Six miles before landmark Bixby Creek Bridge, you can tour 1889 **Point Sur Lightstation** (☏831-625-4419; www.pointsur.org; adult/child from $12/5). Check online or call for tour schedules, including seasonal moonlight walks, and directions to the meeting point.

Monterey

Working-class Monterey is all about the sea. It lures visitors with a top-notch aquarium that's a veritable temple to Monterey Bay's underwater universe. A National Marine Sanctuary since 1992, the bay begs for exploration by kayak, boat, scuba or snorkel. Meanwhile, downtown's historic quarter preserves California's Spanish and Mexican roots.

Monterey Bay Aquarium Aquarium (☏info 831-648-4800, tickets 866-963-9645; www.montereybayaquarium.org; 886 Cannery Row; adult/child $35/22; ☉9:30am-6pm Mon-Fri, to 8pm Sat & Sun Jun-Aug, 10am-5pm or 6pm daily Sep-May; ☎♿) ⚑ Give yourself at least half a day to see sharks and sardines play hide-and-seek in kelp forests, observe the antics of frisky otters,

Big Sur

419

Coastal Intrigue

If you like the stunning ocean scenery at Big Sur, don't miss these other waterfront charmers.

Mendocino Some 160 miles north of San Francisco, Mendocino is a salt-washed historical gem perched on a gorgeous headland. A headland walk passes berry brambles and wildflowers, where cypress trees stand guard over dizzying cliffs. Nature's power is evident everywhere, from driftwood-littered fields and cave tunnels to the raging surf.

Santa Barbara Life is certainly sweet in this coastal Shangri-La, where the air is perfumed with citrus and jasmine, flowery bougainvillea drapes whitewashed buildings with Spanish-style red-tiled roofs, and the coast is cradled by pearly beaches. State St, the main drag, abounds with bars, cafes, theaters and boutique shops.

Santa Cruz SoCal beach culture meets NorCal counterculture in Santa Cruz. The UCSC student population makes this old-school radical town youthful, hip and lefty-political. It's also a surfer's paradise.

meditate upon psychedelic jellyfish and get touchy-feely with sea cucumbers, bat rays and other tide-pool creatures.

Monterey State Historic Park   Historic Site

(🎧 audio tour 831-998-9458; www.parks.ca.gov) Downtown, Old Monterey boasts a cluster of lovingly restored 19th-century brick-and-adobe buildings, including novelist Robert Louis Stevenson's one-time boarding house and the Cooper-Molera Adobe, a sea captain's home. Admission to the gardens is free, but individual buildings' opening hours, admission fees and tour schedules vary. Pick up walking-tour maps and check current schedules at the **Pacific House** (📞 831-649-7118; www.parks.ca.gov; 20 Custom House Plaza; admission $3, incl walking tour $5; ⏱ 10am-4pm Fri-Mon), a multicultural historical museum.

Asilomar Conference Grounds   Lodge $$

(📞 888-635-5310, 831-372-8016; www.visitasilomar.com; 800 Asilomar Ave; r incl breakfast $115-175; @ 🛜 🏊 👶) Coastal state-park lodge preserves buildings designed by architect Julia Morgan, of Hearst Castle fame. Historic rooms are small and thin-walled, but charming nonetheless.

Passionfish   Seafood $$$

(📞 831-655-3311; www.passionfish.net; 701 Lighthouse Ave; mains $16-26; ⏱ 5-9pm Sun-Thu, to 10pm Fri & Sat) Eureka! Finally, a perfect, chef-owned seafood restaurant where the sustainable fish is dock-fresh, every preparation fully flavored and the wine list affordable. Reservations strongly recommended.

The Best of the Rest

Hawaii (p422)
An island getaway with idyllic beaches, mighty volcanoes and magical sunsets.

Alaska (p426)
Rugged and beautiful, with soaring peaks, massive glaciers and awe-inspiring wildlife.

Rocky Mountains (p430)
Grizzlies, geysers, alpine meadows, snow-covered mountains and farm-fresh food.

Texas (p434)
Historic sites, world-class barbecue and one of America's finest live-music scenes.

Philadephia (p438)
Colonial history, heritage buildings, excellent museums and a burgeoning dining scene.

Niagara Falls (p440)
Waterfalls dividing New York and Canada.

Mount Rushmore (p442)
Four-faced icon of the US's great presidents.

Top: Grizzly bear cubs, Alaska (p426);
Left: Yellowstone National Park (p433)

Hawaii

HIGHLIGHTS

1 Haleakalā National Park (p426) Catch dawn over Maui's 'house of the rising sun.'

2 Hanauma Bay (p424) Snorkel with tropical fish in stunning Oahu.

3 Hana Highway (p425) Drive Maui's twisting seaside highway past jungle valleys and waterfalls.

4 Waikiki Frolic in the waves and stroll the powdery sands.

Surfer at Waikiki Beach
ANN CECIL/GETTY IMAGES ©

Hawaii, as tourist bureaus and Hollywood constantly remind us, is 'paradise.' Push past the hype and you may find they're not far wrong. Hawaii is diving coral-reef cities in the morning and listening to slack-key guitar at sunset. It's biting into juicy *liliko'i* (passion fruit) with hibiscus flowers in your hair. These Polynesian islands are an expression of nature's diversity at its most divine, from fiery volcanoes to lacy rainforest waterfalls to crystal-clear aquamarine bays.

O'ahu

O'ahu is the *ali'i* (chief) of Hawaii's main islands – so much so that others are referred to as 'Neighbor Islands.' Honolulu is the center of state government, commerce and culture, while nearby Waikiki's beaches gave birth to the whole tiki-craze fantasia. If you want to take the measure of Hawaii's diversity, O'ahu offers the full buffet in one tidy package: in the blink of an eye you can go from crowded metropolis to turquoise bays teeming with sea life – and surfers.

🛈 Getting There & Around

Honolulu International Airport (HNL; 📞808-836-6411; http://hawaii.gov/hnl; 300 Rodgers Blvd, Honolulu) is Hawaii's major air hub. From the US mainland, round-trip fares start around $400 from California. **Roberts Hawaii** (📞808-441-7800, 800-831-5541; www.airportwaikikishuttle.com) runs 24-hour airport shuttles to/from Waikiki (one way/round trip $13/24).

HONOLULU & WAIKIKI

Among its many museums, historical sites and cultural offerings, Honolulu is also a foodie haven dishing up everything from cheap noodles to gourmet Hawaii Regional Cuisine. Saunter over to Waikiki Beach to lounge on the sand, play in the water, hear Hawaiian music and watch hula dancers sway after sunset.

Sights

Neighboring downtown Honolulu, **Chinatown** lends itself to exploring on foot. Bring an appetite – you'll be grazing pan-Asian marketplaces and cafes between antique and lei shops, temples and art galleries.

Bishop Museum   Museum

(☏ museum 808-847-3511, planetarium 808-848-4136; www.bishopmuseum.org; 1525 Bernice St; adult/child $20/15; ◷ 9am-5pm Wed-Mon; P ♿) ⌖ Ranked among the world's best Polynesian anthropological museums, Bishop Museum boasts impressive cultural displays such as the triple-decker Hawaiian Hall. The family-oriented Science Adventure Center puts kids virtually inside an erupting volcano.

'Iolani Palace   Palace

(☏ info 808-538-1471, tour reservations 808-522-0832/0823; www.iolanipalace.org; 364 S King St; grounds admission free, adult/child basement galleries $7/3, self-guided audio tour $15/6, guided tour $22/6; ◷ 9am-5pm Mon-Sat, last entry 4pm) In the heart of downtown Honolulu, this historical site where the monarchy was overthrown offers a glimpse into the Kingdom of Hawai'i's final decades.

Sleeping & Eating

Hotel Renew   Boutique Hotel $$

(☏ 888-485-7639, 808-687-7700; www.hotelrenew.com; 129 Pa'oakalani Ave; r from $180; P ❄ @ 🛜) ⌖ Just a block from the beach, this eco-savvy, gay-friendly boutique hotel satisfies sophisticated urbanites and romantic dreamers alike with sleek rooms, attentive staff and loads of little niceties.

Roy's
Waikiki   Hawaii Regional Cuisine $$$

(☏ 808-923-7697; www.royshawaii.com; 226 Lewers St; mains $30-42, 3-course prix-fixe menu without/with wine pairings $47/67; ◷ 11am-9:30pm Sun-Thu, to 10pm Fri & Sat) Groundbreaking chef Roy Yamaguchi doesn't actually cook here, but his signature *misoyaki* butterfish, blackened ahi (tuna), macadmadia nut–encrusted mahimahi and deconstructed sushi rolls always appear on the menu. Reservations essential.

🎯 Activities

It's all about loooong **Waikiki Beach**. Catamarans and outrigger canoes pull right up onto the sand, while concession stands offer surf lessons and rent boards. For a swim without the tourist crowds, head to mile-long **Ala Moana Beach Park** (1201 Ala Moana Blvd; P ♿), just west of Waikiki.

Hanauma Bay (p424), O'ahu
LYNN GAIL/GETTY IMAGES ©

DIAMOND HEAD & SOUTHEAST O'AHU

O'ahu's southeast coast abounds in dramatic scenery and outdoor activities. For windy 360-degree panoramas, make the 0.8-mile climb up **Diamond Head** (www.hawaiistateparks.org; off Diamond Head Rd btwn Makapu'u & 18th Aves; admission per pedestrian/car $1/5; ⏰6am-6pm, last trail entry 4:30pm; 🚹), the 760ft extinct volcano tuff cone visible from Waikiki.

Go eyeball-to-mask with tropical fish at **Hanauma Bay** (📞808-396-4229; www.honolulu.gov/parks/facility/hanaumabay; Hanauma Bay Rd, off Hwy 72; adult/child $7.50/free; ⏰6am-6pm Wed-Mon Nov-Mar, to 7pm Wed-Mon Apr-Oct; 🚹), a turquoise bathtub set in a rugged volcanic ring. For the best snorkeling conditions, arrive early. You can rent snorkel gear on-site. Parking costs $1, but when the lot fills, often by mid-morning, all cars are turned away. From Waikiki, take bus 22 ($2.50, 45 minutes, no service Tuesday).

HALE'IWA & NORTH SHORE

O'ahu's North Shore is legendary for the massive 30ft winter waves that thunder against its beaches. The gateway to the North Shore, **Hale'iwa** is the region's only real town – along its main drag you'll spot art galleries, shops selling surf gear and bikinis, and rusty pickup trucks with surfboards tied to the roof. When the surf's up, folks drop everything to hit the waves. They don't have to go far: in-town **Hale'iwa Ali'i Beach Park** gets towering swells.

Outside town, **Waimea Bay Beach Park** has a split personality. In summer the water can be as calm as a lake and ideal for swimming and snorkeling; in winter it rips with the island's highest waves.

Team Real Estate (📞800-982-8602, 637-3507; www.teamrealestate.com; North Shore Marketplace, 66-250 Kamehameha Hwy; studio/1br/2br/3br/4br from $60/95/150/165/250) rents accommodations, from studio apartments to beachfront luxury homes, along the North Shore; book in advance. Food trucks park alongside the Kamehameha Hwy and on the south side of Hale'iwa town.

Maui

According to some, you can't have it all. Perhaps those folks haven't been to Maui, which consistently lands atop travel-magazine reader polls as one of the world's most romantic islands. And why so? With its sandy beaches, deluxe resorts, gourmet cuisine, fantastic luau, world-class windsurfing, whale-watching, snorkeling, diving and hiking, it leaves most people even a little more in love than when they arrived.

ℹ️ Getting There & Around

US mainland and inter-island flights land at **Kahului** (OGG; 📞808-872-3830; www.hawaii.gov/ogg; 1 Kahului Airport Rd). From the airport, bio-diesel **Speedi Shuttle** (📞877-242-5777; www.speedishuttle.com) charges from $30 to Kihei and $50 to Lahaina.

LAHAINA & WEST MAUI

For the megahotel and resort experience, bunk down in West Maui, with its prime sunset beaches. For historical atmosphere, entertainment and dining out, make time for Lahaina, a 19th-century whaling town rich in old-timey architecture.

◎ Sights & Activities

The focal point of Lahaina is its bustling small-boat harbor, backed by the **Pioneer Inn** and **Banyan Tree Square**, home to the USA's largest banyan tree. Oceanside Front St is chock-a-block with art galleries, shops and restaurants.

For those world-famous beaches, head north and keep going: between Ka'anapali and Kapalua, one impossible perfect strand follows another. Three top-ranked gems are **Kahekili Beach**, **Kapalua Beach** and **DT Fleming Beach Park**. Nearly all water sports are possible, and gear rental and tour outfitters abound.

INGMAR WESEMANN/GETTY IMAGES ©

 Don't Miss
Scenic Drive: Road to Hana

One of Hawaii's most spectacular scenic drives, the **Hana Highway** (Hwy 360) winds its way past jungle valleys and back out above a rugged coastline. The road is a real cliff-hugger with 54 one-lane bridges and head-spinning views. Gas up and buy snacks and drinks in Pa'ia before starting out.

Waterfall swimming holes, heart-stopping vistas and incredible hikes call out almost nonstop along the way. Detour to explore coastal trails and the black-sand beach at **Wai'anapanapa State Park** (www.hawaiistateparks.org; off Hwy 360). For basic tent camping (sites $18) and rustic housekeeping cabins ($90), advance reservations are required. Book online with Hawaii's **Division of State Parks** (www.hawaiistateparks.org).

Sleeping

Ka'anapali Beach Hotel Resort **$$**
(☏808-661-0011, 800-262-8450; www.kbh-maui.com; 2525 Ka'anapali Pkwy; r from $169; P ❄ @ ☏ ≋ ♣) While not the fanciest, newest or biggest, this low-key Ka'anapali resort hotel has an enviable beach location and, most of all, genuine aloha. Take free kid-friendly lessons in ukulele, hula and Hawaiian crafts.

Plantation Inn B&B **$$**
(☏800-433-6815, 808-667-9225; www.theplantationinn.com; 174 Lahainaluna Rd; r/ste incl breakfast from $158/$248; P ❄ ☏ ≋) Forget cookie-cutter resorts – if you want a taste of Old Hawaii, book a romantic if small room at Lahaina's genteel oasis, furnished with antiques and Hawaiian quilts on four-poster beds.

Eating

Mala Ocean Tavern   Seafood **$$$**
(☎808-667-9394; www.malaoceantavern.com;
1307 Front St; mains lunch $12-26, dinner $19-45;
🕙11am-9:30pm Mon-Fri, 9am-9:30pm Sat, 9am-
9pm Sun) For Lahaina's best waterfront
fine dining, stop searching. Mala marries
Mediterranean and Pacific Rim influences
with organic, farm-fresh ingredients and a
bounty of just-caught seafood.

Drinking & Entertainment

Around sunset, catch the free torch-
lighting and cliff-diving ceremony at
Pu'u Keka'a (Black Rock) on northern
Ka'anapali Beach.

Hula Grill & Barefoot Bar   Bar
(www.hulagrillkaanapali.com; Whalers Village,
2435 Ka'anapali Pkwy; 🕙11am-11pm) It's your
Maui postcard: sunset mai tais, sand be-
neath your sandals and the lullaby sounds
of Hawaiian slack-key guitar.

Old Lahaina Luau   Luau
(☎800-248-5828, 808-667-1998; www.old
lahainaluau.com; 1251 Front St; adult/child
$98/68; 🕙from 5:15pm or 5:45pm; 👪) For a
night to remember, this beachside luau
is unsurpassed for its authenticity and
aloha – the hula is first-rate and the feast
darn good. Book ahead.

HALEAKALĀ NATIONAL PARK

No trip to Maui is complete without visit-
ing this sublime **park** (☎808-572-4400;
www.nps.gov/hale; 3-day entry per car $10).
From the towering volcano's rim near the
summit, there are dramatic views of a
lunarlike surface and multicolored cinder
cones. For an unforgettable (and chilly)
experience, arrive in time for sunrise – an
event Mark Twain called the 'sublimest
spectacle' he'd ever seen.

Alaska

HIGHLIGHTS

1 **Anchorage** Explore culture-rich
museums and hike scenic trails
outside town.

2 **Juneau** (p429) Gaze over snow-
covered peaks from the US's
prettiest state capital.

3 **Glacier Bay National Park** (p428)
Take a scenic cruise and hike a
captivating icy wonderland.

Mendenhall River, Juneau (p429)
DAGNY WILLIS/GETTY IMAGES ©

Big, beautiful and wildly bountiful. Far away, rurally isolated and very expensive. Alaska is a traveler's dilemma. No one can deny there are few places in the world with such grandeur and breathtaking beauty.

Anchorage

Anchorage offers the comforts of a large US city but is only a 30-minute drive from the Alaskan wilderness.

 Sights & Activities

Anchorage Museum   Museum
(www.anchoragemuseum.org; 625 C Street; adult/child $15/7; ⊙9am-6pm; 🏛) A $106-million renovation has made this Alaska's best cultural experience. Spend an afternoon viewing paintings by Alaskan masters, including Sydney Laurence, on the 1st floor and then check out the incredible Smithsonian exhibit on the 2nd.

Alaska Native Heritage Center   Cultural Center
(📞800-315-6608, 330-8000; www.alaskanative.net; 8800 Heritage Center Dr; adult/child $25/17; ⊙9am-5pm) This center is spread over 26 acres and includes studios – with artists carving baleen (the filter-feeder system found inside the mouths of whales) or sewing skin-boats – a small lake and five replica villages. Other than traveling to the Bush (where many native Alaskans live), this is the best place to see how humans survived – even thrived – before central heating.

Flattop Mountain Trail   Hiking
A three- to five-hour, 3.4-mile round trip of Alaska's most-climbed peak starts from a trailhead on the outskirts of Anchorage. Maps are available at the Alaska Public Lands Information Center (📞866-869-6887, 907-644-3661; www.alaskacenters.gov; 605 W 4th Ave, suite 105; ⊙9am-5pm) and the Flattop Mountain Shuttle (📞907-279-3334; www.hike-anchorage-alaska.com; round-trip adult/child $22/15) will run you to the trailhead (and they also run a hike/bike combo).

Tony Knowles Coastal Trail   Cycling
On the other side of the creek from the Flattop Mountain trail, beginning at the west end of 2nd Ave, this 11-mile trail is the most scenic of the city's 122 miles of paved path.

Downtown Bicycle Rental   Cycling
(www.alaska-bike-rentals.com; 333 W 4th Ave; 3hr/24hr rental $16/32; ⊙8am-10pm) Anchorage has been called a 'Bike Utopia.' Rent a bike and find out why.

Tours

Rust's Flying Service   Scenic Flight
(📞907-243-1595; www.flyrusts.com; 4525 Enstrom Circle) Has 30-minute tours ($100), a three-hour flight to view Mt McKinley in Denali National Park ($385) and a 1½-hour tour of Knik Glacier ($245).

🛌 Sleeping & Eating

Puffin Inn   Motel $$
(📞907-243-4044; www.puffininn.net; 4400 Spenard Rd; r $125-165; 📶) Arriving on the red-eye? This motel offers free 24-hour airport shuttle as well as four tiers of fine rooms, from 26 sardine-can economy rooms to full suites.

Snow City Café   Cafe $$
(www.snowcitycafe.com; 1034 W 4th Ave; breakfast $8-15, lunch $10-15; ⊙7am-3pm Mon-Fri, to 4pm Sat & Sun; 📶) This hip and busy cafe serves healthy grub to a mix of clientele that ranges from the tattooed to the up-and-coming. Surrounding all of them are walls adorned with local art. It's worth reserving a table on the weekend.

Snow Goose & Sleeping Lady Brewing Co   Brewery
(717 W 3rd Ave) If the sun is setting over Cook Inlet and the Alaska Range, head to the rooftop deck of this brewpub. Only the beer is better than the view.

🛈 Getting There & Away

Ted Stevens Anchorage International Airport (ANC; www.dot.state.ak.us/anc; 📶) has frequent inter- and intra-state flights.

KIM HEACOX/GETTY IMAGES ©

★ Don't Miss
Glacier Bay National Park & Preserve

Eleven tidewater glaciers that spill out of the mountains and fill the sea with icebergs of all shapes, sizes and shades of blue have made Glacier Bay National Park and Preserve an icy wilderness renowned worldwide. This can be an expensive side trip from Juneau but, for most people who include it on their itinerary, well worth the extra funds.

Gustavus (www.gustavusak.com) is a weekly stop ($33, 4½ hours) for the **Alaska Marine Highway** ferry (AMHS; ☎800-642-0066; www.dot.state.ak.us/amhs/pubs/). Alaska Airlines (p489) has daily flights between Gustavus and Juneau.

Food, lodging and transportation to Bartlett Cove in the park is available in Gustavus. **Annie Mae Lodge** (☎907-697-2346; www.anniemae.com; Grandpa's Farm Rd; s $160-220, d $170-230; ☎) has 11 rooms, most with private entrances and bathrooms.

The **park headquarters** (☎907-697-2230; www.nps.gov/glba; 1 Park Rd; ⊙8am-4:30pm Mon-Fri) in Bartlett Cove maintains a free campground and a **visitor center** (☎907-697-2627; ⊙6am-9pm) at the dock, which provides backcountry permits and maps. You can stay at **Glacier Bay Lodge** (☎888-229-8687; www.visitglacierbay.com; 199 Bartlett Cove Rd; r $199-224), the only hotel and restaurant at Bartlett Cove.

To see the glaciers, board the *Fairweather Express* operated by **Glacier Bay Lodge & Tours** (☎888-229-8687, 907-264-4600; www.visitglacierbay.com; adult/child $190/95) for an eight-hour cruise up the West Arm of Glacier Bay. The only developed hiking trails are in Bartlett Cove, but there is excellent kayaking; rent equipment from **Glacier Bay Sea Kayaks** (☎697-2257; www.glacierbayseakayaks.com; single/double kayaks per day $45/50).

Alaska Shuttle (☎907-338-8888, 907-694-8888; www.alaskashuttle.net) offers door-to-door transportation between the airport and downtown and South Anchorage (one to three people $50) and Eagle River ($55).

Juneau

The first town to be founded after Alaska's purchase from the Russians, Juneau became the territorial capital in 1906 and today is the most scenic capital in the country. Its historic downtown clings to the gap between snowcapped mountains and a bustling waterfront. The rest of the city spreads north into the Mendenhall Valley. Juneau is also Alaska's cruise-ship capital and the gateway to many attractions, including Tracy Arm and Glacier Bay National Park.

Sights

Mendenhall Glacier   Glacier
Juneau's famous 'drive-in' glacier is one of the most picturesque attractions in Southeast Alaska. This frozen river and its informative **USFS Visitor Center** (Glacier Spur Rd; adult/child $3/free; ☉8am-7:30pm) is 12 miles from the city. **Mendenhall Glacier Transport** (MGT; ☎789-5460; mightygreatrips.com; round trip $16) runs buses from downtown.

 Activities

Hiking   Hiking
Hiking is the most popular activity in the area, and some trails access USFS cabins. **Juneau Parks & Recreation** (☎907-586-0428; www.juneau.org/parksrec) organizes free hikes. **West Glacier Trail**, which sidles along Mendenhall Glacier, has the most stunning scenery. The **Mt Roberts Trail** is the most popular hike to the alpine country above Juneau.

Taku Glacier Lodge   Scenic Flights
(☎907-586-6275; www.wingsairways.com; adult/child $297/250) The most popular tours in Juneau are flightseeing, glacier viewing and salmon bakes and a trip to this historic camp combines all three. You reach it via a floatplane that includes flying across a half-dozen glaciers. At the log lodge you enjoy an incredible meal of wild salmon to the view of Taku Glacier.

Alaska Boat & Kayak Center   Kayaking
(☎907-364-2333; www.juneaukayak.com; 11521 Glacier Hwy; single/double kayak $50/70; ☉9am-5pm) Rents boats and offers a self-guided Mendenhall Lake paddle ($109).

Orca Enterprises   Whale Watching
(☎888-733-6722, 907-789-6801; www.alaskawhalewatching.com; adult/child $119/59) Uses a 42ft jet boat for three-hour whale-watching tours.

Sleeping & Eating

Silverbow Inn   Boutique Hotel $$$
(☎907-586-4146; www.silverbowinn.com; 120 2nd St; r $189-219; @ 🛜) A wonderful boutique inn on top of a downtown bagel shop. Along with 11 rooms, there's an outdoor hot tub with a view of the mountains.

Tracy's King Crab Shack   Seafood $$
(www.kingcrabshack.com; 356 S Franklin St; crab $13-30; ☉10:30am-8pm) Squeezed between the library parking garage and the cruise-ship docks, this little hut serves up crab, from outstanding bisque to mini-cakes. A bucket of king crab pieces ($60) is 2lb of the sweetest seafood you'll ever have.

 Getting There & Away

The main airline serving Juneau is **Alaska Airlines** (p489).

Rocky Mountains

HIGHLIGHTS

1 Denver Head off on a hike into the mountains, followed by dinner in one of the city's culinary gems.

2 Rocky Mountain National Park (p432) Take in the sweeping views from a soaring mountain peak.

3 Yellowstone National Park (p433) See geysers, alpine scenery and an awesome variety of wildlife.

Dancers by Jonathan Borofsky, Denver
RICHARD CUMMINS/GETTY IMAGES ©

The high backbone of the lower 48, the Rockies are nature on steroids, with rows of snowcapped peaks, rugged canyons and wild rivers running buckshot over the Western states. With its beauty and vitality, it's no wonder that 100 years ago, it beckoned ailing patients with last-ditch hopes for cures.

Locals love a good frozen, wet or mud-spattered adventure and, with plenty of climbing, skiing and white-water paddling, it's easy to join in. Afterwards, relax by soaking in hot springs under a roof of stars, sipping cold microbrews or feasting farm-to-table style.

Denver

Denver's mile-high gravity is growing, pulling all objects in the Rocky Mountain West toward its glistening downtown towers, hopped-up brewpubs, hemped-out cannabis dispensaries, trails, toned-and-tanned mountain warriors, and growing Western cosmopolitanism that's fostered a burgeoning arts scene, and brought great restaurants and hip bars to a cow-town gone world-wide crazy.

Top that off with back-door service to the Rocky Mountains, one of the best off-road bike trail systems in the US, and plenty of parks, open spaces, riverfronts and sunshiney perches for a sky-high psychedelic carpet ride.

◉ Sights & Activities

Denver Art Museum　　Museum
(DAM; ☏ ticket sales 720-865-5000; www.denverartmuseum.org; 100 W 14th Ave; adult/child/student $13/5/10, 1st Sat of each month free; ☺10am-5pm Tue-Thu, Sat & Sun, to 8pm Fri; 🅿 🛜 🚻; 🚌9, 16, 52, 83L RTD) ✿ The DAM is home to one of the largest Native American art collections in the USA, and puts on special avant-garde multimedia exhibits.

Confluence Park　　Park
(2200 15th St; 🚻; 🚌10 RTD) ✿ **FREE** Where Cherry Creek and Platte River meet is the nexus and plexus of Denver's sunshine-loving culture. It's a good place for an

Best Mile-High Day Hikes

There are hundreds of day hikes within an hour of Denver. Many people choose to head up to Boulder's Mountain Parks or Colorado Springs for a day.

Jefferson County Open Space Parks (www.jeffco.us/openspace; ⓘ) Top picks include Matthews Winters, Mount Falcon, Elk Meadow and Lair o' the Bear.

Golden Gate Canyon State Park (☎303-582-3707; www.parks.state.us/parks; 92 Crawford Gulch Rd, Golden; entrance/camping $7/24; ⏱5am-10pm) Located halfway between Denver and Nederland, this massive 12,000-acre state park can be reached in about 45 minutes from downtown Denver.

Staunton State Park (☎303-816-0912; www.parks.state.co.us/parks) Colorado's newest state park sits on a historic ranch site 40 miles west of Denver. It is accessed from Hwy 285 between Conifer and Bailey.

Waterton Canyon (☎303-634-3745; www.denverwater.org/recreation/watertoncanyon; Kassler Center) South of the city, just west of Chatfield Reservoir, this pretty canyon has an easy 6.5-mile trail to the Strontia Springs Dam. From there, the **Colorado Trail** (CTF; ☎303-384-3729; www.coloradotrail.org; ⏱9am-5pm Mon-Fri) will take you all the way to Durango!

Buffalo Creek Mountain Bike Area (www.frmbp.org; Pine Valley Ranch Park) If you're into single-track mountain biking, this area has about 40 miles of bike trails.

afternoon picnic, and there's a short white-water park for kayakers and tubers.

Sleeping

Curtis
Boutique Hotel **$$**

(☎303-571-0300; www.thecurtis.com; 1405 Curtis St; d $159-279; ❄ @ 🛜; 🚌15 RTD) It's like stepping into a doobop Warhol wonderworld at this temple to post-modern pop culture. Attention to detail – be it through the service or the decor in the rooms – is paramount at the Curtis, a one-of-a-kind hotel in Denver.

Queen Anne Bed & Breakfast Inn
B&B **$$**

(☎303-296-6666; www.queenannebnb.com; 2147 Tremont Pl; r incl breakfast $135-215; 🅿❄🛜) 🌿 Soft chamber music wafting through public areas, fresh flowers, manicured gardens and evening wine tastings create a romantic ambience at this ecoconscious B&B in two late-1800s Victorian homes.

Eating & Drinking

Beatrice & Woodsley
Tapas **$$**

(☎303-777-3505; www.beatriceandwoods-ley.com; 38 S Broadway; small plates $9-13; ⏱5-11pm Mon-Fri, 10am-2pm & 5-10pm Sat & Sun; 🚌0 RTD) Beatrice and Woodsley is the most artfully designed dining room in Denver. Chainsaws are buried into the wall to support shelves, there's an aspen growing through the back of the dining room and the feel is that of a mountain cabin being elegantly reclaimed by nature.

Steuben's Food Service
American **$$**

(☎303-803-1001; www.steubens.com; 523 E 17th Ave; mains $8-21; ⏱11am-11pm Sun-Thu, to midnight Fri & Sat; ⓘ) 🌿 Although styled as a midcentury drive-in, the upscale treatment of comfort food (mac and cheese, fried chicken, lobster rolls) and the solar-powered kitchen demonstrate Steuben's contemporary smarts.

Forest Room 5 — Bar

(📞303-433-7001; www.forestroom5.com; 2532 15th St; ⏰4pm-2am) One of the best damned bars in Denver, this LoHi (that's Lower Highlands) juggernaut has an outdoor patio with fire circles (where you can smoke!), streams and a funked-out Airstream.

ℹ Getting There & Away

Denver International Airport (DIA; 📞information 303-342-2000; www.flydenver.com; 8500 Peña Blvd; @ 🛜) is served by around 20 airlines and offers flights to nearly every major US city. Public Regional Transit District runs a SkyRide service to the airport from downtown Denver hourly ($9 to $13, one hour).

Amtrak's *California Zephyr* runs daily between Chicago and San Francisco via Denver. Trains arrive and depart from a **temporary station** (1800 21st St) behind Coors Field until light-rail renovations at **Union Station** (📞Amtrak 800-872-7245; www.denverunionstation.org; cnr 17th & Wynkoop Sts; 🚌31X, 40X, 80X, 86X, 120X RTD) finish in 2014.

Rocky Mountain National Park

Rocky Mountain National Park showcases classic alpine scenery, with wildflower meadows and serene mountain lakes set under snowcapped peaks. There are more than four million visitors annually, but many stay on the beaten path. Hike an extra mile and enjoy the incredible solitude. Elk are the park's signature mammal – you will even see them grazing hotel lawns, but also keep an eye out for bighorn sheep, moose, marmots and black bear.

◎ Sights & Activities

With over 300 miles of trail, traversing all aspects of its diverse terrain, the park is suited to every hiking ability.

Those with the kids in tow might consider the easy hikes in the Wild Basin to Calypso Falls or to Gem Lakes in the Lumpy Ridge area, or the trail to Twin Sisters Peak south of Estes Park, while those with unlimited ambition, strong legs and enough trail mix will be lured by the challenge of summiting Longs Peak.

Regardless, it's best to spend at least one night at 7000ft to 8000ft prior to setting out to allow your body to adjust to the elevation. Before July, many trails are snowbound and high water runoff makes passage difficult.

🛏 Sleeping & Eating

Aside from campgrounds, there are no lodging options in the park. The following are in nearby Estes Park.

YMCA of the Rockies – Estes Park Center — Resort $$

(📞970-586-3341; www.ymcarockies.org; 2515 Tunnel Rd; r & d from $109; cabins from $129; P ❄ 🛜 ♿ 👪) Estes Park Center is not your typical YMCA boarding house. Instead it's a favorite vacation spot. There are upmarket motel-style accommodations and cabins set on hundreds of acres of high-alpine terrain. Book ahead.

Stanley Hotel — Hotel $$$

(📞970-577-4000; www.stanleyhotel.com; 333 Wonderview Ave; r from $199; P 🛜 🏊 ♿) The white Georgian Colonial Revival hotel stands in brilliant contrast to the towering peaks of Rocky Mountain National Park that frame the skyline. A favorite local retreat, this best-in-class hotel served as the inspiration for Stephen King's famous cult novel *The Shining*.

Ed's Cantina & Grill — Mexican $$

(📞970-586-2919; www.edscantina.com; 390 E Elkhorn Ave; mains $9-13; ⏰11am-late Mon-Fri, 8am-10pm Sat & Sun; ♿) With an outdoor patio right on the river, Ed's is a great place to kick back with a margarita and one of the daily $3 blue-plate specials (think fried, rolled tortillas with shredded pork and guacamole).

ℹ Getting There & Around

There are two entrance stations on the east side, Fall River (US 34) and Beaver

Meadows (US 36). The Grand Lake Station (also US 34) is the only entry on the west side.

In summer a free shuttle bus operates from the Estes Park Visitor Center multiple times daily, bringing hikers to a park-and-ride location where you can pick up other shuttles.

Yellowstone National Park

They grow their critters and geysers big up in Yellowstone, America's first national park and Wyoming's flagship attraction. From shaggy grizzlies to oversized bison and magnificent packs of wolves, this park boasts the lower 48's most enigmatic concentration of wildlife. Throw in half the world's geysers, the country's largest high-altitude lake and a plethora of blue-ribbon rivers and waterfalls, all sitting pretty atop a giant supervolcano, and you'll quickly realize you've stumbled across one of Mother Nature's most fabulous creations.

 Sights & Activities

Yellowstone is split into five distinct regions, each with unique attractions. All the visitor centers have information desks staffed by park rangers who can help you tailor a hike to your tastes, from great photo spots to the best chance of spotting a bear.

Geyser Country   Geysers, Hiking
With the densest collection of geothermal features in the park, Upper Geyser Basin contains 180 of the park's 250-odd geysers. The most famous is **Old Faithful**, which spews from 3700 to 8400 gallons of water 100ft to 180ft into the air every 1½ hours or so. For an easy walk, check out the predicted eruption times at the brand-new visitor center and then follow the easy boardwalk trail around the Upper Geyser Loop.

Mammoth Country   Springs, Hiking
Known for the geothermal terraces and elk herds of historic **Mammoth** and the hot springs of **Norris Geyser Basin**,

Mammoth Country is North America's most volatile and oldest-known continuously active thermal area. The peaks of the Gallatin Range rise to the northwest, towering above the area's lakes, creeks and numerous hiking trails.

Roosevelt Country   Wildlife, Hiking
Fossil forests, the commanding **Lamar River Valley** and its tributary trout streams, **Tower Falls** and the Absaroka Mountains' craggy peaks are the highlights of Roosevelt Country, the park's most remote, scenic and undeveloped region. Several good hikes begin near **Tower Junction**.

Canyon Country   Lookouts, Hiking
A series of scenic overlooks linked by hiking trails highlight the colorful beauty and grandeur of the Grand Canyon of the Yellowstone and its impressive **Lower Falls**. South Rim Dr leads to the canyon's most spectacular overlook, at Artist Point. **Mud Volcano** is Canyon Country's primary geothermal area.

Lake Country   Lakes, Boating
Yellowstone Lake, the centerpiece of Lake Country and one of the world's largest alpine lakes, is a watery wilderness lined with volcanic beaches and best explored by boat or sea kayak.

Sleeping

Reservations are essential in summer. Contact the park concessionaire **Xanterra** (☏ 307-344-5395; www.yellowstonenational parklodges.com) to reserve a spot at its campsites, cabins or lodges.

Plentiful accommodations can also be found in the gateway towns of Cody, Gardiner and West Yellowstone.

Roosevelt Lodge Cabins   Cabin **$$**
(☏ 866-439-7375; www.yellowstonenationalpark-lodges.com; cabins $69-115; 🎒) These cabins are good for families. With a cowboy vibe, the place offers nightly 'Old West dinner cookouts,' during which guests travel by horse or wagon to a large meadow 3 miles from the lodge for open-air buffets (book ahead).

Old Faithful Inn   Hotel **$$**
(☎ 866-439-7375; www.yellowstonenationalpark-lodges.com; old house d with shared/private bath from $103/140, standard from $164; ☺ early May-early Oct) Next to the signature geyser, this grand inn is the most requested lodging in the park. A national historic landmark, it features an immense timber lobby, with its huge stone fireplaces and sky-high knotted-pine ceilings.

ℹ Information

Park entrance permits (hiker/vehicle $12/25) are valid for seven days for entry into both Yellowstone and Grand Teton National Parks. Summer-only visitor centers are evenly spaced every 20 to 30 miles along Grand Loop Rd.

Albright Visitors Center (☎ 307-344-2263; www.nps.gov/yell; ☺ 8am-7pm Jun-Sep, 9am-5pm Oct-May) Serves as park headquarters. The park website is a fantastic resource.

ℹ Getting There & Away

The airport (WYS) in West Yellowstone, MT, is usually open June to September. It's often more affordable to fly into Billings, MT (170 miles), Salt Lake City, UT (390 miles) or Denver, CO (563 miles) and rent a car.

Texas

HIGHLIGHTS

1 **Austin** Take in the fabled live-music scene of Texas' free-spirited capital.

2 **San Antonio** (p436) Saunter along the riverfront and visit the famed Alamo.

3 **Lockhart** (p437) Feast on tender morsels of perfection in the state's celebrated barbecue capital.

The Alamo (p436), San Antonio
ETHEL DAVIES/GETTY IMAGES ©

Cue the theme music, and make it something epic: Texas is as big and sweeping a state as can be imagined. If it were a country, it would be the world's 40th largest. And as big as it is geographically, it is equally large in people's imaginations. With a state this big, there's room for Texas to be whatever you want it to be.

Austin

Austin is about the experience. Bars, restaurants, even grocery stores and the airport have live music. And there are outdoor activities galore. A full day might also include shopping for some groovy vintage clothes, sipping a margarita at a patio cafe and lounging on the shores of Barton Springs.

Sights & Activities

Bob Bullock Texas State History Museum
Museum
(☎512-936-8746; www.thestoryoftexas.com; 1800 Congress Ave; adult/4-17yr $9/6, Texas Spirit film $5/4; ⏰9am-6pm Mon-Sat, noon-6pm Sun) This is no dusty old historical museum. It's a big and glitzy ramble through the Lone Star State's history, all the way from when it used to be part of Mexico up to the present, with high-tech interactive exhibits and fun theatrics.

Barton Springs Pool
Swimming
(☎512-867-3080; 2201 Barton Springs Rd; adult/child $3/2; ⏰9am-10pm Fri-Wed mid-Apr–Sep) Even when the temperature hits 100, you'll be shivering in a jiff after you jump into this icy-cold natural-spring pool.

Zilker Park
Hiking, Cycling
(☎512-974-6700; www.austintexas.gov/department/zilker-metropolitan-park; 2100 Barton Springs Rd) This 350-acre park is a slice of green heaven, lined with hiking and biking trails. The park also provides access to the famed Barton Springs natural swimming pool and Barton Creek Greenbelt. Find boat rentals, a miniature train and a botanic garden, too.

Lady Bird Lake
Canoeing
(☎512-459-0999; www.rowingdock.com; 2418 Stratford Dr; ⏰6:30am-8pm) Get out on the water at the Rowing Dock, which rents kayaks, canoes and paddle boards for $10 to $20 per hour, and paddle boats for slightly more.

Bicycle Sport Shop
Bicycle Rental
(☎512-477-3472; www.bicyclesportshop.com; 517 S Lamar Blvd; per 2hr from $16; ⏰10am-7pm Mon-Fri, 9am-6pm Sat, 11am-5pm Sun) The cool thing about Bicycle Sport Shop is its proximity to Zilker Park, Barton Springs and the Lady Bird Lake bike paths, all of which are within a few blocks.

Sleeping

Hotel San José
Boutique Hotel $$
(☎512-444-7322; www.sanjosehotel.com; 1316 S Congress Ave; r $165-285, with shared bathroom $95-145; P❄🛜🐾) Local hotelier Liz Lambert revamped a 1930s-vintage motel into a chic SoCo retreat with minimalist rooms in stucco bungalows, native Texas gardens and a very Austin-esque hotel bar in the courtyard that's known for its celebrity-spotting potential.

Austin Motel
Motel $$
(☎512-441-1157; www.austinmotel.com; 1220 S Congress Ave; r $84-139, ste $163; P❄🛜🐾) 'Garage-sale chic' is the unifying factor at this wonderfully funky motel that embodies the spirit of the 'Keep Austin Weird' movement.

Eating & Drinking

Moonshine Patio Bar & Grill
American $$
(☎512-236-9599; www.moonshinegrill.com; 303 Red River St; dinner mains $11-21; ⏰11am-10pm Mon-Thu, to 11pm Fri & Sat, 9am-2pm & 5-10pm Sun) Within its exposed limestone walls, you can enjoy upscale comfort food, half-price appetizers at happy hour or a lavish Sunday brunch buffet ($16.95). Or chill on the patio under the shade of pecan trees.

Bouldin Creek
Coffee House

Vegetarian $

(☏512-416-1601; 1900 S 1st St; meals $5-9; ☉7am-midnight Mon-Fri, 8am-midnight Sat & Sun; 🛜📶) You can get your veggie chorizo scrambler or organic oatmeal with apples all day long at this vegan-vegetarian eatery. It's got an eclectic South Austin vibe and is a great place for people-watching, finishing your novel or joining a band.

East Side Showroom

Bar

(☏512-467-4280; 1100 E 6th St; ☉5pm-2am) With an ambience that would feel right at home in Brooklyn (in the late 1800s), this bar on the emerging east-side scene is full of hipsters soaking up the craft cocktails and bohemian atmosphere.

⭐ Entertainment

Continental Club

Live Music

(☏512-441-0202; www.continentalclub.com; 1315 S Congress Ave; ☉4pm-2am) No passive toe-tapping here; this 1950s-era lounge has a dance floor that's always swinging with some of the city's best local acts.

Broken Spoke

Live Music

(www.brokenspokeaustintx.com; 3201 S Lamar Blvd; ☉11am-midnight Tue-Thu, to 1am Fri & Sat) With sand-covered wood floors and wagon-wheel chandeliers that George Strait once hung from, Broken Spoke is a true Texas honky-tonk.

ℹ Getting There & Around

Austin-Bergstrom International Airport (AUS; www.austintexas.gov/airport) is off Hwy 71, southeast of downtown.

The downtown **Amtrak station** (☏512-476-5684; www.amtrak.com; 250 N Lamar Blvd) is served by the *Texas Eagle* that extends from Chicago to Los Angeles.

San Antonio

In most large cities, downtown is bustling with businesspeople dressed for office work hurrying to their meetings and luncheons. Not so in San Antonio. Instead, downtown is filled with tourists in shorts consulting their maps. In fact, many people are surprised to find that two of the state's most popular destinations – the Riverwalk and the Alamo – are right smack dab in the middle of downtown, surrounded by historical hotels, tourist attractions and souvenir shops.

◎ Sights & Activities

The Alamo

Historic Building

(☏210-225-1391; www.thealamo.org; 300 Alamo Plaza; ☉9am-5:30pm Mon-Sat, from 10am Sun) FREE Find out why the story of the Alamo can rouse a Texan's sense of state pride like few other things. For many, it's not so much a tourist attraction as a pilgrimage and you might notice some of

Cowboy boots for sale, Texas
HERMAN AGOPIAN/GETTY IMAGES ©

Lockhart Barbecue

In 1999 the Texas Legislature adopted a resolution naming Lockhart – 33 miles south of Austin – the barbecue capital of Texas. Of course, that means it's the barbecue capital of the *world*. You can eat very well for under $10 at these places:

Black's Barbecue (215 N Main St; sandwiches $4-6, brisket per pound $11; ⏱10am-8pm Sun-Thu, to 8:30pm Fri & Sat) A longtime Lockhart favorite since 1932, with sausage so good Lyndon Johnson had Black's cater a party at the nation's capital.

Kreuz Market (☎512-398-2361; 619 N Colorado St; brisket per pound $11.90, sides extra; ⏱10:30am-8pm Mon-Sat) Serving Lockhart since 1900, the barnlike Kreuz Market uses a dry rub. This means you shouldn't insult it by asking for barbecue sauce – Kreuz doesn't serve it, and the meat doesn't need it.

Smitty's Market (208 S Commerce St; lunch plates $6, brisket per pound $11.90; ⏱7am-6pm Mon-Fri, 7am-6:30pm Sat, 9am-3pm Sun) The blackened pit room and homely dining room are all original (knives used to be chained to the tables). Ask to have the fat trimmed off the brisket if you're particular about that.

the visitors getting downright dewy-eyed at the description of how a few hundred revolutionaries died defending the fort against thousands of Mexican troops.

Riverwalk Waterfront
(www.thesanantonioriverwalk.com) A little slice of Europe in the heart of downtown San Antonio, the Riverwalk is an essential part of experiencing this city. This is no ordinary riverfront, but a charming canal and pedestrian street that is the main artery at the heart of San Antonio's tourism efforts.

Mission Trail Historic Site
(www.nps.gov/saan) Spain's missionary presence can best be felt at the ruins of the four missions south of town: Missions Concepción (1731), San José (1720), San Juan (1731) and Espada (1745–56) make up **San Antonio Missions National Historical Park**. Stop first at Mission San José (6701 San José Dr; ⏱9am-5pm), which is also the location of the main **visitor center**. Known in its time as the Queen of the Missions, it's certainly the largest and arguably the most beautiful.

Rio San Antonio Cruises Boat Tour
(☎210-244-5700, 800-417-4139; www.riosanantonio.com; adult/under 5yr $8.25/2; ⏱9am-9pm) One of the best ways to experience the Riverwalk is with these 40-minute narrated cruises that give you a good visual overview of the river and a light history lesson.

 Sleeping

Hill Country Inn & Suites Hotel $
(☎210-599-4204, 800-314-3424; www.stayhci.com; 2383 NE Loop 410; d incl breakfast $65-99; P ❄ 🛜 ♒ 👪) Just north of downtown, this anachronistic place feels like it belongs in the Hill Country more than off an interstate, with cabin-style rooms, ranch-style porches and country-style furnishings.

Noble Inns B&B $$
(☎210-223-2353, 800-242-2770; www.nobleinns.com; d incl breakfast from $139; P ❄ 🛜 ♒) This collection of three inns has something for everyone – at least everyone who likes antiques and Victorian style.

🍴 Eating & Drinking

Monterey American **$$**
(📞210-745-2581; www.themontereysa.com; 1127 S St Marys St; brunch $7-12, mains $10-17; 🕐5-11pm Tue-Thu, to midnight Fri & Sat, 10am-2pm Sun) Despite the small number of options, the menu will please most foodies and you'll be dazzled by the choices available when it comes to its extensive selection of microbrews and wine. A great all-round place to hang out, day or night.

**Mi Tierra
Cafe & Bakery** Tex-Mex **$$**
(📞210-225-1262; www.mitierracafe.com; 218 Produce Row; mains $12-16; 🕐24hr) Dishing out traditional Mexican food since 1941, this 500-seat behemoth in Market Sq sprawls across several dining areas, giving the busy wait staff and strolling mariachis quite a workout.

Friendly Spot Ice House Bar
(📞210-224-2337; 943 S Alamo St; 🕐3pm-midnight Mon-Fri, from 11am Sat & Sun; 👶🐾) What could be friendlier than a big, pecan tree–shaded yard filled with colorful metal lawn chairs? Friends (and their dogs) gather to knock back some longnecks, while the kids amuse themselves in the playground.

ℹ️ Getting There & Away

San Antonio is served by the **San Antonio International Airport** (SAT; 📞210-207-3433; www.sanantonio.gov/sat; 9800 Airport Blvd), about 9 miles north of downtown. The *Sunset Limited* (Florida–California) and *Texas Eagle* (San Antonio–Chicago) trains stop a few days a week (usually late at night) at the **Amtrak Station** (www.amtrak.com; 350 Hoefgen Ave).

Philadelphia

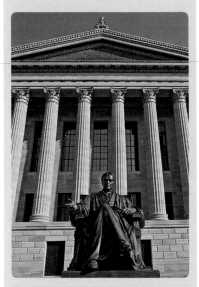

HIGHLIGHTS

① **Independence National Historic Park** Peer back in time at Revolutionary War–era Philadelphia.

② **Philadelphia Museum of Art** Climb the steps, Rocky-like, then explore the galleries of Philly's superb art showcase.

③ **Italian Market** Browse, shop and eat to your heart's content.

Philadelphia Museum of Art
DAVID ZANZINGER/GETTY IMAGES ©

Although it may seem like a little sibling to NYC, which is less than 90 miles away, Philadelphia is more representative of what East Coast city living is like. And in the minds of many, it offers every upside of urban life: burgeoning food, music and art scenes, neighborhoods with distinct personalities, copious parkland and, just as importantly, relatively affordable real estate. The older, preserved buildings in historic Philadelphia provide a picture of what colonial American cities once looked like – based on a grid with wide streets and public squares.

◉ Sights & Activities

The L-shaped **Independence National Historic Park**, along with Old City, has been dubbed 'America's most historic square mile.' Once the backbone of the US government, it has become the backbone of Philadelphia's tourist trade. Stroll around and you'll see storied buildings in which the seeds for the Revolutionary War were planted and the US government came into bloom. You'll also find beautiful, shaded urban lawns dotted with plenty of benches and costumed actors wandering about.

Philadelphia Museum of Art   Museum
(☏ 215 763 8100; www.philamuseum.org; 2600 Benjamin Franklin Pkwy; adult/child $20/free; ⊙10am-5pm Tue, Thu, Sat & Sun, to 8:45pm Wed & Fri) It's one of the nation's largest and most important museums, featuring excellent collections of Asian art, Renaissance masterpieces, post-impressionist works and modern pieces by Picasso, Duchamp and Matisse. The grand stairway at its entrance was immortalized when Sylvester Stallone ran up the steps in the 1976

flick *Rocky*. Music, food and wine Friday nights.

Italian Market   Market
(S 9th St, btwn Wharton & Fitzwater Sts; ⊙9am-5pm Tue-Sat, to 2pm Sun) These days, the country's oldest outdoor market is as much Mexican as Italian and you'll probably find more taquiles than prosciutto; however, it's still a highlight of South Philadelphia. Butchers and artisans still hawk produce and cheese and a handful of authentic old-school Italian shops sell homemade pastas, pastries and freshly slaughtered fish and meats. **Anthony's** (915 S 9th St; gelato $3.50; ⊙7am-7pm), a small cafe, is a good place to take a break with an espresso or gelato.

🛏 Sleeping

Morris House Hotel   Boutique Hotel **$$**
(☏ 215-922-2446; www.morrishousehotel.com; 225 S 8th St; r incl breakfast from $179; ❄ 🛜)
Upscale colonial-era boutique, this Federal-era building has the friendly charm and

Old City, Philadelphia
RICHARD CUMMINS/GETTY IMAGES ©

intimacy of an elegant B&B and the professionalism and good taste of a designer-run 21st-century establishment.

Penn's View Hotel
Hotel **$$**

(☎215-922-7600; www.pennsviewhotel.com; cnr Front & Market Sts; r from $149-329; ❋ 🛜; Ⓢ2nd St) Housed in three early-19th-century buildings overlooking the Delaware waterfront, Penn's View is ideal for exploring the Old City.

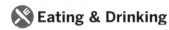 Eating & Drinking

Silk City Diner
Diner **$$**

(435 Spring Garden St; mains $13; ⊙4pm-1am, from 10am Sat & Sun) Cocktails have replaced milkshakes at this classic-looking diner on the edge of the Old City and Northern Liberties.

La Locanda del Ghiottone
Italian **$$**

(☎215-829-1465; 130 N 3rd St; mains $16; ⊙5-11pm Tue-Sun) The name means 'the Place of the Glutton,' and chef Giussepe and Joe the head waiter encourage overeating. Try the gnocchi, mushroom crepes and mussels. BYOB.

North 3rd
Gastropub

(www.norththird.com; 801 N 3rd St; ⊙4pm-2am) A Northern Liberties gem equally recommended for drinks like huge mojito martinis as for its tremendous food like steamed clams and pork chorizo in a tomato and cilantro broth.

ℹ Getting There & Away

Bus

Greyhound (☎215-931-4075; www.greyhound.com; 1001 Filbert St) and Peter Pan Bus Lines (www.peterpanbus.com; 1001 Filbert St) are the major bus carriers; Bolt Bus (www.boltbus.com) and Megabus (www.us.megabus.com) are popular competitors.

Train

Beautiful 30th St Station (☎215-349-2153; www.30thstreetstation.com; cnr 30th & Market Sts) is one of the biggest train hubs in the country. Amtrak (www.amtrak.com) runs the train service.

Niagara Falls

HIGHLIGHTS

❶ Horseshoe Falls Cross the border and catch the photogenic panorama from the Canadian side.

❷ Goat Island Gaze over the thundering falls from this superb vantage point.

❸ Maid of the Mist Take a memorable (and wet!) boat ride around the base of the falls.

Maid of the Mist tour boat, Niagara Falls
EMILY RIDDELL/GETTY IMAGES ©

It's a tale of two cities and two falls, though either side of this international border affords views of an undeniably dramatic natural wonder. There are honeymooners and heart-shaped Jacuzzis, arcades, tacky shops and kitsch boardwalk-like sights, but as long as your attention is focused nothing can detract from the majestic sight. For good reason, the Canadian side is where almost everyone visits, though it's easy to stroll back and forth between the two (bring your passport).

◎ Sights & Activities

The falls are in two separate towns: Niagara Falls, New York (USA) and Niagara Falls, Ontario (Canada). The towns face each other across the Niagara River, spanned by the Rainbow Bridge, which is accessible for cars and pedestrians.

You can see views of the **American Falls** and their western portion, the **Bridal Veil Falls**, which drop 180ft from the **Prospect Point Observation Tower** (716-278-1796; admission $1, free from 5pm; 9:30am-7pm). Cross the small bridge to **Goat Island** for close-up viewpoints, including Terrapin Point, which has a fine view of Horseshoe Falls and pedestrian bridges to the Three Sisters Islands in the upper rapids. From the north corner of Goat Island, an elevator descends to the **Cave of the Winds** (716-278-1730; adult/child $11/8), where walkways go within 25ft of the cataracts (raincoats provided).

The **Maid of the Mist** (716-284-8897; www.maidofthemist.com; 151 Buffalo Ave; adult/child $15.50/9; 9am-7pm summer) boat trip around the bottom of the falls has been a major attraction since 1846 and is highly recommended. Times vary so check the website. Boats leave from the base of the Prospect Park Observation Tower on the US side and from the bottom of Clifton Hill on the Canadian side.

Canadian Niagara Falls

When people say they are visiting the falls they usually mean the Canadian side, which is naturally blessed with superior views. Canada's **Horseshoe Falls** are wider and especially photogenic from Queen Victoria Park; at night they're illuminated with a colored light show. The **Journey Behind the Falls** (905-354-1551; 6650 Niagara Pkwy; adult/child Apr-Dec $15.95/10.95, Dec-Apr $11.25/6.95; 9am-10pm) gives access to a spray-soaked viewing area beneath the falls. **Niagara on the Lake**, 15km to the north, is a small town full of elegant B&Bs and a famous summertime theater festival.

Sleeping

Giacomo   Boutique Hotel **$$**
(716-299-0200; www.thegiacomo.com; 220 First St; r from $150; P ❋ ☎) While the majority of floors are taken up by high-end condos, the three-dozen spacious rooms are luxuriously appointed and the 19th-floor lounge offers spectacular falls views.

❶ Getting There & Around

The **Amtrak train station** (27th St, at Lockport Rd) is about 2 miles northeast of downtown. From Niagara Falls, daily trains go to New York City (nine hours). **Greyhound** (www.greyhound.com; 303 Rainbow Blvd) buses are run out of the Daredevil Museum.

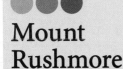

Mount Rushmore

HIGHLIGHTS

1 **Presidential Trail** Go eye-to-eye (or eye-to-nose, rather) with four legendary statesmen.

2 **Nature trail** Walk through a peaceful pine forest en route to the viewing area.

3 **Sculptor's Studio** See how the mountain was carved and gain insight into the artist behind the monument.

Glimpses of Washington's nose from the roads leading to this hugely popular monument never cease to surprise and are but harbingers of the full impact of this mountainside sculpture once you're up close (and past the less impressive parking area and entrance walk). George Washington, Thomas Jefferson, Abraham Lincoln and Theodore Roosevelt each iconically stare into the distance in 60ft-tall granite glory.

It's hugely popular, but you can easily escape the crowds and fully appreciate the **Mount Rushmore National Memorial** (www.nps.gov/moru; off Hwy 244; parking $11; 8am-10pm summer, to 5pm other times) while marveling at the artistry of sculptor Gutzon Borglum and the immense labor of the workers who created the memorial between 1927 and 1941.

The **Presidential Trail** loop passes right below the monument for some fine nostril views and access the worthwhile **Sculptor's Studio**. Start clockwise and you're right under Washington's nose in under five minutes. The **nature trail** to the right as you face the entrance connects the viewing and parking areas, passing through a pine forest and avoiding the crowds and commercialism.

Sleeping & Eating

The nearest lodging and restaurants to Mt Rushmore are in Keystone, South Dakota, a one-time mining town now solely devoted to milking the monument. Gaudy motels vie with fudgeries for your attention, however you can get great sandwiches at **Teddy's Deli** (236 Winter St; mains from $5; 9am-9pm summer, shorter hours other times).

ⓘ Getting There & Away

Rapid City Airport, 32 miles northeast of Mt Rushmore, has regional connections. Once here, you'll need a car – there is no public transport to Mt Rushmore.

Rock climber, South Dakota
TYLER STABLEFORD/AURORA OUTDOOR COLLECTION/GETTY IMAGES ©

Mount Rushmore

JOHN ELK/GETTY IMAGES ©

USA
In Focus

Bull elk, Yellowstone National Park (p433)
KRAIG LIEB / GETTY IMAGES ©

Greenmarket Farmers Market (p67), New York City

> *Although Obama declared his support for same-sex marriage, the federal government remained opposed*

belief systems
(% of population)

51	24	2	2	21
Protestant	Roman Catholic	Mormon	Jewish	Other

if the USA were 100 people

65 would be white
15 would be Hispanic
13 would be African American
4 would be Asian American
3 would be other

population per sq mile

 ≈ 11 people

AUSTRALIA USA CANADA

Obama 2.0

Democrats cheered his victory, but President Barack Obama returned to office without being surrounded by quite the same hope and optimism as the first time. Times had changed, and the US, like much of the world, had struggled through tough years. In 2013 the unemployment rate was about what it had been during his first inauguration, back in 2009 (around 8%), though economic growth seems at last to be on a solid foundation.

Obama's ambitious healthcare reform has passed through Congress, becoming the most significant healthcare expansion since Medicare and Medicaid in 1965. Whether it will be a success or failure is still hotly debated; the outcome probably won't be clear for years.

Going to Pot

In 2012 voters in Colorado and Washington state approved ballot measures to legalize marijuana. This has created tension with the federal

riage, sometimes leaving it up to voters to decide. By 2013, 13 states had legalized same-sex marriage.

A major breakthrough occurred in June 2013, when the Supreme Court ruled that the discriminatory *Defense of Marriage Act* – the law barring the federal government from recognizing same-sex marriages legalized by the states – was unconstitutional. The ruling, which came just days before scheduled Gay Pride parades nationwide, added to particularly exuberant and well-attended celebrations.

HUW JONES/GETTY IMAGES ©

government, which still treats marijuana as an illegal substance.

The prevailing attitude across the US is one of relaxing restrictions on cannabis. Some 18 states have supported the legalization of marijuana for medicinal use and a handful have also decriminalized it, making possession of small amounts a misdemeanor rather than a felony. How Colorado and Washington will handle the taxing and selling of marijuana come 2014 (when the law goes into effect) is the big unknown.

Marriage for All

Another hot topic is gay marriage. Although Obama declared his public support for same-sex marriage in 2012, the federal government remained tacitly opposed to it. National polls continued to show a majority of Americans support legalized marriage for all. Some states had set their own rulings about gay mar-

Unhealthy Appetites

No one could deny that the US has an obesity problem – shows like *The Biggest Loser* and Eric Schlosser's book *Fast Food Nation* shine a spotlight on the nation's deadly eating habits. Americans have been doing some soul-searching and changes big and small are happening across the country. New York City has helped lead the way, banning the use of trans fats and requiring fast-food restaurants to post the calorie content of all menu items (however, an attempt to ban the sale of sugary beverages over 20oz failed).

Michelle Obama has been one of the nation's most vocal advocates of healthy eating, targeting childhood obesity (an alarming one in three US children is obese) and encouraging parents to make more informed decisions about eating. Apps such as the government's MyPlate – a food diary and calorie counter that's popular on social media sites such as Pinterest – are among an increasing number of tools helping diners make better choices.

History

Cannons at a Civil War battlefield, Virginia

Demagogues, visionaries and immigrants all contribute to the American story. Early colonists arrive in the 1600s, planting the seeds of independence, which later blossom into full nationhood. Westward expansion follows, along with bloody Civil War and the emancipation of slaves. In modern times, the US struggles through the Great Depression and horrific wars, and enacts great changes during the Civil Rights movement. After the USSR's demise, the US becomes the world's leading superpower.

Enter the Europeans

In 1492 the Italian explorer Christopher Columbus, backed by the monarchy of Spain, voyaged west by sea, looking for the East Indies. With visions of gold, Spanish explorers quickly followed: Hernán Cortés conquered much of today's Mexico; Francisco Pizarro conquered Peru; Juan Ponce de León wandered through Florida looking for the fountain of youth. Not to be left out, the French explored Canada and the Midwest,

8000 BC

Widespread extinction of Ice Age mammals. Indigenous peoples hunt smaller game and start gathering native plants.

while the Dutch and English cruised North America's eastern seaboard.

Of course, they weren't the first ones on the continent. When Europeans arrived, between two million and 18 million Native American people occupied the lands north of present-day Mexico and spoke more than 300 languages. European explorers left in their wake diseases to which indigenous peoples had no immunity. More than any other factor – war, slavery or famine – disease epidemics devastated indigenous populations, by anywhere from 50% to 90%. By the 17th century, Native North Americans numbered only about one million, and many of the continent's once-thriving societies were in turmoil and transition.

In 1607, English nobles established North America's first permanent European settlement, in Jamestown, Virginia. Eventually the colony came to be run by a representative assembly of citizens, and it brought the first African slaves to the continent to work the tobacco fields.

In 1620, a boatload of radically religious Puritans established a colony at Plymouth, Massachusetts. Their settlement – intended to be a religious and moral beacon to the world – was notable for its 'Mayflower Compact,' an agreement to govern themselves by consensus. Sadly, the harmony did not extend to the colonists' relationships with local Native American tribes, and their eventual falling out led to bloody warfare.

Thus, at Jamestown and Plymouth, the seeds of the 'American paradox' were sown: white political and religious freedom would come to be founded through the enslavement of blacks and the displacement of Native Americans.

The Best...
Colonial Sites

1 Independence National Historic Park (p439), Philadelphia

2 Freedom Trail (p175), Boston

3 Strawbery Banke Museum (p194), Portsmouth, NH

4 Colonial Williamsburg (p250), Virginia

IN FOCUS HISTORY

The American Revolution

For the next 150 years, European powers – particularly England, France, Portugal and Spain – competed for position and territory, bringing all their Old World political struggles to the new one. In the south, English businessmen developed a cotton and tobacco plantation economy that became entirely dependent on the use of forced labor, and slavery was eventually legalized into a formal institution. By 1800, one out of every five persons in America was a slave.

7000 BC–100 AD
During the 'Archaic period,' the agricultural 'three sisters' (corn, beans, squash) and permanent settlements become established.

1492
Italian explorer Christopher Columbus 'discovers' America, eventually making three voyages throughout the Caribbean.

1607
Jamestown is founded, though life there is grim: 80 of 108 settlers die the first year.

The Best... Historic Homes

1 Mount Vernon (p122), Alexandria, VA

2 Paul Revere House (p167), Boston

3 Hearst Castle (p397), California

Meanwhile, in the 1760s – after winning the Seven Years' War with France and finally gaining control of the eastern seaboard – England started asking the American colonies to chip in to the Crown's coffers. Up to then, Britain had mostly left the colonists alone to govern themselves, but now England raised new taxes and stationed a permanent army.

This didn't sit well, to put it mildly. Colonists protested and boycotted English policies (arguing for 'no taxation without representation'), and openly questioned the benefits of monarchy. Who needed a king imposing rules from abroad when they were doing quite well without one?

In 1774, fired by increasing conflict and the era's Enlightenment ideas of individualism, equality and liberty, the colonists convened the First Continental Congress in Philadelphia to decide what to do. Before they could agree, in April 1775, British troops skirmished with armed colonists in Massachusetts, and both sides were at war.

It wasn't until July 4, 1776, that the Revolutionary War's ultimate treasonous goal – independence from England – was first articulated in the Declaration of Independence. Unfortunately, the Continental army, led by George Washington, was underfunded, poorly armed, badly trained and outnumbered by Britain's troops, who were the largest professional army in the world. If not for a 1778 alliance with France, which provided the materials and sea power that eventually won the war for the colonists, America might very well have been a short-lived experiment.

Westward Expansion

After winning independence, the Founding Fathers came to the hard part: fashioning a government. The US Constitution wasn't adopted until 1787. While the democratic government it created amounted to a radical political revolution, economic and social relationships were not revolutionized: rich landholders kept their property, including slaves; Native Americans were excluded from the nation; and women were excluded from politics. As a result, following the ratification of the Constitution, US life has pulsed with the ongoing struggle to define 'all' and 'equal' and 'liberty' – to take the universal language of America's founding and either rectify or justify the inevitable disparities that bedevil any large society.

It would be 70 years before the first real troubles surfaced. In the meantime, America looked west, and its ambitions grew to continental size. Believers in 'manifest

1620

The *Mayflower* lands at Plymouth with 102 English Pilgrims. Native Americans save them from starvation.

1773

Bostonians protest British taxes by dumping tea into the harbor, called the 'Boston Tea Party.'

Statue of Sam Adams, Boston

destiny' felt that it was divinely fated that the United States should occupy all the land from sea to shining sea – and through wars, purchase and outright theft, they succeeded. Particularly after the discovery of gold in California in 1848 (the Spanish explorers just hadn't known where to look), groaning wagon trains brought fevered pioneers west, a motley collection of miners, farmers, entrepreneurs, immigrants, outlaws and prostitutes, all seeking their fortunes on the frontier. This made for exciting, legendary times, but throughout loomed a troubling question: as new states joined the USA, would they be slave states or free states? The nation's future depended on the answer.

The Civil War

The US Constitution hadn't ended slavery, but it had given Congress the power to approve (or not) slavery in new states. Public debates raged constantly over the expansion of slavery, particularly since this shaped the balance of power between the industrial North and the agrarian South.

Since the founding, Southern politicians had dominated government and defended slavery as 'natural and normal,' which an 1856 *New York Times* editorial called 'insanity.' The Southern pro-slavery lobby enraged Northern abolitionists. But even many Northern politicians feared that ending slavery would be ruinous. Limit slavery, they reasoned, and in the competition with industry and free labor, slavery would wither without inciting a violent slave revolt – a constantly feared possibility. Indeed, in 1859, radical abolitionist John Brown tried unsuccessfully to spark an uprising to free the slaves at Harpers Ferry, West Virginia.

The economics of slavery were undeniable. In 1860, there were more than four million slaves in the US, most held by Southern planters, who grew 75% of the world's cotton, accounting for over half of US exports. Thus, the Southern economy supported the nation's economy, and it required slaves. The 1860 presidential election became a referendum on this issue, and the election was won by a young politician who favored limiting slavery: Abraham Lincoln.

In the South, even the threat of federal limits was too onerous and, as President Lincoln took office, 11 states seceded from the Union and formed the Confederate States of America. Lincoln faced the nation's greatest moment of crisis. He had two choices: let the Southern states secede or wage war to keep the Union intact. He chose the latter.

The war began in April 1861, when the Confederacy attacked Fort Sumter in Charleston, South Carolina, and raged for the next four years in some of the most gruesome combat the world had known. By the end, more than 600,000 soldiers – nearly an entire generation of young men – were dead, and Southern plantations and cities (most notably Atlanta) lay sacked and burned. The North's industrial might

1781
General Washington leads his ragtag troops to victory at Yorktown as the British surrender.

1787
US Constitution establishes a democratic form of government, with power vested in the hands of the people.

1803–06
France sells the US the Louisiana Purchase; Lewis and Clark then trailblaze west through it to reach the Pacific Ocean.

provided an advantage, but its victory was not preordained; it unfolded battle by bloody battle.

As fighting progressed, Lincoln recognized that if the war didn't end slavery outright, victory would be pointless. In 1863, his Emancipation Proclamation expanded the war's aims and freed all slaves. In April 1865, Confederate General Robert E Lee surrendered to Union General Ulysses S Grant in Appomattox, Virginia. The Union had been preserved, but at a staggering cost.

Immigration & Industrial Revolution

The Civil War ended an economic system of forced labor. But American society remained largely, and often deeply, racist. During Reconstruction (1865–77), the civil rights of ex-slaves were protected by the federal government, which also extracted reparations from Southern states, creating Civil War grudges that lingered for a century.

After Reconstruction, Southern states developed a labor system of indentured servitude (called 'sharecropping') and enacted laws aimed at keeping whites and blacks 'separate but equal.' The South's segregationist 'Jim Crow' laws (which remained in place until the 1960s Civil Rights movement) effectively disenfranchised African Americans in every sphere of daily life.

Meanwhile, with the rapid, post–Civil War settlement of the West, the US appeared like a mythic 'land of opportunity' to immigrants, who flooded in from Europe and Asia. In total, about 25 million people arrived between 1880 and 1920. Poles, Germans, Irish, Italians, Russians, Eastern Europeans, Chinese and more fed an urban migration that made the late 19th century the age of cities. New York was transformed into a buzzing, multi-ethnic 'melting pot,' and the nation's undisputed capital of commerce and finance.

America's industrialists became so rich, and so effective at creating monopolies in steel, oil, banking and railroads, that they became known as 'robber barons,' and not always disparagingly. These paragons of capitalism fueled the industrial revolution, even as choking factories and sweatshops consigned many to lives of poverty and pain. Through the turn of the century, the rise of labor unions and progressive reformers, such as President Woodrow Wilson, led to new laws that broke up the monopolies and softened workplace abuses.

After the US's brief involvement in WWI, the prosperity of the 'roaring' 1920s led to a wave of optimism and good times. The Jazz Age bloomed: flappers danced the Charleston, radio and movies captivated millions, and stock prices went up, up, up.

1849

An epic cross-country gold rush sees 60,000 'Forty-Niners' flock to California's Mother Lode.

1865

The Civil War ends, though celebration is curtailed by President Lincoln's assassination five days later.

1880–1920

Millions of immigrants flood in to the US's cities from Europe and Asia, fueling a new age of urban living.

Great Depression, the New Deal & World War II

In October 1929, investors, worried about a gloomy global economy, started selling stocks. But all that selling caused everyone to panic, until they'd sold everything. The stock market crashed, and the US economy collapsed like a house of cards.

Thus began the Great Depression. Frightened banks called in their dodgy loans, people couldn't pay, and the banks folded. Millions lost their homes, farms, businesses and savings, and as much as 50% of the American workforce became unemployed in certain parts of the country (the overall rate at its peak was nearly 33%). In 1932, Democrat Franklin D Roosevelt was elected president on the promise of a 'New Deal' to rescue the US from its crisis, which he did with resounding success.

When war once again broke out in Europe in 1939, the isolationist mood in the US was as strong as ever. But the extremely popular President Roosevelt, elected to an unprecedented third term in 1940, understood that the US couldn't sit by and allow victory for fascist, totalitarian regimes. Roosevelt sent aid to Britain and persuaded a skittish Congress to go along with it.

On December 7, 1941, Japan launched a surprise attack on Hawaii's Pearl Harbor, killing more than 2000 Americans and sinking several battleships. As US isolationism transformed overnight into outrage, Roosevelt suddenly had the support he needed. Germany declared war on the US, and America joined the Allied fight against Hitler and the Axis powers, putting almost its entire will and industrial prowess into the war effort.

Initially, neither the Pacific nor European theaters went well for America. Fighting in the Pacific didn't turn around until the US unexpectedly routed the Japanese navy at Midway Island in June 1942. In Europe, the US dealt the fatal blow to Germany

Americans Get a New Deal

America reached its lowest point in history during the Great Depression. By 1932, nearly one-third of all US workers were unemployed. National output fell by 50%, hundreds of banks shuttered, and great swaths of the country seemed to disappear beneath enormous dust storms.

Franklin D Roosevelt, elected president in 1932, helped rescue the nation from collapse. He bailed out banks, saved homeowners from foreclosure and added millions of jobs. He created massive projects like the Civilian Conservation Corps, which planted more than two billion trees, and the Works Progress Administration, a 600,000-strong workforce that built bridges, dams and other infrastructure.

1917
President Woodrow Wilson plunges the US into WWI, pledging that 'the world must be made safe for democracy.'

1920
The 19th Amendment is passed, giving US women the right to vote.

1920s
The Harlem Renaissance inspires a burst of African American literature, art, music and cultural pride.

with its massive D-Day invasion of France on June 6, 1944. Germany surrendered the following year.

Nevertheless, Japan continued fighting. Rather than invade the country, President Harry Truman chose to drop experimental atomic bombs (created by the government's top-secret Manhattan Project) on Hiroshima and Nagasaki in August 1945, destroying both cities. Japan surrendered, but the nuclear age was born.

The Red Scare, Civil Rights & the Wars in Asia

In the decades after WWII, the US enjoyed unprecedented prosperity but little peace.

Formerly wartime allies, the communist Soviet Union and the capitalist USA soon engaged in a running competition to dominate the globe. The superpowers engaged in proxy wars – notably the Korean War (1950–53) and Vietnam War (1959–75) – with only the mutual threat of nuclear annihilation preventing direct war. The UN, founded in 1945, couldn't overcome this worldwide ideological split and was largely ineffectual in preventing Cold War conflicts.

Little Rock Central High School, Arkansas, site of pivotal events of the Civil Rights movement

1941–45
The US enters WWII, deploying over 16 million troops and suffering about 400,000 deaths.
WWII soldiers on patrol

1954
In Brown v Board of Education, the Supreme Court ends segregation in public schools.

Meanwhile, with its continent unscarred and its industry bulked up by WWII, the American homeland entered an era of growing affluence. In the 1950s, a mass migration left the inner cities for the suburbs, where affordable single-family homes sprang up. Americans drove cheap cars using cheap gas over brand-new interstate highways. They relaxed with the comforts of modern technology, swooned over TV, and got busy, giving birth to a 'baby boom.'

Middle-class whites did, anyway. African Americans remained segregated, poor and generally unwelcome at the party. Echoing 19th-century abolitionist Frederick Douglass, the Southern Christian Leadership Coalition (SCLC), led by African American preacher Martin Luther King Jr, aimed to end segregation and 'save America's soul': to realize color-blind justice, racial equality and fairness of economic opportunity for all.

Beginning in the 1950s, King preached and organized nonviolent resistance in the form of bus boycotts, marches and sit-ins, mainly in the South. White authorities often met these protests with water hoses and batons, and demonstrations sometimes dissolved into riots, but with the 1964 Civil Rights Act, African Americans spurred a wave of legislation that swept away racist laws and laid the groundwork for a more just and equal society.

Meanwhile, the 1960s saw further social upheavals: rock and roll spawned a youth rebellion, and drugs sent Technicolor visions spinning in their heads. President John F Kennedy was assassinated in Dallas in 1963, followed by the assassinations in 1968 of his brother Senator Robert Kennedy and of Martin Luther King Jr. Americans' faith in their leaders and government was further tested by the bombings and brutalities of the Vietnam War, as seen on TV, which led to widespread student protests.

Yet President Richard Nixon, elected in 1968 partly for promising an 'honorable end to the war,' instead escalated US involvement and secretly bombed Laos and Cambodia. Then, in 1972, the Watergate scandal broke. A burglary at the Democratic

The Civil Rights Movement

From the 1950s, a movement got underway in African American communities to fight for equality. Rosa Parks, who refused to give up her seat to a white passenger on a bus, inspired the Montgomery bus boycott. There were sit-ins at lunch counters where blacks were excluded; massive demonstrations led by Martin Luther King Jr in Washington, DC; and harrowing journeys by 'freedom riders' aiming to end bus segregation. The work of millions paid off: in 1964, President Johnson signed the Civil Rights Act, which banned discrimination and racial segregation by federal law.

1959–75
The US fights the Vietnam War, supporting South Vietnam against communist North Vietnam.

1963
President John F Kennedy is assassinated while riding in a motorcade in Dallas, Texas.

1974
President Richard Nixon resigns after the Watergate scandal erupts.

The Best... Ethnic & Cultural Sites

Party offices was, through dogged journalism, tied to 'Tricky Dick,' and in 1974 he became the first US president to resign from office.

The tumultuous 1960s and '70s also witnessed the sexual revolution, women's liberation, struggles for gay equality, energy crises over the supply of crude oil from the Middle East and, with the 1962 publication of Rachel Carson's *Silent Spring*, the realization that the USA's industries had created a polluted, diseased environmental mess.

Pax Americana & the War on Terror

In 1980, Republican California governor and former actor Ronald Reagan campaigned for president by promising to make Americans feel good about America again. The affable Reagan won easily, and his election marked a pronounced shift to the right in US politics.

Reagan wanted to defeat communism, restore the economy, deregulate business and cut taxes. To tackle the first two, he launched the biggest peacetime military build-up in history, and dared the Soviets to keep up. They went broke trying, one of the many factors that led to the eventual dissolution of the USSR at the end of the decade.

Reagan's military spending and tax cuts created enormous federal deficits, but these were largely erased during the 1990s high-tech internet boom, which seemed to augur a 'new US economy' based on white-collar telecommunications. These hopes and surpluses vanished in 2000, when the high-tech stock bubble burst. That year, after one of the most divisive elections in modern US politics, President George W Bush enacted tax cuts that returned federal deficits to amounts greater than before.

On September 11, 2001, Islamic terrorists flew hijacked planes into New York's World Trade Center and the Pentagon in Washington, DC. This catastrophic attack united Americans behind their president as he vowed revenge and declared a 'war on terror.' Bush soon attacked Afghanistan in an unsuccessful hunt for Al-Qaeda terrorist cells, then he attacked Iraq in 2003 and toppled its anti-US dictator, Saddam Hussein. Meanwhile, Iraq descended into civil war.

Bush's second term was marred by scandals and failures – torture photos from Abu Ghraib, the federal response in the aftermath of Hurricane Katrina and the inability to bring the Iraq War to a close.

1989
The 1960s-era Berlin Wall is torn down, marking the official end of the decades-long Cold War.

1990s
The internet revolution creates the biggest boom and bust since the Great Depression.

2001
The September 11 terrorist attacks destroy NYC's World Trade Center and kill nearly 3000 people.

Promising hope and change, Democrat Barack Obama was elected as the nation's first African American president in 2008, in itself a hopeful sign that the US's long-standing racial divides were healing. However, Obama's New Deal–style initiatives – such as a massive economic stimulus bill and an overhaul of the broken US health-care system – were met with widespread protests from a growing anti-government, conservative 'Tea Party' movement.

President Obama won reelection in 2012, aided in large part by the most ethnically and racially diverse coalition in American history. Over 90% of African Americans and nearly 70% of Latinos voted for the man who described himself as 'a mutt.'

As of 2013, one of Obama's biggest successes has been the passing of the Affordable Care Act (aka 'Obamacare'), making health insurance more affordable and accessible to all. But scandals have marred his presidency, including the Snowden affair, which revealed that the US and UK intelligence communities had been spying not only on foreign nations but on allies as well as American citizens.

Taos Pueblo (p330)

2005
Hurricane Katrina ruptures levees, flooding New Orleans and killing more than 1800 people.

2008–12
Financial mismanagement and a housing market crash cause the US's worst recession since the Great Depression.

2012
Hurricane Sandy devastates the East Coast. More than 80 Americans die (plus 200 more in other countries).

Family Travel

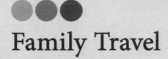

Amusement park, Santa Monica Pier (p382)

LONELY PLANET/GETTY IMAGES ©

The USA generally welcomes families with young travelers. From coast to coast, you'll find superb attractions for all ages: theme parks, zoos, eye-popping aquariums, natural-history exhibits and hands-on science museums. There's also bucket-and-spade fun to be had at the beach, hikes in wilderness reserves and plenty of other activities to wow the young ones. Wherever you go, traveling with children can bring an exciting new dimension to the American experience.

Planning

Weather and crowds are all-important considerations when planning a US family getaway. The peak travel season across the country is June to August, when schools are out and the weather is warmest. Expect high prices and abundant crowds, meaning long lines at amusement and water parks, fully booked resort areas and heavy traffic on the roads; you'll need to reserve well in advance for popular destinations. The same holds true for winter resorts during January to March.

Lodging

Motels and hotels typically have rooms with two beds, which are ideal for families. Some also have roll-away beds or cribs that can be brought into the room for an extra charge, but keep in mind that these are usually 'Pack 'n' Plays,' which not all children sleep well in.

Some hotels offer 'kids stay free' programs for children up to 12 or even sometimes 18 years old. Be wary of B&Bs, as most don't allow children; ask when booking.

Dining with Children

The US restaurant industry seems built on family-style service: children are not just accepted almost everywhere, but are usually catered to, with special children's menus offering smaller portions and lower prices. In some restaurants children under a certain age even eat for free. Some restaurants may also offer crayons and puzzles and, occasionally, live performances by cartoon-like characters.

Restaurants without children's menus don't necessarily discourage kids, though higher-end restaurants might. Even at the nicer places, if you show up early enough (right at dinner-time opening hours), you can usually eat without too much stress – and you'll likely be joined by other foodie couples with kids. You can ask if the kitchen will make a smaller order of a dish (also ask how much it will cost). Chinese, Mexican and Italian restaurants are the best bet for finicky young eaters.

Farmers markets are widespread in the USA, and every sizable town has at least one a week. This is a good place to assemble a first-rate picnic, sample the local specialties and support independent growers in the process. After getting your stash, head to a park or waterfront; there should be at least one nearby.

The Best...
Theme Parks & Animal Spotting

Driving

Every car-rental agency should be able to provide an appropriate child seat, since these are required in every state, but you need to request it when booking and expect to pay around $10 more per day.

Be particularly conservative planning road trips. Distances in the USA can be long, and kids often need extra 'transition time' when traveling. With kids, it can be hard to hit the road early, to drive far without stopping and to keep to regular mealtimes – all of these things can throw off a trip schedule. So keep distances short, don't string driving days together, and always try to arrive an hour before mealtime, so everyone can unwind.

Planes & Trains

Domestic airlines don't charge for children under two. Those aged two and over must have a seat, but discounts are unlikely. Very rarely, some resort areas (like Disneyland) offer a 'kids fly free' promotion. Amtrak and other train operators occasionally run similar deals (with kids up to 15 years old riding free) on various routes.

Need to Know

○ **Change facilities** Found in most public buildings and restaurants.

○ **Cribs (cots)** Available at most hotels.

○ **High chairs** Available at most restaurants, as are booster seats.

○ **Diapers (nappies)** Widely available.

○ **Health** Pack basic medicines; standard of hospital care is excellent.

○ **Children's menus** Often available, and many restaurants are willing to improvise to make a kid-friendly meal.

○ **Strollers** Bring an umbrella stroller.

○ **Transport** Major car-rental firms can supply car seats.

Discounts

Child concessions often apply for tours and admission fees, with some discounts as high as 50% off the adult rate. However, the definition of 'child' can vary from under 6 to under 16 years. Some popular sights also have discount rates for families, which will save a few dollars compared to buying individual tickets. Most sights offer free admission to children under two years.

Helpful Resources

Family Travel Files (www.thefamilytravelfiles.com) Ready-made vacation ideas, destination profiles and travel tips.

Kids.gov (www.kids.gov) Eclectic, enormous national resource; download songs and activities, or even link to the CIA Kids' Page.

Travel with Children For all-around information and advice, check out Lonely Planet's *Travel with Children*.

Local Tips

To find family-oriented sights and activities, accommodations, restaurants and entertainment, just look for the child-friendly icon (⊞) in our reviews.

Food & Drink

California cuisine: shrimp kebabs with tomato and zucchini

BRENT WINEBRENNER/GETTY IMAGES ©

Long before the dawn of competitive cooking shows, molecular gastronomy and organic farm stands, Wampanoag tribes people brought food to help the Pilgrims stave off certain famine over the winter of 1620, thus kicking off the very first Thanksgiving. Since then Americans have mixed myriad food cultures to create their own distinct culinary traditions, based in part on the rich bounty of the continent.

Staples & Specialties

These days you can get almost every type of food nearly everywhere in the US, but regional specialties are always best – sometimes unrecognizably better – in the places they originated.

NYC: Culinary Powerhouse

They say that you could eat at a different restaurant every night of your life in New York City and not exhaust the possibilities. Considering that there are more than 23,000 restaurants in the five boroughs, with constant openings and closings, it's true. Owing to its huge immigrant population and an influx of 50 million tourists annually, New York captures the title of America's greatest restaurant city, hands down. Its diverse neighborhoods serve authentic Italian food and thin crust–style pizza, all manner of Asian food, French *haute cuisine*, and classic Jewish deli food, from

The Best... Local Temptations

1 Boston clam chowder

2 Maine lobster

3 Cajun crawfish

4 Memphis barbecue

5 Chicago deep-dish pizza

6 Santa Fe chili stew

bagels to piled-high pastrami on rye. And the list goes around the globe: Moroccan, Indian, Vietnamese, Russian, Cuban, Brazilian and more. Plus, Manhattan boasts street-cart dining that puts some city restaurant scenes to shame.

Mid-Atlantic: Global Cooking, Crab Cakes & Cheesesteaks

Washington, DC, has a wide array of global fare – not surprising given its ethnically diverse population. In particular, you'll find some of the country's best Ethiopian food. DC also makes fine use of its position near the Chesapeake Bay, offering top crab cakes and seafood. In Philadelphia you can gorge on 'Philly cheese steaks': thin sautéed beef, fried onions and melted cheese on a bun.

New England: Clambakes & Lobster Boils

New England's claim of having the nation's best seafood is hard to beat, because the North Atlantic offers up clams, mussels, oysters and huge lobsters, along with shad, bluefish and cod. New Englanders love a good chowder (seafood stew) and a good clambake, an almost ritual meal where the shellfish are buried in a pit fire with corn, chicken, potatoes and sausages. Fried clam fritters and lobster rolls (lobster meat with mayonnaise served in a bread bun) are served throughout the region. There are excellent cheeses made in Vermont, cranberries (a Thanksgiving staple) harvested in Massachusetts, and maple syrup from New England's forests. Maine's coast is lined with lobster shacks, while baked beans and brown bread are Boston specialties.

The South: Barbecue, Biscuits & Gumbo

No region is prouder of its food culture than the South, which has a long history of mingling Anglo, French, African, Spanish and Native American foods in dishes such as slow-cooked barbecue, which has as many meat and sauce variations as there are towns in the South. Southern fried chicken is crisp outside and moist inside. Breakfasts are as big as can be, and treasured dessert recipes tend to produce big layer cakes, or pies made with pecans, bananas and citrus. Light, fluffy biscuits are served hot and well buttered, and grits (ground corn cooked to a porridge-like consistency) are a passion among Southerners, as are refreshing mint julep cocktails.

Louisiana's legendary cuisine is influenced by colonial French and Spanish cultures, Afro-Caribbean cooking and Choctaw Indian traditions. Cajun food, found in the bayou country, marries native spices such as sassafras and chili peppers with provincial French cooking. Creole food is more urban, and centered on New Orleans, where dishes such as shrimp remoulade, crabmeat ravigote, crawfish étouffée and beignets are ubiquitous.

The Southwest: Chili, Steak & Smokin' Hot Salsa

Two ethnic groups define Southwestern food culture: the Spanish and Mexicans, who controlled territories from Texas to California until well into the 19th century. While there is little actual Spanish food today, the Spanish brought cattle to Mexico, which the Mexicans adapted to their own corn- and chili-based gastronomy. The result is tacos, tortillas, enchiladas, burritos and chimichangas filled with everything from chopped meat and poultry to beans. Don't leave New Mexico without trying a bowl of spicy green-chili stew. Steaks and barbecue are always favorites on Southwestern menus, and beer is the drink of choice for dinner and a night out.

Pacific Northwest: Salmon & Starbucks

The cuisine of this region draws on the traditions of the local Native Americans, whose diets traditionally centered on game, seafood – especially salmon – and foraged mushrooms, fruits and berries. Seattle spawned the modern international coffeehouse craze with Starbucks, while the beers and wines from both Washington and Oregon are of an international standard, especially the Pinot Noirs and Rieslings.

California: Farm-to-Table Restaurants & Taquerías

Owing to its vastness and variety of microclimates, California is the US's cornucopia for fruits and vegetables. The state's natural resources are overwhelming: wild salmon, Dungeness crab and oysters; robust farm produce year-round; and artisanal products such as cheese, bread, olive oil, wine and chocolate. Starting in the 1970s and '80s, star chefs such as Alice Waters and Wolfgang Puck pioneered 'California cuisine' by incorporating the best local ingredients into simple yet delectable dishes. The influx of Asian immigrants, especially after the Vietnam War, enriched the state's urban food cultures with Chinatowns, Koreatowns and Japantowns, along with huge enclaves of Mexican Americans who maintain their own culinary traditions across the state. Don't miss the fist-sized burritos in San Francisco's Mission District and the fish tacos in San Diego.

Wine, Beer & Beyond

Americans have a staggering range of choices when it comes to beverages. A booming microbrewery industry has brought finely crafted beers to every corner of the country. The US wine industry continues to produce first-rate vintages – and it's not just Californian vineyards garnering all the awards.

Craft & Local Beer

Craft beer production is rising meteorically, accounting for 11% of the domestic market in 2010. There are more than 1500 craft breweries across the USA, with Vermont boasting the most per capita. In recent years it has become possible to 'drink local' all over the country.

Vegetarian & Vegan Dining

Some of the most highly regarded US restaurants cater to vegetarians and vegans. Exclusively vegetarian and vegan restaurants abound in major US cities, though not always in small towns and rural areas away from the coasts. Eateries that have a good selection of vegetarian options are noted in our reviews using the vegetarian icon (🥬). Browse restaurants online at www.happycow.net.

Wine

US wines have made an even more dramatic impact: the nation is the world's fourth-largest wine producer, behind Italy, France and Spain. Today almost 90% of US wine comes from California, and Oregon, Washington and New York wines have achieved international status. According to the *LA Times*, 2010 marked the first year that the US actually consumed more wine than France.

The Great Outdoors

Rafting the Colorado River (p304), Grand Canyon National Park

JOHN ELK/GETTY IMAGES ©

Snow-covered peaks, alpine lakes, lunarlike deserts and a dramatic coastline of unrivaled beauty: the USA has no shortage of spectacular settings for a bit of outdoor adventure – and so far, we've described just one state (California). In the other 49 lie an astounding collection of natural wonders, from red-rock canyons and lush rainforests to soaring mountains and vast stretches of wilderness devoid of people but full of endless possibility.

The Land

The USA is big, no question. Covering over 3.5 million sq miles, it's the world's third-largest country, trailing only Russia and its friendly neighbor to the north, Canada. The continental USA is made up of 48 contiguous states ('the lower 48'); Alaska, its largest state, which is northwest of Canada; and the volcanic islands of Hawaii, the 50th state, lying 2600 miles southwest of the mainland in the Pacific Ocean.

It's more than just size, though. The US feels big because of its incredibly diverse topography, which began to take shape around 50 to 60 million years ago.

National Parks

National parks are the big backyards of America. Cross-country road trips connect the dots between the USA's big-shouldered cities, but don't always reach its national parks. There you'll encounter remarkable places, rich in unspoiled wilderness, rare wildlife and rich history.

Some parks look much the same as they did centuries ago, when this nation was just starting out. From craggy islands off the Atlantic Coast, to prairie grasslands and buffalo herds across the Great Plains, to the Rocky Mountains raising their jagged teeth along the Continental Divide, and onward to the tallest trees on earth – coastal redwoods – standing sentinel on Pacific shores, you'll be amazed by the natural bounty.

Wildlife

The USA is home to creatures great and small, from the ferocious grizzly bear to the industrious beaver, with colossal bison, snowy owls, soaring eagles, howling coyotes and doe-eyed manatees all part of the great American menagerie. The nation's varied geography – coastlines along two oceans, mountains, deserts, rainforests and massive bay and river systems – harbor ecosystems where an extraordinary array of plant and animal life can flourish.

Currently, more than 1300 plants and animals in the USA are listed as either endangered or threatened. Although all endangered species are vital to the ecosystem, if it's brag-worthy animals you're keen to see (and photograph), here are places to spot them before (gulp) it's too late:

Bighorn sheep Zion National Park, UT

California condor Big Sur, CA, and Grand Canyon National Park, AZ

Florida panther Everglades National Park, FL

Gray wolf Yellowstone National Park, WY

Manatee Everglades National Park, FL

The Best... Jaw-Dropping Scenery

1 Grand Canyon National Park (p300)

2 Yosemite National Park (p415)

3 Acadia National Park (p198)

4 Zion National Park (p321)

5 Olympic National Park (p355)

6 Death Valley National Park (p396)

Hiking

Fitness-focused Americans take great pride in their formidable network of trails – literally tens of thousands of miles of them. There's no better way to experience the countryside up close and at your own pace.

The wilderness is amazingly accessible for easy exploration. National parks are ideal for short and long hikes; if you long for nights in remote places beneath star-filled skies, plan on securing a backcountry permit in advance (especially in places like the Grand Canyon, where spaces are limited, particularly during summer).

Top Hiking Trails in the USA

Ask 10 people for their top hiking trails and no two answers will be alike. The country is so varied and the distances so enormous, there's little consensus. That said, you can't go wrong with the following all-star sampler.

Appalachian Trail (www.appalachiantrail.org) Completed in 1937, the country's longest footpath is over 2100 miles long, crosses six national parks, traverses eight national forests and hits 14 states from Georgia to Maine.

Pacific Crest Trail (PCT; www.pcta.org) Follows the spines of the Cascades and Sierra Nevada, traipsing 2650 miles from Canada to Mexico, passing through six of North America's seven ecozones.

John Muir Trail (Yosemite National Park, CA) Has 222 miles of scenic bliss, from Yosemite Valley up to Mt Whitney.

Enchanted Valley (Olympic National Park, WA) Magnificent mountain views, roaming wildlife and lush rainforests – all on a 13-mile out-and-back trail.

South Kaibab/North Kaibab Trail (Grand Canyon National Park, AZ) A multiday cross-canyon tramp down to the Colorado River and back up to the rim.

Tahoe Rim Trail (Lake Tahoe, CA) This 165-mile all-purpose trail circumnavigates the lake from high above, affording glistening Sierra views.

Beyond the parks, you'll find troves of trails in every state. Almost anywhere you go will have great hiking and backpacking within easy distance. Just bring a sturdy pair of shoes (sneakers or hiking boots) and a water bottle.

Here are some resources to assist your planning.

American Hiking Society (www.americanhiking.org) Find local hiking clubs or take a 'volunteer vacation' and help build trails.

Backpacker (www.backpacker.com) Premier national magazine for backpackers, from novices to experts.

Rails-to-Trails Conservancy (www.railstotrails.org) Converts abandoned railroad corridors into hiking and biking trails; publishes free trail reviews at www.traillink.com.

Survive Outdoors (www.surviveoutdoors.com) Dispenses safety and first-aid tips, plus helpful photos of dangerous critters.

Wilderness Survival (Gregory Davenport; Stackpole Books, 2006) Easily the best book on surviving nearly every contingency.

Cycling

Cycling's popularity grows by the day in the USA, with many cities (including New York) adding more cycle lanes and becoming more bike-friendly, and an increasing number of greenways dotting the countryside. You'll find die-hard enthusiasts in every town, and numerous outfitters offering guided trips for all levels and durations. For the best advice on rides and rentals, stop by a local bike shop or Google the area you plan to visit.

For our money, these are the country's top cycling towns:

San Francisco, CA A pedal over the Golden Gate Bridge lands you in the stunningly beautiful, and stunningly hilly, Marin Headlands.

Austin, TX This indie rock–loving town has nearly 200 miles of trails and great weather year-round.

Portland, OR A trove of great cycling (on- and off-road) in the Pacific Northwest.

Mountain Biking

Mountain-biking enthusiasts will find trail nirvana in Moab, UT, and Marin, CA, where Gary Fisher and friends bunny-hopped the sport forward by careening down the rocky flanks of Mt Tamalpais on home-rigged bikes.

A few great rides include the following:

Kokopelli's Trail, UT One of the premier mountain-biking trails in the Southwest, the trail stretches 140 miles on mountainous terrain between Loma, CO, and Moab, UT. Other nearby options include the 206-mile, hut-to-hut ride between Telluride, CO, and Moab, UT.

Sun Top Loop, WA A 22-mile ride with challenging climbs and superb views of Mt Rainier and surrounding peaks on the western slopes of Washington's Cascade Mountains.

Porcupine Rim, UT A 30-mile loop from Moab, this venerable high desert romp features stunning views and hairy downhills.

Scuba Diving & Snorkeling

On the continental USA, Florida has the lion's share of great diving, with more than 1000 miles of coastline subdivided into 20 unique undersea areas. There are hundreds of sites and countless dive shops offering equipment and guided excursions. South of West Palm Beach, you'll find clear waters and fantastic year-round diving with ample reefs. In the Panhandle (the northern part of the state), you can scuba in the calm and balmy waters of the Gulf of Mexico; off Pensacola and Destin, there are fabulous wreck dives; and you can dive with manatees near Crystal River.

The Florida Keys, a curving string of 31 islets, are the crown jewel; expect a brilliant mix of marine habitats, North America's only living coral garden and the occasional shipwreck. Key Largo is home to the John Pennekamp Coral Reef State Park, with over 200 miles of underwater bliss.

There's also terrific diving and snorkeling (and much warmer water) just off the mangrove swamps of the Florida Keys, boasting the world's third-largest coral system.

Surfing

The best surf in continental USA breaks off the coast of California. There are loads of options – from the funky and low-key Santa Cruz, to San Francisco's Ocean Beach (a tough spot to learn!) and bohemian Bolinas, 30 miles north. South, you'll find strong swells and Santa Ana winds in San Diego, La Jolla, Malibu and Santa Barbara, all sporting warmer waters, fewer sharks of the great white variety, and a saucy SoCal beach scene. The best conditions are from September to November. Along the coast of Oregon and Washington, you'll find miles and miles of crowd-free beaches and pockets of surfing communities.

Huntington Beach, CA – aka Surf City, USA – is the quintessential surf capital, with perpetual sun and a 'perfect' break, particularly during winter when the winds are calm. A selection of other fine breaks:

Black's Beach, San Diego, CA This 2-mile sandy strip at the base of 300ft cliffs in La Jolla is known as one of the most powerful beach breaks in SoCal, thanks to an underwater canyon just offshore.

Rincon, Santa Barbara, CA Arguably one of the planet's top surfing spots; nearly every major surf champion on the globe has taken Rincon for a ride.

Steamer Lane & Pleasure Point, Santa Cruz, CA There are 11 world-class breaks, including the point breaks over rock bottoms, at these two sweet spots.

Coast Guard Beach, Eastham, MA Part of the Cape Cod National Seashore, this family-friendly beach is known for its consistent shortboard/longboard swell all summer long.

Rock Climbing

Scads of climbers flock to Joshua Tree National Park, an otherworldly shrine in southern California's sun-scorched desert. Amid craggy monoliths and the country's oldest trees, they pay pilgrimage on more than 8000 routes, tackling sheer verticals, sharp edges and bountiful cracks with aplomb. Or not. Fortunately, the top-notch **Joshua Tree Rock Climbing School** (www.joshuatreerockclimbing.com) offers classes for all levels, with local guides leading beginners to experts on 7000 different climbs in the park.

In Zion National Park, UT, multiday canyoneering classes teach the fine art of going *down*: rappelling off sheer sandstone cliffs into glorious, red-rock canyons filled with trees. Some of the sportier pitches are made in dry suits, down the flanks of roaring waterfalls into ice-cold pools.

Surfers at Santa Barbara (p420), California
HUTCH AXILROD/GETTY IMAGES ©

Top National Parks

Acadia, ME (p198) Rocky coastlines and end-of-the-world Atlantic islands.

Everglades, FL (p279) Home to crocs, panthers, manatees and more.

Grand Canyon, AZ (p300) Ancient, colorful chasm carved by the Colorado River.

Great Smoky Mountains, TN (p237) Southern Appalachian woodland with thickly forested ridges.

Mt Rainier, WA (p353) Alpine meadows, high snowfields and a glacier-covered, rumbling giant.

Olympic, WA (p355) Primeval rainforests, mist-clouded mountains and wild Pacific Coast beaches.

Rocky Mountain, CO (p430) Jagged mountain peaks, lakes, streams and pine forests.

Yellowstone, WY (p433) North America's largest intact ecosystem.

Yosemite, CA (p415) Verdant valleys featuring thunderous waterfalls and Sierra Nevada peaks.

Zion, UT (p321) Stunning desert oasis in the heart of red-rock country.

Horseback Riding

Horseback riding is a mighty pleasurable way to survey the landscape. West of the Mississippi River in particular, many national parks are serviced by outfitters offering trail rides. Most last an hour or two; overnight pack trips require reservations. Some great places to saddle up include Grand Canyon National Park, Zion National Park, Bryce Canyon National Park, Yellowstone National Park and Rocky Mountains National Park.

Water Sports

In summer, national parks are great places for getting your feet wet in rivers and lakes. At Maine's Acadia National Park and Washington's San Juan Islands, sea kayaking is one of the highlights. Meanwhile, Everglades National Park offers unforgettable canoeing.

The People

Native American dancer

Native American dancer

JOHN ELK/GETTY IMAGES ©

Many people point to the election of President Barack Obama as proof of the US's multicultural achievements. It's not just his personal story (white mother, black father, Muslim name), or that he's the first African American to be elected president – it's the belief that America is a land of possibility. If you apply yourself you can achieve your dreams: as simplistic as it sounds, it's the core of the national psyche.

Population

'The times they are a-changin', Bob Dylan famously sang, and it could be the theme song for the US's demographics. During the next few decades the country's population will undergo two major shifts: it will become far more Hispanic/Latino, and it will become significantly older. The nation's elderly population will more than double by 2050. One in five Americans will be aged over 65 by then, creating a new challenge: how will the country take care of all of its older citizens?

Multiculturalism

From the get-go, America was called a 'melting pot,' which presumed that newcomers blended into the existing American fabric. It might not be quite that easy but the US hasn't let go of the sentiment completely. On the one hand, diversity is celebrated (Cinco de

Mayo, Martin Luther King Jr Day and Chinese New Year all get their due) and on the other, Americans from all different backgrounds celebrate Independence Day and Thanksgiving.

Immigrants currently make up nearly 13% of the US's population. About one million newcomers immigrate each year – the majority from Mexico, followed by Asia and Europe. Another 11 million or so are in the country illegally. This issue makes many Americans edgy, and immigration is a hot political topic.

Culture Wars

America's biggest schism isn't between religions or even between faith and skepticism: it's between fundamentalist and progressive interpretations within each faith. At the forefront are questions on abortion, contraception, gay equality, stem-cell research, the teaching of evolution, school prayer and government displays of religious icons. The country's Religious Right (the oft used term for evangelical Christians) has pushed these issues onto center stage. This effort has prompted a slew of court cases that have tested the nation's principles on separation of church and state. The fundamentalist-progressive divide remains one of the US's biggest culture wars, and it plays a prominent role in politics, especially during elections.

The Best... Places to See Native American Art

1 National Museum of the American Indian (p105), Washington, DC

2 Heard Museum (p309), Phoenix

3 Wheelwright Museum of the American Indian (p324), Santa Fe

4 Acoma Pueblo (p329), Arizona

Native Americans

Today there are more than three million Native Americans (a fraction of their pre-Columbian numbers) from 500 tribes, speaking some 175 languages and residing in every region of the US. Not surprisingly, North America's indigenous people are an extremely diverse bunch with unique customs and beliefs, molded in part by the landscapes they inhabit – from the Inuit living in the frozen tundra of Alaska, to the many tribes of the arid, mountainous Southwest.

Native Americans today follow diverse paths, as they inherit a legacy left by both their ancestors and the cultures that invaded from outside. Some may be weavers who live on reservations, others may be web designers living in Phoenix. Some plant corn and squash, others seek to harvest the sunshine in solar-energy farms.

Culturally speaking, America's native peoples grapple with questions about how to prosper in contemporary America while protecting their traditions from erosion and their lands from further exploitation, and how to lift their people from poverty and a variety of social and health problems while still maintaining their sense of identity and ties to sacred culture.

The Tribes

The Cherokee, Navajo, Chippewa and Sioux are the largest tribal groupings in the lower 48 (ie barring Alaska and Hawaii). Other well-known tribes include the Choctaw (descendants of a great mound-building society originally based in the Mississippi River

Unbreakable Code

The Navajo's Athabascan tongue is the most spoken Native American language, despite its notorious complexity. In the Pacific Theater during WWII, Navajo 'code talkers' sent and received military messages in Navajo. Japan never broke the code, and the code talkers were considered essential to the US victory.

Valley), the Apache (a nomadic hunter-gatherer tribe that fiercely resisted forced relocation) and the Hopi (a Pueblo people with Southwest roots dating back 2000 years). The Navajo Nation in Arizona is by far the largest reservation by size, though the highest percentage of Native Americans (about 25%) live in California and Oklahoma.

Arts & Crafts

Encyclopedias have been written about the artistic traditions of America's indigenous peoples, which span from ancient rock art to contemporary paintings and literature. In places like the Southwest, Native American art is as intrinsic to the landscape as sagebrush and slot canyons.

An essential feature of most Native American crafts is that everyday function and spiritual beliefs are intertwined. Decoration is not merely pretty, but woven with ceremonial meaning. This is in keeping with Native American religions, which see the entire natural world as infused with living spirit. Some of the most famous crafts include Navajo rugs and turquoise-and-silver jewelry, Southwestern pueblo pottery, Hopi katchinas, Zuni fetishes, Sioux beadwork, Inuit sculptures and Cherokee wood carvings, to name only a few.

Jack Kerouac St, North Beach (p400), San Francisco

RICHARD CUMMINS/GETTY IMAGES ©

The US has always been a chaotic, democratic jumble of high and low cultures: Frank Lloyd Wright and Frank Sinatra, Georgia O'Keeffe and A Chorus Line, The Great Gatsby and Star Wars. Like so much else, America's arts are a pastiche, a crazy mix-and-match quilt of cultures and themes, of ideas borrowed and stolen to create something new, often leaving dramatic new paradigms along the way.

Music

No other US art has been as influential as popular music: blues, jazz, country, rock and roll, and hip-hop are the soundtrack of America's 20th century. The rest of the world has long returned the love, and American music today is a joyful, multicultural feast, a freewheeling blend of genres and styles. To witness it, head to the country's best live-music scenes, in New York City, Nashville, New Orleans, Memphis, Chicago and Austin.

The South is the mother of American music, most of which has roots in the frisson and interplay of black-white racial relations. Blues was the seminal sound, and nearly all subsequent American music has tapped this deep well. It developed out of the work songs of slaves, and black spiritual songs and their 'call-and-response' pattern, both of which were adaptations of African music. Famous musicians include Robert Johnson, Bessie Smith, Muddy Waters, BB King, John Lee Hooker and Buddy Guy.

The birthplace of jazz is New Orleans, where ex-slaves combined African-influenced rhythms with the reed, horn and string instruments of Creole musicians. This fertile cross-pollination has produced a steady stream of innovative sounds: ragtime, Dixieland jazz, big-band swing, bebop and numerous jazz fusions. Major artists include Duke Ellington, Louis Armstrong, Billie Holiday, John Coltrane, Miles Davis and Charles Mingus.

True fiddle-and-banjo country music developed in the Appalachian Mountains, the product of Scottish, Irish and English immigrants. In the Southwest, 'western' music was distinguished by steel guitars and larger bands. These styles merged into 'country-and-western' music in the 1920s, becoming centered on Nashville, TN, while bluegrass music mixed country with jazz and the blues. For the originals, listen to Bill Monroe, Hank Williams, Johnny Cash, Patsy Cline and Loretta Lynn.

Rock and roll, meanwhile, combined guitar-driven blues, rhythm and blues, and country-and-western music. Most say rock and roll was born when Elvis Presley started singing. From the 1950s, it evolved into the anthem for a nationwide social revolution in youth culture.

Finally, hip-hop emerged from 1970s New York, as DJs spun and mixed records, calling out rhymes with a microphone, to spur dance parties. Synonymous with urban street culture, it had become the defining rebel sound of American pop culture by the 1990s.

Classic American Films

WESTERN

High Noon (1952), Fred Zinnemann

The Searchers (1956), John Ford

MUSICAL

42nd Street (1933), Lloyd Bacon

Singin' in the Rain (1952), Stanley Donen & Gene Kelly

GANGSTER

The Maltese Falcon (1941), John Huston

The Godfather trilogy (1972–90), Francis Ford Coppola

Goodfellas (1990), Martin Scorsese

Pulp Fiction (1994), Quentin Tarantino

DRAMA

Gone with the Wind (1939), Victor Fleming

Citizen Kane (1941), Orson Welles

Rear Window (1954), Alfred Hitchcock

Rocky (1976), John Avildsen

COMEDY

The Gold Rush (1925), Charlie Chaplin

Some Like It Hot (1959), Billy Wilder

Dr Strangelove (1964), Stanley Kubrick

Annie Hall (1977), Woody Allen

Film & TV

What would the US be without movies and TV? They are like the nation's mirror, where America checks its hair and profile before going out. That's fitting, as both mediums were essentially invented here.

Though France was developing similar technology, Thomas Edison is credited with creating the first motion pictures and the first movie studio, in New Jersey in the 1890s. Early films including *The Great Train Robbery* (1903) and *Birth of a Nation* (1915) introduced much of cinema's now-familiar language, such as the fade, close-up and flashback. In the 1920s, Hollywood established itself as the home of the film studios, and the rest, as they say, is history – very glamorous, celebrity-studded, Cinemascope-size history.

The first commercial TV set was introduced at the 1939 New York World's Fair. By the 1950s and 1960s, TV outshone the movies, nearly killing the film studios, and by the 1990s, the handful of original stations had multiplied into hundreds. For a long time, TV was looked down on as the doughy middle of US culture – the 'boob tube' – yet today many TV programs exhibit depth and storytelling that surpass that of cinema.

Literature

The greatest American novel remains *Huckleberry Finn* (1884), written by Samuel Clemens (aka Mark Twain), whose satirical humor and vernacular style came to define American letters.

After WWI, American novelists came into their own. They were revolutionary in style, and became often sharp critics of a newly industrialized, and later suburbanized, 20th-century American society. There are too many excellent, important writers to name, but a short list of those who are essential for understanding American literature include Ernest Hemingway (*The Sun Also Rises*, 1926), John Steinbeck (*The Grapes of Wrath*, 1939), William Faulkner (*The Sound and the Fury*, 1929), Zora Neale Hurston (*Their Eyes Were Watching God*, 1937), Flannery O'Connor (*Wise Blood*, 1952), Allen Ginsberg (*Howl*, 1956), Jack Kerouac (*On the Road*, 1957) and Toni Morrison (*The Bluest Eye*, 1970). Notable contemporary writers include Don DeLillo, Dave Eggers, Jonathan Lethem and Michael Chabon.

Visual Arts

Painting in the US did not draw much attention until the advent of abstract expressionism. Exposed to the shockwaves of European modernism in the early 20th century, America's artists found their voice after WWII. New York painters Franz Kline, Jackson Pollock and Mark Rothko pushed abstract expressionism to its extremes, throwing color and movement across epic canvases. In the 1960s, the US's other definitive style – pop art – developed in response to this: Jasper Johns, Robert Rauschenberg and Andy Warhol playfully blurred the line between art and commerce. Pop art co-opted media images, comics, advertising and product packaging in a self-conscious ironic wink that is now the media age America lives and breathes.

Minimalism followed, swinging back toward abstraction and emphasizing mixed media and installation art; major artists included Sol LeWitt, James Turrell, Richard Serra and Richard Tuttle. By the 1980s, civil rights, feminism and AIDS activism had made inroads in visual culture. Artists not only voiced political dissent through their work but embraced a range of once-marginalized media, from textiles and graffiti to video, sound and performance. To get the pulse of contemporary art in the US, check out works by artists such as Jenny Holzer, Kara Walker, Chuck Close, Martin Puryear and Frank Stella.

The Best...
Art
Museums

1 Metropolitan Museum of Art (p72), NYC

2 Museum of Modern Art (p67), NYC

3 National Gallery of Art (p105), Washington, DC

4 Art Institute of Chicago (p137)

5 Museum of Fine Arts (p169), Boston

6 Los Angeles County Museum of Art (p379)

Baseball game, Fenway Park (p177), Boston

What really draws Americans together – sometimes slathered in blue body paint or with foam-rubber cheese wedges atop their heads – is sports. It provides an important social glue, so whether a person is conservative or liberal, married or single, Mormon or pagan, chances are that come Monday at the office they'll be chatting about the weekend performance of their favorite team.

Seasons

The fun and games go on all year long. In spring and summer there's a baseball game nearly every day. In fall and winter, a weekend or Monday night doesn't feel right without a football game on, and through the long days and nights of winter, there's plenty of basketball to keep the adrenaline going.

Baseball

Despite high salaries and steroid rumors dogging its biggest stars, baseball remains America's favorite pastime. It may not command the same TV viewership (and subsequent advertising dollars) as football, but baseball teams have 162 games over a season, versus 16 for football.

Besides, baseball isn't to be experienced on TV – it's all about the live version: being at the ballpark on a sunny day, sitting in the bleachers with a beer and hot dog and indulging in the seventh-inning stretch, when the entire park erupts in a communal sing-along of 'Take Me Out to the Ballgame.' The final play-offs, held every October, still deliver excitement and unexpected champions. The New York Yankees, Boston Red Sox and Chicago Cubs continue to be the favorite teams, even when they're abysmal (the Cubs haven't won a World Series in over 100 years).

Tickets are relatively inexpensive – seats average about $15 at most stadiums – and are easy to get for most games. Minor-league baseball games cost half as much, and can be even more fun, with lots of audience participation, stray chickens and dogs running across the field and wild throws from the pitcher's mound. For more information, go to www.minor leaguebaseball.com.

Football

Football is big, physical and rolling in dough. With the shortest season and least number of games of any of the major sports, every match takes on the emotion of an epic battle, where the results matter and an unfortunate injury can deal a lethal blow to a team's play-off chances.

Football's also the toughest because it's played in fall and winter in all manner of rain, sleet and snow. Some of history's most memorable matches have occurred at below-freezing temperatures. Green Bay Packers fans are in a class by themselves when it comes to severe weather. Their stadium in Wisconsin, known as Lambeau Field, was the site of the infamous Ice Bowl, a 1967 championship game against the Dallas Cowboys where the temperature plummeted to 13°F below zero – mind you, that was with a wind-chill factor of -48°F.

Different teams have dominated different decades: the Pittsburgh Steelers in the 1970s, the San Francisco 49ers in the 1980s, the Cowboys in the 1990s and the New England Patriots in the 2000s. The pro league's official website (www.nfl.com) is packed with information. Tickets are expensive and hard to get, which is why many fans congregate in bars to watch televised games instead.

Even college and high-school football games enjoy an intense amount of pomp and circumstance, with cheerleaders, marching bands, mascots, songs and mandatory pre- and post-game rituals, especially 'tailgating' – a full-blown beer-and-barbecue feast that takes place over portable grills in parking lots where games are played.

The rabidly popular Super Bowl is pro football's championship match, held in late January or early February. The other 'bowl' games (such as the Rose Bowl and the Orange Bowl) are college football's title matches, held on and around New Year's Day.

Start Your Engines

Nascar – officially, the National Association for Stock Car Auto Racing – has played an unusual role in US culture. It flew under the radar for years, mostly thrilling fans in the southeast, where it originated. Money started to flow in during the 1990s, and it burst onto the national scene in a big way in 2002.

The Sprint Cup is the top-tier tour, with the Daytona 500 being the year's biggest race, attracting more than 180,000 spectators.

The Best...
Places to See
a Pro Game

1 Fenway Park, Boston

2 Wrigley Field, Chicago

3 Dodger Stadium, Los Angeles

4 Yankee Stadium, NYC

5 Sun Life Stadium, Miami

6 Nationals Park, Washington, DC

Basketball

The teams bringing in the most fans these days include the Chicago Bulls (thanks to the lingering Michael Jordan effect), the Detroit Pistons (a rowdy crowd where riots have broken out), the Cleveland Cavaliers, the San Antonio Spurs and, last but not least, the Los Angeles Lakers, who won five championships between 2000 and 2010. Small-market teams such as Philadelphia and Portland have true-blue fans, and such cities can be great places to take in a game.

College-level basketball also draws millions of fans, especially every spring when March Madness rolls around. This series of college play-off games culminates in the Final Four, when the four remaining teams compete for a spot in the championship game. The games are widely televised, and bet upon – this is when Las Vegas bookies earn their keep – and their Cinderella stories and unexpected outcomes rival the pro league for excitement.

Survival Guide

Cyclists on the Vera Katz Eastbank Esplanade along the Willamette River, Portland (p358)

ANTHONY PIDGEON/GETTY IMAGES ®

A-Z
Directory

Accommodations

For all but the cheapest places and the slowest seasons, reservations are advised. In high-season tourist hot spots, hotels can book up months ahead. Online travel booking, bidding and comparison websites are another good way to find discounted hotel rates – but they are usually limited to chain hotels. You can also check out **Hotels.com** (www. hotels.com), **Hotwire** (www. hotwire.com) and **Booking. com** (www.booking.com).

B&Bs

In the USA, many Bed & Breakfasts are high-end romantic retreats in restored historic homes that are run by personable, independent innkeepers who serve gourmet breakfasts. The owners of these B&Bs often take pains to evoke a theme – Victorian, rustic, Cape Cod and so on – and amenities range from merely comfortable to indulgent. Rates normally top $100, and the best run are $200 to $300. Some B&Bs have minimum-stay requirements, and most exclude young children.

Some online resources:

Bed & Breakfast Inns Online (www.bbonline.com)

BedandBreakfast.com (www.bedandbreakfast.com)

BnB Finder (www.bnbfinder. com)

Select Registry (www. selectregistry.com)

Book Your Stay Online

For more accommodations reviews by Lonely Planet authors, check out http://hotels. lonelyplanet.com. You'll find independent reviews, as well as recommendations on the best places to stay. Best of all, you can book online.

Hotels

Hotels in all categories typically include in-room phones, cable TV, private baths and a simple continental breakfast. Many midrange properties provide minibars, microwaves, hairdryers, internet access, air-conditioning and/or heating, swimming pools and writing desks, while top-end hotels add concierge services, fitness and business centers, spas, restaurants, bars and higher-end furnishings.

Even if hotels advertise that children 'sleep free,' cots or rollaway beds may cost extra. Always ask about the hotel's policy for telephone calls; all charge an exorbitant amount for long-distance and international calls, but some also charge for dialing local and toll-free numbers.

Motels

Motels – distinguishable from hotels by having rooms that open onto a parking lot – tend to cluster around interstate exits and on main routes into town. Some remain smaller, less-expensive 'mom-and-pop' operations; breakfast is rarely included, and amenities might be a phone and TV (maybe with cable). Motels often have

Climate

New York City

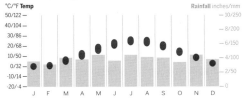

New Orleans

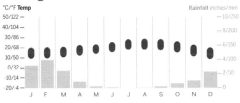

Los Angeles

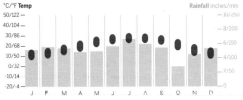

●●●
Electricity

120V/60Hz

120V/60Hz

a few rooms with simple kitchenettes.

●●●
Customs Regulations

For a complete list of US customs regulations, visit the official portal for **US Customs & Border Protection** (www.cbp.gov).

Duty-free allowance per person is as follows:

o 1L of liquor (provided you are at least 21 years old)

o 100 cigars and 200 cigarettes (if you are at least 18)

o $200 worth of gifts and purchases ($800 if you're a returning US citizen)

o If you arrive with $10,000 in US or foreign currency, it must be declared.

There are heavy penalties for attempting to import illegal drugs. Forbidden items include drug paraphernalia, lottery tickets, items with fake brand names, and most goods made in Cuba, Iran, North Korea, Myanmar (Burma) and Sudan. Fruit, vegetables or other food or plant material must be declared or left in the arrival area bins.

●●●
Food

See p461 for everything you need to know about food culture in the USA.

Food Prices

Rates for main meals in Eating sections are:

$ less than $10

$$ $10 to $20

$$$ more than $20

Gay & Lesbian Travelers

It's never been a better time to be gay in the USA. Gay, lesbian, bisexual and transgender (GLBT) travelers will find lots of places where they can be themselves without thinking twice. Beaches and big cities typically are the most gay-friendly destinations.

Hot Spots

Manhattan has loads of great gay bars and clubs, especially in Hells Kitchen, Chelsea and the West Village. Other East Coast cities that flaunt it are Boston, Philadelphia, Washington, DC and Massachusetts' Provincetown on Cape Cod.

In Florida, Miami and the 'Conch Republic' of Key West support thriving gay communities. Of course, everyone gets their freak on in New Orleans.

In the Midwest, seek out Chicago. Further west, you'll find San Francisco, probably the happiest gay city in America. There's also Los Angeles and Las Vegas, where pretty much anything goes.

Lastly, for an island idyll, Hawaii is generally gay-friendly, especially in Waikiki.

Attitudes

Most major US cities have a visible and open GLBT community that is easy to connect with.

The level of acceptance varies nationwide. In some places, there is absolutely no tolerance whatsoever, and in others acceptance is predicated on GLBT people not 'flaunting' their sexual preference or identity. Bigotry still exists. In rural areas and conservative enclaves, it's unwise to be openly out, as violence and verbal abuse can sometimes occur.

Resources

Advocate (www.advocate.com) Gay-oriented news website reports on business, politics, arts, entertainment and travel.

Gay Travel (www.gaytravel.com) Online guides to dozens of US destinations.

Gay Yellow Network (www.glyp.com) Yellow-page listings for more than 30 US cities.

National Gay & Lesbian Task Force (www.thetaskforce.org) National activist group's website covers news, politics and current issues.

Purple Roofs (www.purpleroofs.com) Lists gay-owned and gay-friendly B&Bs and hotels.

Health

Planning

The USA offers excellent health care. The problem is that, unless you have good insurance, it can be prohibitively expensive. It's essential to purchase travel health insurance if your regular policy doesn't cover you when you're abroad.

Bring any medications you may need in their original containers, clearly labeled. A signed, dated letter from your physician that describes all medical conditions and medications, including generic names, is also a good idea.

If your health insurance does not cover you for medical expenses abroad, consider supplemental insurance. Check the Travel Services section of the **Lonely Planet** (www.lonelyplanet.com/usa) website for more information. Find out in advance if your insurance plan will make payments directly to providers or reimburse you later for overseas health expenditures.

Availability & Cost Of Health Care

In general, if you have a medical emergency the best bet is for you to find the nearest hospital and go to its emergency room. If the problem isn't urgent, you can call a nearby hospital and ask for a referral to a local physician, which is usually cheaper than a trip to the emergency room. Stand-alone, for-profit urgent-care centers can be convenient, but may perform large numbers of expensive tests, even for minor illnesses.

Pharmacies are abundantly supplied, but you may find that some medications that are available over the counter in your home country (such as Ventolin, for asthma) require a prescription in the USA and, as always, if you don't have insurance to cover the cost of prescriptions, they can be shockingly expensive.

Insurance

No matter how long or short your trip, make sure you have adequate travel insurance, purchased before departure. At a minimum, you need coverage for medical emergencies and treatment, including hospital stays and an emergency flight home if necessary. Medical treatment in the USA is of the highest caliber, but the expense could bankrupt you.

You should also consider getting coverage for luggage theft or loss and trip cancellation.

If you will be driving, it's essential that you have liability insurance. Car-rental agencies offer insurance that covers damage to the rental vehicle and separate liability insurance, which covers damage to people and other vehicles.

Worldwide travel insurance is available at http://www.lonelyplanet.com/travel-insurance. You can buy, extend and claim online anytime – even if you're already on the road.

Internet Access

Travelers will have few problems staying connected in the tech-savvy USA.

This guide uses an internet icon (@) when a place has a net-connected computer for public use and the wi-fi icon (📶) when it offers wireless internet access, whether free or fee-based. These days, most hotels and some motels have either a public computer terminal or wi-fi (sometimes free, sometimes for a surcharge of $10 or more per day); ask when reserving.

Big cities have a few internet cafes and even wi-fi-connected parks and plazas, but in smaller towns, you may have to head to the public library or a copy center to get online if you're not packing a laptop or other web-accessible device. Most libraries have public terminals (though they have time limits) and often wi-fi.

Legal Matters

In everyday matters, if you are stopped by the police, bear in mind that there is no system of paying traffic or other fines on the spot. Attempting to pay a fine to an officer is frowned upon at best and may result in a charge of bribery. For traffic offenses, the police officer or highway patroller will explain the options to you. There is usually a 30-day period to pay a fine. Most matters can be handled by mail.

If you are arrested, you have a legal right to an attorney, and you are allowed to remain silent. There is no legal reason to speak to a police officer if you don't wish to, but never walk away from an officer until given permission to do so. Anyone who is arrested is legally allowed to make one phone call. If you can't afford a lawyer, a public defender will be appointed to you free of charge. Foreign visitors who don't have a lawyer, friend or family member to help should call their embassy; the police will provide the number upon request.

As a matter of principle, the US legal system presumes a person innocent until proven guilty. Each state has its own civil and criminal laws, and what is legal in one state may be illegal in others.

Drinking

Bars and stores often ask for photo ID to prove you are of legal drinking age (ie 21 or over). Being 'carded' is standard practice; don't take it personally. The sale of liquor is subject to local government regulations; some counties prohibit liquor sales on Sunday, after midnight or before breakfast. In 'dry' counties, liquor sales are banned altogether.

Driving

In all states, driving under the influence of alcohol or drugs is a serious offense, subject to stiff fines and even imprisonment.

Drugs

Fifteen states treat possession of small amounts of marijuana as a misdemeanor (generally punishable with a fine of around $100 or $200 for the first offense).

Practicalities

○ **Electricity** AC 110V is standard; buy adapters to run most non-US electronics.

○ **Newspapers & Magazines** National newspapers: *New York Times, Wall Street Journal, USA Today.* Mainstream news magazines: *Time, Newsweek, US News & World Report.*

○ **Radio & TV** Radio news: National Public Radio (NPR), lower end of FM dial. Broadcast TV: ABC, CBS, NBC, FOX, PBS (public broadcasting). Major cable channels: CNN (news), ESPN (sports), HBO (movies), Weather Channel.

○ **Video & DVD Systems** Videos are NTSC standard (incompatible with PAL or SECAM). DVDs are coded for Region 1 (US and Canada only).

○ **Weights & Measures** Weight: ounces (oz), pounds (lb), tons. Liquid: oz, pints, quarts, gallons (gal). Distance: feet (ft), yards (yd), miles (mi).

at least one credit card, if only for emergencies. Visa and MasterCard are the most widely accepted.

If your credit cards are lost or stolen, contact the issuing company immediately:

American Express (☎ 800-528-4800; www.americanexpress.com)

Diners Club (☎ 800-234-6377; www.dinersclub.com)

Discover (☎ 800-347-2683; www.discover.com)

MasterCard (☎ 800-627-8372; www.mastercard.com)

Visa (☎ 800-847-2911; www.visa.com)

In addition, Colorado and Washington have legalized marijuana – though it is still illegal to smoke in public in either state. Colorado's first retail marijuana stores opened in 2014.

Aside from marijuana, recreational drugs are prohibited by federal and state laws. Possession of any illicit drug, including cocaine, ecstasy, LSD, heroin, hashish or more than an ounce of pot, is a felony potentially punishable by a lengthy jail sentence. For foreigners, conviction of any drug offense is grounds for deportation. The exception is if it is your first conviction and it is for possessing 30 grams or less of marijuana for your own use.

Money

Most locals do not carry large amounts of cash for everyday use, relying instead on credit cards, ATMs and debit cards. Smaller businesses may refuse to accept bills larger than $20. Prices quoted in this book are in US dollars and exclude taxes, unless otherwise noted.

ATMs

ATMs are available 24/7 at most banks, and in shopping centers, airports, grocery stores and convenience shops. Most ATMs charge a service fee of $2.50 or more per transaction and your home bank may impose additional charges.

Credit Cards

Major credit cards are almost universally accepted. In fact, it's almost impossible to rent a car or make phone reservations without one (some airlines require your credit-card billing address to be in the USA – a hassle if you're booking domestic flights once there). It's highly recommended that you carry

Currency Exchange

Banks are usually the best places to exchange foreign currencies. Most large city banks offer currency exchange, but banks in rural areas may not. Currency-exchange counters at the airport and in tourist centers typically have the worst rates; ask about fees and surcharges first.

Taxes

Sales tax varies by state and county, and ranges from 5% to 9%. Hotel taxes vary by city from about 10% to over 18% (in NYC).

Tipping

Tipping is *not* optional; only withhold tips in cases of outrageously bad service.

Airport & hotel porters $2 per bag, minimum per cart $5

Bartenders 10% to 15% per round, minimum per drink $1

Hotel maids $2 to $4 per night, left under the card provided

Restaurant servers 15% to 20%, unless a gratuity is already charged on the bill

Taxi drivers 10% to 15%, rounded up to the next dollar

Valet parking attendants At least $2 when handed back the keys

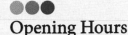

Opening Hours

Typical normal opening times are as follows:

Bars 5pm to midnight Sunday to Thursday, to 2am Friday and Saturday

Banks 8:30am to 4:30pm Monday to Thursday, to 5:30pm Friday (and possibly 9am to noon Saturday)

Nightclubs 10pm to 2am or 4am Thursday to Saturday

Post offices 9am to 5pm Monday to Friday

Shopping Malls 9am to 9pm; stores 10am to 6pm Monday-Saturday, noon to 5pm Sunday; supermarkets 8am to 8pm, some open 24 hours

Public Holidays

On the following national public holidays, banks, schools and government offices (including post offices) are closed, and transportation, museums and other services operate on a Sunday schedule. Holidays falling on a weekend are usually observed the following Monday.

New Year's Day January 1

Martin Luther King Jr Day Third Monday in January

Presidents' Day Third Monday in February

Memorial Day Last Monday in May

Independence Day July 4

Labor Day First Monday in September

Columbus Day Second Monday in October

Veterans' Day November 11

Thanksgiving Fourth Thursday in November

Christmas Day December 25

During spring break, high school and college students get a week off from school so they can overrun beach towns and resorts. This occurs throughout March and April. For students of all ages, summer vacation runs from June to August.

Safe Travel

Despite its seemingly apocalyptic list of dangers – violent crime, riots, earthquakes, tornadoes – the USA is actually a pretty safe country to visit. The greatest danger for travelers is posed by car accidents (buckle up – it's the law).

For the traveler it's not violent crime but petty theft that is the biggest concern. When possible, withdraw money from ATMs during the day, or at night in well-lit, busy areas. When driving, don't pick up hitchhikers, and lock valuables in the trunk of your car before arriving at your destination. In hotels, you can secure valuables in room or hotel safes.

Telephone

The US phone system comprises regional service providers, competing long-distance carriers and several mobile-phone and pay-phone companies.

Cell Phones

In the USA cell phones use GSM 1900 or CDMA 800, operating on different frequencies from other systems around the world. The only foreign phones that will work in the USA are GSM tri- or quad-band models. If you have one of these phones, check with your service provider about using it in the USA. Ask if roaming charges apply, as these will turn even local US calls into pricey international calls.

It might be cheaper to buy a compatible prepaid SIM card for the USA, like those sold by AT&T, which you can insert into your international mobile phone to get a local phone number and voicemail.

If you don't have a compatible phone, you can buy inexpensive, no-contract (prepaid) phones with a local number and a set number of minutes, which can be topped up at will. Virgin Mobile, T-Mobile, AT&T and other providers offer phones starting at US$10, with a package of minutes starting around $40 for 400 minutes. Electronics stores such as Radio Shack and Best Buy sell these phones.

Dialing Codes

All phone numbers within the USA consist of a three-digit area code followed by a seven-digit local number. If you are calling long distance, dial 🕽1 plus the area code plus the phone number.

○ 🕽1 is the international country code for the USA if calling from abroad (the same as Canada, but international rates apply between the two countries).

○ Dial 🕽011 to make an international call from the USA (followed by country code, area code and phone number)

○ Dial 🕽00 for assistance making international calls

○ Dial 🕽411 for directory assistance nationwide

○ 🕽800-555-1212 is directory assistance for toll-free numbers

Pay Phones

Pay phones are an endangered species in an ever-expanding mobile-phone world. Local calls at pay phones that work (listen for a dial tone before inserting coins) cost 35¢ to 50¢ for the first few minutes; talking longer costs more.

Phone Cards

A prepaid phone card is a good solution for travelers on a budget. Phone cards are easy to find in larger towns and cities, where they are sold at newsstands, convenience stores, supermarkets and major retailers.

●●●
Time

The USA uses Daylight Saving Time (DST). On the second Sunday in March, clocks are set one hour ahead ('spring forward'). Then, on the first Sunday of November, clocks are turned back one hour ('fall back'). To keep you on your toes, Arizona (except the Navajo Nation), Hawaii and much of Indiana don't follow DST.

●●●
Tourist Information

The official tourism website of the USA is www.discover america.com. It has links to every US state and territory tourism office and website, plus loads of ideas for itinerary planning.

●●●
Travelers with Disabilities

If you have a physical disability, the USA can be an accommodating place. The Americans with Disabilities Act (ADA) requires that all public buildings, private buildings built after 1993 (including hotels, restaurants,

theaters and museums) and public transit be wheelchair accessible. However, call ahead to confirm what is available. Some local tourist offices publish detailed accessibility guides.

Telephone companies offer relay operators, available via teletypewriter (TTY) numbers, for the hearing impaired. Most banks provide ATM instructions in Braille and via earphone jacks for hearing-impaired customers. All major airlines, Greyhound buses and Amtrak trains will assist travelers with disabilities; just describe your needs when making reservations at least 48 hours in advance. Service animals (guide dogs) are allowed to accompany passengers, but bring documentation.

Some car-rental agencies, such as Budget and Hertz, offer hand-controlled vehicles and vans with wheelchair lifts at no extra charge, but you must reserve them well in advance. **Wheelchair Getaways** (🕽800-642-2042; www.wheelchairgetaways. com) rents accessible vans throughout the USA. In many cities and towns, public buses are accessible to wheelchair riders and will 'kneel' if you are unable to use the steps; just let the driver know that you need the lift or ramp.

Most cities have taxi companies with at least one accessible van, though you'll have to call ahead. Cities with underground transport have elevators for passengers needing assistance; DC has the best network (every station has an elevator); NYC's elevators are few and far between.

Many national and some state parks and recreation areas have wheelchair-accessible paved, graded dirt or boardwalk trails. US citizens and permanent residents with permanent disabilities are entitled to a free 'America the Beautiful' Access Pass. Go online (www.nps.gov/findapark/passes.htm) for details.

Some helpful resources for travelers with disabilities:

Disabled Sports USA (📞 301-217-0960; www.disabledsportsusa.org) Offers sports and recreation programs for those with disabilities and publishes *Challenge* magazine.

Flying Wheels Travel (📞 877-451-5006, 507-451-5005; www.flyingwheelstravel.com) A full-service travel agency, highly recommended for those with mobility issues or chronic illness.

Mobility International USA (📞 541-343-1284; www.miusa.org) Advises disabled travelers on mobility issues

and runs educational international exchange programs.

Visas

Be warned that all of the following information is highly subject to change. US entry requirements keep evolving as national security regulations change. All travelers should double-check current visa and passport regulations *before* coming to the USA.

The **US State Department** (www.travel.state.gov/visa) maintains the most comprehensive visa information, providing downloadable forms, lists of US consulates abroad and even visa wait times calculated by country. Apart from most Canadian citizens and those entering under the Visa Waiver Program, all foreign visitors will need to obtain a visa from a US consulate or embassy abroad.

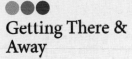

Transport

Getting There & Away

Flights and tours can be booked online at www.lonely-planet.com/booking.

Entering the USA

If you are flying to the US, the first airport that you land in is where you must go through immigration and customs, even if you are continuing on the flight to another destination. Upon arrival, all international visitors must register with the Department of Homeland Security's Office

---

Visa Waiver Program

Currently under the Visa Waiver Program (VWP), citizens of the following countries may enter the USA without a visa for stays of 90 days or fewer: Andorra, Australia, Austria, Belgium, Brunei, Chile, Czech Republic, Denmark, Estonia, Finland, France, Germany, Greece, Hungary, Iceland, Ireland, Italy, Japan, Latvia, Liechtenstein, Lithuania, Luxembourg, Malta, Monaco, the Netherlands, New Zealand, Norway, Portugal, San Marino, Singapore, Slovakia, Slovenia, South Korea, Spain, Sweden, Switzerland, Taiwan and the UK.

If you are a citizen of a VWP country, you do not need a visa *only if* you have a passport that meets current US standards *and* you have gotten approval from the Electronic System for Travel Authorization (ESTA) in advance. Register online with the Department of Homeland Security at https://esta.cbp.dhs.gov/esta at least 72 hours before arrival; once travel authorization is approved, your registration is valid for two years. The fee, payable online, is $14.

Climate Change & Travel

Every form of transport that relies on carbon-based fuel generates CO_2, the main cause of human-induced climate change. Modern travel is dependent on airplanes, which might use less fuel per mile per person than most cars but travel much greater distances. The altitude at which aircraft emit gases (including CO_2) and particles also contributes to their climate change impact. Many websites offer 'carbon calculators' that allow people to estimate the carbon emissions generated by their journey and, for those who wish to do so, to offset the impact of the greenhouse gases emitted with contributions to portfolios of climate-friendly initiatives throughout the world. Lonely Planet offsets the carbon footprint of all staff and author travel.

of Biometric Identity Management program, which entails having your fingerprints scanned and a digital photo taken.

Once you go through immigration, you collect your baggage and pass through customs. If you are continuing on the same plane or connecting to another one, it is your responsibility to get your bags to the right place. There are usually airline representatives just outside the customs area who can help you.

 Air

Airports

The USA has more than 375 domestic airports, but only a handful are the main international gateways.

International gateway airports in the USA:

Logan International Airport (Boston; www.massport.com/logan)

O'Hare International Airport (Chicago; www.ohare.com)

Honolulu International Airport (http://hawaii.gov/hnl)

Los Angeles (LAX; www.lawa.org/lax)

Miami International Airport (MIA; www.miamiairport.com)

John F Kennedy (JFK; New York; www.panynj.gov)

Liberty International (EWR; Newark; www.panynj.gov)

San Francisco International Airport (SFO; www.flysfo.com)

Seattle-Tacoma International Airport (SEA; www.portseattle.org/Sea-Tac)

Dulles International Airport (Washington, DC; www.metwashairports.com/dulles)

Tickets

Flying midweek and in the off-season (usually fall to spring, excluding holidays) is always less expensive, but fare wars can start any time. To ensure you've found the cheapest possible ticket for the flight you want, check every angle: compare several online travel booking sites with the airline's own website. Engage a living, breathing travel agent if your itinerary is complex.

Meta sites like **Kayak** (www.kayak.com) and **Hipmunk** (www.hipmunk.com) are good for price comparisons, as they gather from many sources (but don't provide direct booking).

Bidding for travel can be very successful, but read the fine print carefully before bidding. Try **Hotwire** (www.hotwire.com), **Skyauction** (www.skyauction.com) and **Priceline** (www.priceline.com).

Getting Around

✈ Air

When time is tight, book a flight. The domestic air system is extensive and reliable, with dozens of competing airlines, hundreds of airports and thousands of flights daily. Flying is usually more expensive than traveling by bus, train or car, but it's the way to go when you're in a hurry. Overall, air travel in the USA is very safe (much safer than driving out on the nation's highways); for comprehensive details by carrier, check out **Airsafe.com** (www.airsafe.com).

The main domestic carriers:

AirTran Airways (☎ 800-247-8726; www.airtran.com) Atlanta-based airline; primarily serves the South, Midwest and eastern US.

Alaska Airlines (800-252-7522; www.alaskaair.com) Has direct flights to Anchorage from Seattle, Chicago, Los Angeles and Denver.

American Airlines (800-433-7300; www.aa.com) Nationwide service.

Delta Air Lines (800-221-1212; www.delta.com) Nationwide service.

Frontier Airlines (800-432-1359; www.flyfrontier.com) Denver-based airline with nationwide service, including to Alaska.

Hawaiian Airlines (800-367-5320; www.hawaiianair.com)

JetBlue Airways (800-538-2583; www.jetblue.com) Nonstop connections between eastern and western US cities, plus Florida, New Orleans and Texas.

Southwest Airlines (SWA; 800-435-9792; www.southwest.com) Service across the continental USA.

Spirit Airlines (801-401-2200; www.spiritair.com) Florida-based airline; serves many US gateway cities.

United Airlines (800-864-8331; www.united.com) Nationwide service.

US Airways (800-428-4322; www.usairways.com) Flies between Flagstaff, AZ, and Sky Harbor International Airport in Phoenix.

Virgin America (877-359-8474; www.virginamerica.com) Flights between East and West Coast cities and Las Vegas.

Bicycle

Regional bicycle touring is popular. It means coasting winding backroads (because bicycles are often not permitted on freeways), and calculating progress in miles per day, not miles per hour. Cyclists must follow the same rules of the road as automobiles, but don't expect drivers to respect your right of way. **Better World Club** (www.betterworldclub.com) offers a bicycle roadside assistance program.

For epic cross-country journeys, get the support of a tour operator; it's about two months of dedicated pedaling coast to coast.

For advice, and lists of local bike clubs and repair shops, browse the website of the League of American Bicyclists (www.bikeleague.org). If you're bringing your own bike to the USA, be sure to call around to check oversize luggage prices and restrictions. Amtrak trains and Greyhound buses will transport bikes within the USA, sometimes charging extra.

It's not hard to buy a bike once you're here and resell it before you leave. Every city and town has bike shops; if you prefer a cheaper, used bicycle, try garage sales, bulletin boards at hostels and colleges, or the free classified ads at **Craigslist** (www.craigslist.org). These are also the best places to sell your bike, though stores selling used bikes may also buy from you.

 Bus

To save money, travel by bus, particularly between major towns and cities. Gotta-go middle-class Americans prefer to fly or drive, but buses let you see the countryside and meet folks along the way. As a rule, buses are reliable, cleanish and comfortable, with air-conditioning, barely reclining seats, lavatories and no smoking.

Bus Fares & Times

Here are some sample standard one-way adult fares and trip times on Greyhound:

SERVICE	PRICE ($)	DURATION (HR)
Boston–Philadelphia	57	7
Chicago–New Orleans	149	24
Los Angeles–San Francisco	59	8
New York–Chicago	119	18
New York–San Francisco	269	72
Washington, DC–Miami	155	25

Greyhound (📞 800-231-2222; www.greyhound.com) is the major long-distance bus company, with routes throughout the USA and Canada. To reach country towns on rural roads, you may need to transfer to local or county bus systems; Greyhound can usually provide their contact information. Greyhound often has excellent online fares – web-only deals will net you substantial discounts over buying at a ticket counter.

Competing with Greyhound are the 75-plus franchises of **Trailways** (📞 703-691-3052; www.trailways.com). Long-distance bus lines that offer decent fares and free wi-fi (that doesn't always work) include **Megabus** (📞 877-462-6342; www.megabus.com) and **BoltBus** (www.boltbus.com); both operate routes primarily in the Northeast and Midwest.

Many bus stations are clean and safe, but some are in dodgy areas; if you arrive in the evening, it's worth spending the money on a taxi. Some towns have just a flag stop. If you are boarding at one of these, pay the driver with exact change.

Costs

For lower fares on Greyhound, purchase tickets at least seven days in advance (purchasing 14 days in advance will save even more). Round trips are also cheaper than two one-way fares.

Reservations

Tickets for some Trailways and other buses can only be purchased immediately prior to departure. Greyhound,

Megabus and BoltBus tickets can be bought online. You can print all tickets at home or in the case of Megabus or BoltBus, simply show ticket receipts through an email on a smartphone. Greyhound also allows customers to pick up tickets at the terminal using 'Will Call' service.

Seating is normally first-come, first-served. Greyhound recommends arriving an hour before departure to get a seat.

🚗 Car & Motorcycle

For maximum flexibility and convenience, and to explore rural America and its wide-open spaces, a car is essential. Although petrol prices are high, you can often score fairly inexpensive rentals (NYC excluded), with rates as low as $20 per day.

Automobile Associations

The **American Automobile Association** (AAA; www.aaa.com) has reciprocal membership agreements with several international auto clubs (check with AAA and bring your membership card from home).

A more ecofriendly alternative, the **Better World Club** (📞 866-238-1137; www.betterworldclub.com) donates 1% of revenue to assist environmental cleanup, offers ecologically sensitive choices for every service it provides and advocates politically for environmental causes.

WIth organizations, the primary member benefit is 24-hour emergency roadside assistance anywhere in the USA. Both also offer trip planning, free travel maps,

travel-agency services, car insurance and a range of travel discounts (eg on hotels, car rentals, attractions).

Driver's License

Foreign visitors can legally drive a car in the USA for up to 12 months using their home driver's license. However, an International Driving Permit will have more credibility with US traffic police, especially if your home license doesn't have a photo or isn't in English. Your automobile association at home can issue an IDP, valid for one year, for a small fee. Always carry your home license together with the IDP.

To ride a motorcycle in the USA, you will need either a valid US state motorcycle license or an IDP specially endorsed for motorcycles.

Insurance

Rental-car companies will provide liability insurance, but most charge extra. Rental companies almost never include collision-damage insurance for the vehicle. Instead, they offer an optional Collision Damage Waiver (CDW) or Loss Damage Waiver (LDW), usually with an initial deductible cost of between $100 and $500. For an extra premium, you can usually get this deductible covered as well. Paying extra for some or all of this insurance increases the cost of a rental car by as much as $30 a day.

Many credit cards offer free collision damage coverage for rental cars, if you rent for 15 days or less and charge the total rental to your card. This is a good way to avoid paying extra fees to the

Driving Distances & Times

200 km
120 miles

CANADA

MEXICO

Vancouver
Seattle
Portland
Eugene
San Francisco
Reno
Las Vegas
Spokane
Boise
Butte
Billings
Salt Lake City
St George
Flagstaff
Phoenix
Yellowstone National Park
Grand Junction
Denver
Cheyenne
Rapid City
Bismarck
Fargo
Sioux Falls
Minneapolis/St Paul
Omaha
Lincoln
Santa Fe
Albuquerque
El Paso
Fort Stockton
San Antonio
Houston
Dallas
Abilene
Amarillo
Oklahoma City
Kansas City
St Louis
Chicago
Detroit
Toronto
Niagara Falls
Buffalo
Cleveland
Charleston
Lexington
Nashville
Memphis
Birmingham
Atlanta
New Orleans
Tallahassee
Savannah
Orlando
Miami
Raleigh
WASHINGTON, DC
New York
Boston
Portland
Montreal
Great Smoky Mountains National Park

130/3
175/3
110/2
285/5
430/8
320/5
220/4
195/4
510/9
410/7
435/7
365/5
520/8
350/6
225/4
380/6
535/8
275/4
465/7
380/6
125/2
305/6
270/6
145/2
440/7
330/5
65/1
290/5
390/6
270/4
450/8
240/4
325/5
200/3
240/4
185/3
210/4
460/7
470/7
240/4
345/5
605/10
455/7
60/1
480/7
255/4
575/9
410/7
240/4
190/3
350/6
250/4
285/5
305/5
385/5
395/6
355/6
345/6
390/6
260/4
280/5
325/6
230/4
275/5
365/6
495/8
240/4
215/4
300/6
270/4
415/7
410/7
355/6
110/2
290/6
385/7
375/7
215/4
465/8
325/6
245/5
355/6
30/0.5

NOTE:
- Driving distances are in miles
- Times are estimates and rounded to the nearest hour

Example: 380/6 represents 380 miles and 6 hours

Fueling Up

Many gas stations in the USA have fuel pumps with automated credit-card pay screens. Most machines ask for your ZIP code after you swipe your card. For foreign travelers – or those with cards issued outside the US – you'll have to pay inside before fueling up. Just indicate how much you'd like to put on the card. If there's still credit left over after you fuel up, just pop back inside, and the attendant will put the difference back on your card.

rental company, but note that if there's an accident, sometimes you must pay the rental-car company first and then seek reimbursement from the credit-card company. There may be exceptions that are not covered, too, such as 'exotic' rentals (eg 4WD Jeeps, convertibles). Check your credit-card policy.

Rental

Car rental is a competitive business in the USA. Most rental companies require that you have a major credit card, be at least 25 years old and have a valid driver's license. Some major national companies may rent to drivers between the ages of 21 and 24 for an additional charge of around $25 per day.

Car-rental prices vary wildly so shop around. The average daily rate for a small car ranges from around $30 to $75, or $200 to $500 per week.

Road Conditions & Hazards

America's highways are thought of as legendary ribbons of unblemished asphalt, but they're not always. Road hazards include potholes, city commuter traffic, wandering wildlife and, of course, cell-phone-wielding, kid distracted and enraged drivers. Caution, foresight, courtesy and luck usually gets you past them. For nationwide traffic and road-closure information, click to www.fhwa.dot.gov/traf-ficinfo/index.htm.

In places where winter driving is an issue, many cars are fitted with steel-studded snow tires; snow chains can sometimes be required in mountain areas. Driving off-road, or on dirt roads, is often forbidden by rental-car companies, and it can be very dangerous in wet weather.

In deserts and range country, livestock sometimes graze next to unfenced roads. These areas are signed as 'Open Range' or with the silhouette of a steer. Where deer and other wild animals frequently appear roadside, you'll see signs with the silhouette of a leaping deer. Take these signs seriously, particularly at dusk and dawn.

Road Rules

In the USA, cars drive on the right-hand side of the road. The use of seat belts and child safety seats is required in every state. Most car-rental agencies rent child safety seats for around $13 per day, but you must reserve them when booking.

On interstate highways, the speed limit is sometimes raised to 75mph. Unless otherwise posted, the speed limit is generally 55mph or 65mph on highways, 25mph to 35mph in cities and towns and as low as 15mph in school zones (strictly enforced during school hours). It's forbidden to pass a school bus when its lights are flashing.

Unless signs prohibit it, you may turn right at a red light after first coming to a full stop – note that turning right on red is illegal in NYC. At four-way stop signs, cars should proceed in order of arrival; when two cars arrive simultaneously, the one on the right has the right of way. When in doubt, just politely wave the other driver ahead. When emergency vehicles (ie police, fire or ambulance) with sirens/flashing lights approach from either direction, pull over safely and get out of the way.

In an increasing number of states, it is illegal to talk on a handheld cell (mobile) phone while driving; use a hands-free device instead.

The maximum legal blood-alcohol concentration for drivers is 0.08%. Penalties are very severe for 'DUI' – driving under the influence of alcohol and/or drugs. Police can give roadside sobriety checks to assess if you've been drinking or using drugs. If you fail, they'll require you to take a breath test, urine test or blood test to determine the level of alcohol or drugs in your body. If you refuse to be tested you'll be treated the same as if you'd taken the test and failed.

In some states it is illegal to carry 'open containers' of alcohol in a vehicle, even if they are empty.

Local Transportation

Except in large US cities, public transportation is rarely the most convenient option for travelers, and coverage can be sparse to outlying towns and suburbs. However, it is usually cheap, safe and reliable. In addition, more than half the states in the nation have adopted ☎511 as an all-purpose local-transportation help line.

Airport Shuttles

Shuttle buses provide inexpensive and convenient transport to/from airports in most cities. Most are 12-seat vans; some have regular routes and stops (which include the main hotels) and some pick up and deliver passengers 'door to door' in their service area. Costs range from $15 to $30 per person.

Bicycle

Some cities are more amenable to bicycles than others, but most have at least a few dedicated bike lanes and paths, and bikes can usually be carried on public transportation.

Bus

Most cities and larger towns have dependable local bus systems, though they are often designed for commuters and provide limited service in the evening and on weekends.

Costs range from free to between $1 and $3 per ride.

Subway & Train

The largest systems are in New York, Chicago, Boston, Philadelphia, Washington, DC, Chicago, Los Angeles and the San Francisco Bay Area. Other cities may have small, one- or two-line rail systems that mainly serve downtown.

Taxi

Taxis are metered, with flagfall charges of around $2.50 to start, plus $2 to $3 per mile. They charge extra for waiting and handling baggage, and drivers expect a 10% to 15% tip. Taxis cruise the busiest areas in large cities, otherwise, it's easiest to phone and order one.

Tours

Hundreds of companies offer all kinds of organized tours of the USA; most focus on either cities or regions.

Backroads (☎ 800-462-2848, 510-527-1555; www.backroads.com) Designs a range of active, multisport and outdoor-oriented trips for all abilities and budgets.

Gray Line (☎ 800-472-9546; www.grayline.com) For those short on time, Gray Line offers a comprehensive range of standard sightseeing tours across the country.

Green Tortoise (☎ 800-867-8647, 415-956-7500; www.greentortoise.com) Offering budget adventures for independent travelers, Green Tortoise is famous for its sleeping-bunk buses. Most trips leave from San

Francisco, traipsing through the West and nationwide.

Road Scholar (☎ 800-454-5768; www.roadscholar.org) For those aged 55 and older, this venerable nonprofit offers 'learning adventures' in all 50 states.

🚆 Train

Amtrak (☎1800-872-7245; www.amtrak.com) has an extensive rail system throughout the USA, with Amtrak's Thruway buses providing connections to and from the rail network to some smaller centers and national parks. Compared with other modes of travel, trains are rarely the quickest, cheapest, timeliest or most convenient option, but they turn the journey into a relaxing, social and scenic all-American experience.

Amtrak has several long-distance lines traversing the nation east to west, and even more running north to south. These connect all of America's biggest cities and many of its smaller ones. Long-distance services (on named trains) mostly operate daily on these routes, but some run only three to five days per week. See Amtrak's website for detailed route maps, as well as the Getting There & Around sections in this guide's regional chapters.

Commuter trains provide faster, more frequent services on shorter routes, especially the northeast corridor from Boston, MA, to Washington, DC. Amtrak's high-speed Acela Express trains are the most expensive, and rail passes are not valid on these trains.

Classes & Costs

Amtrak fares vary according to the type of train and seating; on long-distance lines, you can travel in coach seats (reserved or unreserved), business class, or 1st class, which includes all sleeping compartments. Sleeping cars include simple bunks (called 'roomettes'), bedrooms with en-suite facilities and suites sleeping four with two bathrooms. Sleeping-car rates include meals in the dining car, which offers everyone sit-down meal service (pricey if not included). Food service on commuter lines, when it exists, consists of sandwich and snack bars. Bringing your own food and drink is recommended on all trains.

Various one-way, round-trip and touring fares are available from Amtrak, with discounts of 15% for seniors aged 62 and over and for students with a 'Student Advantage' card ($20) or an International Student Identity Card (ISIC), and 50% discounts for children aged two to 15 when accompanied by a paying adult. AAA members get 10% off. Web-only 'Weekly Specials' offer deep discounts on certain undersold routes.

Generally, the earlier you book, the lower the price. To get many of the standard discounts, you need to reserve at least three days in advance. If you want to take an Acela Express or Metroliner train, avoid peak commute times and aim for weekends.

Amtrak Vacations
(☏800-268-7252; www. amtrakvacations.com) offers vacation packages that include rental cars, hotels, tours and attractions. Air-Rail packages let you travel by train in one direction, then return by plane the other way.

Reservations

Reservations can be made any time from 11 months in advance up to the day of departure. Space on most trains is limited, and certain routes can be crowded, especially during summer and holiday periods, so it's a good idea to book as far in advance as you can; this also gives you the best chance of fare discounts.

Train Passes

Amtrak's USA Rail Pass offers coach-class travel for 15 ($439), 30 ($669) or 45 ($859) days, with travel limited to eight, 12 or 18 one-way 'segments,' respectively. A segment is *not* the same as a one-way trip. If reaching your destination requires riding more than one train (for example, getting from New York to Miami with a transfer in Washington, DC) that one-way trip will actually use two segments of your pass.

Present your pass at an Amtrak office to pick up your ticket(s) for each trip. Reservations should be made by phone (call ☏1800-872-7245, or ☏215-856-7953 from outside the USA) as far in advance as possible. Each segment of the journey must be booked. At some rural stations, trains will only stop if there's a reservation. Tickets are not for specific seats, but a conductor on board may allocate you a seat. Business-class, 1st-class and sleeper accommodations cost extra and must be reserved separately.

All travel must be completed within 180 days of purchasing your pass. Passes are not valid on the Acela Express, Auto Train or Thruway motorcoach connections or the Canadian portion of Amtrak routes operated jointly with Via Rail Canada. Fares can double if you don't buy them at least three or four days in advance.

Train Fares & Times

Sample standard, one-way, adult coach-class fares and trip times on Amtrak's long-distance routes:

Service	Price ($)	Duration (hr)
Chicago–New Orleans	127	20
Los Angeles–San Antonio	182	29
New York–Chicago	101	19
New York–Los Angeles	248	68
Seattle–Oakland	163	23
Washington, DC–Miami	179	23

Behind
the Scenes

Our Readers

Many thanks to the travelers who used the last edition and wrote to us with helpful hints, useful advice and interesting anecdotes: Arno Jose Booy, Eleonor Content, Greg Cummins

Author Thanks
Regis St Louis

This book is dedicated to all the amazingly talented editors I've worked with at Lonely Planet during the past 11 years. Special thanks to Suki Gear and Kathleen Munnelly, who have helped create many great books over the years. Your dedication, creativity and good humor will be sorely missed.

Acknowledgments

Climate map data adapted from Peel MC, Finlayson BL & McMahon TA (2007) 'Updated World Map of the Köppen-Geiger Climate Classification', Hydrology and Earth System Sciences, 11, 1633¬44.

Illustrations p78-9, p110-11 by Javier Martinez Zarracina; p404-4 by Michael Weldon.

Cover photographs: Front: Monument Valley, Arizona, Kerrick James/Corbis; Back: The Capitol, Washington, DC, David R Frazier Photolibrary Inc/Alamy

This Book

This 2nd edition of Lonely Planet's *Discover USA* guidebook was coordinated by Regis St. Louis, and researched and written by Amy C Balfour, Sandra Bao, Michael Benanav, Greg Benchwick, Sara Benson, Alison Bing, Catherine Bodry, Celeste Brash, Gregor Clark, Lisa Dunford, Ned Friary, Michael Grosberg, Adam Karlin, Mariella Krause, Carolyn McCarthy, Brendan Sainsbury, Caroline Sieg, Adam Skolnick, Ryan Ver Berkmoes, Mara Vorhees and Karla Zimmerman. This guidebook was commissioned in Lonely Planet's Oakland office and produced by the following:

Commissioning Editor Suki Gear
Coordinating Editors Kirsten Rawlings, Luna Soo
Senior Cartographer Alison Lyall
Book Designer Katherine Marsh
Associate Product Director Sasha Baskett
Senior Editors Karyn Noble, Catherine Naghten
Assisting Editor Kate James
Cover Research Naomi Parker
Thanks to Ryan Evans, Larissa Frost, Genesys India, Jouve India, Elizabeth Jones, Clara Monitto, Wayne Murphy, Mazzy Prinsep, Alison Ridgway, Jessica Rose, Wibowo Rusli, Dianne Schallmeiner, John Taufa, Angela Tinson, Juan Winata

SEND US YOUR FEEDBACK

Things change – prices go up, schedules change, good places go bad and bad places go bankrupt. So if you find things better or worse, recently opened or long since closed, or you just want to tell us what you loved or loathed about this book, please get in touch and help make the next edition even more accurate and useful. We love to hear from travelers – your comments keep us on our toes and our well-traveled team reads every word. Although we can't reply individually to postal submissions, we always guarantee that your feedback goes straight to the appropriate authors, in time for the next edition. Each person who sends us information is thanked in the next edition – the most useful submissions are rewarded with a selection of digital PDF chapters.

Visit lonelyplanet.com/contact to submit your updates and suggestions or to ask for help. Our award-winning website also features inspirational travel stories, news and discussions.

Note: We may edit, reproduce and incorporate your comments in Lonely Planet products such as guidebooks, websites and digital products, so let us know if you don't want your comments reproduced or your name acknowledged. For a copy of our privacy policy visit lonelyplanet.com/privacy.

Index

INDEX M

N

Nags Head 245
Nantucket 186-7, **180**
Napa Valley 371, 413-14
Nascar 477
Nashville 20, 207, 232-6
Natchez Trace Pkwy 237
National Archives 109
National Cherry Blossom Festival 42
National Civil Rights Museum 227
National Mall 98, **110-11**
national & state parks 22, 465, 469
  Acadia National Park 198-9, 200
  Andrew Molera State Park 419
  Arches National Park 322
  Bahia Honda State Park 285
  Bill Baggs Cape Florida State Park 281
  Bryce Canyon National Park 29, 319
  Canyonlands National Park 322
  Crater Lake National Park 365
  Death Valley National Park 396-7
  DL Bliss State Park 418
  Ecola State Park 365
  Emerald Bay State Park 418
  Everglades National Park 26, 257, 279-80
  Glacier Bay National Park & Preserve 428
  Grand Canyon National Park 12, 300-7, **302**
  Great Smoky Mountains National Park 207, 237-8
  Haleakalā National Park 426
  Indian Key Historic State Park 283
  Indiana Dunes State Park 153
  John Pennekamp Coral Reef State Park 281
  Joshua Tree National Park 392
  Julia Pfeiffer Burns State Park 418
  Lignumvitae Key Botanical State Park 283
  Lime Kiln Point State Park 356
  Malibu Creek State Park 382
  Mesa Verde National Park 320
  Moran State Park 357
  Mt Rainier National Park 31, 337, 353
  Nickerson State Park 182
  Olympic National Park 337, 355-6
  Pfeiffer Big Sur State Park 419
  Rocky Mountain National Park 432-3
  Wai'anapanapa State Park 425
  Yellowstone National Park 433-4
  Yosemite National Park 23, 371, 415-17
  Zion National Park 29, 295, 321
Native Americans 471-2
  art 471, 472
  etiquette 297
  museums 309
Native American sites 27, 297, 329
  Bandelier National Monument 328-9
  Canyon de Chelly National Monument 322, 324
  Monument Valley Navajo Tribal Park 295, 323
  Navajo Nation 322-4
Navy Pier 140
New England 15, 157-201, **158-9**
  beaches 162
  food 162, 462
  highlights 160-1
  historic sites 162
  internet resources 163
  itineraries 164-5
  outdoor activities 163
  planning 163
  travel within 163
New Orleans 13, 203, 206, 212-23, **214-15**
  accommodations 219-20
  children, travel with 220
  courses 218
  drinking 222
  entertainment 222-3
  food 220-2
  highlights 217
  live-music venues 223
  sights 212-18
  tourist information 223
  tours 218-19
  travel to/within 223
New York City 11, 46, 51 93, **62**, **68**, **80**
  accommodations 75, 81-2
  Brooklyn 93
  Central Park 76-9
  children, travel with 75
  drinking 87-9
  entertainment 90-1
  food 55, 56, 82-7, 461-2
  galleries 56, 92
  highlights 54-5
  internet resources 57
  itineraries 58-9
  jazz venues 89
  museums 56
  nightlife 57, 87-9
  performing arts venues 91
  planning 57
  Queens 87
  shopping 91-2
  sights 60-1, 64-7, 70-4
  sports 90-1
  tourist information 92
  tours 74-5
  travel to/within 57, 92-3

000 Map pages

Y

Z

How to Use This Book

These symbols give you the vital information for each listing:

✐	Telephone Numbers	🛜	Wi-Fi Access	T	Boston T
☉	Opening Hours	☒	Swimming Pool	🚌	Bus
P	Parking	✔	Vegetarian Selection	🚢	Ferry
⊖	Nonsmoking	👪	Family-Friendly	M	Metro
✳	Air-Conditioning	🐾	Pet-Friendly	S	Subway
@	Internet Access	B	BART	🚋	Tram

Look out for these icons:

FREE No payment required

🌿 A green or sustainable option

Our authors have nominated these places as demonstrating a strong commitment to sustainability – for example by supporting local communities and producers, operating in an environmentally friendly way, or supporting conservation projects.

All reviews are ordered in our authors' preference, starting with their most preferred option. Additionally:

Sights are arranged in the geographic order that we suggest you visit them, and within this order, by author preference.

Eating and Sleeping reviews are ordered by price range (budget, mid-range, top end) and within these ranges, by author preference.

Map Legend

Sights
- 🏖 Beach
- ☸ Buddhist
- 🏯 Castle
- ✝ Christian
- 🕉 Hindu
- ☪ Islamic
- ✡ Jewish
- ❶ Monument
- 🏛 Museum/Gallery
- ⊗ Ruin
- ⊗ Winery/Vineyard
- 🦁 Zoo
- ◎ Other Sight

Activities, Courses & Tours
- 🤿 Diving/Snorkelling
- 🛶 Canoeing/Kayaking
- ⛷ Skiing
- 🏄 Surfing
- 🏊 Swimming/Pool
- 🚶 Walking
- 🏄 Windsurfing
- ➕ Other Activity/Course/Tour

Sleeping
- 🛏 Sleeping
- ⛺ Camping

Eating
- ✕ Eating

Drinking
- 🍷 Drinking
- ☕ Cafe

Entertainment
- 🎭 Entertainment

Shopping
- 🛍 Shopping

Information
- ✉ Post Office
- ❶ Tourist Information

Transport
- ✈ Airport
- ⊗ Border Crossing
- 🚌 Bus
- Cable Car/Funicular
- Cycling
- 🚢 Ferry
- Monorail
- P Parking
- S Taxi
- Train/Railway
- Tram
- ⊖ Tube Station
- U U-Bahn
- M Underground Train Station
- ● Other Transport

Routes
- Tollway
- Freeway
- Primary
- Secondary
- Tertiary
- Lane
- Unsealed Road
- Plaza/Mall
- Steps
- Tunnel
- Pedestrian Overpass
- Walking Tour
- Walking Tour Detour
- Path

Boundaries
- International
- State/Province
- Disputed
- Regional/Suburb
- Marine Park
- Cliff
- Wall

Population
- ✪ Capital (National)
- ◉ Capital (State/Province)
- ● City/Large Town
- ● Town/Village

Geographic
- 🏠 Hut/Shelter
- 🗼 Lighthouse
- 👁 Lookout
- ▲ Mountain/Volcano
- 🌴 Oasis
- 🌳 Park
-)(Pass
- 🌲 Picnic Area
- 💧 Waterfall

Hydrography
- River/Creek
- Intermittent River
- Swamp/Mangrove
- Reef
- Canal
- Water
- Dry/Salt/Intermittent Lake
- Glacier

Areas
- Beach/Desert
- Cemetery (Christian)
- Cemetery (Other)
- Park/Forest
- Sportsground
- Sight (Building)
- Top Sight (Building)

MARA VORHEES

Boston & New England Born and raised in St Clair Shores, Michigan, Mara traveled the world (if not the universe) before finally settling in the Hub. She now lives in a pink house in Somerville, MA, with her husband, two kiddies and two kitties. She is the author of Lonely Planet guides *New England* and *Boston*, among others. Follow her adventures online at www.havetwinswilltravel.com.

KARLA ZIMMERMAN

Chicago A life-long Midwesterner, Karla is well-versed in the region's beaches, ballparks, breweries and pie shops. When she's not home in Chicago watching the Cubs (or writing for magazines, websites and books), she's exploring. For this gig, she curled in Minnesota, caught a wave in Michigan, heard the curds squeak in Wisconsin and drank an embarrassing number of milkshakes in Ohio. Karla has written for several Lonely Planet guides to the USA, Canada, the Caribbean and Europe.

MICHAEL GROSBERG

New York City, The Best of the Rest Thanks to an uncle and aunt's house upstate on the Delaware River in the southern Catskills, Michael has had a base to explore the region for two decades – when not home in Brooklyn, NYC, that is. No matter his love for the city, getaways are necessary and he has taken every opportunity to range far and wide in New York, New Jersey and Pennsylvania, from cross-country skiing in the Adirondacks or pitching a tent on an island in the St Lawrence to chowing down on ballpark food at a Pirates game in Pittsburgh and finding a classic diner in Jersey's Pine Barrens.

ADAM KARLIN

Washington, DC, New Orleans & the South Adam was born in Washington, DC, raised in rural Maryland and lives in New Orleans – a city he discovered on assignment for Lonely Planet. His love of travel stems from a love of place that was engendered by the tidal wetlands of the Mid-Atlantic. That need for wandering has pushed him overseas and across the world, and in the process he has written some 40 guidebooks for Lonely Planet, from the Andaman Islands to the Zimbabwe border.

MARIELLA KRAUSE

Florida, The Best of the Rest This is Mariella's fourth go-round with a USA guide, but her first time taking on two whole states. Having written both the Florida chapter and the Texas section, she now considers herself an expert on places with panhandles. Mariella will always consider Texas home, and she still sprinkles her language with Texanisms whenever possible, much to the amusement of those who don't consider 'y'all' a legitimate pronoun.

CAROLYN MCCARTHY

The Best of the Rest Carolyn fell for the Rockies as an undergraduate at Colorado College, where she spent her first break camping in a blizzard in the Sangre de Christo Range. For this title she sampled the craft beers of four states, tracked wolves and heard even more Old West ghost stories. Carolyn has contributed to more than 20 Lonely Planet titles, specializing in the American west and Latin America, and has written for *National Geographic*, *Outside*, *Lonely Planet Magazine* and other publications.

BRENDAN SAINSBURY

The Pacific Northwest An expat Brit from Hampshire, England, now living near Vancouver, Canada, Brendan is a Nirvana-loving, craft beer–appreciating, outdoors-embracing, art-admiring, bus-utilizing coffee addict who had no problem finding like-minded souls in Seattle. He's been writing Lonely Planet guides for the past nine years and collecting notes on Seattle since 2009. He is the author of Lonely Planet's current guide to Seattle, and has contributed to each edition of this book.

CAROLINE SIEG

Boston & New England Caroline Sieg is a half-Swiss, half-American writer. Her relationship with New England began when she first lived in Boston and she began heading up to Maine for foodie treats and windswept coastal walks. She was delighted to return to the land of lobster and blueberry pies for Lonely Planet.

Read more about Caroline at:
lonelyplanet.com/members/carolinesieg

ADAM SKOLNICK

New Orleans & the South Adam writes about travel, culture, health, and politics for Lonely Planet, *Outside*, *Men's Health*, and *Travel & Leisure*. He has coauthored more than 20 Lonely Planet guidebooks to destinations in Europe, the US, Central America and Asia. He drove 5990 miles during his research trip for this guide, and will from here on blame the state of Kentucky for his growing bourbon dependency. Read more of his work at www.adamskolnick.com. Find him on Twitter and Instagram @adamskolnick.

RYAN VER BERKMOES

The Best of the Rest Ryan first drove across the Great Plains with his family in the 1960s. Among his treasured memories are a pair of Wild West six-shooters he got at Wall Drugs in South Dakota and which he still has (in a box someplace, not under his pillow). Through the years he has never passed up a chance to wander the backroads of America's heartland, finding beauty and intrigue where you'd least expect it. Find more at www.ryanverberkmoes.com; @ryanvb.

GREG BENCHWICK

The Best of the Rest A Colorado native, Greg's been all over the Centennial State. He has taught skiing in Vail, walked through fire pits in campsites across the state and attended journalism school in Boulder. He calls Denver's Highlands home.

Read more about Greg at:
lonelyplanet.com/members/gbenchwick

SARA BENSON

California, The Best of the Rest After graduating from college in Chicago, Sara jumped on a plane to San Francisco with just one suitcase and $100 in her pocket. She has bounced around California ever since, in between stints living in Asia and Hawaii and working as a national park ranger. The author of 55 travel and nonfiction books, Sara summited Sierra Nevada peaks, uncovered the Lost Coast and survived Death Valley while researching this guide. Follow her adventures online at www.indietraveler.blogspot.com and @indie_traveler on Twitter.

Read more about Sara at:
lonelyplanet.com/members/sara_benson

ALISON BING

California During more than 15 years in San Francisco, Alison has done everything you're supposed to do in the city and many things you're not, including falling in love on the Haight St bus and quitting a Silicon Valley day job to write 43 Lonely Planet guidebooks and commentary for magazines, mobile guides and other media. Join further adventures as they unfold on Twitter @AlisonBing.

CATHERINE BODRY

The Best of the Rest Catherine has spent the bulk of her life escaping her suburban upbringing, and after 13 years considers Alaska home. She loves mountains and road trips, and spends a lot of time running the trails in the Chugach Range. Catherine has contributed to several Lonely Planet guides including *Alaska*, *Thailand*, *Canada* and *Pacific Northwest's Best Trips*.

CELESTE BRASH

The Pacific Northwest Locals have a hard time believing it, but the beauty of the Pacific Northwest is what coaxed Celeste back to the US after 15 years in Tahiti. She was thrilled to explore and imbibe the treasures of her new backyard for this book: hiking snowy peaks, looking for orcas and getting in touch with her cowboy and Indian roots. Find out more about Celeste and her award-winning writing at www.celestebrash.com.

GREGOR CLARK

Boston & New England Gregor fell in love with Vermont at age 16, while working as a summer conservation volunteer in the state's southwestern corner. He's made his home there since 1997, during which time he's explored the state from top to bottom. A lifelong polyglot with a degree in Romance languages, Gregor has written regularly for Lonely Planet since 2000, focusing on Europe and Latin America. He lives with his wife, two daughters, five cats and two chickens in Middlebury, VT.

LISA DUNFORD

The Grand Canyon & the Southwest As one of Brigham Young's (possibly thousands of) great-great-granddaughters, Lisa was first drawn to Utah by ancestry. But it's the incredible red rocks that have kept her coming back for 10 years. She feels at home hiking through pinkish sand around Zion or Arches until her shoes are permanently stained, rounding a bend and being accosted by purple- crimson- and rose-colored cliffs, or witnessing brilliant wildflowers among the hardened dunes of the Grand Staircase-Escalante National Monument (GSENM). Lisa coauthored Lonely Planet's Zion & Bryce Canyon National Parks.

NED FRIARY

Boston & New England Ned's college days were spent in Amherst, and traveling around his old stomping grounds always feels like a homecoming of sorts. He now lives on Cape Cod and has explored the region from one end to the other, searching out the best lobster roll, canoeing the marshes, and hiking and cycling the trails. His favorite moment while researching this book was catching the sunset over the Connecticut River valley from the summit at Skinner State Park.

Our Story

A beat-up old car, a few dollars in the pocket and a sense of adventure. In 1972 that's all Tony and Maureen Wheeler needed for the trip of a lifetime – across Europe and Asia overland to Australia. It took several months, and at the end – broke but inspired – they sat at their kitchen table writing and stapling together their first travel guide, *Across Asia on the Cheap*. Within a week they'd sold 1500 copies. Lonely Planet was born.

Today, Lonely Planet has offices in Melbourne, London and Oakland, with more than 600 staff and writers. We share Tony's belief that 'a great guidebook should do three things: inform, educate and amuse'.

Our Writers

REGIS ST LOUIS

Coordinating Author A Hoosier by birth, Regis grew up in a sleepy riverside town where he dreamed of big-city intrigue. In 2001, he settled in New York, which had all that and more. He has also lived in San Francisco and Los Angeles and has crossed the country by train, bus and car, while visiting remote corners of America. Favorite memories from his most recent trip include village-hopping and seafood overindulgence in Long Island, mountainside rambles in the Catskills and crab feasting on the Chesapeake Bay. Regis has contributed to more than 40 Lonely Planet titles, including *New York City* and *Washington, DC*.

AMY C BALFOUR

New Orleans & the South, The Grand Canyon & the Southwest A southerner of Scots-Irish descent, Amy has hiked, biked, paddled and gambled her way across the US. She's been visiting the Outer Banks since she was a child and never tires of running down Jockey's Ridge. In Arizona she enjoyed a return trip to Phantom Ranch, hiking down the South Kaibab Trail and up the Bright Angel. Amy has authored or coauthored more than 15 books for Lonely Planet and has written for *Backpacker*, *Every Day with Rachael Ray*, *Redbook*, *Southern Living* and *Women's Health*.

SANDRA BAO

The Pacific Northwest Sandra has lived in Buenos Aires, New York and California, but Oregon has become her final stop. Researching the Beaver state has been a highlight of Sandra's 14-year-long authoring career with Lonely Planet, during which she has contributed to dozens of guidebooks covering four continents. She's come to appreciate the wondrous beauty of her home state, how much it has to offer both travelers and locals and how friendly people can be in tiny towns in the middle of nowhere.

MICHAEL BENANAV

The Grand Canyon & the Southwest Michael came to New Mexico in 1992, fell under its spell, and moved to a village in the Sangre de Cristo foothills, where he still lives. Since then he's spent years exploring the state's mountains, deserts and rivers as a wilderness instructor. Aside from his work for Lonely Planet, he's authored two nonfiction books and writes and photographs for magazines and newspapers. Check out his work at www.michaelbenanav.com.

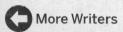 **More Writers** ··

Published by Lonely Planet Publications Pty Ltd
ABN 36 005 607 983
2nd edition – May 2014
ISBN 978 1 74220 584 7
© Lonely Planet 2014   Photographs © as indicated 2014
10 9 8 7 6 5 4 3 2 1
Printed in China